REVOLUTION

Translated and annotated by Bernhard A. Uhlendorf

IN AMERICA

Confidential Letters and Journals
1776-1784 of Adjutant General
Major Baurmeister of the
Hessian Forces

RUTGERS UNIVERSITY PRESS · NEW BRUNSWICK, NEW JERSEY · 1957

973.3
B328r

To my dear friends

Professor and Mrs. Albert Easton White

Note on the Illustrations

For the eighteenth century water color drawings of Hessian regimental groups in this volume, the publishers are indebted to Mrs. John Nicholas Brown of Providence, Rhode Island. Mrs. Brown has taken a special interest in our search for illustrative materials and has generously allowed us to reproduce plates from a book in her collection: *Hochfürst. Hessiches Corps*, circa 1784 (n.p.), by J. H. Carl, who made most of the drawings, and J. C. Müller, the engraver.

The three French prints appeared in a small volume published in Paris, probably in 1784: *Recueil d'Estampes Représentant les Différents Evénemens de la Guerre qui a procuré l'Indépendence aux Etats Unis de l'Amérique*—Paris chez M. Ponce, Graveur de Mgr Comte d'Artois, et chez M. Godefroy, Graveur de Sa Majesté Impériale. M. Niquet, Scrip. A.P.D.R. The volume is in the New York Public Library.

Four of the illustrations and the endpapers are taken from the Phelps Stokes, Emmet, and Spencer Collections of the New York Public Library. "The *Phoenix* and the *Rose*," one of the very few naval prints of the Revolutionary period and the first to show ships in action, was published April 2, 1778, by J. F. W. Des Barres in the *Atlantic Neptune*, the superb collection of maps and views issued by the British Admiralty, 1763-1784. Another outstanding naval print of the period, and the only important large one engraved in America, is the aquatint of the British attack on Mud (Mifflin) Fort, published in Park Street, Philadelphia, February 17, 1787. Archibald Robertson's drawing of the arrival of Lord Howe's fleet is one of the important group of Revolutionary views that he made during his service with the British headquarters troops. Lord Rawdon's water color of the "Landing of the British forces in the Jerseys" may possibly be the work of Captain Thomas Davies, who made a very similar drawing of the British and Hessian attack on Fort Washington.

The line engraving on the endpapers was published by William Lane, Leadenhall Street, London, January 1, 1789. The Convention Army, consisting of Burgoyne's force which surrendered to Gates at Saratoga in 1777, should by the terms of the convention have been returned to England. Among this army were many Germans, mainly Brunswickers under Baron von Riedesel. They were first quartered near Cambridge, Massachusetts, but at the end of 1778 were forced to march south to an encampment in Charlottesville, Virginia. The trip took them two months, and they had to build their own barracks and lay out gardens and poultry yards.

Preface

The letters and journals published in this volume are part of the Von Jungkenn Papers in the William L. Clements Library of The University of Michigan. The author's purpose in preparing an English translation of these significant personal accounts of the American Revolution was twofold: first, to make available to the general reader an interesting narrative by an active participant in a great historical event; second, to throw some new light on that great struggle which brought political independence to the American colonies.

Contemporary American and British accounts which portray this struggle have long furnished valuable data for scholarly works as well as background material for popular accounts dealing with the various phases of that period. But the narratives of the German troops who were hired by Great Britain to subjugate the colonists have failed to receive the attention they deserve.

While the correspondence and journals of Baron and Baroness von Riedesel have been regarded as valuable source materials for nearly a century, the diaries of Krafft, Pausch, Popp, and Wiederholdt have enjoyed but scant recognition. (Only one of the authors of these accounts, namely, Andreas Wiederholdt, served with the Hessian troops.) One explanation for this neglect is the fact that they are mainly records of day-to-day occurrences within certain localities and within relatively short spans of time. Another diary, that of Döhla, is even less known than the other four, although it is more extensive and more interesting and has appeared in print twice—in Germany in 1912 and in this country in 1917. The Hessian diaries and letters published in *The Siege of Charleston* (translated and edited by the author) are of course limited both as to time and locality.

This volume, on the contrary, covers almost the entire Revolution, for it presents a virtually continuous narrative of events from May 22, 1776, to April 23, 1784. It is told by Adjutant General Major Baurmeister, a Hessian officer who participated in the events which he describes, who knew much of what went on behind the scenes, who was a keen observer and a shrewd interpreter, and who had a knack for telling what he saw and heard.

Baurmeister's letters and journals comprise nearly one third of the Von Jungkenn Papers. These papers consist of letters, journal-like accounts, diaries, and a few printed items—a total of 760 folio and 1280 quarto pages (not counting the printed matter)—sent to Baron von Jungkenn by the Hesse-Cassel officers. The collection as a whole takes in the period from March, 1776, to April, 1784, from embarkation for England to disembarkation in Germany.

Since most of the officers were personally acquainted with von Jungkenn, who was also a professional soldier, with the rank of colonel at the time the troops left Germany and that of lieutenant general when they returned, the correspondence is devoid of the cold official tone characteristic of most military papers; besides, since the Hessians had no patriotic feelings either for England or America, their accounts were in many respects less biased than those of either British or American soldiers. They merely described what they did, what they saw, what they heard, and what they felt.

The papers were acquired in 1932 from the firm of Emil Hirsch, antiquarian book dealers of Munich, Germany. How Hirsch gained possession of the papers is not known, and in view of the circumstances that had led to their discovery a few years before, it is just as well that their whereabouts between 1929 and late in 1931 are clouded in mystery.

The circumstances are these: In 1923 the Government of Westphalia announced that it would soon pass a law requiring the Westphalian nobility to surrender their family papers to the state archives. To prove to the government that they could take care of their possessions themselves, the Westphalian nobility, under the leadership of Count Max von Landsberg-Velen und Gemen, formed the United Archives of the Westphalian Nobility. According to the plans that were formulated, the nobility were not to give up title to their papers; their collections were merely to be sorted and roughly inventoried by the curator of the new archives, whose headquarters were to be in an archives building to be constructed by Count Max within the confines of his castle. Thus, these long-buried treasures were to be made available for scholarly research.

The archives building was constructed and furnished, and Dr. Heinrich Glasmeier, archivist of the United Archives, brought together in this building the family papers from sixty-seven castles belonging to various branches of the Landsberg family. These papers were said to occupy about one and three-quarter miles of shelf space in 1929.

While searching for hitherto unknown collections, Dr. Glasmeier in the spring of 1929 called at Schloss Hüffe, District of Minden, Westphalia, where the aged Baroness von Vely-Jungkenn, the last of her line, lived in retirement. In the sacristy of her castle, Dr. Glasmeier found in an old chest, probably unopened for nearly a century and a half, the papers that were ultimately to be deposited in the Clements Library.*

Upon arrival of the collection in the library, the present author assisted in inventorying the papers and subsequently spent a week appraising their value from the point of view of the historian of the American Revolution. His report, dated January 26, 1932, helped to procure the necessary funds for the acquisition of the collection, and the notes he took furnished the late Dr. Randolph G. Adams, Director of the Clements Library, with material

* See H. R. Knickerbocker's article in the *New York Evening Post,* June 29, 1929, section 3, pp. 1–3.

for an article which appeared in the *New York Times Magazine* on July 3, 1932.

Baroness von Vely-Jungkenn was the great-great-grandniece of Baron von Jungkenn, the foremost figure at the court of the Landgrave of Hesse-Cassel during the War of American Independence. Friedrich Christian Arnold, Baron von Jungkenn, Müntzer von Mohrenstamm, was Lord High Chamberlain and Minister of State. He was born at Colgenstein on May 1, 1732, the youngest son of the Colgenstein line of the von Jungkenn family. At an early age von Jungkenn entered the military service in a Prussian regiment commanded by one of his cousins, and became an ensign at the age of twenty-one. Four years later he obtained a commission as second lieutenant in a Hessian regiment, whose titular commander was the hereditary prince of Hesse-Cassel. This regiment was then serving on the side of Prussia and her allies (including England) in the Seven Years' War, and the young officer took part in the campaigns of Silesia and Bohemia in 1758.

When, in 1760, Prince Frederick succeeded to the throne of Hesse-Cassel, von Jungkenn followed him to the court. He was commissioned captain in the First Regiment of Guards and appointed third adjutant general to His Most Serene Highness. He became a major in 1761, a lieutenant colonel in 1764, and a colonel in 1766. In 1777 he was promoted to the rank of major general and in 1781 to that of lieutenant general.

During the twenty years in which he advanced from a captaincy to a lieutenant generalcy, von Jungkenn also gained in influence at the court and in the affairs of the state. At the time the Landgrave's Minister of State, Baron Martin Ernst von Schlieffen, was bargaining for terms with the agent of George III, he held the court title of Lord High Chamberlain. In 1779 he received a seat in the privy council of the Landgrave, and the following year he succeeded Baron von Schlieffen as Minister of State. Apparently he performed his manifold duties, which embraced those of a minister of war, to the satisfaction of his sovereigns—Frederick II died in 1785 and was succeeded by his son, William I. After von Jungkenn had asked three times for permission to retire,

his resignation was finally accepted in 1789. He withdrew from
the court and took up residence in Schloss Hüffe, Kreis Minden,
Westphalia. In this castle, which he himself had acquired, he died
on November 11, 1806, without issue.

In an anonymous account of the city of Cassel (the modern
spelling in Kassel) and its court, entitled *Briefe eines Reisenden
über den gegenwärtigen Zustand von Cassel,* published in 1781
and attributed to Friedrich Justinian Günderode, we read the following: "The youngest in years among the ministers is General
Jungkenn-Müntzer, a most industrious worker, which is proved by
the fact that he conscientiously manages the several departments
entrusted to him, of which the military is the most important. . . .
He is highly esteemed, is beloved by the Landgrave, the court,
and the military, and it is justly said of him that he willingly aids
all those who turn to him for help." *

It was originally planned to publish a transcript of this narrative together with the translation, so that the student of history
might have the joy of reading and quoting the documents in the
language in which they were written. However, since the transcript (together with photostats of the originals) has been deposited in the William L. Clements Library, where it as well as
the originals may be consulted by interested and qualified readers,
it was decided to issue the translation only.

The manuscripts were sometimes difficult to decipher. Baurmeister himself did not write a clear, legible hand, and the ten
scribes he employed frequently up to July, 1780, and once thereafter (they are denoted by the letters A to J in the chronological
list of copyists following the text) apparently could not always
make out his rough copy. There are many grammatical errors and
numerous misspelled words, even judging by contemporary
orthographic usage. Terminating syllables and inflectional endings
are often indicated only by tail-like strokes. Somewhat confusing
also are the many dialectic variations between Baurmeister's way

---

* Fritz Herrmann, *Die Familie Jungkenn* . . . (printed as Manuscript, Op-
penheim, a.Rh., 1931). The above quotation is taken from page 77, and refers to
page 206 of Günderode's account.

of speaking and writing and that of several of the scribes; moreover, there is always a certain amount of carelessness, especially
toward the end of long accounts, probably owing to fatigue and,
sometimes, to the pressure of time.

The task of translation, partly because of the difficulties just
noted, was rather trying at times. Nevertheless, except for nine
passages, where a variant translation or an explanatory note is
given in the footnotes, the translation is believed to be accurate
and faithful, both as to content and spirit. A more literal translation could have been prepared only at the expense of readability.

What proved to be quite vexatious is the misspelling of
proper names, especially English ones, which, moreover, do not
always appear in the same variation. Every effort was made to
verify personal and geographic names. At times positive identification could not be made, and in a few cases the search was
entirely fruitless. Personal names are recorded in the index in the
form verified, and when for other reasons a footnote was considered desirable, the correct form is given there as well. Eighteenth-
century geographic names no longer in use today have been retained in the text, but are identified in the footnotes.

Accounts of military and naval movements and encounters
and of nonmilitary events were likewise verified whenever possible. Sometimes no corroborative evidence could be found except, perhaps, in a none-too-trustworthy account in one of the
loyalist newspapers, in which case the probable source is cited
in a footnote. However, agreement of a statement by Baurmeister
with one by Gaine or Rivington, the New York loyalist printers,
might point only to a common source. This is certainly true if
corroborative evidence was found only in Almon's *Remembrancer,*
which was published in London.

As a general practice, aside from that just noted, annotations
are given only if explanatory or corroborative information was
found only after laborious searching, or if the text is in disagree-
ment with more authentic records, or if more specific information
seemed desirable to prevent misinterpretation or confusion. It is
hoped that the notes will meet the needs of the general reader as
well as those of the historian.

Bibliographical references are given in full only the first time they appear. For frequently cited titles, subsequent references give only the author or a short descriptive title. These are explained in a key following the text.

Baurmeister, as well as some of the scribes, frequently wrote long accounts without paragraphing them; however, for the sake of readability, the use of paragraphs has been considered advisable.

The late Edna Vosper, for several years Curator of Manuscripts in the Clements Library, who collaborated in the publication of the Baurmeister letters describing the Philadelphia campaign,* assisted also with the editorial work of this volume. Her contribution lies in the verification of a large portion of the personal and geographic names and in the checking of some of the passages against rare published and manuscript source materials. Her painstaking work is gratefully acknowledged.

The author desires to express his gratitude also to Dr. William Warner Bishop, late Director Emeritus of The University of Michigan General Library, to the late Dr. Randolph G. Adams, Director of the William L. Clements Library, and to his successor, Professor Howard H. Peckham, for their interest in the preparation of this volume; to the several state, county, and local historical societies, especially those of New York, Pennsylvania, and New Jersey, which were extremely cooperative in supplying information requested; to the Library of Congress for procuring a photostatic copy of a much-needed volume of the Hesse-Cassel yearbook, † and to its Divisions of Manuscripts and Maps for ever-willing assistance; to the State Library of Hesse-Cassel for obtaining from the state archives biographical data on Baurmeister; to the late Helen A. Wolter, Medical Librarian of The University

* "Letters of Major Baurmeister to Colonel von Jungkenn written during the Philadelphia Campaign, 1777 to 1778," *Pennsylvania Magazine of History and Biography*, October, 1935, and January and April, 1936; Offprint: Historical Society of Pennsylvania. *Pamphlet Series: Narratives and Documents*. No. 3, ix, 77 pp. (with frontispiece map and index). The letters are here republished, with corrections and some additions, by permission of Dr. Julian P. Boyd, former editor of the magazine.

† *Hochfürstlich Hessen-Casselischer Staats- und Adress-Calender auf das Jahr Christi 1779*, Cassel [1779]. 1 vol. bound in 2. [382] pp.

of Michigan, who kindly assisted the author in checking and re-checking the translation against the transcript and the photostats; and to the Executive Board of the Horace H. Rackham School of Graduate Studies and to Dr. Richard G. Folsom, Director of the Engineering Research Institute, both of The University of Michigan, for making available funds for the photostating of the original manuscripts and the preparation of maps and other materials.

BERNHARD A. UHLENDORF

Ann Arbor, Michigan
March, 1956

Bibliographical Abbreviations

Carleton Calendar: Gt. Brit., Hist. MSS Comm. *Report on American Manuscripts in the Royal Institution of Great Britain*, vols. 2–4, Dublin, 1906–09.

Clowes: W. L. Clowes, *The Royal Navy*, London, 1897–1903, 7 vols.

Dawson: H. B. Dawson, *Battles of the American Revolution*, New York, 1876.

Eelking-Rosengarten: Max von Eelking, *Die deutschen Hülfstruppen im nordamerikanischen Befreiungskriege, 1776 bis 1783*, Hannover, 1863, 2 vols. in 1; abridged and translated by J. G. Rosengarten as *The German Allied Troops in the North American War of Independence*, Albany, N. Y., 1893.

Fitzpatrick's *Calendar*: J. C. Fitzpatrick, *Calendar of the Correspondence of George Washington*, Washington, 1915, 4 vols.

Heitman: F. B. Heitman, *Historical Register of the Officers of the Continental Army*, Washington, 1914.

Staats-Calender: *Hochfürstlich Hessen-Casselischer Staats- und Adress-Calender*, Cassel, 1779, 2 vols. in 1. (Photostats in Library of Congress.)

Stryker: W. S. Stryker, *The Battles of Trenton and Princeton*, Boston, 1898.

Contents

The Hessians and the Revolution

In the summer of 1775, when the British in Canada had already surrendered Crown Point and Ticonderoga, and the patriot investment of Boston had commenced in earnest in spite of American losses at Breed's Hill and Bunker Hill, the King of England, George III, had at the most eighteen thousand effective land troops stationed in various garrisons of Great Britain. Attempts at recruiting brought very little result; the class of people from which recruits would ordinarily have come was not unsympathetic toward the struggle of the colonists, for more liberties for the colonists might eventually also mean more liberties for the poorer classes of Britain. Hence, if the rebellion was to be put down by force, it could be done only by resorting once more to the age-old practice of hiring foreign troops.

Overtures were made to Catherine the Great of Russia for a loan of twenty thousand men. The Empress had the troops available, for her country had just fought a successful war against the Turks. She expressed her desire to have the continued good will of the King of England, but made no mention of supplying soldiers. The English envoy did not comprehend the significance of her shrewd remarks, and when a formal request for troops was made, the Empress, largely owing to pressure brought to bear by Frederick the Great of Prussia, refused to send any help whatever and expressed the hope that the American conflict might be settled by peaceful means.

Germany was the next potential source of aid. Her petty princes had for many years been supplying troops to fight under foreign flags, especially under that of Great Britain.

As Elector of Hanover, the King made himself a loan of five battalions of Hanoverians, a total of 2,365 men, which were sent to Gibraltar and Minorca to relieve a like number of British troops for military duty in England. He also directed that four thousand additional men be recruited in his hereditary domain for service in the British regiments, but only about two hundred and fifty Hanoverians served on the North American Continent.

Within weeks after the news of the Battle of Breed's Hill and Bunker Hill had appeared in the German press, three of the almost three hundred petty princes reigning within the German Empire approached King George with offers of military aid. One was the Count of Hesse-Hanau, a nephew of the King; the others were the Prince of Waldeck and the Markgrave of Anspach-Bayreuth, whose offers certainly were not motivated by family loyalty.*

Although none of these offers were accepted at the time, they did, in a way, serve as a basis for future negotiations. For this purpose Colonel William Faucitt was sent to Germany by Lord Suffolk, Minister of State, in August, 1775, as minister plenipotentiary. Colonel Faucitt had served on German soil during the Seven Years' War and knew of the avarice of some of the German princes and of the impoverished conditions of their lands. Upon arriving on the Continent, his first duty was to muster in the five Hanover battalions, which were ready to sail September 1, 1775, but for lack of British transports were detained until October 2nd and 6th.

In the meantime Sir Joseph Yorke, the King's ambassador at The Hague, who supposedly had a better knowledge of conditions on the Continent than any of the other representatives of the Crown, reported to Lord Suffolk in September that five German princes were ready to supply troops at small costs, and on Novem-

---

* For the correspondence between these princes and George III and Lord Suffolk, which was carried on in French, see Friedrich Kapp, *Der Soldatenhandel deutscher Fürsten nach Amerika*, 2nd ed., Berlin, 1874, pp. 243–48.

ber 24th Lord Suffolk authorized Colonel Faucitt to see what he could accomplish at the courts of Brunswick and Hesse-Cassel.

The sovereign of Brunswick was Duke Charles I, who shared his monarchical duties with his son Prince Charles William Ferdinand, a brother-in-law of George III. The Prince became ruler in 1780, upon the death of his father. He alone of the six princes whose troops fought for Great Britain permitted his subjects to stay in America upon the conclusion of the war; in fact, he ordered that there be left behind all those who were guilty of crime or disorderly conduct or were bodily unfit for military duty. After some haggling between Colonel Faucitt and Feronce von Rotenkreuz, the Duke's representative, and additional instructions from London, an agreement was reached January 9, 1776.

This treaty, which in its general aspects followed precedents established in 1755 in a treaty between England and Russia, stipulated the following: (1) The Duke was to furnish four thousand three hundred officers and men, well equipped, and was to keep them in uniforms, accouterments, and arms; he was to receive slightly over seven pounds sterling (thirty crowns banco) for recruiting expenses and a subsidy of nearly twelve thousand pounds per year until the return of his troops and twice that amount per annum for two years thereafter; moreover, he was to be paid a sum equal to the levy money for each soldier killed, incapacitated, or taken prisoner, and, "according to custom," the same amount for every three wounded. (2) The officers and men were to receive the same pay and maintenance as the British (which certainly were better than anything to which they had been accustomed).

The treaty stated further that the King would make restitution for any extraordinary losses due to pestilence, shipwreck, siege, or battle (in conformity with an article of a treaty of 1702); that all pay was to begin two months in advance of the troops' departure from their homeland, the subsidy beginning the day the treaty was signed; and that all travel was to be at the King's expense.

Brunswick sent altogether 5,723 officers and men, of whom only 2,708 returned to Germany. The four thousand infantry and some three hundred dismounted dragoons (the horses were to be furnished in America) delivered in 1776 were by no means the best troops. Their uniforms were so bad that the British Commissariat advanced five thousand pounds for the purchase of new ones in Portsmouth, England. This contingent and the 224 recruits sent in March, 1777, were commanded by Major General Baron von Riedesel,* who with General John Burgoyne and about five thousand men, after two decisive battles, surrendered at Saratoga on October 17, 1777. The respective commanding generals, Burgoyne and Horatio Gates, had agreed in a convention that the captives were to be sent to England; however, the Americans did not live up to the terms of the convention, since the return of the troops to England would have freed an equal number of fresh British garrison troops for service in America.† (Of the fate of the Convention troops Baurmeister has much to say.)

From Brunswick Lord Suffolk's agent went to the court of Hesse-Cassel, where he negotiated with the Minister of State, General Baron Ernst Martin von Schlieffen. The Landgrave, Frederick II, was in a much more favorable position to bargain than was the Duke of Brunswick, for although most of his subjects lived in poverty, partly because of high taxes, he and his court lived in a state of luxury unparalleled in other German principalities. He, too, was related to the King of England by marriage, his first wife having been Princess Mary, a daughter of George II. But when the Landgrave embraced Catholicism, she left him and retired to the court of Hesse-Hanau, where she lived with her son, the hereditary prince of Hesse-Cassel.

The treaty was signed January 15, 1776. It was the sixth time within one hundred years that a sovereign of Hesse-Cassel had entered into a treaty for the sole purpose of hiring out his troops. England had been the best customer. Hessians had fought for George II on the Continent in 1739, 1740, and 1742, and, together with Dutch troops, on British soil in 1746 in the Battle of Culloden, where they helped to bring victory to the Duke of Cumberland.

* Riedesel was only a colonel prior to taking over this command. He was promoted to a generalcy at the request of Colonel Faucitt, who followed instructions from London.

† A British historian considers the violation of the Saratoga convention "a blot on the lustre of the American Revolution."

In the bargaining that preceded the execution of the treaty, Baron von Schlieffen won out on every point, for the Landgrave had money and could wait, while the King of England needed troops and could not wait. Many of the details of this agreement were essentially the same as those of the Brunswick treaty, but the amount per man to be paid to the Landgrave as subsidy was more than twice as high. He was to receive virtually one hundred and ten thousand pounds annually for twelve thousand men until one year after his troops had returned to Cassel. To his credit it must be said that he spent some of this money for the maintenance of charitable institutions and for the promotion of the arts and sciences.

The treaty differed from the one concluded with Brunswick in that it was a treaty of military alliance; in that it did not contain the blood-money clause, that is, the clause relative to payments to be made to the German prince for killed, maimed, and wounded; in that it permitted the Landgrave to have his own paymaster general;* and in that it stipulated that the sick and wounded were to be treated by Hessian physicians and surgeons and in Hessian hospitals.

While negotiations were in progress, Baron von Schlieffen succeeded also in obtaining British recognition of a fourteen-year-old, formerly disallowed claim of forty-two thousand pounds for hospital service in the Seven Years' War.

The troops furnished by Hesse-Cassel were superior to those sent by any other of the German principalities. Among the twelve thousand five hundred supplied in two divisions in 1776 (only twelve thousand were called for in the treaty) were some of the Landgrave's best garrison regiments—all drilled on the Prussian system, well disciplined, and in good physical condition. Before the war ended, Hesse-Cassel sent across the sea 16,992 officers and men, out of a total population of less than three hundred thousand,

---

* This concession, which had to be obtained from London, made it possible for the officers, and perhaps for the Landgrave, to pocket pay for soldiers no longer alive, for payment was made for the number of men at the last annual muster. Some time prior to November, 1779, this practice had become somewhat risky, and the economy measures introduced by the British Commissary General, Brook Watson, in 1782 put an end to this practice altogether.

or approximately one out of every four able-bodied male inhabitants of military age.

More than one third of the virtually seventeen thousand men who left Hesse-Cassel did not return. Some had been killed in action or had died of their wounds or of disease, but by far the greatest number had deserted or else had "escaped" from American prisons to settle in the country and could not be induced to return to their homeland at the close of the war.

The third treaty concluded was with Baron von Malsburg in behalf of Duke William of Hesse-Hanau, who had offered to come to the aid of King George in the summer of 1775. The Duke was the son of Frederick II of Hesse-Cassel by his marriage to Princess Mary, daughter of George II. When in 1785, upon the death of his father, he succeeded to the throne of Hesse-Cassel, he became also the recipient of his father's last annual subsidy.

The treaty, concluded February 5, 1776, contained the shameful blood-money clause, and, as did the treaties with Brunswick and Hesse-Cassel, it restricted the employment of Hesse-Hanau subjects to the North American Continent. The Duke furnished in 1776 one regiment of infantry (668 men) and one company of artillery (120 men). He had counted on obtaining additional subsidy for the artillery, as was customary at the time, but his request was not granted. A total of 2,422 officers and men left their homeland, some 400 of whom were recruits sent in 1781 and 1782. Most of the Hanauers served in Canada. Only about 1,400 returned to their homeland. The Duke's subsidy amounted to some ten thousand pounds per year.

Of the six sovereigns who sent troops across the sea, Duke William and his father were the only ones to lower the taxes of those of their subjects who had a father, a son, or a husband in British pay.

From Hanau, Colonel Faucitt went to the court of Prince Frederick of Waldeck. The entire male population of his domain, excepting university students, had for many years been subject to compulsory military service—not to defend their own little country but rather to defend Holland's colonial possessions. In spite of having two regiments stationed in Holland at the time, Prince

Frederick had written to Lord Suffolk on November 3, 1775, that he would regard it as a favor if the King would accept a regiment of six hundred men in case he should have need for them.

When Faucitt arrived in Waldeck, there were only about two hundred men in uniform in the entire principality. Nevertheless, whether by the recall of troops from Holland or by ruthless conscription, a sufficient number of men were brought together to start negotiations. The treaty was signed on March 17, 1776.

Waldeck sent 1,225 men; one regiment of infantry and some artillery sailed with the second Hesse-Cassel division, arriving at New Rochelle October 23, 1776. They served for several years in the two Floridas, where many died because of the unhealthful climate. Only about 40 per cent saw their fatherland again.

The fifth German principality visited by Colonel Faucitt was Anspach-Bayreuth. The two formerly independent countries, Anspach and Bayreuth, had been united in 1769 under Markgrave Charles Alexander. He had offered two battalions to the King of England in the fall of 1775, and a year later, when it was apparent that the American war would continue for at least another year, this offer was renewed by the Markgrave's London representative. But it was not until January 14, 1777, that Faucitt was instructed to enter into negotiations with the Markgrave's plenipotentiary. The treaty, signed February 1, 1777, called for two regiments of infantry of 570 men each, 101 jägers (chasseurs), and 44 artillery, that is, a total of 1,285 officers and men. The treaty was much the same as those with Hesse-Hanau and Waldeck, except that it did not contain the blood-money clause.

The troops were embarked at Ochsenfurth-on-the-Main on March 9, 1777, and were to go by boat all the way to the Dutch coast. Their quarters were so miserable that many went ashore, and the next day both regiments mutinied. It was not until the Markgrave arrived the following day and threatened that all those who would not willingly embark should forfeit all their earthly possessions, as well as his favor, that peace was restored and the boats could cast off.

A later contingent was to be sent by way of Brandenburg, but Frederick the Great, the Markgrave's uncle, refused to let the troops pass through his territory. In 1791, incidentally, Charles Alexander sold his country to his uncle for a pension; this he spent in England, where he died in 1806.

Anspach-Bayreuth supplied 2,353 mercenaries, including from 152 to 318 recruits per year between 1777 and 1782. Almost half of them did not see their native land again.

The last princeling with whom a treaty was concluded was Prince Frederick August of Anhalt-Zerbst, a brother to Catherine the Great. The little domain over which he ruled had only about twenty thousand inhabitants and, due to famine and war and a purely agricultural economy, was probably the poorest of the poor countries within the German Empire. The Prince had also offered troops to George III, but, it is said, the letter was so clumsily written and the penmanship so poor that the King could not get any sense out of it and therefore did not reply. The Prince then sought the assistance of the courts of Hesse-Hanau and Bruns-wick, and finally of Sir Joseph Yorke, the King's ambassador in Holland. On April 29, 1777, Faucitt was authorized to start ne-gotiations, and late in October the treaty, based on that with Anspach-Bayreuth, was concluded, to become effective when the troops were actually mustered in by Faucitt. The small principal-ity furnished 1,152 men, of whom 420 were sent in April, 1781. All but 168 returned to their misery in the fatherland—an astound-ing fact, indeed.

The treaties entered into with the four last-named powers were not so favorable for the princes as was the agreement with Hesse-Cassel, nor so favorable for the King as that with Bruns-wick.

All the treaties stipulated that the troops when being mus-tered in had to swear allegiance to the King of England, without, however, renouncing their allegiance to their German monarch. Legal jurisdiction was reserved to the latter.

Negotiations were also begun with the Duke of Würtemberg and the Elector of Bavaria, at their own instigation. But since their troops would have had to march either through one or two of the territories of the princes who were already under contract and were filling their quotas by whatever means they could, or through

Prussian territory, which Frederick the Great refused to permit, no treaties resulted.

In 1776, the first year of actual war, almost twenty-two thousand German auxiliary troops (including Hanoverians) entered the British service, and virtually twenty thousand arrived on the North American Continent. This force remained at about twenty thousand throughout the war and nearly equaled the number of British regulars in America.

Because the Hesse-Cassel troops constituted over one half the total number of German mercenaries and perhaps also because English tongues had no difficulty in pronouncing the word Hessian, all the German auxiliaries (Brunswickers, Hanauers, Waldeckers, Anspachers, and Anhalters) have usually been called erroneously by that name.

Reactions on this traffic in soldiers varied. Frederick the Great, the most enlightened ruler within the German Empire, looked with displeasure on the German princes who trafficked in human blood. In a letter to his friend Voltaire (June 18, 1776), he says: "If the Landgrave had come out of my school, he would not have sold his subjects to the English as one sells cattle to be taken to the slaughter house. . . . Such conduct is motivated only by selfish greed. I pity the poor Hessians who will end their lives unhappily and uselessly in America." And to his nephew, the Markgrave of Anspach-Bayreuth, Frederick wrote on October 24, 1777: "I must admit to your Serene Highness that I never think of the present war in America without being struck with the eagerness of some German princes to sacrifice their troops in a quarrel which does not concern them." *

In spite of these apparently sincere expressions of disapproval, it is not unlikely that Frederick refused the passage of mercenaries through his territories because several of the princes who were selling their troops, notably his nephew, had been favoring Austria rather than Prussia in the struggle for political ascendency within the German Empire. Besides, the recruiting of men

* The entire letter, written in French, appears in Kapp's *Der Soldatenhandel deutscher Fürsten*, p. 259.

for service in America interfered with the recruiting for the Prussian army. The King was a friend of the Americans primarily because they were the enemies of his enemies. In this respect he was guided by the same policy that was pursued by France when it entered the war against Great Britain.

Nothing has been found in German journals which might indicate that the idea of soldiers being considered a merchandisable commodity was revolting to the German mind at that time. In 1776 an outstanding periodical, *Schlözers Briefwechsel meist historischen Inhalts,* began to appear in Göttingen, Hanover. It was edited by August Ludwig Schlözer, a professor of political economy at the University of Göttingen. During the seven years of its existence it carried sixty-five contributions relating to America. Among them were many letters from Brunswick, Hessian, and Waldeck officers; but Schlözer's editorial comments do not contain one word which might lead one to infer that he disapproved of the traffic. A professor at a university in Hanover probably did not dare publish anything detrimental to the interests of the country's hereditary ruler, George III. *

In 1783, the year when most of the German troops returned to their homelands, Friedrich Schiller, Germany's greatest dramatic poet of the classical period, protested eloquently against the traffic in his play *Kabale und Liebe* (Act II, Scene 2). The final words in his denunciation are: "At the very city gates they turned and cried, 'God help you, wife and children! Long live our father, the Duke! We shall be back for the *Day of Judgment.*' "

Another poet, Johann Gottfried Seume, left a grim description of his impressment into Hessian service, when as a nineteen-year-old student of theology he passed through a corner of Hesse-Cassel territory. †

* The letters from the Germans serving in America were translated by both W. L. Stone (*Letters by Brunswick and Hessian Officers during the American Revolution,* Albany, 1891) and R. W. Pettengill (*Letters from America, 1776–1779,* Boston, 1924).

† See *Neue Literatur- und Völkerkunde,* ed. by J. W. Archenholtz, II, 362–81, Oct. 1789, and *Mein Leben,* Seume's autobiography.—The present author found among the Von Jungkenn Papers a letter by Seume and two manuscript poems, one written on the sea and the other in camp near Halifax, probably his earliest poetic compositions. See B. A. Uhlendorf, "Some Unpublished Poems of J. G. Seume: A Contribution to the Washington Bicentennial," *The Germanic Review,* VII, 320–29 (1933).

Finally, we have proof that at least one of the negotiating plenipotentiaries, Baron Reinhard von Gemmingen of Anspach-Bayreuth, experienced a feeling of shame at being involved in his sovereign's unsavory business. "It is always very difficult for me to deal in troops," he wrote to the Landgrave's London representative, "but the Landgrave is determined to put his affairs in order at any cost, and to pay off all his debts as well as those of his predecessors. So the benefits that may result from such a treaty of subsidy may far outweigh the hatefulness of this business." *

The treaties, of course, did not become effective until they were ratified by the British Parliament. The German princes had been warned that the opposition party, as was inevitable in a constitutional monarchy, would not mince words in attacking the treaties.

The treaties with Brunswick, Hesse-Cassel, and Hesse-Hanau were debated in the House of Commons on February 29, 1776, and in the House of Lords on March 5th. Lord North, the King's first minister, asserted in Commons that the emergency made the hiring of foreign troops necessary; that the German soldiers cost less than English recruits; that on the present occasion they cost less than they had cost at any previous time; and that the combined British and German forces would be able to subdue the colonies perhaps without further bloodshed.

Members of the opposition party maintained that the troops cost about half again as much as would have to be paid for Englishmen; that in view of the fact that one hundred and fifty thousand Germans are already settled in North America, desertion and perhaps mutiny would be inevitable; that it was unthinkable to hire German slaves to subdue the sons of Englishmen and of freedom; and that the offensive-defensive alliance concluded with the Landgrave of Hesse-Cassel might embroil all Europe in a costly war.

It is of interest to note that Lord Suffolk, in defending the treaties for which he was responsible, stated quite bluntly that the section of the Hesse-Cassel treaty relative to the alliance was merely a lot of pompous words. In the end, the Ministry won in the House of Commons by a vote of 242 to 88.

* Translated from Kapp, *Der Soldatenhandel*, pp. 108-109.

In the House of Lords the Duke of Richmond moved that a humble address be presented to the King, praying that he would be graciously pleased to countermand the marching order for the foreign troops and give directions for the immediate suspension of hostilities in America. The address submitted to the Lords for their approval called attention to the possibility that France, Spain, and Prussia, as well as other powers, might come to the aid of the Americans, and, finally, it asserted that never before had Great Britain entered into a treaty so expensive, so unilateral, so dishonorable, and so dangerous in its consequences.

After a lengthy debate it came to a vote, which supported the Ministry 100 to 32.*

American reactions to the hiring of German soldiers by Great Britain are perhaps best summarized by quoting the passage from the Declaration of Independence in which the King is assailed for "transporting large armies of foreign mercenaries to complete the works of death, desolation, and tyranny already begun with circumstances of cruelty and perfidy scarcely paralleled in the most barbarous ages, and totally unworthy the head of a civilized nation."

Since Hesse-Cassel furnished more than half of the total number of German auxiliaries, and since they participated in every major engagement after their arrival on American soil, a few details concerning these troops may be helpful.

The rank and file of these troops, many of whom had seen service in the Seven Years' War, were regulars, although some, especially in the later years of the war, were conscripted or secured by press gangs. The officers were career soldiers, most of whom had taken part in one or more campaigns. Many were of the lesser nobility, probably younger sons of the landed gentry; others had been or were subsequently elevated to the nobility for meritorious service.

From the letters and diaries in the Von Jungkenn Papers and from other manuscript as well as printed sources, we may judge that most of the Hessian officers had received a fairly good educa-

* Parliamentary Register, 1st series, III, 341–60, and V, 174–216.

tion. Since about half of them were of the nobility, it may be assumed that they had benefited from educational advantages not enjoyed by most people at that time. Some had received instruction from Jacob Mauvillon at the Collegium Carolinum at Cassel. Mauvillon was a well known writer on military science and economic theory. Many had some knowledge of Latin and a conversational familiarity with French, but only a few knew English. Lack of familiarity with the English language must have been a decided handicap and a source of embarrassment to the Hessians and other auxiliaries during the early years of the war.

The Hesse-Cassel troops were the only auxiliaries who by agreement were to be employed as a unit under their own commanding general * and to be separated only when the necessities of war so demanded. The Landgrave sent fifteen regiments of light infantry to America. Each regiment consisted of six hundred and fifty officers and men and was divided into five companies. While in service on the European Continent, a regiment was made up of two battalions, one of fusiliers and one of musketeers, the names indicating the types of firearms they carried. Distributed among the two battalions were about one hundred and twenty grenadiers. Heeding a British request that the British military system be adopted insofar as feasible, the grenadiers were drawn from the regiments, and, together with two companies taken from the Landgrave's bodyguard, were organized into four battalions, each five hundred and twenty-four officers and men. Sometimes, when the infantry regiments were weak due to losses, illness, or desertion, they, too, were referred to as battalions, which in fact they were.

The regiments and battalions were named after their chiefs, either one of the princes or the colonel in charge, except that one regiment was called Leib (bodyguard) Regiment. When a colonel was transferred, or on the death of a colonel, the name of his command was changed to that of the new chief. During periods when

* The three successive commanding generals were Lieutenant General Leopold Philipp von Heister, Lieutenant General Wilhelm von Knyphausen, and Lieutenant General Baron Friedrich Wilhelm von Lossberg. Von Heister was recalled because he could not get along with General Howe, and von Knyphausen was replaced by von Heister after active hostilities had ceased.

a regiment or battalion had no colonel or lieutenant colonel at its head, the unit in question was called "vacant," sometimes followed by the last commander's name.

In addition to infantry and grenadiers, there was also a corps of jägers. The name *Jäger* indicates that the men were recruited from among the hunters, gamewardens, and foresters. The English called them "chasseurs," and sometimes the Germans did too. They were light troops, both foot and horse, and carried rifles. During several campaigns in America some hundred were mounted. One company arrived with Lieutenant General von Heister in August, 1776, and another with Lieutenant General von Knyphausen in October of the same year. Since they were found to be especially effective against American riflemen, a request for more jägers was sent to London immediately after the Battle of Long Island, and in December, 1776, the number of jägers to be furnished by the Landgrave was raised by a separate treaty from two hundred and sixty to one thousand and sixty-seven, provided, however, that "experienced chasseurs, all well-trained marksmen" could be obtained. It is doubtful that the total number of effective jägers in America ever exceeded seven hundred, and not all these were Hessians.

The Jäger Corps, which was organized in the summer of 1777 and put under the command of Colonel Ludwig Johann Adolph von Wurmb of the Hesse-Cassel forces, included some Hesse-Hanau and Anspach jägers. The jägers usually operated as detachments rather than a corps. These detachments were employed to great advantage in reconnoitering and patrol duties and in guarding foraging parties and headquarters. During several campaigns, jäger detachments served as adjuncts to infantry regiments. When a large body of British and auxiliary troops marched in column formation, the jägers either led the van or flanked both sides of the column; when the troops were deployed to give battle, the jägers usually formed the flanks; and when they were pursued by the enemy, the jägers covered the retreat. During siege operations, they occupied the front trenches, making their own approaches, like sappers and miners. Because of their accurate fire and their valor, they were greatly feared by the Americans.

Among the Cassel troops were also three companies of artillery, numbering together five hundred and eighty-eight men. Also, each regiment and battalion and each jäger company had two fieldpieces as supporting weapons. These proved so effective that General Guy Carleton in July, 1782, ordered all British regiments to be equipped with two light cannon and a complement of artillerymen.

The proportion of officers to men was quite normal when compared with present-day armies, but perhaps slightly high for the time. A regiment of infantry, for example, had twenty-one commissioned officers, sixty noncommissioned officers, five noncombatant officers, and, in addition, twenty-two musicians.

The Hesse-Cassel infantry regiments were organized into four brigades, and the grenadier battalions into one brigade. The corps had its own general staff and its own hospital and supply train. The officers were allowed as many servant men as they could afford, and some had their wives with them, as did also some rank and file. For example, with the first contingent of Brunswickers, consisting of 2,282 men, there were 77 soldiers' wives, and with 1,164 Anhalt-Zerbst troops, 34. The soldiers' wives usually worked as washerwomen.*

The several services—infantry, grenadiers, dragoons, jägers, and artillery—had distinctive uniforms and arms. Like all eighteenth-century uniforms, they were very colorful but definitely not suited to field duty, especially when it involved, as it did in America, long marches in rough terrain and under a hot sun, and maneuvering and fighting in woods and fenced-in fields.

The infantry wore tricornered hats, some with pom-poms at the corners; the grenadiers, high mitre-shaped brass or white-metal caps, with scrolls and heraldic emblems in front; the dragoons, large, high, rimless hats adorned with horse-hair or feather plumes; and the jägers, cocked hats with a twig of oak leaves. The coats were long and had turned-back skirts; the vests were also

---

* Baroness von Riedesel, in *Die Berufs-Reise nach Amerika*, 2nd ed., Berlin, 1801, states that through the carelessness of officers' wives the enemy frequently received advance information of troop movements.

long and sometimes belted; and the breeches were tight and fitted into high gaiters or boots.

The color of the coats (except that of the jäger coats) was a medium blue; but the breeches and vests of the various units or corps, and the lapels, cuffs, and collars, as well as the facings and trim, were of distinguishing colors. For example, the Landgraf Regiment wore light yellow breeches and vests, and their coats had facings and collars of scarlet, trimmed in gold; the Erb Prinz Regiment, white breeches and vests, their coats having facings and cuffs of pink, trimmed in silver; the Regiment von Knyphausen, straw-colored breeches and vests, the facings and cuffs of their coats being of black velvet, trimmed in gold; the Jäger Corps, green vests trimmed in gold, and green coats with crimson collars, cuffs, and facings (their winter breeches were green, their summer breeches, white); and the Engineer Corps, straw-colored breeches and vests and blue coats with gold braid and with black facings, collars, and cuffs.*

The uniforms of the commissioned officers were even more colorful. Aside from colored, gold, or silver trim and additional lacings, they included sashes of various colors, worn from the right shoulder to the left side, and many of the higher officers, when in dress uniform, wore gorgets, that is, small ornamental plates suspended from chains around the neck. Their footwear consisted of high riding boots, usually reaching well above the knee in front.

The arms of the several services naturally differed also. Most of the foot troops carried muskets, although some regiments carried fusils. The muskets were heavy flintlock firearms, in which a slow-match (punk) served to ignite the powder; the fusils were lighter than muskets and were of the flintlock variety. In addition, the foot troops were fitted out with short-swords and bayonets. The mounted troops—those serving in America were all dragoons, mounting heavy horses—carried short carbines, a pair of pistols, and long, heavy swords. The jägers were equipped with long rifles and long bayonets. The cartouche boxes and powder pouches

---

* *Hochfürstlich Hessen-Casselischer Staats- und Adress-Calender auf das Jahr Christi 1779,* Cassel [1779].

were attached to belts slung from the left shoulder to the right hip, and the firearms, to slings crossing the belts.

As was customary at the time, the soldiers' hair was heavily larded and strewn with white powder. It was either tied or braided and was worn either hanging down or turned up, but within any one unit always in the same manner.

It is obvious that soldiers so uniformed and with such accouterments were not the most effective soldiers, but in general they differed very little from the British, except in the colors of their coats. Other German auxiliaries were fitted out much the same as were the Hessians. Only the two hundred Brunswick dragoons who served under Baron von Riedesel in Canada differed from most of the German troops in that their uniforms, accouterments, and arms were extraordinarily ill-suited to the type of warfare being waged in America, especially while the dragoons were still serving as foot soldiers, that is, before they had had an opportunity to procure horses from American farms. A Brunswick dragoon's outfit included high, heavy riding boots with large spurs, thick leather breeches, long gauntlets, a large hat with a thick tuft of feathers, a clumsy sabretache, a huge saber, and a heavy carbine.

Neither the German soldiers nor their officers probably knew much about the causes of the war, and whatever they did know was very likely colored by British views. To them the Americans were rebels, who refused obedience to their lawful king. Now that the Germans had sworn allegiance to this same king, they were bound to fight for him against the benighted rebels. The sense of duty instilled in them since childhood and their respect for authority made them good soldiers, and as well-trained and well-disciplined soldiers, they fought for a cause in which they had no concern.

As we know, Hesse-Cassel troops took part in every major engagement of the War after their arrival in America. For instance, ten regiments and battalions (about six thousand men) participated in the attack on Fort Washington, which surrendered to the German commander in chief and was in his honor renamed

Fort Knyphausen; nine took part in the Battles of Long Island and Brandywine; seven were at White Plains; six at Newport and Charleston; and five at Springfield. Jäger detachments participated in all the engagements except some minor skirmishes in the South.

Two Hessian colonels who had given proof of military leadership and personal valor in the battles on Long Island and New York Island were fatally wounded before the end of the campaign of 1777. Colonel Johann Gottlieb Rall lived not much more than a month after the attack on Fort Washington, during which he had particularly distinguished himself. While in command of a brigade of Hessians quartered in a cordon extending from Bordentown through Princeton to Trenton, his post was attacked by General Washington in the early morning hours of the 26th of December, 1776. Although Rall had received intelligence which indicated the possibility of an attack, he was so disdainful of the military abilities of the Americans that he did not take the necessary precautions. He was mortally wounded, and a large portion of his brigade taken prisoners. The American victory came at a time when, following a series of defeats and reverses, Washington's army was dwindling rapidly. This first victory was needed to instill confidence in his troops and hope in the hearts of the patriots.

While the British-Hessian army was stationed in and about Philadelphia, ready to retire into winter quarters, General Howe sent Colonel von Donop to take Fort Mercer at Red Bank. The Colonel, then only thirty-seven years old, had fought with great gallantry on Long Island. Before starting out with his Hessian units, he is said to have exclaimed that the fort would either soon be called Fort Donop, or he would have fallen. He did fall, severely wounded by a musket ball, and the fort remained in American possession. He died three days later in the presence of a French engineer, Duplessis du Mauduit. Just before the end came, he is said to have uttered in French: "This is an early end to a fine career, but I die the victim of my ambition and of the avarice of my sovereign." *

* François Jean Marquis de Chastellux, *Travels in North-America in the Years 1780, 1781, and 1782. . . .* Translated from the French, London, 1787, I, 266. Chastellux was acquainted with Mauduit and quotes him in reporting Donop's death.

The Hessians, as will be seen from the accounts of Major Baurmeister, certainly were not the ogres many schoolbooks paint them to be. In the beginning of the war they were feared by the civilian population—patriot propaganda had not been in vain—but later on they were generally better liked and more civilly treated than were the British. When prisoners of war, the Hessian officers and even the common soldiers were frequently shown favors not bestowed upon their British comrades—chiefly to cause them to desert after being exchanged.

Legends of the Hessians being guilty of a great deal of plundering have survived to this day, even in history books. Of course, the common soldier, some noncommissioned officers, and even some subaltern commissioned officers appropriated many valuables on excursions into enemy-held territory; but this type of looting was then generally considered to be a more or less legitimate way for the soldier to reward himself for his services. The Hessians, however, looted no more than did the British—or the patriots, when Tory property was concerned.

In the letters and diaries which follow there occur repeated remarks about pillaging, marauding, and plundering—always uttered in condemnation of the offense. There are also statements about rightfully earned booty and allotment of spoils. The words pillaging, marauding, and plundering are synonymous, as are also the words booty and spoils; but there is a decided difference between the first group of three words and the second group of two, particularly as they were used in the eighteenth century and earlier.

The *Oxford English Dictionary* and *Grimms Wörterbuch* are substantially in agreement in defining the word booty (*Beute*) as collective spoils, which are distributed. For example, when an enemy ship with a valuable cargo was seized, everyone who took part in the capture shared in the returns from the sale of her cargo (see letter dated September 2, 1776), and when Charleston, South Carolina, surrendered in May, 1780, the troops participating in the siege expected to share in the booty, that is, the confiscated property.

The two dictionaries also agree that the word plunder (*Plunder*) signified at that time the appropriation of valuables by forceful means and in a systematic manner. Both the British and Hessian troops were frequently warned that anyone found guilty of plundering would be severely punished. Baurmeister reports that General Howe on one occasion (August 27, 1777) ordered one soldier guilty of this offense to be hanged and six others to be flogged mercilessly, and that General von Knyphausen caused ten men of one brigade to run the gantlet for some "excesses." But Howe in his orders of the day praised the commanders of one of the Hessian regiments and of the Jäger Corps for observing the "best discipline." On another occasion Baurmeister says that plundering such as was done on a foraging expedition of Lord Cornwallis's from Philadelphia across the Schuylkill had done infinitely more to maintain the rebellion than to smother it. Finally, in his account of the withdrawal of the combined British-Hessian forces from Philadelphia through New Jersey, he says the following: "There was much plundering, which disturbed General Clinton. There was much new evidence of it in Jersey. It has made the country people all the more embittered rebels. There was no pillaging and plundering on the part of the Hessians, but it is my duty to report to your Lordship that we had many deserters." It is obvious that plundering could not be entirely prevented in spite of cruel punishment.

Washington on one occasion, according to Baurmeister, ordered the return of loot to Staten Island, whence it had been taken during an excursion from New Jersey. (See letter of March 26, 1780.)

The lives of the German officers and soldiers who returned to their native land were enriched by many new experiences. They had endured the hardships of two long ocean voyages, during which at least some of them must have received indelible impressions of the grandeur of the sea and the sky above; they had experienced life in a young, robust country; some Waldeck troops, on their way to West Florida, had even spent a few days on Jamaica, owing to their ships having been scattered by a storm. On their return to the fatherland they were received amid demonstrations of joy, like heroes returning from a victorious campaign.*

The experience gained during the war in America proved to be valuable during the French campaigns, 1792–1794. We are told by a writer on military history, a Prussian general, that of all the nationalities that went to war against France, the Hesse-Cassel troops were the best disciplined and that they excelled all others by their ready acceptance of hardships and their proclivity for war.†

One of the Hessian officers frequently lauded by Baurmeister for his daring exploits and military strategies, Captain Johann Ewald of the Jäger Corps, later a lieutenant general in the service of Denmark, drew upon his American experiences in several publications, of which the most important is *Belehrungen über den Krieg, besonders über den kleinen Krieg*, published in 1798, 1800, and 1803. The three volumes, now extremely rare, are an important source for the military history of the Revolution. Among the Von Jungkenn Papers is also a short unpublished treatise by Ewald on the subject of what an officer needs to know of the use of mounted troops in the field.

The writer of the letters and diaries presented here, Carl Leopold (later von) Baurmeister, was born at Rinteln, in Hanover, May 5, 1734, the son of Colonel Friedrich Andreas Baurmeister and Louise Sibylle, née von Unger. He entered the military service in an Anhalt regiment and became an ensign in 1756, a lieutenant and an adjutant to the Prince of Anhalt in 1758, and a staff captain in 1762. It is very likely that he saw service with this regiment during the Seven Years' War, since but few standing regiments escaped service in one campaign or another.

About this time he seems to have entered the service of Frederick II, the Landgrave of Hesse-Cassel. He was first attached

---

* The author has in his possession a small leaflet consisting of a title page plus three pages containing a twelve-stanza poem, which was recited, and perhaps also composed, by a Baron von Reizenstein, to celebrate the entry of the returning Bayreuth troops into the small town of Culmbach.

† See Georg Wilhelm, Freiherr von Valentini, *Erinnerungen eines alten preussischen Offiziers aus den Feldzügen von 1792, 1793, und 1794, in Frankreich und am Rhein*, Glogau, 1833, pp. 17–19.

to the Prinz Carl Regiment, and then to the Regiment von Mirbach, in which he became a captain in February, 1776, almost to the day when his sovereign signed the treaty of friendship and mutual aid with George III. Exactly one year later he was commissioned a major in the same regiment, and in 1782 he was transferred to the Jung von Lossberg Regiment, also as a major.

Throughout his service in America he was a general staff officer, serving as first adjutant to all three Hessian commanders in chief, von Heister, von Knyphausen, and von Lossberg, and for some time between 1779 and 1782 as aide-de-camp to Sir Henry Clinton. Only once did he command a body of troops, namely at Edge Hill, during the Philadelphia campaign, when von Knyphausen asked him to take charge of von Minnigerode's Grenadier Battalion. In 1783 he was authorized by Generals von Lossberg and Carleton to negotiate in person with Congress for the return of German prisoners and deserters who had settled in the Philadelphia area or were employed in an iron mill at Mount Hope, New Jersey.

Two years after his return to Cassel, probably partly as compensation for his services in America, Baurmeister was elevated to the nobility and commissioned a lieutenant colonel. He participated in the campaigns in France and on the Rhine and was wounded near Hondschoote (Holland) in August, 1793, a short time after he had been promoted to the colonelcy of the Erb Prinz Regiment. The same year he commanded the rear guard of the Hessian corps on its retreat from Holland to Westphalia. In 1793 von Baurmeister received the rank of major general and was further honored by being appointed to the most important position within the diplomatic service, that of resident minister to London. He died in London, April 8, 1803, at the age of 68. His wife, née Friederike Diefenbach, outlived him by sixteen years.

Obituary notices appeared in the *Gentleman's Magazine, European Magazine, Cobbett's Weekly Political Register,* and *Annual Register,* all reporting his age as 63 instead of 68. "[April] 8th. At his house, in Jermyn-street, in his 63rd year, general de Baurmeister, resident minister from the court of Hesse-Cassel. His remains were deposited in the Savoy chapel. In the death of this distinguished personage, the Landgrave of Hesse-Cassel has lost an able general and a faithful minister. His excellency's military career has shown itself most conspicuously in the German, American, and the late continental wars; and he bore to his grave the honourable wounds he received in those contests. His services were principally with his Britannic majesty's troops. His suavity and mildness of manners endeared him particularly to their majesties and the royal family, to most of the nobility, and to all those who had the honour of his acquaintance. His excellency's illness was long and painful; during which time, the attention of his excellency's secretary, N. G. Lewis, esq. and a number of friends, was unremitted; which must afford much consolation to his relatives abroad." ("Chronicle" of *Annual Register*, 1803, XLV, 504.)

When the present editor, in collaboration with the late Edna Vosper, published an English translation of the Baurmeister letters and journals covering the Philadelphia campaign, Mr. Clifford Lewis, Jr., of Philadelphia, contributed the following interesting note:

"The house of Ellis Lewis, located on the westerly side of Second Street between Walnut and Spruce, was occupied by Major Baurmeister as his headquarters during the period covered by his letters of 1777–1778 (the old number was 140; the new number, 244). This house was built in 1693 by Edward Shippen, first mayor of Philadelphia under the Charter of 1701. Generally known as 'Great House,' or 'Governor's House,' it was occupied from time to time by various executives of the Province. The following is quoted from Leach's *Old Philadelphia Families:* 'At the time of the occupation of the city by the British, 1777–78, Ellis Lewis then being deceased, the widow and children were compelled to give quarters to Major Baurmeister, a Hessian officer. According to one authority, Lord Cornwallis was located there for a time, also. A son of General Knyphausen, a Lieutenant, though only thirteen years of age, came frequently to the house, and, taking off his sword, would play with the widow's son, young David Lewis, then twelve years old, and the younger children.'

"A memoir of David Lewis (1766–1840) by his son David (1800–1895) mentions the fact that 'the Hessian Major was an

agreeable gentleman and propitiated his unwilling hosts by little
kind presents, some of which still remain in the family.' A small
plain gold pin, given by Major Baurmeister to young David Lewis,
has passed down to his descendants. The tradition is that the gift
of the pin followed a reconciliation between the boys after young
David (a Quaker) had declined to salute the young lieutenant
[von Knyphausen]. The pattern of the pin is revealed in the por-
trait of David Lewis painted by Rembrandt Peale *circa* 1830. The
pin itself is now in the possession of the writer, great-great-grand-
son of David Lewis, and is framed with an old faded inscription
in the handwriting of David Lewis (1800–1895), son of 'young
David,' reading as follows: 'Given by Major Baurmeister of Hessian Army to D. Lewis in 1777.' "

Baurmeister's letters and journals constitute a nearly consecu-
tive account of American events, not only military, but social and
economic as well. They are unusual, in comparison with almost
all other personal accounts of the Revolutionary War, in that they
contain a great deal of information about the movements and
activities of the naval forces, especially in the West Indies. It was
there that the Americans obtained a large portion of the manufactured wares for which they were dependent on Europe. Even
unscrupulous British merchants supplied British manufactured
products to the West Indies, particularly the Dutch island of St.
Eustatius, for transshipment to American ports. Baurmeister, as
Adjutant General, was in a good position to collect the news which
he reports, for the admirals of the fleet and the commanding generals were naturally under orders to keep each other informed of
their plans and activities.

How he chronicled the events of the Revolution, which as
general staff officer and for some time one of Clinton's aides he
was in an enviable position to do; how he criticized British laxity
and negligence and the interrelations of British commerce and
warfare; how he depicted the social and economic conditions in
America; what he had to say about sectional jealousies, about
Washington and his fellow officers, about Congress, the disunity
between Congress and Washington, and about American suspi-

cions of French sincerity; how he tried to differentiate between truth and mere hearsay and propaganda; how he apologized when he let his sentiments influence his reports; how he interceded with von Jungkenn in behalf of his fellow officers, who had to pay dearly for their care and that of their servant men during long sieges of illness—all this must be read in Baurmeister's own words.

At the time his accounts begin (summer of 1776), Howe's army coming from Boston by way of Halifax had just disembarked on undefended Staten Island and was waiting for reinforcements. These arrived with the fleet of his brother Admiral Lord Howe, among them the first division of Hesse-Cassel troops and Major Baurmeister. Prior to this time, hostilities had been confined to some activities around Boston and in regions near the present Canadian border, as well as an attempt against Charleston, South Carolina.

British troops stationed in Boston under the command of General Thomas Gage had sustained considerable losses at nearby Concord and Lexington (April 19, 1775), but they had driven the Americans from entrenchments on Breed's Hill and Bunker Hill, with heavy casualties on both sides (June 17, 1775). Washington, who had arrived before Boston on July 2nd, eventually managed to mount cannon on a peninsula facing the city, and General William Howe, who had succeeded Gage, decided that it was time to withdraw his soldiers and ships from Boston (March 7, 1776).

In the meantime some New England forces had taken Fort Ticonderoga and Crown Point (May 10 and 11, 1775), and an expedition sent by Washington had forced the British garrison of Fort St. Johns to surrender (November 2, 1775). Other patriot forces had brought about the capitulation of Montreal (November 13, 1775). But General Guy Carleton, the commander of the British forces in Canada, foiled an attempt against Quebec (December 31) and forced the withdrawal of American troops from Montreal. Thus, while the campaign in the north was a failure, it temporarily prevented the enemy from invading the colonies by way of the Hudson River.

While still in Boston, Howe had dispatched Sir Henry Clinton and a naval squadron to reduce Charleston, South Carolina. Before Clinton returned from this fruitless expedition to rejoin the main body of Howe's forces, the thirteen colonies had declared their independence, and the war was about to begin in earnest.

1776

: | :

Right Honorable Lord,
Gracious High and Mighty Colonel:

Although I am convinced that your Lordship receives news of our experiences from the best of sources, I am anxious not to be the last to inform you of the fate of the corps, which, after departing from St. Helen's on the Isle of Wight at six o'clock in the evening of the 6th of May, has now safely reached land.

Without burdening your Lordship with detail, I shall simply tell what distinguished one day from another, beginning with the 12th of August, when the first division assembled at Sandy Hook. After a long voyage the entire division encamped on Staten Island on the 14th and 15th of August.

From the 22nd to the 30th of May constant storms endangered the passage of the greater part of the first division. Owing, however, to the excellent preparations that had been made in England, we could not find fault either with the adequacy of the ships or with the quality and quantity of the provisions. The first fleet, carrying the greater part of the first division, consisted of ninety-

31

two sail. Twenty-six more sail joined it at Sandy Hook, completing the division. Only 132 men out of the entire division had to be sent to the hospital established on Staten Island—most of them sick with scurvy and a rash. Fifteen men died on the voyage, among them an ensign of von Donop's Regiment, von Stoedell, who was buried at sea near Halifax. Lieutenant Kleinschmidt accidentally shot and killed Count zur Lippe [1] of the Leib Regiment on the deck of the *Unanimity* on the 4th of June. I shall say no more of this unfortunate occurrence. The fleet celebrated the birthday of the King of England. The seven men-of-war and the frigates acting as convoy fired a salute. There was also music and much cheering on all the ships and unlimited quantities of punch. Eleven hundred English Foot Guards under Brigadier General Mathew and Colonel Osborn joined Lieutenant General von Heister's command at Portsmouth. The Colonel has been made Hessian muster commissary.

General Howe, after his enforced departure from Boston, sailed with his army to Halifax, where he disembarked all the sick and the women, about thirteen hundred in all, and from there without loss of time to Staten Island, which lies opposite New York. His brother, Admiral Howe, left Portsmouth on the 10th of May and arrived at Halifax on the 2nd of July, where the first division was to rendezvous. But when he failed to find General Howe, he issued new orders directing the fleet to rendezvous at Staten Island, too. This resulted in a loss of three weeks' time. We arrived at Halifax on the 7th of July, but had to sail on without being able to provide ourselves with fresh water. We had the good fortune, however, to find Major General Stirn there with fourteen transports that had been separated from the fleet off Newfoundland during a fog lasting eight days. The *Malaga* transport, carrying Captain Waldenberg of the Leib Regiment, had the good luck, after losing the fleet on the 1st of June, to capture an American provision ship and take her into Halifax harbor. Her cargo was destined for Martinique to be exchanged for gunpowder.

---

[1] Count zur Lippe was killed by Kleinschmidt in a duel. Max von Eelking, *Die deutschen Hülfstruppen im nordamerikanischen Befreiungkrieg*, Hannover, 1863, I, 26.

Captain Waldenberg received twelve thousand Reichsthalers for himself and his company. A part of the proceeds of the cargo was given to Governor Arbuthnot of Halifax [2] on the King's account, and the rest to Commodore Hotham, the commander of our fleet.

We found the English troops which had been driven out [3] encamped on Staten Island on nine different heights: (1) at Amboy Ferry, Lieutenant General Clinton with two brigades and half of an artillery brigade; (2) between Amboy Ferry and the Old Blazing Star,[4] Brigadier General Leslie with three brigades and half of an artillery brigade; (3) at the Old Blazing Star, Brigadier General Farrington [5] with two brigades and two 12-pounders and also half a troop of light dragoons to carry dispatches; (4) at the New Blazing Star,[6] Brigadier Generals Smith, Robertson, and Agnew with three brigades, one and a half artillery brigades, and the other half of the troop of light dragoons; (5) at Musgrower's Lein,[7] Lieutenant General Percy and Brigadier General Erskine with two brigades and four 6-pounders and one officer and twenty-five light dragoons; (6) at the point opposite Elizabethtown Ferry, Major General Grant with one brigade, two light guns, and fifteen dragoons; (7) at the Morning Star,[8] Lieutenant General Cornwallis with two and a half brigades, six 12-pounders, four howitzers, and fifteen dragoons; (8) at Decker's Ferry,[9] Major General William James with the 37th and 52nd Regiments and two light guns; (9) to the right of Decker's Ferry, in a country house close to the shore opposite New Jersey, Major General Vaughan with six grenadier battalions, the 46th Regiment, the rest of the disembarked artillery, the rest of the light dragoons, and General Howe's headquarters.

[2] Rear Admiral Marriot Arbuthnot was lieutenant governor of Nova Scotia, 1776–1778.

[3] I.e., out of Boston.

[4] The Old Blazing Star, now Rossville.

[5] Sir Anthony Farrington was a captain of artillery in 1776. No other Farrington, of superior rank, could be identified.

[6] The New Blazing Star, on Long Neck, in modern Linoleumville.

[7] Not identified; Musgrave's Lane?

[8] Morning Star, the country seat of Henry Holland, on the northern side of the island.

[9] Decker's Ferry, now Port Richmond.

Lieutenant Colonel Dalrymple was in command of the trenches thrown up on Staten Island, which is fifteen English miles long and five wide. The inhabitants are loyalists and have furnished five hundred militia. Richmond Town is the parish seat of the island, which, like Long Island, is under the government of New York. The English hospital was still on shipboard. Thirty-eight warships and 439 transports lay in the New York channel. Forty-two of the latter are now preparing to sail to Ireland for fresh provisions.

The situation of the English troops is none too good. The battalions are not full strength; they fly before the riflemen, and their maintenance is not especially good. But much can be expected of their generals, from the highest to the lowest. Encouraged by the reinforcement of the national as well as the auxiliary forces, they are determined to undertake anything. Hence we shall probably be able to put down the rebellion. The English warships have accomplished nothing as yet. New York is well fortified, and Long Island appeared to be so strongly fortified and entrenched that it should have been much more formidable than will be seen in this narrative. Neither a frigate, nor a fireship, nor any other vessel could be seen around New York, in spite of the fact that two British frigates, the *Rose* and the *Phoenix*, were stationed, or rather bottled up, in the Hudson River above New York, twenty-four miles from Decker's Ferry, and did not dare to pass the many batteries thrown up before New York and join the fleet.

However, at three o'clock in the morning of the 18th of August the two frigates, favored by fog, set sail and stood 382 shots, which they answered with a continuous fire. The two frigates had only one sailor killed and five wounded, while the ships themselves suffered no damage at all. The Americans, on the other hand, had thirty-five men wounded, nine killed, and five guns dismounted. On the same day an engineer attempted to swim to our shore at Decker's Ferry. Although Lieutenant General Cornwallis sent a boat to the man's assistance, the man perished with all his papers. We learned that his name was Freudenberg [10]

[10] Cf. Brigadier General Wm. Heath's letter to George Washington, Aug. 24, 1776: ". . . On the 21st Instant the Body of a man was taken up at Burditt's

and that the American General Washington was greatly pleased when he drowned.

On the 23rd of August all the English troops, the three Hessian grenadier battalions, and the jägers under Colonel von Donop embarked. The brigade of Major General Stirn, who made his headquarters in Richmond Town, occupied the nine posts vacated by the English troops. The disloyal inhabitants of Staten Island had their arms taken from them, and the militia were assigned stations in case of an attack from New Jersey on the nine posts. General von Heister stayed on the far side of Staten Island with the remaining regiments under Major General von Mirbach. General Howe went on board the warship *Preston,* sixty guns, to join his brother, Admiral Howe.

At ten o'clock in the morning of the 24th a landing was effected on Long Island. Each battalion had eight or nine transports, the frigates keeping to the outside of them. The Scottish Highlanders, landing without opposition, were the first. This regiment and the English grenadiers were under the command of Brigadier General Erskine. They were followed by the Hessian grenadiers and the jägers under Colonel von Donop, and, lastly, by the English infantry and General Howe and his staff. Barns, grain stacks, and the lighthouses built here and there were immediately set on fire.[11]

Ferry, The Commanding officer there not being able to find any Civil Authority appointed a Court of Enquiry to consider the Cause of his Death, who reported the Enclosed [missing]. The Body was afterwards Buried, and the money and Effects are in the Hands of Col: Ward. It since appears that Hardenbrook (for that was his Name) was by Occupation a Carpenter belonging to the City of New York, who had been heretofore Employed by Dunmore and Tryon and for whom he retained an Affection,-That upon the Day of the Ships falling down the River he attempted to get on Board of them But found a Watery Grave, the reward of such unrighteousness, I am told that he has a Brother in the City who is a Staunch friend to American Liberty, and who I suppose is as yet Unacquainted with the Fate of his Brother. . . ." (Washington MSS, Library of Congress.) One of the nearly 1,000 loyalists who signed an address to Admiral and General Howe, dated New York, Oct. 16, 1776, is John Hardenbrook. (See New York City Mercantile Library Association, *New York City during the American Revolution,* New York, 1861, p. 127 and note.)

[11] I.e., by the Americans. They ordered cattle to be removed, mills dismantled, and all grain and hay destroyed. Cf. Greene to Washington, Aug. 15, 1776, and Resolutions of the New York Convention, Aug. 24, 1776. (Washington MSS, Library of Congress.)

General Howe took quarters at Gravesend, one English mile from the place of debarkation, and there the entire English infantry encamped without tents. All the grenadiers, the jägers, the Scottish Highlanders,[12] and the light dragoons, however, moved further inland, through New Utrecht to Flatbush. There, at six o'clock in the evening, the Hessian jägers met for the first time the much-feared riflemen, who were setting fire to five of the loyalists' houses. Nine riflemen and one Hessian jäger were killed. Lieutenant General Cornwallis, though he had been unable to induce General Howe to march the troops further, gave orders to attack at sunrise on the 25th some posts occupied by five hundred men. The enemy deserted them without offering resistance, for they had no guns, and the two light pieces, which accompany the jägers wherever they go, sufficed to chase away this lot of rabble which parades under the name of riflemen. They withdrew to the woods which separate the Flatbush country from Natt Island[13] or the Brooklyn country.

These woods, three English miles long and one English mile wide, are thickly grown with large trees and are full of gullies and ravines, which make it impossible for even three men to walk abreast, not to mention a platoon. Hence we were compelled to follow the example of the English, that is, to form in columns, two men abreast and rather far apart, as if lined up for someone to run the gantlet.

It was decided that at four o'clock in the morning of the 27th we should fall upon the enemy force entrenched in these woods. General Clinton was to command our left, Lieutenant General Cornwallis our right, and Lieutenant General von Heister the center. At retreat on the 26th the English infantry left its encampment at New Utrecht and set out to penetrate the left of the woods. They took only their fieldpieces along and did not break camp.

12 The Scottish Highlanders is the 71st (Highland) Regiment of Foot.

13 Perhaps a misreading by Baurmeister's amanuensis of a poorly written "Nassau Island" (an old name for Long Island), or possibly a confusion with Nutten Island, now Governor's Island. The word is clearly and unmistakably written in Roman script.

At the same time, General Cornwallis also advanced to the edge of the woods, while the Hessian jägers and grenadiers under Colonel von Donop were ordered to remain on his left, half an English mile beyond Flatbush. The latter did not begin to move until six o'clock in the morning of the 27th, after the fire on both wings had begun to be effective.

Lieutenant General von Heister had ordered the Erb Prinz Regiment to support the Hessian Grenadier Battalions von Linsing and von Minnigerode, and von Donop's to support the Grenadier Battalion Block. Von Mirbach's Regiment followed von Donop's to the last height on the left of the woods; Rall's Regiment took position to the left of Mirbach's; and finally, on its left, the Regiment von Knyphausen, which was to be supported from the rear by the 250 men under Colonel von Heeringen,[14] who had broken camp on the morning of the 26th.

With this alignment the left wing of von Knyphausen's Regiment was less than a mile from the right wing of the English infantry. To enable us to move the fieldpieces, we leveled all the roads we could find, the jägers and Hessian grenadiers, who had kept on the wide road from Flatbush to New York, accomplishing the most. They fired into the woods directly in front of them and were followed by the several battalions, first in columns, then deployed. The jägers soon occupied a deserted trench, in which they found three brass 6-pounders and one howitzer, all spiked, as well as two overturned munition wagons. All the riflemen fled, abandoning their strongest posts and throwing away their rifles. The enemy made their most stubborn resistance on our right wing, where they were attacked by the Scottish Highlanders and the English grenadiers, but even there they were compelled to fall back, leaving behind over four hundred killed and wounded.

If the courageous Scottish Highlanders and grenadiers had made their attack as did the Hessian and other regiments, namely, by sending their artillery ahead and continually beating their

[14] Colonel Henrich Anton von Heeringen died September 25, 1776. He was a knight of the order Pour la Vertu Militaire. See *Hochfürstlich Hessen-Casselischer Staats- und Adress-Calender*, Cassel, 1779. (Future references to this state yearbook will be abbreviated *Staats-Calender*.)

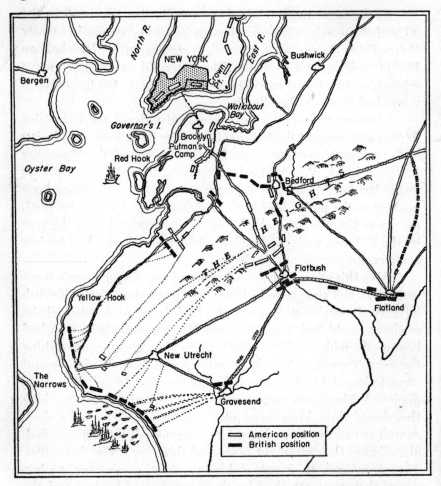

Plan of the Battle of Long Island. (Redrawn from a section of William Faden's "Plan of New York Island, with Part of Long Island . . . , London, October 19, 1776.")

drums, they would not have had 334 killed and wounded. The Hessian troops had one grenadier killed and three officers and twenty-two rank and file wounded, most of them severely. But the Hessian officers, namely, Major Pauli of the Artillery, Captain O'Reilly,[15] and Lieutenant von Donop, were only slightly wounded. This day we took eleven hundred prisoners, and on

[15] See 1778, note 122.

the 28th picked up another 426. The total of their killed and wounded is not yet known, since they lie scattered in the woods, where many of the wounded will perish miserably. We captured two generals, Stirling and Sullivan, nine colonels, and some fifty officers,[16] most of whom are artisans and poorly equipped.

They wear black, white, or purple linen blouses with fringe on their sleeves and collars in Spanish fashion. Their guns, having rifled barrels five feet long, are much too heavy for one to aim well without support. They have a kind of cartridge box, from which hangs a powder horn and in which is a wooden frame holding twenty-three cartridges.

The enemy retreated in small groups and in great confusion toward the Brooklyn lines, where they have built fortifications strong enough to withstand an assault of fifty thousand men. On both wings they have zigzag trenches, casemated and supplied with provisions for 350 men. In front of these fortifications is a picketed double trench. In this manner they have raised one work behind another as far as the sea. On their right wing, moreover, is a woods with many trenches and strong abatis. On the highest spot of a small peninsula called Red Hook, they have raised a battery to keep the New York channel clear and prevent us from occupying the woods. In his orders of the 29th, General Washington stated that for the time being he found it necessary to fall back before the cruel enemy and evacuate Long Island. We had no knowledge of this, however, until four o'clock in the morning of the 30th. In the several trenches we found three brass and eleven large iron guns, all spiked, but no ammunition. In all his orders, General Washington had charged his troops to be as sparing as possible with their powder. They would have had none at all had they not captured 1,500 tons with several companies of Scottish Highlanders in Boston harbor early in June. The captured ships maintained that they had not known of General Howe's departure.

The entire American army has fled to New England, evacuating also New York, where the demoralized troops abandoned

---

[16] Following eighteenth-century usage, Baurmeister frequently employs the term "officer" to designate low-ranking officers, i.e., officers below the rank of major, and sometimes below that of colonel.

more than six thousand sick. Their commanders, who have come together from all the provinces, are constantly quarreling and do not know what to do. On the 31st, day before yesterday, the English headquarters, all the English troops, and Colonel von Donop's brigade moved from Bedford to Newtown; and Brigadier General Erskine advanced further to the right into Long Island with the light dragoons and Scottish Highlanders to bring in wagons and forage. On this occasion he surprised and captured one colonel, two majors, and 153 riflemen who had lost their way during the engagement of the 27th and were unable to withdraw. The part of Long Island into which Brigadier General Erskine moved is called Jamaica. The island is divided into three counties, namely, King's, Queen's, and Suffolk counties.

The men-of-war are drawing as close to New York as possible and would come closer if the rebels had not sunk so many ships there and made the approach impossible. The tops of the masts can be seen in the water and only rowboats can pass between them. I must add that the rebels, after having vacated everything except an island one English mile long, called Governor's Island, on which four hundred Pennsylvanians were encamped, have now embarked these men, too, in spite of a battery thrown up in front of us, and taken them to New York on small vessels under cover of a two-masted frigate. We sank only two of these boats. They carried no more than about forty men, but these perished miserably.

The enemy's abandoned camp within the Brooklyn lines was made of wooden structures instead of tents. Their gun coverings were also made of wood. Behind their front they had just completed some hospitals, but everything was burned before the first Hessian regiment moved in.

Generals Washington and Putnam are praised by friend and foe alike, but all their mastery in war will be of no avail with a mob of conscripted, undisciplined troops. The two Adamses are men of excellent judgment, who have so far promoted the rebellion with the assistance of the wealthy Hancock and other equally rich merchants. I wish the Hessian troops could have taken as much in coin as they did in paper money (which had to be turned in at the English headquarters). Time alone will show whether any of it will be redeemed.

Congress intended to distribute in the Hessian camp several thousand printed leaflets, dated August 14th, informing us in high-sounding phrases of their just cause, and promising property to deserters. A few came into the possession of the brigade on Staten Island, which has been commanded by Colonel von Lossberg [17] since the 25th of August, when Lieutenant General von Heister and Major Generals von Stirn and von Mirbach also crossed over to Long Island with all the other regiments. So far I have been unable to obtain one of these handbills; if I do, I shall enclose it in some future letter together with the exact *ordre de bataille* of the English troops. They consist of six battalions of light infantry, seven brigades of artillery, the 5th, 35th, 49th, 28th, 23rd, 57th, 64th, 44th, 43rd, 63rd, 54th, 22nd, 15th, 45th, 27th, 4th, 17th, 46th, 55th, 40th, 71st (three battalions), 37th, 52nd, 38th, 10th, 42nd (two battalions), and 33rd Infantry Regiments, [18] and, lastly, ten battalions of grenadiers.

We came into possession of eleven enemy flags with the motto "Liberty." General Burgoyne is approaching with some Indians. At General Howe's quarters I met two chiefs of the Mohawk and Iroquois tribes, [19] who have since returned to meet General Burgoyne. A good deal is expected from the friendship of these Indians, and there is already some talk of an early peace and a speedy return to the fatherland.

I have not had time to continue my journal and have a clean copy made for your Lordship beyond this point. I hope this account will meet with your Lordship's approval and that I shall

[17] Colonel (later Major General, then Lieutenant General) Friedrich Wilhelm, Freiherr von Lossberg, who in May, 1782, became commander in chief of the Hessian forces.

[18] The fact that in the above list the 71st and the 42nd Regiments are stated to consist of three and two battalions, respectively, is an indication of the weakness of the other regiments. Hence, the words regiment and battalion are frequently used rather indiscriminately. However, the grenadiers, both English and German, were organized as battalions.

[19] The Mohawk chief was Captain Joseph Brant (cf. letter dated Aug. 27, 1779, No. 40).

be permitted to furnish more in the future. I have just learned that General Howe has sent three frigates [20] to Hell Gate to observe the enemy.

I commend myself to your Lordship's grace and remain with the greatest esteem

Your Lordship's

Most obedient servant

Baurmeister

[*Addressed*]
A Monsieur
Monsieur le Baron de Iunckheim
Collonel dans le Premier Bataillon
des Gardes aide de Camp General et
Grand Chambellan de S. A. S^me. Mon-
seigneur le Landgrave de Hesse Cassel

^p Londrs.   ^a Cassell

[20] The *Brune* and the *Niger,* the third being a bombardier (see following letter).

: 2 :

In the hope that my journal of the 2nd instant has safely arrived and met with your Lordship's approval, I am sending the continuation of my account by the next packet.

With the exception of Major General Grant's brigade and Major Generals Stirn's and von Mirbach's Hessian brigades, which remained at Bedford across from New York under the command of his Excellency General von Heister, the army has been encamped between Newtown and the peninsula of Red Hook. Captain Pitter's [22] English artillery brigade has been stationed behind the enemy's works in order to keep in check the rebels in the city and the redoubts outside. To do this more effectively, a captain and one hundred men were ordered to occupy Governor's Island toward noon of the 2nd of September. Here they found ten spiked iron guns, four 18- and six 32-pounders, many empty shells, several thousand cannon balls, and some barrels of flour and salt meat. This post had been relieved every twenty-four hours.

[21] A translation of this letter was printed in the *Magazine of American History*, I, 33.

[22] Identification was impossible, though a Captain Bitter is mentioned in a contemporary account of the same month.

Pickets detached from the English and Hessian regiments occupied the shore from Hell Gate to Red Hook. Two frigates, the
Brune and the *Niger,* both thirty-two guns, and a bombardier lay
at anchor before Hell Gate. On the shore to the left of these ships,
we threw up a battery of two 24-pounders, four 12-pounders, and
two howitzers. Blackwell's Island was also occupied by a captain
and one hundred English infantrymen.

In the night of the 2nd–3rd of September, the *Rose* frigate,
thirty-two guns, and thirty boats left the fleet, sailed to the right
of New York up the East River without the least interference, and
anchored along the shore in Wallabout Bay and at Bushwick. All
the captured guns were made fit for use and mounted in the old
and newly erected batteries on the height to the left of the Ferry
village [23] and along the shore to a point opposite Governor's
Island. The rebels, to be sure, fired repeatedly on these batteries
from their works, especially from the large Bunker Hill fort,[24]
but without effect. Their outposts were regularly relieved at six
in the morning.

The enemy army was encamped in the large woods between
Crown Point [25] and Bloomingdale. To keep their rear clear and
maintain communications with the mainland, they had their
strongest posts along the Harlem River. Several times rebels have
come to the English camp at night in small boats to join our army.
They were assigned to Colonel De Lancey's new brigade, which
is now two thousand strong. The Colonel's ancestors settled on
New York Island, and he has suffered much from the rebels. Several hundred of the prisoners taken in the action of the 27th of
August have also been mustered into this brigade.

On the 4th of September the English vacated Blackwell's
Island, and the rebels immediately occupied it with such a large

[23] Brooklyn Ferry village, Long Island. Brooklyn itself was inland.

[24] Bunker Hill fort, a battery on Bunker Hill, or Bayard's Mount, later known
also as Mount Pleasant. Bayard's Mount, to use its older name, was the highest
hill on the southern end of Manhattan. Leveling it away began in 1802 and continued until no evidence of a hill remained. The corner of Grand and Center
streets marks the approximate site of the fort. Cf. Mary L. Booth. *History of the
City of New York,* New York, 1867, p. 494, and I. N. Phelps Stokes, *Iconography
of Manhattan Island,* New York, 1915–28, III, 541.

[25] Corlaer's Hook.

force that our outposts along the shore were exposed to constant fire, which even the large battery could not prevent. On the 5th of September each regiment was supplied with five wagons and draft horses for its guns. At Newtown a forage magazine was erected. The inhabitants of Long Island, except those of Suffolk County, recognized the sovereignty of the King. There are still several thousand rebels scattered throughout Suffolk County who are waiting for an opportunity to fight against us.

Why Brigadier General Erskine with his strong detachment proceeded no farther than nine English miles beyond Jamaica and was ordered to return again on the 6th of September, I do not know; but it is not unlikely that that region, the best part of Long Island, is to be preserved for part of our winter quarters, for the army has stripped the country of everything on its march—produce, cattle, and even horses, all these having been declared rebel property. At present, there is no English regiment without its full quota of horses, and soon the Hessian regiments will also be fully supplied, because an officer can acquire them for little money and often for nothing. I myself procured three horses in this manner.

The prosperity of the inhabitants, whose forebears were all Dutch, must have been great indeed. Everywhere one sees real quality and abundance. One sees nothing useless or old, certainly, nothing dilapidated. The inhabited regions resemble the Westphalian farming districts, where the people live on scattered farms. The houses are beautiful and are furnished in better taste than any we are accustomed to in Germany. At the same time everything is so clean and neat that no description can do it justice. The women are generally beautiful and delicately brought up. They dress becomingly according to the latest European fashions, wearing Indian calicoes, white cotton goods, and silk crêpes. There is not a single housewife who does not have an elegant coach and pair. They drive and ride with only a negro on horseback for an escort. Near the dwellings are the cabins of the negroes, their slaves, who cultivate the fertile land, herd the cattle, and do all the rough housework. They are Christians and are purchased on the Guinea Coast, and sold again among the white people for from 50 to 120 New York pounds a head. Twenty New York shillings make a pound, and thirty-seven New York shillings make a guinea.

On the 7th the fleet anchored closer to New York, between Red Hook and Governor's Island. The baggage of the Hessian corps, which, for the most part, was still on shipboard, was loaded on the transports for the greater convenience of each regiment. This alleviated much of the trouble caused by the frequent loading and unloading made necessary by the shortage of boats. General Howe had ordered the Brooklyn line to be demolished, but when his Excellency General von Heister pointed out that the troops could not be expected to do this work, which would take four weeks, without remuneration, General Howe revoked his order.

Finally, on the 8th, preparations were made on the English right wing to dislodge the rebels from Blackwell's Island. This was accomplished on the 9th in spite of a very stubborn resistance. The English had five killed and eleven wounded, while the loss of the rebels was considerably heavier. They vacated Buchanan's and Montresor's Islands, which were occupied by the 71st Regiment under the command of Brigadier General Erskine. The Hessian grenadier brigade and the jägers under Colonel von Donop, who had held a quiet post on the left of the English camp below Newtown, went into the camp vacated by the 71st.

Brigadier General Erskine advised the rebels to cease their musketry and confine themselves to vigilance as he did, unless they wanted his guns to demolish all their houses on the shore opposite Montresor's Island, where he had mounted four 12-pounders. This proposal was accepted and quiet was restored. The river between these posts is not quite as wide as the River Fulda in Hesse, but much deeper and full of rapids.

The captured General Sullivan returned early this morning to Admiral Howe, who was on board the warship *Eagle*. The day before, he had arrived in New York from Philadelphia with the necessary equipage for himself and some for General Stirling. On the 10th of September Colonel von Lossberg was advised by Admiral Howe that a boat flying a white flag would arrive from New

York at his post at Amboy on Staten Island at six o'clock in the morning of the 11th and that it was to be admitted without interference. At this hour not only the expected boat arrived, but also Admiral Howe, accompanied by three sea captains. On the New York boat were three representatives from Congress, namely, Adams, Franklin, and Rutledge, who were received by the Admiral. Their conference lasted two hours. However, the proposals of the rebels, who called themselves deputies of the United American Independent States, were hardly listened to, much less answered.[26] The Americans were served breakfast, and then, without having accomplished anything, both parties sailed back.

After this day we could clearly observe that the heavy pieces in the New York batteries opposite Governor's Island were being removed and that their sick were being transported from the city to Powles Hook. The inhabitants, who had long ago removed their most valued possessions, took their last belongings, even their cattle, from the city to the best land in New York during the night. The loyalists were plundered and maltreated, and many of them dragged off. The artillery in Bunker Hill fort played but little on our works. Evenings, however, the enemy doubled their posts along the shore between New York and Crown Point, where General Washington could often be seen. This provoked Captain Krug of the Artillery to fire two shots at him and his suite, and he would have fired a third if only their horses had not kept moving.

In the night of the 11th–12th, thirty-six boats left the fleet, sailed up the river undisturbed, and anchored along the shore above Bushwick. During the day a frigate and five provision ships returning from Ireland joined the fleet. They had left Halifax on the 7th of August. We were given permission to move the Hessian

---

[26] It will be remembered that Lord and Admiral Howe had been instructed to restore peace between the colonies and the mother country. The captured General Sullivan was sent to Philadelphia on parole to urge Congress to send representatives to confer with the Howe brothers. After some pleasantries exchanged between Lord Howe and Dr. Franklin, who had become acquainted in England, and some further remarks concerning the status of Benjamin Franklin, John Adams, and Edward Rutledge, Lord Howe discoursed at length on the British conditions for the termination of hostilities. The American commissioners found the British proposals unacceptable.

sick from the ships to Brooklyn, thus saving the lives of many men. Had this been done earlier, many more lives would have been spared. Dysentery, which is caused by unripe fruit and a lack of good bread, is increasing.

In the night of the 12th–13th of September, forty boats took the same course and went to the same place as had the thirty-six on the 12th. General Howe wanted to land on New York Island on this day, because it was the eighteenth anniversary of General Wolfe's victory at Quebec, though, to be sure, he paid for the victory with his life. Consequently, the watchword was "Quebec" and the countersign "Wolfe." However, the frigates were too dilatory for this attack. Not until five o'clock in the evening of the 14th did four frigates, the *Phoenix, Roebuck, Orpheus,* and *Carysfort,* all thirty-two guns, leave the fleet to sail up the East River and anchor above Bushwick. The rebels fired on the frigates from all directions, but, covered by our batteries, the ships sailed past without damage.

The battery on Governor's Island cannonaded the point of New York with great effect. The wooden guardhouse on the island suffered all the damage the rebels intended for the battery, but in spite of this not a man was lost.

Toward evening his Excellency General von Heister received orders to have Major General Stirn's brigade set out for Bedford at two o'clock in the morning of the 15th, leaving behind baggage and fieldpieces. He was to join Major General Grant's brigade, and at four o'clock in the morning both brigades were to march to the shore above Wallabout Bay to make a second landing with several English brigades, all under the command of Lieutenant General Percy. The first landing was made with eighty-four boatloads of English infantry and Hessian grenadiers under Lieutenant General Clinton. This landing was superintended by Commodore Hotham. Five frigates had previously anchored close to the shore in Kipp's Bay above Crown Point and cannonaded the enemy outposts and the extensive woods for three hours. A red flag was the signal for the departure of the boats, a blue one for a delay in the passage, while a yellow one was to be flown if the boats were compelled to withdraw.

While the troops were landing, the rebels under the command of General Putnam, their front deployed, first withdrew on their left from the shore toward the woods between Crown Point and Bloomingdale and then advanced on their right. But when our regiments formed along the shore and the drums gave the signal to advance in line, the rebels did not wait in formation for our arrival, but fled into the woods. Although General Putnam did his utmost to check his men, his efforts were in vain. He himself was lucky to be able to escape on a horse which had been captured from the English light horse in Boston.

One rebel regiment, confronted by Block's Grenadier Battalion, which had sent its skirmishers ahead, showed signs of surrender, but after a few shots from the skirmishers, the enemy battalion fell back in the direction of the main body of their army with arms shouldered. However, they fired one round, which killed seven and wounded sixteen in von Block's Grenadier Battalion. The enemy, on the other hand, lost their colonel, a major, several captains, some subalterns, and more than fifty men, all taken prisoners, besides many killed and wounded who remained on the field, the number of which I was unable to learn.

At seven o'clock in the morning the warship *Renown*, forty guns, and two frigates, the *Repulse* and the *Pearl*, thirty-two guns each, left the fleet, proceeded up the North River, and anchored above Bloomingdale. The rebels cannonaded them from Powles Hook without effect, while the ships fired several broadsides at the New York shore in passing. This so frightened the enemy that they abandoned the city as well as the Bunker Hill fort. Toward half past ten a white flag was raised, and at eleven o'clock the Admiral's flag flew over the tip of New York. Admiral Howe then sent some hundred marines into the city to take possession and post watches in the principal streets. This prevented all plundering and no one suffered any loss.

On the 16th the enemy went into camp in good order in front of Fort Washington. Their left wing extended as far as Harlem. A line of trenches runs from Fort Washington to Kings Bridge, behind which the enemy can retreat under cover of the fort. The English light infantry, which had pursued the retreating enemy too heedlessly, fell into an ambuscade of four thousand men at Hogeland's Hill.[27] If the English and Hessian grenadiers and especially the Hessian jägers had not come to their assistance in the nick of time, none of these valiant light troops would have escaped. They had twenty killed and two hundred and ten wounded. The enemy must have lost many, for all the jägers and the Scottish Highlanders ran out of shot and powder. Lieutenant Hinrichs of the Jäger Corps was wounded in the left side.[28] Four other jägers were also wounded.

In the orders of the 17th, in which he expressed his satisfaction at the successful landing, General Howe deemed it necessary to commend this corps, which had so far been under General Leslie's command, for its caution and bravery. The English encamped in two lines near Bloomingdale. We have come into possession of several enemy baggage and flour wagons.

Major General Robertson [29] has been appointed Commandant of New York. The garrison consists of the 54th and part of the 5th Regiment. All the marines have returned to the fleet. The houses of the rebels, now deserted, have all been marked G.R. and confiscated. The new government is taking over all the enemy's papers and other effects, while the fleet is erecting magazines in the city.

Many subjects are returning to their lawful government, and on Long Island the villages of Gravesend, New Utrecht, Flatbush, Brooklyn, and the Ferry are filled with returned fugitives. Most of them, however, find their houses empty, their belongings destroyed, and windows broken; nor will they ever recover their cattle. These loyalists must distinguish themselves from the rebels by wearing red ribbons on their hats.

On this same day General von Heister left the Brooklyn line with von Mirbach's brigade and went into camp at Hell Gate. Brigadier General Erskine with the 71st Regiment (three battalions), still posted on Buchanan's and Montresor's islands, was put under von Heister's command, as was also Major General

[27] Usually called the action of Harlem Plains.

[28] For a biographical sketch of Johann (von) Hinrichs, later a lieutenant general in the Prussian service, see B. A. Uhlendorf, tr. and ed., *Siege of Charleston,* University of Michigan Press, 1938, pp. 8–12.

[29] Brigadier General James Robertson.

Robertson's brigade, consisting of the 4th, 15th, 27th, and 45th Regiments, which are quartered in the houses of the Hell Gate district. These seven battalions [30] have only 1,812 effectives, which shows the weakness of all the English regiments, excluding, however, the regiments of Foot Guards, numbering eleven hundred men.

On the 18th two frigates drove five rebel ships from the Hudson River. Some enemy troops decamped from Powles Hook, and the rebels posted on the right of New York Island withdrew further back.

On the 19th the Hessian baggage ships moved into the East River, closer to the army, and some frigates and boats left the fleet and sailed up the North River. They were cannonaded from Powles Hook, but sailed past without answering the fire.

At half past twelve in the night of the 19th–20th a terrible fire started in the northern part of the city of New York. Picked incendiaries, who are still hidden in the city, and a colonel with forty more rogues, who had come from Powles Hook by boat with a favorable west wind, set fire at the same time to many parts of this beautiful city. The weather and the carelessness, not to mention the inadequacy, of the watch favored in every way, as it were, this calamity, which brought about the destruction of 560 houses, including the greater part of the best. An English church also fell a prey to this madness of the rebels, who committed this atrocious crime believing it fully justifiable in times of war.

Nine of the miscreants who were caught in the act have been arrested, and others thrown into the flames. One fanatical rebel, whose wife and five children could not persuade him to refrain from this murderous arson, mortally injured his wife with a knife when she tried to extinguish the fire with buckets of water. The man was seized by some sailors, stabbed to death, and then hung by his feet in front of his own home. He was left hanging there until the 20th at four o'clock in the afternoon.

The English guard which was covering General Howe's headquarters was sent into the city to put out the fire. The sailors from

---

[30] Seven battalions, viz., the three battalions of the 71st Regiment and the four regiments mentioned, which were only battalion strength.

the fleet did the best work, but rewarded themselves for their labors by plundering other houses which had not burned. New York in this state of desolation is a horrible sight.

On the 21st all was quiet. So was it on the 22nd, save that two English brigades and Major General Stirn's, all under the command of Lieutenant General Percy, left the second division of the army and marched far below Bloomingdale to a place almost opposite Powles Hook, where they were to attempt to land and take post (three frigates had already proceeded to the New Jersey shore), but a strong northwest wind made this expedition fruitless. However, at two o'clock in the afternoon of the 23rd, Lieutenant General Percy left camp with the same troops, except that the English light infantry took the place of Major General Stirn's brigade. The enemy deserted their post, which was then occupied by the English.

This morning at four o'clock five enemy boats with one hundred men were bold enough to attack our post on Montresor's Island. While still on board, many were killed and wounded, and a major and twelve men of those who landed were taken prisoners. This visit cost the 71st English Regiment four men killed and eight wounded.

The 24th, 25th, and 26th are the days appointed for a muster of the troops, which Colonel Osborn is undertaking in the Hessian corps. I shall not fail to send your Lordship the continuation of this journal.

With the greatest esteem I remain [*etc.*]

P.S. The 2nd division has not arrived yet. We have only uncertain news about General Burgoyne, but the rebels, who have more reliable reports, are much alarmed and are beginning to desert. Some officers have even returned to their estates.

: 3 :

NEW YORK
NOVEMBER 27, 1776

His Excellency General von Heister had hardly taken quarters in the city when we were advised, late last night, by Adjutant General Paterson that a packet is to sail tomorrow. Though I have a great many notes for continuing the journal sent in my last, I have not had time to make a clean copy. But I shall not miss an opportunity (they come all too rarely) to pen this part for your Lordship, even though I shall not be able to retain a copy for myself.

Begging you to be kind enough to excuse the mistakes and commending myself to your further gracious protection, I am with unalterable reverence [*etc.*]

P.S. Major von Biesenrodt,[31] who has been very ill, is well on the way to recovery. I wish Major General von Mirbach were doing as well, but the recurrence of the paralytic strokes gives us little hope. On the other hand, Major von Wurmb is again taking part in the expedition with his regiment. He has been very ill.

---

[31] Probably Hans Moritz von Biesenrodt of the Regiment von Mirbach. The *Staats-Calender* for 1779 has Biesenrod, though it lists also a Colonel and a Captain von Biesenroth.

: 4 :

. . . .[32] In spite of this, I shall go back to the occupation
. . . [of] Powles Hook, which took place on the 25th of September. The enemy evacuated this post, leaving two iron 12-pounders, and the 57th English Regiment took possession of it. Two battalions of New Jersey militia disbanded completely, as did also a battalion of Riflemen under Colonel Webbe [33] at Kings Bridge, without anyone attempting to hold the disgruntled rebels in check. On the other hand, we have received news that four thousand men of General Lee's force have joined their army and that the General himself will soon arrive.

On the 26th General Sullivan was exchanged for General Prescott, who was captured at Boston last year, and General Alexander, who goes under the name of Lord Stirling among the rebels, for two majors, Browne and Skinner. The former had

[32] MS torn.
[33] Probably Colonel Samuel B. Webb, 7th Connecticut Continentals.

been governor of Providence,[34] which he defended with little glory.

Burgoyne's Dragoons [35] have landed near New York. They lost fifty-eight horses on their voyage, which lasted thirteen weeks. With each troop were forty dismounted dragoons, whose accouterments were the same as those of the mounted ones, except that they wore leather boots and carried pistols and rifled guns instead of their regular side arms. After a rest of one week they began active service again. De Lancey's corps of volunteers has assembled at Hempstead on Long Island, where it is to be completed.

A captain named Rapelje,[36] who was recruiting in Suffolk County, was fatally shot on a street in Flushing. The culprit has been hunted in vain. I should not be surprised if many more such acts were committed, for there are but few loyalists on the entire island. They have been gathering in Brooklyn the last few days to swear allegiance before Governor Tryon of New York and acknowledge the King of England for their sovereign. For his cause they have sworn to fight against the rebels, betray their plots, and conceal neither accouterments, ammunition, nor provisions.

Since the action at Flatbush, Suffolk County has sent 340 young men to join the rebel forces and has delivered to Congress for paper money all the cattle and sheep that could be dispensed with—all this without the least arrangement being made on the county's behalf. The Earl of Dunmore,[37] who has been in Virginia, one of the most zealous Englishmen, gained nothing at headquarters . . . to England, whither he sailed on the first ship.

In the night of the 27th–28th the Admiral ordered forty transports to get under sail to follow two warships and three frigates

[34] I.e., New Providence, now Nassau, Bahama Islands. Montfort Browne, Governor of the Bahamas (1774–1780), was captured in the American attack on New Providence, March 3, 1776, and exchanged for General Stirling. Other accounts do not mention Skinner in this exchange.

[35] The 16th (or Queen's) Regiment of (Light) Dragoons.

[36] Jeronimus Rapelje, whose wife is said to have informed the British of the American evacuation of Long Island (W. Irving, Life of George Washington, New York, 1857–59, II, 334–35).

[37] John Murray, 4th Earl of Dunmore, the last royal governor of Virginia.

into the North River. They came to anchor along the right shore close to Baron Bayard's [38] summer home. The entire Halifax garrison now serving in the army was ordered to prepare for embarkation, and on the 29th the requisite ships unloaded their cargoes in New York.

Furthermore, the treasury and the large English hospital were moved to the city. General Howe appointed a town major, an adjutant, a quartermaster, and a barrack master to serve under General Robertson. All the quarters were listed; the existing barracks were enlarged, and new ones were built in the fire-ravaged northern part of the city. Wood and coal magazines were also erected, and forage brought in. The flour brought from Ireland was put into storehouses to dry. In short, the entire town was prepared to serve as a *place d'armes* and winter quarters for six thousand men. All the captured guns, ammunition, provisions, and flags in the army were carefully listed, and the list turned over to the Commandant of New York, General Robertson.

No one received the slightest remuneration, and when the question of rewards came up, we were told there would be none in this war. Otherwise, much of the remuneration would have been due to the First Company of Hessian Jägers. On the 30th General Howe promoted many officers in the army, for he is authorized to fill all vacancies from a colonelcy down.

In the night of the 1st–2nd of October fifteen rebel deserters came in boats to Barren Island.[39] Their reports agreed that General Washington had detached ten thousand men to White Plains and that the enemy was storing provisions at Mamaroneck. On the 3rd they stripped the village of Harlem of all available forage, occupied the trenches thrown up before it on the seaward side, and returned unmolested. . . .

On the 4th thirty men and one officer who had deserted from the enemy arrived on Montresor's . . . [From them] Colonel Erskine [40] learned . . . that the enemy were on the far side of

[38] William Bayard, whose country estate was near Greenwich.
[39] Ward's Island.
[40] Sir William Erskine, promoted to brigadier general in America only, April 23, 1776. Cf. Baurmeister's first letter, wherein Erskine is called brigadier general.

the village, but that they had posted a picket of twenty men to give the alarm in case we should attempt a landing. To obtain more reliable information, Colonel Erskine detached one staff officer and 150 men with a regimental piece to the opposite shore under cover of a frigate. Before five o'clock in the evening this detachment destroyed its entrenchments, filled up the ditches, and burned everything without the slightest interference, after which it returned to camp on Montresor's without loss.

The 2nd and 6th English brigades under Major Generals Agnew [41] and Leslie [42] left Long Island, marched through New York, crossed in flatboats over to the Ferry, and encamped at Bedford on Long Island.

On the 7th General von Heister with Major General von Mirbach's brigade broke camp at Hell Gate and marched to Newtown, where he encamped. On the 8th he was to proceed to Jamaica, and the two English brigades were to leave Bedford and put themselves under his command. He received new orders, however, commanding him to remain at Newtown with the Hessian regiments, and therefore he had the English go into camp at Jamaica alone.

On the 9th two battalions of the 71st English Regiment vacated Barren Island and Montresor's (leaving only the 3rd Battalion of this regiment to occupy both islands) and also encamped at Jamaica. Preston's Dragoon Regiment,[43] scattered in detachments over Long Island, assembled at Flushing. On the 10th General von Heister's entire corps received six days' provisions, whereupon he left his camp in front of Newtown and went to Jamaica, too. At six o'clock in the morning of the 12th, this corps broke camp, marched through Flushing to Whitestone on the East River, and embarked on fifty-three flatboats awaiting it. Toward eight o'clock in the morning we could, from our place of rendezvous, distinctly see them landing on Throg's Neck, a peninsula of Westchester.

[41] Brigadier General James Agnew, Colonel of the 44th Regiment of Foot.
[42] Alexander Leslie, a brigadier general at this time. Cf. letter dated Sept. 2, 1776 (No. 1), where Baurmeister refers to him as a brigadier general.
[43] The 17th Regiment (Light) Dragoons.

In the night of the 11th–12th General Howe embarked . . .
Lieutenant General Lord Percy . . . brigades under Major Generals Grant, Jones, and Stirn occupying the lines. The landing was
effected without mishap, save that a flatboat with four brass 6-
pounders and four English artillerymen foundered in the whirl-
pool at Hell Gate.

General von Heister did not cross over to Throg's Neck until
half past two in the afternoon. Admiral Howe, who was present
in person and who had advised landing at New Rochelle, was
greatly displeased to see the army in a narrow encampment on
the peninsula without having effected its purpose, for the narrow
road leading past the so-called Red Mill to the East Chester country was occupied by a strong force and was, moreover, bordered
by a morass on both sides. The grenadiers of the army were not
permitted to advance, and the Hessian jägers were barely able to
take post this side of the narrrow road.

In the night of the 12th–13th the enemy had time to make
everything still more unapproachable. They cannonaded the camp
of the 71st Regiment, which lost six killed and three wounded. If
the rebels had accurately aimed their guns, the balls of which
flew over English headquarters, they could have annihilated the
Guards and the 33rd Regiment in the reserve.[44] On the 12th also
Colonel von Lossberg's brigade, excepting the Regiment von
Trümbach, embarked on thirteen transports at Staten Island and
remained on board ship until the 17th.

These troops had scarcely vacated the island, leaving only
the trenches occupied, when the rebels crossed over at Amboy
and Elizabethtown. They made the roads to Richmond unsafe,
burned some houses, set fire to the old camps, and captured a
strong patrol which Lieutenant Colonel Dalrymple had needlessly
sent from the trench to the said village. Lieutenant Clewe [45] and
eight men of von Trümbach's Regiment were among those captured. The Lieutenant got away, but the eight soldiers were taken
to Philadelphia, where they were well treated and promised

---

[44] Action of Throg's Neck, or Harlem Heights.
[45] Name could not be verified in the *Staats-Calender*.

great rewards if they would enlist in the rebel army. Four of the oldest of these prisoners are said to have entered their service. We learned this from a commissary who was sent to Philadelphia at the beginning of this month to effect an exchange of prisoners, in which, however, he was unsuccessful. The rebels want to keep their prisoners and want us to keep ours to increase our burdens.

On the 14th twenty-six provision ships arrived in New York from England with a package of Hessian letters of very old date and six hundred English recruits under a major named Donkin.[46] They were immediately assigned by lot to the various regiments and turned over to them on the 16th. The recruits under the name of Scheither Corps [47] were also allotted to the English regiments. These low-spirited people have received nothing besides their German thaler pocket money, their two shillings at Portsmouth, and their daily rations, and, moreover, they have no prospect of getting anything. Some have even been engaged as officers, but will never be able to serve in that capacity here, not even as noncommissioned officers. At our request, General Howe turned over to us all the Hessian deserters discovered among them.[48] The Hessians found among the rebel prisoners are also to be returned to their respective regiments.

Early in the morning of the 17th, all the grenadiers of the army, the reserves, the Hessian Jäger Company, and the artillery of the park embarked on flatboats in the East River in front of

[46] Major Robert Donkin.

[47] Scheither Corps—250 Hanoverian volunteers under Lieutenant Colonel Georg Heinrich Albrecht von Scheither for distribution in the English regiments. They left Germany March 26, 1776, with Baron von Riedesel and his Brunswickers, and sailed from England in the same fleet as Burgoyne and Phillips, April 3, 1776, arriving at Quebec June 1. See Eelking, *Die deutschen Hülfstruppen*, and the abridged translation thereof by J. G. Rosengarten, *The German Allied Troops in the North American War for Independence*, Albany, 1893, p. 88. (Further references to this work will be abbreviated Eelking-Rosengarten.)—The article in the *Allgemeine deutsche Biographie* states that he organized a corps of volunteers, called Scheither Corps in Brunswick in 1762, and that in 1775 he was authorized to raise a corps of 4,000 men for service in North America, but that he gave up when by the end of the year he had raised only 150 men.

[48] On their march from Hesse-Cassel through the Duchy of Hanover to the place of embarkation (Bremerlehe), which took usually four days, many soldiers deserted. (See, for example, MS diary, of Friedrich von der Malsburg in the Library of Congress.)

Captain Smith's house,[49] and, after a short roundabout passage, landed on the Westchester coast in the district called Pelham Manor, a stretch of solid land twenty-one English miles wide, between New Rochelle on the right and East Chester on the left. The 2nd and 6th English Brigades remained at the disembarkation place,[50] and the rest of the army marched across Throg's Neck to the shore opposite the intended landing place.[51] They were to cross over in a direct line in the same flatboats as soon as the above-mentioned division of the army had landed. The Hessian artillery occupied the shore on this side [52] to prevent the enemy from interfering with the landing.

It was beautiful to see the flatboats arriving. Two frigates followed by Admiral Howe's sloop sailed ahead and cannonaded the Westchester coast, as did also the Hessian artillery. About fifty rebels were keeping watch on the shore, but they fled back to their largest contingent, consisting of approximately one thousand men who had advanced from the three rebel camps on the East Chester heights. Inside an hour and a half the entire army had landed in Westchester and set out to march in a single column. The jägers occupied the woods on the right and did not allow the rebels to get a foothold. The enemy intended to withdraw behind lines of piled-up stones and fences. Captain von Wreden and forty Hessian jägers silenced a gun, which was meant to be used with effect. The jägers occupied the ground in front of us and gained the road to New Rochelle.[53]

Colonel von Lossberg's brigade also joined the army, which stayed in the fields without tents until the 19th, when the baggage arrived and the troops pitched camp. But lack of room prevented them from making a regular camp; besides, there was no necessity to guard against an attack. The Hessian Leib Regiment marched to Rochelle [54] without encountering any rebels, though it found a

---

49 Not identified; perhaps the house of Claudius Smith and his son Richard.
50 I.e., where the army had disembarked on Throg's Point from New York.
51 The landing place on Pell's Point.
52 This side is the Pelham side.
53 Action of Pelham Manor, or New Rochelle.
54 I.e., New Rochelle.

Quaker church filled with salt. Rogers' Corps [55] took post beyond Rochelle on the Boston roads. This corps, as well as the New York and Grant's volunteer companies have repeatedly risked being fired upon, but since they resemble in many ways the rebels who have no uniforms, the latter could not distinguish between friend and enemy.

On the 20th the greater portion of the army marched into the East Chester country. Only General von Heister with Lossberg's and Mirbach's brigades remained encamped. He extended the line of his camp in such a way that the Leib Regiment before Rochelle constituted his right wing. The 6th English Brigade came from Throg's Neck into position beyond the Leib Regiment at a like distance. The 2nd English Brigade joined the army, leaving only the 28th English Infantry Regiment posted on Throg's Neck.

On the 21st the grenadiers, Rogers' Corps, and the 1st Jäger Company were detached from the army to advance to Mamaroneck; but the enemy did not await their arrival, and abandoned their magazine. However, lack of wagons, complete ignorance of the enemy's strength, and the fear that they might have doubled back made the detached troops destroy these badly needed provisions. After Rogers' Corps had occupied a good position, the rest of the detachment returned to camp.[56]

On the 22nd an English officer spread a false alarm of the approach of an enemy corps under General Lee. The grenadiers and all the reserve were ordered to take up arms and proceed to the right wing of the army, but they waited in vain for the enemy until eleven o'clock at night. After another hour the corps quietly returned to the army.

On the 23rd General von Knyphausen's [57] corps and the Waldeck Regiment, which we had long expected, finally landed at New Rochelle. Though they had spent twenty-one weeks on

[55] The corps of Robert Rogers was called the Queen's Rangers. Rogers had earned some renown during the French and Indian War. He was a typical partisan, who sided with the British in spite of the fact that he had given his word to Congress not to fight against the colonies.

[56] Action at Mamaroneck.

[57] Lieutenant General Wilhelm, Freiherr von Knyphausen.

board ship, the troops still looked well. Their sick had been disembarked and sent to the hospitals at Brooklyn and the Ferry.
They went into camp before Old Rochelle at the place where the
6th English Brigade (which had marched to Mamaroneck under
General Agnew and had Rogers' Corps for an outpost) had encamped on the right of the Leib Regiment, for not a single rebel
dared approach there.

The 2nd Jäger Company received orders to join the 1st immediately. On its way it attempted an attack upon the enemy
outposts at Mile Square, but since Captain Ewald advanced too
far to the left, not knowing the lay of the land and being, very
likely, badly advised, he was compelled to fall back with a loss
of two killed, two wounded, and two missing.[58] Lieutenant von
Rau received a severe wound in the ankle. Though the bullet could
not be located, he is now supposed to be out of danger.

On the 24th the 28th English Regiment also left Throg's
Neck, and on the 25th the army advanced six English miles, so
that it had Mile Square [59] on the left and the East Chester heights
along its entire front. This was the very first time the army
marched according to written orders.

On the 26th Brigadier General Erskine reconnoitered the
enemy's right wing with the 2nd Hessian Jäger Company, one
hundred of Preston's Dragoons, one light infantry battalion, and
Rall's Regiment. The enemy vacated their camp, making their
tents useless. We dispensed the wine and rum we could not take
with us in bottles and destroyed the flour magazine. The dragoons
captured one officer and twenty-nine men. We also found the two
jägers who had been missing since the attack of the 23rd. They
could not praise enough the good treatment they had received.

[58] Captain Johann (later von) Ewald met part of Lee's division. Cf. *Heath's
Memoirs of the American War*, ed. by R. R. Wilson, New York, 1904, p. 86: "Oct.
24. . . . at 5 oClock, A. M. a firing of small-arms was heard to the southward. It
was a skirmish between 200 men of Gen. Lee's division, and 250 Hessians—10 of
the latter were killed, and two taken prisoners." For a biographical sketch of (von)
Ewald, later a lieutenant general in the Danish army, see Uhlendorf, *Siege of
Charleston*, pp. 6–8.
[59] Mile Square is now part of the city of Yonkers. A tract of land one mile
square was sold in 1676 by Elias Daughty, of Flushing, to Francis French, Ebenezer Jones, and John Westcott.

They had even been given companions who could speak German and who promised them great rewards if they would enter the rebel service and urge their countrymen to do likewise. One of them had been shot in the leg.

On the 27th Brigadier General Erskine made another reconnaissance to this place. This time he had with him only forty of Burgoyne's Dragoons and the 29th Regiment. He brought back nine prisoners and the assurance that all the rebels had left this part of the country and gone to White Plains, and that no more than six thousand men remained at Kings Bridge.

On the 28th the army advanced along the road to White Plains, marching in the same two columns as on the 25th. The Hessian Jägers formed the van of both columns and after an hour's march encountered some enemy outposts. General Clinton found a way on the right to pass around a hill occupied by the enemy, which they abandoned since they could no longer hold it without guns. Our right wing then occupied the hill, for it was strategically situated. The second column experienced greater hardship in making its advance. The narrow and poor road necessitated marching in file. However, the 2nd English Brigade filed out, marched ahead of the column, and took a position under General von Heister's command, whereupon the rebels were compelled to remain on the far side of the Bronx, a stream fourteen feet wide, of varying depth, and with banks of varying height.

General Washington had posted the Marylanders [60] and the North and South Carolinians on rising ground on the far side of the river, the right wing resting on a woods, and the left extending across open fields along the broad road to White Plains. The woods, which extended to the slope of the river bank, were filled with pickets, and three guns were mounted in front of their left wing. This position was held by the enemy up to the time of the attack. Meanwhile, the second column, still marching in file, had advanced to some cleared lowland in front of the junction of two dense woods. The Leib Regiment marched across this lowland unmolested. The Prinz Carl Regiment and von Dittfurth's, which were next in the column, marched to the right of the lowland and

[60] Smallwood's battalion of Maryland militia.

took a position on the right of the 2nd English Brigade, where they had a woods in front of them. Rall's and von Knyphausen's followed the Leib Regiment, while Lossberg's joined the Regiment von Dittfurth.

This breakup of the Hessian brigades was the result of hurried orders to occupy the most advantageous places as quickly as possible. The Leib Regiment, and, somewhat to the left of it, Rall's and von Knyphausen's crossed the Bronx River. After these three regiments had ascended the slope, they maneuvered into line on the left. Their fieldpieces, however, were mounted on rising ground this side of the river, where they could rake the woods occupied by the rebels. The terrain on which the 2nd English Brigade had taken position was too narrow to allow them to form in line with the above-mentioned Hessian regiments. Hence General von Heister had the guns of the Leib Regiment and Rall's and von Knyphausen's Regiments support the left wing. Then he had two English 6-pounders mounted beside the left wing of the Lossberg Regiment, and not far from there, this regiment's cannon. To the right of the Lossberg Regiment was von Dittfurth's, on its right, the Prinz Carl Regiment, and behind the Lossberg and von Dittfurth's, the 2nd English Brigade.

General Howe ordered the Hessian grenadier brigade to move out of the first column and come up closer to support the attack. Von Lossberg's Regiment left its position and marched into the lowland of the Bronx River. Then followed, on its right, the entire 2nd English Brigade, the right wing of which took position in the greater part of the woods occupied by the enemy. Von Dittfurth's and Prinz Carl's followed as soon as there was enough room. All these movements were covered by a very lively cannonade of the regimental pieces.

The Regiment von Lossberg had much trouble fording the river, many wading through water above their knees. On the far side is a steep slope, where the right wing had to halt while the left maneuvered to the front, under a severe musketry fire. The 2nd English Brigade, however, withstood an even hotter fire of grapeshot. The enemy guns defended only the woods, from which the approaches to their position were not so steep. But the English were not disturbed and kept on marching, and von Lossberg's Regiment had already climbed half the height when it received a round of musketry. Three platoons of its left wing passed a charcoal fire that the enemy had built.

Von Minnigerode's Grenadier Battalion followed to support the attack, but because it had crossed the river too far to the left, it was compelled to advance by companies through brushwood and over rocks. Therefore Rall's and von Knyphausen's came more quickly to the aid of the Lossberg Regiment, which attacked the enemy and drove them from their position. This regiment had some forty wounded, and the Rall Regiment lost one man killed. Lieutenant Mühlhausen of Rall's was wounded above the left hand, and the regiment will feel his absence all the more since Colonel Rall was pleased with his services as adjutant.

The artillery, being short of horses, had great difficulty getting the pieces from one hill to another, for all the fields are enclosed with log and rail fences. This gave the enemy time to fall back to their camp at White Plains, which had been well fortified. Toward five o'clock in the afternoon the left wing halted, the right remaining in its old place. The 2nd Jäger Company occupied a woods along the left wing, and the whole army remained in the fields without tents throughout the night. The baggage and tents finally arrived on the 29th. On this day each corps transported its wounded to Rochelle, whence Lieutenant General von Knyphausen had marched the previous day and occupied the place where Brigadier General Erskine had reconnoitered on the 26th.

On the 29th von Knyphausen proceeded to Kings Bridge, leaving Wissenbach's and Huyn's at Valentine's Hill [61] under General Schmidt.[62] The Waldeck Regiment, however, remained at Rochelle. Eighteen men of this regiment went marauding in the region around Mamaroneck, where they were surprised and attacked by forty rebels and disarmed. One subaltern and twelve soldiers were captured and hurriedly sent away. Two men remained on the field, wounded. At General Washington's behest the most intelligent of the prisoners were treated like the Hessian

---

[61] Now part of the city of Yonkers.
[62] Major General Martin Conrad Schmidt of the Hessian army.

grenadiers.[63] On the 30th the enemy evacuated Fort Independence, situated this side of Kings Bridge, and also the large fortification across the river from it called Spuyten Duyvil. The rebels
burned all their barracks and demolished the bridge at Kings
Bridge and those called Dyckman's bridge and Williams' bridge.
Lieutenant General von Knyphausen had them repaired and sent
the Grenadier Battalion Köhler and Wutginau's and Stein's Regiments across the river to encamp at places where they would be
safe from the fire of the rebels' batteries. The rest of his corps
encamped behind Fort Independence, whither Major General
Schmidt also sent von Wissenbach's Regiment and the Regiment
von Waldeck, excepting fifty men who remained at Rochelle.

On the 31st the enemy were to be attacked at White Plains,
while Lieutenant General von Knyphausen was to make an attack
on Fort Washington. But a heavy rain, fortunately perhaps for the
army, frustrated all our plans. The enemy, well advised of everything, were prepared and ready to repulse us, sleeping on their
arms that night. Much might have been done on our left wing
to mislead them. For example, we might have built some bridges
and constructed roads to them—but nothing was done. On the contrary we did not even interfere when the enemy, on one side of
our front, set fire to all the houses of the Hunt family, who have
unanimously spoken against Congress. These unfortunate people
then sought refuge in places where the army had left nothing, for
it had taken all cattle and horses and had so stripped the houses
of their contents that the inhabitants were reduced to nakedness.

On the night of the 31st of October to the 1st of November
the enemy left the village of White Plains in flames, abandoning
the fortifications on the right of it and the hill before their abatised
camp. As soon as day permitted, the Hessian grenadier brigade
took possession. On the 2nd the army received six days' provisions
from Rochelle, which we completely evacuated.

On the 3rd it was again planned to attack the enemy in their
camp, but once more our trouble was in vain. Our right wing ad-

---

[63] Baurmeister is probably thinking of the grenadiers of von Trümbach's Regiment (above). The most intelligent were, no doubt, expected to be the most likely
to use convincing arguments in urging their countrymen to desert.

vanced slowly through White Plains, while our left occupied a height opposite the flank of the enemy's camp. Two battalions formed in line on this hill, and the Hessian grenadier brigade held the center between the two wings. The enemy, however, remained calm, did not break camp, and permitted us to hear and see that all their batteries were well manned and that we could not get at them. Two 32-pounders killed four men in Dittfurth's, Rall's, and the Leib Regiments, and three were severely wounded. General Howe abstained from further attempts and ordered all the regiments to return to camp by the nearest roads.

On the 4th General Grant's brigade and most of the heavy artillery left the army and proceeded to Valentine's Hill. This brigade had left Long Island on the 30th of October, embarked at Turtle Bay, and, going by way of Rochelle, joined the army at nine o'clock on the 31st. On the 5th the entire army marched toward the North River to encamp at Dobbs Ferry, where it did not arrive until ten o'clock in the morning of the 6th, for the baggage, which preceded the columns, could make but little headway. The mountains were endless—all the worse for the two-horse wagons, which were the only kind we had. Not a single rebel dared approach our rear guard.

It was not until the second day that a corps under General Stirling advanced one mile from White Plains, but its outposts did not scout far enough at any time to be reached by the jägers. In Jersey, across the river from Dobbs Ferry, the enemy had a small camp which high shrubs prevented us from seeing entirely, and in front of which, behind an embankment, they had posted an 18-pounder, which fired on a frigate and two transports that lay at anchor close to our shore.

On the 7th General Howe detached the following troops from the army to Kings Bridge under cover of a battalion of light infantry and fifty jägers commanded by Captain Lorey: a train of heavy artillery together with Brigadier General Cleaveland, and all the engineers. There, at Kings Bridge, we had started work on some batteries. One of them had been staked out beyond Kings Bridge on the left of the York road under cover of the von Wissenbach Battalion, while two more had been begun on this side of Kings Bridge far below the left wing of the camp of von Knyphausen's corps.

On the 8th the jägers unexpectedly molested the enemy outposts; the rebels had one engineer and five men killed, and some men wounded, whom they carried off. Our loss was two jägers killed. Two more were killed on the 9th, when the enemy, one hundred strong, attacked a post commanded by a noncommissioned officer, killing Lieutenant Schwein [64] as he was about to reoccupy the post. After the enemy had withdrawn and set fire to two houses, Lieutenant General von Knyphausen not only strengthened this post, but advanced it even farther. A rebel brigade major [65] who was sent from the fort with dispatches for Congress deserted and asked to be taken to General Howe. From his papers we learned that the garrison [66] was discouraged, that it was expecting reinforcements, and that Lieutenant General von Knyphausen's corps was believed to be twelve thousand strong. On the 10th the Mirbach brigade marched to Kings Bridge under Colonel Rall, and the army was ordered to be ready to march at a moment's notice. The provisions had been landed at Morrisania, whence the army got them as needed.

On the 11th the army advanced in two columns, the one on the left under Lieutenant General Cornwallis to Cortlandt manor,[67] and that on the right under General von Heister on the New York road along the North River, the opposite shore of which is a high cliff three English miles long. On the top of this smooth, rocky wall, with which Nature has little to compare, is a dense woods of oak and chestnut, which descends, at each end of the cliff, into hills of moderate height.

[64] Lieutenant Schwein, Regiment von Stein. (See Eelking, *Die deutschen Hülfstruppen*, I, 32.) Eelking-Rosengarten, curiously enough, gives Swein, probably following Gaine's *New-York Gazette and Weekly Mercury*, March 17.

[65] William Demont, adjutant to Colonel Magaw. Cf. Justin Winsor, *Narrative and Critical History*, New York, 1923, VI, 287, 341, and E. F. Delancey, "Capture of Mount Washington, 1776, the Result of Treason," *Magazine of American History*, I, 186.

[66] I.e., the garrison of Fort Washington.

[67] Not the Van Cortlandt manor at Croton-on-Hudson, but the Van Cortlandt house, now in Van Cortlandt Park.

The right column made camp above Philipsburgh, a large mansion, at present inhabited by the family of Major Philipse, who has a large estate and an annual income of six thousand York pounds and is now held prisoner by the rebels. The manor house stands on level ground close to the North River, and its courtyard is half surrounded by a bay. On the left of it are two mills, which are driven by the high and low tides. Above the bay is a church, and on the right of the main building is a large garden with all ornamentation in the Dutch manner.

On the 12th the entire army assembled near Kings Bridge in three unequal lines extending from the rear of Fort Independence to De Lancey's Mill, which served as headquarters. General Agnew left Mamaroneck at the same time that General Grant left Valentine's Hill, and both brigades encamped with the army. Rogers' Corps, however, took position on the Rochelle road on both sides of Mile Square and was there reinforced by the New York companies and Captain Grant's.

On the 13th we received confirmation of the report that Colonel Knox was no longer in command of the rebels in Fort Washington, and on the 14th we learned that Colonel Magaw [68] had arrived that day with considerable reinforcements. General Howe, who had supposed all along that the enemy would evacuate the fort, now realized that they were determined to defend it.

On the 15th he sent Adjutant General Paterson to the fort with a formal summons. The enemy requested two hours for deliberation, but before this time was up, they sent word that they would defend it no matter who or how many undertook the fruitless assault upon their fort. Hence, on the 16th, toward half past eleven in the morning, the attack upon Fort Washington began.

Lord Percy attacked the lines from the New York side, and Lieutenant General von Knyphausen undertook the main assault with two columns as soon as he heard Percy's fire. Meanwhile, the

[68] American accounts show Magaw in command at Fort Washington from September until his surrender. Cf. Washington's orders, Sept. 18, 1776 (*Writings*, ed. by J. C. Fitzpatrick, Washington, 1931–44, VI, 71); G. W. Greene, *Life of Nathanael Greene*, New York, 1872, I, 252, 263–64; and *Heath's Memoirs of the American War*, ed. by R. R. Wilson, p. 90.

English Guards and two English light infantry battalions had embarked at Kings Bridge with orders to land, under cover of the two batteries on this side, on the left of the main attacking force at the edge of a wooded slope, on top of which was a road leading directly to the fort. Lieutenant General von Knyphausen had a narrow strip of woods, in which his columns formed for the attack, the distance between this wood and the enemy being too short to form in line.

The right column was led by Major Dechow, who had under him one hundred and fifty men selected from all the regiments and forty jägers under Captain Lorey. Then followed the Grenadier Battalion Köhler and then Rall's, von Lossberg's, and the Waldeck Regiments. The left column had a vanguard of one hundred men commanded by Captain Medern,[69] who were followed by the Wutginau, von Huyn, von Knyphausen, and von Bünau Regiments. Wissenbach's and Stein's remained behind to cover the camp and the batteries. The short but very steep road leading to the enemy, who were firmly entrenched on their hill behind strong lines and two batteries, enabled them to pour a very effective fire, especially from their first battery, against Wutginau's Regiment, which suffered heavy loss.

The column on the right, which went up the hill just as rapidly, could not be reached by the enemy's second and highest battery. Hence the rebels took flight, setting fire to their entire supply of powder. The attack of the English to the left of this column was also successful, so that we then filed on the fort from all the heights. Finally, when Lord Percy, his skirmishers meeting with but little resistance, ascended to their lines, all the rebels hastily withdrew into the fort. Colonel Rall, who had advanced with his regiment to within thirty paces of the fort, in which the enemy, through anxious embarrassment, did not defend themselves, then summoned the garrison to surrender. Colonel Magaw immediately surrendered the fort and the entire garrison to Lieutenant General von Knyphausen.

[69] Captain Medern of the Wutginau (later Landgraf) Regiment was wounded in the attack. See *New-York Gazette*, March 17, 1777.

The enclosed list [70] notes all our losses, to which must be added, however, nine Englishmen wounded and five killed, and four killed and eleven wounded in Lord Percy's corps. Among the latter was one soldier of the Erb Prinz Regiment. The rebels must have lost some two hundred men, besides the three thousand taken prisoners. In the fort we found thirty-two iron guns, two large mortars, and two howitzers, very little powder for guns and small arms, but many filled cartridges for small arms, great quantities of filled shells, hand grenades, bullets, flints, several barrels of slow-matches, quantities of provisions such as rum, flour, oil, butter, vinegar, salt meat, and fish, and fifty-three barrels full of potatoes. In the batteries facing Lieutenant General von Knyphausen's attacking column and that of the English, we took eleven guns of various caliber. On the other hand, Lord Percy's corps captured no more than two guns, which Lieutenant von Nagel's skirmishers had taken along with fourteen prisoners.

On the 17th the prisoners, guarded by von Mirbach's Regiment, were in Harlem, whither they had been escorted the previous night by the two battalions of English light infantry. On the 18th they were taken to New York by two battalions of General Jones's brigade and were quartered in the churches and large warehouses. Colonel von Lossberg's brigade and the Regiments von Wutginau, Bünau, and Huyn of the Knyphausen corps left the army this same day under von Lossberg's command and encamped before the city of New York. These regiments, two English brigades, and a train of heavy artillery are ready to embark under General Clinton and Lord Percy.

On the 19th, at nine o'clock in the evening, General Cornwallis left the army with the English and Hessian grenadiers, both jäger companies, two battalions of English light infantry, and the Guards, marched to Philipsburgh, crossed the North River in the night, and advanced along steep footpaths to the heights of Jersey. The enemy, who were expecting an attack on Powles Hook rather than on Jersey, deserted their camp.[71]

[70] Missing from the Von Jungkenn Papers. Probably removed by recipient for comparison with official returns.

[71] Rest of MS missing. It covered the period November 20–27. The following journal recapitulates the more important events.

: 5 :

[*NEW YORK*

NOVEMBER 25 TO

DECEMBER 27, 1776]

At the conclusion of my journal of the 27th of November, 1776, I said that the 6th and 2nd English Brigades and General Mirbach's had landed in Jersey under the command of Colonel Rall on the 26th. Things were quite different; the 2nd and 4th English Brigades crossed the North River under Fort Knyphausen on the 25th of November, while the 6th English Brigade marched down in front of Harlem, where it is still encamped and will remain until the Hessian hospital can be moved from that quarter to this place—which has not yet been done. Nor have the Regiments von Trümbach, Stein, and Wissenbach at Fort Knyphausen been quartered in barracks, for these are still unfinished. These three Hessian regiments, the 6th English Brigade, one battalion of the 71st Regiment, and Colonel Rogers' Corps are encamped on both sides of the fort under Lieutenant General von Knyphausen.

On the 25th of November, the 4th Brigade went into camp at New Bridge, while the 2nd occupied the camp at English

Neighborhood,[72] which Colonel von Donop had just evacuated to march to Hackensack. On the 26th General Cornwallis forded the Passaic with his entire corps and remained during the night without tents near the village of Acquackanonk, where the 4th Brigade under General Grant came up on the 27th, which was a day of rest.

On the 28th the corps set out on its march again. The right column under Colonel von Donop encamped in the Newark Mountains,[73] while the left column was marched to the Newark region by General Cornwallis himself. Not until the 28th did General von Mirbach's brigade, under the command of Colonel Rall, cross the North River under Fort Knyphausen in boats and encamp at English Neighborhood in Jersey—without tents.

On the 29th this brigade went into camp in Hackensack, a town which extends four English miles along the highway. General Cornwallis also set out with his corps on this day and went into cantonment in and around Elizabethtown. One battalion of light infantry and the 1st Hessian Jäger Company held outposts at Rahway, where on the 30th the corps went into cantonment, extending to Woodbridge. One light infantry battalion was at Amboy, and another, together with the 2nd Hessian Jäger Company, was quartered at Connecticut Farms Meeting.[74]

On the 1st of December they set out on a march through Bonhamtown and Piscataway to New Brunswick [75] without being harassed by the enemy. Colonel von Donop, who took the road this side of the Raritan River as far as the heights and drove the rebels before him, had Captain von Weitershausen [76] and four

---

[72] English Neighborhood is modern Fairview, New Jersey.

[73] The Newark Mountains are shown on Clinton Map No. 246 (John Hill's) as First Mountain and Second Mountain, two long ridges west of Newark, now in Orange County. The U. S. Geological Survey calls them First Watchung Mountains and Second Watchung Mountains.

[74] Union, New Jersey.

[75] At that time usually called Brunswick. This is the only time Baurmeister calls it New Brunswick.

[76] Cf. "On the third instant Capt. Weitershausen, of the grenadiers, was shot at Brunswick bridge by a rebel, who had concealed himself under the bridge. The Capt. had wrote by the last packet to his wife desiring her to follow him to America." Extract from an anonymous Hessian diary captured at Trenton and printed in the *Pennsylvania Evening Post*, July 26, 1777, reprinted in *Newspaper Extracts*, I, 432–33 (*New Jersey Archives*, 2nd Series).

grenadiers wounded, of whom the Captain and one grenadier died on the 2nd. The Captain was buried at Brunswick on the 3rd.

Colonel Rall was ordered to deposit all dispensable baggage on Staten Island and follow General Cornwallis's corps as far as Newark. Here Colonel Rall doubled his pickets when he learned that a considerable body of rebels under General Williamson [77] was approaching. His patrols also brought in a prisoner, who had been attempting to drive away cattle.

On this same day General Howe went to Jersey and ordered the Waldeck Battalion to embark at the King's Wharf in this city and sail to Amboy. General Stirn's brigade was also garrisoned here, partly in barracks and partly in uninhabited houses. The houses are provided with ship's mattresses, fireplaces, several benches, a common table in each room, kettles, and a few iron pots —certainly making rather poor quarters. While there is no shortage of wood, coal, light, and provisions, there is a decided lack of the comfort which the soldier expects, desires, and needs in winter quarters.

On the 6th Colonel Rall's brigade went into cantonment in Elizabethtown and relieved two hundred English infantrymen who joined the corps in Brunswick. In Springfield and in Morris County the rebels under General Lee increased.

On the 7th Colonel Rall continued his march as far as Maidenhead,[78] leaving von Lossberg's Regiment in Elizabethtown until the Waldeck Battalion should come to relieve it. At first Colonel Rall had instructions to march to Brunswick, but after he had started out he received orders to proceed to Maidenhead— a very fatiguing march of twenty-six English miles. The regiments were compelled to spend two nights without quarters or tents, though they finally sought shelter in scattered houses.

This same day, General Howe marched to Princeton with the entire contingent and on the 8th to Trenton on the Delaware. The enemy held the opposite bank with thirty-six guns and six mortars. There were no boats on this side of the river, so not even half a battalion could cross. Up to the 10th, nothing was done.

[77] Brigadier General Matthias Williamson, New Jersey militia.
[78] Maidenhead is modern Lawrenceville, New Jersey.

The brothers, Admiral Howe and General Howe, issued a proclamation promising a pardon to any rebel who would come in as a faithful subject within sixty days. A great many came to headquarters in Trenton, were accepted, and dismissed with a protection. Unfortunately, it was not discovered until too late that many, on the other hand, had come only to look around and spy. On the 12th the rebels were bold enough to come down the Delaware with fifteen galleys which fired on our outposts.

On the 14th General Lee was taken prisoner on the other side of Morristown by Lieutenant Colonel Harcourt of Burgoyne's Regiment. The Lieutenant Colonel had sent some men to scout around General Lee's quarters, then he himself with one officer and not more than nine dragoons went there in a very roundabout way. A rebel of the General's watch, who was not on duty, seized his musket and fired. A dragoon cut him down. This discouraged the others from coming out of their barn. An officer who gallantly defended the doorway was shot and killed, and when the Colonel hurriedly ordered his dragoons in a loud voice to set fire to the house, General Lee and a French officer ran out and surrendered. They were immediately taken to Brunswick on the dragoons' horses. The Frenchman, whose name is Roche de Fermoy,[79] showed us a pass from St. Germain, Minister of State,[80] giving him permission to serve in the army of the United North American Provinces. He will be taken to England on a man-of-war. General Lee has been given a public hearing as a deserted lieutenant colonel.[81]

On the same day Colonel Rall relieved Colonel von Donop in Trenton. The former was again given von Lossberg's Regiment,

[79] A curious statement. M. de Gaiault, not Roche de Fermoy, was captured with Lee. For an account of Lee's capture see *The Lee Papers*, IV, 387–94 (*New York Historical Society Collections*, 1874). De Fermoy was, however, supposedly in the region. See Washington's orders to Mercer, Stirling, Stephen, and de Fermoy, Dec. 14, 1776, J. C. Fitzpatrick's *Calendar of the Correspondence of George Washington*, Washington, 1915, p. 220. There is a strange disappearance of de Fermoy's name from American military papers during the latter part of December, though there is no mention of his capture or exchange.

[80] Claude Louis, Comte de Saint-Germain, Minister of War for France.

[81] Lee had served in the British army prior to the outbreak of actual hostilities.

for the Waldeck Battalion had moved from Amboy to Elizabeth-town on the 12th. Colonel von Donop left Lieutenant von Grot-hausen and fifty jägers behind to cover the right wing of Rall's post, and on its left wing detachments were posted to maintain communication with Colonel von Donop, who was stationed in Bordentown and was in command of the entire cordon along the Delaware. Colonel Rall was also given an officer and twenty dra-goons from Burgoyne's, who were to patrol the neighborhood.

At Bordentown Colonel von Donop had the Grenadier Bat-talions von Minnigerode and von Linsing. The houses along the road to Trenton were occupied only by Captain Stamford's [82] company. Block's Grenadier Battalion was quartered in Black Horse,[83] and Captain Eschwege's [84] grenadier company of Wut-ginau's Regiment in the houses between Black Horse and Borden-town. Bordentown is a good eight English miles from Trenton, Black Horse seven miles from Bordentown, and Burlington four-teen miles from Black Horse. The 1st Jäger Company and Captain Lorey with twelve mounted jägers occupied an outpost before Burlington, while the 2nd Jäger Company was posted in a mill between Bordentown and Black Horse. General Grant was the commander in chief in Brunswick; General Leslie remained in Princeton; and the rest of the contingent went into quarters in Amboy, Elizabethtown, Hackensack, and Bergen.

General Howe and General Cornwallis returned to this city [85] on the 16th. The latter is preparing to sail for England on Ad-miral Lord Shuldam's ship, on which Colonel Dalrymple and the officers of the 6th and 14th Regiments have also embarked. The small remainder of these two battalions, noncommissioned officers and soldiers, have been distributed among the regiments of the first division.

[82] Captain Ludwig Friedrich von Stamford, Grenadier Battalion von Linsing, a cousin of Major von Baurmeister.

[83] Now Columbus, Burlington County, New Jersey.

[84] Captain Friedrich von Eschwege, who testified at the court of inquiry, January, 1782, concerning the surprise at Trenton (W. S. Stryker, *The Battles of Trenton and Princeton*, Boston, 1898, p. 414).

[85] I.e., New York.

Two regiments, namely, the 7th and the 26th,[86] have finally been exchanged for the same number of rebels. We still have more than three thousand rebel prisoners in the churches of this city. Many unmarried men who were tired of being held in captivity have entered our service and embarked for Gibraltar.

His Excellency General Howe thought fit to take Köhler's Grenadier Battalion from General von Knyphausen on the 20th of December and have it embark at the King's Wharf with a train of heavy artillery for Amboy in Jersey to reinforce Colonel von Donop. In return the Regiment von Trümbach, which has been in garrison here since the 7th of December, set out to join General von Knyphausen.

On the 17th we finally received the news that General Clinton's corps had landed in three divisions on Rhode Island on the 8th of December and quietly taken possession of everything. Colonel von Lossberg had taken quarters with the Leib Regiment, Prinz Carl's, and von Dittfurth's in Newport, where Colonel Campbell of the 22nd Regiment has been made commandant. The fleet, under the command of Peter Parker, *chef d'escadre*, consisted of six men-of-war, five frigates, thirty-two transports, and three storeships, following with provisions.

The passage of the fleet was as follows: Between the 25th of November and the 1st of December the ships gathered beyond Hell Gate. On the 1st the fleet weighed anchor and, divided in three divisions, sailed past Brothers and Blackwell's islands and cast anchor in the Sound in Whitestone Bay, where it remained until the 4th because of bad winds. On that day it set sail again in spite of a rough sea, and passed City Island and the Bay of Saybrook, where some of the ships that had sailed ahead rejoined the fleet. They had discovered some enemy ships far away which headed for Rhode Island and undoubtedly reported the advent of the English fleet, for in the night of the 6th–7th of December, six hundred rebels with twenty guns and quantities of cattle escaped on ships to Boston. On the 7th the fleet passed Block Island and ran safely into the harbor of Newport the same eve-

---

[86] These two regiments had been captured at Chambly and St. Johns, Quebec, October 18 and November 3, 1775.

ning. On the 18th Colonel von Lossberg sent a second report, according to which everything is the same, save that several men-of-war are cruising in the direction of Boston.

I should be happy to be able to finish this journal, too, with some good news, but the misfortune of Rall's brigade is too sad. On the 25th of December the enemy attempted an attack on Rall's brigade, which was saved by the watchfulness of the outposts.

But on the 26th, an hour after sunrise, Lossberg's, Knyp-hausen's, and Rall's Regiments were surprised in Trenton by more than ten thousand rebels. They were badly treated and made prisoners, losing their guns, colors, and all equipage. The post at headquarters, consisting of one hundred men of Rall's brigade, Lieutenant von Grothausen, and the English dragoons, and as many as three hundred men of the three battalions, escaped to Colonel von Donop. Moreover, seventy-five picked men under Lieutenant von Winzingerode of Lossberg's Regiment are sta-tioned here, and an even greater number are in the hospitals. Many officers escaped and are sick, but many others died with Colonel Rall, though I cannot furnish at this time a list of the killed and wounded.

Today an officer and a regimental quartermaster of von Knyphausen's Regiment are leaving for Philadelphia to carry money and minor equipment to the prisoners. Why the surprise was so sudden and so disastrous for the brigade I cannot explain in detail, but this much is certain: The day before, Colonel Rall wrote to Colonel von Donop that his brigade was extremely fa-tigued because of the miserable weather and continuous service and was in no condition to defend the post without relief and rein-forcements; that only two officers in his regiment were fit for duty; and that the other regiments had the same complaints, above all the gallant Regiment von Lossberg, which had suffered more than any other through the whole campaign. My brother-in-law, Lieu-tenant Colonel Bretthauer, is also said to have been killed.[87] I hope to be able to send a more detailed report with Captain Em-

---

[87] Lieutenant Colonel Balthasar Bretthauer, Regiment von Rall, was not killed, but died a prisoner of war at Dumfries, Virginia.

merich,[88] who is in command of all the Guides and sails in a week and will go to England as fast as his ship will carry him. Colonel von Donop evacuated the bank of the Delaware and withdrew to Princeton as soon as he heard of Rall's misfortune. He was compelled to leave twenty sick grenadiers behind in Bordentown.

[88] Captain, later Lieutenant Colonel, Andreas Emmerich was in command of a corps of volunteers which he had raised in Germany. He had gone there from America, where he had settled after the Seven Years' War. His knowledge of the country and the English language made him especially valuable for reconnaissance excursions (Eelking-Rosengarten, p. 121).

1777

1777

: 6 :

NEW YORK

FEBRUARY 16, 1777

Right Honorable Lord,
Gracious High and Mighty Colonel:

Since the 9th of this month, when I respectfully dispatched my last journal,[1] the six English regiments under the command of Colonel Butler have landed at Amboy, the disembarkation taking place on the 14th of this month. Consequently, his Excellency General Howe will embark this evening to be present in person at the attack on the rebels in Jersey. General Washington has moved his quarters from Morristown to Princeton. Several days ago he sent in a bank note, in the name of Congress, for the maintenance of General Lee, which, however, was promptly re-

---

[1] There is no letter dated February 9. In view of the Trenton disaster it seems likely that there was also at least one January letter. Upon receipt of the first reports the Landgrave of Hesse-Cassel ordered a thorough investigation to be made as soon as the officers who were taken prisoners had been exchanged. Since many were not exchanged until after Cornwallis's surrender, the court of inquiry was not held until January, 1782, and the report of the Hessian War Commission, which was based on the records of the court, was dated Cassel, April 15, 1782. It seems reasonable to assume that von Jungkenn made the missing letters available to the War Commission.

turned. This eminent rebel has been questioned several times in the presence of General Robertson.

The day before yesterday a patrol of four light dragoons, who had advanced from Fort Independence over Williams' bridge too far to the right, fell into an ambuscade of nine rebels who had come from East Chester. One dragoon was killed and another severely wounded. The regimental quartermaster, Müller, has not yet returned. He is being detained in Philadelphia. It is said, unfortunately, that the captured officers have been sent to Baltimore, and the noncommissioned officers and privates to Virginia. However, this is not credited by his Excellency General Howe, who is hoping for an exchange of prisoners in the near future.

This moment Adjutant General Captain von Münchhausen informs me that Colonel Erskine has attacked the rebels in their quarters near Shrewsbury, Monmouth County, killing many and taking seventy prisoners.[2] This attack occurred on the 12th of this month. I hope to be able to send good news with the next packet.

Enclosing a kind of pocket almanac printed here,[3] I remain with the greatest respect [etc.]

[2] The raid on Shrewsbury was led by Major Andrew Gordon, 26th Regiment. See the account in the *New-York Gazette*, Feb. 17, 1777, reprinted in *Newspaper Extracts*, I, 287 (*New Jersey Archives*, 2nd Series).

[3] Not in the Von Jungkenn Papers. Hereafter absence of enclosures in the collection will be indicated by "[missing]" following or close to the text reference.

: 7 :

NEW YORK

JUNE 2, 1777

Hoping that Captain von Kutzleben [4] has communicated to your Lordship my last account, dated the 19th of May,[5] I now take this opportunity to send your Lordship a copy of my journal:

Everything is ready for the opening of the campaign. On the 29th of May the Hessian Prinz Carl and Leib Regiments and the 63rd English Battalion, which had been stationed on Rhode Island, encamped before this city along the East River. These troops had embarked on the 18th of May with one company of negroes and forty light dragoons, leaving twelve dragoons, three English battalions, and the Landgraf,[6] Dittfurth, Huyn, and Bünau Regiments on the said island. Colonel von Lossberg re-

---

[4] Captain (later Major) Karl August von Kutzleben was Hessian resident minister in London.

[5] This account as well as others that may have been sent between February 16 and May 19 is not in the Von Jungkenn Papers. By the end of March Baurmeister might well have had an unofficial request for more, and perhaps more specific, information on the Trenton debacle. The letters containing such information might likewise have been submitted to the Hessian War Commission.

[6] The Landgraf Regiment is the old Wutginau.

85

mained with these Hessian regiments, but the English Major General Prescott commands the whole.

On the 27th of May Major General Agnew embarked in the North River with the 64th, 44th, and 23rd Regiments and landed at Amboy on the 28th of May. At present the following regiments are ready to embark: the 27th, 15th, and 4th, as well as the Hessian Leib Regiment, Donop's, and Mirbach's.

On the 31st of May the Prinz Carl Regiment marched to camp below Fort Independence. A corps of provincials is posted along the Harlem River on the right of this camp. The Regiments von Trümbach, von Stein, and von Wissenbach are also encamped at the fort, and Lieutenant General von Knyphausen and Major General Schmidt are to remain with them. The English Major General Jones is commandant of the fort, and Major General Pigot commandant of New York. The 63rd, 45th, and 28th English Regiments and the Hessian Regiment Erb Prinz remained behind as a garrison. This last regiment had so many sick and dead that it was unable to march, as were Stein's and Wissenbach's.

Since the 19th of May the troops occupying Brunswick have been encamped seven miles along the Raritan River, where on the 21st of May the Amboy garrison also encamped. The rebel force in Jersey has increased to ten thousand men since the beginning of May and has been harassing our quarters from all sides in spite of their continual losses. While our loss has been negligible, the troops have been much fatigued.

The 42nd English Regiment greatly distinguished itself on the 10th of May, when its quarters near Bonhamtown were attacked by 1,500 rebels under Generals Maxwell and Stephen.[7] However, it was a disorderly attack. In spite of their great number, they continually exposed either their right or their left wing, and so this superior force was compelled to fall back with great loss. Furthermore, on the retreat they were pursued by a battalion of English light infantry. The attack cost them forty-eight men killed and many wounded. The English had one major, three

[7] Brigadier General William Maxwell and Adam Stephen, then a major general.

officers, and seventeen soldiers wounded, and one officer and six men killed.[8]

On the same day the enemy attacked the jäger post at Raritan Landing, but were quickly turned back, the jägers having one noncommissioned officer killed. Captain Lorey of the Hessian jägers, who, with some of his men, has procured mounts again, is greatly feared by the rebels. Two weeks ago he succeeded in posting himself in an ambush between Princeton and Bonhamtown and surprised a troop of the enemy, falling upon them so suddenly that six of their most prominent men asked for pardon—and not in vain. Some of the enemy fell in the first onrush; others escaped. The jägers proceeded as far as Bound Brook, cutting down everyone they encountered. They then returned to their outpost at Raritan Landing. Because it had grown dark, the rebels in Bound Brook, having recovered from their fear, believed it was still not safe in the village and fired at each other in all the streets until far into the night, greatly alarming all the rebel outposts nearby. General Howe himself expressed his thanks to Captain Lorey.

The enemy likewise has been stirring in Jersey since the 25th of May. They have their heavy baggage in a camp between Morristown and Quibbletown,[9] and some of their artillery is already across the Delaware. They will probably not wait for us to attack them. Nor can anyone guess what General Howe's intentions are. The enemy is gathering fresh provisions to replace those we destroyed at Peekskill and at Danbury in Connecticut.

We have no reliable information about the movements of Carleton's army, but it is not very far from here. In and around Albany the loyalists and the rebels are taking care of each other. Their prisons are full, and one hears of very cruel deeds. In Boston nothing is to be had any more, not at any price, and Philadelphia has been ravaged. All the regions which the rebels thought untenable are desolate. Thus they prepare their own destruction.

---

[8] Major Simon Frazer, 71st Regiment, and Lieutenant William Stuart, 42nd Regiment, were wounded. See diverse accounts of losses in *New Jersey Archives,* 2nd Series, I, 377–79, 383, 386; and Lieutenant Stuart's memorial in Sir William Howe's letter to Barrington, May 10, 1777. Public Record Office, War Office, Series I, vol. 10, folio 365 (photostat in the Library of Congress).

[9] Now New Market, Middlesex County, New Jersey.

The English ships have been so active that this harbor is full of prizes. The Delaware is almost entirely blocked. Every ship that the fleet can dispense with has been made ready to cruise. The English regiments are getting many recruits and are expecting the rest of their reinforcements any day, as is also the Hessian corps. Sickness in the corps has completely subsided. The Erb Prinz, Stein, and Wissenbach Regiments, and some companies of Köhler's Grenadier Battalion have the most invalids; otherwise, the Hessian troops look well, and the grenadier brigade could not be finer. The regimental quartermaster Müller has again departed to take money to the prisoners.

On the 24th of March Lieutenant Colonel Bretthauer sent an unsealed letter from Dumfries [10] to his Excellency General von Heister, which, however, conveyed no information save that Captain Brübach of the Regiment vacant Rall [11] had died. The bearer carried a passport signed by General Washington himself. He brought also a written reply to General von Heister's letter in which he had requested the passport. The noncommissioned officers and soldiers are still at Lancaster, while the officers are at Dumfries. There is no mention of any exchange of prisoners. Some rebel officers who had been sent to Long Island and had seized an opportunity to escape from there, were sharply reprimanded by General Washington on their arrival and even ordered to return. [12]

Some time ago five French officers were brought in on a prize and, after a thorough examination, sent to England, for they were determined to obtain commissions and serve in the rebel army. Tomorrow General Lee will be taken from his confinement to the warship *Centurion*.

On Rhode Island the troops are encamped as follows: the three English battalions, the 22nd, 43rd, and 54th, as well as the Landgraf and Dittfurth Regiments at Quaker Hill, and the Huyn

---

[10] In Virginia.

[11] German regiments were called vacant ——, and sometimes simply Vacant, when they had no chief. Von Rall's Grenadier Battalion was successively commanded by von Woellwarth, von Trümbach, and d'Angelelli.

[12] The rebel officers must have been prisoners taken by the British and, very likely, paroled to Long Island. They were subject to punishment for breaking their parole.

and Bünau Battalions on the hill above the city of Newport. In addition, there is a post of sixty chasseurs [13] on Conanicut Island.

I shall not fail to continue this journal, especially as it is beginning to be more interesting; so I commend myself to your Lordship's grace and remain with the greatest respect [etc.]

P.S. I take the liberty of enclosing a detailed report [missing] of prisoners, killed, wounded, and those who died of their wounds. Since I have had great difficulty in obtaining approximately correct figures, I have resolved to pursue a different course in future campaigns to forestall all difficulty. I shall then enclose a list of all increases and losses with each journal. In order to fill its vacancies as far as possible, the Erb Prinz Regiment has enlisted negroes. Some of them have run away, and others have been claimed by their owners. The experiences of the provincial battalions are sufficient proof that it is useless to enlist the Germans among the rebel prisoners, for as soon as they are fully equipped, they run away.

Many Hessians are arriving with the Scheither recruits.[14] Some of the 1st Battalion of Guards from Lieutenant General von Bardeleben's [15] companies were in the last shipment. We have repeatedly requested that these people be returned to us, but the fact that the English need them and, to some extent, the expense involved make this transfer infinitely difficult. However, they are not refusing our requests, which gives us cause to be hopeful.

Today transports were ordered to be held in readiness to embark the Hessian grenadier brigade and part of the English battalions encamped at Amboy, where, as at Powles Hook, only a small post is to be maintained. We cannot guess what General Howe's intentions may be. Between Bedford and Brooklyn, Long Island, 240 two-horse wagons are ready to follow the army. Some

[13] I.e., jägers.
[14] See 1776, note 47.
[15] Lieutenant General Ernst Christoph Wilhelm, Freiherr von Bardeleben did not serve in America. He was a member of the Hessian War Commission, which on April 15, 1782, reported to the Landgrave of Hesse-Cassel on the surprise at Trenton.

pontoons are already in Jersey; others are still on large transports. Things will develop soon, however.

Lieutenant von Rau is able to walk again without crutches; he can also ride a horse, and there is no more doubt that he will completely recover. It has been decided to use the North Church of this city for a Hessian hospital after the troops depart. Sickness is letting up considerably. Scurvy has been the worst. The English Dr. Morris [16] has often visited our sick and been satisfied with their treatment and care. Now that the sick get fresh vegetables and breathe pure air, any disease can be fought more easily. No one can praise enough the English care, good provisions, beer, vinegar, and rum; and herein the Hessians have a great advantage over the English.

I remain [*etc.*]

P.S. Since there was time to write more, I opened this letter, and in pulling it out, tore the enclosed return a little, for which I ask a thousand pardons. On the 3rd of June the Anspach troops arrived here; likewise, the Hessian recruits, and Lieutenant von Wangenheim with some jägers. Their voyage from Portsmouth took not much more than eight weeks. The recruits are being allotted to the various regiments. The King's birthday was celebrated at General Howe's with great solemnity. All the troops have embarked save those at the English and Hessian headquarters. The first lap of their voyage will take them to Amboy. If the packet remains here longer and if anything noteworthy occurs, I shall write a separate letter. I am yours most respectfully.

[16] Dr. Michael Morris, physician and Inspector of Regimental Hospitals.

: 8 :

For lack of time I am unable to write a complete journal; but since a packet is being made up, I do not want to miss an opportunity to send your Lordship at least a summary report: General Clinton, having returned to New York from England, was ordered to take over the command at Kings Bridge, which he did on the 14th of July, when his Excellency General von Knyphausen left that post. The latter remained in New York until the 16th, when he embarked on the warship *Nonsuch* with Lieutenant Colonel von Cochenhausen,[18] Major du Puy, and Captain Phipps.[19] Captain Griffith [20] of this ship commanded the fleet on the voyage.

[17] Elk Ferry on the western shore of the Elk River, approximately eight miles from Elkton, and now a part of Oldfields Point farm, owned by Dr. G. Harlan Wells and Mr. R. H. Thatcher of Philadelphia. A portion of the ferry landing and the Oldfields Point farmhouse used by General Howe's staff for quarters still exist.

[18] Johann Friedrich Cochenhausen (not Kochenhausen, as given in Stryker, *The Battles of Trenton and Princeton*).

[19] Captain the Hon. Henry Phipps, one of Clinton's aides-de-camp.

[20] Captain Walter Griffith; killed in action in the West Indies, December 18, 1779.

The general's suite, however, was assigned to the *Elizabeth* transport, where everyone lived comfortably.

The two chaplains of the general's staff remained in New York. Brigade Major von Wilmowsky and his adjutant, Lieutenant Führer, also remained with General Clinton, whose corps at Kings Bridge consists of the following troops: 120 English artillerymen in the trenches thrown up before the seven forts above Kings Bridge; fifty Pioneers of Major Holland's corps; the entire 17th Regiment of Dragoons; the 7th, 26th, 36th, and 38th Regiments under Major General Vaughan; then the following provincial battalions under Major General Governor Tryon of New York: one Fanning's, one Browne's, one Bayard's, De Lancey's 2nd, and four companies of New Yorkers, each 120 strong; under Major General Schmidt: one battalion Köhler's Hessian Grenadiers, one Prinz Carl, one Trümbach's, one Stein's, and one Wissenbach's.[21]

On Long Island was De Lancey's 1st Battalion. The three hundred provincials under Colonel Skinner were posted at the Elizabethtown ferry on Staten Island. On this island also, under the command of Brigadier General Campbell, were the 52nd English Regiment, one Bayreuth battalion, the Waldeck Regiment, and sixteen English artillerymen in the two main trenches. A battalion of Anspachers has also recently been ordered to march into the camp at Kings Bridge. At Powles Hook are six hundred provincials. All these troops and the New York garrison are under the command of General Clinton.

[21] Cf. "Fishkill, Aug. 14. By several deserters from the British army at Kingsbridge, examined at Peekskill, we have the following information.—That Col. Rholler's regiment, stationed between Col. Cortlandt's and the North river, consists of about two hundred and fifty men, with two other Hessian regiments, three hundred men each; one regiment at fort Washington and another at fort Independence, 300 men each; the whole commanded by Gen. Smith a Hessian; they keep a picket of fifty men advanced about a mile from their main body.—That they have two field pieces to each battalion. That Brown's corps consists of about four hundred and fifty, stationed at Kingsbridge, De Lancey's four hundred and fifty, Bayard's two hundred and eighty, col. Fanning's four hundred and sixty, the New-York volunteers commanded by col. Grant, one hundred and fifty, the 35th British regiment of two hundred and fifty men lie at mount Mifflin; and col. Robinson's lying at Morrissania, contains about three hundred. Gen. Clinton has the command of British troops, and gen. Smith, the Hessians; a great number of Hessians are sick in the New-York hospital." *Pennsylvania Evening Post*, Aug. 19, 1777.

At present Major General Jones is commandant of New York, for Major General Pigot has been dispatched hurriedly to Rhode Island to take over Major General Prescott's command. General Prescott seems to have selected poor quarters in Rhode Island, for he was captured again at the end of June.

On the 19th of July the fleet was ready to sail. All the Hessian troops who had participated in the Jersey expedition were embarked much too early, and their ships had to ride at anchor before Staten Island for two weeks. Consequently, their store of fresh provisions diminished greatly, which was very unfortunate, for they were on board ship altogether five weeks with contrary winds and excessive heat.

On the 20th the fleet weighed anchor. A little below Sandy Hook the transports formed in six divisions. Each division was commanded by a lieutenant of the navy and all were under Sea Captain Bourmaster, [22] who took his orders from, and made his reports to, the warship *Nonsuch*. The principal men-of-war sailed ahead of and along both sides of the fleet, which numbered 265 ships. They were: the frigate *Liverpool*, which led the fleet; then came the *Eagle*, sixty-four guns, on board which were the Howe brothers; behind the *Eagle* and to its right, the *Augusta*, sixty-four guns; to its left in the same relative position, the *Raisonnable*, sixty-four guns; in the center, right and left respectively, the *Somerset*, sixty-four guns, and the *Isis*, fifty guns. The last ship in the fleet was the *Nonsuch*, which had for its couriers the *Swift* and the *Dispatch*, both sixteen guns. Nine frigates sailed around the fleet at some distance. Several of these were dispatched far out but finally joined the fleet again.

The daily thunderstorms did much damage to the ships. Lightning struck the masts of the transport *Britannia*, on which General Howe's entire suite had embarked, and also those of the *Henry*, carrying part of the horses of the 16th Regiment of Dragoons. On the former, two servants were lamed; and on the latter, seven horses were rendered unfit for duty. The wind was unfavorable all the way. The fleet spent three days before the mouth of the Delaware, plying to and fro. The frigates *Roebuck* and

[22] Captain John Bourmaster, master of the *Fanny*.

Janny [23] are still stationed in the river near Reedy Point, beyond which the rebels have some fireships. Besides, they have many guns mounted on the right bank near the entrance.

During the voyage several prizes were taken on our left. Of these I know nothing certain, however. On the other hand, many rebel ships smartly escaped our best frigate. On the 9th of August the fleet finally reached the lowest point of Chesapeake Bay. At five o'clock in the evening, when we took the first sounding, we found sixty-two fathoms of water. From the 10th to the 12th of August the fleet ran into the bay with a moderate wind, sailing closer to Fort Henry than to Fort Charles. Both shores of Virginia were visible, but they were more distinct after the fleet was able to get on the right course. During the passage up the bay we sounded bottom at twenty-one and from sixteen to nine fathoms. On the 18th of August the fleet passed the broad Wicomico River, the point of which, called by the same name, is the border line between Virginia and Maryland. Where the river enters the bay it has a rather strong current, which was on our left.

Finally, on the 22nd of August the fleet cast anchor between the Sassafras and Elk rivers in water varying from nine to six and one-half fathoms. The warships were compelled to remain farther behind. On the 23rd and 24th we took soundings in the Elk River.

[23] Possibly a confusion of the *Roebuck's* sloop *Stanley* or a miscopying by Baurmeister's amanuensis of a badly written *Fowey*. Admiral Howe's dispatch to Philip Stephens, Secretary of the Admiralty, August 28, 1777, lists the *Pearl, Liverpool, Camilla,* and the sloop *Merlin* as being stationed in the Delaware and states that the *Roebuck* was under orders to return there. The *Stanley* was at the mouth of the Elk attending the operations of the army. The *Roebuck* and *Stanley,* which had been stationed in the Delaware throughout the summer of 1777, were withdrawn by Admiral Howe when his fleet reached its mouth, and the *Liverpool* substituted for them because of the intimate knowledge of Captain Hamond (*Roebuck*) of the Chesapeake. See PRO, Admiralty Papers, Secretary's Office—Letters from the Admirals, vol. 487, *passim* (photostats in the Library of Congress). The *Fowey,* which had been stationed in the Delaware off and on during 1776 and the spring of 1777, was at this time in Irish waters and did not return to America until late December, 1777. See the log of the *Fowey,* PRO, Admiralty Papers. Mr. Hilary Jenkinson of the Public Record Office has kindly informed me that an examination of the log of the *Roebuck* failed to reveal a clue to the identity of the *Janny.* There was a transport *Fanny,* but it seems scarcely credible that Baurmeister could have confused this with a frigate. Major André in his description of the Mischianza, the farewell party given to the Howe brothers in Philadelphia (*Gentleman's Magazine and Historical Chronicle,* Aug., 1778) mentions an armed ship *Fanny.* Cf. previous note.

Some people of Maryland, to the right of the fleet, brought fowl, fruits, and milk to several of our ships, for which they were well paid. Neither enemy ships nor rebels were in sight, though on the 17th of August we had seen and pursued an armed galley below Wicomico River.

In the city of Annapolis on the left shore of Maryland we saw a provincial flag, but sailed past without firing at it. This city is situated in a valley not far from the shore. With field glasses we could distinctly make out the streets, a large church, and other new, beautiful buildings which belong to the tobacco manufacturers—so the pilots told us. On both shores were tobacco fields, a few grain fields, large pastures with cattle, and a great deal of woods. Already, the water in the entire bay was sweet. The springs along the shores are clearer and colder than any in Germany.

On the 25th we disembarked on the left bank of the Elk River, in Cecil County, the last county in Maryland. The grenadiers, the jägers, the light infantry, and the 1st Artillery Brigade were the first to go ashore. There was no interference at all. The people, who live in scattered houses, were amazed to see so many ships in a river where large transports had not been before. When they learned that they were English ships, they left their homes, their goods and chattels, and their cattle. In the first onrush the rigid orders against plundering were not strictly observed. This made General Howe sentence some to be hanged on the spot and others to be flogged within an inch of their lives. On the other hand, the Hessian troops under Colonel von Donop and Lieutenant Colonel von Wurmb were warmly thanked in the orders of the 28th [24] for observing the necessary discipline in every way.

On the 26th Lieutenant General von Knyphausen went ashore; also, enough wagons were unloaded for the horses which the army had brought along. General Howe made his headquarters at Elk Ferry. A strange incident occurred on the 26th of August when a Pennsylvanian produced a new kind of protection to be signed by us. Many thousand copies had been printed in New York, both in English and in German. None of us had known of it, or previously given any. It has caused a thorough in-

---

[24] In the following journal Baurmeister refers to these orders as of August 27.

vestigation to be started, and now a different kind of protection is given. It is, however, an ominous indication that the men at the head of the revolution were informed all too soon of our activities.

General Howe intended to move forward with a part of the army on the 27th, but did not set out until four o'clock in the morning of the 28th. He took with him the following troops: (1) the dismounted jägers, who were preceded by a noncommissioned officer and twelve mounted jägers; (2) two battalions of light infantry, the Queen's Rangers and Ferguson's Corps (these are English chasseurs), the English grenadiers, and the 1st Artillery Brigade with ten guns; (3) the Hessian grenadiers, the 2nd Artillery Brigade with ten guns, the baggage belonging to the generals and staff officers, the hospital wagons, and one wagon with entrenching tools; (4) three companies of the 16th Regiment of Dragoons, all the dismounted dragoons of this regiment, the mounted and dismounted jägers; and lastly, the brigade of Foot Guards and the Scottish 71st Regiment.

Quartermaster General Erskine posted this last regiment two to two and one-half miles from the old camp to the new, along the road to the Head of Elk or Iron Hill, in order to maintain communication with the rest of the army, which remained behind under his Excellency Lieutenant General von Knyphausen and consisted of the 3rd Artillery Brigade with ten guns, Major General Grey's English infantry brigade, Major General Agnew's, Major General Stirn's, and the rest of the 16th Regiment of Dragoons. On the 30th of August at five o'clock in the morning, Major General Grey's brigade broke camp and, furnished with two days' provisions, marched in the direction of Elk Town. General von Knyphausen, who has been ordered to follow the army, will depart shortly.

With the greatest respect, I remain [etc.]

: 9 :

I have not been able to write for some time, for we embarked at New York on the 16th of July and after a very difficult passage finally landed the 26th of August on the east bank of the Elk River far above Turkey Point in Cecil County, Maryland. During most of the voyage we had contrary wind and intense heat, which was accompanied almost daily by terrific thunderstorms, causing much suffering among men and horses and damage to the masts and sails.

On the 6th of July General Clinton returned from England and on the 14th relieved General Knyphausen at Kings Bridge. The latter went to New York and embarked on the warship *Nonsuch* with Lieutenant Colonel von Cochenhausen, Major du Puy, and Captain Phipps. The rest of the suite and I went on board the *Elizabeth*. General Howe joined Admiral Howe on the *Eagle*, and General Howe's suite went on board the *Britannia*.

On the 20th of July the fleet, consisting of 264 sail, weighed anchor before Staten Island, sailed past Sandy Hook, and formed

[25] This journal was enclosed in the letter of Oct. 26 (No. 10).

in six divisions, each commanded by a lieutenant of the navy, the whole being under the command of Captain Bourmaster, who received and gave out all orders.

The Commodore, Captain Griffith of the *Nonsuch,* whose ship sailed astern of the fleet, had at his command two sloops of war, the *Swift* and the *Dispatch.* The *Eagle,* preceded by the frigate *Liverpool,* thirty-two guns, led the fleet. Four men-of-war, the *Raisonnable, Somerset, Augusta,* and *Isis,* kept in the center, while nine frigates circled around the fleet at some distance. These frigates took some prizes.

We had the following troops with us: one company of English Riflemen under Captain Ferguson, one provincial battalion (Wemys), two battalions of English grenadiers and two battalions of light infantry, the Hessian and Anspach jägers, three Hessian grenadier battalions under Colonel von Donop, the three battalions of the 71st Highland Regiment, the brigade of English Guards, the 1st English Brigade (General Cornwallis), the 2nd (General Grant), the 3rd (General Grey), and the 4th (Brigadier General Agnew), and General Stirn's Hessian brigade consisting of the Leib Regiment, Mirbach's, Donop's, and the Combined Battalion [26] under Colonel von Loos. Then we had three artillery brigades with their trains and one wagon of tents for each company. There were also five hospital ships in the fleet, three of which have recently taken in the Hessian sick, amounting at present to about three hundred.

During our passage twenty-seven men and one hundred and seventy horses died, and about one hundred and fifty horses were disembarked totally unfit for duty—a natural consequence of spending more than five weeks on a voyage which in good weather can be made in six or eight days. Moreover, the troops were ordered to embark on the transports immediately after the Jersey expedition and so had lain before Staten Island more than two weeks.

[26] After the total defeat of von Rall's brigade at Trenton, the remainder of the regiments of his brigade, namely his own, von Lossberg's, and von Knyphausen's, were reorganized to form the Combined Battalion, which was put under the command of Colonel (later Brigadier General) Johann August von Loos. See also 1777, note 78.

When on the 28th of July we reached the mouth of the Delaware, we all supposed that we would run up into it and land, but the *Roebuck* frigate brought the news from the river that two English frigates had ascended as far as Reedy Point and anchored there to keep watch above the point. The frigates found a rebel fireship stationed there and ascertained that the banks could be easily defended by batteries, so landing there would be extremely hazardous. Hence, on the 1st of August we set out for Chesapeake Bay, which we reached on the 9th.

With Cape Henry to the west and Cape Charles to the east, we ran into the bay on the 14th. On the 18th of August the fleet passed the mouth of the Wicomico River, which separates Virginia from Maryland. Tobacco plantations, pasture lands, cultivated fields, and large woods border the shores as far as Annapolis, a city beautifully situated on the west coast. Adjacent to this city are two high batteries flying rebel flags. Many houses are scattered throughout this region. The fleet sailed past, and no boats were permitted to put out for shore.

On the 22nd of August the ships cast anchor in the middle of the mouth of the Elk River in four and one-half fathoms. Because of shallow water the men-of-war were compelled to remain fourteen English miles behind. On the 23rd and 24th the Elk River was sounded, and on the 25th and 26th a landing was effected under cover of the frigates *Roebuck* and *Vigilant* without the slightest interference.

Elk Ferry was made headquarters. Most of the inhabitants had fled from their homes, taking with them the best of their belongings; but they had also destroyed a great deal and driven their cattle into the woods. In spite of the strictest orders, marauding could not at first be entirely prevented. Several men in the most advanced English troops were caught by General Howe himself. One of these marauders was hanged, and six others were flogged within an inch of their lives.

Colonel von Donop and Lieutenant Colonel von Wurmb, however, were praised in the orders of the 27th of August for maintaining the best discipline among their troops. General von

Knyphausen made ten men of Stirn's brigade run the gantlet for some excesses. Good order and discipline have now been almost entirely restored. I must also boast to your Excellency of the especially good harmony existing between the Commander in Chief and General von Knyphausen, from which the entire army derives much satisfaction.

Our land operations now begin:

Early in the morning of the 28th of August General Howe with all the light troops, two brigades of artillery, the 1st and 2nd English Infantry Brigades, the English Guards, the 71st Regiment, and half of the 16th Regiment of Dragoons, dismounted, set out on their march and took a position between Elk Town and Iron Hill. The rest of the army remained behind under the command of General von Knyphausen. The 71st Regiment was posted by battalions at strategic places between the two encampments to maintain communications.

On Iron Hill [27] General Howe's troops encountered about six hundred rebels, whom they scattered, and in the Elk River about sixteen enemy boats were taken. The greater part of their cargoes, which consisted of tobacco, Indian corn, coffee, sugar, and flour, was distributed among the army, but the flour and corn were delivered to the English commissariat. On this day we learned that on the 24th of August the enemy army had marched through Philadelphia 8,500 strong with a vanguard of something over 2,000, that the said army was then at Wilmington, that three brigades under General Stirling had taken position at Christiana Bridge,[28] and that an advanced post of this corps, namely, 560 volunteers commanded by Brigadier General Maxwell, was occupying the ford across the little Gosch River [29] below Iron Hill.

[27] Washington and Captain Montresor both name Grey's (now Red) Hill as the height from which the Americans were dislodged on August 28. See Washington to Nelson, Sept. 2, 1777 (*Writings*, Fritzpatrick ed., IX, 164); and the *Journal of Capt. John Montresor*, ed. by G. D. Scull (*New York Historical Society Collections*, 1881). Grey's Hill is about a third of the way from Elkton to Iron Hill and lay directly on Howe's route.

[28] Now Christiana, Delaware.

[29] Gosch—one of Baurmeister's ways of spelling Cooch. Probably the small tributary of the Christiana just south of Iron Hill. The eminent Delaware historian, Hon. Edward W. Cooch of Cooch's Bridge, informed me that he had never heard of a name for this stream, and that though it ordinarily is fordable its entire length,

Therefore, General Howe ordered the 3rd English Infantry Brigade under General Grey, the rest of the 16th Regiment of Dragoons, and the 1st Battalion of the 71st Regiment to cross the Elk at Elk Ferry early in the morning of August 30th and encamp at Cecil Church,[30] approximately four English miles from the right bank of the Elk River.

On the 31st General von Knyphausen followed the same road with the rest of the troops. We joined General Grey at Cecil Church, where we made camp. The houses were empty here, too. The cattle were driven in and delivered to the English commissariat, which had already acquired a large cattle and sheep park, wherefrom it furnished the army twice weekly with fresh meat, instead of salt provisions, in addition to the flour and good rum.

On the 2nd of September Lieutenant General von Knyphausen proceeded with his corps to Mill Dam [31] in accordance with the orders given the troops on the 1st of September: "Tomorrow morning by five o'clock camp must be broken and the regiments must be at the front ready to march. The old pickets will have been previously withdrawn. The new pickets of the English regiments will make up the vanguard and take along two of Lieutenant Willson's 3-pounders; then will follow the English dragoons, except that one noncommissioned officer and six dragoons will march at the head of the pickets; then all the quartermasters and officers' men from the battalions of the 71st Regiment; then the 3rd and 4th English Infantry Brigades by half companies; then the Hessian Leib Regiment, Mirbach's, the Combined Battalion, and half of von Donop's Regiment, then the baggage (the wagons of the generals first and the rest in the same order as the regiments). The baggage will be followed by the cattle, and the guards assigned to it will keep the drovers in order. The Hes-

---

after heavy rains it swells considerably. There were heavy rains on August 26 and 27, 1777.

There was also a ford across the Christiana at the Welsh Tract Baptist Church under the northeastern slope of Iron Hill on the old Great Road to Elk, to which Baurmeister may refer here, but inasmuch as the ford and road fell into disuse after the building of Cooch's Bridge, prior to the Revolution, this seems less likely.

[30] Now known as St. Augustine Church, St. Augustine, Maryland.

[31] Lum's Pond, about one mile southwest of Kirkwood, Delaware.

sian pickets will patrol along both sides of the baggage and cattle train, keeping particularly close watch on the right. Lieutenant Colonel Heymell [32] will form the rear with the other half of von Donop's Regiment, which is to be preceded by Lieutenant Willson's two remaining 3-pounders. Everyone is warned against setting fire to houses, barns, or other buildings along the line of march. At each building a double post will be left, which is to be relieved by each successive battalion until the rear guard. In addition, one officer and fifteen dragoons will follow the rear guard." This marching order was maintained up to Mill Dam. The dragoons preceding the vanguard fell in with some Maryland militia, some of whom they took prisoners.

Early in the morning of the 3rd of September Lieutenant General von Knyphausen's corps set out from Mill Dam and Carson's Tavern [33] and marched to Aiken's Tavern [34] in Pencader Hundred, joining the army on the high land beyond this tavern. General Howe had left Elk Town on this morning, leaving General Grant behind with four battalions. The enemy had made an attempt on the outposts which had been sent out from Elk Town and stationed under Iron Hill, but they were driven back with a few wounded on both sides. General Howe's vanguard consisted of the Hessian foot jägers under Lieutenant Colonel von Wurmb. They encountered the enemy outposts at Cooch's Bridge and attacked them. On the far side of the river, on the heights along the main Philadelphia road, the rebels were said to have many strong posts.

Captain von Wreden gained a patch of woods on the enemy's left flank, from which he made a spirited attack. When his jägers cannonaded their front with some amusettes and charged with bayonets, the enemy withdrew in the direction of Christiana Bridge, leaving behind thirty killed—among them five officers— but taking their wounded with them. General Cornwallis and

---

[32] Lieutenant Colonel (later Colonel) Carl Philipp Heymell.

[33] Also known as the Buck Tavern. About one hundred yards south of the Chesapeake and Delaware Canal and one quarter of a mile north of the village of Summit Bridge.

[34] Now Glasgow, Delaware.

Colonel von Donop posted pickets on the terrain vacated by the enemy and occupied the road to Christiana Bridge or Philadelphia and the one to Fisher's Mill [35] and Newark. The army went into camp at Aiken's Tavern, which was used as headquarters. General Howe expressed his satisfaction with the good behavior of the vanguard in general orders as follows:

"The spirited manner in which Lieutenant Colonel von Wurmb opposed the advanced corps of the main body of the rebel troops deserves the special acknowledgments of the Commanding General." [36]

This advanced enemy corps is said to have consisted of 650 men under Colonel Maxwell and to have been detached from the three brigades stationed at Christiana Bridge, whither General Stirling is said to have marched from Wilmington as early as the 25th of August. General Washington himself is reported to be at Wilmington with the main army, the strength of which is reputed to be fifteen thousand regulars, not counting the militia under Generals Armstrong and Potter,[37] said to number another fifteen thousand men.

The army remained encamped through the 7th of September, during which time all tents and other heavy baggage and the sick were taken to Elk Town and put on transports, so that the provision train could be strengthened, which, on the 8th of September, when the army set out in three divisions, consisted of 276 wagons loaded with rum, flour, and salt meat.

When General Howe learned that the enemy would not go into a regular camp at Wilmington and had withdrawn all but fifty men from Christiana Bridge, and when he had obtained further information of the real strength of the enemy's force from

[35] On Christiana Creek, about a mile and a half northwest of Cooch's Bridge, toward Newark.

[36] Howe MS Orderly Book (William L. Clements Library) gives the following: "The spirited manner in which Lieutenant Colonel von Wurmb & the officers and men yesterday engaged & defeated the chosen advanced corps of the enemy deserves the highest encomiums & calls for the General's fullest acknowledgments."

[37] Brigadier General John Armstrong and Brigadier General James Potter, both Pennsylvania militia. Potter was in command of the militia during the Philadelphia campaign.

a captured German officer named von Uechtritz, [38] he set out with
the army on the 8th of September to march by way of Newark to
the heights called Society Hills. These hills are situated this side
of New Garden Meeting House at the intersection of the Newark–
Lancaster road with the Chester road. The enemy had not expected this move and were compelled to quit all their posts in the
neighborhood of Wilmington. Leaving behind one brigade of
Maryland militia, they crossed Brandywine Creek at Chadd's
Ford. The main army occupied the hills on the far side of the
creek, while a detachment under Brigadier General Greene, composed of a thousand volunteers from the regular battalions, among
them perhaps some fifty light dragoons, remained this side of the
creek taking post as far as Welch's Tavern, four English miles
from Chadd's Ford.

At one o'clock in the afternoon of the 9th of September, after
General Howe had obtained sufficient information about the
enemy, the army set out on the march in two columns. The Commanding General remained with the first column, which was led
by General Cornwallis, and marched about two miles on the right
of the second column, which was led by Lieutenant General von
Knyphausen. The marching orders were such that both columns
would arrive at the place of rendezvous at Welch's Tavern at the
same time.

The column on the left under Lieutenant General von Knyphausen, in the middle of which was the entire provision train and
all the artillery and cattle, marched along the New Garden road
through continuous narrow defiles. The van reached Kennett
Square several hours after nightfall. General Howe, who with the
van of the first column had arrived at the Quaker church in Marl-
borough Township, did not think it advisable to proceed further
and ordered the army to halt in column formation. He posted the
grenadiers between the two columns and the 3rd English Infantry

[38] Louis Augustus, Baron de Uechtritz (according to F. B. Heitman, *Historical
Register of the Officers of the Continental Army*, Washington, 1914), who served
in Ottendorff's Pennsylvania Battalion, which was later merged with Armand's
partisan corps, in which de Uechtritz served as captain. Eelking-Rosengarten (p.
110) has von Üchtritz and states that he was formerly an officer in the army of
Saxony.

Brigade to the rear of the second column and had this column's provision train and baggage drawn up at Kennett Square. All this was accomplished in a steady downpour, and by the time it was finished and the rear guard had finally come up, day was breaking.

On the 10th of September the army pitched a regular camp in two lines at Kennett Square. The Hessian jägers and the light troops occupied the approaches, but they saw none of the enemy save some light dragoons. The enemy patrols could advance farther than ours because they were known and feared by the inhabitants, whereas ours risked being shot from ambush or cut off at every house, bush, woods, and fence—which has happened more than once.

We learned that the rebels, after much discussion between Washington and the other generals, especially one Du Coudray, have changed their position on the hills beyond Brandywine Creek, so that their right wing extends to Terrenton [39] and Edward Brand's [40] mill, and their left to Dilworth, with the Brandy-

[39] Both times this word is used, it is clearly written in Roman script. Probably a corruption of Thornton, in Thornbury Township, Delaware County, or of Darlington, the name of a prominent family in Birmingham Township, Chester County.

Thornton lies three miles northeast of Dilworth. Its location as well as its tradition indicates it to be the Terrenton referred to below, through which the Americans retreated to Chester after the battle. But, if, as Baurmeister says, the American left was at Dilworth, the right could not have been at Thornton, unless Baurmeister was thinking, contrary to his usual practice, of the American right as the wing opposite his own right.

Darlington's Corners lies approximately two miles northwest of Dilworth, while Abraham Darlington's house was located about two miles west of Dilworth not far from Caleb Brinton's mill on the Brandywine. Both these places fit Baurmeister's statement on this page, but cannot be the Terrenton through which the Americans retreated *after* the battle, the first being in the wrong direction and the second lying within the battlefield.

[40] Undoubtedly Brinton (sometimes spelled Branton), the name of a prominent Chester County family. Two mills were owned by members of this family in 1777: one by Caleb Brinton at Brinton's Ford, one mile above Chadd's Ford on the Brandywine, and the other by William Brinton on the site of the present Brinton Lake Club between Dilworth and Thornton. Edward Brinton (d. 1779) was the largest landholder of Chester County at this time, but I can find no record of his owning a mill in 1777.

For this and the above note, I am deeply indebted to Mr. Chester F. Baker of the Delaware County Historical Society and to Dr. Henry Pleasants, Jr., of the Chester County Historical Society, as well as to the *Proprietary and other Tax Lists of the County of Chester for the years 1774, 1779, 1780, 1781 and 1785*, ed. by Wm. Henry Egle; J. Smith Futhey and Gilbert Cope, *History of Chester County, Pennsylvania . . .*, Philadelphia, 1881; B. J. Lossing, *Pictorial Field Book of the*

wine Creek in front and the main Chester road in the rear; [41] that they have thrown up batteries covering both fords of the creek at Chadd's Ford; that four deputies from Congress have approved this position and charged General Washington to defend it to the utmost; and, furthermore, that they sought to admonish the common soldiers to remain steadfast by all sorts of chimera. They have even ordered religious services to be held in each battalion and the clergy to exhort the men to believe that the British army, though parading under the name of parliamentary regulars, is made up of nothing but discontented stragglers; that this army is so weak that it was compelled to evacuate the Jerseys last June with great loss; that in desperation it was now making a last attempt to maintain a foothold in America (for which reason it embarked on ships) and, being repelled in the Delaware, found it necessary to sail into Chesapeake Bay and land on the east bank of the Elk in Maryland; that it had lost more than one third of its men through sickness; and that nothing was more certain than that the small remainder would now be annihilated—the fruit of their last victory. [42] The result will be seen:

At sunrise on the 11th of September, in accordance with an order received the previous day, the army set out in two columns to march along two different roads. General Howe remained with the column on the left, which was led by General Cornwallis. Lieutenant General von Knyphausen commanded the column on the right.

Cornwallis's column consisted of the Hessian Jäger Corps, both mounted and dismounted, the light infantry, all the grena-

---

American Revolution, New York, 1855; and Bowen and Futhey's Plan of the Battle of Brandywine, September 11th, 1777. Compiled from an actual Survey made during the Summer of 1846.

[41] Detailed accounts of the American positions are given in Sullivan's testimony before the Court of Inquiry, New Hampshire Provincial and State Papers, XVII, 192. Inasmuch, however, as they were taken after the receipt of the intelligence Baurmeister reports here, they cannot be identified with the line from Dilworth to Terrenton and Edward Brand's mill.

[42] For an interesting parallel to parts of this long sentence, see Washington's general orders, Wilmington, Sept. 5, 1777, as printed in the Pennsylvania Evening Post, Sept. 9, 1777.

diers of the army, the British Guards, the 3rd and 4th Brigades of English Infantry, the 3rd Brigade of Heavy Artillery, and half of the 16th Regiment of Dragoons.

The column under Lieutenant General von Knyphausen was made up of Captain Ferguson's British Riflemen, one battalion of the Queen's Rangers, the 71st Highland Regiment (which consisted of three battalions), the 1st and 2nd English Brigades under General Grant, General Stirn's brigade (i.e., the Leib Regiment, Donop's, Mirbach's, and the Combined Battalion), the other half of the 16th Regiment of Dragoons, two brigades of heavy artillery, the entire artillery and provision train, the baggage, and the cattle.

The 1st and 2nd Battalions of the Scottish Highlanders flanked both sides of the train, while the 3rd Battalion formed the rear guard.

This column marched along the main Chester road, which between Welch's Tavern and Chadd's Ford, has many defiles between hills and woods. When our vanguard, i.e., the Riflemen and the Queen's Rangers, arrived at Welch's Tavern, it encountered the first enemy troops. It drove them back and became master of the defile without delaying the march of the column. The skirmishing continued to the last hills of Chadd's Ford. Heretofore the enemy had been repulsed by our vanguard alone, but now the engagement became more serious. The van had arrived at a place where the road passes through some swampy land. On both sides of this lowland are hills and woods, and beyond it a road turns off to the left from the main road and runs through this lowland for about half an English mile. This road, which leads to a ford on Brandywine Creek, was enfiladed by an enemy battery situated beyond the creek. All the woods were full of enemy troops.

Captain Ferguson posted his Riflemen behind a house beyond the lowland and was supported by a hundred men under Captain Le Long from Stirn's brigade. The English 49th Regiment, two heavy guns, and two 3-pounders were detached to the right of the column and posted on an elevation directly above the Riflemen. In the meantime the Queen's Rangers had proceeded to the left and after a short but very rapid musketry fire, supported by the

23rd English Regiment, which had filed out of the column to the left, quickly drove the rebels out of their woods and straight across the lowland. Under cover of a continuous cannonade, the 28th English Regiment filed out of the column to the right, and the rebels, who had been shouting "Hurrah" and firing briskly from a gorge in front of us and the heights behind it, where they had a small flèche, were quickly put to flight.

Meanwhile the Riflemen and the Queen's Rangers had also advanced toward the left flank of the enemy, who were by this time constantly yielding ground. The 28th, 23rd, 55th, and 40th English Regiments, the Leib Regiment, and Mirbach's were formed in line on the height beyond the lowland and the road to the ford; the Combined Battalion and Donop's Regiment took position in column formation along this road, and the 5th, 49th, 27th, and 4th English Regiments this side of the lowland, on the heights along the creek. All these movements were covered by the gunfire of the English artillery, the various pieces having been mounted with all possible haste in strategic places and on high ground.

The enemy's fire was also heavy, especially that from the battery of four guns and one howitzer situated just beyond the ford. But although the balls and grapeshot were well aimed and fell right among us, this cannonade had but little effect, partly because the battery was placed too low. We pushed our light troops and outposts close to the creek, for the enemy on this side were completely dispersed. Then we straightened our line, posted one battalion of the 71st Regiment and the Queen's Dragoons [43] on the height on our right flank where the enemy troops had held a flèche, and drew up the baggage under cover of the two other battalions of the 71st Regiment on the rising ground where we first skirmished with the enemy.

These movements were completed by half past ten, and Lieutenant General von Knyphausen thought it wise to maintain this position until the left column should begin its attack upon the enemy's right wing, when he would attempt to cross the creek.

[43] The 16th (or the Queen's) Regiment of (Light) Dragoons.

The small-arms fire ceased entirely, although our cannon fired from time to time, each shot being answered by the enemy. The purpose of our gunfire, however, was only to advise the second column of our position.

The enemy apparently thought that we were maneuvering to approach their formidable position and were likely hesitating about fording the creek. Hence, they directed all their attention to the fords between them and us, especially to one very strategically situated, in front of which the 4th English Regiment was posted and which was covered by two guns on the nearest hill.

Toward half past one, however, the patrols of their right wing must have informed them of the approach of the second column. We saw several battalions, some artillery, and some troops of dragoons file to the right to reinforce their right wing and other changes in the line being made to give the necessary defensive strength to their left wing, which had been weakened by the removal of some of these troops.

Finally, toward four o'clock we heard the attack of the left column. Lieutenant General von Knyphausen gave orders to advance; the artillery began a fearful cannonade; the 1st Battalion of the 71st Regiment pushed toward the ford and crossed the stream; it was followed by the Riflemen and the Queen's Rangers, the 4th English Regiment led by his Excellency General von Knyphausen himself, the 5th and all the English regiments of this brigade according to their rank, and, lastly, Stirn's brigade.

The crossing was effected on our right wing, about 250 paces from the enemy's battery, which lay a little to the left of the ford. After crossing, the troops attacked them furiously, partly with the bayonet. The enemy's left wing began to fall back, and we took the battery. Our regiments, which pushed across one by one, gained one height after another, from which the enemy withdrew. They withstood one more rather severe attack behind some houses and ditches in front of their left wing. Finally, we saw the entire enemy line and four guns, which fired frequently, drawn up on another height in front of a dense forest, their right wing resting on the Chester road.

By the time it grew dark, the van of the left column and General Howe had joined us. General Howe made Dilworth his headquarters. The British army, complete masters of the so-called Brandywine Hills, which the enemy had had infinite hope of holding and believed to be impregnable, took position on them in excellent order. The enemy, however, gained the road to Chester in considerable confusion. Had not the darkness favored their retreat, we might have come into possession of much artillery, munitions, and horses.

The march and attack of the left column was as follows: It set out on its march at the same time as our column. Two miles from camp it fell in with a small hostile detachment, which it repulsed. The march to James Trimble's ford, where it arrived at eleven o'clock, was uneventful. Here, eight miles from the old camp, it forded one of the two forks of the Brandywine and two miles farther, the other, at Jefferis' Ford. Between the east and west Brandywine fords, it halted until all had crossed. At Birmingham Meeting House the column was to re-form and advance upon the enemy's right flank and rear. It was then about two o'clock in the afternoon, and the Meeting House lies seven miles from Chadd's Ford, where Lieutenant General von Knyphausen's column crossed the Brandywine.

Meanwhile, the enemy's position had been reconnoitered by advance patrols. On the hill beyond the Meeting House they had seen a corps of about one thousand men and a party of enemy cavalry somewhat nearer our left wing. They had observed, furthermore, that a corps of two thousand men and five guns was making for these hills in great haste to join the one thousand men already posted there. Then several more enemy battalions followed. Bordered with cannon, they formed quite a formidable front, on the right wing of which there appeared a little later the van of another column coming from the Dilworth road. General Howe dispatched some of the Hessian jägers close to the aforesaid Meeting House, where they occupied an advantageous post. During this time the troops had been formed in three columns for an attack:

LEFT COLUMN	CENTER COLUMN	RIGHT COLUMN
4th English Infantry Brigade	All the dismounted jägers 2 battalions of light infantry 2 battalions of English grenadiers 3 battalions of Hessian grenadiers Artillery	Brigade of Guards English and Hessian cavalry

The 3rd English Infantry Brigade stayed behind to cover the baggage.

At four o'clock in the afternoon the columns advanced to attack, the center column along the main road, and the other two on both sides through valleys and woods. When they had come close enough, they formed in line and advanced upon the enemy, who received them with a heavy fire of cannon and small arms. Our men, however, made a spirited attack with bayonets and drove them back into the woods, following close upon their heels.

Colonel von Donop with the Hessian grenadiers supported the English brigade of Guards throughout, as he had been ordered to do. Three companies of light infantry threw themselves against the flank of the enemy's right wing, which seemed to be outflanking our line, and after turning it back, rejoined their battalion. The Hessian grenadiers joined the English grenadiers in the line.

General Agnew, however, in spite of great efforts, was unable to align completely the 4th Brigade, forming the left wing, because of the rough terrain. Thus the left flank of the 2nd English Grenadier Battalion was unsupported for some time and was compelled to fall back a little before the enemy's attack. General Agnew arrived just in time to support this battalion, and the enemy withdrew all along the line from one height to another. Though they fought stubbornly all the way, they were compelled to escape through Terrenton [44] toward Chester. By five o'clock in the evening the entire column had gained a victory and ad-

[44] See 1777, note 39.

vanced far enough to join our column on the Brandywine Hills at nightfall.

The enemy's loss in killed, wounded, and prisoners is said to be more than one thousand men. We had about five hundred killed and wounded in the two columns. Our first column captured six brass cannon, and the second, four more and one howitzer. The howitzer had been cast in Philadelphia in 1777. The cannon consisted, for the most part, of French 4-pound Couleuvrines made at Douay in 1737, and two new Hessian 3-pounders which the rebels had taken at Trenton, one of which they had rebored to make a 6-pounder of it. Moreover, some munition wagons, a quantity of muskets, most of which were made in the French style and had, perhaps, been furnished by French factories, and many entrenching tools fell into our hands.

On the morning of the 12th of September we buried the dead and transported the wounded to Dilworth, where we found a flour magazine, from which the army was provisioned for two days.

Major General Grant marched with the Queen's Rangers, the 1st and 2nd English Infantry Brigades, and three troops of dragoons to within a half-mile of Chester without meeting any of the enemy. General Sullivan was posted behind Chester Creek with a corps of two thousand men, and the main body of the enemy had gone beyond Darby in its retreat.

Our army pitched camp so that the right wing extended to the lower Chadd's ford and the left to Dilworth, where the grenadiers covered headquarters. The Hessian jägers, however, were posted behind Dilworth. Toward evening the baggage train and provision wagons joined the army after fording the Brandywine. The 71st Regiment, which had covered them and which, having been composed of three battalions heretofore, was now formed into two, marched to Wilmington, dispersed some enemy militia, and found seven iron guns in a trench.

When this came to the knowledge of General Howe, who had been assured by Admiral Howe that he would have several ships at Wilmington on the 15th of September at the latest, Colo-

nel von Loos with the Combined Battalion was ordered to escort
all the sick and wounded to Wilmington early on the 14th, to
establish a hospital there, and to remain until further orders.
This was accomplished without the least interference, in spite of
the fact that the road through Kennett Square was made rather
unsafe by scattered hostile parties.

Each regiment had given three wagons for the transport of
the invalids; on these wagons von Loos's men loaded all the flour
found at Wilmington and in the houses along the road. On the
15th of September they again joined the army, which was a little
short of flour and rum, although it had fresh meat in abundance.
General Howe gave permission to the rebels to send their own
doctors and surgeons to care for their wounded.

On the 16th of September the army broke camp and took the
road to the Turk's Head,[45] whither patrols of Hessian jägers had
advanced from Dilworth. This was also the objective of General
Cornwallis, who was approaching from the Chester district. He
had joined General Grant on the 14th with the English grenadiers
and light infantry, having taken the road past Coob's [46] Meeting
House, where his patrols captured two enemy staff officers. After
both columns had effected a junction, General Howe had General
von Knyphausen advance to the Boot Tavern. The army was to
encamp beyond the White Horse [47] on the Valley Hills along the
Lancaster–Philadelphia highway.

In the meantime the rebels had continued their retreat as far
as Germantown, but on the 14th had started out again and passed
the Schuylkill at Swedes Ford [48] and Yellow Springs. They had
left their heavy baggage and their hospital behind at this last
crossing, and encamped at the White Horse. Generals Wayne and
Maxwell with about two thousand men have been detached forward to observe our movements between Chester and Dilworth.

[45] West Chester, Pennsylvania.
[46] Cobbs?
[47] White Horse Tavern in East Whiteland Township, Chester County, Pennsylvania. The present village of White Horse preserves the old name. For an account of this important tavern, see " 'The Sign of the Whitehorse' in East Whiteland" in J. F. Sachse, The Wayside Inns on the Lancaster Roadside between
Philadelphia and Lancaster, Lancaster, Pa., 1912–14, pp. 185–201.
[48] Norristown, Pennsylvania.

This enemy corps arrived toward one o'clock on the 16th in front of our right column at a time when both our columns were making a halt behind the Boot Tavern and while Colonel von Donop was reconnoitering the road in front with a part of the jägers of the vanguard. Colonel von Donop was almost cut off, but he joined the vanguard again with all possible speed after skillfully executing some maneuvers to his left. All the jägers, mounted and dismounted, and the Hessian grenadiers formed in a few minutes, left the column, and advanced in line to the right against the rebels, who were posted on high ground covered with a corn field and orchards. The jägers, dodging behind the fences around the fields and woods, had an opportunity to demonstrate to the enemy their superior marksmanship a .d their skill with the amusettes, and the enemy, who soon retired to a dense forest, left behind many killed and wounded.

I wish I could give a description of the downpour which began during the engagement and continued until the next morning. It came down so hard that in a few moments we were drenched and sank in mud up to our calves.

But since General Howe and Lord Cornwallis had also moved to the right, the enemy detained us on our march and thus succeeded to some extent in their designs. General Washington probably realized by this time that he would be unable to take the open road to Lancaster with his entire army. He therefore recrossed the Schuylkill and took position at Swedes Ford, leaving General Sullivan with six brigades and a suitable number of artillery at Yellow Springs.

Congress left Philadelphia and, insofar as the new constitution permitted, took along all well-to-do inhabitants, mostly Quakers. The enemy army hospital was established at Bethlehem.

On the 17th of September General Cornwallis went into camp at the White Horse. Lieutenant General von Knyphausen's column also marched to this place. After a respite of two hours, the entire army continued its march another six miles and encamped on the Valley Hills in West Whiteland Township, Chester County. Tredyffrin was headquarters.

The Hessian Jäger Corps covered the flank of the right wing along the roads which lead eastward to Swedes Ford and Philadelphia and northward to Valley Forge, whither the 1st Battalion of Light Infantry and the English grenadiers and Guards had previously been detached. Here they had taken a flour magazine of four thousand tons, many iron implements, as well as other goods like soap and candles. Over twenty thousand broadaxes and a great quantity of horseshoes and horseshoe nails were distributed to the army. They also found many iron cannon balls of various sizes; they kept some of these and scattered the rest. Finally, they destroyed the smithy and all the tools.

Early in the morning of the 21st of September the army got under way again, making a halt in its old camp. The Hessian Leib Regiment and von Donop's were posted at various places along the Philadelphia road to cover the army's march.

In the meantime General Sullivan had detached General Wayne from Yellow Springs by way of the White Horse to harass our left flank. However, General Grey had set out with the 3rd Brigade and the 2nd Battalion of Light Infantry at ten o'clock on the evening of the 20th to surprise this enemy corps. He encountered it at half past twelve at night, guns in hand and ready to march. General Grey, having forbidden a single musket to be loaded, attacked their right wing with the bayonet. His men deployed so fast that they massacred it. The enemy artillery, which was already hitched up, succeeded in escaping with most of the munition wagons along the road to the White Horse, and the rest of the enemy followed, but in such confusion that many threw away their muskets. Some one hundred men were bayoneted, some seventy wounded, and eighty-two taken prisoners, and ten wagons were captured. General Grey rejoined the army after this fortunate coup.

When day came, General Howe sent a troop of dragoons to the place of encounter, with orders to destroy all the enemy's abandoned muskets, which numbered about one thousand. The wounded were taken to nearby houses. General Washington was advised of this by a flag of truce and given permission to send surgeons to dress their wounds.

General Wayne retired across the Schuylkill before sunrise with the rest of his men, while General Sullivan left Yellow Springs and joined General Washington's army, which is posted behind Swedes Ford on Swamp Creek.[49] Our army was not molested on its march on this day. It crossed Valley Creek at the Forge,[50] where the right wing took position; the rest of the line extended past the Bull's Head Tavern, across Pickering Creek and as far as French Creek, with the Schuylkill in front. This region is in Charlestown Township, Chester County.

Towards noon on the 22nd of September our right wing attempted to cross the Schuylkill at Fatland Ford.[51] After firing a few cannon shots, the enemy withdrew from the opposite bank, and the English Guards, a battalion of light infantry, six guns from the park, and twenty-five dragoons took post on the other side of the ford. Colonel von Donop, on our left wing, was also ordered to attempt to cross the Schuylkill at Schef's Ford [52] toward five o'clock in the evening. Captain Lorey with twenty horse and Captain von Wreden with sixty dismounted jägers crossed the river, while four fieldpieces cannonaded the enemy posted on the opposite bank. Captain von Westerhagen followed with a hundred grenadiers, while another hundred grenadiers under Captain Schimmelpfennig remained behind to support them in case of need. The enemy deserted their post and withdrew into a woods, whence they marched during the night to join General Washington's army. One mounted jäger was slightly wounded, as were also Captain Lorey's horse and the horses of two other jägers.

On the night of the 23rd of September at moonrise the army began its march, defiling to the right to Fatland Ford and there crossing the Schuylkill. The jägers and grenadiers recrossed at Scheff's Ford without being further annoyed by the enemy and joined the left wing of the army, which, in a split column, had crossed before eight o'clock in the morning. General Grant, who had remained behind with an English infantry brigade to cover

49 The first tributary of the Perkiomen above its mouth.

50 I.e., Valley Forge.

51 Fatland Ford was about half a mile below Valley Forge.

52 Gordon's Ford, at modern Phoenixville. Schef (Scheff) may possibly be a linguistic corruption of Jeff (i.e., Jeffrey), perhaps Jeffrey Gordon.

the baggage, artillery, and provisions train, then also crossed the river, and the army continued its march till three o'clock in the afternoon, when it arrived at Norriton and made camp—seventeen English miles from Philadelphia.

On the 25th of September the army, moving in two columns, advanced as far as Germantown, five English miles from Philadelphia. The right wing extended through the town toward Frankford Creek and the left as far as the Wissahickon. The Hessian Jäger Corps was posted by a stone bridge over the latter to form an outpost toward the Schuylkill.

At eight o'clock on the morning of September 26th Lord Cornwallis set out for Philadelphia with two English and two Hessian grenadier battalions (von Linsing's and von Lengerke's),[53] six 12-pounders, and four howitzers, and arrived at eleven. He posted strong guards in the central part of the city, a battalion of English grenadiers below it on the Delaware, and above it along the Schuylkill, von Linsing's Battalion, the other English grenadier battalion, and von Lengerke's. The artillery was divided between these last two posts.

Two enemy frigates, which have never been to sea and are said to have only part of their complements and no guns, have gone up the Delaware to Bristol along with some other boats, while two other frigates, the *Delaware*, twenty-eight guns, and the *Province*,[54] thirty-two guns, have anchored close to the city.

Philadelphia is rather a lovely city of considerable size and is laid out with parallel streets. The public squares are beautiful. For the most part, ordinary houses are moderately large and built of brick in the Dutch style. Classical architecture and its embellishments are met with only in the churches and in a few public buildings, of which the city hall, where Congress has been holding its sessions, is one of the most noteworthy.

The city is very charmingly situated in level, fertile country on the Delaware and Schuylkill rivers. At present it is only sparsely populated, because many inhabitants left with the enemy army,

---

[53] Lengerke's is the old Grenadier Battalion Block.

[54] Baurmeister means the province ship *Montgomery*. Cf. Hazelwood's orders for this attack, *Pennsylvania Archives*, V, 637.

but there are still many people left, especially Quakers. Commerce is increasing again considerably, for merchants receive cash for their goods, and paper money no longer circulates.

On the 27th of September the two frigates anchored near the city, and the *Fly*, a sloop of eight guns, cannonaded the battery of two 12-pounders which we had thrown up close to the city, but without any effect. Our battery did enough damage to the *Delaware* frigate to oblige her to strike her sails, while the *Province* and the *Fly* made for Bristol. Then a row galley loaded with ammunition confronted our battery. She was immediately cannonaded, and her masts were so shot to pieces that when she came near the *Delaware* frigate, her crew was compelled to leave her and escape in boats to the Jersey coast. We captured the crew and manned the frigate with a lieutenant and fifty sailors from the warship *Roebuck*. They had to come by land to Philadelphia from Chester, where this warship lay. The *Delaware* now serves to cover the city and observe other hostile vessels.

On the night of the 28th–29th of September the 1st English Grenadier Battalion, the 42nd, and the 10th Regiment, under the command of Colonel Stirling, crossed over to the Jerseys to capture the fort at Billingsport across from Mud Island. At the approach of our troops the rebels vacated the fort, abandoning eleven spiked iron cannon and leaving five killed and thirteen wounded, and retreated to Mud Island in the Delaware.

On the 30th of September two battalions of the 71st Regiment left Wilmington to occupy Chester, where large quantities of provisions were unloaded from the ships and transported overland to Philadelphia, because our ships could not pass Mud Island on account of the stockade built by the enemy in the Delaware and covered by a battery which they held on that island.

On the 2nd of October we established a complete bakery at Philadelphia.

We learned from enemy deserters that on the 28th of September General Washington, who was stationed with his army at Pottstown, ordered a *feu de joie* because General Burgoyne had been completely defeated by General Gates at Stillwater. Moreover, Washington is said to have distributed rum to all his troops and started the rumor that he would attack our army. On the 1st of October, after he had been reinforced with eight battalions of fresh militia from Virginia and all the troops which had been posted at the magazines between Reading and Lancaster, he marched to Norriton.

October 4. General Washington with his whole army set out before sundown yesterday on his march to surprise our army at Germantown at sunrise. He detached General Potter with two thousand men and two guns to take the Philadelphia road this side of the Schuylkill and attack our army's left wing on Wissa-hickon Creek, where the Hessian jäger picket was posted. General Washington with the main body of his army followed the road from Norriton to Germantown as far as Chestnut Hill, two miles beyond Beggars Town, where he halted toward midnight. He ordered General Wayne to march with one column to the left toward the Abington road and proceed along it and enter the center of Germantown at daybreak. This town is five English miles long. General Washington then continued his march to Beggars Town, where he arrived toward three o'clock in the morning. Here he made another halt to allow the troops detached to the right and left to gain their ground.

Shortly before sunrise a Hessian jäger patrol from our left wing encountered three hundred enemy troops one English mile from our most advanced outpost, and by daybreak we were convinced of the actual approach of the enemy army. It was so foggy on this morning that one could hardly see fifty paces.

Meanwhile the enemy had driven back the advanced pickets of the 2nd Battalion of Light Infantry posted between Germantown and Beggars Town. General Washington had so deployed his own column that one part would enter Germantown on the left, the second on the right, and the center by the street running through the city; thus he could attack our army along its entire front. General Wayne was to proceed by way of the Abington road and fall upon our right flank. The center column attacked the 2nd Battalion of Light Infantry with such vigor and superior strength that it was compelled to withdraw and leave behind one gun.

Colonel Musgrave, who was posted a little further to the rear with the 40th Regiment under orders to support the light infantry in case of attack, then advanced. But he saw the light infantry, continually charged by the enemy, withdraw quickly toward Germantown. Thus he was in danger of being cut off by the enemy columns deploying to the right and left, and so resolved to throw himself and his regiment into a stone house [55] on the right side of the street. Having accomplished this, he barricaded the doors and windows on the ground floor (the windows also had strong shutters).

On this floor he posted as many men as were necessary to hold back with the bayonet any who might gain an entrance to the house. With the rest of his men he went to the second floor, from which he fired with great effect upon the troops now completely surrounding the house. They, however, cannonaded the building with four 6-pounders and were determined to push the attack with all their strength. This and our especially courageous defense delayed their advance an hour and a half. Although cannon balls had torn open both outside doors, the bayonets kept the enemy from entering. In this attack they lost over one hundred men killed and one hundred and fifty wounded.

By this time the entire army was in motion and formed as follows: The 1st and 2nd Brigades, leaving the Abington road on their right, marched toward the road leading to the Frankford Creek bridge. The 3rd and 4th Brigades and the Hessian Leib Regiment advanced from their encampment and took position in Germantown. Von Minnigerode's Grenadier Battalion remained at its post on the left to support the jägers, who were to be reinforced by von Linsing's Grenadier Battalion from Philadelphia. Similarly, the English grenadier battalion advanced to strengthen the right wing. Von Donop's Regiment marched a little to the front and to the right toward the town to maintain communication with the left wing and support the pickets of the 3rd and 4th Brigades on that side of Germantown and also the Leib Regiment and von Donop.

The enemy, who had already penetrated far into Germantown and were firing from gardens and behind houses (which

[55] The house of Justice Benjamin Chew.

here are set far apart), were now attacked so fiercely that they gave up the attack on the house defended by Colonel Musgrave, abandoned the cannon they had captured from the light infantry, and made their retreat through the several streets in great haste.

General Potter and his column had come so close upon our left wing that while our right was making its attack, he rushed upon the jäger picket at the bridge so furiously that it was compelled to fall back a little; but after a company of jägers had advanced to its support, our men regained their post this side of the bridge. General Potter withdrew in the greatest haste and was pursued three English miles by Lieutenant Colonel von Wurmb.[56]

General Howe pursued the enemy with the right wing along the road leading to the bridge across Frankford Creek, while the Leib Regiment and two English regiments from the 4th Brigade pursued them along the left of this road. About four English miles from Germantown they encountered an enemy corps, which fired from a woods while retreating and wounded slightly several men of the Leib Regiment. General Stirn received a light contusion from a musket ball.

Finally, all the brigades in pursuit of the enemy aligned and halted this side of Chestnut Hill. The Leib Regiment and the 40th English Regiment were sent ahead to take post along the Reading Pike. Von Donop's Regiment now set out from Germantown along the above-mentioned road and posted small bodies of troops along it to maintain communications. The army maintained this disposition for several hours, but after the enemy had completely withdrawn, it moved back into its old encampment.

While Colonel Musgrave was defending the house, he lost nineteen killed and wounded in the 40th Regiment. The light infantry and those English regiments which were first engaged by the enemy in Germantown also had some losses. Major General Agnew [57] and Colonel Bird [58] remained on the field, and Colonel Walcott [59] was severely wounded. Our total loss probably amounts

[56] Probably with the Jäger Corps, which he commanded.
[57] Brigadier General James Agnew, Colonel of the 44th Foot.
[58] Lieutenant Colonel John Bird, 15th Foot.
[59] Lieutenant Colonel William Walcott, 5th Foot.

to some four hundred men, which is, however, only a guess. The Hessian Jäger Corps had six severely and four slightly wounded.

Nor can I give definite figures of the enemy's loss. Their killed and wounded, which are estimated at about eight hundred, are said to include several generals [60] and staff members. There are some forty officers among the three hundred and eighty prisoners. Von Linsing's and the English battalions which had come from Philadelphia to reinforce the army returned to the city, where the 23rd English Regiment and von Lengerke's Grenadier Battalion had been stationed during their absence.

Although everything has remained quiet in Philadelphia, several inhabitants were arrested because they had aroused suspicion of being well disposed toward the enemy. Later it was announced in the city and in the country that everyone must surrender his arms within a definite time, those failing to do so and later found with arms in their possession being threatened with very severe punishment. We are told that a great quantity of arms has already been surrendered.

On the 5th of October the wounded were transported to Philadelphia.

The army shifted its camp this morning so that the right wing extended further beyond Germantown, while on this side there remained only the 4th English Brigade and the two Hessian regiments, which were ordered to move forward. The Battalion von Minnigerode also moved slightly forward on the left wing. The jägers remained in their old camp.

On the 6th of October the regiments sent to Jersey rejoined the army.

On the 7th of October sixty jägers under Captain Ewald foraged as far as Plymouth without meeting any of the enemy.

On the 10th of October a packet arriving in the fleet brought letters from Europe dated in the month of June. It also brought the news that the rebels had made an attack on Staten Island, Long Island, and Kings Bridge on the 22nd of August, but were driven back with some loss.

[60] Brigadier General Francis Nash, of the Continental Army, died on October 7 of wounds received during the battle.

On the 11th we learned from deserters that General Washington was again approaching with his army to attack us. Moreover, a jäger picket of one noncommissioned officer and three men had been captured by the enemy the previous night on the road to Barren Hill and Swedes Ford. Therefore, the army turned out before daybreak; but since everything remained quiet, it returned to camp again toward nine o'clock in the morning.

The enemy, however, did intend to surprise the troops detached to Chester and Wilmington and for this purpose sent a corps under General Potter across the Schuylkill. Hence, the 71st Regiment was ordered from Chester to Wilmington to embark with the troops posted there.

October 12. Since the 9th of October we have been engaged in opening communications with the fleet in the Delaware and clearing this river of all enemy ships, so that we may soon break up the stockade sunk by the enemy at Mud Island. To accomplish this, we have raised batteries on Greenwich Island, Province Island, and Carpenter's Island to bombard the enemy's fort on Mud Island and their ships, consisting of some thirty sail, row galleys, and floating batteries.

In spite of repeated attacks on our batteries, during which Captain von Wurmb [61] (on the 8th) and Captain von Stamford (on the 10th) particularly distinguished themselves, our undertaking is progressing so well that we have hopes of hearing shortly of its final success.

On the 15th of October the enemy General Potter withdrew from the neighborhood of Wilmington and Chester. He camped yesterday at Foxhall, six English miles from our jäger outposts, and has since apparently withdrawn further.

Since I have been informed of the sailing of the packet, I must now close, hoping to report in the future as much as possible about further events.

[61] Captain Philip von Wurmb of the Jäger Corps.

HAMILTON'S HOUSE
NEAR PHILADELPHIA
OCTOBER 26, 1777

Right Honorable Lord,
Gracious High and Mighty Major General: [62]

I humbly thank your Lordship for your gracious letter of the 16th of June of this year. I send you herewith the continuation of my journal extending to the 17th of this month. Since I have time to write an appendix, I wish my account could be more favorable; but fortune in war is very fickle.

Before I begin, I humbly congratulate your Lordship on your recent promotion. It is my desire that continued health accompany your Lordship's merited good fortune and that I may further enjoy your efficacious protection, which I flatter myself I have had up to now. I cannot more honestly desire anything, as I myself will gain much from it.

I have stated that General Potter had to fall back as far as Foxhall. Of the 1,240 men with whom he had been detached from the enemy army, he had hardly one-half when he arrived there,

[62] This is the first time von Jungkenn is addressed as Major General.

the rest having disbanded and in groups of twenty to thirty men plundered their way home. Hence, an entire brigade, consisting of five battalions of Pennsylvanians, had been sent to Foxhall on the 14th to reinforce him.[63]

On the 15th Colonel von Loos and those under him embarked at Christiana Creek at Wilmington. Previously, on the 12th of October, the prisoners and wounded, as well as the sick rebels and the British hospital, had embarked and set sail for New York—as had the army's sick who had remained with the fleet the whole time. The Hessian Dr. Eskuche [64] also went to New York with the invalid fleet.

On the 18th Colonel von Loos and his regiments, and also the English and Hessian convalescents, disembarked at Chester, proceeded to the bank of the Schuylkill, and on the 19th built a bridge at Gray's Ferry, one and a half miles from Philadelphia. On the same day, the army encamped at Philadelphia behind the ten redoubts that had been thrown up between the Delaware and the Schuylkill. The Hessian grenadiers covered the right of the camp; the Hessian Jäger Corps, the left; and the English grenadiers and light infantry, the center.

On the 20th a hundred wagons of ammunition and a train of heavy artillery with eighteen pieces were brought up from Chester for Colonel von Loos's corps. They were escorted by Brigadier General Mathew with the English Guards, one battalion of the 71st Regiment, and the 10th Regiment. Some troops from Patterson's Corps, who had lost their way in the woods, opened an insignificant fire on this escort.

On the 21st Colonel von Donop with the Hessian Jäger Corps, the Hessian grenadiers, the Regiment von Mirbach, and two howitzers was detached to Jersey with orders to take the fort at Red Bank. The place vacated by Mirbach's Regiment, which had gone to the other side of the Schuylkill, was occupied by the 10th, the 27th, and the 28th English Regiments, while the English

[63] Washington's army had been reinforced by about 1,200 Rhode Island troops and nearly 1,000 from Virginia, Pennsylvania, and Maryland.

[64] Eelking-Rosengarten, p. 287, has Dr. Estarch. Both forms of the name appear to be garbled.

Guards took the place of the Hessian grenadiers on the right wing, and one battalion of the 71st Regiment occupied the camp of the Hessian jägers on the left wing, where Lieutenant Mertz and twenty mounted jägers were left behind as a scouting party.

On the 22nd, toward nine o'clock in the evening, Colonel von Donop attacked the fort at Red Bank, but failed completely. Von Lengerke's Battalion covered the artillery and the crossing, so that the enemy could not creep up from the bank of the Delaware, while the Jäger Corps covered the rear. The other two grenadier battalions and von Mirbach's Regiment suffered a tremendous loss; 377 killed and wounded is a heavy loss indeed. Especially regrettable is the loss of so many worthy officers. Never again will the Regiment von Mirbach be under Lieutenant Colonel von Schieck. Of this regiment, Captain von Bogatzky and Lieutenants von Wurmb and Riemann were killed, Lieutenant Schutten and Ensign Berner severely wounded, and Lieutenant Reifforth [65] slightly wounded; von Linsing's Battalion had Captain von Gröning and Lieutenant du Puy killed, and Captain von Eschwege, Captain von Stamford, Lieutenant von Weitz,[66] Lieutenant Rodemann, and Lieutenant von Gottschall severely wounded, the last being in an especially critical condition.

Lieutenant Colonel von Minnigerode is wounded, as are also Captains Hendorff [67] and Wachs. Lieutenants von Offenbach and Hille remained on the field.

Colonel von Donop, Captain Wagner, and Lieutenant Heymell with practically one hundred wounded were taken prisoners. Lieutenant von Heister was sent with a flag of truce to inquire about Colonel von Donop. With the permission of Commodore Hazelwood, Captain Roberson [68] of the navy took him ashore to

[65] Apparently Christoph Philipp Reuffurth, listed as a staff captain in Knyphausen's Regiment in 1779 (*Staats-Calender*). Eelking-Rosengarten, p. 312, calls him Christoph Philip Renfurth.

[66] Eelking-Rosengarten lists a Waitz von Eschen, of the Grenadier Battalion von Linsing, as having been wounded at Red Bank. Waitz von Eschen can be no other than Wilhelm Waitz, Freiherr von Eschen, a first lieutenant in the 3rd Battalion of the Hessian Regiment of Guards, which, however, did not come to America as a unit (*Staats-Calender*, p. 25).

[67] Eelking-Rosengarten, probably erroneously, gives Stendorff.

[68] Captain Isaiah Robinson of the *Andrew Doria*?

the Colonel, who lay in a house about a mile from the fort at Red Bank. He has a dangerous musket-shot wound in the thigh; the bone is said to be broken, and there is little hope for his recovery. Captain Wagner seems to have no chance whatsoever, since both his legs were shot to pieces and another bullet entered his mouth and came out through his cheek. Lieutenant Heymel, on the other hand, will recover.

Yesterday, the 25th, Lieutenant Schutten had his right arm amputated above the elbow. He is my sister's only son and was adjutant to his regimental chief. Not being permitted to remain with a sick man,[69] he accompanied his regiment. The regiment can vouch that it has always been satisfied with him. The loss of Captain von Bogatzky is a great blow to this regiment, too. Major von Wilmowsky is sick with dysentery. A few days ago his condition was still rather serious, but now he seems to be improving. Colonel von Borck is in charge of the regiment for the time being.[70]

On the 23rd all the wounded were brought to Philadelphia, and the English light infantry was ordered to Jersey to cover the retreat of the corps in case it should be attacked. On the night of the 23rd–24th all the troops arrived on this side of the Delaware, so the Hessian corps moved back into its old position on the left of the camp, and the Grenadier Battalion von Lengerke encamped beside the English Guards. The other two grenadier battalions, out of which only 190 men are fit for duty, have gone into barracks together with the Regiment von Mirbach, which had 112 killed and wounded. On the 22nd of October Colonel von Loos was ordered to break his camp on the other side of the Schuylkill. Late in the evening he encamped behind the right wing.

On the 23rd there was a terrible cannonade at Mud Island. The rebels sent five fireships, one by one, against the English ships, but without effect. We were so unfortunate, however, as to have two warships blow up, the *Augusta*, sixty-four guns, and

[69] I.e., Colonel Carl Emil Curt von Donop.

[70] Colonel Henrich von Borck belonged to the von Knyphausen Regiment, whereas the sick Major von Wilmowsky was of the Mirbach Regiment. Officers were frequently assigned to temporary duty with regiments other than their own.

the *Pearl*, thirty-two guns. This must be attributed to the careless handling of ammunition.[71] The *Roebuck*, forty guns, then weighed anchor and sailed off to Chester, whence she is now returning with more ships.

On the 25th of October Major General Grey marched to Billingsport with eight hundred English troops, that is, four brigades of two hundred men each. Heavy artillery will follow him, so that he may take Red Bank in good form and also make an attack on Mud Island from that side. Everyone wishes for good results.

Major von Eschwege will be able to tell your Lordship a good deal about all this in person. I have to admit that I am sensitive and let things affect me, especially our wounded, so that I do not know where I am. We are very short of necessary help. The main hospital is in New York and also the commissariat. Badly needed things are still on board ship. In the meantime, everything happens that can happen. It is truly to be desired that this miserable war will soon end. We hear more contradictory statements every day, and because of the great distance, the truth, unfortunately, is often never found out.

For the present I commend myself, as I have ever done, to your kind benevolence and remain with the greatest respect [*etc.*]

P.S. What we hear about General Burgoyne and what General Clinton's adjutant reported to us on the 17th of October, your Lordship will hear from Major von Eschwege. I shall send another report by the next packet. Since the 24th of October we have had a bridge again across the Schuylkill and have thrown up on the other side a kind of *tête de pont* to maintain the Chester road. Should we remain in Philadelphia and the Schuylkill not be open, we could then get provisions overland with a strong escort.

[71] The *Augusta* blew up, but not the *Pearl*. The sloop *Merlin*, sixteen guns, which was fired, was abandoned after the misfortune to the *Augusta*.

: II :

Herewith another part of my journal—up to the —— of November.[72] We are still quietly encamped before Philadelphia. No rebels are to be seen, except on our right wing toward Frankford, although on our left a patrol of dragoons has been approaching every other day to the four-mile stone. There are only about three hundred enemy infantrymen in Germantown.

Washington continues to be quiet in Whiteland Township,[73] fifteen English miles from our camp. All the deserters tell us that he has fallen out with Congress and that General Gates is now esteemed much more.[74] It is said with much assurance that as soon as a division of our army advances, General Washington will proceed to the Susquehanna, whither all heavy baggage and the greater portion of his heavy artillery had been sent by the 16th of November.

[72] Date omitted; apparently it was to have been filled in on completion of the letter.

[73] Washington was at Whitemarsh, a township of Montgomery County. See Fitzpatrick's *Calendar of the Correspondence of George Washington, sub* Dec. 1, 1777.

[74] A result of the so-called Conway Cabal, in which Generals Gates, Mifflin, and Conway connived.

The corps under General Potter withdrew as far as Yellow Springs and the White Horse on the Lancaster Pike as early as the 14th of November, leaving the region on the other side of the Schuylkill unoccupied far beyond Chester and Wilmington. This corps allowed the people to keep but few of their belongings. However, there is still a stretch of land between Wilmington and Elk Town about ten English miles square called Big Neck, where some of the troops might get winter quarters after an expedition. General Sullivan has really resigned from the rebel service.

Our unfortunate prisoners have not been exchanged yet. Last spring several thousand rebel prisoners were released from New York. They arrived in the rebel camp poorly provisioned and half sick, and few of them survived. They make their number very inconsistent, but are willing to let it pass, provided General Lee is exchanged for General Prescott. The Howe brothers cannot be moved, however, and so all our hopes are in vain.

Two new major generals for the English troops have lately arrived from England; Wilson [75] for the infantry and Pattison [76] for the artillery in place of General Cleaveland. General Cornwallis is to go to London, where he will remain until next May. Admiral Howe has already taken quarters in Philadelphia and has been working with his brother and private secretary.

On the 26th of November the Hessian hospital ship had the misfortune to run into a stockade and was damaged considerably, although the sick and the equipage were saved. These miserable hospital ships have killed many a soldier. Of five sick in my company only one has recovered. A hospital is now being set up in Philadelphia. Many of those wounded at Red Bank have returned to their companies. On the other hand, Captain Wagner died on the 22nd of November and Lieutenant von Gottschall on the 25th, both having been severely wounded.

[75] Major General Sir Thomas Spencer Wilson.
[76] Brigadier General James Pattison. He did not become a major general until 1779, when Sir Henry Clinton appointed him to that rank. See Sir Henry Clinton to Lord Barrington, Feb. 2, 1779, Gt. Brit., Hist. MSS Comm., *Report on American Manuscripts in the Royal Institution of Great Britain*, vol. I. (Volumes II–IV of this set, being a calendar of the Carleton Papers, will hereafter be referred to as *Carleton Calendar*.)

Colonel von Donop had a negro boy about thirteen years old whom he bequeathed to your Lordship. Chaplain Köster of von Donop's Regiment has given him instruction in the German language and also in the Christian religion. When the chaplain was transferred to the grenadier brigade, he gave something for the boy's maintenance and left him behind with the understanding that he should be sent to Hesse at the first opportunity.

All the Hessian troops in General Howe's army, noncommissioned officers as well as the rank and file, have received new shoes. General Pigot, who has been stationed in Rhode Island, is being relieved by General Robertson, the former going to New York to his old post of commandant.

The entire shore at Philadelphia is being fenced off, so that no one without business there can approach the ships lying at the wharves. The night watch at the ships consists of 250 marines. There is now a chain extending from the first trench on the right wing of our camp across the Delaware to the Jersey shore. The frigate *Delaware* is anchored on the right; one row galley covers the center, and another the left. When the transports have unloaded the victuals, the greater part of the ships will go to the mouth of the Delaware, where there will be less danger of ice floes.

The Hessian regiments encamped here are impatiently waiting for their winter clothing. All the woolen breeches were left in New York. This is one reason the wounded suffered so much. Philadelphia was depleted of everything, and the regimental surgeons had left even their medicines aboard ship. No respectable hospital could be established, and all expenses were defrayed by the companies out of their pay. The Society of Friends helped out a great deal in the hospitals by furnishing many bandages and caring for the wounded.

Lieutenant Schutten has completely recovered, but has lost his right arm. May I commend this only son of my sister, the Widow Schuttin,[77] to your Lordship's gracious care? I have the greatest confidence in him. He knows a great deal besides military

[77] Schuttin is a now rarely used feminine form of either Schutt, Schutte, or Schutten.

science. He now writes with his left hand as well as he did with his right. Completely resigned to his fate, he is anxious to serve his master and the ruler of his land to his last moments.

The Combined Battalion was ordered to hold itself in readiness to march, and only the new accouterments for all the captive officers, noncommissioned officers, and privates were permitted to come to Philadelphia; but these orders have been changed. The Regiment von Mirbach is to sail to New York. Since his Excellency General Howe would like to drop the word "Combined" and wishes to have the strongest regiment [78] separated from the two weaker ones, I suppose this will be done.

Lieutenant Colonel von Minnigerode and Captains von Stamford and Hendorff are out of bed already, as is also Ensign Berner, whose wound in the left leg at first seemed very threatening.

With deep reverence and the greatest respect I have the honor to be [etc.]

P.S. Billingsport is still occupied by 150 Scottish Highlanders, and the shore covered by two frigates.

[78] Another example of the rather indiscriminate use of the words "regiment" and "battalion," though here with more justification (see 1777, note 26). At Clinton's request the Combined Battalion was reorganized by putting the two weaker ones under Colonel von Loos and the strong one under Colonel von Woellwarth. At the time of the evacuation of Philadelphia the former's command is called a brigade. The brigade which he commanded sometime later consisted of the Knyphausen, Lossberg, and Mirbach Regiments. See Plan of Distribution enclosed in letter dated Nov. 9, 1778 (No. 27.)

: 12 :

I have had the pleasure of sending your Lordship my journal up to the 1st of this month. Since Lord Cornwallis and Colonels Osborn and Stuart [79] are leaving the army and sailing for London, I take this opportunity to make another report.

Up until the 4th nothing important occurred, except that the rebel commander of the captured frigate *Delaware* escaped from prison on the 2nd with two midshipmen and eighteen sailors, and none of them has since been seen. At his Excellency General Howe's command, the Hessian troops and English battalions here have been provided with new tent blankets and woolen mittens. They are also to receive woolen gaiters very soon. In each of the ten redoubts, guardhouses are being built. They are all fully supplied with artillery and ammunition.

On the other side of the Schuylkill, where a bridge has been built at the Middle Ferry, many men are busy cutting firewood for the magazines. They are covered by a captain with one hundred men. A patrol on our left wing, and mounted jägers at that,

[79] Probably Lieutenant Colonel Charles Stuart, like Colonel Sir George Osborn, a member of Parliament.

advanced too far to engage an enemy picket and fell into an ambush; two jägers were wounded and another was fatally shot along with his horse.

On the 3rd of December the army was to have set out in accordance with orders previously given. We do not yet know the cause for this delay. The reports coming into the English headquarters are always uncertain and undependable.

The highways from Philadelphia to Germantown and Frankford, and the road to Trenton by way of Jenkintown, are open to anyone. Some Philadelphians have been appointed to give passes to loyalists, who are then permitted to pass the pickets. When returning, these people always bring foodstuffs with them. The rebel light dragoons frequently carry the women's packages on their horses as far as their vedettes. From these people we receive most of the news about the rebels.

It seems to be true that between the 28th of November and the 2nd of December their heavy baggage and the large artillery train followed Congress to Carlisle, and that less than a third of the new militia, whose term of service was to have begun the 1st of December, have actually come in. General Potter's militia corps, which was stationed between the White Horse and Yellow Springs, has completely disbanded. This compelled Washington to leave his favorable post at Whitemarsh in Whiteland Township [80] and secure the roads to Reading and Lancaster. I suppose we were to attack them in this condition and run them down. We had made all the necessary preparations, but, unfortunately, the enemy is informed of everything as soon as our generals get their orders.

In the night of the 4th–5th of December our army set out to march in the following order:

VANGUARD UNDER GENERAL CORNWALLIS

1) Two battalions of light infantry
2) The Hessian dismounted jägers
3) The Hessian grenadiers

[80] Whitemarsh is in Whitemarsh Township, Montgomery County; Whiteland Township is in Chester County.

4) The 4th English Brigade
5) Two troops of the 16th Regiment of Dragoons
6) Two 12-pounders and two howitzers

THE MAIN CORPS UNDER HIS EXCELLENCY GENERAL VON KNYPHAUSEN

1) The Hessian Leib Regiment and von Donop's
2) The 1st English Brigade with two light 12-pounders
3) The Brigade of English Guards
4) One troop of the 16th Regiment of Dragoons
5) The 5th and 27th Regiments with two light 12-pounders
6) The 7th and 26th Regiments and the 3rd English Brigade
7) Two troops of the 17th Regiment of Dragoons
8) Hospital provisions, one hundred empty wagons, and the 71st Regiment
9) The Hessian mounted jägers and one troop of the 17th Regiment of Dragoons
10) The Queen's Rangers, who marched on the right of the train

Under General Leslie's command there remained in Philadelphia and in the trenches Colonel von Woellwarth with his brigade, the Mirbach Regiment, the 63rd Regiment, and two battalions of Anspachers, while fifty dragoons remained to patrol the other side of the Schuylkill as far as Darby and Chester.

The rebel Colonel Morgan, who had held the main outpost at the Rising Sun, withdrew by way of Germantown before sundown on the 4th, leaving behind twelve light dragoons. Hence, we met with no interference on our march.

At eight o'clock on the 5th, the van of the column arrived at the ten-mile stone near Chestnut Hill. Our left wing extended as far as the Wissahickon, and our right took position with its full front facing the enemy camp, which was about four miles from our lines on a range of hills. Both their wings were fortified by strong abatis; the center approaches were completely covered by several batteries; the whole position was strongly fortified by fifty-two heavy pieces, and the slopes were patrolled by many pickets.

Before our arrival they had increased their fires, lighting many large ones in straight and deep lines, so that it looked as if fifty thousand men were encamped there. By day we could see that this was merely a trick to deceive us. However, we could obtain no information, for we saw no deserters, or any people living in the neighborhood. Their right wing began to stir, and on their left we could distinctly make out their works. Their ammunition wagons, which had been in the center, scattered to all parts of the camp.

Brigadier Irvine [81] attacked the British light infantry and grenadiers, who were supported by the Hessian grenadiers. Everyone believed that this was the beginning of a general attack. But after Irvine had fallen wounded from his horse and his detachment had probably some thirty killed, the enemy withdrew. We were satisfied with having made Irvine and some twenty men prisoners. Each side sent out pickets and our army pitched tents and built fires. On the night of the 6th–7th General Howe had the army break camp as quietly as possible and march off to the right in the following order:

THE VANGUARD UNDER GENERAL CORNWALLIS

1) The British light infantry and grenadiers
2) The Hessian grenadiers
3) The 4th English Brigade

THE MAIN CORPS UNDER HIS EXCELLENCY GENERAL VON KNYPHAUSEN

1) Two light 12-pounders and two howitzers ⎱ under the com-
2) The Brigade of English Guards and the 1st Brigade ⎰ mand of
3) The 7th and 26th Regiments — General Grant
4) Two light 12-pounders
5) The Hessian Leib Regiment and von Donop's
6) One officer and twenty horse of the 17th Regiment of Dragoons
7) All the wagons of the army, flanked on the left by the dismounted dragoons

THE REAR GUARD UNDER GENERAL GREY

1) The 3rd English Brigade
2) The entire Hessian Jäger Corps
3) The Queen's Rangers

[81] Brigadier General James Irvine, Pennsylvania militia.

We marched in the direction of Germantown. In the center of this town the column turned off to the left on the Abington road and reached Jenkintown, two and a half miles to the left of the enemy's camp, at daybreak. Jenkintown is on the road from Philadelphia to Trenton. We arrived at the same time as the provision train from Philadelphia. As soon as the army had taken position in three lines, rum and biscuits were distributed. We then executed some forward movements, which exposed the British light infantry on our right wing and the Hessian Jäger Corps on our left to some musketry. The rebels retired as far as their new abatis and hastened to blockade every approach. Their right wing blocked the Trenton road behind them, so that this road could not be forced except by heavy artillery.

Lieutenant Colonel von Wurmb was completely successful in driving the enemy within the narrowest confines of their camp. General Grey followed with the troops that had formed the rear guard and so secured our left wing. General Grant gained the heights called Edge Hill, driving the enemy before him. The army formed in line on these hills in front of the enemy's left wing, but this was thought, after a thorough reconnaissance, to be a very disadvantageous position from which to attack them. The British grenadiers, who were to be followed by the Hessian grenadiers in the attack and who had already advanced to within a pistol shot of the enemy's abatis, could see how strong their fortifications were.

General von Knyphausen was kind enough to entrust me with the command of von Minnigerode's Battalion,[82] while he put von Lengerke's Battalion under Captain von Eschwege, for von Lengerke [83] had injured his right arm in a fall.

I went in front of the English grenadiers and found the rebels entrenched as follows: Before and behind their strongest abatis, which went up the slope of the hill, they had dug trenches with embrasures every two to three hundred paces. There were no

[82] Baurmeister, being a general staff officer, did not ordinarily have a command.

[83] Colonel George Emanuel von Lengerke, who in 1777 became chief of Block's Grenadier Battalion.

batteries behind the abatis, but on the entire flank I counted nine uncovered pieces, all of which were manned by French officers and soldiers. The Marylanders, whom I recognized by their grey uniforms with white trim, stood in a dense line between the artillery. They were all determined to wait for whatever might come, but at the same time there was much excitement among them. I do not know even yet why their artillery remained silent. They could not only hear us approach through the woods, where the leaves rustled, but their advanced posts and our skirmishers exchanged many a shot.

At half past three in the afternoon the entire line received orders to rendezvous near Jenkintown. The rebels were still silent and were silent also on the 8th of December, when the army marched back again in three columns to Philadelphia. A troop of light dragoons hung on the right of the column until the Hessian Jäger Corps's artillery drove them back. At half past ten at night the entire army was back in the old camp in Philadelphia.

During this expedition the Jägers lost two killed and eight wounded; but they took seventeen prisoners and killed many rebels. The English light infantry had one officer killed, three wounded, and forty-two soldiers killed and wounded. The rebel accounts mention over one hundred killed and twice as many wounded. An officer and five men of the 9th Pennsylvania Battalion, who had deserted from a picket on the night of the 7th–8th of December, brought an exact list of the enemy's strength. It gave a total of eleven thousand two hundred fit for duty, and confirmed the number of heavy pieces to be fifty-two, and that with two hundred and fifty French artillerymen, more than fifty officers of that nation were serving in the Army.

On the night of the 9th–10th [84] of December General Cornwallis was sent across the Schuylkill to make a general foraging expedition beyond Darby. He had with him 3,500 men and almost all the dragoons and mounted jägers. Washington, who was immediately informed of this, left Whitemarsh with the greater

---

[84] André gives the time of Cornwallis's departure at 3 A.M., December 11. See André's *Journal*, Boston, 1903, *sub* Dec. 1777.

part of his army and twenty-two pieces of artillery at four o'clock in the afternoon of the 9th.

Attempting to get ahead of General Cornwallis before Darby, several thousand of his militia had already crossed a bridge above Swedes Ford toward eleven o'clock on the 10th. Since the dragoons and jägers came too close, they hastily withdrew in very great confusion and demolished the bridge,[85] which no one prevented them from doing, for General Cornwallis had intended to do this very thing, principally to be able to forage more quietly.

Washington in the meantime formed his troops *en ordre de bataille* on the other side of the bridge. General Cornwallis did likewise on a height which would allow him a safe retreat. On the 11th he stopped foraging after having collected about two thousand head of cattle and sheep. He arrived in camp with these on the evening of the 12th without any loss. Washington also left the other side of the Schuylkill and moved again into his regular camp at Whitemarsh.

His Excellency General Howe was exceedingly satisfied with General Cornwallis's conduct, but not with those who did the foraging and drove in the cattle. They all thought first of themselves and not of the commonweal. In fact, many deserve being openly accused and punished without consideration. In this, as well as in several other things, we have been going too far and have done infinitely more to maintain the rebellion than to smother it. These excesses, though we gain but little by them, may have very serious consequences.

On the 12th a scouting party of one noncommissioned officer and ten soldiers which had been detached from the one hundred men who cover the woodcutters on the far side of the Schuylkill was captured on the Chester road. Captain von Urff was in command of this detail; the noncommissioned officer and six of the men are from the Leib Regiment and the other four from Donop's.

Lieutenant Dickson of the navy[86] sailed out of the Dela-

---

[85] This bridge was a makeshift one of wagons and planks, according to Albigence Waldo. See W. S. Baker, "Itinerary of General Washington," *Pennsylvania Magazine*, XIV, 275.

[86] Probably Captain Archibald Dickson, master of the *Greyhound*. See journal, May 18 to June 11, 1778 (No. 18).

ware for Rhode Island with some thirty transports on which to
embark Burgoyne's prisoners at Providence and take them to
Gibraltar. We hope that Ticonderoga will hold out. The rebels
are exerting themselves to the utmost to get possession of it again.
At Kings Bridge all is quiet, except that Captain Emmerich was
sent two miles above Dobbs Ferry to fire nineteen houses which
the rebels planned to use for magazines. On the other hand, General De Lancey has suffered at the hands of the rebels, who maltreated his family and ransacked and burned his beautiful home
near Bloomingdale on New York Island.

Quarters for twenty-six battalions are now being established
in Philadelphia; headquarters, quarters for the generals and their
suites, and the necessary hospitals and storehouses all require
space, food, and provisions. With so little room in the desolate
city of Philadelphia and with no firm foothold in Jersey, General
Howe is probably worrying as much about the procurement of
these necessities as he is about the defense of the extensive banks
of the Delaware and Schuylkill should we suddenly have cold
weather. The English battalions have not increased in strength,
and the Hessian regiments have become quite weak, as your Lordship, no doubt, knows from our reports. There are more sick every
day; none are being discharged as recovered, and many die. Admiral Howe and most of the warships will spend the winter in
Rhode Island.

The situation of the rebels is certainly not the best. Virginia
wants to hear no more of independence; her militia makes no
haste to join the mob. There is a great shortage of everything.
Congress is quite severe, but it has no power, except paper money.
Furthermore, much discord has arisen among the members of
Congress. Many officers have resigned and are again living at
home. Trade and barter among the several provinces are paralyzed, and manufacturing has ceased. I believe twelve thousand
men generaled in the German way plus the present army, full
strength, could make a very fortunate campaign.

His Excellency General von Knyphausen is in the best of
health. We are waiting for the new uniforms from New York.

Everyone is preparing to make the winter tolerable, but we would welcome an order to embark and sail home.

I have the honor to be with the greatest respect
Your Lordship's

Most obedient servant
Baurmeister

Philadelphia
December 16, 1777

P.S. Today the 71st and von Mirbach's are leaving Chester. They embarked yesterday at high tide and sailed through the stockades (for they had not yet been entirely removed at Mud Island). These troops are going into winter quarters in New York.

1778

: 13 :

Right Honorable Lord,
Gracious High and Mighty Major General:

My last account covered the events up to the 16th of December, when Lord Cornwallis departed for England. By this packet I send a continuation, which will show how little has been accomplished in the present war in spite of considerable losses, on both sides.

The last campaign furnished sufficient proof that the stubborn and inexperienced rebels are too lucky. The English army, active as it is, has got no farther than Philadelphia, is master of only some parts of the banks of the Delaware and Schuylkill, and has no foothold whatsoever in Jersey, from where, as well as from Germantown in front and from Wilmington, Darby, and Chester in the rear, it is being watched and constantly harassed by the enemy's main posts.

General Washington not only cautiously supports these posts from time to time, but also covers Lancaster, Reading, and the bank of the Susquehanna. With the greater part of his army he occupies a stationary camp at Valley Forge, where the soldiers have been encouraged with cash rewards to build solid huts. They have been told, moreover, that their steadfastness and patience through one more campaign will secure their independence once and for all. They also enjoy the generous support of foreign powers, who have their staple in Boston. Furthermore, they have more means of their own to keep up this war than was at first supposed.

The Americans are bold, unyielding, and fearless. They have always lived in plenty, and we cannot block their resources. Then their indomitable ideas of liberty, the main springs of which are held and guided by every hand in Congress! Good for nothing and unimportant as most of these men may have been before these disturbances (because they were incompetent and without wealth) they now resort to every means, for more than one reason, to weaken the rich and the loyalists within and stubbornly resist the English without.

This short exposition is meant only to show the state of things here, and that England, though she has not lost the game so far, nevertheless may lose everything. With little show, the Americans will exert themselves to the utmost to gain complete freedom, and they are by no means conquered. If only one province, for example, Jersey, could be subdued and a tolerable government set up without interference, then, everyone believes, all provinces would prefer peace to war.

Except for minor attacks which scouting parties of dragoons successfully made on enemy outposts in front of our line, nothing occurred between the 16th and the 21st of December last. In order to remain master of the main highway to Lancaster, General Washington moved on the 18th into the above-mentioned stationary camp at Valley Forge, where General Potter had been stationed with the Pennsylvania and Virginia militia. These militiamen and all the rest from other regions have since disbanded.

Reports agree that Washington's force is less than seven thousand strong, for the standing militia in Jersey have been reinforced with some troops, including the greater part of the dragoons, and General Sullivan has been detached to Wilmington with two

Map of Pennsylvania and New Jersey at the Time of the Revolution. (Redrawn from various sources.)

thousand men to cover Darby and Chester. Springfield has been occupied from Valley Forge. Scouting parties of dragoons come from all three places to the opposite bank of the Schuylkill.

A scanty supply of forage and fresh food—the former was always neglected and thought of only when almost too late—finally induced General Howe to cross the Schuylkill on the 22nd with the larger part of the army and encamp on the left of the main road this side of Darby in a line four and a half English miles long. This enabled the troops to forage over the entire expanse between this line and the Delaware.

Inasmuch as this enterprise was very successful, the Hessian grenadiers were ordered to encamp beyond Darby. To make their right flank secure against a possible attack from Springfield, the English light infantry took position on the Springfield road. A scouting party of one officer and twenty horse of the 17th Regiment of Dragoons followed the Darby road toward Wilmington with such utter heedlessness that at four o'clock in the afternoon of the 23rd of December they fell into an ambush. After firing one round, thirteen horses and eleven dragoons were captured.

Eight English battalions, the Queen's Rangers, one officer and twenty-four English dragoons, and Stirn's and Woellwarth's brigades remained in the lines before Philadelphia under the command of his Excellency Lieutenant General von Knyphausen.

At half past six on the evening of the 24th the rebels attempted to attack our redoubts. While they approached by two routes from Germantown, several row galleys sought to approach our frigates. But after a few cannon shot from the 5th Redoubt and the *Camilla* frigate, everything became quiet again. Since then it has been so empty and desolate on our front toward Germantown and beyond that it is almost useless to send patrols in that direction.

On the 28th we stopped foraging. Most of the hay was loaded on ships, and a great deal was taken over Gray's Ferry Bridge across the Schuylkill, over which the 450 sheep and 180 head of cattle were also driven. This forage will probably last eighty days, beginning with the 1st of January, and would allay the fears of every English commissary if our close quarters did not compel us to keep all our wagons and horses in one place, for after the first campaign we sent everything to Long Island, even the horses of the heavy and light artillery.

General Howe returned with the army on the 28th of December in a heavy snowstorm. Some detachments of the English light infantry which were in the rear guard and had made an ambuscade, captured two officers and thirty-four soldiers who had been trailing them.

On the night of the 26th–27th of December General Washington sent two brigades under General Stirling from Valley Forge to Springfield, while he himself advanced to the left with many troops as far as Harford.[1] Neither division, however, made a main attack. On the 29th Washington and Stirling retired to camp again, while the English army returned to its winter quarters in Philadelphia on the 30th of December.

We have taken up our quarters in such a way that from the battalion alarm places, each brigade can march into the city (as well as conditions and order will permit) and also behind the redoubts outside the city. To explain this arrangement more fully, I shall describe how the several brigades daily move into the eleven redoubts along the line from their quarters. The redoubts are numbered, beginning on the Delaware. The 1st, 2nd, and 3rd are occupied by the English Guards and the Queen's Rangers, the 4th by the 1st English Brigade, the 5th by the 2nd, the 6th by the 4th, the 7th by the 3rd, the 8th by the 5th and the 2nd Battalion of Anspachers, the 9th by Stirn's brigade, the 10th by Woellwarth's, and the 11th by the Hessian grenadiers.

The Hessian dismounted jägers have their quarters on the Neck, which is the point of land where the Schuylkill flows into the Delaware. The main part of this corps is on Gloucester Point [2] and faces Province Island. The English dragoons and the mounted jägers have their headquarters in the center of the city.

The daily duty in the city is performed by two captains, ten subalterns, thirty-seven noncommissioned officers, ten drummers,

---

[1] Ravenford? Baurmeister was, of course, misinformed. Washington remained at Valley Forge.

[2] Now Girard Point.

and three hundred and sixty-two privates, of whom one captain and a hundred men are detached across the Schuylkill to cover the woodcutters. Each regiment and the Hessian General Staff must procure and transport its own firewood. It takes three-eighths of a cord per week for one fireplace, and a cord costs five shillings sterling, cash. Light is furnished, and once a week we get provisions as well as rum of the best quality.

The city market is full of fresh meat, all kinds of fowl, and root vegetables. The residents of the city lack nothing except flour and firewood. What they sell and what they earn by working for so many people gives enough money to everyone to pay for even the most expensive things. If the English merchants would accept the accredited English paper money, trading would be greatly facilitated. People come from Jersey and the most distant parts of Pennsylvania to sell food for hard money. While there is nothing remarkable about that, there is something very remarkable about the falling off of high prices. We can now get things at one-third the price we used to pay for them.

During the month of December, 256 deserters came in, and so far in January, 63. It is not so much their lack of clothing as homesickness that drives them to desertion. This is such a dominant passion with them that General Washington keeps his troops constantly moving.

Congress is now holding its sessions in York Town, on the other side of the Susquehanna. General Wayne with his brigade is now in that region to protect Congress and enforce its orders more quickly among the inhabitants, for the plans of Congress, whose members are no longer all in attendance, meet with endless resistance. Even the people of New England are tired of contributing so much in man power, money, and provisions. I still believe that if we could subdue only one province, the rest would surrender. The rebels are spending enough money, but I have never heard of a generous, and therefore alluring, reward being given. If any people worships money, it is the Americans, for everyone is in business; even the most pious Quaker can give lessons to a Feidell.[3]

[3] Probably a shrewd merchant of Cassel. Veithel?

The severe cold, which lasted from the 1st to the 3rd of January and froze the Schuylkill over solidly and the Delaware from the banks nearly to the middle, let up on the 4th, and on the 5th the high tide brought ice floes. The rebels then threw barrels filled with combustibles into the Delaware, hoping to set our ships on fire. However, trees placed in front of our ships prevented any damage. The sight of some fifty of these little machines exploding one by one was as beautiful as the enemy's designs were destructive.

The commissaries at Wilmington are sending cattle once a week for the captive rebels and, from time to time, clothing. On the 16th, Regimental Quartermaster Kitz of Woellwarth's Regiment[4] was sent to the prisoners at Winchester to deliver money and equipment to the officers. Now and then one or more soldiers return from captivity. They have no complaints about their treatment and even less about lack of food. There seems to be some hope that within the near future the officers will be paroled, especially since it would bring about the exchange of Generals Prescott and Lee.

The 71st Regiment and von Mirbach's made the voyage from here to New York in ten days, landing there on the 25th of December last. On the 17th and 18th of December the 71st foraged near Chester.

At present there are quartered in New York the 38th, 52nd, and 57th English Regiments and the Hessian regiments Erb Prinz, Prinz Carl, Trümbach, Wissenbach, and Stein. Von Mirbach's Regiment is posted in scattered houses along the North River as far as Bloomingdale. At its right wing, near Jones's[5] house, is a detachment of four hundred men from New York, who are relieved every four weeks. The daily duty in the city is being done by one captain, six subalterns, twenty-eight noncommissioned officers, seven drummers, and two hundred and fifty-seven privates.

---

[4] Woellwarth's Regiment is part of the Combined Battalion (see 1777, note 78); it consisted mainly of what was left of von Rall's Regiment.

[5] Woodlawn, the home of Nicholas Jones. It stood a little west of the present corner of 107th St. and 11th Ave. (*Magazine of American History*, VIII, 48).

The 45th Regiment, all the provincials, Köhler's Grenadier Battalion, and Emmerich's Chasseurs are stationed at Kings Bridge under Major General Tryon. The 1st Battalion of the 71st Regiment, the 35th Regiment, and all the dispensable train are on Long Island under Colonel McDonnel,[6] and the 2nd Battalion of the 71st and the Waldeck Regiment are posted on Staten Island under the command of Brigadier Campbell.

Letters dated New York, January 6th, report that everything continues quiet. There are still over a hundred Hessians in the hospital at New York and almost three hundred here. They are not suffering from any dangerous or contagious disease; most of them are weak and lame from scurvy. Some of those who were severely wounded at Red Bank are still in Princeton.

I do not know whether General Burgoyne's captured troops have been embarked at Providence, Rhode Island, or why Admiral Howe is spending the winter on the said island, or when he will set sail for New York. Meanwhile, the commission's private secretary,[7] who ordinarily never leaves the Admiral, has been stationed here.

Only a few prizes are being taken. I almost believe that the English ships do not cruise and cannot stay at sea because they constantly fear an attack on Rhode Island. I am strengthened in my belief by the fact that many French ships have safely reached Boston.

Some time ago Major St. Ouary,[8] a Frenchman whom we captured while scouting, assured us that forty-two French officers were looking forward to leaving the rebels forever. However, neither the Boston nor the Albany newspapers, which frequently come to us in a roundabout way, say a single word about their returning to France. Now it is known for certain that General Lee has been paroled in New York and is no longer looked upon as a deserter. General Prescott is expected back, and so the exchange

---

[6] Lieutenant Colonel John McDonnel, 76th Regiment.

[7] Ambrose Serle, Lord Howe's secretary, who appears to have served as secretary to the Howe Commission, had embarked for Newport, Rhode Island, on December 21, 1777. See *The American Journal of Ambrose Serle*, ed. by E. H. Tatum, Huntington Library, 1940, p. 334.

[8] Major Bernde St. Ouary.

of all prisoners will finally come about. Captains von Westerhagen and von Eschwege will be able to report more in person.

Commending myself to your Lordship's gracious remembrance, I have the honor to be with the greatest respect [*etc.*]

P.S. The spectacle of Hessian troops on watch, church, and pay parades in completely new uniforms is applauded by everyone. The English troops also have new equipment, although several regiments lost theirs when the rebels stopped some ships, which they unloaded and burned. This must be blamed on the ships' masters, who were heedless and chose a poor time for their passage.

: 14 :

PHILADELPHIA

MARCH 24, 1778

Since a packet is speedily making ready to carry new letters to London, I again have the honor to send an account of American events. My last letter, which I finished on the 6th of this month,[9] was dispatched on a boat which set sail with a favorable wind on the 9th.

At retreat time on the 6th, two hundred dragoons under Major Crewe of the 17th Regiment of Dragoons were detached to Chestnut Hill by way of Germantown in order to surprise some Continental troops who, coming from Fatland Ford by way of Norriton, had roamed that far in an attempt to raise militia and burn forage and grain. They consisted of 260 men whom General Wayne had turned over to Governor Livingston before leaving Jersey on the 24th of February.

On the 4th of March they had crossed the Delaware near Burlington with twenty-five of Pulaski's dragoons and proceeded to Fatland Ford on the Schuylkill, whence they advanced to Chestnut Hill, terrorizing the country people. When they heard of the approach of the British dragoons however, they assembled

[9] Not in the Von Jungkenn Papers.

154

on the right bank of the Wissahickon, followed the footpaths along this creek to Schuylkill Falls, and crossed the river without our dragoons being able to pursue them. Our troops killed five men and captured one officer and seventeen soldiers who were too late to cross in safety.

Of the seven transports loaded with hay which were on their way from Rhode Island, two were stopped and burned on the 8th by nine armed galleys and boats in the Delaware between Reedy Island and Christiana Creek. At the same time, the schooner *Alert*, which had been put under the command of Captain Montresor of the Engineers,[10] was captured by Captain Barry of the rebel navy. The schooner had much baggage on board from New York for Captain Montresor and other English officers, all of which was lost.

Counsellor of War Lorentz[11] had sent by this schooner a package of letters from New York addressed to Paymaster Schmidt. On the 10th all these letters were returned from Valley Forge under a flag of truce with a very courteous letter from General Washington to his Excellency Lieutenant General von Knyphausen. All the letters were opened, but returned intact. Among them was one with £1,900 sterling on the paymaster's account. The English letters, however, were not returned.

The empty schooner was brought in by the warship *Experiment*, the frigate *Brune*, and the *Dispatch* and *New York* sloops of war, which arrived here on the 12th. At this same time, the five remaining hay ships and eleven provision ships from Ireland also cast anchor alongside the city.

On the 11th the following troops embarked under Colonel Marth:[12] the 17th, the 27th, and 46th Regiments, the Queen's

---

[10] Captain Barry's report to Washington, March 9, 1778, states that the *Alert* was "in the Engineering Department," and the articles of capitulation enclosed in the same letter are between "Capt. Moore of the Schooner Alert in His Britanick Majesty's service & Capt. John Barry on the part of the United States." Washington MSS, Library of Congress.

[11] Johann Georg Lorentz. Eelking-Rosengarten calls him Counsellor of War and Commissary General; in the *Carleton Calendar* (Gt. Brit., Hist. MSS Comm., *Report on American Manuscripts in the Royal Institution of Great Britain*, vols. II–IV) he is called Commissary General of Hessian forces.

[12] I.e. (Charles) Mawhood (see following letter).

Rangers, and one hundred Royal Pennsylvania Militia.[13] They took with them four heavy pieces and two howitzers and provisions for two weeks. Six empty transports followed them to Salem to take on forage and cattle, the *Camilla* frigate acting as convoy.

On the 14th the *Diamond* frigate arrived with dispatches from Admiral Howe to the English headquarters, and on the 15th the *Brune* frigate departed for Rhode Island with letters for Admiral Howe. From Rhode Island we received the news that at the end of February twenty transports under cover of the *Juno* and *Cerberus* frigates sailed to Boston to embark at last General Burgoyne's captive troops.

These prisoners, whose officers were in Cambridge, barely escaped being murdered. A colonel had plotted with his officers to have the prison guards commit this dastardly deed during the night. The plot was discovered and the colonel arrested. General Heath was obliged to make a thorough investigation, for General Burgoyne, who has lodged a bitter complaint and has much incriminating evidence that leaves no doubt of the wicked designs of this plot, demands revenge. Another report, namely, that Congress has detached General Lafayette to Canada with five thousand men and a train of heavy artillery to support a new revolt there, still needs confirmation.

On the 15th of February General Wayne advanced to Bristol in Jersey [14] with four hundred men and on the 9th of March penetrated still deeper into the province from the bank of the Delaware in order to burn grain and forage and collect horses and cattle. He assembled at Haddonfield three hundred and fifty Jersey militia under Colonel Ellis,[15] from which an alarm watch has been detached as far as Cooper's Ferry [16] opposite this city. General Wayne has joined General Washington again. He ordered Brigadier General Pulaski, who was then in Trenton, to follow him at a moment's notice with the eighty dragoons and one hun-

[13] Pennsylvania Loyalists.
[14] Bristol is in Pennsylvania, across the Delaware from Burlington, New Jersey.
[15] Colonel Joseph Ellis of Newcomb's New Jersey militia.
[16] Camden, New Jersey.

dred Continental troops under him. General Washington's army, exceedingly weakened by desertion and disease, is prepared to approach Lancaster. The whole country around Valley Forge is devastated.

On the 17th a detachment of light infantry surprised a troop of rebels on the Westfield road, on the other side of the Schuylkill, killing four and taking eighteen prisoners. As usual, detachments are being sent out on the evening before a market day to protect the country people who venture everything to bring fresh food to the city. Enemy parties are always looking for these people and maltreat those they catch and take their goods away. Often the farmer pays them for safe conduct, in which case the food is sold for that much more in the market.

On this day three rebel staff officers escaped from prison. The following morning fifty-seven were removed from this building and put into the new city prison. Moreover, they lost, once for all, the privilege of walking about, under escort, an hour each day. On the same day, eight provision ships arrived from Ireland, having made the voyage from Cork in fifty-one days.

At the Gulph Ferry Mill, fifteen miles from here, is a strong enemy outpost detached from Valley Forge. On the night of the 19th–20th this post sent out a party of sixty men, who crept up close to the Schuylkill opposite the 10th Redoubt, where they collected some cattle and set fires. The wing adjutant, Captain von Münchhausen, with forty mounted Hessian jägers under Lieutenant Mertz was so fortunate as to catch up with this party the following morning just before they reached the Black Horse.[17] He captured one officer and ten men and killed and wounded several more. The rest of the rebels were lucky to be able to hide behind a swamp. The jägers had only one horse killed.

Since the rebels are devastating the land and carrying off everything, a train of wagons covered by 150 light infantry went to Chestnut Hill and Germantown on the 21st to collect leather and forty hogsheads of vinegar and bring them into the royal

[17] The Black Horse Tavern on the Lancaster Pike, about five miles northwest of Philadelphia. George Baker, "The Camp by the Old Gulph Mill," *Pennsylvania Magazine*, XVII, 423.

stores of this city. The owners were paid cash for the merchandise.

It seems that the prisoners will soon be exchanged. According to a public notice, the rebel war secretary, Thomson,[18] will bring all those of the British army to Lititz [19] near Lancaster at the end of this month. Every one hopes and wishes that nothing will cause further delay. Ensign Knoblauch of von Donop's Regiment and two English officers, who had been taken prisoners at Germantown on the 4th of October last year, were paroled at Reading and arrived here on the 18th.

The British grenadiers and light infantry have been raised to full strength from the battalions. Thirty men of each light infantry battalion are now mounted. They are learning to ride, together with the recently created Philadelphia troop of 112 horse.

With the greatest respect, I have the honor to be [*etc.*]

[18] Charles Thomson, Secretary of Congress. Richard Peters was Secretary of the Board of War.

[19] See John W. Jordan, "The Military Hospitals at Bethlehem and Lititz during the Revolution," *Pennsylvania Magazine*, XX, 147.

: 15 :

My last account was put on a packet on the 24th of March. The said packet, however, cast anchor this side of Reedy Island to await Admiral Howe's arrival. Since Admiral Howe has not arrived yet, in spite of leaving the harbor of Rhode Island long ago, I fear my account of the 24th of March will be very long in getting to your Lordship. In the orders of day before yesterday the departure of another packet was announced, by which I shall send the following account.

On the 25th of March General Lee arrived here from New York by way of Jersey in company with Major Williams. Several days later he was paroled to General Washington's army. General Prescott arrived in New York under the same conditions. It made me very happy to be present when the said Major Williams, the former commander of Burgoyne's artillery, gave General Howe unequivocal testimony of the valor of all the German troops he had learned to know. I was especially happy because, aside from General Burgoyne's reports, no straightforward account had ever been given.

On the 28th of March twelve Hessian and five English officers were released from confinement by the rebels and have since arrived here. The staff officers and captains as well as the noncommissioned officers and soldiers are still being held.

On the 31st of March the following commissioners met at Germantown: Colonel Stephens, Lieutenant Colonel O'Hara, and Captain Fitzpatrick for the British, and Colonel Grayson, Lieutenant Colonels Harrison and Hamilton, and a jurist by name of Boudinot for the rebels. After all the credentials were recognized as valid, there was nothing more to do in my opinion except to effect the exchange. Mr. Boudinot, however, presented a vast amount of papers and discoursed on irrelevant topics.

Then the meeting adjourned to Newtown beyond Springfield, where the rebel commissioners declared that they would continue to hold the men they had taken prisoners, which amount to almost eight thousand men (including Burgoyne's), and that they could afford to do without the twelve hundred we had taken. Then they demanded £500,000 sterling for maintenance already provided. They declared, moreover, that they did not owe us another man in return for those taken at Fort Knyphausen [20] and released immediately after the first convention, although we have received prisoners in exchange for only half of them. They also made the bold assertion that they could not possibly lose the game. We still do not know whether the prisoners released on parole may remain or whether they have to return.

On the 29th of March the corps of Colonel Mawhood (whom I called Marth in my last journal) returned from Salem. He brought with him thirty-eight ships loaded with hay, which, together with the forage brought from Rhode Island, will probably last until the end of May this year. The said colonel had no difficulty anywhere. On the contrary, the people showed themselves well disposed. The Queen's Rangers made twenty-one militiamen prisoners.

While the English troops were posted at Salem, the small vessels which were following them had the good luck to take some armed boats in some of the small tributaries of the Delaware. The

[20] I.e., Fort Washington, renamed Fort Knyphausen.

English are taking many prizes now, especially Captain Lee,[21] who took eleven foreign ships of considerable size in Massachusetts Bay which were brought to anchor at New York.

On the 30th one of the twenty-eight transports unfortunately ran into the chevaux-de-frise below Mud Island. Little or nothing of it could be saved. Since then, a detachment of 140 marines and an agent have been stationed on this island to assist incoming ships.

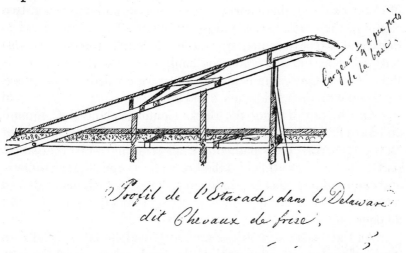

Sketch of a Cheval-de-Frise, Enclosed in Letter of April 18, 1778. The Americans had sunk many such chevaux-de-frise in the Delaware River to stop passage of British ships.

On the 2nd of April the rebels completed the bridge across the Schuylkill at Fatland Ford. They have chosen a good place, for the current of the river is hardly noticeable there. On the bank this side they have erected a *tête de pont* with four cannon and manned it with 250 men. They intend to use this bridge in proceeding from the recently fortified camp at Valley Forge to Whitemarsh and Bristol and, after crossing the Delaware, to Jersey.

Lately Trenton has been occupied by a stronger force, and the rebel ships and galleys anchored at Burlington are on their guard so they will not be easily surprised.

21 Not identified.

In the night of the 4th–5th of April five hundred British grenadiers under Lieutenant Colonel Abercromby [22] crossed over to Jersey on flatboats at Gloucester Point in order to surprise a strong enemy post at Haddonfield Meeting House. The enemy, however, having learned of our approach through scouting dragoons and two deserted sailors, left the meeting house and withdrew to Woodbury, five English miles behind Haddonfield.

Lieutenant Colonel Abercromby, who was to return by way of Cooper's Ferry, there encountered an outpost of one major, two captains, three subalterns, and forty soldiers. The major, the captains, and two of the subalterns did not belong to the detachment, but had come to reconnoiter the bank, the ships, and the city of Philadelphia. One captain and nine men were killed; the rest were captured with their field glasses and brought in.

On the 8th of April the Bucks County Volunteer Company and forty Pennsylvania dragoons under Captain Thomas advanced to the Old York crossroad, drove all scouting and observation parties as far as Smithfield, killed one officer and fifteen soldiers, and captured one officer and nine men. These detachments always return in this manner without loss, though inflicting considerable damage on the enemy.

All the fields and gardens around Philadelphia, especially in the inhabited piece of land called the Neck, where the Schuylkill empties into the Delaware, are being fenced in again and sown and cultivated. This region can justly be called most charming and fertile.

Last Thursday, the 9th of this month, there came to anchor before this city a packet which safely made the voyage from Falmouth in fifty-three days. Since then it is being said with much assurance that General Howe and his brother, the Admiral, will leave America. General Clinton is said to be coming from New York to take over the command of the army, while General Jones, who departed day before yesterday, is to take over General Clinton's command at New York.

General Howe has always enjoyed love and obedience, and Admiral Howe, high esteem and trust. Both know America and

[22] Lieutenant Colonel Robert Abercromby (later Sir Robert), 37th Regiment.

the minds of the people and have always agreed on the measures to be used against them. This alone is a great advantage when two, entrusted with equal power, act against one enemy. To begin with, even the most accurately prescribed plan is not always understood the same way; then, the enemy have to be attacked under great difficulty, now on the sea and again on land.

Furthermore, there can be no doubt that if the reinforcements called for by the two brothers in every dispatch arrive in good time, the rebellion will come to a happy end with good terms for both parties. To conquer the Americans completely and impose arbitrary terms is thought to be impossible.

At General Howe's request, a chasseur battalion of three hundred men was to be drawn from the Hessian regiments at New York and Philadelphia and commanded by Captain von Münchhausen. Now that General Howe is to leave, Captain von Münchhausen has abandoned his quest, and all orders given to that effect have been countermanded.

On the 14th of this month a frigate arrived from England with dispatches for the English headquarters, whereupon, on the 15th, printed proclamations were posted everywhere announcing that England for the present was giving up all taxation of America and that in the future the several provinces would be taxed according to their ability to pay. Everyone doubts that this will make an impression. Commissioners are expected from England who will make a formal declaration. General Howe will not depart until they, as well as General Clinton, have arrived.

Colonel Kospoth has arrived here from Rhode Island and has taken over the command of the Hessian grenadier brigade.

The Hessian troops, including the artillery, are holding daily drills in firing. At present there are only fifteen wounded and twenty-five sick in the hospital. It is difficult to conceive of an army in such excellent condition and such order as the army in the city.

I have the honor to be with the greatest respect [etc.]

: 16 :

For four and one-half months the Hessian troops have received no news from the Fatherland. Convinced, as we are, that we are graciously and warmly remembered, we are at a loss to understand why we have had no assurance of it for so long. We have been sending letters with every packet. I myself find much comfort in writing, for I cannot think day after day of our distant homeland without becoming sentimental. Since the departure of another packet has been announced, I send herewith an account of the events that took place between the 18th of April and this day.

According to an emphatic Congressional edict, no one living within six English miles of Philadelphia has been permitted to come to the city since the 15th of April, nor have any of the residents been permitted to go into the country. Any communication with Jersey is even more emphatically forbidden.

Consequently, the militia were ordered to collect in strong detachments in front of our lines at the following posts: (1) Between Bristol and the Crooked Billet Tavern, fifteen English miles from here; (2) at Springhouse, this side of Whitemarsh, thirteen

164

miles from here, whence a temporary post of 250 men is to be detached to Germantown; (3) at Barren Hill near the Schuylkill Falls, ten miles from here. Beyond the Schuylkill there is to be a temporary post in Darby, also at Reedy Tavern and the Gulph Mill, with an observation post at Springfield. All this militia was raised in the lower counties of Pennsylvania. These posts will certainly greatly hinder bringing in fresh food. However, the country people are still experiencing but little difficulty in coming to the city.

In Jersey only the bank of the Delaware is occupied by the levies, for Governor Livingston can raise only a few militia. Pulaski is no longer in Trenton. He is engaged in raising a volunteer corps of six hundred men, for whom the war council granted only arms and two hundred and forty horses. Their food and pay they must get through their own bravery.

Everything is progressing very slowly, however, and we get descriptions of much cruelty in every place where the militia is now being raised. House and property are being burned and devastated if the owner refuses to go along or fails to get a substitute. No recruits can be got for less than £60 cash, Pennsylvania currency. Many of the farms have been desolate since the beginning of the second campaign, for even the farmers have been taken along by force.

Virginia now gives almost no militia. Congress, frightened by the refusal of the Virginians, proceeds more leniently there than in other provinces. The least Virginia planter has fifty negroes, the wealthier two hundred and fifty, and the richest four to eight hundred souls. The number of negroes owned by twenty of them is greater than General Washington's army, including the militia raised so far. Maryland can contribute but little or nothing. The people of this province have always lived a life of ease and luxury and consequently have never been hardened for war. Those who took up arms two years ago have died with but few exceptions. The products of these two provinces are tobacco, wheat, and Indian corn. Much of the land is no longer cultivated, and trade is completely paralyzed. Hence, neither provisions nor money, which were formerly obtained from these provinces, are furnished any longer. Scarcity and want have made a veritable wilderness out of them.

The English ships are very busy and are not searching the coast in vain. They are taking many rich prizes. Of forty ships they have recently taken, thirty-four are French vessels. Chesapeake Bay is so empty that even the smallest sloop will not venture out of a creek.

When I concluded my last journal on the 18th of April, three of the parties that had been sent out to engage the rebels at some of their posts had not yet returned. Fifty dragoons had taken the Germantown Road as far as Flourtown, where they encountered Jersey militia from Monmouth County. Of these, sixteen men were killed, some twenty were left wounded, and eighteen taken prisoners. The Pennsylvania dragoons and two hundred and fifty light infantry had advanced as far as Bristol, where they met a much stronger force of Bucks County Militia, whom, however, they did not recognize as such because the militiamen had neither uniforms nor arms. They dispersed with the loss of only a few men who were cut down. But the watch, consisting of one officer and thirty-two Continental soldiers, and also two staff officers and nine subalterns, were captured. A little plundering concluded this Bristol visit.

At the same time the entire Hessian Jäger Corps had crossed the Schuylkill and advanced five English miles beyond Darby. Captain von Wreden covered this corps on the right during this march in the dark. His pickets marching directly in front of him encountered an infantry patrol of one officer and eighteen men. Several rifle shots betrayed the presence of the jägers, one of whom was slightly wounded in an exchange of fire. One rebel was captured. We could learn from him almost nothing, except the strength of the scouting party. We could not find out from him whether a larger force of rebels had followed the patrol.

While returning on the 18th, during the daytime, this corps picked up a grenadier by name of Christoph Bachmann from Captain von Blessen's company, who, after having been shot through the right hand and wounded in the nape of the neck at Red Bank, was cured by the rebels. He had won the good will of the doctor and, feigning lameness, was discharged as unfit for duty. He is completely cured and is doing duty.

Finally, on the 20th of April, the rest of the Hessian officers returned from their long imprisonment. In exchange for them we paroled the following day as many rebel officers of the same rank. General Lee has retired to his estates in Virginia. The English officers who returned at this time and later are selling their commissions.

On the 24th a captain and 150 light infantry marched out as far as the Schuylkill Falls. They were met by a rebel deserter, who told them that he had left the post at Barren Hill with one captain, one officer, and sixty men in complete safety. The captain made use of this information and surprised the rebels by advancing on them from two directions. Three men of the watch were killed and one wounded. The captain and five men escaped through the Schuylkill, but all the rest, including the officer, were brought in.

On the 26th Captain De Lancey of the Dragoons [23] and fifty horse surprised a post at Springhouse. Only a few of the rebels escaped; twelve were taken prisoners.

On the 29th General Erskine and Captain Montresor of the Engineers crossed the Delaware under cover of six British grenadier companies. Landing in Jersey, at Cooper's Ferry, they searched beyond the ferry for a suitable place to erect a strong camp for one brigade. They all returned again toward evening. Several Hessian jäger detachments have lately crossed the Schuylkill, but have come back without meeting any of the enemy. During these excursions the corps has had several deserters.

On the 30th the rich and influential Quakers returned from their prisons, in which they had been confined from the time the rebels, after the action at Brandywine, were obliged to leave this city, and in which they were treated in no gentle manner. I cannot but tell your Lordship that the wives of four of these Quakers asked permission at the English headquarters to go and beg for the release of their husbands. General Washington, in camp at

[23] Captain Oliver De Lancey, Jr., commissioned major, 17th Regiment of Dragoons, June 3, 1778.

Valley Forge, received these courageous Quaker women in the most cordial manner, kept them to dinner, and for the rest of the day they were entertained by the General's wife. Through this lady's kindly intercession, all Quakers were released.

The joy among the members of this powerful sect over the unexpected return to their brethren is extremely great. But how Congress treated them, and, according to good information, how many unworthy and previously worthless men make up this august body is shown by the fact that it completely forgot its dignity. Congress could not pass silently over this insult, yet, at the same time it could not praise enough the great justice of General Washington. And this praise is not unique; everyone is captivated by this general.

Two days previously there had been a meeting of the commissioners for the exchange of prisoners, which had accomplished nothing. The French volunteer Lafayette had come to this meeting to see Captain Fitzpatrick, whose acquaintance he had made in Paris several years before. After a long conversation he was asked by his English friend how he could bring himself, first, to leave France, and then, in America, to choose by no means the best company and surroundings. Lafayette replied that he, Captain Fitzpatrick, might rather ask him how he could ever deliberately make up his mind to sail away from America, ever regretting afterwards, in the society of his frivolous countrymen, the loss of his rare and pleasant associations with General Washington. How he would ever be able to bear this loss, he himself did not know.

On the night of the 1st–2nd of May there assembled between the 1st and 2nd redoubts fourteen companies of British grenadiers and light infantry, the Queen's Rangers, and 120 dragoons under Major Crewe,[24] the entire detachment being under the command of Lieutenant Colonel Abercromby. After a forced march along the Old York Road, they encountered, at the Crooked Billet Tavern, twelve English miles from our lines, Brigadier Lacey's militia brigade of five hundred men, busily engaged in throwing up fortifications on the road in order to make Bristol and all of Bucks County secure. Major Crewe, without waiting for all the grena-

[24] Major Richard Crewe, 17th Regiment of Dragoons.

diers, made a quick attack and scattered the disconcerted troops. Between eighty and a hundred were killed; the wounded were left on the field; and fifty-eight were taken prisoners. Eight four-horse wagons were brought in full of field requisites, entrenching tools, and provisions; three wagons were burned and only the horses taken. Several grenadiers were so embittered that they burned nine rebels. Besides, everything that had already been fortified with fascines was burned and ruined. Brigadier Lacey [25] and the officers were the first to flee, which put all Bristol to flight again. Only one lieutenant was captured.

On the 3rd two English infantry regiments, the 55th and the 63rd, crossed over to Jersey and encamped behind Cooper's Ferry. Since then working parties have been detached from this city each day to fortify their camp. With them is an officer and thirty dragoons for patrolling the country. This is being done with the intent of acquiring fresh food and forage more easily from the country people and also of cutting firewood and bringing it to the local magazines. All this is being accomplished without interference.

On the 4th all the Hessian troops near here turned out, formed in line two deep, and were reviewed by General and Admiral Howe. The weather was good, and the two brothers as well as many thousand onlookers were truly satisfied. The Leib Regiment distinguished itself especially, though no fault could be found with the appearance and marching of any other unit. The strength of the assembled troops was as follows:

	Officers	Noncommissioned Officers	Musicians	Soldiers	Horses
The Jäger Corps	18	67	17	574	90
The Grenadier Brigade	41	120	60	871	
Woellwarth's Brigade	23	99	21	536	
Von Donop's Regiment	15	55	22	432	
The Leib Regiment	15	58	22	408	
Artillery	7	13	3	164	
TOTAL	119	412	145	2,985	[90]

[25] Brigadier General John Lacey. Lacey's report of this attack was published in *Pennsylvania Archives,* vol. VI, and his memoirs (covering the year 1777) may be found in the *Pennsylvania Magazine,* vol. XXVI.

In his orders General Howe publicly expressed his satisfaction to Lieutenant General von Knyphausen and his thanks to all the troops without distinction, adding that he would personally render to His Majesty the King of Great Britain a most faithful report of the good condition of the Hessian troops.

On the 5th Brigadier General Erskine advanced with a dragoon patrol too far in the direction of Hackenfield [26] in Jersey. He was driven back with the loss of three dragoons and was almost captured himself.

On the 7th Brigadier General Leslie with two Pennsylvania battalions joined the regiments that had gone to Jersey on the 3rd and took over the command of the entire detachment.

Your Lordship can learn Congress's answer to the declaration of the British Parliament more clearly from the enclosed newspaper [missing]. On the 2nd of May the rebels had a *feu de joie* at Valley Forge to celebrate the news that France and Spain had recognized the independence of America and concluded commercial treaties for thirty years.

On the 6th of May the arrival of some of the Hessian and British recruits was celebrated at Wilmington with three running fires. The rest of the ships will cast anchor by and by. The rebel General Wayne is in Jersey to observe the troops posted at Cooper's Ferry. Hence a battalion of light infantry has joined General Leslie.

On the 7th General Clinton arrived here at exactly the same time as an English frigate, which had made the passage in two days less than five weeks.

With the greatest esteem, I commend myself to your Lordship's gracious benevolence and have the honor to be [etc.] [27]

26 Haddonfield?

27 The following page of the MS letter has some notes, probably in von Jungkenn's hand, for a letter to Baurmeister acknowledging receipt of four letters, including one dated March 6, 1778, which is missing from the collection.

: 17 :

I had the honor of receiving your Lordship's esteemed letters
of the 13th of November of last year and of February 15th of this
year on the 21st of May. I am very grateful for your remembering
me so kindly and still more for your Lordship's gracious benevolence toward Captain Schutten, my nephew. I suppose he will be
able to leave New York with Major General von Mirbach.

I herewith enclose the news I have collected. Captain von
Münchhausen, who is about to leave for Europe, will, to be sure,
give a better account in person. I do not like, however, to inter-
rupt the sequence of my reports and hope that this part will not
be superfluous.

In concluding, I commend myself to your further grace and
am with the greatest respect, so long as I live [etc.]

P.S. The negro boy intended for your Lordship has been well
taken care of and is now with his Excellency General von Knyphausen, who meant to send him with Captain von Münchhausen.
The Captain, however, had sufficient excuses for not taking him.
I believe that if we return to New York there will still be an oppor-

tunity to send him. I shall gladly take care of everything. Ferguson, the commissary of prisoners, is visiting me while I close this letter. He informs me that one hundred American dragoons are roaming through Virginia in search of the Hessian prisoners who are quartered here and there with the residents, that they can be brought together only with great difficulty, that many do not want to come, and that many are being concealed by the inhabitants.

Lord Cathcart, captain in the 17th Regiment of Dragoons, now adjutant to General Clinton, returned from Congress day before yesterday late in the night. No one can get any news. It is said that Congress insists upon American independence. If we are to advance through Jersey to New York without knowing what has been decided, we shall meet with numerous obstacles such as demolished bridges and barricaded roads in the woods. However, I cannot give accurate information. Once more I commend myself.

: 18 :

I was unable to send a report with the packet which sailed on the 22nd of May this year. The confusion that prevailed at the time and still prevails makes all news so indefinite that it is like a vexatious riddle even to those who are here.

On the 24th of May General Howe boarded his ship and surrendered the command to General Clinton. The artillery park fired a last salute of nineteen guns, and General Clinton gave "Brandywine" as the password and "Howe" as the countersign.

Since the 21st of May we have been loading the heavy baggage, all the heavy artillery, and the greater part of the train on board the ships. The heavy artillery of a few of the redoubts was replaced by fieldpieces. Only a few provisions were left on land. On the 3rd of this month the last of the loaded ships sailed to Chester, where all the ships were to rendezvous.

The English merchants were informed of the evacuation of Philadelphia and took their wares, which were considerable, on board the ships. The smaller merchants followed their example. Also the people in the service of the government embarked with their families and possessions.

Thus Philadelphia at present greatly resembles a fair during the last week of business. Prices are going up from day to day. The Society of Friends has endless worries. They are expecting an unbearable fate should the army completely withdraw from the city.

Between the 7th and 9th, the 2nd Light Infantry Battalion under Major Maitland burned many ships at Burlington belonging to the residents. Two American frigates, the *Effingham* and the *Washington,* and some smaller vessels had the same fate.[28] At the peak of the high tide, the rebels turned all these ships toward the Jersey shore and anchored them without masts, so that none of them could be rescued. Twenty-five more ships only half built, which are lying at the wharf and also belong to the residents, are likewise to be burned when we leave the city.

On the 1st the corps at Cooper's Ferry was reinforced by two English regiments, while the 15th Regiment joined the post at Billingsport. On the 3rd of this month the 3rd British Brigade crossed over to Jersey, for General Smallwood[29] with the Wilmington garrison had joined General Maxwell in Jersey on the 25th of May. General Dickinson commands the militia of this province, which is gathering near Trenton, though in small numbers and unwillingly. General Washington and his army, which is said to be no more than eight thousand strong, remain quietly at Valley Forge. He is following our example and sending all his dispensable heavy baggage and even his heavy artillery across the Susquehanna. His troops are fortifying the camp and making gardens. Every ten days they receive the necessary provisions from the small magazine at Lancaster, which is then replenished from York Town.

In spite of the apparent preparations to evacuate Philadelphia, three hundred men are working in the lines every day. Our wood and hay magazines and our cultivated gardens and fenced-in meadows are being carefully guarded and kept up. In

---

28 These vessels were burned by the Americans to prevent their falling into British hands.

29 Brigadier General William Smallwood did not go into Jersey; he was ordered to cover stores at Head of Elk and send his First Brigade to Valley Forge. See Washington's letter to Smallwood, May 25, 1778.

the meantime, Washington is not receiving any reinforcements from New England. These provinces want General Gates to be made commander in chief of all the American land forces, while the provinces around here, especially Virginia, exalt Washington above everyone else. General Lafayette and all the French volunteers also sincerely revere Washington.

I now wish that I could give an account with all the details of General Howe's last unsuccessful expedition: As early as the 18th of May, General Howe had learned that some three thousand rebels under General Lafayette had left Valley Forge with eight guns, intending to cross the Schuylkill at Fatland Ford and take position at Barren Hill. Ten days' provisions followed this corps, and it had for its vanguard sixty Indians and a hundred and fifty Carolina riflemen. A strong detachment of British dragoons, which had advanced by way of the Schuylkill Falls to Barren Hill church very early in the morning of the 19th of May and which had met many obstacles on the way, confirmed the presence of the rebels in its reports.

General Lafayette had hardly encamped and protected his right wing with strong pickets posted on the road leading to the Schuylkill Falls when he detached the Indians to the left through Germantown into the woods, from which they could observe the three main roads to Philadelphia. The riflemen remained beyond Germantown with orders not to fire and to fall back before all patrols. At the approach of the British they were to assemble half an English mile from the left wing and offer resistance until further orders. With Lafayette's corps were only sixty dragoons, but many French volunteers.

At retreat on the 19th General Howe sent out Generals Grant and Erskine, both dragoon regiments, the Guards, the Queen's Rangers, the light infantry, the English and Hessian grenadiers, and Captain Ewald with a hundred dismounted jägers. Except for a few fieldpieces, there was no artillery. The corps had strict orders to attack the enemy only with the bayonet. Even before daybreak on the 20th the British light infantry was in front of the rebel camp, where the pickets had already been withdrawn and great confusion prevailed as they retreated on the several roads.

General Howe set out at half past five on the morning of the 20th of May. Unfortunately, General Washington was informed immediately of this, so he put the rest of his army under arms and repeatedly dispatched orders to General Lafayette to withdraw quickly and have his men rendezvous on the other side of the Schuylkill on the highway in Charlestown Township, since the bridge at Fatland Ford would be demolished.

General Grant neither attacked nor pursued the rebels, for he believed that the retreat had been planned in advance and that General Washington was likely to be there in person; thus he would be caught in a cross fire. But their retreat was as certain as it was quick. When General Howe had advanced one and a half miles beyond Germantown, he met General Erskine, who reported that the rebels had recrossed the Schuylkill and that their loss was one French officer and six riflemen killed and one French officer and nine men captured, while they themselves had two light infantrymen and one dragoon horse wounded.

Toward two o'clock in the afternoon General Howe and the rest of the army, accompanied by Generals Clinton and von Knyphausen, returned to Philadelphia, where only von Woellwarth's brigade had remained as a reserve for the watches and pickets in the lines.

General Howe had good reasons to suspect that the enemy corps would be supported by the rest of the army and that thus a general engagement would take place between Barren Hill and Fatland Ford, where the vanguard of the British army could easily occupy the higher ground of the country, and where on its right the roads to Whitemarsh were partly covered and on the left the highway from Norriton to Barren Hill was already outflanked.

Washington, although he is not a good strategist and does not always follow through, gained in this manner his previous advantages, which, however, mean nothing when taken as a whole.

Toward evening General Grant's troops returned to their quarters. The weather was hot, and a fruitless march totaling forty English miles fatigued the men very much. The Indians, who enjoyed undisturbed rest, returned unmolested across the Schuylkill in the night of the 20th–21st of May.

That the rebels retreated in confusion and were much fatigued is shown in General Lafayette's report, which states that one hundred and twenty-six men were drowned in the Schuylkill, that about one thousand muskets and rifles were thrown away, and that two guns which had been left in the camp had been found and brought in again, since the enemy did not pursue. He also asks for new provisions in his report since theirs had been abandoned.

A rebel general, Baron Steuben, wrote to General von Knyphausen after this expedition requesting that the captured French officer not be treated unkindly.

The English ships have lately been extremely fortunate at sea. The *Greyhound* recently captured a French ship carrying twenty guns. Captain Dickson, the commander, who had captured two armed American schooners two days before and had about fifty men from these two ships in irons, was fervently asked by the prisoners for permission to work at the guns during the attack on the French ship. Their fearlessness and good work proved that they were in earnest. After the French ship had been taken, Captain Dickson rewarded all the Americans for their services by putting them at liberty on a seaworthy, well-provisioned schooner and letting them sail away.

On the 18th of May twenty-three British staff officers gave a fête in General Howe's honor. Seven hundred and fifty invitations were issued. Behind a house not far from the Neck a great salon was built and decorated with mirrors and candelabra and chandeliers. Two rows of tables and benches were provided for the guests. The house was made ready for a reception and ball. In front of the house a display of fireworks had been prepared, which was set off at ten o'clock in the evening.

In the center of the great lawn, which extended down to the Delaware, was a triumphal arch. The part of the lawn near the house was lined with an appropriate guard displaying all the British and Hessian colors. On the other side of the arch a tournament was held. It consisted of only two quadrilles faultlessly executed by the Knights of the White Rose and of the Burning Mountain.

The festivities began toward four o'clock in the best of weather with a parade of many boats on the river. The frigate *Roebuck* greeted the sloop of the brothers Howe with a salute of nineteen guns, and many transports responded. Soon field music was heard everywhere. The ladies and gentlemen disembarked in front of the festive country house. Accompanied by continuous field music from the place of the tournament, the Howe brothers and fifty-two ladies and officers then passed through the triumphal arch and moved into the circle, which was completely surrounded with flags. It was a spectacle one will never forget. Tea and refreshments were served in good order and without crowding. Dancing began as early as eight o'clock in the evening and continued, except during the display of fireworks, until the banquet.

The tables were laid with 330 covers and were loaded with 1,040 plates, dishes, etc. The finest fruit that can be obtained here and in the West Indies in the spring was served. Many negroes and other servants quickly and in excellent order satisfied every desire before one could express it. Music and song alternated, and the toasts were the following: (1) the King, (2) the Royal Family, (3) the sea and land forces, (4) the Howe brothers, (5) the noble ladies of the order of the White Rose and the Burning Mountain, and (6) the originators of the festival to all present. There was no lack of huzzas, and the dance, resumed after the banquet, lasted until six o'clock in the morning.

The staff officers paid 3,312 guineas for this fête. The great English shop of Coffin and Andreson [30] took in £12,000 sterling for silk goods and other fine materials, which shows how much money was lavished on this affair and how elegantly the ladies were dressed. There was not the least disorder nor any unfortunate incident, in spite of the fact that the majority of the army and the residents were spectators.[31]

[30] A storekeeper by name of Coffin is mentioned in *Kemble Papers,* I, 228, Jan. 3, 1776 (*New York Historical Society Collections,* 1884), and in *Report on American Manuscripts in the Royal Institution of Great Britain,* I, 6–7, July 2, 1775. Perhaps Anderson (?) became associated with Coffin after 1776.
[31] The above account of the Mischianza parallels in many details André's description in *Gentleman's Magazine,* Aug., 1778.

On the 4th of June the birthday of the King of Great Britain was celebrated as usual. At high noon the cannons on land fired a salute, and at one o'clock those on the ships did the same. All the generals and staff officers who were in the city had dinner with General Clinton.

On the same day we received a confirmatory report that the Indians living in the extreme west near the confluence of the Ohio and the Monongahela have taken Fort Pitt and are approaching the Susquehanna in great mobs to come to the aid of the King beyond the Great Water (so they call the King of Great Britain), spreading horror everywhere, and that, on the other hand, General Washington has sent fifteen hundred men to the said fort. Fort Pitt is situated three hundred English miles west of Philadelphia.

Since everyone was talking of evacuating the city, and all our boats had left, and the packet was ready to depart, I concluded my journal. However, on the 5th, at ten o'clock in the evening, a boat came in with the news that General Cornwallis and new commissioners had arrived in the Delaware. They landed here on the 6th and have already taken quarters. The magazines are again being stocked with provisions, and the departure of the packet has been postponed. On the 7th the English artillery park greeted the commissioners by firing a salute. Their names are as follows: Admiral Lord Howe, General Sir Henry Clinton, Lord Carlisle, Mr. Johnstone (the former governor at Pensacola in West Florida), and Mr. Eden.[32]

On the 9th at two o'clock in the morning, the two battalions of Anspachers embarked at the wharf near the Swedish Church. Their dispensable equipage, the wagons, the horses of the officers, and the fieldpieces are still here under a guard of three men per company. Where these battalions will go and when they will rejoin the army are not known to date.

On the 10th a secretary of the new peace commissioners departed with dispatches for Congress. Although he was permitted to pass the first outpost at Valley Forge, he was sent back by the

---

[32] The British peace commissioners were Sir Henry Clinton; Frederick Howard, Earl of Carlisle; George Johnstone, formerly Governor of West Florida; and William Eden, later Lord Auckland.

second. The following day General Washington wrote to General Clinton that such commissioners would not be permitted to pass unless they had passes or special permission from Congress. On the 11th Admiral Howe resigned as commissioner, but decided definitely to retain command of the fleet. We have every reason to suspect that the army will move again, but do not know whether it will be to Jersey or to Valley Forge. The prisoners taken at Trenton and since then are expected any day.

: 19 :

NEW YORK
JULY 7, 1778

After a difficult march through Jersey, which took from the 17th of June to the 1st of July and fatigued the army considerably, his Excellency General von Knyphausen landed here safely day before yesterday at six o'clock in the evening.

On the 14th of June [33] I sent your Lordship by Captain von Münchhausen another part of my journal so that the continuity would not be interrupted, though I am well aware that the said Captain von Münchhausen can furnish a better account in person. This time I dutifully report the following:

On the 15th of June all the half-built ships at the wharves of Philadelphia were burned on the bank of the Delaware. Stirn's and Loos's brigades crossed the Delaware at Cooper's Ferry and encamped three English miles beyond the ferry. The 17th Regiment of Dragoons and the last section of the artillery followed on the 16th.

On the 17th his Excellency General von Knyphausen crossed over with the Hessian grenadiers, the Jäger Corps, and the Queen's Rangers and proceeded to Haddonfield, where he posted

[33] The journal has the superscription "Philadelphia, June 15, 1778."

the Jäger Corps and two Hessian grenadier battalions. The two British regiments he sent to Gloucester to cover the landing of the army.

On the night of the 17th–18th General Clinton moved into the lines. This caused Washington to believe that we would attack him at Valley Forge after all. Since the 14th he has been posted with seven thousand men in a clearing three English miles in front of his camp, with his right wing covering the Lancaster road and his left wing in touch with a strong detached post close to the Gulph Mill.

General Mifflin with six hundred men occupied an outpost at the Sorrel Horse, seven English miles from our bridge across the Schuylkill, and sent a constant string of patrols through Germantown toward our lines. It was these patrols who discovered that General Clinton, between five and six in the morning, had retired by brigades through Philadelphia to Gloucester Point, whence he crossed on flatboats to Gloucester without interference. One enemy patrol which had come by way of Bush Hill passed between our 9th and 10th redoubts and advanced to Seventh Street in Philadelphia. At the corner of Erd [34] and Second streets it finally came upon our last patrol and exchanged some shots with them, after which we evacuated Philadelphia entirely, leaving the rebels positively nothing but empty redoubts and houses.

This was reported to General Washington by General Mifflin after he had occupied the city with his detachment from the Sorrel Horse at half past eight in the morning. Only a few British officers and their servants, who had inquired too late about the last orders, were found in the houses of their tender acquaintances and taken prisoners.

The army assembled at Haddonfield. Major General Leslie with the Hessian Jäger Corps and three English regiments marched to Fostertown, whither headquarters followed on the 19th with General Cornwallis's corps, which consisted of the greater part of the dragoon regiments, the Guards, all the grena-

[34] Third Street? or Elfreth's Alley? The latter runs from First to Second streets, north of Arch Street.

diers, and the 3rd and 4th Brigades of Light Infantry. His Excellency General von Knyphausen remained at Haddonfield to await the arrival of the Billingsport garrison, which had been met halfway by two English regiments, but had encountered no difficulty.

On the 20th headquarters and General Cornwallis's corps advanced to Mount Holly, and his Excellency General von Knyphausen, to Moorestown. The artillery park, the provision train, and twenty-four pontoons made a long halt. On the 21st his Excellency General von Knyphausen also marched to Mount Holly. Up to this time the drizzly weather had been very good for marching over deep sand roads; but from this time on, the extreme heat caused great suffering among the troops. A patrol detached from the Jäger Corps to Rancocas Creek burned two two-masted and four single-masted American ships on this stream and appropriated all the flour in a mill.

On the 22nd the army marched in one column as far as Black Horse,[35] and on the 23rd headquarters arrived at Crosswicks, where General Cornwallis's corps halted. General Leslie had pushed on halfway to Allentown. General von Knyphausen, who had kept further to the right, advanced to Recklesstown, where he encountered many obstacles at Black's Creek, an arm of Rancocas Creek,[36] for Brigadier General Maxwell and his detachment of six hundred infantrymen and Colonel Moylan with one hundred and fifty horse had demolished all the bridges they could. They did not have much trouble in accomplishing this, in spite of the few troops. Washington had not expected the British army to keep so far to the right, but supposed it would pass through Burlington to Kingston and then take the road over Rocky Hill to Brunswick.

Consequently, in the night of the 18th–19th, Washington had General Lee and Colonel Morgan cross the Delaware cautiously at Gorell's or Howell's Ferry [37] and take post in Jersey at Collwell's

---

[35] Columbus, New Jersey.

[36] Black's Creek flows into the Delaware on the south side of Bordentown and not into the Rancocas.

[37] Going up the Delaware, the ferries above Trenton were Yarley's, Howell's, McConkey's (Washington Crossing), Coxe's, Coryell's (New Hope), Wells or

house behind Wickecheoke Creek. On the 20th he detached General Gates [38] with two brigades and Morgan's Riflemen along the north side of the Raritan to Brunswick. He himself followed with the rest of the army on the 21st and encamped before Pennington as early as the 23rd. Here he had General Dickinson join him with the Jersey militia.

Then he ordered General Gates [39] and Brigadier General Maxwell to join him at Cranbury early on the 26th. He reinforced Colonel Moylan's troop with two hundred more dragoons, so that he could march as closely as possible on our left and observe our activities from day to day. Between Allentown and Cranbury and as far as Brunswick, Governor Livingston had a thousand-yard-wide strip of the finest woods cut down in order to barricade all the roads passing through.

General Clinton marched to Allentown on the 24th, where General Leslie had attempted to force the nearest roads the previous evening, but had been compelled to desist because they were occupied by too strong a force. The enemy withdrew, however, during the night. On the 25th General Clinton moved even further to the right in Monmouth County, thus avoiding all obstacles as far as possible and all major engagements, as had been positively ordered by higher authority.

His Excellency General von Knyphausen found the bridge across Crosswicks Creek at Waln's mill completely demolished, which delayed his march to Imlaystown, where he was to arrive on the 24th, for five and one-half hours. He arrived in Monmouth Township on the 25th, when General Cornwallis's corps was still a march of two and a half English miles away. Headquarters remained along the road, in the Rising Sun. General Leslie was also in the rear guard.

Hence, on the 26th his Excellency General von Knyphausen formed the van in the march to Freehold or Monmouth Court-

Gorell's, and Howell's. This last was on the Pennsylvania side opposite the mouth of Wickecheoke Creek. Stryker states that Lee's and Wayne's advanced divisions reached Coryell's Ferry Friday night, June 19, and crossed Saturday afternoon and evening. Stryker, p. 69.

[38] Wayne. See following letter, where Baurmeister corrects this statement.

[39] Wayne. See preceding note.

house. Headquarters were one mile in the rear. The army needed a day of rest, which was granted on the 27th. Three hundred and twenty horses had already arrived in the artillery park, in the train, and with the baggage, while as many, if not more, were picked up along the march. All the cattle and sheep we could get hold of were also taken along. For these the country people were paid cash by the Commmissary General of War. Many ailing and sick followed in wagons.

Although the men were never in need of salt or fresh provisions, there was much plundering, which disturbed General Clinton. There is much new evidence of it in Jersey. It has made the country people all the more embittered rebels.

There was no pillaging and plundering on the part of the Hessians, but it is my duty to report to your Lordship that we had many deserters. This, however, can best be seen from the return sent to our sovereign, His Most Serene Highness the Landgrave. The total is at least two hundred. This cannot be attributed to the fatiguing march, but rather to our long stay in Philadelphia and the many kinds of temptation, which need not be very alluring to blind the common soldier and make him break his oath. I believe that since this vice had never been known or even suspected among us, we had no cause to be particularly watchful and therefore were probably careless in one way or another. Much as most of them will repent it, they will not be able to return, for the rebels will guard them as prized possessions.

The English had from eighteen to twenty-one deserters per brigade. In other words, in the five brigades, not counting the Guards, the grenadiers, the light infantry, the Queen's Rangers, and the dragoons, they had more than a hundred. The most remarkable of all this is that all the English deserters were returned prisoners and that among the Hessians there were more native Hessians than foreigners.[40]

On the 27th the enemy reconnoitered the left wing of General von Knyphausen's corps, advancing as far as the picket of Loos's brigade; indeed, this picket had to fall back until one of the

[40] Foreigners, i.e., subjects of sovereigns other than the Landgrave of Hesse-Cassel. Many of these were impressed on the way to the port of embarkation.

brigade's cannon induced the rebels to withdraw in haste. It was an advance troop of Washington's vanguard, which was on the march mid-distance between Cranbury and Freehold.

Early in the morning of the 28th his Excellency General von Knyphausen set out and moved along the road to Middletown. The van of the army had already advanced five English miles, and the artillery park and the train were well under way, when, at the very spot where the pickets of Loos's brigade had been harassed the previous day, the rebels pushed forward on an open space to the left of the column and made an attempt on the baggage. Several skirmishers got between the wagons and maltreated the drivers and some patrols alongside them.

General Clinton was then forced to believe the many reports that Washington was determined to make a general attack on the marching column in order to divide the army and then defeat each part separately. According to our spies, his army had increased to almost twenty-five thousand.

Hence, General Clinton, without first ordering General von Knyphausen to discontinue his march, had the 1st Battalion of Light Infantry take a roundabout route to oppose the enemy's left flank and the greater part of their cannon. This battalion had to wade through a morass; but it would have been late anyhow, for General Clinton immediately attacked in person with the Guards and the 42nd Battalion as well as the front permitted. He had ordered only the British grenadiers and the Queen's Rangers to follow as a reserve and commanded the Hessian grenadiers to form his left flank.

The rebels, who anticipated nothing less than an orderly defense, gained an elevation in the rear under an effective cannonade of fourteen pieces. Finally, their artillery also withdrew to this elevation, abandoning its ammunition in order to escape more easily. The Guards and the 42nd Regiment, after firing so often that they could scarcely hold their guns, completely routed the rebels with the bayonet.

General Clinton marched back to Freehold, and the rebels to two miles beyond Freehold toward Cranbury. Those who did not reach the elevation took all the wagons they could for the slightly wounded. Sixty-two severely wounded remained in the field with a flag of truce. The British outdid themselves in bravery in this unexpected action. They had one hundred and twelve killed and one hundred and seventy-four wounded; sixty-two died from the heat. Moreover, the dragoons lost twenty-four horses.

General Clinton, in the thickest fire, was saved by one of his adjutants, Captain Sutherland,[41] when a rebel colonel aimed at him, but missed. Captain Sutherland's horse was wounded. Another adjutant, Lloyd,[42] stabbed the colonel. Likewise, Captain Wilson, captain of horse of the dragoons of the light infantry, stabbed General Lee's adjutant. Captain von Wilmowsky lost his horse in this action. Colonel Monckton [43] of the British Grenadiers was killed, a great loss indeed. Major Gardiner [44] was again wounded in the foot, and several other British officers, who greatly distinguished themselves, were also wounded.

The loss of the rebels amounts to six hundred killed and wounded, according to their own account in a Trenton newspaper of June 30th, which adds that this loss has finally gained everlasting liberty for the Americans. The unreliable militia scattered at the very beginning and will not be brought together very soon. Washington's force totaled no more than twelve thousand men, over five thousand of whom did not take part in the engagement. It is said that Washington came as close as he did to our line of march to please the French. This was also the reason for his firing a victory salute on the 4th of this month in his camp between Englishtown and Brunswick. (*no, 4th of July !!*)

In the night of the 28th–29th General Clinton followed his Excellency General von Knyphausen as far as Middletown, whence the army proceeded on the night of the 30th of June to the 1st of July to the heights of Shrewsbury. On the 2nd the

[41] Captain William Sutherland, 55th Regiment, aide-de-camp to Sir Henry Clinton. Cf. "Stephen Kemble's Orderly Book," *New York Historical Society Collections*, 1884, pp. 468, 587.

[42] Lieutenant Thomas Lloyd, 7th Regiment, appointed adjutant to Sir William Howe, Oct. 13, 1777, *ibid.*, p. 517.

[43] The Hon. Lieutenant Colonel Henry Monckton, 45th Regiment.

[44] Major William Gardiner, 10th Regiment of Foot.

embarkation began near Sandy Hook. His Excellency General von Knyphausen embarked on the 4th and disembarked at New York with General Clinton on the 5th at six o'clock in the evening. A salute of seventeen guns was fired in their honor. A bridge across the narrowest part of Shrewsbury [45] facilitated the crossing of the army to Sandy Hook, where all embarked without interference.

Cautious with his little army, General Washington had much reason to fear being cut off from the Delaware on the Elizabethtown side, so he did not pursue us. He retired to Brunswick and is beginning to send detachments across the North River at Peekskill in order to occupy the strong post at White Plains before we can get there.

Our army, after part of it has rested close to the South Wharf in front of this city and another part on Long Island, will occupy a new position, and we shall see what happens.

Major General von Mirbach and many other officers ordered to return to Hesse are ready to embark with the first convoy, with which, or earlier if an opportunity offers, I shall send the next part of my journal. I ask a thousand pardons for being obliged to send this without having it copied. We have very little time to devote to anything except necessary duty, and I have to write this in very great haste so that it will not miss the packet.

Concluding this account, I commend myself to your Lordship's gracious benevolence and remain with the greatest respect [*etc.*]

p.s. Your Lordship probably knows of General Pigot's successful expedition from Rhode Island to the mainland, which was undertaken the end of May.

[45] In 1778 Sandy Hook, which had previously been connected with the rest of Shrewsbury Township by a narrow bar, became an island. Along the old bar and over the new opening of Shrewsbury Inlet, the British built a pontoon bridge. Cf. W. Stryker, p. 231.

: 20 :

I sent my last report on a packet which sailed on short notice on the 7th of this month. From it your Lordship will have seen that General Clinton evacuated Philadelphia on the 18th of June and marched the army through Jersey by way of Haddon-field, Mount Holly, Allentown, Freehold, and Middletown to Sandy Hook, where it arrived July 1st.

On the 28th of June it decisively beat back an enemy attack at Freehold, and as early as the 2nd of July all the baggage and train, followed by the army itself, went into camp on Staten, Long, and York islands.

At present the army is encamped as follows: on Staten Island, the 2nd British Brigade; on Long Island, the 3rd, 4th, and 5th British Brigades, Governor Browne's provincials, and the 17th Regiment of Dragoons; on York Island, the 1st British Brigade, the three battalions of Philadelphia militia, the three new corps (Lord Rawdon's, Emmerich's, and Sutherland's Caledonians [46]), the Guards, the British Artillery Corps, and the Hessian Jäger Corps. Above Fort Independence are posted the Hessian grenadier

[46] Also known as Sutherland's Highlanders.

189

brigade and Stirn's, Schmidt's, and Loos's brigades. The Anspachers, Fanning's Provincial Corps, and the 38th Regiment have been sent to Rhode Island. The 15th and the 44th Regiments are stationed at Sandy Hook in the redoubts thrown up beside the lighthouse. And the 23rd Regiment is presently on board ships to reinforce the marines on the warships, for on the 7th of this month a French fleet of twelve ships of the line and four frigates was sighted twenty leagues off Cape Henry.

This fleet had first headed for the Delaware, but as soon as it learned of the departure of the English fleet and the evacuation of Philadelphia, it sailed into Chesapeake Bay, where many French and American merchantmen with full cargoes had assembled in the rivers emptying into this bay to wait for safe convoy to France.

On the 11th the French fleet anchored five English miles off Sandy Hook, and on the 16th a hospital was built at Shrewsbury in East Jersey for the numerous sick sailors. Fourteen British vessels that did not know of the presence of the French fleet have already been stopped. Moreover, the admiral, Count d'Estaing, hoisted the English flag and used the signals Admiral Howe had given the cruising ships to notify them on their return whether to run into a given harbor or remain on the high seas.

Admiral Howe made use of thirteen hundred volunteers from the transports to raise to full complement six sixty-four-, four fifty-, and one forty-gun ships of the line as well as fourteen frigates of from thirty to twenty guns. The fleet is anchored in two lines between Sandy Hook and the narrow entrance to the harbor. Two men-of-war of sixty-four guns are expected to arrive from Rhode Island through Hell Gate at any hour, while on the East River a warship of seventy guns is being made ready. As soon as Admiral Howe has assembled the fleet, he is expected to attack.

There is much talk of the impending arrival of the English fleet under Admiral Byron, which we fervently hope is true. Our fleet could then successfully engage the foreign fleet and pursue the many merchantmen destined for France with cargoes worth several millions. These cargoes would more than pay for what the Americans have received on credit since the beginning of the rebellion. It is estimated that our provisions will last to the end of October. Fresh victuals can now be obtained only from Long Island; nothing comes in anymore from East Chester and Westchester by way of Kings Bridge.

Since the 2nd of this month General Gates has been at White Plains with the following Continental regiments: Putnam's, Webb's, Eno's, Meigs's, Sheldon's, Nixon's, Sherburne's, Graham's,[47] Wyllys's, the Albany battalion under Brigadier Hoocker,[48] and 150 dragoons.

On the 11th of this month General Washington's army, tremendously fatigued, having lost almost a thousand men on the 28th of June and having been deserted by most of the Carolina, Virginia, and Maryland militia, left the remainder of the Jersey militia under Generals Wayne [49] and Maxwell at Elizabethtown, Newark, and Amboy and then proceeded by way of Hackensack to the North River. It crossed the river on flatboats at King's Ferry and is now stationed at White Plains. General Gates thereupon went to Philadelphia to take over the duties of War President.[50] (I find it necessary to advise your Lordship that where in my journal of the 7th I said Gates, I should have said Wayne.) The total strength of the rebels cannot be ascertained, since only a few deserters are coming in.

Congress desires to possess Rhode Island again. For this reason Washington is making movements to his left. He is expecting the complete cooperation of the French fleet. To be sure, the said island is occupied by a strong force, and General Pigot, who is always on his guard, has made two sorties that were unfortunate for the rebels. It would be too great a stroke of luck for the enemies of England to succeed in such an undertaking.

On the 17th of this month five hundred Hessian prisoners were finally turned over to us at Elizabethtown. All of them look

[47] A Lieutenant Colonel John Graham commanded a regiment of New York militia, and a Captain John Graham served in Colonel Goose Van Schaick's 1st New York Regiment.

[48] Not identified.

[49] Brigadier General William Winds of the New Jersey militia, not Wayne.

[50] General Gates was appointed President of the Board of War, November 27, 1777.

well. The rest are expected any day, and so the Regiments Lossberg, Knyphausen, and the vacant von Woellwarth [51] will soon
be full strength again. The English artillery park is giving each
regiment two fieldpieces.

The trial instigated by General Washington against General
Lee immediately after the attack of the 28th of June has turned
out to the satisfaction of the former. Washington has all the members of the eastern governments on his side, besides General Gates
and his followers. Since then, the enemy army has been divided
into two hostile camps: even a duel has been fought between
General Conway and Colonel Cadwallader, in which the former
was mortally wounded.[52] The local newspapers are full of it.

In one of them I read General Washington's report to Congress concerning the attack at Freehold. In the action this general
had his army occupy an open field, where there was hardly enough
room for his vanguard to engage the front of one battalion and
where the English Guards, stationed on the road to Middletown,
had just enough room to attack with two companies of the left
wing of the 1st Battalion, which permitted the center of the battalion and then the right wing of the 2nd Battalion of the Guards
to gain the abandoned open field.

General Clinton could then see what the enemy's plans were.
He ordered the 1st Battalion of Light Infantry to execute a quick
flanking movement around the enemy's left wing in order to capture the fourteen pieces of artillery which Washington had placed
on his front. Just then General Lee's corps, in a disorderly retreat,
met the main corps. This completely disheartened the troops.
Washington was compelled to remove to an elevation on the left
of Freehold and ordered his artillery to do likewise.

In order to be able to move faster, the artillery threw away
their ammunition chests, all of which would have come into the
possession of our light infantry had these brave troops not been
stopped by a morass. The spirited behavior of the Guards, the

[51] See 1777, note 11.

[52] General Conway was not mortally wounded. The so-called Conway Cabal,
in which Gates was almost equally guilty, ended in Conway's return to France,
where he had served as a colonel. He had resigned his American commission, April
28, 1778. He died in 1800.

light infantry, the British grenadiers, the 33rd Regiment,[53] and the Queen's Rangers cannot be praised too highly.

Washington states in his account that he intended to attack again on the 29th of June. However, he was by no means able to do so. His army, which numbered hardly twelve thousand men, greatly fatigued, and forsaken by twice as many militia, could not attack us from any place of vantage along the route of march.

General Clinton calmly continued his march until the 29th of June, and by this emphatic proof showed the rebels sufficiently that when he had orders to attack, none of Britain's enemies was safe in any field. General Arnold has the command at Philadelphia in place of Mifflin, who is ill.

This account will go by packet. Only a stiff east wind, however, can now take our ships through Hell Gate and then to the open sea off Rhode Island between nightfall and dawn. From there on the safe passage of a packet is said to depend merely on the wind.

With the greatest respect I have the honor to be [*etc.*]

P.S. The 17th Regiment of Dragoons has been raised to full strength by men and horses taken from the 16th. The rest of this regiment and the Guards are ready to be embarked and taken to England. General von Mirbach and the other officers are still here. Admiral Gambier [54] promises to equip a ship for them at the next opportunity.

[53] The 33rd Regiment did not take part in the Philadelphia campaign. Baurmeister probably means the 23rd Regiment.

[54] Rear Admiral James Gambier, who was second in command under Admiral Lord Howe.

: 21 :

On the 7th and 20th of July I had the honor to send your Lordship reports from New York about the activity of the army up to those days. Since then the following events have taken place: On the 22nd of July the French fleet disembarked at Shrewsbury the rest of the sailors who were dangerously ill, and Governor Livingston had them taken to Middletown, where the French established a hospital. The fleet took in as much fresh meat and water as was practicable and weighed anchor late the same evening. The next morning nothing more was to be seen of the foreign ships.

Lord Howe was also late in learning of the sojourn and further intentions of this fleet, and even then knew only that it had sailed to Rhode Island (where it was sighted by the troops of occupation on the 30th of July) in order to attack that island from the sea, while General Sullivan attacks from the land. The rebels gathered there are ten thousand strong and are said to be well provided with all necessities.

194

On the other hand, including the marines, there are at present nine thousand men on the island, eighty 12-pounders, thirty-six 24-pounders, and many 9-pounders and fieldpieces. Two frigates are anchored in the harbor so close to the shore that they can prevent any landing. Only frigates can lie off the shore of the island to bombard it, but batteries have been erected (opposite these places) to fire upon them.

Any enterprise will therefore meet with commensurate opposition, and Lord Howe will have sufficient time to engage the French fleet. He left New York harbor on the 1st of August and sailed into the open sea off Sandy Hook with sixteen ships of the line, six frigates, and four fireships. There he found contrary wind until the 4th, but on the 5th the ships set sail again. Two miles above Block Island they were compelled to stop again and there they remained until the 9th. On the 10th the fleet was able to take a direct course to Rhode Island. Nothing further has been heard to date. A frigate is ready to sail as soon as anything decisive occurs at Rhode Island. No one doubts that the French fleet will be completely annihilated, and that General Pigot will defend the island in a very spirited manner.

On the 28th of July we had news that Admiral Byron's fleet was near. Though at first everywhere confirmed, it was soon denied. However, a seventy-four-gun ship from that fleet ran into New York harbor on the 30th of July, and then Lord Howe was informed how far Admiral Byron had come. This ship as well as three others of equal strength which had arrived since the 7th of August joined Admiral Howe's fleet.[55]

It is surmised that three ships of the line, two frigates, and one fireship of this new fleet have sailed to Chesapeake Bay to capture the merchantmen lying at anchor here and there with full cargoes, for shortage of sailors has kept most of them from sailing. The rest of Admiral Byron's fleet is said to be stationed outside Boston harbor awaiting further orders.

Great faith can be put in Lord Howe's wise dispositions. He alone can save America for England, not the army, and even less

[55] Contradicted in following letter.

the very yielding propositions of the present commissioners, with whom Congress will treat no more.

On the 11th of July these peace messengers wrote Congress asking what the alliances between the provinces and the Crown of France embraced, and in spite of the fact that they received no answer, they even confirmed that the favorable conditions they offered for peace with England would continue to hold even though France should be defeated in this war.

General Washington's army took a long time to cross the North River at King's Ferry, the last troops passing over on the 26th of July. Not until the 27th did a corps leave White Plains to reinforce General Sullivan at Rhode Island. Moreover, four complete battalions were detached from White Plains to Albany. Dissatisfied with the strength of the camp at White Plains, Washington is having it fortified more and more.

An enemy corps occupies a hill at Dobbs Ferry and has pushed an outpost of three hundred men as far as Philipse's house. At retreat this post withdraws to Fowler's,[56] two miles beyond Philipse's and to the right of the highway as we look at it. Lieutenant Colonel von Wurmb, who is posted with the Jäger Corps on the last height of North Hill,[57] sends out patrols and observation posts in that direction. Captain von Münchhausen will be able to show you where the Jäger Corps is stationed, for one of the Van Cortlandt houses stands on this hill.

A second enemy outpost, consisting of 360 men and two fieldpieces, is stationed as far away as Valentine's Hill. It is relieved every four days and withdraws each night to Tuckahoe. The Queen's Rangers under Lieutenant Colonel Simcoe, posted half a mile in front of Fort Independence, send patrols and observation posts there.

A third and last enemy outpost is stationed beyond East Chester and consists of four hundred men with two fieldpieces and twenty dragoons. It is relieved every four days, and its infantry withdraws each night to Stephen Ward's house. The dra-

[56] Clinton Map No. 184 shows Young Fowler's and Old Fowler's property adjoining on the east side of the Albany road.
[57] I.e., Spuyten Hill. Cf. "Journal of Lt. John Charles Philip von Krafft, 1776–1784," New York Historical Society Collections, 1882, p. 57.

goons, however, are posted on the many roads this side of East Chester to observe the least movement we may make.

Lieutenant Colonel Emmerich's Corps is posted in front of the 4th and 5th redoubts on the road to De Lancey's house and mill. It patrols as far as Morrisania and from there to the Bronx, and then, touching the last outpost of the Queen's Rangers, returns to camp. The redoubts are well manned, and all outposts beyond Kings Bridge are under the inspection of a staff officer.

Since the 24th of July his Excellency General von Knyphausen has been in command on this island.[58] The troops have not been shifted since I wrote my last letter, except that the 3rd British Brigade under General Leslie has come over from Long Island.

The British grenadier and light infantry battalions were reorganized at Bedford, Long Island, on the 2nd of August, each of the detached companies having returned to its regiment after the retreat from Philadelphia. One of these light infantry battalions and the 42nd Regiment were embarked at Brooklyn Ferry. On the 9th of August the ships sailed with a good wind through Hell Gate sound, and it is said that they have joined Lord Howe's fleet. The further destination of these troops is not known.

General Tryon is stationed at Huntington in the outermost part of Long Island, where he guards the coast with eleven hundred provincials, so that the rebels will not continue to come from Connecticut, burn forage, devastate fields, and drive away cattle. The rebel flatboats are stationed in Fairfield Bay.[59] When intending a landing on Long Island, the only place fresh provisions can be procured, they proceed along their shore as far as Elizabeth Point, whence they quickly cross over to Eaton's Neck. Prices are going up every day.

On the 3rd of August there was, unfortunately, another fire, which destroyed sixty-four of the finest houses in the city, and the next day lightning blew up a powder ship loaded with 248 tons in the East River, shaking all the houses along the river and

[58] I.e., York Island (New York Island, Manhattan Island), sometimes called City Island.

[59] Probably the inlet at the mouth of the Pequonnock River, near which the town of Fairfield is located.

damaging them greatly. A considerable stock in wet and dry and also yard goods was burned.

Almost four hundred Hessians are still held prisoners. Lieutenant Colonel von Speth,[60] who is in the Brunswick service, is receiving the Brunswick prisoners and those of Hesse-Hanau. They are being quartered on Long Island. These prisoners are the ones taken by the rebels before the complete surrender at Saratoga.

On the 10th, 11th, and 12th of this month the Hessian troops were mustered. I sincerely wish that your Lordship could see the excellent condition of these regiments. The von Wissenbach and von Seitz Battalions [61] and Köhler's Grenadier Battalion can be matched against any other command. Lieutenant Colonel Schlemmer's [62] death will be a distinct loss to von Seitz's Battalion.

I wish I could conclude with a report on the outcome of the struggle for Rhode Island—it must be decided in the near future. The packet is to be closed, however. This much is certain: Everyone has good reasons for expecting the best.

The New York papers are full of accounts of the daring deeds of one John Butler, who, with fire and sword and a strong force of Virginia loyalists and savages, has roamed through the Wyoming district on the Susquehanna (this district comprises eight townships) and destroyed completely the large rebel magazine at Carlisle. It is said, moreover, that he has made prisoners of two Continental battalions. The deserters arriving from White Plains tell us that the savages and Tories are raising havoc in South Carolina and especially in Virginia, and that General Washington has found it necessary to send troops there. In time we shall know how much of this is true. I shall then report more in detail.

With the deepest respect I have the honor to be [etc.]

---

[60] He had served in an infantry regiment under Baron von Riedesel and was captured at Stillwater. Because of ill health he was permitted to come to New York (Eelking-Rosengarten, p. 146).

[61] The von Seitz Battalion is the former Regiment von Stein, its chief, Lieutenant General Johann Ludwig Ferdinand von Stein, having died Feb. 4, 1778.

[62] Lieutenant Colonel Arnold Schlemmer. Cf. New-York Gazette, Aug. 5, 1778, quoted in Eelking-Rosengarten, p. 316.

P.S. The French ships have been driven away from Rhode Island. I cannot tell what their loss was, or whether there was also an attack from the land. The frigate is lying in wait to leave immediately. Your Lordship's letter of the 15th of January with the enclosure for Captain von O'Reilly,[63] who is very well [64]

[63] See 1778, note 122.
[64] Sentence incomplete.

: 22 :

Today a packet is to sail for London with the news that on the 9th of this month the French fleet off Rhode Island raised the siege, which was to facilitate an attack from the land. Admiral Howe's fleet weighed anchor on the same day above Block Island and came so close to the departing foreign ships, which were carrying a press of sail, that it could effectively fire whole broadsides at this squadron, which was also being cannonaded from the land batteries. Many French ships were damaged, especially the *Languedoc*.

The enemy fleet had a stiff breeze, and so, in accordance with their plan, they slipped away from a general engagement. Admiral Howe could not catch up with them, in spite of the fact that he gave lively chase.

Subsequently a continuous storm from the 10th to the 15th of this month confounded the ships of both nations about twelve leagues off Long Island. On the 16th, after the wind had driven them together, they went into separate actions. The *Isis*, fifty guns, engaged a French ship [65] of seventy-four guns for four hours, pursuing her until darkness separated them.

[65] The *Zélé*. See letter dated Sept. 13, 1778 (No. 24).

On the 17th the *Isis* arrived off Sandy Hook, where she joined the fleet which Admiral Howe had assembled there. Besides having her masts and sails greatly damaged, she lost one officer, fifteen marines, and nine sailors. Admiral Howe thanked her commander, Captain Raynor, and held him up as an example for all commanders to follow.

The frigate *Apollo* was completely disabled by the storm, but has been repaired again. The *Monmouth,* a seventy-four-gun ship of Admiral Byron's fleet, has also run in here, and nine more fireships are ready to sail with her any hour.

The French fleet cast anchor off Cape May and, like the rebels, has not given up the conquest of Rhode Island. On the 19th the *Experiment* man-of-war and two frigates left New York for Rhode Island, but one of the two frigates, returning in great haste through Hell Gate sound, reached New York very late on the 22nd with the news that the greater part of the French fleet and five American frigates had again anchored before Rhode Island, that they had disembarked two thousand French troops, and that the garrison was being assailed on all sides.

When the French fleet appeared again before Rhode Island, necessity demanded sinking the frigate *Flora* and burning the frigates *Orpheus, Cerberus,* and *Lark* together with fourteen transports and two sloops of war before they could be completely unloaded.[66]

Where Admiral Byron is and where the provision ships have been all this time, I do not know. The English reports that three of Byron's warships joined the fleet here on the 7th of this month are false. Besides the *Cornwall,* seventy-four guns, one such warship, the *Monmouth,* came into port on the 18th. They give out no information.

The rebels are also threatening a landing on Long Island in Suffolk County. We have increased our watchfulness so as not to lose anything on that island, for we can ill afford to lose another foot of ground. On the 19th General Clinton sent a train of heavy artillery from New York to Rhode Island, perhaps to erect bat-

[66] For a more complete list of ships burned and abandoned see W. L. Clowes, *The Royal Navy,* London, 1897–1903, IV, 109.

teries which, in the worst event, could prevent a disembarkation. Nothing further has happened since the 14th, when I had
the honor of writing last.

The army at White Plains lives in plenty. A week ago it de-
tached some thousand men to Pennsylvania to check the raids of
Colonel Butler, who is feared by everyone as far as Philadelphia.
A French officer named Armand has, under the title of colonel,
raised a volunteer battalion of three hundred men in Boston.
About eighty of these are Frenchmen, and the rest are Bruns-
wickers and Hesse-Hanauers, among them an officer named
Siebert. This corps has been serving in the rebel army since the
15th of this month. So far twenty-six Brunswickers and ten
Hesse-Hanauers have deserted to our outposts.

Your Lordship will see from the reports that Ensign Führer
of the Regiment von Knyphausen and Ensign Kleinschmidt [67] of
the Regiment vacant von Woellwarth have gone over to the rebels.
It is a pity that these nice-looking fellows think so little of the
service and of their future.

May I humbly beg your Lordship to recall my sister Bretthauer's three boys at some propitious moment, for this poor
family cannot possibly subsist on a pension of six thalers a month.
I know that the unhappy father of these innocent children is in
bad repute and that the punishment meted out to him by His
Serene Highness is just, but I also know that His Highness will
have pity and not permit these boys to be impoverished through
his anger.[68] My sister wrote a touching letter to me. I will help
her, but in the near future I shall be able to give but little
assistance. Will your Lordship please pardon this very humble
request. I hope that, if it is possible, my plea will not be in vain.

With the deepest respect, I remain for life [etc.]

[67] Johann Philipp von Krafft, in his "Journal" (*New York Historical Society
Collections*, 1882), says that he deserted because of debts. Probably the same
Kleinschmidt who killed his adversary in a duel on board ship (see 1776, note 1).

[68] Lieutenant Colonel Balthasar Bretthauer was severely wounded at Trenton.
All the senior officers were suspected of neglect of duty.

: 23 :

In addition to my letter mailed on the 24th of August, the following further account can now be sent by the same packet.

Not all the French ships attempted to rendezvous before Cape May; most of them cast anchor off Rhode Island again on the 17th, while two of the largest frigates had never sailed away. By the 19th Count d'Estaing had reassembled all his ships and once more discharged all his sick, who were sent overland to Providence as quickly as possible.

On the 20th [69] of August the rebel General Greene landed on Rhode Island with five thousand Continental troops, and by the 23rd [70] ten thousand New England militia had joined him, all crossing over at Bristol and at Howland's ferries. The rebels were now firmly resolved to become masters of the island with the assistance of the French. This is proved by the fact that they landed this large force and brought up a train of thirty-six brass

---

[69] The Americans began crossing over to Rhode Island on August 9. Baurmeister corrects this statement in the following letter.

[70] Also corrected later.

and forty-two heavy iron cannon and a thousand wagons of ammunition, timber, and entrenching tools.

General Pigot, whose lines were sufficiently provided with the best means of defense, had so massed his forces that the greater part of his troops benefited from his vigilance. The first news of these events was brought to New York on the 22nd of August by a frigate which was to have sailed to Rhode Island on the 19th with the warship *Experiment*. Admiral Howe could not leave Sandy Hook until the night of the 25th–26th of August.

General Clinton embarked at Long Island with the 3rd and 4th English Brigades, one light infantry battalion, one of British grenadiers, and forty dragoons. On the 27th they were ready to sail, but the wind remained unfavorable until the 29th. Finally, on the 31st of August they anchored off Rhode Island, where on the preceding night not a single rebel was to be found, however.

The enemy had withdrawn from their lines at ten o'clock in the evening of the 30th of August in complete safety and retreated over Bristol and Howland's ferries. The Continental troops had taken position at the last-named ferry, but the militia was dissatisfied and disbanded. Nor did Count d'Estaing wait for Admiral Howe. He had departed for Boston on the 27th with the greater part of his strongest ships and ordered the remaining weaker part to run into Portsmouth harbor under the urgent pretext that these badly damaged and poorly manned ships must be repaired and re-manned.

Admiral Howe has started in pursuit of him, and General Clinton is expected on Long Island any hour. Earl Cornwallis has taken quarters on that island, and General Vaughan has been ordered to go to Bedford, whither General Tryon had retreated from Huntington after collecting the forage and dispensable grain, cattle, and sheep from the eastern part of the island and bringing it all to safety.

On the 29th of August six men-of-war from Admiral Byron's fleet again came to anchor off Sandy Hook. They immediately disembarked almost two thousand sick on Staten Island. Admiral Byron is at Halifax with three ships. The *Albion* was compelled to return to England, for she had suffered too greatly in a storm to be able to stay at sea much longer.

On the 31st of August the Queen's Rangers, Emmerich's Corps, and Lord Cathcart's Light Dragoons [71] surprised the enemy outpost at De Voe's house, one and a half miles this side of Valentine's Hill. It was a corps of Indians of the Stockbridge tribe and was commanded by their chief, Nimham.[72] They fell upon the front and both flanks of this outpost so quickly that only two men escaped. The chief, his son, and the common warriors were killed on the spot. About two hundred Continental troops hastened to their support, but withdrew as quickly, losing twelve men and one captain. Our loss was five dragoons killed, sixteen of the Queen's Rangers killed and wounded, and nine horses killed.[73]

On the same day the Hessian Jäger Corps sent a strong patrol halfway to Philipse's house. One hundred and fifty rebels lying in ambush fortunately rushed out into the open road onto the head of the patrol. The rebels discharged their rifles, killing three jägers and wounding as many, and were resolved to continue the attack with the bayonet, but meeting with resistance, they withdrew, suffering the same loss as the jägers. Captain von Donop, who commanded this patrol, halted and did not return with the jägers until his flanking patrols found no more of the enemy and he could therefore return quietly.

On the 2nd of this month all the outposts on this island marched out again. Although they proceeded far beyond Philipse's house and as far as the road to Old Rochelle, they met none of the enemy. But they found many newly started watchfires, which indicates that the enemy is avoiding further engagements and will reoccupy its posts as soon as our patrols have withdrawn.

On the 1st of this month ten deserters from Armand's Corps came in. They were two Hessian jägers who had been taken at sea, seven Brunswickers, and one Hesse-Hanauer. Since then

[71] 17th Regiment of Light Dragoons, in which Lord Cathcart was then a captain.

[72] Daniel Nimham, a Wappinger chief.

[73] Often called the action at Indian Field, or Indian Bridge.

several more deserters have arrived, all of whom agree that on the
28th of August an order was issued that the Continental battalions
should no longer draw on the militia, and that for the time being
they should not recruit on their own behalf.

The English commissary for prisoners is daily expecting a
notice to return to Elizabethtown in Jersey to receive the rest of
the Hessian and the greater part of the English prisoners.

With deepest respect, I have the honor to be [*etc.*]

P.S. We have just received the confirmed report that Admiral
Howe has sailed through the Southern Channel to the vicinity
of Cape Cod, thirty leagues from Boston. He took a different
route from that of the French ships, which are keeping to the
right and consequently will arrive a week later at the place where
the English ships will already be anchored.[74] The *Ariel* has
captured an American armed ship and brought it into New York.
On board were some twenty pilots who were on their way to the
French fleet. Admiral Gambier will send three ships of the line to
Admiral Howe, who has urgently requested them, not later than
tomorrow. In great haste [75]

[74] Howe thus endeavored to intercept d'Estaing. See his letter of Aug. 25,
1778, printed in Almon's *Remembrancer*, VII, 47.
[75] Sentence incomplete.

: 24 :

Since the French and American ships are now cruising more, packets are dispatched more frequently than heretofore. It has been announced that an armed ship is ready to depart. This gives me a good opportunity to report that Admiral Howe's fleet is again anchored near Rhode Island, for all the French warships have run into Boston harbor to refit. The *Languedoc* and the *Zélé* were greatly damaged, and more than one third of the men in the fleet have been lost. The English ships lost as many men, most of them in Byron's fleet, but they have been replaced by the sailors of the four frigates and the transports burned at Rhode Island. The transports sunk there are being raised again.

We do not know what Admiral Howe has decided to undertake, or what his orders are in respect to further activities; but the safe escape of the French fleet has caused much anxiety and discontent.

It is, by the way, almost unbelievable that we should know so little and receive so much wrong information about the activities on our side. This is the reason we do not get a complete picture of the counter activities of the French and the rebels. We can only guess at the course of events from accounts and circumstances.

So far we have received no reports from the troops on Rhode Island, but this is not their fault. Only those who see them sail know of outgoing and incoming ships. Because of this, the officers, recruits, and field requisites destined for Rhode Island have now been lying in wait in New York over five months, notwithstanding repeated requests.

It was not from the 20th to the 23rd of August that the rebels became masters of the greater part of Rhode Island, but as early as the 9th,[76] on which day they occupied the northern part of the island with the cooperation of some French men-of-war.

On the 14th of August General Sullivan assembled sixteen thousand to eighteen thousand men, including the artillery and its train, at Quaker Hill, and on the 15th of August the enemy corps marched in three narrow columns to within one and a half English miles of the English fortifications, where they formed in two lines and a reserve. The light infantry was under the command of Colonel Livingston, the right wing of the first line under General Greene, and the left under General Lafayette. The entire second line was commanded by General Hancock, and the reserve by Colonel West.[77]

General Pigot had the singular good fortune to stop this strong rebel force with a continuous artillery fire, for the harbor was not being forced by any French ships. Count d'Estaing also sailed away on the 15th to meet the English fleet arriving off Block Island, exposing his ships on the way out to many broadsides from the land batteries. It was the time of the gale, and, as I have reported before, both fleets were at the mercy of the wind.

Unwilling to have the reputation of opening the war,[78] they separated on the 17th of August. Only the French ship *Zélé* and the English ship *Isis* cannonaded each other violently at close

[76] Baurmeister corrects here an earlier statement.

[77] Colonel (later Brigadier) William West, Rhode Island militia.

[78] Though the British government considered the announcement of the French treaty of amity and commerce with the United States tantamount to a declaration of war, neither France nor England made a formal declaration—a fact that aroused comment at the time. Cf. *Gentleman's Magazine*, Aug., 1778; and the letters to the printer in Rivington's *Royal Gazette*, Nov. 4 and 11, 1778. Presumably Baurmeister had not heard of the action off Cape Ushant, the first general engagement between English and French forces in the war.

range after the sea became calm. When darkness compelled them to let up, they separated with much damage on both sides.

The chief place of rendezvous for the French ships was and remained Rhode Island, and by the 19th of August Count d'Estaing had his ships assembled again before Newport, no more than two having anchored off Cape May. This greatly pleased the rebels and made them even more eager for the French admiral to take possession of the harbor, for he had promised to disembark a thousand of his troops and storm Newport while the Americans made an attack on the British lines.

Then, on the 23rd of August they began to have doubts about the serious cooperation of their ally, who informed them that Lord Howe, reinforced by Admiral Byron, was approaching with a full press of sail, so that d'Estaing, having already sustained much damage to his ships and equipment, was compelled to weigh anchor as soon as possible and sail to Boston, although he expected to return soon and be that much more effective on the sea. He informed them further that General Sullivan had advanced far enough to be able to overcome the few obstacles alone.

General Sullivan was now convinced that the British fleet would arrive with fresh reinforcements. He sent away all his heavy brass artillery, baggage, and cattle in the night of the 24th–25th of August, and was even more on his guard. By the 27th of August there was nothing left on our front except his troops and twenty fieldpieces.

On the 28th [79] General Pigot decided to march out of his fortifications in two columns and attack the rebels. General Smith led the first on the right, which was made up of all the British regiments. The grenadier and light infantry companies formed the van, and then followed Fanning's Provincial Corps.

General von Lossberg led the second (the left column), which marched close to the first and consisted of Hessian troops. Captain von der Malsburg [80] formed the vanguard with the chasseurs. The Anspachers remained as a reserve in front of the lines,

---

[79] Pigot's letter to Clinton (Almon's *Remembrancer*, VII, 34) says August 29.
[80] Friedrich Wilhelm von der Malsburg, Regiment von Dittfurth, who kept an exceedingly interesting and historically valuable diary.

and the sailors stayed within the fortifications. The heads of both columns came upon heavily manned redoubts, which, however, mounted no guns. The British wing companies, supported by Fanning's Provincial Corps, advanced too far. The rebels were reinforced and rushed in between the provincials and the 22nd and 43rd British Regiments, causing disorder and consternation. Captain von der Malsburg had the good fortune to take a trench immediately, and the rebels flew from two other redoubts at the first onrush of the Hessian chasseurs. This gave von Huyn's Regiment enough room to execute a flanking movement to the right. After an effective fire, they attacked the rebels with the bayonet, routed them, and forced them to flee, which enabled the right column to recover in good order.

Nevertheless, the rebels were unwilling to fall back, and General Pigot formed his troops *en ordre de bataille* in front of the three redoubts which Captain von der Malsburg had taken. Here the troops were out of range of the enemy batteries thrown up to cover the retreat over Howland's and Bristol ferries. Inasmuch as everything had previously been removed, the last rebels left the island at ten o'clock in the night of the 30th of August, taking along not only their wounded but also their dead.

Although they had brought with them between twelve thousand and thirteen thousand head of cattle, they did not touch our straw and hay magazines, or molest anyone in any way, so certain were they of taking the island. On their retreat they did not have enough room to burn the magazines without endangering themselves, or enough time to carry them off. On Conanicut many curious persons had gathered to see the impending surrender.

General Pigot's total loss amounts to 270 men. The Hessian chasseurs had six killed and between twenty and forty wounded; von Huyn's Regiment had Captain von Schaller [81] and four men killed, fifty-eight wounded, and seven taken prisoners.

The enemy's loss must have been considerable.

[81] Captain Georg Friedrich von Schaller, though killed on August 30, 1778 (cf. Almon's *Remembrancer*, VII, 33–34), is still carried on the roll of Huyn's Regiment in 1779.

General Sullivan reported to General Washington that since the French ships had sailed away, unwilling to force the harbor or land at Newport, it was impossible for him to wait longer, especially since his force had been considerably weakened by sickness and by great numbers of militia deserting and returning to their homes; that his only satisfaction was that he had made a stand against the English when they unexpectedly attacked his retreating corps, that he had captured two guns, but lost them again during a spirited attack of the Hessians; that, moreover, after bringing off the wounded, he had had enough time to collect the dead; and that, after leaving the island, the New England militia disbanded and returned dissatisfied to their homes.

On the 1st of the month General Clinton had his reinforcements sail into the harbor, but only the General and his suite disembarked. General Pigot made an oral report [82] of everything that had happened and gave the best testimony of the Hessian troops. He said that Fanning's Provincial Corps and still more the 22nd and 43rd Regiments bore the liveliest gratitude toward the Regiment von Huyn, since by this regiment's action at the right moment, as spirited as it was quick, they escaped the rebels who had already surrounded them.

On the 3rd General Clinton and his suite sailed to New York and left General Grey in command of the above-mentioned reinforcements with orders to land at New London and burn the pirate ships which had been harassing all vessels that arrived at, or departed from, Rhode Island alone.

Hence General Grey, accompanied by three men-of-war, sailed to New London early on the 5th, but he found only three small ships and no enemy. Therefore he did not land, but set sail and ran into the Dartmouth River.[83] Landing in Buzzard's Bay, he marched to Bedford,[84] burned many ships and large magazines there and at the mills above, and then doubled back to

---

[82] Pigot's reports to Clinton of August 31 and September 6 are printed in Almon's *Remembrancer, loc. cit.*

[83] Probably the Apponagansett River. Grey's report to Clinton, dated Whitestone, September 18, 1778 (Almon's *Remembrancer*, VII, 36), says that they ran into Clark's Cove.

[84] I.e., New Bedford, Massachusetts.

Fairhaven, where he demolished an abandoned earthwork and destroyed eleven iron guns and large stores of ammunition.

At noon on the 6th the English troops boarded their ships again at Sconticut and returned to Rhode Island, whence General Grey will bring them to Long Island and land them at Whitestone Point. The number of one-, two-, and three-masted ships burned amounts to seventy. Loss of ships is felt more by the rebels than any other loss. They must finally become docile, for a burned child shuns the fire.

Colonel Simcoe, chief of the Queen's Rangers, and Emmerich's and Lord Cathcart's light troops patrolled from late in the night of the 7th to the 8th of this month. Simcoe went to Mamaroneck and New Rochelle and on his return passed close to the left wing of the enemy light infantry under General Scott in the vicinity of Valentine's Hill, where he captured one corporal, five dragoons, and a commissary. General Scott's report so stirred the entire camp at White Plains that the men took down their tents and packed their baggage, and Washington reinforced all outposts with artillery.

On the 1st of September the rebels had two hundred slain at Shamokin in another encounter with Colonel Butler. He is now enjoying the cooperation of a savage chief and loyalist named Brant,[85] who burned Cochecton, advanced from there along the Minisink to the Delaware,[86] and is now threatening to invade all of Sussex County in Jersey. Colonel Butler has taken the precaution to erect a large magazine in an Indian settlement at Niagara, so that he has shelter and food at least during the winter in case he can no longer obtain support.

Colonel Simcoe seriously proposed to march through Jersey with twelve hundred men, one hundred dragoons, and several fieldpieces to join Colonel Butler and cooperate with him, but he was not given permission. I believe they would be the King's best commissioners.

[85] Captain Joseph Brant, a Mohawk chief. He did *not* burn Cochecton—mere rumors and fears.

[86] Should read: "advanced from there to Minisink on the Delaware"; perhaps garbled by the scribe in making the clean copy.

Congress is in despair over the unexpected behavior of the French fleet and expressed its displeasure to the French emissary in no uncertain terms. Congress wants either a different admiral or different conduct. I enclose a news sheet [*missing*] concerning it.

General Lee has been suspended for a year. He has written violently against this action and therefore was sent home at the end of last month without ceremony. He is said to have a heart wilder than an Indian's. Much might be done with such desperate people.

On the 5th and 6th of this month some twenty transports arrived from Cork. They brought eight months' provisions and English, Anspach, and Hessian recruits, many of whom were sick and have been taken to the hospitals. Moreover, nineteen Hessian recruits died at sea.

In the camp at White Plains a great many are sick with dysentery, which is very common this time of the year. Most of them are half naked and without tents, and so are doubly exposed to the extremely cold nights and dampness. The regiments of the local army are not wanting for tents, bed straw, and good covers; the provisions are good and adequate, and desertion has stopped.

A hundred transports are ready to take English troops on board the moment orders are given. Only time will tell what their destination is.

With the deepest respect, I have the honor to be [*etc.*]

P.S. Admiral Howe returned alone from Rhode Island to New York. Johnstone, one of the King's commissioners, is about to leave for London. Congress refuses to answer any communication bearing his signature. On the 11th of this month sixteen transports left for Quebec to procure flour and grain. Lieutenant Colonel von Speth received orders to embark on these ships with his troops and those from Hesse-Hanau, and has accordingly done so.

: 25 :

Admiral Byron finally arrived in New York on the 16th of this month and departed again for Rhode Island on the 18th. Admiral Howe is in a great hurry to embark on his ship in order to sail to England with the first wind. The ship's chaplain, Mr. Oborne, who is taking leave of me this moment, will take charge of this letter.

I have the honor to acknowledge herewith the receipt of your Lordship's esteemed letter of the 20th of April. A transport that came in at the same time that Admiral Byron arrived brought us many Hessian letters dated in the month of April this year. I dispatched my last to your Lordship on the 13th of this month.

Although General von Mirbach has hopes of sailing on the 23rd, I do not want to miss this opportunity to inform your Lordship that on the 16th of this month the light troops in the outposts of this island, supported by three English battalions, surrounded all the enemy outposts, causing the greatest alarm amongst them, and captured three officers and thirty-one soldiers.[87] Such visits to their front, then the attack on their left

[87] This engagement is commonly referred to as the action at Westchester.

wing as far as Bedford, which General Grey recently made with such success, compelled the rebels to leave the camp at White Plains on the 17th and 18th of this month and encamp on the other side of the Croton River on the right of the road to Fishkill. The militia are going home. What is most remarkable, however, is the great dissatisfaction in Boston with the French fleet. Captured British sailors who had the liberty of walking about in the city had a fight with some French ship hands. When the former got the worst of it, many of the residents were so aroused that they attacked the French, who then retreated to their ships.

On the 17th of this month General Grey arrived safely on Long Island. A storm of six hours in the night of the 16th–17th forced him to jettison all his artillery and saddle horses. He took a herd of six thousand sheep to our troops on Rhode Island, who were in great need of them.

Yesterday, the 10th, 45th, and 52nd English Regiments were distributed among ten other British regiments. Everyone wonders whether the troops who are ready to embark will sail to the West Indies or whether something will be undertaken against Boston.

The correspondence between the King's commissioners and Congress is in full sway. No information is being given out. The rest of the prisoners taken at Trenton have not yet returned. Each day increases the number of sick here. They are getting excellent care in the hospitals.

With the greatest respect, I have the honor to be [etc.]

: 26 :

I had the honor to send my last letter to your Lordship on the 21st of September this year, when Admiral Howe departed. I should have sent another by General von Mirbach, but it was impossible. Now, just when I am in New York on business, eleven London ships lie ready to sail at any moment. Since all the officers of the 10th, 45th, and 52nd English Regiments are to leave on them, it may be wise not to wait for the ordinary packet, but to take this opportunity to put the continuation of my journal in good hands and have it posted in London.

On the 22nd General Cornwallis and Major Generals Grey and Mathew with two British brigades, the grenadiers, the light infantry, the Guards, two hundred dragoons, Lord Rawdon's Irish battalion, and two hundred provincials landed at Fort Lee in Jersey and marched to the Liberty Pole.[88] Their vanguard immediately encountered some militia and fifty dragoons, who lost twenty-nine prisoners and fourteen killed, while the British had one dragoon and two horses killed.

[88] Liberty Pole, at the head of English Neighborhood Creek.

On the 23rd of September the following troops marched out under the command of his Excellency General von Knyphausen: the British light troops under Colonel Campbell to Hunt's bridge [89] over the Bronx; the Hessian Jäger Corps to Philipse's house; the 71st Regiment to Valentine's Hill to support the advanced posts; and two Hessian brigades, von Stirn's and the grenadiers, to the left of Van Cortlandt's house. On the 24th Colonel von Hachenberg's brigade, six British regiments, and Generals Grant, Leslie, and Erskine marched to Philipse's house, where headquarters were established. The left wing was stationed at the twenty-mile stone on the road to Dobbs Ferry, the center rested on Sawmill Creek, and the right wing extended to the Bronx.

Beginning with the left wing, the troops were posted as follows: Donop's, the Leib Regiment, the Erb Prinz, Wissenbach's, Köhler's Grenadiers, Minnigerode's, Lengerke's, Linsing's, the 7th, 26th, 28th, 49th, 63rd, 71st, and 4th British Regiments.

Lieutenant Colonel von Wurmb covered the left wing; the *Phoenix* man-of-war, fifty guns, stationed in the North River, afforded sufficient protection for the flank; Captain von Wreden with two companies of dismounted jägers was posted along Saw-mill Creek and covered the center of the front; and Colonel Sim-coe had his huts across the Bronx built in such a way that he could keep continual watch on the roads between our right wing and the East River which lead from Mamaroneck and New Rochelle to Morrisania, the heights of Kings Bridge, and Fort Independence.

A daring troop of two hundred dragoons could at any time have alarmed the redoubts and the country, for only Colonel von Loos's brigade and two companies of De Lancey's Volunteers remained posted at Fort Knyphausen, and they did duty in the redoubts as well. No troops could be spared from New York, for von Seitz's Regiment had already left the garrison with two brigades [90] of De Lancey's New York Volunteers and two Penn-

---

[89] The second bridge across the Bronx north of Williams's bridge (cf. Clinton Map No. 184).

[90] Battalions. Probably the scribe's error.

sylvania battalions, namely, Chalmers' and Allen's,[91] and embarked on the 8th to reinforce the garrison at Halifax.

On the 24th of September the corps under General Cornwallis encamped between New Bridge and Fort Lee, occupying a stretch eight English miles long, with Hackensack and Hackensack Creek in front. They threw up five redoubts. The bridge across the Hackensack had not been demolished, and the patrols met many militia, both mounted and dismounted, who had been sent hither and yon to urge the country people to remove their cattle, grain, and forage. It was General Clinton's intention to procure all these necessities either by paying for them outright or by giving receipts.

Contrary to expectations, General Cornwallis found an abundance of these provisions in the district he occupied, though at Mamaroneck, on this side of the North River, no more than fifty tons of hay were found. The camp at White Plains and even more the destitute population allow no surplus. Besides, the entire region is quite mountainous, even more so than the Cologne Sauerland.

General Clinton was in Jersey. At ten o'clock on the night of September the 25th he called on his Excellency Lieutenant General von Knyphausen, and on the 26th he set out to follow Captain von Wreden's strong patrol as far as Tarrytown. He met this patrol on its way back at Dobbs Ferry. Captain von Wreden brought with him from Tarrytown three eminent rebels who have long been hunted and were the only ones he saw.

Moreover, he brought positive news that General Scott was posted at North Castle, and under him, Colonels Butler,[92] Gist, and Sheldon; that General Scott had posted Major Lee [93] of the Dragoons in King's Street in such a position that he could keep strict watch over Tarrytown on the right and White Plains on the left as well as the road to Horse Neck [94] and beyond. General

---

[91] Chalmers' Maryland Loyalists and Allen's Pennsylvanians.

[92] Colonel Richard Butler. Not to be confused with Colonel John Butler, the Tory Indian leader.

[93] "Light Horse Harry" Lee, 1st Continental Dragoons.

[94] Horse Neck, the peninsula of West Greenwich, Fairfield County, Connecticut.

Washington is encamped between Fishkill and Danbury, his left wing covering Hartford and Bedford.[95] Behind his front at Quaker Hill are two large iron works, where ship cannon, shells, and cannon balls are now being cast. Von Wreden also learned that General Gates, who had started out for Boston with three strong brigades and thirty guns, has been ordered back, and that the Carolina militia refused to march to New England and has therefore been sent to reinforce Forts Clinton, Montgomery, and Defiance. All this has been confirmed by later reports.

In addition we have learned that the extravagance of the French fleet in Boston is a heavy drain on the magazines, that flour and grain can be brought from the southern provinces only with the greatest difficulty, and that General Sullivan is compelled to remain in a stationary camp near Providence in order to succour Boston, for the rebels are mainly concerned about an expedition from New York against Boston.

The French fleet sailed into Boston harbor on the 29th of July,[96] and since the 1st of August [97] the French marines and regiments alone have occupied the harbor. They have usurped the police duty, have cleared the entrance of the harbor of all sunken vessels, have raised strong redoubts on Georges Island, are fortifying all high points, and are giving work to between four hundred and five hundred Americans. Five of their largest ships, completely dismantled, are careened for repairs from top to bottom.

On the 3rd of this month a lieutenant of the French fleet arrived in New York. His business has been kept secret. He was allowed to go about in the city, and, after taking care of his business, he sailed back. He confirmed the report that there had been a fight between some English prisoners and French sailors. He

[95] New Bedford, Massachusetts. Cf. Washington to Congress, Sept. 23, 1778: "These several posts appear to be the best we can occupy in the present doubtful state of things, as they have relation to the support of West Point . . . and are also in the communication to the Eastward, if the Enemy point their operations that way." See also Rivington's *Royal Gazette*, Oct. 31, 1778: "It is reported that Mr. Washington is now posted in Hartford, in Connecticut, jealous of an attack from hence, on their Most Christian allies' fleet in Boston Harbor."

[96] August 29. Baurmeister corrects this date in the following letter.

[97] September 1 (cf. note above).

said that one of the French officers died of his wounds and was buried with military honors, but that the affair left no bad impression; that two churches had obligingly been assigned to them, so that they could have their religious services quietly; and that the residents did not show any indignation on that account.

In the night of the 27th–28th of September the 71st Regiment under the command of Colonel Campbell as well as Colonel Simcoe embarked on twenty-five flatboats at Philipse's house and let themselves be carried by the tide to the mouth of Tappan Creek on the Jersey shore. Colonel Campbell landed his troops on the left of this creek and marched by a short roundabout route as far as Harrington.

At the same time, General Grey marched by a circuitous route on the right from New Bridge to Old Tappan. Twelve dragoons and Maitland's light infantry battalion, who formed his vanguard, surprised Lady Washington's Dragoon Regiment of 120 horse, which had recently arrived from Virginia under Colonel Baylor.[98] Sixty dragoons, among them five officers, were cut down in some barns, and fifty-seven dragoons and nine officers were wounded and taken prisoners. Three dragoons who were on guard duty escaped. The colonel, the major, two officers, the doctor, and the paymaster were left behind on parole, since with their severe wounds they could not be transported. The men and horses show what Virginia has to offer. Not a single dragoon was younger than eighteen or older than twenty-six.

Colonel Campbell, not so fortunate as to keep his march a secret, was discovered by General Heard,[99] who escaped with four hundred militia between Old Tappan and Harrington. Late in the night of the 28th of September this detachment returned to our camp.

On the 30th of September his Excellency General von Knyphausen again sent patrols to the front from both wings of his camp. Captain von Donop occupied the road to Dobbs Ferry with fifty dismounted jägers and had Lieutenant Mertz ride ahead

---

[98] Colonel George Baylor commanded the 3rd Regiment of (Continental, Light) Dragoons, sometimes called "Mrs. Washington's Guards."

[99] Brigadier General Nathaniel Heard, New Jersey militia.

with fifteen mounted jägers. This side of Dobbs Ferry these mounted jägers encountered some rebels and saw many more in ambush on their right. This discovery made it necessary to recall Lieutenant Bickell, who had been detached to a hill on the left of the road. When Lieutenant Mertz set out to do this, the enemy cut in on the road behind him. He attacked the superior troop of dragoons and beat his way through. Making a short halt, he was again engaged. After a heated skirmish, during which he received several cuts about the face, he was obliged to surrender as a prisoner. Two jägers were killed, one was left severely wounded, and one escaped.

Lieutenant Bickell, who proceeded on foot along the North River, fared much better; he had one noncommissioned officer and one jäger wounded. It was Colonel Butler with 250 men on foot and Major Lee with 200 dragoons who had crept up by way of Horse Neck, proceeded thence to the right to the North River, and waited in ambush, hoping to surprise the entire Jäger Corps. Had the rebel infantry been quieter, and if Captain von Donop had advanced half an English mile further, he, too, would have been cut off and taken prisoner.

Captain Hanger [100] was sent after the rebels with a flag of truce to take equipage and servants to Lieutenant Mertz. However, Major Lee procured the lieutenant's release because he had so gallantly defended himself in both attacks, and he returned with Captain Hanger. His wounds, which are across the nose and on both cheeks, are not dangerous. He has already been exchanged for another lieutenant.

On the 3rd of this month six men, who had been sent to New England by Lieutenant Colonel Emmerich in the month of May of this year to buy horses and recruit men for his corps, arrived at our outposts with eleven dragoon horses. They had been discovered and imprisoned in Peekskill, but found an opportunity to break loose. On their way back they untied eleven of Colonel Sheldon's dragoon horses on King's Street and came off with them.

[100] The Hon. George Hanger, later Baron Coleraine. In 1771 he was gazetted ensign in the Foot Guards, but resigned in disgust at promotions made over his head. He then applied to the Hessian Court and was appointed captain in the Jäger Corps in February, 1776.

A patrol of one hundred horse pursued the fugitives as far as Sawmill Creek, and about nine o'clock the same morning they bounded forth in front of Köhler's Grenadier Battalion; but before Captain von Wreden could get there, they were gone, and they have not returned.

On the 7th Colonel Simcoe patrolled with a strong force between White Plains and Horse Neck. He fell in with a dragoon post and captured six men and nine horses. The enemy officer hid in a magazine, which was set on fire; since no one knew that he was there, he lost his life in the flames. Two large smithies were also burned down.

On the 9th General Clinton again called on his Excellency General von Knyphausen and ordered him to march all his troops back to the old camp at Kings Bridge the next day, the 10th. Not until the 12th did a strong rebel force patrol as far as the Hessian Jäger Corps's abatis to learn whither we had marched.

General Cornwallis left Jersey on the 13th of this month. He had no enemy opposing him, for the Jersey militia have disbanded to the last man. General Grant is at present embarking with ten British regiments, each one of which has been raised to full strength (five hundred men) from the 10th, 45th, and 52nd Regiments. The regiments under him are the 4th, 5th, 17th, 27th, 28th, 40th, 46th, 35th, 49th, and 55th. When they will depart, and whether they will sail directly to the West Indies, is still unknown. But then, nothing can be said with certainty.

Four provincial battalions and the vacant von Woellwarth and the Wissenbach Regiments will be embarked within the next few days for St. Augustine in East Florida. They will take along all their heavy and light baggage, artillery, one horse for each staff officer, and all their sick, as did the Regiment von Seitz.

The rebels made some attacks on St. Augustine from Carolina and Georgia last spring, but without effect. The St. Augustine garrison consists of two battalions of the Royal American, by number the 60th Regiment, and one provincial regiment under Colonel Innes.[101] It is a little further south from New York than Halifax is north.

[101] Colonel Alexander Innes, South Carolina Royalists.

5th Regt.
ot 17th

See troop
dispositions
on pages
279-80
289-91
293

Among the many respectable prizes brought in several days ago was the frigate *Raleigh* of thirty-two guns, which was captured in the Bay of Boston. Of the Irish fleet which set sail at the first of the month, two ships were captured by privateers hiding in Egg Harbor. This made Admiral Byron decide upon the destruction of this harbor. Commodore Hotham was therefore ordered there with several ships, while Captain Ferguson with three hundred volunteers burned everything on land near the harbor and completely ruined the large salt works near Cape May. The ships and galleys that were not brought back were burned.

The peace commissioners are tired of working without results. On the 3rd of this month they issued the enclosed proclamation [*missing*], which was posted everywhere and sent to Congress, to General Washington, and to Governor Trumbull of Connecticut. However, the proclamations have been returned with the solemn declaration that they would never have any effect on the Americans.

General Pigot has returned to New York from Rhode Island, surrendering his command to General Prescott. Admiral Byron also came into New York harbor from Newport with a small squadron of warships, but has already set sail again. The British and Hessian prisoners have not yet arrived. Up to the end of September of this year, eighty-one rebel officers held on Long Island have escaped.

General Clinton's former adjutant, now Major Sutherland, has been sent to the Bermudas with all the invalids of the British regiments who are still fit for service. The rebel Generals Putnam and Mifflin have retired. A certain Allen of Philadelphia, a wealthy and esteemed man who also owns several estates above Albany in the vicinity of Bennington called the Hamsteden Flats,[102] there declared his domain, along with five other counties, independent, not only of Great Britain, but even more so of Congress. Colonel Butler [103] is said to have gone to Canada. More with the next packet.

[102] Probably the New Hampshire Grants. Baurmeister apparently has confused Ethan and Ira Allen with William Allen of Philadelphia in reporting this rumor.
[103] Colonel John Butler, the Tory Indian leader.

With the greatest respect, I have the honor to be [*etc.*]

P.S. In the evening of day before yesterday I had the honor to receive your Lordship's letter of the 22nd of July. All the letters mentioned in it have arrived safely.

Yesterday a flag of truce came to our outposts. It was the Marquis de Lafayette's adjutant with a letter from Count d'Estaing to Admiral Byron, which he had orders to deliver in person. When this was refused, he rode off with the letter, asking permission to stop in Horse Neck for two days. He undoubtedly wanted to know whether Admiral Byron was already at sea or still in New York. He was sent away once and for all by Colonel Simcoe without having received any information. Again I have the honor to commend myself. Your Lordship's [*etc.*]

: 27 :

On the 21st of October I had the honor to send my last journal. Another packet will sail within the next few days, supposedly to report that the corps under General Grant departed on the 1st of this month and that the 71st Regiment of Scottish Highlanders, the Waldeck Regiment, the two Hessian garrison battalions von Woellwarth and Wissenbach, and some provincials have embarked for the two Floridas to join the forces there. One warship of seventy-four guns, two of sixty-four, and four frigates carrying from twenty-eight to thirty-two guns each are convoying the transports.

The French have taken the Island of Dominica in the West Indies, which was garrisoned by about eighty men. All the English inhabitants are to retain possession of their estates and the revenues thereof. General Grant will reoccupy it without difficulty and also take St. Lucia.

Admiral Barrington [104] has already arrived there with his fleet and found no French warships. It is still doubtful whether this

---

[104] Rear Admiral Samuel Barrington, who was commander in chief in the West Indies until January, 1779.

expedition is intended immediately for the West Indies or for
Charleston in South Carolina, for most of the inhabitants of that
state, tired of war and the total cessation of commerce, will readily
embrace the advantages of our new offer as soon as they can throw
off the yoke of Congress.

On the whole, it may be said that the proclamation issued on
the 3rd of October had a great effect in all the provinces. Washington himself went before Congress, and because his army is grow-
ing weaker every day, his troops have been posted since the 22nd
of October as follows: two brigades of Carolina troops under
General Heath at Forts Montgomery, Clinton, and Defiance; one
brigade of eight battalions of Continental troops under General
Stirling at Fishkill; and two brigades at Danbury.

General Washington's headquarters, under cover of five brigades, are at Hartford, where, according to the latest news, General Gates is also still stationed. General Sullivan is now at Boston
with three brigades made up of very weak battalions.[105] Officers
from Maryland and Virginia have returned home, and many
French officers are going back to France.

The light corps under General Scott, and under Butler, Gist,
Sheldon, Lee, and Armand are still at their temporary posts between the North and East rivers, namely, Tarrytown, King's
Street, North Castle, Ward's house, Mamaroneck, New Rochelle,
and Horse Neck. Their patrols are good, cautious, and quick-
footed. Enjoying the affection of the residents, they know all our
movements. An ambush laid for them on the night of the 3rd–4th
of this month was immediately discovered. An advance patrol of
Armand's, consisting of one officer, one corporal, and four Brunswickers who had been taken prisoners and subsequently enlisted,
commended themselves to their officer, rode over to us, and told

---

[105] An interesting example of confused intelligence. Putnam, not Heath, commanded in the Highlands, while the latter was in Boston during the period from
October 22 to November 7. Sullivan was not in Boston, but at Providence, and
Stirling took over the post at Elizabethtown, New Jersey, October 15. True, Gates
moved from Danbury to Hartford October 25, but he went on to Boston at the
end of the month. Washington's headquarters were at Fredericksburg (now Patterson, Putnam County, New York). Cf. Fitzpatrick's *Calendar of the Correspondence
of George Washington*. The *Royal Gazette* (Oct. 27 and 31, 1778), however, reported Washington and Gates in Hartford, thus paralleling Baurmeister's statement.

the jägers that they were waiting in vain, for all knew of their ambush.

From the enclosed plan of distribution [106] your Lordship will see that the strip beyond Kings Bridge, representing the cordon, is occupied by detachments inferior in strength to closed battalions, which could cover the redoubts. The worst of all regrettable events certainly would not be the loss of some closed battalions by a surprise attack.[107] For my part, I am certain that since the rebels are still of the opinion that we will evacuate New York entirely, they will, on discovering an established garrison, exert themselves to the utmost against Kings Bridge and Fort Knyphausen, for all the New England militia, including the third levy, have recently been ordered to hold themselves in readiness to march.

The French fleet in Boston harbor is ready to sail, but is closely watched by Admiral Byron. There is good reason to suspect that it intends to sail for Europe, for it has taken all its invalids and artillery on board again. Nevertheless, their behavior is that of an American ally, for which they have been met with British hatred and bitterness. I made a mistake in my last journal, that of October 21st, when, instead of noting the arrival of the French warships in Boston harbor under the 29th of August, I said that the same had occurred on the 29th of July.

From the reports of his Excellency General von Knyphausen your Lordship [must have seen?] [108] that Lieutenant Juliat [109] has returned again. I shall not be able to tell many details. He

---

[106] See end of this letter.

[107] Baurmeister's reasoning seems to follow this line: An attack on the outlying redoubts must be expected; they are covered only by small detachments, which could definitely not withstand an attack; closed battalions might ward off defeat, even though the battalions might be lost. On the other hand, perhaps the original is garbled.

[108] MS torn along edge.

[109] Charles (i.e., Franz Karl Joseph) Juliat, recommended for Pulaski's Legion. He was involved with Lieutenants Führer and Kleinschmidt in a scheme to raise a corps of volunteers for the American service from German deserters. Apparently too poor to wait until Congress took action, he returned to the Hessian service, thus causing considerable embarrassment to Führer and Kleinschmidt. Cf. *Journals of the Continental Congress*, ed. by J. C. Fitzpatrick, *sub* Sept. 3, 1778, and *Royal Gazette*, Nov. 7, 1778.

[has?] deserted. Youth and his embarrassment for letting the rebels persuade him to go over to them could let him make no better resolve than to leave the nefarious rebels, in spite of having to face much danger, for like the old Romans they now talk seriously about extraordinary deeds and inflict much more cruel punishments without any consideration. Moreover, on the 30th of October of this year Congress issued a countermanifesto threatening every Englishman.

On the 27th of October, 279 of the Trenton prisoners finally returned; 132 have not yet come back. About forty men have been retained in Philadelphia as tailors for the army, while some twenty remained there on account of sickness. But of the rest, probably not many will return.

The light-minded officers, Führer and Kleinschmidt, now captains in a corps of German volunteers, are persuading many to take service. Besides [some?] have married. In these cases it is necessary to be patient for the time being. Once the provinces are subjugated, their return can be effected with greater authority. The Hessian jägers of Lieutenant Mertz's patrol who were taken prisoners on the 30th of September have been exchanged.

Lord Cornwallis has been paid the value of the frigate *Delaware*, which was captured when we took possession of Philadelphia. Since both British and Hessian grenadiers were at that time under his command, he gave the Hessian grenadiers, from privates up to noncommissioned officers, some £820 sterling. The *Harriot* packet,[110] which left Falmouth on the 7th of September this year, was captured by a French privateer on the 17th of the same month. Consequently all the European letters on this packet were consigned to the sea. Captain [Reuting] [111] of the Grenadier Company Prinz Carl has been made Town Major in New York in consideration of the Hessian garrison.

With the greatest respect, I have the honor to be [*etc.*]

---

[110] The *Harriot* packet, sixteen guns and forty-five men, was taken by the privateer *Vengeance*, Wingate Newman, commander, September 17, and sent to Newburyport. See *Royal Gazette*, Nov. 4, 1778.

[111] Name given in following letter.

Plan of Distribution [112]

CITY OF NEW YORK	LONG ISLAND

English and Hessian headquarters
Brigade of Guards
The 23rd Regiment
Volunteers of Ireland
Hessian grenadier brigade

ON YORK ISLAND TO
FORT INDEPENDENCE

7th ⎫
17th ⎪
26th ⎬ British regiments
44th ⎪
57th ⎪
63rd ⎭

Lossberg's ⎫
Knyphausen's ⎬ Loos's brigade
Mirbach's ⎭

Leib Regiment ⎫
Donop's ⎬ Gosen's brigade
Trümbach's [113] ⎭

Lastly, Emmerich's Corps

LONG ISLAND

Light infantry and grenadiers
                    to Jamaica
33rd Regiment   to Bedford
42nd Regiment   to Newtown
Queen's Rangers
                    to Hallet's Cove [114]
British Legion   to Jericho
17th Dragoons with three
        battalions of De Lancey's
                    to Hempstead
Hessian Erb Prinz   to Brooklyn
Prinz Carl   to Bushwick
Anspach and Hessian jägers
                    to Flushing

ON STATEN ISLAND

Hessian Grenadier Battalion
        Köhler
37th Regiment
Skinner's 4th Battalion
The 64th Regiment at Powles
        Hook

---

[112] Enclosed with letter dated Nov. 9 (No. 27).

[113] Von Trümbach is the new chief of von Woellwarth's, formerly von Rall's Regiment; the old Trümbach Regiment is now von Bose's.

[114] Hallet's Cove, later Astoria, now part of Brooklyn, New York.

Astoria is part of Queens /

: 28 :

On the 10th of this month a frigate put out after General Grant's expedition with orders to accompany the transports a certain distance and then sail for England. This frigate is carrying a large packet of letters, among them one which I had the honor to write your Lordship on the 9th. Since his Excellency General Clinton, wind permitting, will dispatch another packet with letters to Spithead tomorrow, I take this opportunity to inform your Lordship that Admiral Byron's fleet, unable to stay off Boston Bay any longer because of the many gales, anchored at Sandy Hook yesterday morning, and that the French fleet likewise departed from Boston harbor and has doubtless taken a course for the West Indies, where the French have taken not only Dominica, but also St. Vincent.

The rebels have sent several brigades and also General Scott to Virginia, for Burgoyne's prisoners have been taken to that part of the country. General Clinton had remonstrated against their removal and offered to send the necessary provisions for them to Boston, but to no avail.

Four brigades under General Gates have been sent into winter quarters in New England as far as Albany, and General Washington has left Hartford with two brigades, two dragoon regiments, and the artillery park to spend the winter in Fredericksburg.[115] He has asked for his discharge and has recommended Generals Sullivan and Greene as his successors. General McDougall has taken over the command of the post of light troops in Scott's place.

On the 12th of this month Lieutenant Colonel Simcoe marched through East Chester, New Rochelle, Mamaroneck, and Rye, turned off to the left in the direction of the sawmill, and assaulted the house of the rebel Colonel Thomas.[116] Thomas had one officer and five men with him and was determined to defend himself. However, the house was forced. The Colonel and three men were found defenseless in the corners, but the officer and two men were killed.[117] The prisoners would have received a pardon if one of Simcoe's men had not been shot with a pistol. For two years Colonel Thomas, the rebel most feared in that region, has cleverly escaped being captured.

On the 20th of this month his Excellency General von Knyphausen will take quarters in New York. For the time being General Tryon, Governor of New York, and the titular Brigadier O'Hara [118] will retain the command here. The Hessian regiments are moving into miserable quarters in huts. There is much delay in delivering the most necessary materials and tools to build quarters, and they are supplied in insufficient quantities; nor are there many boards, nails, and entrenching tools in the magazines.

[115] Fredericksburg, now Patterson, Putnam County, New York.

[116] Colonel Thomas Thomas, Westchester County militia.

[117] Cf. *Simcoe's Military Journal*, New York, 1844, p. 92: "the man who fired was the only person killed."

[118] Colonel Charles O'Hara, 2nd Foot (Coldstream) Guards, was named brigadier by Clinton. "The necessity of paying particular Attention to Sandy Hook whilst the French Fleet lay off this Harbour, inclined me to appoint Colonel O'Hara to that Command; and as the Duty was extraordinary and the Trust great, I thought the appointing him to the Rank of Brigadier General but a just Recompence. . . ." Clinton to Barrington, PRO, War Office, I, vol. 10, folio 571. A photostat is in the Library of Congress, and copies are in the Clinton and Carleton MSS, William L. Clements Library.

Meanwhile, the whole situation and crowded condition remain unchanged.

Another large provision fleet of thirty-two sail has safely arrived from Cork. A newspaper containing the countermanifesto and the reply to it is enclosed [*missing*]. I also take the liberty to enclose a letter to my wife, of whom I have heard nothing since the 31st of May this year. I hope that your Lordship will not take this amiss.

With the greatest respect, I have the honor to be [*etc.*]

P.S. If the former adjutant Captain Phipps [119] should sail with the peace commissioners before the end of the month, he will take with him some seeds of a genuine North American magnolia, which he will deliver into Major von Kutzleben's care. The magnolia is one of the most fragrant tree blossoms in this part of the country. There will also be some seeds of the West India magnolia. The trunks of these trees grow into wood for three years, and the trees frequently get no taller than dwarf fruit trees. They grow in rich swampy soil where they get abundant sunshine or along quiet brooks, but they do still better close to ponds. I hope that they may give pleasure.

[119] The Hon. Henry Phipps (later Earl of Mulgrave), 1st Regiment of Foot Guards.

: 29 :

If my letter of the 16th of this month arrives safely, your Lordship will see that I hope to have the honor to send you some magnolia seeds in care of Major von Kutzleben. I filled two glass bottles with them. In the bottom of one are twenty-four seeds of the West India magnolia, which can be easily distinguished because they are larger than the seeds of the North American variety. The seed should be planted in damp, rich soil near quiet brooks or ponds. This flowering tree will not grow on high ground; nevertheless, it needs sunshine. The trunk grows for three years before the blossoms appear. The flower is white, greatly resembles a tulip just opening, and has a very pleasant fragrance. On the top in the other bottle are twelve seeds of the West India magnolia.[120] If these seeds grow, I shall take the liberty of asking in time for a few trees for my little property in Rothenburg.

On the 4th of this month the French fleet left Boston harbor, sailing before a strong wind. Since then Admiral Byron has sent

[120] Should read: "North American magnolia" (cf. postscript to previous letter).

233

in thirty prizes, although he has not been able to give positive information about the course the enemy ships have taken.

In the last storm the warship *Somerset*, sixty-four guns, ran ashore not far from Boston Bay [121] with a loss of thirty sailors drowned. I am enclosing several newspapers worth reading [*missing*]. The two regiments vacant von Woellwarth and the Wissenbach as well as the 71st Regiment Highland Scots suffered much in the storm and have come to anchor in damaged ships at Sandy Hook. They had to change transports and will put to sea again as soon as possible. Two other transports, on which provincial troops are embarked, have not arrived to date.

Tomorrow his Excellency General von Knyphausen will take up quarters in New York. General Governor Tryon and the titular Brigadier O'Hara have the command here. Captain Reuting has been made Town Major of New York at the request of his Excellency General Clinton. Inasmuch, however, as a very good knowledge of the English language is required, he has, in accordance with instructions, resigned. His place has been given to Captain O'Reilly,[122] who will fill it well.

I have the honor to be with deepest respect [*etc.*]

P.S. On the 20th instant his Excellency General Clinton gave a large ball in honor of Mrs. Eden, wife of one of the peace commissioners. Everyone was invited. However, his Excellency General von Knyphausen permitted Colonel von Cochenhausen and myself to go to the city. The rest of his suite remained here with him, thirty-eight ladies and *chapeaux*.[123] Three times as many gathered at the English headquarters at eight o'clock in the eve-

---

[121] The *Somerset* was driven ashore on Cape Cod in Massachusetts Bay. Cf. following letter and Clowes, *Royal Navy*, IV, 110.

[122] A letter in French addressed to von Jungkenn, signed "O'Reilly," is in the collection. The *New-York Gazette*, Nov. 30, 1778, calls him von Oreilly, as did also Baurmeister in his letter dated Aug. 14, 1778 (No. 21). Both Heinrich Wilhelm Reuting and O'Reilly were captains in von Lengerke's Grenadier Battalion, though Captain Reuting seems to have been in command of the grenadier company of the Prinz Carl Regiment for some time. The *Staats-Calender* has Maximilian Wilhelm Oreilly.

[123] Escorts, admirers, "gentlemen friends"; not an uncommon word at the time, used for example, by Goethe in *Die Leiden des jungen Werther*.

ning. It was after two o'clock in the morning when the festivity was over.

The frigate on which the commissioners are sailing had to be specially fitted out for this voyage. However, of the total expense, only £562 sterling were charged to the King's account.

: 30 :

On the 22nd of last month I had the honor to dispatch for your Lordship by Captain Phipps, who was about to sail to England, the last part of my journal and two glass bottles filled with magnolia seeds, which are to be forwarded by Major von Kutzleben. The ships, however, did not set sail until the 26th, i.e., four days later, for Lord Carlisle and Mr. Eden, the two peace commissioners, were detained by business. After a dinner at General Clinton's quarters, to which were invited as many Englishmen and Hessians as the dining room would hold, they went on board on the 25th, accompanied by Generals Cornwallis and Grey.

On the 23rd of November the Hessian General Staff went into winter quarters in this city, and by the end of the month each regiment was quartered in accordance with the plan of distribution previously enclosed. They were to have remained the entire winter, but it was thought necessary to send the 26th Regiment to Staten Island to reinforce General Leslie and to quarter four companies of Mirbach's Regiment in Harlem, so that only one company of this regiment remained at McGown's Pass, near Harlem.

The Barracks Office has supplied each regiment with sufficient mattresses, straw sacks, sheets, covers, lights, straw, and

woolen gloves. The huts have been built so solidly and made so
weatherproof that most of them are to be preferred to the drafty
houses. The Leib Regiment, it seems, takes precedence in the art
of building these. All its huts stand in a row, and the officers'
quarters, built in front of the company huts, are as regular as they
are comfortable.

The rebels, still of the opinion that next spring at the latest
the British and their auxiliary forces will leave all of America, have
had a wide cordon of about eight thousand Continental troops
ready since the 24th of November to occupy our narrow quarters
as soon as we leave them. General Washington has taken up headquarters in Morristown. In the west their right wing extends to
Elizabethtown; Fishkill, on the North River, is considered the
center of their quarters, while their left wing reaches as far eastward as Hartford in Connecticut. Brigadier General McDougall
commands less than three hundred light troops between White
Plains and Mamaroneck. His patrols have never advanced as far
as Williams's bridge, two miles from Fort Independence.

The country people come a distance of twenty miles from
Kings Bridge with droves of cattle, which they sell, and buy whatever they need with the proceeds. They are not disturbed either
on the way or here. On the contrary, expensive as farm products
are, we are glad that fresh victuals are still brought in, for everything indicates that soon nothing more will be obtainable. Prices
are so high that things can hardly be bought. We hope that the
provision ships will arrive soon. The various troops and even the
many privateers which have lately put to sea have sadly depleted
our stores.

We still do not know when and where General Grant landed,
or whether the reinforcements sent at the same time to Halifax
and East and West Florida arrived safely. The everlasting gales,
which, with little intermission, still prevail, caused nine transports
and one frigate to return to Staten Island on the 19th of November. After changing to other ships, the troops finally put to sea
again on the 26th. Among them were the Regiments von Woellwarth and von Wissenbach.

On the 2nd of November the *Somerset*, sixty-four guns, foundered off Cape Cod. Some sixty men drowned, and over four hundred were taken to Boston as prisoners. The store ship *Martha* ran aground on her way here from Halifax at Barnegat, fifteen leagues north of Egg Harbor.[124] When the frigate *Daphne*, which was to assist her, arrived, the Americans had already taken her crew and cargo. To prevent the rebels from taking the ship, too, she was set on fire.

On the 8th of November this frigate had the good fortune to capture the richly laden merchantman *Sophie* near the mouth of the Delaware. Mr. Gérard [125] of Philadelphia had sent this ship to Bordeaux with a cargo of indigo and dispatches for Paris. The package of letters was thrown into the sea, but a sailor from the *Daphne* jumped in after it and brought it aboard. Many of the letters written in code have not been deciphered yet, although we have learned the following: Count d'Estaing's fleet, with scarcely six weeks' provisions, left Boston with a favorable but high wind on the 4th of November, expecting to reach its destination within that time. Two British frigates, the *Active* and the *Minerva*, were captured in the West Indies, and their crews disembarked at Cape François.[126] Both frigates are now cruising against Admiral Peter Parker, who has captured two heavily armed French ships and thirteen loaded vessels on their way back from Dominica.[127] An Irish provision fleet has come safely to anchor at Antigua. At Barbados the necessary barracks for the English have been built, and in Jamaica ten thousand militia and two thousand negroes under the famous Captain Cudjoe [128] are under arms to defend the fortifications in case of an attack. The inhabitants of the Bermudas were at first incensed when the English increased the

124 Cf. *Royal Gazette*, Dec. 9, 1778.

125 Conrad Alexandre Gérard de Rayneval, French minister to the United States. The *Sophie* was bound for Bordeaux with Gérard's dispatches (*ibid.*, Nov. 21 and Dec. 2, 1778).

126 Now Old Cape Français, Santo Domingo. Cape François during the eighteenth century was, perhaps, the most important of the French West Indian harbors, and during the Revolutionary War served as the naval base for the French fleet.

127 Cf. *London Chronicle*, Jan. 2–5, 1779.

128 A Captain Cudjoe led slave insurrections on Jamaica in the late eighteenth and early nineteenth centuries.

forces there, but they are now becoming reconciled to these necessary measures.

In a letter to his wife Mr. Gérard writes frankly about the American nation and its financial difficulties. He particularly laments the discord among the members of Congress. Then he says quite bluntly that winning over the Americans and then sharing with them is like making chemical experiments, and that neither side, in spite of doing its utmost, has gained very much.

If the French fleet really has sailed to the West Indies, Admiral Barrington and Sir Peter Parker have enough ships there to resist any enterprise until Admiral Byron arrives. The latter is now anchored at Newport. He has brought in twenty-eight prizes, all from Admiral d'Estaing's fleet, although the warships have not yet come to close quarters. In the beginning, the French fleet also set out in two divisions in a NW [sic] direction.[129] There is not a Frenchman left in Boston.

Shortage of provisions finally induced Congress to send Burgoyne's prisoners from Rutland [130] and Cambridge to the southernmost parts of Virginia. On the 27th, 28th, and 29th of November they crossed the North River at Fishkill by divisions, together with all the enemy field artillery, which was being taken from Fredericksburg [131] to Bound Brook in Jersey, where several brigades are in cantonments as they were last year at Valley Forge, and where the main rendezvous in Jersey is said to be.

Almost forty of Bourgoyne's prisoners and then one noncommissioned officer and twelve artillerymen arrived here on the 1st of this month. Thus it became known who it was that had crossed the North River at Fishkill. General Clinton, believing he could attract even more deserters, had the Guards, one battalion of grenadiers, one battalion of light infantry, Lord Rawdon's Irish corps, and one brigade of artillery unexpectedly embark on the North River on the 2nd of this month at eight o'clock in the evening and sail with the tide up to Tarrytown, while the 7th, 44th, and 57th

---

129 D'Estaing, of course, went to the West Indies.
130 Rutland, Worcester County, Massachusetts. Part of the Convention troops were sent there April 15, 1778. Cf. *Heath's Memoirs of the American War*, p. 173.
131 Now Patterson, New York.

English Regiments and von Mirbach's were ordered to march there by way of Kings Bridge. They were too late, however, and the prisoners' escort was too strong.

On the other side of the river, it seems, they were not so watchful, for reliable information was received at English headquarters that close to four hundred have escaped in large troops to the right to join Butler and Brant. These partisans have gained another victory, this time in Cherry Valley over Colonel Alden,[132] whom Gates had detached there with his battalion and two hundred militia. This district, which is said to be fifty English miles from Albany, is now as devastated as the settlement at Wyoming. This may be said also of German Flats, Springfield, and Ulster. It has caused a great scarcity of food in Tryon, Albany, and Charlotte [133] counties.

On the 7th instant the titular Brigadier O'Hara and Colonel Hyde [134] were sent to Amboy with proposals for a complete exchange of Burgoyne's prisoners. Lieutenant Berdot [135] accompanied them with a small escort. The negotiations were cut short, and all proposals were fruitless. The rest of the Hessian troops are still detained in Philadelphia on shallow excuses. The distance which Burgoyne's troops have to travel from Rutland and Cambridge is reckoned to be six hundred English miles. Ten Brunswick officers under a certain Major Meibom [136] are still here on parole, as are also twenty-six English officers. Congress is willing to release all officers, but General Clinton will not agree. He is asking in vain for all the rebel officers who escaped from prison in Flatbush, Long Island.

I must tell of another bold stroke of Congress: When the boat fitted out by Admiral Gambier arrived in Philadelphia with the package containing the late manifesto, which a sea officer was to deliver to Congress, the officer and the sailors were immediately

---

[132] Ichabod Alden, Colonel 7th Massachusetts, killed at Cherry Valley.

[133] Schoharie?

[134] Colonel West Hyde, 1st Regiment of Foot Guards.

[135] Probably First Lieutenant Leopold Friedrich Bertaud of the Landgraf Regiment (*Staats-Calender*, p. 28). Baurmeister spells his name Perdot later on.

[136] Later the Major's name appears as Maybaum, which is the more likely spelling. English and some German accounts have Meibom, as above.

thrown into prison. Then Congress publicly declared that anyone transmitting similar seductive sheets under a flag of truce would be arrested and would never be released. So far Congress has stubbornly kept its word and has answered all representations with a copy of these resolutions. Any person who is in the least suspected is hanged on the spot. Everyone trembles at the thought of such despotic power. The English themselves are saying that Congress will not become more lenient until it is too late to maintain itself. This reminds me that the English did not become aware of the true wickedness of the Americans and the need for forceful action till it was almost too late.[137]

The printed text of General Clinton's report of the action at Monmouth in Jersey has come here from the rebel newspapers. It is recognized as an exact copy. General Lee took this occasion to have another apologia printed, of which I enclose a copy.[138] I also send another installment of "Memento Mori,"[139] the beginning of which was in the newspaper enclosed in my last, further, a resolution concerning a certain Colonel Connolly, who suffered great hardship in prison[140] and whose release has been requested, and lastly, the answer of the President of Congress to Admiral Gambier[141] concerning the detained ship and officers.[142]

Many more privateers would be equipped if we were not short of sailors. The Americans have lost almost three hundred vessels, whose chief cargoes have been indigo, turpentine, tobacco, and flour. Since sailing has become so great a risk, insurance in Charleston, Baltimore, Philadelphia, and Boston has gone up to 145 per cent. English goods arrive from Europe insured at

[137] Although the last sentence is rather freely translated, it preserves Baurmeister's meaning.

[138] Lee printed a long article in the *Pennsylvania Packet*, Dec. 3, 1778, which was reprinted in *Royal Gazette*, Dec. 12. Presumably the enclosure, which is missing from the Von Jungkenn Papers, was this reprint.

[139] "Memento Mori" appeared in the columns of *Royal Gazette*, Nov. 18 and 25, and Dec. 19.

[140] Colonel John Connolly. See *A Narrative of the Transactions, Imprisonment, and Sufferings of John Connolly, an American Loyalist, and Lieutenant Colonel in His Majesty's Service*. London, 1783 [New York, reprinted for C. L. Woodward, 1889].

[141] See *Royal Gazette*, Nov. 28, 1778.

[142] None of the enclosures is in the Von Jungkenn Papers.

11 per cent with convoy, and at 22 per cent without convoy. The arming of our ships leaves much to be desired.

At the end of October the frigate *Ariel* captured an eight-hundred-ton ship from Boston destined for Toulon with a quantity of masts for warships, of which the local wharves were in dire need. This ship was boarded by some sailors from the *Ariel* and ordered to sail to New York. The frigate then went in pursuit of other prizes and has since come in with two tobacco ships from Maryland, although her first prize has not arrived yet. The *Bedford*, seventy-four guns, and the frigate *Amazon*, thirty-two, are at anchor here simply because they have no masts. All the ships that were anchored alongside the city have been sent to Newtown Bay on the East River for the winter. Because of fear of fire the best measures have been instituted.

The office of the English secretariat has suddenly taken to giving us such short notices for posting our mail that it has been impossible for me to have this copied. I therefore send the original and entrust it to Captain Holefeld.[143] Colonel von Wurmb commends the enclosure to my care.

I have the honor to be with the deepest respect [*etc.*]

[143] Of the Landgraf Regiment. Eelking-Rosengarten spells his name Hohlefeld.

: 31 :

Since the ships destined for England will not sail until tomorrow, and perhaps later, I take this opportunity of sending another letter by Captain Holefeld to inform your Lordship that the packet which left Falmouth on the 14th of October this year cast anchor off Sandy Hook at one o'clock on the 21st of this month and immediately sent its dispatches by a pilot to the English headquarters. Except for some letters which Major von Kutzleben had forwarded in care of his Excellency General von Knyphausen, nothing has been received from Hesse by the corps. Consequently, everyone is waiting anxiously for good news.

I enclose some newspapers [*missing*] containing items which have been confirmed by private reports and authentic accounts that have come into English headquarters, namely, the arrival of Grant's corps at Barbados, Colonel Prevost's march from St. Augustine into Georgia, the great ferment in Congress, the discord among the American generals, and the departure of Byron's fleet from Newport. From deserters brought in from Powles Hook we have learned that on the 19th of this month General Washington gave orders to his troops to hold themselves ready to march.

Whether he will partly evacuate Jersey and proceed to Virginia to protect himself and his estates, time will tell more reliably than these deserters. Count d'Estaing's poorly translated declaration finds no approval. We have had no news from Canada since the 29th of September of this year, nor have the flour ships arrived from there. If the last packet had not raised our hopes that a large provision fleet is near this harbor, we should have good reason to be very discontented. At present we are being furnished biscuits of coarsely ground oats, and for our horses we get poor rough fodder and peas.

His Majesty the King of England remembered General von Knyphausen and his corps with the most gracious expressions in his message of thanks to General Clinton concerning the retreat from Philadelphia and the attack at Monmouth. Humbly commending myself, I have the honor to be with the greatest respect

Your Lordship's

Most obedient servant

Baurmeister

New York
December 26, 1778

1779

: 32 :

Right Honorable Lord,
Gracious High and Mighty Major General:

On the 20th and 26th of December last year I had the honor
to send your Lordship by Captain Holefeld further accounts of
local events. I hope that all the ships, which set sail at the same
time, will reach Europe safely. The storms have been terrible, and
also the subsequent cold spell and the deep snow. All of it was as
strange to us as it was unpleasant.

Some twenty transports and smaller vessels were entirely destroyed by the ice which the ebb tide brought down the North
River into the harbor. As a result, the officers of the 16th Regiment of Dragoons, who were to sail to England, lost the greater
part of their equipage; but even more lamentable is the loss of
seventy-two sailors, of whom there has been a great shortage
anyhow.

How cold it was can be appreciated from the fact that wild
geese and ducks froze to death by the thousands on the shores
of Long and Staten islands. They were most greedily eaten by the
soldiers and the inhabitants, for the provisions had become very

low. There was no more flour, and the small amount of good oat-
meal mixed with the spoiled did not make wholesome biscuits for
the soldiers. However, after a ten weeks' journey a British brigan-
tine finally came in on the 3rd of this month with a cargo of 340
tons of flour. Moreover, on the 8th the much longed-for Cork provision fleet arrived. The Admiral's ship greeted the *Nottingham*,
an Indiaman, under whose convoy the fleet ran into the harbor,
and our guests replied with great satisfaction by firing a salute of
nineteen guns.

The common soldiers, accustomed to getting their provisions
regularly and unable to procure anything extra, were virtually at
the end of their patience, especially since most of them were living in huts during this bitter cold weather and were doing heavy
field duty regardless of privation and hardship. This has even
caused some desertion in spite of the greatest watchfulness, as will
be seen, along with other things, from the reports.

A strong force of Refugees[1] and Westchester militia recently
made an attack on a grain and flour magazine at Young's farm,
three miles beyond White Plains, returning not only with the entire store loaded on thirty-seven wagons, but also with the famous
rebel Captain Williams.[2]

Admiral Barrington's West India fleet, consisting of thirteen
ships of the line and frigates, has picked up many French merchantmen. The harbors of Bermuda, Barbados, and Antigua are
full of them. The rebel reports of the progress of the said admiral
go into such detail that there is no cause for doubt when they
say that this fleet has undertaken an expedition against Martinique
and Guadeloupe.

On the 2nd of this month Congress, in Philadelphia, received
a report from Charleston that Brigadier General Campbell[3] had
landed in Georgia and occupied Savannah and that everyone
recognizes the King's sovereignty, but I have not learned whether

[1] James De Lancey's Refugees, sometimes called De Lancey's Cowboys because of their frequent forage duty.

[2] Captain Daniel Williams of the New York militia. For an account of the capture see *Royal Gazette*, Dec. 30, and subsequent issue. The action on Young's farm
took place December 25.

[3] Lieutenant Colonel Archibald Campbell. Brigadier General John Campbell
was at this time on his way to Pensacola. (See also following letter.)

the English headquarters have received such a desirable report from Brigadier General Campbell. I did learn, however, that on the 14th of November the Seitz Battalion reached Halifax harbor.

The rebels took all the invalids of Burgoyne's army and the greater part of the sailors of the shipwrecked *Somerset* and of other armed ships that had foundered along the coast to Newport by way of Providence. I enclose a newspaper of the 9th of this month [*missing*]. The forces of Butler and Brant were considerably increased by deserters from the divisions of Burgoyne's prisoners on their fatiguing march to the southern part of Virginia. Even some rebels of the escort ran away with them. This has been confirmed by a captain named Höemele,[4] who deserted from Colonel Butler at Cherry Valley and reached English headquarters after traveling a long roundabout route. The conduct of the Indians is very cruel, and the misery of the inhabitants of those settlements is beyond description, all of which gives the greatest embarrassment to Congress.

All the Brunswick and English officers have been turned over to the rebel commissaries at Elizabethtown, whence the greater part have been sent to Easton. Several British officers, however, were permitted to return. In addition to the eighty-five rebel officers who escaped from prisons and whose return has been requested, another 102 rebel officers released on parole are expected to return to us, for General Clinton made it clear once and for all that he will not have Burgoyne's prisoners separated from all their officers.

At present there are few sick in the hospitals, and on Rhode Island there are almost none. Deputy Muster Master Porter,[5] who recently returned from the said island, cannot give enough praise to the Hessian troops quartered there. General von Bose is expected to return to New York from Rhode Island any day, for the continued illness of Generals Stirn and Schmidt demands his presence here. I take the liberty of enclosing a letter for Major von Eschwege.

With the greatest respect, I have the honor to be [*etc.*]

4 Not identified.
5 William Porter, Deputy Commissary of Musters.

: 33 :

I sent my last letter on the 11th of last month and hope that the thirteen accounts which I have sent since the 7th of July last year have all arrived.[6] On the 23rd of last month a packet finally came in with Hessian mail dated in October.

I have the honor to report further that on the 1st of this month an Irish provision fleet of eleven sail arrived. This not only relieved the serious shortage of food but also filled our magazines for nine months. These stores have been further increased by the profitable enterprises of General Erskine, who finally made a thorough search in the eastern parts of Long Island, taking from those inhabitants who are still rebels all the grain, hay, straw, and cattle they did not need. To their own disadvantage they had promised their friends in Connecticut to surrender everything to them or else hide it in the woods. The rest of the inhabitants bring their garden produce and cattle to market. But we must take care not to be too anxious to buy, or else they will bring no more. This is the reason everything is no frightfully expensive.

[6] They did arrive; i.e., Nos. 20 to 32, inclusive, and not counting the letter of July 7 (No. 19).

The situation on this and the neighboring islands is still the same. The severe winter and insufficient stores have rendered the greater part of the rebels in Connecticut and in New England defenseless. Lieutenant Colonel Emmerich's dragoon patrols are surprising and discovering weak posts.

Beyond Kings Bridge the enemy have occupied the following quarters: Brigadier McDougall with fifteen hundred is at Peekskill and environs; four hundred men are on King's Street; four hundred men in Horse Neck; and five troops of dragoons, each of which is said to consist of sixty-five horse, are in Danbury and Fairfield. Putnam is in command of two thousand men. All these troops are under General Gates, who is stationed in Boston, while General Sullivan, who is under Gates, is in Providence.

The garrisons of Boston and Albany are weak, but the one at Ticonderoga is very strong. Much work is being done on Lake Champlain, and new fortifications are being built in addition to the forts on the North River. The militia have orders to be prepared to march to their places of rendezvous at the first alarm.

After the rebels found it necessary to send Colonels Moylan and Woodford with a brigade of South Carolinians and five troops of dragoons into Pennsylvania [7] to confront Colonel Butler and Joseph Brant, who have united and are making incursions as far as Harris's Ferry [8] near Carlisle and to Little York, [9] the remaining troops in Jersey were quartered as follows:

General Washington's headquarters are at Wallace's house, [10] twelve English miles from Brunswick on the far side of the Raritan; Brigadier General Maxwell holds an outpost in Elizabethtown with six hundred infantry and some forty dragoons; between Newark and Spanktown [11] one hundred and fifty men are quartered in huts; the Earl of Stirling with three hundred men has his

[7] Neither Stephen Moylan nor William Woodford could have been sent to Pennsylvania. This statement is apparently based on Rivington's fabrication (*Royal Gazette*, Dec. 19, 1778).

[8] Harris's Ferry, at the site of modern Harrisburg.

[9] Little York, perhaps the present York, Pennsylvania.

[10] Washington's headquarters were at Middlebrook after February 1; Wallace's house could not be identified. Baurmeister's source may have been the *Royal Gazette, loc. cit.*

[11] Spanktown, now Rahway.

quarters at Bound Brook; from there to the Raritan are posted five hundred men and fifty dragoons under Generals Greene and Van Wechter;[12] the artillery under Brigadier General Knox is stationed at Pluckemin, and in order to give them something to do the park was fortified; three hundred men and the hospital are in Middletown; four hundred are in Brunswick, and three hundred in Quibbletown.[13] Most of these places are situated in front of headquarters; the left wing is covered by a range of high mountains, and the right by the Raritan.

The freebooters on our side have been extraordinarily lucky. Between the 1st of January and the 4th of February they have brought forty-six prizes into this harbor alone, and between the 16th of December and the 28th of January, twenty-two into the Bermudas. The warship *Le Lion,* forty guns, with a cargo of fourteen hundred hogsheads of tobacco surrendered to the frigate *Maidstone,* twenty-eight guns, after a three-hour engagement. The cargoes of most of the other prizes are also of great value. On these prizes, moreover, we found some letters from Virginia which complain bitterly that almost all their ships fall prey to the British, that trade is completely paralyzed, and that the plantations are desolate.

On the prizes taken in the Delaware were some letters from Deane to Mr. Franklin in Paris, in which there are more specific complaints about the evil consequences of paper money, the resultant hopeless bad feeling among the Continental troops, the increasing discord among the members of Congress as well as among the highest generals of the army, the shortage of grain, flour, and salt, and the impossibility of erecting large magazines. Deane maintains that the hunger and nakedness in the northern provinces are due to the fact that a hundredweight of wheat flour sells in Boston for two hundred Spanish dollars paper money.

---

[12] Perhaps an error by Baurmeister's amanuensis. According to the *Royal Gazette,* of Dec. 19, Greene's forces were stationed "at Mr. Van Vetchter's on Rariton River." There is no record of a General Van Vechter in the American forces. The Van Vechters were a numerous family in lower New York and New Jersey, figuring frequently in local annals. Both Ephraim Van Vechter and Tunis Van Veghten are listed in the Adjutant General's Office as deputy quartermasters general. (Revolutionary War Records, A.G.O., National Archives.)

[13] Quibbletown, now New Market, Middlesex County.

Then he wonders how, in case France should live up to her promise to send ten thousand men to the harbor and environs of Boston, these troops could be fed, since all hard coin has already been sent to their ally, and since the guinea has an exchange value of thirty-eight and forty and a whole Johan, of one hundred and thirty-six Spanish paper dollars, and particularly since there is no more to be had in spite of the fact that all the debts are not paid yet.[14] The originals of these letters were sent to London by Admiral Gambier.

The number of Refugees so increased that most of them were quartered at Hempstead on Long Island and organized into companies, whereupon they were taken over to Rhode Island to take the place of four companies of light infantry and grenadiers. Lieutenant Colonel Fox of the 38th Regiment brought these wing companies to Long Island, and Major General von Bose took this occasion to come here to take over the command of the brigade which Colonel von Loos had had for some time. The said Refugees had hardly disembarked on Rhode Island when they boldly crossed over to Prudence Island and returned with 120 draft horses without much interference or any loss.

The homeless loyalists who are still here are fitting out forty vessels to cruise under cover of six armed British ships and land anywhere between Rhode Island and Portsmouth and between here and Egg Harbor. They will keep all their booty without exception, which has greatly encouraged them, for all of them had been well-to-do, but have lost everything and are fortunate to be still alive.

The rapid advance of Lieutenant Colonel Archibald Campbell is described in the *Gazette Extraordinary* enclosed herewith [*missing*]. Von Trümbach's Regiment distinguished itself exceedingly in the main attack on the 29th of December last year.[15] Lieutenant Barrington McKenzie of the 71st Regiment Scottish Highlanders, who left Savannah on the 19th of January and arrived here on the 2nd of this month with important news, cannot

[14] The *Royal Gazette*, Dec. 4, 1778, has a deciphered letter from Silas Deane to Jonathan Williams (reprinted in *Deane Papers*, III, 64, *New York Historical Society Collections*, 1887–90), which somewhat parallels Baurmeister's account.

[15] Action at Savannah, Georgia.

praise it enough. Among other things, he says that the rebels at first withstood the fire of the British, who had opened ranks, but that they lost their coolness when the said regiment advanced with closed front and effectively answered their disorderly fire, and that, unable to withstand it longer, the enemy escaped through swamps and creeks to Ebenezer.

General Clinton is now awaiting confirmation of more good news, which was brought in by Sea Captain Butler from Martinique, who had been taken prisoner on the *Delaware* sloop-of-war on the 4th of December and released by Count d'Estaing on the 7th of January. His reports cover the following events:

As soon as the troops under General Grant arrived at Barbados, Admiral Barrington sailed to St. Lucia on the 12th of December last year, in spite of the close proximity of the French fleet. Early in the morning of the following day he anchored in the Grand Cul de Sac, not far south of the harbor of the Carénage. Without encountering any resistance, the greater part of his land force disembarked on the island, occupied the highest hill, and so came into possession of the Governor's house, the barracks, and one of the most complete hospitals. But when the rest of the troops landed on the 14th, the small frigate *Ariadne* came in under a press of sail to inform Admiral Barrington of the approach of the entire French fleet.

Count d'Estaing had no sooner anchored at Martinique on the 8th of December when he embarked four thousand fresh troops to sail with the favorable wind to Grenada and also to capture Dominica, but when, on the 14th, he sailed past St. Lucia and saw the British flag, he gave up his plan and decided to drive the British away. As soon as Admiral Barrington realized d'Estaing's design, he anchored his seven men-of-war across the Grand Cul de Sac, and behind them, his transports. Since the French ships had insufficient wind, their cannonade of the British ships fell short, and it would have been in vain to have answered with a single shot.

On the 15th Count d'Estaing came closer and did considerable damage to the rigging of the *Prince of Wales* [16] and the *Boyne,* killing several sailors. However, Admiral Barrington

16 The *Prince of Wales,* seventy-four guns, Barrington's flagship.

formed his warships and transports in an east-west line in navigable water, thus exposing them only to an attack from the north, which the French were wise enough not to undertake, for it would have exposed each of their ships to whole broadsides before they could have maneuvered into battle formation. The French ships stopped firing, sailed back, and anchored in the bay [17] to windward of the harbor of the Carénage, where they remained until General Løvendal [18] landed with four thousand men on the north side of the peninsula, beyond which, on the south, lies the harbor.[19]

The British Brigadier General Medows stood one English mile inland with thirteen hundred grenadiers and light infantry. His position allowed the enemy an approach barely wide enough for a front of thirty men. Although they attacked fiercely, they were compelled to withdraw quickly, as they also did on the following day, when their force was increased to seven thousand men. The British obtained several fieldpieces, which they fired on their front with unbelievable effect. Everything was quiet through the 24th.

On the 25th another five thousand men arrived from Guadeloupe, but the ensuing general attack was as fruitless as were the first two. Then Count d'Estaing, sighting Admiral Byron's ships, sailed off to Fort Royal in Martinique. The French governor had no longer any choice but to capitulate and recognize the British as masters of the island of St. Lucia. The highest French officers admit that they had 2,900 killed and that the hospitals on Martinique are filled with wounded. The English loss amounts to 150 killed and wounded. Among the killed are mentioned Captain Hay [20] of the grenadiers, and among the wounded, Brigadier General Medows, Major Harris,[21] and five officers.

---

[17] The Anse du Choc, which lies north of the Carénage.

[18] François Xavier Joseph Grève Danneskjold-Løvendal.

[19] Point Vigie, on which Løvendal landed his troops, separates the Anse du Choc and the Carénage (today's Port Custries), forming the north side of the latter's excellent harbor. The above is a rather free translation; literally, it says: ". . . of the peninsula, which extends from the harbor on the south."

[20] According to Grant's casualty list (Almon's *Remembrancer*, VII, 281–82, and *London Chronicle*, March 23–25, 1779), Captain Hay was wounded, not killed.

[21] Grant's list mentions Lieutenant Harris of the 5th Regiment. However, the only Harris in his regiment, according to the *Army Lists*, was Major George Harris.

On the 7th of this month a prize was brought in which had been taken while on her way from Dominica to Philadelphia. From this ship we learned not only that the island of St. Lucia is in possession of the English, but also that they are expecting a visit, for the two admirals, Barrington and Byron, have united and are keeping the French fleet blocked up in Martinique. Another prize coming from Cape François declared that forty laden merchantmen were waiting there to sail to Europe with a convoy, but that they lacked enough armed ships.

From Kingston, Jamaica, we received a report dated December 5th informing us that Brigadier General Campbell [22] had arrived there with eight transports, and that after a short rest he will continue on his expedition to Pensacola. His troops, consisting of sixteen hundred men, are the Regiment Prinz Waldeck, a battalion of Allen's Pennsylvanians, and a battalion of Chalmers' Maryland Loyalists. More with the next packet. I am also enclosing a copy of a letter which Ensign Gessner of Wissenbach's Battalion wrote me [missing].

With the greatest respect I have the honor to be [etc.]

[22] Brigadier General John Campbell.

: 34 :

I sent my last journal, together with all the Hessian letters, on the 14th of this month. A packet is ready to depart, but it does not carry any important news so far as we know.

From Philadelphia we have heard that Major General Lincoln, who had intended to oppose Colonel Archibald Campbell on the South Carolina border, has been beaten back, so the progress of the British continues. No particulars were related, nor has a report appeared from Colonel Campbell. Direct reports from Major General Grant on St. Lucia and information about the blockaded French fleet at Martinique are also lacking.

The prizes brought in from Cape François not only confirm what I have already written but also inform us that the merchantmen at Cape François are expecting a convoy any hour and that there is a great shortage of food at Martinique, on land as well as on water.

On the day before yesterday General Clinton landed in Jersey between Newark and Elizabethtown with twenty-five hundred English infantry. Brigadier General Maxwell immediately abandoned both these towns and withdrew with some other rebels and two cannon to a height in the vicinity of Woodbridge.[23] To be sure, some thirty rebels were taken prisoners, but only a few were wounded or killed. The English, on the other hand, had twelve men killed and one officer and twenty-eight men of the Guards wounded after the magazine and barracks in both towns had been set on fire. Secrecy and order were wanting in this attack. Moreover, the retreat in flatboats did not take place during the high tide. Since the large armed ships could not come close enough to fire artillery and so dampen the rebels' spirit, we had some men killed after they were already in the boats.

Admiral Gambier has been recalled to England and will leave toward the end of March; also the Marquis de Lafayette has left Boston with nine French officers to go to France. All the produce and cattle that can be spared in New England is being stored in Boston, the cattle being slaughtered and salted down. They[24] are expecting French and Spanish ships, but with what justification only time will tell.

General Washington has gone to his estates in Virginia,[25] but before leaving Philadelphia he detached Brigadier General Pulaski with two thousand men and six hundred dragoons to South Carolina. Two members of Congress have received severe prison terms for counterfeiting two millions in paper money and putting it into circulation in Virginia and Maryland. Fourteen of their friends were associated with them.[26]

Major General Arnold, who has served the rebels so well, was not able to escape his enemies. He has been suspended and must submit to a thorough inquiry. The Hessian regiments on this island have again been mustered. A mere description cannot suffice to tell your Lordship of the fit condition of the regiments and

[23] For an account of the descent on Elizabethtown see Frank Moore's *Diary of the American Revolution,* New York, 1863, II, 135, quoting the *New-Jersey Gazette,* March 3, 1779.

[24] I.e., the Bostonians.

[25] Another rumor. Washington did not see Mount Vernon until on his way to Yorktown in 1781.

[26] No intimation of this is to be found in the journals and papers of the Continental Congress, the *Maryland Archives,* or the *Calendar of Virginia State Papers.* The *Royal Gazette,* Feb. 17, 1779, prints a fabricated story about Colonel John Bannister and fourteen accomplices being arrested for counterfeiting.

grenadier battalions and of the good appearance that every soldier makes. Moreover, only a few are sick at present.

Lieutenant Montluisant [27] was so bold as to undertake a journey to Philadephia contrary to orders, although he had free passage to England, the best recommendations from General Clinton's headquarters, and a draft for thirty guineas which Captain von Wreden had advanced him. He was stopped by the last outpost beyond Kings Bridge, but refused to be sent back. Aiming at a noncommissioned officer of the Regiment von Bose,[28] he pulled the trigger of his pistol, which fortunately did not go off. He was arrested in not too polite a manner and was turned over to the grand provost in the new English prison, where he is to remain until a new convoy with transports sails for England.

I shall not enclose a copy of the impudent apologia of the two deserted officers Führer and Kleinschmidt. Its whole content is false and loathsome.

A journal of the two partisans, Brant and Butler, is enclosed herewith [missing]. I am not yet proficient enough to send a translation of it, and I dare not give it to anyone here. Winter took these two capable men to the westernmost part of Pennsylvania, where they are enjoying a rest. However, they will soon advance again with all the more determination.

I also enclose an American Register-Calendar [missing] and have the honor to remain with the greatest respect [etc.]

[27] Lieutenant de Montluisant, a Frenchman serving in the Hessian Jäger Corps, obtained his discharge after hostilities had begun between England and France and attempted to join the Americans. He was caught and sent to England, whence he evidently made his way to France. In May, 1781, he was back in America and applied to Congress for employment in the army, but was refused. See *Journals of the Continental Congress, sub* May 8, 1781; Montluisant's memorial to Congress, Papers of the Continental Congress, No. 78, XVI, folio 187; and Eelking-Rosengarten, p. 266. The documents cited give only his last name.

[28] Von Bose's Regiment was formerly the Regiment von Trümbach.

: 35 :

NEW YORK
APRIL 4, 1779

We have received no news from Hesse since November of last year and sincerely hope that our letters get there more regularly and more quickly. I had the honor to send my last on the 27th of February this year. Admiral Gambier, having been relieved by Commodore Sir George Collier, is ready to depart. The ship on which he sails will also carry letters to Europe.

I obediently hasten to inform your Excellency that General Grant, after a decisive action in which the French had heavy losses, became master of St. Lucia and that the united forces of Admirals Barrington and Byron have completely blockaded Admiral d'Estaing's fleet at Martinique. Many enemy ships attempted to break through, but were immediately captured by the British. The two admirals sent six of their best ships of the line to sea to engage any approaching enemy ships. The English are again in possession of the Island of Dominica. Eight ships of the line which escorted a provision fleet from England recently joined the force of the two admirals. Twenty-nine sail of this provision fleet arrived in New York harbor on the 26th of March under convoy of the *Romulus*, which brought 200,1000 [*sic*] guineas for the war chest.

These ships, which had set sail on the 2nd of January, brought the news that in May at the latest considerable reinforcements would arrive. General Clinton ordered six wing companies of the Halifax garrison to come to New York. One of their ships foundered off Egg Harbor, and of the one hundred and seventy men on board, only twenty-one were rescued.

On the 24th of March we received the news that on the 4th of the same month an action had taken place on the Savannah River,[29] and three days later we read a report of it in the newspapers. On the 31st of March the reports of this fortunate event were confirmed by the arrival of Grenadier Captain Sir James Baird, who had been sent by Colonel Prevost from Savannah thirteen days previously. I enclose a copy of a newspaper [*missing*], which furnishes a more detailed account than I can give here.

It is important to know that the rebels have brought together some three thousand dispirited men with the greatest difficulty and that those who have disbanded and are now unarmed in North and South Carolina have brought back much horror and antipathy toward further war.

Colonel Prevost, who finds it highly necessary to make use of and follow up Colonel Campbell's advantageous activities in Georgia, encamped on his side of the Savannah River after this action and is forming new battalions of the many loyalists coming in. They will be officered by men sent from here. Moreover, Lieutenant Colonel Campbell has formed eight troops of dragoons, of which General Clinton himself is the chief.[30] Whether reinforcements will be sent to Georgia now or in the fall is not yet known.

Sir James Baird does not doubt that the Carolinians will submit to British sovereignty rather than wait for the ruin which has befallen Virginia, Maryland, and Pennsylvania, where the paper money, now virtually of no value at all, is carried about in im-

---

[29] American accounts date the action at Brier Creek March 3. The *Savannah Royal Georgia Gazette*, March 11, 1779, agrees with Baurmeister and may have been one of his sources.

[30] Cf. Germain to Clinton, Dec. 12, 1778, PRO, Am. and W. I., 134, folio 385 (photostats in Library of Congress): "H. M. has been pleased to appoint you Col. in Chief of the Regt. of Loyal Highland Emigrants in room of General Gage, which is put on the Establishment in addition to the Regiment you are already colonel of."

poverished hands, and nothing is to be had for it. The seven pieces of artillery which were taken from the enemy are French 4-pounders. Sir James Baird tells us that the enemy fell back when his light infantry and one battalion of the 71st Regiment rushed them after having fired but one round, that General Elbert,[31] whom he captured, was incensed at the bayoneting of some forty of his officers, and that it was not known whether General Ashe [32] really drowned, although nothing has been heard of him since the action.

I have since had a letter from Major Seelig dated March 6th at Ebenezer, whither two Hessian regiments marched on the 27th of January after leaving three captains, six subalterns, and two hundred men in Savannah. On their passage from New York they had lost the horse transport, which drifted without masts until the 6th of January, when it was captured by a privateer, which threw the horses overboard and disembarked the hostlers on Eily Island, the western point of Florida.[33] Left to their fate, these people roamed about in despair for two days until they found some huts where several families from Norway had recently settled. These kindly people took care of them until they were picked up by a ship destined for Providence.[34] Disembarked at St. Augustine, they finally reached Savannah on the 21st of February.

The expeditions of February 25 and 27 to Elizabethtown in Jersey and to Horse Neck by way of Kings Bridge were unsuccessful. It is a pity that a total of sixty-six men were lost by them. General Clinton can undertake nothing without the cooperation of the fleet. Even the most secret plans have not been kept secret, and this chief has never been on good terms with Admiral Gambier.

[31] Brigadier General Samuel Elbert of the Georgia militia.

[32] Brigadier General John Ashe, North Carolina state troops. After the action at Brier Creek, Ashe escaped through a swamp to Mathew's Bluff. Cf. Brigadier William Moultrie's *Memoirs of the American Revolution*, New York, 1802, I, 323, and particularly the proceedings of the court of inquiry subsequently held to investigate Ashe's conduct, I, 337–53.

[33] Baurmeister must mean Amelia Island, the northeastern point of Florida. Cf. *Boston Gazette*, March 1, 1779, for an account of the capture of the *Sally*, which with nineteen artillery horses on board was bound from New York for Tybee, Georgia, her cargo and men being landed at Beaufort, South Carolina.

[34] New Providence (now Nassau, Bahamas).

The excursion of Captain Willett [35] of De Lancey's Corps from Long Island to Connecticut and his attack on Kebble's five mills at Compo, which he undertook on the 25th of March, were much more successful. A force of no more than twenty-five men was able to burn these mills filled with flour and grain, sink a schooner and five boats, and return with nine prisoners. The flour had been destined for New London, to be loaded on vessels lying ready and to be sent to the French fleet.

In that harbor lie three frigates and some fifty ships, so that single ships cannot pass through the Hell Gate sound. This induced General Clinton to make a landing on the shore of that harbor, as he secretly informed us. He expected to use the troops on Long Island and command them in person. The rebels are gathering six thousand men under General Pattison [36] and doing everything to make a good stand. They have to conceal themselves in miserable huts, for New London is weak.

However, after the fifty-two flatboats and sixteen horse transports which were to land there had suffered for two weeks in the most uncomfortable weather, they returned through the Sound. General Clinton also is leaving Long Island. The intended expedition caused the rebels much trouble and damage.

Two hundred Brunswickers and seventy-eight English of Burgoyne's men recently deserted in Virginia. This brought forth a Congressional resolution investing General Washington with full powers to negotiate with General Clinton for the exchange of these troops, too, which will probably be done very soon.

A British general pardon in favor of deserters has brought very good results. His Excellency General von Knyphausen followed this example and likewise issued a general pardon in printed form, especially since many had previously indicated their repentance and asked from afar remission of their well-deserved punishment.

Captain von Diemar is organizing a troop of hussars of the Brunswick prisoners who took service and then deserted to our

[35] Gilbert Colden Willett of Bucks County, Pennsylvania, 3rd Battalion of De Lancey's Brigade. For an account of this raid see the *Royal Gazette*, Feb. 24, 1779, or the *London Chronicle*, April 10–13.

[36] Baurmeister was misinformed; it was General Israel Putnam. See also below.

lines. This Captain von Diemar was an ensign in von Sydow's Regiment of Hanoverians, in which service his father had been a colonel. He came here as a titular lieutenant in the 60th North American Regiment with a letter of recommendation from his Serene Highness Prince Ferdinand of Brunswick to General Clinton, who received this gracious confidence so well that he gave him a company.

Lieutenant Colonel Simcoe, commander of the Queen's Rangers, is also organizing two companies of hussars. The Legion dragoons [37] under Lord Cathcart have been increased to 350 horse. Lord Rawdon's Irish Volunteers have been raised to full strength, six hundred men, and are one of the finest corps ever seen here. Many refugees have been coming over of late. Between the 8th of September and the middle of last month, 121 privateers have run out of this harbor. They are completely manned and are bringing in many prizes.

I take the liberty to enclose some newspaper clippings, for they give faithful accounts and are worth reading. Among them is a letter to Miss Franks of Philadelphia, the satirical style of which shows the wicked malice of this man.[38] General Arnold has sent his resignation to Congress. With the next packet I hope to be able to report in detail what the provinces have voted in their General Assemblies, also whether General Governor Haldimand is active in Quebec, and what the two partisans, Butler and Brant, are doing.

Brigadier General Maxwell's whole Jersey militia brigade has disbanded. An alarm post only is stationed in Elizabethtown, and the last outpost is at Woodbridge on the Hackensack. There is no longer one in Bergen. Moreover, they do not pursue their deserters to within rifle range of Powles Hook, and they permit

[37] The British Legion, later the 4th American Regiment. It was originally a company of volunteer cavalry which Lord Cathcart had added to the Caledonian Volunteers, a provincial corps he had organized in 1778. Lord Cathcart was both a captain in the 17th Regiment of Dragoons and Colonel of the British Legion, which was later commanded by Colonel Banastre Tarleton. See *Army Lists, Simcoe's Military Journal* (1844 ed., p. 79), and *Dictionary of National Biography*.

[38] General Charles Lee, who was in correspondence with Rebecca Franks of Philadelphia. The clippings are missing.

food to be brought over from Jersey. Droves of cattle are still arriving by way of Kings Bridge.

There is no arable place in all Long Island that has not been sown. Gardens are being laid out around the huts in which the regiments were quartered during the winter, so that the whole resembles a good-sized village. During the entire month of March we had very cold weather and snow or hailstorms every day. In spite of this bad weather, the troops are all well. Anything can be endured except the extremely high prices. I do not care to go into this since it would not be proper. But how the officers can endure it is a greater wonder than the prices themselves.

On the day before yesterday eleven victualers came in from Cork, and on the same day the frigate *Camilla* brought in nine prizes taken in the Bermudas and sent here under her convoy. From this frigate we learned that part of the garrison of Anguilla have landed on the Island of St. Martin and taken possession of it and that the same will be done on St. Bartholomew, that there are but few provisions on Martinique, and that the stores for the fleet and the twelve thousand land troops would not last until the middle of this month. Sixty-two New York privateers are now blockading Chesapeake Bay, and thirty-two the mouth of the Delaware.

On the 25th of last month Major Graff relieved Colonel Köhler, who is already on his way to Savannah. Lieutenant Colonel von Kitzel,[39] who is to go to Halifax, where Colonel von Seitz [40] is very ill, has not arrived yet. The last reports from Halifax were sent by Major von Schaller.[41] Everything is quiet on Rhode Island.

A ship with 190 men of Burgoyne's army who have been ill in Boston arrived here on the 3rd of March. No one would have recognized the Brunswick officers wearing grey cloth jackets and trousers instead of their uniforms. They all agreed that conditions in Boston are quite deplorable and complained most of being

---

[39] Carl von Kitzel, listed in the *Staats-Calender* as lieutenant colonel and commander of the von Seitz Regiment. Stryker lists a Lieutenant Colonel von Kietzell as having been present at the court of inquiry following the Trenton surprise.

[40] Colonel Franz Carl von Seitz, chief of the former von Stein Regiment.

[41] Major Ludwig von Schaller of the von Seitz Regiment.

treated in an unfriendly and suspicious manner. After a rest of one week the officers, but not the privates, were compelled to embark again to be taken to Elizabethtown and delivered to the rebel commissary.

Unfortunately, this Boston ship confirmed the report that on the 9th of October last year fourteen British ships were wrecked near Pensacola during a violent gale, without a single person being rescued. Not until the 6th of January this year did Brigadier General Campbell, with two provincial battalions [42] and the Waldeck Battalion,[43] sail from Port Royal for Pensacola.

Commending myself with the deepest respect, I have the honor to be [etc.]

[42] Allen's Pennsylvanians and Chalmers' Maryland Loyalists. See letter dated Feb. 14, 1779 (No. 33).

[43] Formerly referred to as Waldeck Regiment; it was probably battalion strength.

: 36 :

On the 24th of last month a packet finally arrived from England with Hessian mail. I also had the honor of receiving from your Lordship a gracious communication dated the 20th of November, from which I see that all my narratives up to the 21st of September have been received. I hope that the rest, up to April 4th, will likewise arrive. Admiral Gambier, who left on the 7th of April, took with him the last letters for Hesse. From that time to the day I conclude this, the following has taken place:

Inasmuch as the rebels in Jersey, except some outposts at Elizabethtown, Perth Amboy, and Bergen Neck, are all on the far side of the Raritan, the 64th Regiment, stationed at Powles Hook, has been sending patrols toward the last-named post and recently surrounded the rebels there, returning with one officer and sixteen men taken prisoners.

Between the 10th and 12th of April General Putnam assembled a thousand militia at White Plains. He occupied the roads to Kings Bridge and maintained a large post at Mamaroneck to cover the road to Boston, over which flour and all kinds of other

---

44 Date established from following letter.

provisions were being transported from the southern provinces to the said city, which is suffering from great want.

A cartel ship arrived here from Boston and delivered twenty-one sailors. The master of this ship, who was allowed ashore five hours, gave us terrible descriptions of the general misery in New England. Four artillery companies, lately given French officers, were unwilling to be separated from the rest, and when General Gates had two officers arrested, they refused obedience. The merchants of Boston and Baltimore have given up insurance and called in the rest of their ships. Chesapeake Bay and the Delaware are blockaded, although the latter cannot be completely blocked.

Forty-nine prizes were brought in here between the 8th of April and the 1st of this month, sixteen into the Bermudas up to the 25th of April, according to the report of Captain Orde [45] of the frigate *Virginia*, and eleven to Rhode Island, as well as five more brought into New York by the refugees. The sale of the cargoes of the last increased their treasury by £22,000 sterling. They are refitting the captured ships for their own use.

While stationed near the Bermudas, Captain Orde captured a French ship with a valuable cargo, but two privateers running out of this harbor captured an even more richly laden ship of twenty-two guns called *L'Empereur*, whose cargo is worth £42,000 sterling. The amount of merchandise, the number of rich warehouses, the uninterrupted trade, and the coming and going of the ships cannot be described vividly enough.

The merchants have formed a society to fit out armed ships at their mutual cost for the protection of trade. They are to cover their ships regardless of insurance and to escort the privateers a certain distance, both leaving and returning.

On the 4th of March this year the French frigate *Iphigénie* captured a twenty-eight-gun ship coming from Liverpool, and on the 5th, one of sixteen guns, called the *Renown*, coming from Bristol. An officer and twenty men boarded this prize, which was ordered to proceed to Cape François as soon as the sails and rigging damaged during the attack were repaired. On the night of

[45] Later Admiral Sir John Orde.

the 5th–6th several English mates and thirty sailors who had been in hiding seized the officer and the arms of the French force, which nevertheless put up a desperate fight until the lieutenant and eleven men were killed. The English had thirteen killed and wounded. On the 7th of March the *Renown* came to anchor at Antigua, everyone happy to be at liberty.

Ships from St. Kitts report that on the 20th of February Count de Grasse with four ships of the line and a recruit transport carrying about a thousand men joined Count d'Estaing's fleet at Martinique. On the other hand, the British Commodore Rowley [46] arrived with seven men-of-war to reinforce Admirals Byron and Barrington.[47] Before the arrival of these ships, the combined force of the said admirals consisted of twenty-one capital ships, three of fifty guns, eight frigates, three of twenty guns, nine sloops of war, and five fireships. Provisions at Martinique would have been very scarce if the Dutch of St. Eustatius had not been considerate enough (for cold cash to be sure) to furnish Martinique with food.

On the 13th of April this year some ships coming from Bermuda brought letters to New York which report that it has been learned from St. Kitts that the French fleet, attempting to run the blockade of Fort Royal, has been completely defeated, and the remainder pursued to Guadeloupe. The letters, which were written March 29th and 30th, do not state when this action took place or give any of the details, but they do mention that there was an illumination at St. Kitts.

Neither has one of the two admirals nor General Grant written from the West Indies. Although the latter is not under direct orders from here, promotions in Grant's corps are reserved to General Clinton. Both generals have been instructed from London to inform each other promptly of all events. General Clinton, who has strictly observed these orders, is sending complaints about this delay to the War Office with this packet. It is very likely that, except for a small detachment, General Grant has already left St. Lucia, for he may be needed in other quarters, and the island is

---

[46] Rear Admiral Joshua Rowley.
[47] Rear Admiral Barrington was superseded by Admiral Byron as commander in chief in the West Indies in January, 1779.

supposedly well covered by the warships. He is probably leaving behind a large hospital, for there has been much sickness among his troops, twenty-one officers having already succumbed.

From Georgia we received a report dated March 25th from which we learned that seven hundred savages of the Creek and Cherokee tribes have joined General Prevost's force, that he built a bridge across Brier Creek, and that he is encamped there with two thousand men. This general's force is increased every day by men coming in. Georgia is greatly satisfied with the new government.

In order to strengthen the few Continental troops on the Carolina border, General Lincoln is gathering the militia, who, however, do not stay with him, but come and go. This general wrote to Charleston that if the provinces would send him sufficient troops, he would show General Prevost another Burgoynade, and that it was laughable that after vainly teasing the head of the American snake, the British lion should now begin to play with its tail.

On the 16th of March some British armed ships were attacked by two galleys, but both galleys were captured by Captain O'Farrell, who had fitted out a ship at his own expense and has his establishment in St. Augustine. One of the galleys was manned by 150 Frenchmen, who were serving under the command of a certain Flaire [48] from Guadeloupe.

Since the 19th of March Joseph Brant has been active again. After roaming about in the Wyoming district, he made an incursion into Sussex County in Jersey, where he burned the stores and threatened to massacre the inhabitants indiscriminately as far as the Muskankung and devastate everything if they did not immediately submit. Last year he left this country in peace, for the leaders of the inhabitants had promised to pay tribute and remain faithful to the government. This year, however, he finds this district to be of an entirely different opinion.[49] Nothing definite can

[48] Not identified.

[49] Cf. *New-York Gazette*, April 12, 1779, reprinted in *New Jersey Archives*, 2nd Series, vol. III: "Col. Joseph Brant had sent a flag into Sussex County, in New Jersey, to inform the inhabitants of his having been apprized that many of them who last year pretended Friendship and Attachment to the Cause for which he

be reported of Colonel Butler's movements. Of five men sent to these two partisans, two were seized on the way and hanged. This is the end of all those on whom the least suspicion rests. About twelve days ago three men met the same fate in Hackensack.

Colonel Hyde and Captain André of the Guards [50] were sent to Perth Amboy to negotiate with the rebel commissioners about the proposed exchange of prisoners. This took nine days, and all of them were wasted. They demanded fifteen hundred men for General Burgoyne and as many more because he was chief of the captive troops, fifteen hundred for General Riedesel, and for some lieutenant colonels who had served as brigadiers, such as Phillips, Hamilton, von Specht, and von Gall, as many as for a major general.[51] It seems very likely that they sought something else under this excuse, for it is difficult to conceive why they should be willing one day and unwilling a few days later. It is interesting to note that the American commissioners based their claims on Dutch regulations for the exchange of prisoners.

Immediately after his return, Colonel Hyde embarked with 650 men on the 26th of April and landed at Shoal Harbor in Jersey, east of Middletown. Detaching Captain Ferguson to Shrewsbury, Colonel Hyde advanced with the rest on Middletown. The garrisons of both towns fled, with and without guns, for which reason only twenty-five were taken prisoners. After burning two magazines and destroying all the baggage and arms they found, our troops returned on the 28th of this month.[52] Colonel Hyde will depart for London with this packet.

Since the 28th of April the following troops have embarked under the command of General Mathew of the Guards: the four flank companies of the Guards under Colonel Watson, the 42nd

---

was carrying on Hostilities had since taken up Arms; he now gave them Notice, that no longer any Regard for Professions of that kind would be attended to, for that every Man who did not join him upon his Approach to their Country, should be deemed and treated by him as an Enemy, and that he should soon lay the country waste as low as the Muskankunk."

[50] André served with the 26th and subsequently with the 56th Regiment; neither was a Guard regiment.

[51] The reports of Hyde and André on these negotiations are printed in Almon's *Remembrancer*, VIII, 286.

[52] Read: "28th of last month," i.e., April, for the journal extends to May 3.

Regiment, Lord Rawdon's Irish Volunteers, the Hessian Regiment
Prinz Carl, and a train of light artillery of six pieces. They took
with them thirty days' provisions. It is supposed that they are to
go to Egg Harbor, for the rebels have sixteen strong new privateers and a frigate there, and four weeks ago unfortunately captured six three- and two-masted ships on their way to Georgia and
took them into Boston. Among them was a royal provision ship
carrying Colonel Köhler, Lieutenant Studenroth, and Ensign
Pauli, who were on their way to join von Trümbach's Regiment.
The local insurance company has to stand the loss of £80,000
sterling, for these ships were loaded only with English goods and
wines. If only a single frigate had been sent along as convoy,
everything would have been saved. As it is, only two ships
escaped. Whether they have already cast anchor in Georgia is not
yet known. Admiral Gambier will have to answer for this as well.

The following troops have received orders for another expedition: the Hessian Regiment Erb Prinz, Graff's Grenadier
Battalion,[53] the 7th, 23rd, and 63rd British Regiments [54]

[53] Graff's Grenadier Battalion was formerly Köhler's.
[54] Letter incomplete.

: 37 :

After we had finished our last letters on the 3rd of this month, the packet, which had been ready to sail, departed for England two days later. The ships on which General Mathew and his troops had embarked have also set sail and were accompanied by Sir George Collier himself. During the night prior to their departure, 280 sailors were impressed from the transports riding at anchor. This has given rise to the general assumption that this expedition is headed for Williamsburg to capture two frigates in the James River (each of which is provided with thirty-two guns but not yet manned), to burn another of the same strength lying in dock by the city as well as the entire store of ship's timber, and to seize the large magazines in Virginia on the other rivers emptying into Chesapeake Bay. However, nothing can be said with certainty. Perhaps it will be known before the departure of the next packet, which is already here ready to sail, so that I can report in detail on the success of the expedition.

Several regiments are still under orders to march. On the 12th of this month General Erskine marched back from Hempstead, on the eastern end of Long Island, to Jamaica, where the 17th

Regiment of Dragoons, Lord Cathcart's mounted Legion, and
one battalion of light infantry are encamped at the places where
they first went into winter quarters. The Regiments von Lossberg
and Knyphausen left their huts the same day and moved into
camp before New York, while Major General von Kospoth and the
two Grenadier Battalions Linsing and Lengerke moved out of
New York to occupy the huts of the said regiments.[55] Much work
is being done on the new fortifications on Laurel Hill, this side of
Kings Bridge, the daily working parties consisting of three hundred men, two thirds of whom are Hessians. Half a shilling sterling and additional rum are paid each man for each working day.
His Excellency General von Knyphausen reviewed the drill of all
the regiments on this island on the 5th, 6th, and 7th of this month.
Everyone found the skill in drill, without exception, to be praise-
worthy, likewise the condition of their accouterments, both large
and small. The field requisites have been carefully completed and
are recognized as being well suited for a campaign. Moreover, we
are very fortunate to have few or no sick in the regiments.

Our field artillery as well as the English have been furnished
with powder and balls, so that they can have target practice in
addition to the customary shooting exercises. General Pattison [56]
paid Captain Krug a well-deserved compliment when he told his
officers that he wished they could fire as well. General Clinton
gave the Regiment von Knyphausen a Hessian fieldpiece, which
had been taken at Brandywine with another brass cannon of almost the same caliber, and also an ammunition wagon.

On the 6th of this month Lieutenant von Clüer [57] shot himself in this city. He was in von Lossberg's Grenadier Company
and was esteemed by Colonel von Minnigerode as an experienced
officer who generally deported himself fairly well and had made
many friends. But in spite of these virtues, he had acquired the
reputation of managing his affairs poorly. Finally, he was put

---

[55] This order was rescinded. See postscript to this letter.

[56] Major General James Pattison of the Artillery, Commandant at New York.

[57] Colonel Johann August von Loos, in a letter dated five days after this inci-
dent, calls the lieutenant Gluer, as does also Eelking-Rosengarten, p. 308. The
Staats-Calender lists a Second Lieutenant Ludwig von Gluer in the von Lossberg
Regiment.

under regimental arrest with ordinary provisions and one shilling sterling per day. This must have distressed him and become intolerable. It is a pity that he knew no way out except taking his life. His death is much lamented.

Letters from Georgia of April 17th report that General Howe,[58] who was first encountered at Savannah, made an excursion through North Carolina and brought together at Georgetown [59] five hundred fresh troops with whom he expects to join General Lincoln, that General St. Clair [60] with twelve hundred Virginians had already proceeded as far as Halifax in North Carolina with the same intention, but that after General Ashe's unsuccessful attack [61] and rout became known, the two corps disbanded. General Clinton has received repeated confirmation of the news that the merchants in Charleston are packing their possessions and are ready to flee. The inhabitants of Boston and its environs were very pleasantly surprised to have brought in to them seven richly laden ships that were badly needed in Georgia. It became further known through Colonel Köhler and the officers with him that on one of these ships Lieutenant Colonel Campbell had complete equipage and uniforms for six troops of dragoons. However, it is hard to believe that a sum of piasters equivalent to £ 40,000 was also lost.

General Washington sent a proclamation to all the provinces asking them to arm the inhabitants. Connecticut was assigned a quota of fifteen hundred men, thirty-two wagons and teams, and fifty-six horses. Brigadier General Silliman and his son,[62] a major, were commissioned to collect the quota in Fairfield, but they were captured and brought in without difficulty by six refugees who were taken over from Long Island to Connecticut. These refugees are bold enough to accomplish anything. Last Sunday a troop of

[58] Major General Robert Howe of the Continental Army.

[59] I.e., Georgetown, South Carolina.

[60] St. Clair seems to have been in New Jersey, March 23 to May 31, 1779.

[61] Ashe did not attack; he was attacked (March 3, 1779, at Brier Creek), and the result was a disastrous rout.

[62] Brigadier General Gold Selleck Silliman, Connecticut militia, and his son, William Silliman, Brigade Major. The Sillimans were exchanged in 1780. See *Records of the State of Connecticut*, II, 466.

twenty-one landed in Jersey and invaded Closter.[63] They shot and killed five militia and returned with ten prisoners. On their way back they lost their commanding officer, who, though dead, was stripped and hanged in Closter. It must be remarked that the rebels have posted printed notices that no deserter can expect pardon.

The negotiations at the last unsuccessful meeting of the commissioners for the exchange of prisoners have appeared in print. I enclose a newspaper containing them [missing]. Congress now wants the greater part of the 352 rebel officers at Flatbush to be released and will not recognize the additional prisoners in Georgia, which is a sure sign that we shall keep our prisoners as long as possible and shall not mind the lamentations of their miserable officers, many of whom are taking up their old trades again, such as tailoring and cobbling, for their fellow prisoners.

On the 17th of April a French packet ran into Boston harbor, making the passage from Brest in thirty-nine days. This ship had specific orders to go to that harbor, and from there the dispatches for Mr. Gérard were taken to Philadelphia by land. Though their contents may have been important, they certainly were not pleasant. Mr. Gérard did not, as he had always done, deliver his report to Congress in open session, but had some private conferences with some of the members, after which he went to see General Washington in Morristown, where in his honor nearly four thousand men quartered in that vicinity paraded in uniforms made in France.

General Erskine is settling his accounts in the Quartermaster General's office and will set out for London by the end of this month at the latest. The army will miss in him an experienced and very well-liked man, but he followed the sincere advice of his warmest friends, who urged him to retire from this important position which demanded his constant attention all day and always made him late for supper. Major Drummond of the Artillery, General Clinton's first aide-de-camp, will succeed him.

[63] For an account of this raid see *New Jersey Archives*, 2nd Series, III, 359. The refugees were commanded by Lieutenant Colonel Van Buskirk, of Skinner's Brigade.

General Vaughan will command the second expedition. The ships are ready, and after impressing many sailors day before yesterday, there are two hundred more on them than are needed.

Late yesterday more English provision ships and merchant-men came in, as well as thirteen prizes. Among them was a ship from Georgia which brought the pleasant news reported in the accompanying supplement [*missing*]. The Cork fleet will return toward the 22nd of this month. I hope that in the meantime I shall be able to report further confirmation of this and other news.

I have the honor to be with the greatest respect and venera-tion [*etc.*]

p.s. Because rainy weather began this morning, orders were issued that until further notice, the Regiments von Knyphausen and von Lossberg should remain in their huts and the Hessian Grenadiers in New York.

: 38 :

On the 3rd and 14th of May I had the honor to send two more parts of my journal. With this next packet, which is ready to sail, I shall report on the events from the 17th to date, which, as far as they are known, are as follows:

General Leslie remained alone on Staten Island with the 26th and 37th Regiments, Lieutenant Colonel Graff's Grenadier Battalion, and half of Skinner's Battalion; [64] half of Skinner's Battalion was stationed at Powles Hook and Hoboken; [65] one battalion of De Lancey's, [66] 360 Refugees, [67] 150 Long Island Dragoons, and 250 Hessians of the Erb Prinz Regiment under Major von Fuchs [68] were left on the last-named island [69] as a garrison; and the Erb Prinz, von Lossberg's, and von Knyphausen's Regi-

[64] Should read: "Brigade."
[65] Abraham Van Buskirk's Battalion (the 3rd of Skinner's Brigade) was stationed at Hoboken.
[66] I.e., Oliver De Lancey's Brigade of New York Volunteers.
[67] James De Lancey's Refugees.
[68] Matthias von Fuchs. In the Hessian Muster Rolls (William L. Clements Library), he signs himself Matthew von Fuchs.
[69] I.e., Long Island.

278

ments and the English Guards have been encamped before New York under orders of Colonel von Hachenberg since the 17th of May to do the necessary garrison duty. Generals Tryon and Mathew also remained in the city. The latter will become temporary commandant as soon as General Jones sails. He is ready to depart, along with Generals Stirn and Schmidt.

Since the 25th of May the Hessian General Staff has been quartered again in Morris's house. By the 28th of May the following troops under Generals Erskine, Vaughan, Pattison, and von Kospoth had been assembled at Philipsburgh and beyond Valentine's Hill: the 17th Regiment of Dragoons, Lord Cathcart's Legion, Colonel Simcoe's Queen's Rangers, Emmerich's Corps, Robinson's,[70] Ferguson's, and the Anspach and Hessian Jäger Corps, 2,200 British light infantry and grenadiers, the Hessian grenadier brigade and von Bose's Regiment, then the 7th, 17th, 23rd, 33rd, 63rd, and 64th Regiments of British infantry. There was also an artillery train of eight light 12-pounders and four 24-pounders with two companies of English Artillery and Colonel Morris's corps.[71] Lieutenant Colonels Simcoe, Abercromby, and Webster served as brigadiers.

On the 29th General Mathew returned to New York harbor from the Virginia expedition. Only the commander landed; the rest remained aboard ship and sailed as far as Philipse's house on the 30th of May. Taking advantage of an excellent wind, General Clinton also sailed to the said house and turned the command on this and the other two islands over to his Excellency General von Knyphausen. General von Bose, who commands under him on York Island, has detached the Leib Regiment, von Donop's, and von Mirbach's by companies to the banks of the North and East rivers, and Colonel Donkin with the 44th and 57th Regiments to a similar position beyond Fort Knyphausen.

[70] From the sources consulted it could not be definitely established whether this is Beverly Robinson's Guides and Pioneers or his Loyal American Regiment, both provincial corps. However, from the next reference to this corps (see following letter), it can be determined that it was his Loyal American Regiment. Cf. Otto Hufeland, *Westchester County during the American Revolution* (White Plains, N. Y., 1926), which quotes Pattison's letter of June 9, 1779.

[71] Colonel John Morris's corps was made up of New Jersey volunteers and constituted one of Skinner's battalions.

It was generally assumed that General Clinton would encamp this side of the Bronx between Philipse's house and Mile Square and wait for the reinforcements which were certain to arrive, but in the night of the 30th–31st of May, instead of permitting the troops of the Virginia expedition to disembark, most of the infantry went on board ship and sailed to within eight English miles from Verplanck's Point. He brought about the capitulation of Fort Lafayette [72] on the 1st of June, this current month. He let General Vaughan take post there with all the grenadiers and light infantry, the 33rd Regiment, Ferguson's Corps, the Legion, and two hundred Hessian jägers under Major von Prueschenck.[73]

On the other hand, General Pattison took position at Stony Point, on the west shore of the North River, with one hundred Hessian jägers under Captain Lorey, the 17th, 63rd, and 64th Regiments and sixty British Artillerymen with six light 12-pounders. Stony Point is not more than twelve hundred yards from Fort Lafayette, measuring from shore to shore, so that now King's Ferry is in our possession. Hence, in spite of their fortified West Point and Forts Clinton, Defiance, and Putnam, the rebels must take a circuitous route of one hundred English miles if they wish to maintain their communications.

On the 5th of June General Clinton returned with the troops no longer needed to occupy the posts to Philipse's house and established his headquarters there. General Erskine had remained behind here on the 31st of May with all the cavalry, the rest of the Hessian Jägers, Colonel Simcoe's and Emmerich's Corps, and the 7th, 23rd, and von Bose's Regiments under orders to advance between Dobbs Ferry and Tarrytown in order to surround White Plains. This was done without meeting anyone except some inhabitants of East Chester and Westchester who had been driven away and were taking a thousand head of cattle and sheep and some eighty farm horses to the Croton River, where they would be safe from us. However, the 17th Regiment of Dragoons and the mounted Hessian jägers chased the drivers away and made prisoners of fourteen armed inhabitants. The cattle and sheep

[72] At Verplanck's Point.
[73] Ernst Carl von Prueschenck of the Jäger Corps.

were brought in and put out to various pastures on this island, so that we now can provide fresh meat for the expected reinforcements and the hospitals, although there are at present no more than 160 sick in New York, counting all nationalities.

General Clinton had his troops encamp in a line as follows: between Philipse's house [74] and Sawmill Creek, the 42nd Regiment, Lord Rawdon's Volunteers of Ireland, and the Queen's Rangers, with the Hessian jägers in front; on the right as far as Valentine's Hill, the 7th and 23rd Regiments; this side of Mile Square, the four wing companies of the British Guards, who have taken such a position that the flank of the right wing of their camp is covered in respect to the Rochelle and Mamaroneck [road?] [75] and who have, moreover, Emmerich's Corps in front. All the cavalry goes to pasture at Van Cortlandt's Ridge.[76]

The rebels in Connecticut have brought together no more than one thousand men. New London and Providence are only weakly manned, and Boston is said to have a garrison of only five hundred men. In this last city, as well as in Providence, Fishkill, and Albany, are their magazines. They have their largest magazine, however, at Upper Cohos [77] near Lake Champlain, for like the French, they are ever of the flattering opinion that General Clinton will be compelled to leave New York and have the garrison sail, part to Quebec and part to Halifax, where they think they can finally crush Great Britain's last strength within this year. They have been untiring with their work on Lake Champlain, have appeased the often disillusioned inhabitants of all the provinces, and have convinced themselves in Congress of the certainty of the best termination of this war.

It is likely, however, that this vexatious war will terminate by making America probably the most desolate country in the world and proving very expensive for England, too. Colonel Peters,[78] the commander of the refugees assembled above Albany, with

[74] Probably the Philipse house near Kings Bridge. Philipse manor house was at the mouth of the Sawmill.
[75] MS torn.
[76] The ridge in present Van Cortlandt Park.
[77] Now Coos, New Hampshire.
[78] Lieutenant Colonel John Peters of the Queen's Loyal Rangers.

the help of the Indians burned the American magazines at the end of March and cut the roads. The American allies in the West Indies have lost St. Lucia and are blockaded in the harbor of Martinique. They themselves have lost Georgia, and this province, by a public resolution of Congress, has been given up. Charleston is about to surrender, perhaps has already surrendered. Their commerce has suffered tremendously, and they have no money and even less credit. And, finally, they find more or less opposition in every province.

In the early part of March the rebels were so imprudent as to detach fifteen hundred men to Onondaga Castle [79] under Brigadiers Clinton and Van Schaick [80] to destroy a savage settlement. In this they succeeded. As soon as the savages heard of it, they took up the tomahawk and have since been committing indescribable cruelties under Joseph Brant, Colonel Butler, Governor Hamilton, and Colonel Peters. Some time ago the last named proceeded as far as Mombaccus, sixteen [miles [81]] from Esopus,[82] and burned everything; he then invaded the rich district of Stone Arabia, forty-five miles west of Albany, marking each step with the most savage behavior. Butler has devastated Wyoming and the district thirty miles around it. Whoever escaped the sword and scalping knife has left the banks of the Susquehanna.

In vain did General Washington have fifteen hundred men assemble at Minisink in the early part of April to cover some defenses. Not half of them returned; they were defeated by Joseph Brant, who appropriated all the possessions of everyone disloyal to the government. General McIntosh likewise abandoned the strong Fort DuQuesne on the Ohio when Governor Hamilton approached.[83] This governor brought with him a considerable

[79] Onondaga, New York. The Onondaga towns extended ten miles along Onondaga Creek.

[80] Colonel Goose Van Schaick's expedition to the Onondaga towns took place April 18–24. Clinton did not accompany this expedition, though he later participated in the Indian campaign of 1779. Cf. Justin Winsor, *Narrative and Critical History*, VI, 639.

[81] MS torn along edge.

[82] Now Kingston, New York.

[83] Lieutenant Colonel Henry Hamilton, Lieutenant Governor at Detroit, did not capture Pittsburgh, but was himself taken at Vincennes by George Rogers Clark February 25, 1779. This story of the capture of Pittsburgh appears in both *Royal*

detachment of regular troops and five hundred savages from Canada. He had to make his own roads between the two lakes, Michigan and Erie, in order to cross the River Des Miamis;[84] and from there he turned left as far as the Chianouske[85] River and followed the Indians' hunting paths along this stream through valleys and woods to DuQuesne, which is also called Pittsburgh.

From the rebels we learn, by way of Jersey, that Fort Stanwix[86] on the Mohawk River has been taken, although to date no reports concerning its capture have reached English headquarters. It is supposed, however, that we shall learn any day that Governor Haldimand has moved from Canada.

During this last winter General Washington's force in Jersey never amounted to more than five thousand men. On the 2nd of this month he detached a little more than two thousand men from Middlebrook to Tappan and Haverstraw, while he himself set out from Morristown on the 5th for Warwick in Ulster County by way of Pompton and New Windsor, presumably to reinforce General St. Clair in case we should attack the forts at West Point, which are garrisoned by eight brigades of Carolina and Virginia troops, all in all, not more than three thousand men.[87]

General Wayne, who is near Albany in the upper parts of the Highlands and commands only two brigades of regulars be-

---

Gazette, May 15, 1779, and *New-York Gazette*, May 17, and may have come from Lieutenant Colonel Bolton at Niagara, who reported to Haldimand April 9, 1779, that Pittsburgh had fallen (*Canadian Archives*, 1886, p. 691). In 1778 Hamilton had proposed going to Pittsburgh, a plan to which Haldimand assented only on condition that large stores were proved to be there (*ibid.*, 1887, pp. 201, 205, 209).

[84] Miami of the Lakes or Maumee River.

[85] This river is commonly shown on French maps of the 1740's and 1750's and is placed anywhere from the Monongahela (Poilly, 1755) to the Wabash. Its source is usually shown near present Sandusky. An anonymous manuscript map in the Service Hydrographique de la Marine (4044B8F), dated 1755 and entitled "Cours de l'Ohio Depuis sa Source jusqu'à sa Jonction avec la Rivière d'Ouabache Et du Pais Voisin," identifies it with the Yenanquekonnen, an old name for the Muskingum. Copies of this map are to be found among the Karpinski series of photographs of manuscript maps relating to America in the William L. Clements Library and the Library of Congress.

[86] Cf. end of letter dated Dec. 13, 1779 (No. 44), where Baurmeister states that the news of the surprise of the fort was premature.

[87] The manuscript volume of returns for Washington's army (William L. Clements Library) shows 2,400 at West Point and 2,321 in the Highlands on the east side of the Hudson.

sides the militia when it assembles in case of need, writes pitiful
reports to General Washington. He complains of the miserable
condition of his troops and of his inability to resist the strong
parties of savages or General Haldimand, should he approach. He
further states that everyone submits to the laws of the government
in accordance with the demands of the Indian leaders and shows
but little obedience to him.

Since my last letter of the 14th of May, eighteen large and
richly laden prizes have been brought in, among them eleven
French ships from Cape François. Furthermore, on the 5th of June
the frigate *Daphne* attacked the rebel frigate *Oliver Cromwell,*
twenty guns, about nineteen leagues off Sandy Hook and boarded
her after an engagement of two hours. The *Daphne* had left London only on the 2nd of June,[88] and so far has brought in at least
nine New York privateers and close to twenty other ships. The
captured frigate was immediately manned and is already in use
in our service.

On the 9th of this month a deserter came from Fort Putnam
to Stony Point. He was a Brunswicker who had been taken prisoner and then enlisted. Familiar with the whole region and the
fort, he gave us exact information about the forts and particularly
about the garrison. After making the necessary preparations, a
large train left New York on the 12th and proceeded up the North
River. Since the packet is to be closed, the ensuing events must
be described at the next opportunity.

Herewith I enclose a newspaper [*missing*] giving exact accounts of the Virginia expedition and the preparations made for
the capture of Fort Lafayette. The troops which advanced as far
as Suffolk returned with tremendous riches. What is still left is
now being sold so that everyone may receive his share. The Regiment Prinz Carl got no further inland than Portsmouth. Although
it was praised by General Mathew for good conduct, everyone
will enjoy his well-deserved and rightful share of booty, which
will not be small. The greatest loss for the rebels is probably the
destruction of their shipyards and all the materials stored in them.
We should do well to pay similar visits to their wharves at Balti-

[88] Must be May 2, not June 2.

more and Portsmouth in New Hampshire, for here lie the fountain-heads which must be stopped if this rebellion is to dry up.

General Prevost's reports have not come in, for very good reasons; but from the rebels we have learned how close to Charleston he is, and that he is perhaps already in possession of it, as is said by some, for his army has grown to seven thousand men and is welcomed by the Carolinians. He has, moreover, been fortunate in meeting with but little opposition from Generals Lincoln and Moultrie as well as Pulaski, whose total strength is no greater than his and who are constantly falling back. General Clinton is very anxious to know the actual situation.

Three rebel frigates, the *Confederacy*, thirty-six guns, the *Warren*, thirty-two, and the *Deane*, twenty-eight, and two twenty-gun ships are cruising between the Delaware and Egg Harbor and frequently approach to within two leagues of Sandy Hook. We have only four frigates of much weaker armament cruising between the eastern end of Long Island and Capes Henry and Charles on the Delaware,[89] while three armed ships lie in the Sound of the East River. Commodore Sir George Collier is often greatly embarrassed at the thought of having to defend the harbors against strong enemy ships.

The letters recently arrived from the West Indies and the Bermudas report no further change except that the two fleets are watching each other and that the British frigates are taking many prizes. So far they have not stopped any Dutch ships, which are still supplying Martinique with provisions. The Spanish are more discreet now; they frequently refuse to give French ships needed assistance.

The captured French merchants brought along from Virginia have lost their ships, their merchandise, and all their money. Their lamentations are as just as they are ridiculous, and they cannot be calmed, now that they are ruined for the rest of their lives.

We are expecting two British regiments and the Landgraf Regiment from Rhode Island.

[89] Chesapeake Bay, of course.

I shall not fail to send further accounts whenever I know of a safe opportunity, and in the meantime I commend myself to your benevolence and remain with the deepest respect [*etc.*]

P.S. Major Fuchs has returned from Long Island to join his regiment encamped at New York. No more than one hundred men remain entrenched before Brooklyn.

: 39 :

Regardless of the fact that Generals Stirn and Schmidt, who embark today and will probably sail tomorrow, will soon arrive in Europe and can give an excellent verbal account of American events, I send this written report, which continues where my journal of the 14th of this month left off. Generals Erskine and Jones will also leave us with this fleet.

On the 15th of this month the Jersey newspaper published a very contradictory report which a courier from Philadelphia had spread in Morristown while carrying dispatches to General Washington at Smith's Tavern [90] in Ulster County, approximately fourteen miles from Fort Clinton. It soon became known, however, that General Lincoln did not defeat General Prevost and so stop his advance, and that the latter is already in possession of the islands and the whole south side of Charleston harbor, even Mount Pleasant.

The enclosed newspaper [*missing*] contains everything that is known to date of General Prevost's operations. Even General

[90] In Smith's Clove, The Clove. Cf. Washington's correspondence and *New-York Gazette*, Aug. 9, 1779.

Clinton is much surprised, for he had not ordered any of these movements and has received no direct reports, this news having come from Savannah. However, since a London packet sailed directly to Savannah, arriving there the latter part of March, there is no doubt in the English headquarters that General Prevost was advised, among other things, to do this if he saw fit. We are therefore expecting important news from there as well as from the West Indies. The French fleet and the Island of Martinique are suffering from great want. Brigadier General Medows will attempt a landing on Martinique with the greater part of the garrison of St. Lucia. He expects to land at the same place where the Dutch continually land and deliver food.

The Dutch have finally brought it upon themselves that their ships carrying such cargoes are stopped. It is therefore not unlikely that the French will come to a bad end on this island. Brigadier General Prescott is in command of all the West India troops, for General Grant has received permission to return to England.

General Washington remains motionless at Smith's Tavern with no more than four thousand men. He can keep his small force together only with great difficulty and can get provisions only from the two magazines at Morristown and Trenton. He has recalled General Sullivan (who has again raised six battalions at Minisink) and has ordered him to proceed to the Susquehanna, both sides of which are being fearfully ravaged by the Indians. The great number of deserters, however, have reduced his force to not much more than eight hundred men. Generals McDougall and Nixon [91] are now posted between Peekskill and Fishkill with five thousand men, counting Continentals and militia.

Their patrols have come no closer than fifteen English miles from Fort Lafayette, thus avoiding even the slightest engagement. The outpost at Byram Bridge,[92] nearly twenty miles from Kings Bridge and two miles this side of Horse Neck, has been surprised for the third time, the enemy having each time no less than thirty killed, wounded, and captured. As late as yesterday Emmerich's dragoons surprised this post and brought in one officer and eleven

[91] Brigadier General John Nixon.
[92] The bridge on the Boston Post Road over the Byram River.

men, the rest remaining on the field, killed or wounded. The prisoners complain that they are ruthlessly coerced, for which reason most of them immediately take service on our ships.

Above Albany, and especially in the regions west of it, the young men are joining Butler and Brant to prevent their paternal homes from being plundered by the Indians. This has caused General Washington a great deal of worry, especially since, because of the situation in New England, he does not expect much confidence or many recruits there and since he may soon expect to be met by General Clinton. Besides, if he were to withdraw all the troops from Jersey, the banks of the Delaware would be unprotected, which would, in turn, necessitate the evacuation of Philadelphia.

If only their sea force, instead of constantly increasing, were on the decline, too. Of the one hundred and twenty-one New York privateers reported in April, to which some twenty have since been added, sixty-one have been captured. They have three strong frigates and five armed ships in addition to thirty-one privateers cruising between Sandy Hook and the Delaware and Chesapeake Bay. New London maintains nineteen privateers, one frigate, and six armed ships, while two frigates, nine armed ships, and twenty-two privateers are running out of Boston. These last are cruising along the Halifax route and capturing many ships. I have this from Lieutenant Colonel Campbell, who arrived here on parole on the 26th of this month by way of Kings Bridge after he had been taken prisoner along with Colonel Köhler. He brought letters to General von Knyphausen from Colonel Köhler, who is quartered with his officers at Rutland, where all the Brunswickers captured at Bennington are domiciled.

On the 27th Generals Pattison and Vaughan left their post on the North River with some of the troops and were taken on flatboats to Philipsburgh, where they landed last night. They then marched into camp on Hunt's Hill, taking a position on the right wing of the troops already encamped there. Hunt's Hill is a little less than three English miles from New Rochelle. Lieutenant Colonel Johnson remained behind at Stony Point with the 17th Regiment and half of Ferguson's Corps. Colonel Webster re-

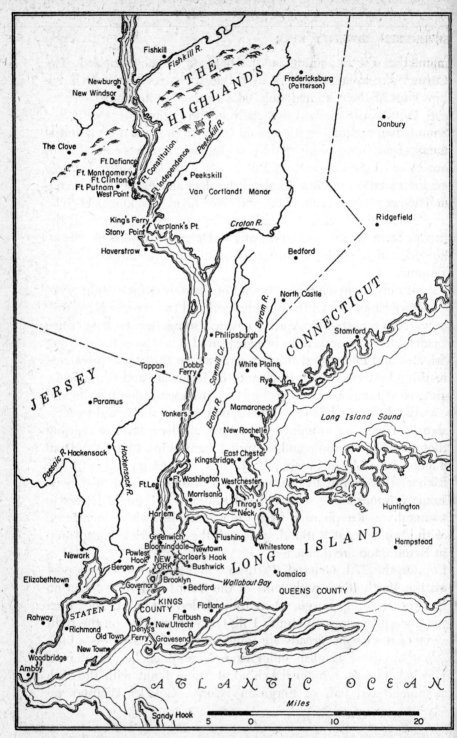

Map of Lower New York During the Revolution. (Redrawn from a section of C. J. Sauthier's "Chorographic Map of the Province of New York . . ., London, William Faden, 1779.")

mained in Fort Lafayette with the 33rd Regiment, Robinson's Corps,[93] and the other half of Ferguson's.

Yesterday afternoon the 54th Regiment, Fanning's Provincial Battalion, and the Landgraf Regiment sailed through the Sound down the East River to New York. They will disembark today and join the army. Graff's Grenadier Battalion is still under orders to be ready to embark at the first command. We have received no reports from the Hessian regiments either in Georgia or Halifax.

I shall send this communication with a packet that is ready to sail. Most obediently commending myself, I have the honor to be with the greatest respect [etc.]

p.s. I forgot to mention that on the 24th of this month the Legion, the Queen's Rangers, and the Hessian Jäger Corps marched out to the Bronx above White Plains and advanced as far as the Croton River, which Lieutenant Colonel Tarleton crossed with the Legion. He surprised the rebel Colonel Drake in Crompond in Westchester County and returned with forty-seven prisoners and many head of cattle and sheep.

His Excellency General Clinton just this moment paid us a short visit on his way to Philipse's house. We learned from them [94] that the two French warships mentioned in the enclosed newspaper [missing] really have foundered at the entrance to the harbor of Martinique and that Brigadier Medows has started out from St. Lucia for Charleston under cover of three men-of-war with five regiments to aid General Prevost in getting possession of the said city, for the strong batteries on Sullivan Island have so far hindered his progress. I do not know whether this news is from direct reports. I beg a thousand pardons for writing on the margin, but the embarkation presses and I must deliver this letter quickly.

93 Robinson's Loyal American Regiment.
94 I.e., Clinton and his suite.

: 40 :

On the 22nd of this month Admiral Arbuthnot's fleet was finally sighted off Sandy Hook, and by the 25th all the ships were in the harbor. On the 26th the troops arriving with this fleet disembarked on Long Island. The 78th,[95] 80th, and four companies of the 82nd Regiment were marched into camp at Bedford, and the recruits for thirteen regiments, to Bushwick. Two hundred and twenty artillerymen, three hundred and fifty men to reinforce the Guard detachments, and about two hundred Anspach recruits remained in New York.

The warships and frigates will weigh anchor as soon as possible and sail to join Admiral Byron, who has gathered the fleet at St. Kitts to refit. While he was convoying a strong fleet of merchantmen to the latitude of the Bermudas in June, Admiral d'Estaing, reinforced at Martinique by seven ships of the line and nine frigates under La Motte Picquet,[96] promptly set sail and took possession of St. Vincent and then Grenada.

[95] A mistake of the copyist, no doubt. From internal evidence it must be deduced that this is the 76th Regiment.

[96] Lieutenant General Toussaint-Guillaume Picquet, Comte de la Motte Picquet de la Vinoyère.

On the 6th of July they came into close action not far from the last-named island. The French with twenty-six ships of the line and ten frigates could not gain an advantage over eighteen ships of the line and four frigates and therefore withdrew from the engagement. Admiral Byron, who had the greater part of the garrison of St. Lucia with him on transports, gained the advantage of being able to disembark the 4th and 40th Regiments at Barbados, one battalion of the 60th at Antigua, the other battalion of the 60th and Colonel Dalrymple's (called the Liverpool Blues) at Jamaica (where ten thousand militia are under arms), and lastly the 15th, 28th, and 55th Regiments at St. Kitts, whither he himself accompanied them. The 27th, 35th, and 49th Regiments had remained at St. Lucia. Since the Admiral had lost many marines—some were killed in the last engagement, but many more had died before of illness—the 5th and 46th Regiments were distributed over the fleet. A transport carrying four companies and the lieutenant colonel of the 4th Regiment was captured by a French frigate; otherwise nothing was lost. Count d'Estaing is refitting in the Bay of Grenada.

On the 16th of this month General Clinton communicated a detailed report from General Prevost, beginning with the 29th of April, on which day he set out from Purysburg to march on Charleston, where he arrived on the 11th of May. The following day he summoned the city to surrender, though in vain. Thereupon he withdrew to James Island and from there, in the night of the 27th–28th of May to Johns Island, where he built a bridge across Stono Ferry to the mainland. On the other side he posted the 1st Battalion of the 71st Regiment and von Trümbach's.

Since he did not receive his promised provisions, which fell into the rebels' hands through lack of convoy, and since he could maintain neither the spirit nor the health of his troops with but scant fresh meat, rice, foul water, and no rum or medicine, he decided on the 15th of June to retreat to Beaufort. He was detained because the ships in Stono Inlet were not ready to sail, and on the 20th of June a rebel force of 5,500 men made an attack on the pickets at Stono Ferry, but got no further than the front of the abatis.

Before reinforcements could come over from Johns Island, Lieutenant Colonel Maitland was in pursuit of the rebels, who were in full retreat. Much praise was bestowed on the said lieutenant colonel, who, in turn, gave due credit to von Trümbach's Regiment. This regiment had six men killed and thirty-eight wounded; Major Endemann, Lieutenant Wiedekind, and Lieutenant Engelhard of the Artillery were slightly wounded, and Lieutenant von Greisheim [97] severely.

From the reports sent on this packet your Lordship will see that the regiments, unfortunately, are much weakened by illness and desertion. The English had 207 deserters on this expedition, in which the following troops participated: the 16th Regiment, the 1st Battalion and three grenadier companies of the 60th Regiment, the two battalions of the 71st, one battalion of De Lancey's, one of Skinner's, Governor Browne's, the New York Volunteers, the South Carolina Royalists and Governor Wright's Georgia Volunteers,[98] and von Trümbach's and von Wissenbach's Regiments, making 4,200 men in all.

The retreat was effected during the last part of June without the loss of another man. Lieutenant Colonel Maitland remained at Beaufort with twelve hundred men, among them von Trümbach's; Purysburg and Ebenezer were also occupied, and von Wissenbach's Regiment was sent to Savannah. The fleet is stationed between St. Helena Sound and Phillips Point.[99] General Prevost had scarcely made these dispositions, when some hundred rebels, most of whom were mounted, appeared between Purysburg and Savannah. He ordered Grenadier Captain Müller [100] of the 60th Regiment to pick out fifty men who could ride after them on horseback and attempt to cut them off on a road leading through rice swamps. Each man was given a Hessian short-sword. However, the said captain fell into an ambush him-

---

[97] The *Staats-Calender* has Friedrich von Griesheim, First Lieutenant, Regiment von Trümbach.

[98] Probably Georgia Loyalists, James Wright, Major.

[99] U. S. Coast Survey, "Sketch of the Sea Coast of South Carolina and Georgia" (1863), gives Phillips' Island, though earlier maps call the southern tip Phillips' Point. Its present name is Bay Point Island.

[100] Lieutenant John K. Müller, 2nd Battalion of the 60th Regiment.

self, and an untimely resistance cost him and some thirty of his
men their lives. The rest were taken prisoners. The short-swords
were paid for at a guinea apiece.

Doubtless more troops will have to be sent there. Von Lossberg's and von Knyphausen's and also three British regiments
were ordered some time ago to be ready, for which purpose the
two Hessian regiments were mustered yesterday. At present, however, there is nothing more to report about this.

Nor do we know what has occurred at Penobscot since it
was taken by the British troops. Three rebel frigates and twenty
armed ships, supposedly carrying seventeen hundred men, set
sail for Penobscot from Boston to dislodge Brigadier General
McLean. Thereupon Sir George Collier set sail from here with all
the frigates to frustrate their designs. It is known from rebel
newspapers that the rebels, after landing in Penobscot Bay, took
two batteries consisting of seven 18-pounders, which had been
spiked, and that, being unable to attack the main fort, they sent
a request to Boston for heavy artillery.

On the 20th of this month, very early in the morning, Major
Lee of the rebels came to Powles Hook from Brunswick with
about four hundred men. The previous evening Lieutenant Colonel Van Buskirk [101] had set out from there with a patrol of one
hundred and fifty in an attempt to capture a rebel detachment at
the far end of Hackensack,[102] for General Stirling, who is in command in Jersey while Brigadier Maxwell is away with General
Sullivan, has called out and put under arms the last militia levy,
amounting to twelve hundred men, and posted them in the district
between Brunswick, Amboy, and Hackensack. Major Lee found
the drawbridge down and the sentinels asleep. Captain von
Schaller,[103] Ensign Kress, and forty privates had been detached
there the night before. A major named Sutherland, formerly an
adjutant to General Clinton, who moreover has his post at the
head of the invalids in the Bermudas, recently undertook this

---

[101] Abram Van Buskirk of Skinner's Brigade of New Jersey Volunteers.

[102] Other contemporary accounts state that they proceeded to English Neighborhood, which is situated in the southern extremity of Hackensack Township.

[103] Captain Henrich Sebastian von Schaller, of the Erb Prinz Regiment.

command at Powles Hook. He had one noncommissioned officer and fifteen Hessian privates stationed at the second blockhouse and as many British at the first, while he himself remained with the rest of Captain von Schaller's command.

This main post became aware of this unexpected visit almost too late, for after a few shots at the noncommissioned officer's post, the men were captured, and the blockhouses as well as the batteries, from which neither the officer nor a single artilleryman had time to escape, were occupied by the enemy. The rebels then repeatedly summoned Captain von Schaller to surrender, but in vain. He saved his ammunition, and the enemy, impressed by his firmness, left Powles Hook without damaging either the guns or the drawbridge. They were satisfied with having made some sixty prisoners.

Colonel Gordon [104] of the Guards was immediately dispatched from New York with two hundred men in boats to support our troops, but he was too late. Ninety men of the Guards were ordered to pursue, but only one noncommissioned officer and six men were brought in by Lieutenant Colonel Van Buskirk. Major Lee got out of the Colonel's way by turning off to the left toward Brunswick in order not to lose any prisoners, many of whom were still intoxicated. Major Sutherland was courtmartialed, and Captain von Schaller and his subaltern were warmly thanked by General Clinton. Five men of the Hessian noncommissioned officer's post ran away when the enemy left Powles Hook. The posts at Stony and Verplanck's points on the North River have been spared further attacks from the enemy.

The light infantry, the Queen's Rangers, and the 17th Regiment of Dragoons have been transferred to Long Island, where the rebels undertake the most devastating landings from Connecticut. They will not leave this district alone in spite of the fact that General Tryon has burned 232 houses, 155 barns, 30 warehouses, 40 stores, 4 mills, and 5 ships. Enclosed is the arrogant answer [*missing*] to the manifesto scattered during the expedition to Connecticut.

[104] Lieutenant Colonel the Hon. Cosmo Gordon, 3rd Regiment of Foot Guards.

General Washington does not stir from his position between New Windsor, Smith's Clove, and the western forts. Thus posted he needs no more than five thousand men. The flatboats built in Philadelphia were taken up the river as far as Trenton, and thence transported to the army on wagons, while the boats built on the Raritan last spring lie at Elizabethtown. To make Staten Island more secure on that side, the 44th Regiment was transferred there.

At the beginning of this month, Colonel Stark [105] was ordered by General Washington to take six hundred men and cover the working parties who are cutting a new road through virgin forest from the Upper Cohos to the Connecticut. However, only a few of the laborers escaped the scalping knives of the Indians, and the said colonel returned to the army without accomplishing his task. At present they are strongly fortifying Ticonderoga.

General Sullivan got no further than Wyoming on his expedition through the western part of Pennsylvania. He started back when the Indians, who had been roaming through Orange County and had advanced between Old Minisink and Sussex, captured a strong convoy for his main magazine at Sunburn or Sunbury.[106] However, he is in such a precarious situation that he will reach the Delaware only with great difficulty. Moreover, all the salt meat in the above-mentioned magazine had become putrid and had to be buried.

So far I have received no information concerning the losses of General Sullivan's detached corps in the engagement with the savages at Freeland's Fort,[107] about seventeen English miles from Sunbury. It is surmised, however, that Joseph Brant has been mortally wounded or killed, for when the rebels were beaten at Lycoming, the savages howled terribly on the battlefield, which

---

[105] Perhaps a colonel of the New York or New England militia or, perhaps, even Brigadier General John Stark (of New Hampshire), who was in command of the Northern Department at this time. It is interesting to note in this connection that Baurmeister's scribe wrote Col. von Starck. Most of the German superior officers were of the lesser nobility, and Stark (Starck) is a German as well as an English name.

[106] Sunbury, Northumberland County, Pennsylvania.

[107] The original report of Captain John McDonell, the British Commander on this raid, is in the Haldimand MSS and has been published by the Department of History, University of the State of New York, in *The Sullivan-Clinton Campaign in 1779,* p. 115.

is said to be a sign that they have lost their commander.[108] We have no confirmation yet. Gurry, his eldest son,[109] is said to be as civilized as the father, whose acquaintance we made during the first campaign.

The rebels are looking forward to being reinforced by eight thousand Frenchmen, who, according to a Philadelphia newspaper, are to be commanded by a certain General Conflans.[110] These auxiliary troops are expected in Boston, where a large grain magazine is being erected. The southern provinces have a good harvest.

In New England twenty thousand militia under General Parsons,[111] General Wolcott,[112] and Governor Trumbull are ready to resist any attack. General McDougall is still posted at Peekskill, this side of the North River, and Armand's and Moylan's independent corps are only rarely seen.

The guard ships stationed from Stony Point to below Fort Knyphausen are so anchored in the North River that when they fire an alarm, the 7th and 23rd Regiments and Lord Rawdon's Irish Volunteers can embark in two minutes and sail to the assistance of the fort, which, we have learned, is to be attacked by a superior force.

The ague has put half of the men in the various regiments to bed, and those suffering from it recover only very slowly. The Hessian hospitals have been greatly helped by the arrival of Dr. Michaelis, for the doctors and surgeons have not been spared by this ugly disease.

[108] Cf. *Philadelphia Gazette*, Aug. 4, 1779, and *Pennsylvania Packet*, Aug. 5. Brant, of course, was not killed.

[109] His name was Isaac Brant, though Gurry might possibly be a corruption of his Indian name.

[110] Conflans, the name of a distinguished French family. Hubert de Brienne Conflans, Comte de Conflans (1690–1777), was both an admiral and a marshal of France, and his rank may have given rise to this rumor. There is no General Conflans listed in either the *Almanach royal* for 1777, or in *Les Combattants français de la guerre américaine*, 1778–1783, published by Ministère des Affaires Étrangères, 1903.

[111] Brigadier General Samuel Holden Parsons, Connecticut militia.

[112] Brigadier General Erastus Wolcott, Connecticut militia, commanded the militia in Parsons' force, while Major General Oliver Wolcott participated actively with Governor Trumbull and Washington in planning the defense of the state.

The new fortifications between Laurel Hill and North Hill [113] will soon be completed. The forts beyond Kings Bridge as far as and including No. 7 are being razed, while No. 8, on the other side of Harlem Creek, opposite Laurel Hill, is being enlarged. We are ready to open the campaign—late, to be sure—but we hope successfully. I shall be happy to be able to report good results.

With the greatest respect I have the honor to be [*etc.*]

P.S. My last letter was dispatched in great haste on the 30th of July this year.[114] Once more I ask your Lordship's pardon for writing so hastily. I enclose another impertinent communication [*missing*] from Congress to show how bold it has become.

[113] See 1778, note 57.
[114] This letter was on the *Sandwich* packet, which was captured (see below).

: 41 :

MORRIS'S HOUSE
SEPTEMBER 22, 1779

The last letters for Europe were of the 27th of August and the 3rd of this month, although they left at the same time. I had the honor to send a letter to your Lordship under the first date, but by the 3rd of September I was suffering from a severe inflammation in the chest, and after it came the ague. Except for his Excellency General von Knyphausen, Captain Beckwith,[115] and five servants, every one of the General's staff has been stricken. On the 19th of this month over two thousand of the army were ill in the hospitals, not counting those that are being nursed by the regiments themselves. It is a universal pestilence and rages still more among the Americans. Hence, General Clinton can undertake nothing. In the meantime he ordered the 26th Regiment to come in and reinforce the 44th Regiment with one hundred men.

The Hessian grenadier brigade has encamped before New York, and the entrance to New York harbor has been fortified along the shores of both Long Island and Staten Island. Likewise the work on the fortifications in the narrow space this side of Kings

[115] Captain George Beckwith, 37th Regiment of Foot Guards.

300

Not in the British Army!

Bridge has been proceeding without interruption, while the redoubts beyond the said bridge, except Nos. 5 and 8, have been demolished. The former will also be razed when all the works this side are occupied, for which no preparations have been made so far. Lieutenant Colonel Emmerich's Corps has been broken up, the cavalry under Captain Hock [116] being incorporated in the Legion, and the infantry under Captain Althaus [117] in the New York Volunteers.

On the 8th of this month the 44th, von Lossberg's, and von Knyphausen's Regiments embarked and immediately sailed out of the harbor, but the strong east wind drove them off their course. Finally they got as far as Block Island and Rhode Island, and now they will probably meet with no more difficulties on their voyage to Quebec. They took all their large and small equipage along. Müller, the regimental quartermaster of Knyphausen's Regiment, remained behind, but will follow with the new uniforms and recruits.

As soon as the illness lets up somewhat, the following troops will be embarked: The light infantry, the British and Hessian grenadiers, including Graff's Battalion, the 7th, 23rd, 33rd, 37th, 54th, and 57th Regiments, the Queen's Rangers, the Legion, the Irish Volunteers, Fanning's Corps, and Diemar's Hussars. Thirty-seven transports, four hospital ships, and twenty-two horse transports and provision ships are ready. Each troop ship has sufficient provisions for ninety days. General Cornwallis is to command this expedition, and Generals Mathew and von Kospoth will be under him. It is generally supposed that this corps of seven thousand men will land in Virginia and then proceed to Carolina, and that Brigadier General Garth will lead the Georgia troops to Charleston over the same route that General Prevost took prematurely and on his own authority. The command in Georgia has been offered to Major General Leslie, who, however, refused it. Fur-

---

[116] Captain Hock could not be identified.

[117] Hufeland, *Westchester County during the American Revolution*, quoting Sergeant Dean's account, has Althaus (as above). Lorenzo Sabine's *Biographical Sketches of Loyalists of the American Revolution*, Boston, 1864, the *Carleton Calendar*, and the *Fort Ticonderoga Museum Bulletin* (II, 173) give several variants. Two references agree on the first name, John.

thermore, two hundred dismounted Hessian jägers under Major von Wurmb and a lieutenant with forty-six Anspachers have subsequently been ordered to take part in the expedition.

These preparations will be reported to London. A packet lies ready for this purpose and will carry these letters. Captain von Wreden is availing himself of this occasion to go to Europe. All the German recruits from England were taken to Canada instead of here; therefore, General Clinton could not keep his word to the said captain.

Your Lordship has probably heard by this time from England that on the 13th of August Sir George Collier completely frustrated the Bostonians' expedition to Penobscot. In the night of the 13th–14th the rebels burned nineteen armed ships, among them six frigates and twenty-four two- and three-masted transports. However, four armed ships came into the possession of the English. The land troops and sailors of the Americans escaped overland. We have no list as yet of the large number of cannon which were dragged out of the water onto the shore and of the many other articles of ammunition and provisions.

Congress had not advised this expedition, but the Bostonians thought they could overcome everything with the eighteen hundred militia they had assembled for this purpose. Brigadier McLean was in no danger of being attacked in his main fort. The rebel General Lovell and Commodore Saltonstall, both inexperienced men, made no essential preparation whatever between the 25th of July and the 12th of August.[118] The Bay of Penobscot is twelve leagues long and not much over one league wide and has a strong NNE current.

If Sir George Collier could have entered the bay without difficulty with all his ships, he would have taken all the rebel ships. The excursion was a very successful coup and brought considerable loss to the rebels. It is said that during the early part of August Captain Cosby of the *Robust* took seventeen sail to Halifax and that, hearing of the danger confronting Brigadier

[118] For an account of this expedition see Almon's *Remembrancer*, VIII, 352 and *Massachusetts Historical Society Proceedings*, 2nd Series, XII, 200–202.

General McLean at Penobscot, he sailed to his assistance only to find that Sir George Collier had made a clean sweep. His return trip to Halifax, however, is said to have been paid for by two French frigates which he encountered and brought in.

Provision ships are still coming in from Cork. On the 10th of this month another seven ships arrived from there with a collier of five hundred tons. From them came the news that the *Sandwich* packet, which sailed on the 4th of August and carried our July letters, has been captured. Assuming that this information is founded on fact, I gave Captain von Wreden a summary of my journal sent on that packet, so that he can tell your Lordship of the events between June 30th and July 30th.

At the beginning of this month General Washington took up his quarters at Moore's [119] house near West Point. He found it necessary to have a brigade of New Englanders come by way of Horse Neck and Fishkill and join him on the 16th. All the troops with him are sick too, and, having detached General Stirling to Amboy and Brunswick, he has but a small force of effective men. General Stirling called out the last levy of Jersey militia, which he posted along the shore facing Staten Island and in Hackensack and Bergen. Major Lee, who recently conducted an ill-managed expedition to Powles Hook, has been arrested and is being court-martialed.[120]

All of Northumberland County has been devastated by the Indians. Those who could escape fled to Lancaster County. Paxtang [121] and Sunbury as well as Carlisle and Lioming [122] have been burned. Thereafter Brant and Butler joined forces and spread their hordes from Chemung to Easton. Maxwell's entire brigade was first annihilated, Maxwell himself remaining on the

---

[119] The Moore house, on the Hudson River, about a mile north of West Point in what is now called Washington Valley. See Hamilton Fish, *George Washington in the Highlands*, Newburgh, N. Y., 1932, *passim*.

[120] Ironically enough, two days after Baurmeister wrote this letter, Congress voted its thanks to Lee for the exploit at Powles Hook. A sketch of the gold medal which it presented to him appears in Lossing's *Pictorial Field Book of the American Revolution*, II, 623. This story of Lee's arrest, however, may be found in the *Royal Gazette*, Sept. 4, 1779.

[121] Modern Paxton.

[122] Lycoming? (or Wyoming?).

field.[123] General Sullivan is now at his wits' end. The southern provinces cannot put another man under arms.

This is the time to march on West Point with eight thousand men, for they would meet with little opposition. Our posts at Stony and Verplanck's points are not being disturbed, in spite of the fact that the 33rd and 64th Regiments and Fanning's Corps have been withdrawn. Our patrols find no rebels, and the latter do not even take the pains to reconnoiter our posts. As soon as the above-mentioned troops have embarked, the new reinforcements will occupy Long and Staten islands, and the garrison duty as well as the occupation of the new fortifications will be regulated.

Lord Rawdon has resigned his office of adjutant general. Nothing is known of the difficulties that have arisen between him and General Clinton. Rawdon is highly esteemed throughout the entire army for his noble deeds, and everyone complains that he has withdrawn from a well-managed office, from which they all derived help and service.

After the decisive naval action at Grenada on the 6th of July, the French fleet withdrew to Nicholas Mole,[124] remained there until the 19th of August, and then sailed to Cape François, whither Admiral Byron followed with twenty-one capital ships. This is all we know for certain from the West Indies.

Our forage and wood magazines are increasing, and those at Brooklyn on Long Island even more. The New Englanders are bringing in such quantities of cattle, sheep, and hogs that we shall have no wants during the coming winter. We sincerely hope that we shall have no visits from enemy ships.

Since it has become known that Spain has entered the war, more New York privateers have been fitted out. However, greater care is being taken that only good loyalists receive permission to do this, for among the first, some forty went over to the rebels and did us considerable damage. I have the honor to commend myself most respectfully [etc.]

---

[123] Again Baurmeister is reporting Rivington's fabrications. Cf. *Royal Gazette* Sept. 1 and 4, 1779, and the reprints in *New Jersey Archives*, 2nd Series, vol. III. Chemung was burned by Sullivan, July 13, 1779.

[124] Now Mole St. Nicolas, Haiti.

in die Hand gekommen. Sie sind noch zu halten, als daß sie selbst zurück gehalten hätte. Klimm
an Bäume. Ich werde künftig damit enthalten, nicht zu einer exacten Ordre de Bataille
der englischen Truppen, dann leicht folgend sind: 6. Bataill. leichte Infanterie, 7. Bri.,
... Artillerie, an Infanterie No. ...; 33. 49. 26. 23. 57. 64. 44. 43. 63. 54.
... 15. 45. 27. 4. 17. 46. 55. 40. 71. 2 te G. Batail. 37. 52. 38. 10. 42. 2 te
Batail. und 33 te Regiment, und leichtl. 10. Grenad. Batallions. Wir haben immer 11. sind
... schwer mit der Devise: Liberty bekommen. Der Gener. Burgoin ist mit dem Militär
an Au Mark. Ich habe 2 Chefs von denen Mohawk und Iroquoisen bei'm General Howe
getroffen, welche wieder zurück dem General Burgoin entgegen gegangen. Man hat
... sich finden ... hat gebracht, so wie man auch für dem Feinde Schütz, und ... Paris hat
... ... Rütteland zurück lassen wollen.

Die Hessen haben gut gewesen ... Räume, ... leicht ... Schießbeller, ...
... zu mittheilen aus den Brouillon mit meiner eigenen
... ... so ... ... werden. Ich
... ... mit der ... gehorsamst erwarte Jetzt, so haben erfahren,
daß der admiral Howe nach Hellgaytes drey Fregatten ...
... um die Feinde zu Observieren! Ich ... mich zum ...
... werthvolles und besseres mit der nächsten ...

Jhr. Hauptquartier

... Land bei New York
on Tag den 21 ten 7 br 1776.

Ganz gehorsamster
Diener

Baurmeister

Erb Prinz Regiment.

Chef und Oberster Se. Hochfürstl. Durchl. der Erb Prinz Wilhelm von Hessen Cassel

Erb Prinz Regiment. Chief and Colonel:
His Serene Highness, the Hereditary Prince
William of Hesse-Cassel.
ANNE S. K. BROWN MILITARY COLLECTION

The Phoenix and the Rose Engaged by t
Enemy's Fire Ships and Galleys on the
Augst. 17
PHELPS STOKES COLLECTI
NEW YORK PUBLIC LIBRA

The PHOENIX and the ROSE Engaged by the ENEMY'S FIRE SHIPS and GALLEYS on the 16 Augst. 177

Engraved from the Original Picture by D. Serres from a sketch of Sir James Wallace's.

iew of the Narrows between Long Island
Staten Island wth our Fleet at Anchor, &
ord Howe coming in, 12th July, 1776. By
rchibald Robertson.

Jäger Corps

Jäger Corps

Regiment von Knyphausen. *Chief: His Excellency, Lieutenant General von Knyphausen.*
ANNE S. K. BROWN MILITARY COLLECTION

The Landing of the British Forces in the Jerseys on the 20th of November 1776 under Cornwallis. Attributed to Lord Rawdon.
EMMET COLLECTION
NEW YORK PUBLIC LIBRARY

presentation of the Action off Mud Fort in
River Delaware, 15th Nov'. 1777. By
:ut. W. Elliott.

ELPS STOKES COLLECTION
W YORK PUBLIC LIBRARY

Prinz Carl Regiment. Chief and Lieutenant
General: His Serene Highness, Prince Carl.
Commander General: Major von Borck.

ANNE S. K. BROWN MILITARY COLLECTION

Drittes Regiment Garde
Chef: Se. Hochfürstliche Durchlaucht der Landgraf

Third Guard Regiment. Chief: His Most Serene Highness, the Landgrave.

The Surrender at Saratoga, October 17, 177

SARRATOGA.

PRISE DE LA DOMINIQUE

*he Capture of Dominica by the French,
*ptember 7, 1778.

*Fusilier Regiment Alt von Lossberg. Chief:
His Excellency, Lieutenant General von
Lossberg.*

*Fusilier Regiment von Alt- Lossberg
Chef. Se Excell. Gen. Lieut: v Lossberg*

General und Ober
Chirurgus.

Auditeur, Regiments
Quartiermeister, oder
Regiments Feldscher
des 1.ten Regiments Garde.

Regiments Feldscher
der Garde du Corps.

Auditeur, Regiments
Quartiermeister oder
Regiments Feldscher
der übrigen Regimente.

Surgeon General and Chief Surgeon. *Auditor, Regimental Quartermaster, or Regimental Surgeon of the First Guard Regiment.* *Regimental Surgeon of the Guard Corps.* *Auditor, Regimental Quartermaster, or Regimental Surgeon of the other regiments.*

ANNE S. K. BROWN MILITARY COLLECTION

The Capture of the Island of Grenada by the French, July 4–6, 1779

PRISE DE L'ISLE DE LA GRENADE.

: 42 :

Since Captain von Wreden embarks today, I take the liberty of obediently informing your Excellency that on the evening of the 22nd of this month the long-awaited recruits finally arrived. After disembarking on the 24th, they were distributed on the 25th. We have every reason to be satisfied with them, especially since many native Hessians were among them. Those for the Jäger Corps were in especially good shape. Only a few are ill, and the number lost on the long voyage is very small. The men assigned to regiments not here will remain with those that are here until an opportunity offers to transport them. Yesterday the unloading of our new uniforms and field requisites was begun, and hence we shall soon receive our private effects and letters, for Colonel Keutel [125] carried with him only the most essential dispatches.

General Cornwallis ran out of the harbor on the 24th of this month without anyone noticing it, taking with him six English regiments, whose flank companies however had not come in yet, the infantry of the Queen's Rangers, the Irish Volunteers and Fanning's Corps. No one knows his destination.

[125] Colonel Keutel, spelled Keytel later on. Eelking-Rosengarten lists a Colonel Heinrich Walrab von Keudell in the Landgraf Regiment.

The residents of Boston and of all Connecticut are taking flight. After West Point had been fortified so as to be almost inaccessible, Washington defiled with the greater part of his army to Morristown. Whether the rest of the troops ready to embark will also go aboard now, cannot be said with certainty. The activity on the East River with the transports and the outfitting of the hospital ships is continuing. Unfortunately, however, this pernicious fever will not let up. More become ill each day, and the number of those recovering is small.

The two frigates captured near Halifax are the *L'Audacieux,* twenty-eight guns, and the *Sullivan,* twenty-four. A ship arriving from Barbados on the 23rd confirmed the news that Admiral Byron has been reinforced by four ships of the line.

With the deepest respect I have the honor to be [*etc.*]

: 43 :

On the 21st of this month [126] I left my bed for the first time after a severe illness. On the 30th of August I was attacked by an inflammation in the chest, which developed into the ague. After recovering from this on the 16th of September, I was seized twelve days later with a hemorrhoidal colic which inevitably would have sent me to the grave if the last medicine of Dr. Amelung, the chief surgeon, had not subdued my dangerously high fever and calmed my turbulent blood.

Even the most faithful description cannot portray the general misery of the patients. We are very fortunate, however, in having only a few Hessians die, although they are creeping around half dead, are prone to have relapses, and recover only very slowly. The English have had from twenty-five to sixty die in each regiment. Colonel von Minnigerode passed away on the 16th of this month after a severe attack of putrid fever.[127] The enclosed

---

[126] October, not November; the journal extends into November.

[127] According to the *New-York Gazette*, Oct. 25, 1779, he was a knight of the Order of Merit, probably the Hessian order Pour la Vertu Militaire.

articles, which I clipped from newspapers, show that his death is generally lamented.

The little leaflet gives a true impression of Congress's and Washington's despair. I am enclosing an embarkation list [128] showing how von Lossberg's and von Knyphausen's Regiments were embarked. On the 12th of September the ships were scattered in a violent gale in latitude 39. Colonel von Borck returned immediately and landed at New York on the 12th, but, convoyed by the *Camilla* frigate as far as the route to Halifax, he finally disembarked there. The *Renown* man-of-war and the agent's ship *Springfield* did everything in their power to get the ships together again, but in vain. The *King George* transport, on which Colonel von Loos had embarked, lost all her masts and was taken in tow by the *Renown*, for the *Springfield* had captured a rebel West India schooner and was, moreover, badly damaged by the storm. By the 16th the worst of the storm had abated.

Major von Stein, his ship on the point of sinking, was captured by freebooters off the Delaware, taken to Trenton, and thence with the entire Leib Company to Philadelphia.[129] On the 1st of October, that is of this month,[130] Lieutenant Colonel Heymell's ship was also seized and towed into Egg Harbor, for it was about to sink. His troops had been on the verge of exhaustion for nine days and had worked their fingers to the bone.

On the 1st of October Colonel von Loos landed in New York harbor with the *Renown*. Their condition was deplorable, as was that of many of the 44th Regiment embarked on the *Favorite* and *Crawford* frigates, the men having been without food for thirteen days. Many of them died later from their hardships. Half of the 44th Regiment and the transport *Adamant*,[131] on which Major von

---

[128] None of the enclosures is in the collection.

[129] Major von Stein and the Guards (Leib Company) of the Regiment von Knyphausen were on the *Triton* which, having suffered great damage in the storm, was forced to surrender and was taken into Egg Harbor (Eelking-Rosengarten, pp. 185–87). According to Andreas Wiederholdt's *Tagebuch* (ed. by M. D. Learned and C. Grosse, New York, 1902), von Stein was on the *Molly*.

[130] Should read "last month," since the letter is dated November 8.

[131] The *Adamant* went down. It carried the Leib Company and the von Lossberg Company of Lossberg's Regiment.

Hanstein [132] had embarked with his company and the Leib Company, are still missing. No news has come in, either from Boston, or New London, or Portsmouth. It was the largest ship and still new. Everyone is pleased to surmise that this ship, like the *Experiment,* which Sir James Wallace commands, has fallen in the path of d'Estaing's fleet, which was torn from its anchors at St. Augustine.

Twelve French capital ships, greatly damaged, have been compelled to cast anchor in the Delaware below Egg Harbor; six others, also in bad condition, got into Chesapeake Bay; but we have no knowledge of the position of the rest of the enemy fleet. Admiral Hyde Parker is not far off Sandy Hook, and Admiral Arbuthnot is prepared to run out on the *Robust* and, being the senior Admiral, take over the command, so the divided French fleet will fare badly.

On the 6th of September the rebels spread the news in Philadelphia that La Motte Picquet had landed in Georgia with four thousand men, had captured Colonel Maitland and nine hundred men at Beaufort, and had driven Brigadier General Garth to Savannah, which, it is said, is about to capitulate. They are beginning to complain in Philadelphia that the French are inactive, although Congress had called for thirty thousand barrels of flour from Pennsylvania, which is to be delivered to the French commissaries at various places on the Delaware. However, since a third of the arable land has been left fallow for two years, and the farmers have only sown enough for their own needs, the entire harvest was less than the quantity of flour demanded.

Each province has been notified of the taxes it is to raise for 1779. Pennsylvania's are fixed at 5,700,000 Spanish dollars, while Maryland and Virginia are to pay only a third of theirs in money and deliver, in place of the rest, six thousand hogsheads of tobacco to the French commissaries, and so begin to pay off the large debt to France. On the 1st of December these are to be

---

[132] A short biographical sketch of Major Ludwig August von Hanstein, Regiment von Lossberg, may be found in Stryker, p. 391. In Lossing's *Pictorial Field Book of the American Revolution,* II, 23, there is a facsimile of his signature, L. A. von Hanstein.

brought to the places along Chesapeake Bay designated by the French commissaries. The Americans, however, accustomed to asserting their independence, will probably refuse to obey.

To show what the people think of Congress I shall mention the following occurrence: On the 11th [133] of this month fifteen persons who had been under arrest and accused of treason were acquitted before a criminal court in Philadelphia. Among them was a German inhabitant named Würtz. He had hardly left the courthouse a free man when he was seized by the populace and dragged through many streets to the house of his attorney,[134] the constantly increasing mob singing and beating him. They tore down the front of this house and maltreated the family. Thereupon some companies of dragoons, made up of the richest citizens, gathered in order to disperse this wild mob. But it came to the worst, and the dragoons opened fire. This was the signal for the raving rabble; they fired back, killed nine dragoons, wounded fifteen, and captured six, and also killed two white boys and a negro boy. Among the wounded were General Mifflin [135] and two colonels of the Artillery. Sixteen men of the mob took the captives to prison in Germantown. Eleven of the insurgents were killed, and some twenty wounded, while seven ringleaders were seized and thrown into the new prison, in front of which four pieces were mounted. Night separated the combatants.

The following morning 119 of the populace appeared before the prison and demanded their confrères. Then a member of Congress (all had locked themselves up in the well-guarded city hall)

[133] October 4, 1779, not 11. For variant accounts of this episode see the *Pennsylvania Packet*, Oct. 5, 1779 *et seq.*; John Sanderson's *Biography of the Signers of the Declaration of Independence*, Philadelphia, 1865, *sub* James Wilson; J. F. Watson's *Annals of Philadelphia and Pennsylvania*, Philadelphia, 1856, I, 425 *et seq.*; and W. B. Reed's *Life and Correspondence of Joseph Reed*, Philadelphia, 1847, II, 151–52.

[134] James Wilson.

[135] Both Watson, *loc. cit.*, and Captain McLane, an eye witness (Reed, *loc. cit.*), state that General Mifflin was in the house. But the *Pennsylvania Colonial Records*, XII, 139 (Records of the Supreme Executive Council), lists but one Mifflin in Wilson's house, John T., under age, who gave bond. Nevertheless, General Thomas Mifflin *was* in the midst of the "Fort Wilson Riot." While he attempted to address the crowd from a second-story window of Wilson's house, someone shot at him but missed. See K. R. Rossman, *Thomas Mifflin and the Politics of the American Revolution*, Univ. of North Carolina Press, 1952, p. 171.

had the courage to appear and address this unruly crowd. After agreeing to the following terms the crowd dispersed: the prisoners of both sides were to be released; the traitors, especially Würtz, were to be taken into custody again, tried before a new criminal court, and punished once and for all. All this has been done, but we do not know yet whether these poor people were found guilty and executed.

The Rhode Island garrison is expected in the Sound any day. It is said to be in no danger of the enemy fleets. The rebels have no one under arms there, and as soon as the British fleet gains the upper hand, Rhode Island will be occupied again without resistance.

Because of the inactivity of the army through sickness, General Clinton must also take every precaution to cover this island and both Staten and Long islands and have enough troops ready to oppose effectively every attempt on the newly fortified line. Hence, most of the troops on Long Island are quartered so as to be able to land on Throg's Neck and gain the enemy's left flank between East Chester and Morrisania while a successful sally is made from the new works.

But Washington, quite likely, will not allow himself to be so trapped. On the contrary, he is probably much pleased that we quietly withdrew from Stony and Verplanck's points on the 21st of this month. He was extremely embarrassed, for he had withdrawn and used up all the stores at Trenton and Morristown. As the western forts had to have supplies, he went to the length of requisitioning all the grain harvested in Dutchess County this year and also enough horses for the three hundred one-team wagons he had brought together since the beginning of September.

Congress, which fears him very much, knows neither how to meet his demands nor how to refuse them. Gates and Wayne are his enemies, the latter openly. All the colonels in the Continental brigades, however, are on Washington's side. Surrounded, moreover, by twelve adjutants, he has nothing to fear. General Lee has won many converts among members of Congress during his idleness in Philadelphia. They are insignificant people who cannot see far and are easily blinded. The less they know about a thing, the greater their fear. Hence Lee, with his exaggerated witticisms, is said to have often remarked publicly that he was now making spectacles for Congress. Mr. Jay, who has been president so far, is to be the ambassador at Madrid, his place being taken by the Hon. Mr. Huntington, a representative from Connecticut.

On the 23rd we learned from several refugees that, under General Howe, the rebels are gathering four thousand men in Connecticut; that six hundred are engaged in binding fascines at Horse Neck; that Generals Parsons, Nixon, and Glover are coming from New England with three Continental brigades, each eight hundred to one thousand strong; that Moylan's and Sheldon's Dragoons, raised to full strength, have already, under Brigadier Wheithe,[136] advanced from Fishkill to Stanwick, where Armand's Corps has been swarming six weeks and whence during this time some forty dragoons have come over to us; that as soon as we vacated Stony and Verplanck's points their strong wagon train was taken across the North River; and that Washington will follow with the effective part of his army, rank and file, and partake in a very important expedition from New London, where 250 flatboats have actually been collected since the 9th of this month.

All these reports make no impression on English headquarters. These movements are taken at the most for strategic maneuvers agreed upon with the French fleet for the devastation of either Rhode Island or Long Island. An attack on our new works requires more than the preparations just described. Besides, they have no magazines on this side. They have no stores either in New London or in Boston. In Boston great embarrassment seems to have arisen for lack of wood. From two hundred to twelve hundred piasters, *hard money*, are being offered as a premium to the first to furnish from two hundred to a thousand cords of firewood.

The Portsmouth region can provide nothing, and Brigadier General McLean is keeping close watch between there and Penob-

---

[136] Possibly Brigadier General William Heath, whose quarters were at Continental Village near Sing Sing until October 24, when he was ordered to camp at Peekskill (*Heath's Memoirs of the American War*, p. 234). The intelligence Baurmeister reports in this paragraph is such a mixture of fact and rumor that it is impossible to make a positive identification.

scot. He has so fortified his position and the Bay with the great number of cannon from the burned rebel ships that he has nothing to fear. He is probably the first Briton who understands the art of winning the confidence of the inhabitants. He has organized militia twenty miles inland, who now occupy posts along the shore, so that no foreign boat can come in, though many an attempt has been made from Portsmouth to get wood from these shores.

On the 26th the Hessian General Staff took quarters in New York. Before I conclude, I hope to be able to enclose a distribution list [137] showing how the troops are quartered and posted.

Nothing further is being said of an expedition by sea, and the many transports had to be stationed in the several bays along the Long Island shore of the East River, so that the North River would be clear. Meanwhile, General Clinton says nothing until he is ready to act. Admiral Arbuthnot is stationed off Sandy Hook with five capital ships, three frigates, one fireship, and nine transports ready to join Hyde Parker, whose fleet is expected in this neighborhood.

On the 27th General Prescott with the entire garrison from Rhode Island arrived in the Sound under a press of sail. To be sure, he had conditional orders to evacuate Rhode Island rather than expose himself to the French fleet. Perhaps his report mentions that this fleet is nearby. Moreover, an order was dispatched five days before, revoking these conditional orders; but the ship missed Prescott's fleet. He left behind over a thousand tons of hay, but the works were all completely demolished. I believe that the whole force will have to return, and I expect to have a definite report before I finish this account.

If only this pernicious ague and putrid fever would let up, General Clinton could undertake a great deal with the troops. But the misery prevailing here cannot be described; it must be seen. Many officers and servants are sick in bed. How the poor subalterns, almost all of whom are in this miserable situation, can stand it is more than I know. Having to pay double to be nursed by strangers, procuring fresh food at the highest prices, and the high cost of medicine—all these are inevitable worries. Of the

[137] See end of this letter.

officers in von Mirbach's Regiment only Major von Wilmowsky,[138] Captain Rodemann, and Lieutenants Wissenmüller and von Biesenroth are well; the rest are deathly ill. Some of them have had from three to five relapses. To increase this misery, the surgeons and women have been taken with fever, too. I distinctly feel the unavoidable cost of my own and my four servants' illness for nine weeks. General Pattison of the British Artillery, at present commandant of New York, can do nothing to bring down the high prices. The Long Islanders bring nothing to market, and force is of no avail.

Nothing is more indiscreet, in my opnion, than to burst forth into immodest complaints, but, since the captains have had their budgets so greatly reduced and the commissariat has given them so little support in the annual balancing of the most important accounts, never failing, however, to make prompt reductions daily, they are no longer in a position (as they formerly were) to give their subalterns the least financial assistance. Full of trust and confidence in your Lordship, I take the liberty of giving a faithful and detailed report of our situation in this respect, for we were astonished to learn that at times there prevailed in the fatherland the erroneous supposition that because of the large appropriations, we caused too much expense. Your Lordship will realize that since we spent nearly five months getting here, the payment was well earned. Then we began to draw the English *douceurs*. Besides, from the very beginning of the operations until the middle of 1778, i.e., while we were marching through the provinces, most of the regiments, being furnished with good provisions, caused no expense. Moreover, many of us secured a great deal of booty. Then the passion for gambling inherent in the British also offered an opportunity to gain money. Nevertheless, it cannot be denied that but few of the Hessians are without debts, and considerable ones. It is tormenting to know that we shall leave nothing but poverty to our families, an evil companion indeed. Who does not love his family dearly enough to hasten to rescue them from this deplorable situation and to dispense with everything possible to

[138] Major Emanuel Ernst Adam von Wilmowsky, Regiment von Mirbach.

help his beloved? Can this faithful description possibly be mis-
understood?

In view of the prevailing regulations it is extremely precarious to continue men on the payroll year in and year out when they
are in the field. It was by no means so in the last two wars. But
the field regulations deny us this profit from one annual muster
to the next. Four reichskronen in German money per man for
small articles of clothing is too little. Our account books prove
that frequently twice as much must be paid per man.

We appreciate, of course, the care shown in sending over
linen, shirts, shoes, and sole leather. The cost is small compared
with the local prices for these articles; for example, five and one-
half shillings sterling for a pair of shoes, two and one-third for a
pair of soles, and twelve and one-half Spanish dollars for a pair of
high boots. On the other hand, the articles sent lose one-third of
their intrinsic worth during the long transportation. Moreover, we
are doing field service and not garrison duty.

I am confident that in view of these just remarks it will be
appreciated that four reichskronen fall far short of being enough.
This is our true situation, and I humbly beg your Lordship not
to take anything amiss, for my intentions are the very best. Far be
it from me to make even the least indiscreet complaint; yet I do
feel compelled to report in detail on this matter, which I believe
has become very grave, for a good manager, if he wants to attend
to his company honestly, must economize on all sides. Unless he
does this conscientiously, what evil consequences will result!

I gave Captain von Wreden, who left here on the 12th of this
month, letters dated the 22nd and 28th of September. He will
deliver them in due course. Had I not become ill again on the
28th, I should have continued my journal to the day of his departure.

On the 29th of this month I was honored by your Lordship's
letter of the 19th of February this year. The *Europe* man-of-war
which should have delivered the packet twelve weeks ago, completely overlooked it, which explains why those letters are acknowledged so late. I humbly thank your Lordship for the gracious
benevolence shown me.

On that same day we first learned of the expedition of Lieutenant Colonel Simcoe, commander of the Queen's Rangers, who had left Staten Island and landed at Perth Amboy in Jersey on the 26th of this month [139] with seventy-two mounted Rangers and six guides. He immediately advanced on Quibbletown,[140] where he found Washington's large stationary camp of last year completely demolished except for a few huts. It was not worth while spending more time there, so Colonel Simcoe hastened to the Raritan and burned all the newly-built rowboats, which could easily have accommodated 150 men at a crossing. There, in the house of one Van Horn, he found six rebel officers, who made written statements acknowledging their imprisonment and gave their word of honor to cross to Staten Island within twelve days.[141] The buildings with the grain and forage collected along the river and the warehouses also were completely burned. Thence the troop proceeded to Somerset,[142] where it opened the prison and freed fifty-two Tories, after which it set fire to the prison. It also caught a notorious gentleman, John Hampton,[143] for whom we have been searching for two years. At daybreak of the 27th Simcoe started back by way of Brunswick over wood roads.

This side of Brunswick he was attacked from the right by 220 rebels, and on the first volley two men were killed and five wounded, and Simcoe's horse was shot from under him. Simcoe fell to the ground and broke his right thigh. His men believed him dead. Under Captain Sandford's [144] command, they pursued the rebels to the plain beyond Brunswick, killing one major, two captains, and several subalterns and taking twenty-eight prisoners. Captain Sandford, while continuing to retreat to Perth Amboy, endeavored to gain one cleared elevation after another, but the rebels following him would not come out into the open. On their retreat the troop set many buildings on fire and took along all the men whom the liberated prisoners declared to be militia.

---

[139] Read "last month"; the letter is dated November 8.
[140] Now New Market.
[141] Simcoe expected to find Colonel Moylan at Van Horn's (Vanhorn's) house.
[142] See *Simcoe's Military Journal*, p. 114.
[143] Captain, New Jersey militia.
[144] Not identified. CAPT, BUCKS COUNTY LIGHT DRAGOONS, ATTACHED WITH THE QUEEN'S RANGERS.

On the 28th Captain Sandford arrived with his men on Staten Island, where Major Armstrong now has the command of the Queen's Rangers, while Colonel Simcoe, suffering from a dangerously fractured leg, lies a prisoner in Brunswick and is unable to obtain his release on parole. It is a real loss.

The Anspach troops were ordered to sail to this city, and today, the 31st, when the packet is to be closed, they are to disembark. The rest of the Rhode Island garrison remained at anchor in Huntington Bay. General Clinton has established his quarters in Denys's house on Long Island. He had himself taken to Sandy Hook to confer with Admiral Arbuthnot, but we have not heard whether Rhode Island is to be occupied again.

General Wayne [145] with two thousand militia and a train of artillery is already on the said island, and Washington, we are told, is making great preparations to undertake something. Since the small area that we occupy is so well fortified and since it is already so cold that his naked militia cannot take the field, all his projects will fall through. Lieutenant Colonel von Schuler [146] has been ordered to command the Grenadier Battalion vacant von Minnigerode for the time being.

Since the packet will not be closed today, this account will continue into November. On the 2nd of November thirty families arrived here from Rhode Island who were unwilling to tolerate General Wayne. We provided quarters for these unhappy people. Unfortunately, we have not yet received any news of the fate of Major von Hanstein of von Lossberg's Regiment. Soon we shall have cause to fear that he and the two companies of the said regiment have perished. Major von Stein has hopes of being released on parole. We still have not received any report from Lieutenant Colonel Heymell; we know of his capture at Egg Harbor on the 1st of October only from a few remarks in the Trenton paper, where the number of those embarked was given correctly.

[145] Probably another confusion of Gates and Wayne. Gates was in command in Rhode Island at this time, while Wayne was stationed in the Highlands, moving down to Paramus in November.

[146] Lieutenant Colonel Henrich von Schuler succeeded Colonel von Minnigerode, who had been wounded at Red Bank and had died October 16.

From the enclosed "Distribution" it will be seen that the rest of the Rhode Island garrison have now also been quartered on Long Island. It seems that with the onset of cold weather the sickness is letting up. The Hessian invalids are being brought together and will depart in ten days. I shall send the continuation of my journal with them.

I have the honor to commend myself most humbly and am with the greatest respect [*etc.*]

P.S. I am unable to find a noncommissioned officer who can make a respectable copy. The best one is ill, and there are only a few who are proficient in writing. I take the liberty of again enclosing a letter to Rothenburg. General Leslie has gone alone to Georgia on a warship, which makes everyone wonder.

Distribution for Winter Quarters
1779–1780

ON YORK ISLAND — LAUREL HILL

1. The brigade of British Guards
2. The Erb Prinz and Prinz Carl Hessian Regiments
3. The entire German Jäger Corps, except for a detachment of one hundred dismounted jägers posted in Harlem
4. Diemar's troop of Hussars
5. Von Mirbach's Regiment at McGown's Pass and in the surrounding houses, some of the companies to be quartered in huts
6. The 64th Regiment in cantonments along the East River from Maston's Wharf to Campbell's Tavern,[147] one and a half miles from New York
7. The Loyal Americans, their left wing extending to Bloomingdale and their right to Jones's house.[148] They are in cantonments and cover the North River
8. Von Bose's Regiment, also in cantonments. Its right wing extends to Bloomingdale and its left to Greenwich

[147] On Corlaer's Hook.
[148] Nicholas Jones's "Woodlawn."

NEAR NEW YORK
IN THE NEW YORK GARRISON

9. Royal Artillery
10. The 42nd Regiment, consisting of two battalions, full strength
11. The two Anspach-Bayreuth regiments
12. Four Hessian grenadier battalions
13. Von Lossberg's Regiment

N.B. This garrison regiment has the suburbs as well as Greenwich for its quarters. Its pickets advance as far as Bunker Hill and along the East River from Campbell's Tavern to the Naval Gate.

ON LONG ISLAND

14. The British Grenadiers ⎱ near Jamaica. All in huts, even their
    The Light Infantry ⎰ commanders and subalterns
15. The 17th Regiment of Dragoons at Hempstead
16. The 23rd ⎱ Regiments at Bedford, in huts
    The 80th ⎰
17. The 33rd Regiment at Denys's house, in huts
18. The 37th ⎱ Regiments in Newtown
    The 54th ⎰
19. The Leib Regiment, Hessians, in cantonments at Hallet's Cove [149] until further orders.
20. The Guides and Pioneers at Hallet's Cove, in huts
21. Von Donop's Regiment, at Bushwick
22. De Lancey's Third Battalion
    The King's American Regiment
    Prince of Wales American Volunteers ⎫ all at Lloyd's Neck
    The New York Loyalists
23. Lord Cathcart's Legion, all in Jericho
24. The 76th Regiment in the new barracks of the works at Brooklyn
25. The 43rd Regiment ⎱ in Huntington
    Von Dittfurth's ⎰
26. The 22nd Regiment at Yellow Hook [150]
27. The companies of the 82nd Regiment between Brooklyn and Red Hook
28. Skinner's Second Battalion in Jerusalem

[149] Hallet's Cove, later Astoria, and now the fourth and fifth wards of Brooklyn.
[150] Situated just north of Denys's Ferry on Long Island.

29. The 38th, the 57th, the Landgraf Regiment, and von Huyn's at
    Flushing and Whitestone, in cantonments under the immediate
    command of Major General von Huyn
30. A detachment of the 7th Regiment under Captain Ferguson in
    New Utrecht, in barracks

ON STATEN ISLAND

31. Von Bünau's Regiment in the huts of the Grenadier Battalion Graff
32. The 7th Regiment in the huts of the 26th Regiment
33. The 63rd Regiment in barracks on the height near the flagstaffs
34. The Queen's Rangers in Richmond
35. Skinner's First and Fourth Battalions in huts at Decker's Ferry
36. Lord Rawdon's Irish Volunteers in the houses along the Narrows.
    However, these quarters are not definitely assigned to them.

: 44 :

NEW YORK
DECEMBER 13, 1779

On the 18th of November, when Hessian letters were again
sent off, it was impossible for me to write even a line, for I was
then suffering for the fourth time from ague and colic, being so
ill that it was almost unbearable. I owe it to Divine Providence
that Dr. Michaelis came to my aid in my miserable condition. His
persevering diligence and his art did so much for me during this
illness (though I was just one of his many patients) that I am
well on the way to complete recovery and feel my lost strength
coming back. Our hospitals are becoming empty, and the most
important duty can now be done with all the requisite relief, for
heretofore the few effective troops in the sentinel huts and at the
outposts could not be relieved.

Your Lordship has probably heard from London of the events
in Georgia, which began on the 3rd of September and ended the
9th of October with great success to British arms. We first learned
of them on the 17th of November, when Governor Tonyn sent a
report from St. Augustine to Admiral Arbuthnot dated November
3rd. In consequence, at five o'clock on the evening of the 19th of

November there was a *feu de joie* here and on all the islands, beginning with a salute of twenty-one guns fired from the ships.

General Clinton did not receive a report from General Prevost until the 10th of this month. The enclosed newspapers [*missing*] give a day-to-day account of the entire siege, the unsuccessful attack by the allied forces, their withdrawal, and their losses. We have good news of West Indian affairs, but since we have received no confirmation of the many favorable accounts, I can say nothing positively.

Count d'Estaing was ill [151] when he boarded his ship on the 20th of October. Two days later he left the Georgia coast with a favorable wind, sailed into Chesapeake Bay with eleven ships of the line, and dropped anchor near Baltimore. In the meantime, four frigates collected flour and fresh and salt meat along the shores of Virginia and Maryland and sent them to their ships of the line, which were in need of major repairs. In order that they might not be exposed to a surprise, two thousand men were disembarked, to throw up some batteries in strategic places. Six more French ships sought the Delaware and anchored at Egg Harbor, as did the others at Baltimore.

Admiral Arbuthnot then sent out some frigates to get exact information of the condition of the enemy ships. Meanwhile, two frigates had been dispatched to Barbados to inform Admiral Hyde Parker of all this and to suggest that he leave his station, if possible, with the greater part of his fleet and sail to New York, in order that a large corps under Lord Cornwallis could be sent to Georgia with as much safety as profit. These troops have had orders to be ready to sail since the 22nd of November.

On the 9th of this month the *Roebuck* man-of-war came to anchor again before the city. However, nothing has come to our knowledge of any reports she may have brought. Circumstances allow us to surmise that Admiral Hyde Parker has not arrived in this vicinity and that the French ships have been repaired and are cruising between Egg Harbor and the route to Boston in order to intercept our provision fleet from Cork, for, while the artillery,

[151] D'Estaing was wounded during the siege of Savannah (see below).

pontoons, ammunition, and equipage for the intended expedition have been taken into the ships, the regiments and battalions under orders to sail have been told to remain quiet.

Only the generals and effective colonels and commanders are allowed to take one horse each on board ship; consequently, it was again advised that each one endeavor to dispose of his horses. General Clinton himself will go on this expedition. Since this has been known, the grenadiers, the light infantry, and the volunteer corps have had good reasons to fear that Lord Cornwallis will remain here. The Hessian grenadier brigade is leaving its new uniforms and heavy equipage behind, while von Huyn's Regiment has put all its belongings on board, for this regiment and its chief will join the two Hessian regiments in Savannah to form a brigade.

Your Lordship will see from the reports how much illness there has been in these two battalions and that they continue to suffer from this devastating evil. The troops are still quartered as they were, except that a month ago the three companies of von Lossberg's went from here to Hempstead Plains on Long Island into the best of quarters.

Unfortunately, Major von Hanstein is still missing. The *Roebuck* was unable to learn anything concerning him in the Bermudas, Barbados, Antigua, or Statia;[152] nor can anything be learned from Boston or the Halifax coast. On the 2nd of this month a ship ran in from Quebec, but again all inquiries were in vain.

We are also as much in the dark about the two and a half companies of the 44th Regiment. We most fervently hope that we shall soon receive good news, and if not, that such accidents will not occur again. The soldiers are now twice as unwilling to board a ship, especially since the British are not keeping the transports in good repair and are overcrowding them. Every transport ready to go on the expedition has been inspected by a special commission authorized by the Admiralty and has been provided with the best of provisions for seventy days.

I send herewith a report [*missing*] which General Lincoln made on the 22nd of October, immediately after returning from

---

[152] I.e., St. Eustatius, at the time also called St. Eustatia and sometimes Statia, for short.

Charleston. According to dependable information direct from Philadelphia, however, the disconcerted members of Congress were unable to conceal the fact that the President deemed it wise to correct it to some extent.

General Lincoln had a heated argument with Count d'Estaing as early as the 13th of September for summoning General Prevost to retire from Georgia in the name of his sovereign, which Lincoln meant to do himself, and which was to have been done in the name of Congress. Count d'Estaing, however, believing that all Georgia was in the possession of the British, thought this a good reason to make the conquest for France.[153] Lincoln's force was too weak, for no militia could be raised, and eight hundred of them, poorly armed, had left him immediately after marching out of Charleston.

General McIntosh, therefore, brought together on the Georgia-Carolina border about nine hundred men, most of them negroes, who swelled his force, to be sure, but only increased the Frenchman's contempt for all Americans. From the first moment when the allied forces encamped between the Savannah and the two roads from Sunbury and St. Augustine, each side despised and hated the other and resolved to have vengeance. The French did not allow any Americans to work with them on the batteries on the left of Tatnall's Hill, about four hundred paces, or yards, from the British lines.

Count d'Estaing has good reason to assert that he received his wounds from the disorderly fire of the Americans. General Lincoln was expected to support both wings when Pulaski, advancing along the Ebenezer road, made the main attack on the British lines and the French advanced on their wing. However, since there was a thick fog during the attack and first one wing and then the other demanded reinforcements from the middle, these troops, as well as their general and officers, became confused and,

[153] Captain Johann Hinrichs of the Jäger Corps, who was at Savannah during the first part of February, 1780, comments similarly on d'Estaing's summoning General Augustine Prevost in the name of the King of France. (See Uhlendorf, *Siege of Charleston*, p. 173.) See also W. B. Stevens, *History of Georgia*, Philadelphia, 1859, II, 207, 224. Cf. letter dated Aug. 11, 1780 (No. 47).

instead of marching to the support of the wings, they fired both right and left, thus killing each other.[154]

The French must have undertaken the attack with the greatest confidence, for they made four attempts. Pulaski was wounded during the first attack, and his corps, called Volunteers of Ireland,[155] exposed to the fire of friend and enemy alike, took flight, leaving many on the field. Count d'Estaing and General Washington had laid out a very dubious plan without consulting Congress. They then communicated to this thoroughly ignorant body a summary report of some parts of their arrangements in a rather arbitrary fashion.

The French officers wounded on the 9th of October who were found before the lines and brought into Savannah made no secret of this to General Prevost and criticized even the indiscreet conduct of their court in this war. It was planned that as soon as Georgia should be taken, General Prevost, if he capitulated, would be allowed to go to St. Augustine with his troops, but, if he made a vain attempt to defend himself and was taken prisoner, then he and his corps would be taken to Virginia and imprisoned like Burgoyne's army. Count d'Estaing was to leave one thousand men in Savannah as a garrison, sail to New York as quickly as possible, and disembark five thousand of his troops and a train of artillery of twenty pieces on the eastern end of Long Island as soon as General Gates with twelve thousand men, twenty guns (not counting fieldpieces), and horses for the French artillery should land on the same shore from Connecticut. Generals Sullivan and Stirling were to land on Long Island from Jersey with five thousand men and sixteen 24-pounders, molest our ships in the narrow entrance to the harbor, and so aid the French in running in.

General Washington with eighteen thousand men intended to advance upon our new works this side of Kings Bridge and storm them without loss of time with all his troops. General Gates

---

154 An anonymous French officer offers a different explanation: "This bad firing was occasioned by a mistake of the ship's steward who had sent to the cannoneers a keg of rum instead of a keg of beer." *The Siege of Savannah as Described in Two Contemporaneous Journals of French Officers in the Fleet of Count D'Estaing,* tr. and ed. by C. C. Jones, Albany, 1874, p. 25.

155 Pulaski's corps was known as the Legion.

had his corps, the artillery horses, and even all the necessary entrenching tools actually ready in Connecticut, for he intended to
land on Long Island, but not begin his operations until Washington should be ready. He had already staked out his camp, which
was to have two lines, for the communication between Connecticut and the East End [156] cannot be stopped.

Throughout October the light dragoons were rounding up
militia from every district, so that General Washington's army
became stronger each day. He had more wagons and horses than
he needed, and since all crops were in, he had enough flour for
sixteen thousand men for at least nine weeks. This whole plan
came to nothing when Congress received General Lincoln's report
on the 28th of October.

Many cannot understand why this well-concerted plan was
given up just because they did not conquer Georgia; but it is clear
to him who realizes that the Americans have learned to know not
only the intentions of their ally but also their own impotence.
They are now beginning to repent seriously of having been so rash
as to turn down the English offer, which the common man has
long accepted, and this gives them but little courage to fight in
earnest. As soon as the events in Georgia became known, the
militia became disheartened and disbanded everywhere. Two
Carolina brigades which are still with Washington's army received
faithful accounts from Charleston, and so the news of the defeat
of their friends spread through the whole region.

Washington, who is always resourceful, went into cantonments in Jersey with five thousand Continentals early this month
between Morristown and Mendham, where his rear and wings are
covered by mountains and his front is so posted that he cannot be
attacked easily, especially during winter. The redoubts at West
Point are still occupied by four thousand men. Gates is posted
this side of the North River near Fishkill. Then they have many
posts as far as the Connecticut border, most of which are occupied
by light corps of mounted troops. This is the way things look in
America at present.

[156] I.e., of Long Island.

Generals Phillips and von Riedesel finally arrived here at the end of November with seven officers. They were brought over from Perth Amboy to Staten Island. General Riedesel had his wife and three merry daughters with him. I cannot keep from remarking that the baroness speaks German only with difficulty and that the children speak English only and do not know a word of their mother tongue. They describe the situation of the Americans to be as defenseless and as hopeless as possible.

We also learned from them that Major von Stein will be paroled, and from a noncommissioned officer and a private, who had been taken prisoner and after working near Philadelphia returned here, comes confirmation that Lieutenant Colonel Heymell and the troops that were on board ship with him have arrived in Philadelphia, that he and all the officers, noncommissioned officers, and soldiers were given their equipage again, and that the noncommissioned officers and soldiers were given permission to hire themselves out to the farmers. So far the said lieutenant colonel has sent no report.

The invalids are about ready to sail. There are four officers with them, Captain Reichel,[157] Lieutenants Spener and Heymell,[158] and Captain Ostwald. Lord Rawdon's retirement from the post of adjutant general of the army turned out very unfortunately for him. He was unable to obtain a command in Georgia, and upon his return he found neglected all those whom he had recommended to General Clinton, who had promised him his support, only to forget it. This conduct as well as some other things dispirited Lord Rawdon and he was displeased to see his recommendations unheeded.

Captain Ostwald recognizes the justice of the judgment pronounced against him but trusts with great faith to find forgiveness and sympathy at our court. Everyone who knows him from the last campaign,[159] during which he conducted himself well at

[157] Original not clearly legible: either Reichel or Reicher. Eelking-Rosengarten has a captain Ludwig Reichell in the Dittfurth Regiment, and the *Staats-Calender*, a staff captain Philip Ludwig Reichel in the same regiment.

[158] Lieutenant Heymell was wounded at Red Bank.

[159] The Seven Years' War? or the campaign of the previous year? Probably the latter.

all times, hopes that his misery will not follow him into old age. A considerable sum of travel money has been collected for him in the corps, and in case the English should not furnish provisions on the journey, his Excellency General von Knyphausen was generous enough to declare that he would pay his maintenance as far as England.

Captain Noltenius, flattered with the hope that Chief Surgeon Bauer [160] will attempt to extricate the lead from his wound, has remained here to undergo the operation. Dr. Bauer has told him that his lameness will disappear as soon as the bullet is removed. The invalids consist of fourteen noncommissioned officers and sixty-six privates.

The news of the surprise of Fort Stanwix was premature. General Clinton must have been of the same opinion, for he had the bearer of this news rewarded with five piasters only, in spite of the fact that this person is known as a Tory in Albany and has therefore exposed himself to double risk in coming here. General Wayne [161] very soon left Rhode Island, leaving behind a colonel with 250 men as a garrison.

I have the honor to commend myself to your Lordship's continued benevolence and remain with the greatest respect,

Your Lordship's

Most obedient servant

Carl Baurmeister

New York
December 13, 1779

[160] Probably Carl Wilhelm Bauer, First Hospital Surgeon. (*Staats-Calender,* p. 43.)

[161] See 1779, note 145. General Gates arrived at Heath's headquarters from Rhode Island, November 23.

1780

: 45 :

NEW YORK
MARCH 26, 1780

Right Honorable Lord,
Gracious High and Mighty Major General:

My last account, which I had the honor to finish on the 13th
of December last year, did not leave until the 24th of that month.
There has been no opportunity since then to send a letter; but
today, the 20th of March, it has been announced that within the
next few days a packet will sail for England. On the 19th of February we were made happy by receiving, by ordinary packet, letters
from Hesse; among them was your Lordship's gracious letter of
August 6th last year, in which my letters up to the 30th of June
were acknowledged.

I wish nothing more than to give your Lordship good news.
Everything worth communicating follows in the order in which
it was brought together. The enclosed list [1] enumerates the troops,
men-of-war, and transports which sailed from here on the 26th of

---

[1] The enclosure, slightly torn and measuring 12 by 14½ inches, gives the names
of the warships and of the 88 transports and shows the distribution of the regiments
and battalions, numbering 8,708 men, and their horses and provisions, among the
transports. The list is reproduced in reduced facsimile in the editor's *Siege of
Charleston.*

December on the expedition to the south under the immediate command of General Clinton. Two days later this fleet was scattered by a violent gale. Most of the horses had to be thrown overboard. Finally, however, the fleet assembled again with the exception of three small ships, namely, the *Lady Crosby* with a cargo of uniforms and tents for the British volunteers at Savannah, the small craft *Swift,* and the sloop *Henry,* which, we later heard, were captured by four rebel frigates two leagues off Cape Hatteras and taken into Charleston harbor. The four frigates were the *Boston,* the *Ranger,* the *Providence,* and the *Queen of France.* These ships and the French warships which Count d'Estaing left behind when he left the coast of Georgia set sail again on the 23rd of January. The French ships are the following: the *Bauvais,* six hundred tons and equipped with sixty-four guns, the *Fovay,*[2] also sixty-four guns, the frigates *Iphigénie* and *Chimère,* and the two captured English packets, the *Providence* and the *Comet,* each twenty guns.

We have no other trustworthy news of this expedition. The rebel newspapers talk of this fleet being in very dire distress, mentioning among other things that a ship with a cargo of heavy guns, six thousand muskets, and ammunition has sunk and that many others have been captured.

Meanwhile, General Lincoln has reported to Congress from Charleston that General Leslie has the command in Savannah, that his troops are quartered over a large area, that General Prevost has taken over the command of St. Augustine, that reinforcements have landed in Georgia, and that he must ask for additional troops if he is to maintain his post. He further wrote General Woodford to gather four thousand Virginia militia without loss of time, supply them with four weeks' provisions, and join him. A similar request was made of General Scott in Petersburg on the James River [3] to hasten the arrival of the militia.

On the 4th of December General Hogun left General Washington's army with the First South Carolina Brigade, and, accom-

[2] The *Bauvais* and *Fovay* are not listed elsewhere as being in d'Estaing's fleet.
[3] Petersburg on the Appomattax. Cf. *New-York Gazette,* March 13, 1780, and *Newport Mercury,* April 5, 1780.

panied by Lieutenant Colonel Washington with half of Moylan's Dragoons,[4] set out to reach Charleston by a forced march.

On the 3rd of February General Hogun reached Halifax in North Carolina in a wretched plight, which he attributed in his account to the bad roads, the lack of food, the crossing of many rivers, and the sparse population of the districts traversed. We shall learn more of this in time.

From the West Indies comes one bit of good news after another through the correspondence of the merchants of St. Kitts, Antigua, Barbados, and the Bermudas with the local merchants. The commanders of the fleet and land forces do not keep each other informed, which, unfortunately, prevents us only too often from taking advantage of extremely favorable situations; for example, on the 22nd of November a ship from Savannah unsuspectingly ran into the harbor of Newport, not knowing that Rhode Island had been evacuated on the 25th of October, a whole month earlier. The ship was not the greatest loss, but rather the sick officers, noncommissioned officers, soldiers, and several commissaries, who were taken prisoners and who are all the worse off since they had left Georgia to regain their health in purer air, if possible.

Vice Admiral La Motte Picquet took over the command of the French fleet at Martinique when Count d'Estaing returned to Europe with several warships, leaving a few ships of the line at various stations for the said vice admiral. While he was assembling his fleet, which was in bad condition, the frigate *Iphigénie* is said to have been captured on her way to Martinique. Hence *Le Fendant* man-of-war left Chesapeake Bay on the 3rd of February for the same destination.

This admiral had, under date of December 29th last year, written the French emissary in Philadelphia that the condition of his fleet was worse than the English could ever describe. He is asking that the lumber dealers in Boston be urged to supply timber. But the agents can accomplish nothing in Boston, for they cannot pay in hard coin, and paper money is not accepted, let

[4] Should read "Baylor's Dragoons" (see Fitzpatrick, *Calendar of the Correspondence of George Washington*, p. 1185).

alone certificates. The merchants of Rhode Island, who still regret the absence of General Prescott's corps but whose greed for gain causes them to pretend to be patriots for the time being, are kind enough to inform us of everything that happens in Boston, New England, New London, and Providence in the hope that we shall soon take possession of the island again.

Vice Admiral Parker has brought in some fifty enemy ships and captured three French frigates since November. The French on Martinique are consequently much worried that the convoy which is expected from France with an escort of five ships of the line under Commodore La Tour Tourvilliers [5] will meet the same fate, especially since five thousand men are said to be coming over with it. Captain Byron of the frigate *Proserpine* was attacked by the French frigate *Sphinx* before the harbor of St. Eustatius. Since Captain Byron was favored by the wind, the *Sphinx* surrendered after an engagement of two hours.

The above-mentioned three enemy frigates are *La Fortunée,* forty guns, *La Blanche,* thirty-two guns, and the *Elise,* twenty-eight guns; the *Sphinx* carried thirty-two guns. The harbor at Barbados is strewn with prizes, and there is not room enough on the shore to unload the valuable cargoes sent over from France, not to mention the large quantities of provisions, war necessities, accouterments, and tents. At present the English ships are cruising before Martinique with the utmost vigilance; they are masters of the sea there and will do everything to keep enemy ships from escaping them.

Count d'Estaing was confronted by too many obstacles to be able to carry out all the excellent plans he confidentially communicated to Count d'Arcourt,[6] the French governor of Hispaniola,

[5] Identification not positive. The ordinary sources give no information. However, an anonymous letter from Barbados mentions a Mons. de la Tour Tourveille commanding "five sail of the French line" in the West Indies (*New-York Gazette,* March 6, 1780); and an extract from a letter from Brest, dated Sept. 25, 1779, refers to a squadron being ready to sail under the command of Mr. de la Touche Traulli (*ibid.,* Feb. 14, 1780).

[6] A. M. Robert d'Argout was military commander at Santo Domingo in the 1760's; a Comte d'Argoult (also spelled Argout) commanded at Martinique in 1777, whence he was tansferred to Santo Domingo—very likely the same person. A copy of a letter of his in the hand of William Bingham is signed "d'Argout" (Stevens's *Fascimiles* No. 247). See also following note.

early in August, who, in turn, thought it necessary to pass the information on to the commander of Havana. A copy,[7] dated August 27th, was found among several intercepted letters on a captured Spanish packet. Its essential matter may be expressed thus: Count d'Estaing intended first to sail to Charleston, South Carolina, to support the city and drive away the royalists stationed before it; then he intended to conquer Georgia and subsequently reduce Halifax; meanwhile some detached ships were to take possession of the Bermudas, where, as well as on Newfoundland, he meant to establish a garrison which would be covered by divisions of his fleet left on the respective coasts; lastly, his entire expedition was to be crowned by the conquest of Jamaica, after which he was to station several warships and frigates at Cape François to protect the merchantmen running in and out.

Congress's plans do not fare much better; all their designs are wrecked. The prescribed taxes, which amount to considerable sums in the various provinces, cannot be levied without great protests in spite of the fact that the demands were couched in the most moving terms. In Jersey they are being raised without the least consideration by unscrupulous collectors. In the province of New York, however, and especially in Albany County, the inhabitants are resisting the ruthless collectors. They took up arms under a certain Daniel Bratt [8] of Hoosick when the militia gathered to help those who are collecting taxes or valuable effects, which they sell in accordance with instructions from Congress.

In Connecticut, New England, and Massachusetts Bay nothing has been levied yet; nor are these districts willing to send a representative to Philadelphia (as Congress has requested each province) to find means of raising the value of the depreciated Continental money and to fix prices for the purchase and sale of wares and victuals. Pennsylvania, the province nearest to the meeting place, has unequivocably declared that this precautionary measure of Congress is too late, now that the piaster is worth

[7] Printed in the *New-York Gazette,* Feb. 28, 1780, with the subscription "D'Arcout."

[8] Cf. *New-York Gazette,* March 13, 1780, for a parallel account of Bratt's activities.

sixty-four dollars Continental in trade and by no means more in exchange.

Because of these bold declarations, Congress believes it is no longer safe in Pennsylvania, and all of Philadelphia has come under black suspicion. Nor does General Washington have the same confidence in the Pennsylvania battalions that he did, and not a single man of these brigades is taken for his bodyguard, which consists of fifty men during the day and a hundred and fifty at night.

Generals Arnold and Sullivan have resigned, although the latter's resignation, in spite of the fact that he is no longer in service, has not yet been accepted. Lee has been dismissed altogether and has been ordered to retire to his estates. Many brigadiers, staff officers, and other officers have resigned their commissions and gone home.

Congress did something very objectionable toward the end of February to a well-to-do resident of Philadelphia named Beekman [9] in paying back to him in Continental money, pound for pound, the sum of sixty thousand dollars which he had advanced in New York currency at the beginning of the rebellion. This American found no hearing, became despondent, and hanged himself. Immediately after this desperate deed, Don Juan de Miralles,[10] agent of the Spanish merchants in the West Indies, seized an opportunity, under the auspices of the French emissary, to demand in no uncertain manner in a public session of Congress that the money he had advanced either be repaid or valid obligations be given. Whether he succeeded and if so, how, I have been unable to learn; nor have I been able to ascertain the amount involved.

On the 9th of March the commissioners met for the third time at Amboy to effect an exchange of all the prisoners. General Washington's views respecting this exchange seem sincere. He has appointed Major General St. Clair and Colonels Hamilton and

[9] Perhaps Gerard William Beekman. Baurmeister's account could not be verified.

[10] A Havana merchant. (Cf. Roscoe Hill's *Descriptive Catalogue of the Documents Relating to the United States in the Papeles procedentes de Cuba*, Washington, 1916.)

Harrison,[11] while we will be represented by Major General Phillips and Lieutenant Colonels Norton and Cosmo Gordon of the Guards. It would be a good thing if these negotiations brought results. In the meantime prisoners are returning every day. On their circuitous routes to our lines, they find many loyalists.

On the 7th of February a report came in from Albany dated January 24th. It contained a description of the apprehensive inhabitants of the city, whither all the adherents of Congress had fled with their movable possessions from the New Hampshire Grants. Colonel Butler and Captain Joseph Brant were approaching this region with five thousand men on their way from Canada to the province of New York. The garrison of Albany consists of Colonel Goose Van Schaick's Battalion, three hundred strong, and the one at Fort Stanwix of Lieutenant Colonel Gansevoort's [12] Battalion, barely two hundred strong.

When this report was dispatched, the people of Albany, urged on by General Schuyler, were engaged in bringing together on sleighs the necessary victuals for the aforesaid fort. However, since the main magazine in Fort Defiance at West Point had been consumed by fire early in February, these provisions, ready to be taken to Fort Stanwix, were sent to Fort Defiance, and on the 22nd of February Colonel Gansevoort was still waiting in vain for provisions.

The severe winter covered the North River with ice early in January; even where the current of the river is swiftest, the ice was eleven feet thick, in spite of the fact that it is 1,800 yards wide between Fort George and Powles Hook. There are 1,760 yards in an English mile. The sound between Staten Island and Jersey was frozen over much earlier. Hence the precaution was taken of sending all dispensable battalions from Long Island to Staten Island and reinforcing the post on Powles Hook. The rebels attempted to get at the ships frozen in and to set them on fire; but they found

---

[11] The three commissioners were Major General Arthur St. Clair, Lieutenant Colonel Alexander Hamilton, and Lieutenant Colonel Edward Carrington. Robert Hanson Harrison was a commissioner in earlier years, but not in 1780 (Fitzpatrick's *Calendar*).

[12] Peter Gansevoort was a colonel at this time (Heitman).

them properly guarded and sufficiently free of ice, so that it was vain to make further attempts.

Meanwhile General Washington put about three thousand men under the command of Major General Lord Stirling;[13] on the 14th of January at five o'clock in the evening this corps assembled at De Hart's Point on the Jersey shore, crossed over with six cannon and two howitzers, and obtained a foothold on Staten Island at the watering place near Decker's Ferry the following morning at daybreak.

The outpost stationed there had advance information of this visit, for five deserters had left their rendezvous and announced that Lord Stirling was in the vicinity. Brigadier General Stirling,[14] who had the command on Staten Island, drew in all his outposts, threw more men into the trenches, and allowed the rebels to advance to the northern height, a gunshot from his trenches, by which position of the rebels his communication with Richmond and the height where the flagstaffs stand was cut off.[15]

But Lord Stirling did not make an attack; he left Lieutenant Colonel Simcoe's corps in Richmond and the detached post at the flagstaff unmolested, and at four o'clock in the morning of the 16th he returned to Jersey by the same roads. He ordered the house at Decker's Ferry to be set on fire and did not interfere when his men maltreated and plundered inhabitants here and there.[16] Some twenty stragglers and as many deserters remained behind on Staten Island. The cold caused the rebels considerable loss; some fifty men froze to death along the road through Elizabethtown, and, according to their own accounts, six hundred men were so frostbitten that they will always have painful memories of this excursion.

General Washington, highly displeased with this unsuccessful expedition, punished very severely those who had plundered the

---

[13] William Alexander, Lord Stirling, of the American army.
[14] Brigadier General Thomas Stirling, of the British forces.
[15] Cf. *New-York Gazette*, Jan. 24, 1780, which also refers to the troops at "the Flag Staff," where according to other accounts Lord Rawdon was stationed.
[16] Lord Stirling, reporting to Washington, complained bitterly about the Jersey inhabitants and rowdies who followed him onto Staten Island and were guilty of plundering excessively.

inhabitants, and ordered all the stolen effects to be returned to Staten Island. The rebel partisan Captain Lockwood [17] undertook an attack with 130 picked militia from Connecticut on the cantonment of the Refugees [18] near Morrisania; he succeeded in capturing one lieutenant colonel, one major, the paymaster of the Refugees, and ten men in De Lancey's mill, all of whom he took off with him in spite of the fact that the alarm was given in all quarters.

Only Major Huggersford [19] escaped in the turmoil, and, finding his men at the alarm place, he quickly decided to pursue the rebels with thirty-five dragoons, ordering twenty-eight infantrymen to follow. He caught up with the enemy at New Rochelle and killed twenty-three; but he captured no more than forty, for Captain Lockwood had been cautious enough to mount his prisoners and send them ahead to Horse Neck with a strong escort. But Major Huggersford would have caught up with these too, if his horses had not been worn out or if his infantry could have followed more quickly. These were the only attempts made by the rebels throughout the winter.

We were not only in the best defensive position but benefited from the fact that the inhabitants of this city are faithful royalists. Within a week's time, as the enclosed list [*missing*] will show, they armed and uniformed over five thousand men, who were joined by the marines and the British commissariat department.

The arrangements made by Generals von Knyphausen and Tryon, which General Pattison was able to effect without loss of time, were highly praised by everyone and doubled the rebels' attention and field duty, the result of which was an extraordinarily heavy desertion among them. However, only a few of the deserters came over to us; they went home instead. Those who came to Staten Island and Powles Hook or Kings Bridge complain about lack of small articles of clothing rather than insufficient provisions, about having to do heavy duty with no rum and but little salt, and

[17] Captain Samuel Lockwood (see Hufeland, *Westchester County during the American Revolution*, p. 323).

[18] I.e., James De Lancey's Refugees.

[19] Huggersford is mentioned in four different sources, but none of them has a given name.

about the greatly depreciated paper money, which buys almost nothing. They all agree that the strength of their army at Morristown is between six and seven thousand men, including one third of the New Jersey militia,[20] who are relieved every six months and are given nothing but ammunition and provisions.

In the night of the 25th–26th of January Major Lumm of the 44th Regiment, at present commandant at Powles Hook, proceeded to Newark with part of his garrison and three hundred infantrymen of the New York garrison; he surprised the post, killed eight men, and returned with thirty-four prisoners, without the loss of a single man.

At the same time Lieutenant Colonel Van Buskirk of Skinner's corps visited the garrison of Elizabethtown from Staten Island. He had only 120 infantry and twelve dragoons with him and fell upon the rebels when they least expected a surprise. He captured two majors, three captains, several subalterns, and forty-seven men, as well as a dragoon patrol of five horse. The double attack made the enemy fire all their alarm cannon; all Jersey took to arms, and everyone believed that a main attack would follow.

Subsequently, some troops of mounted Refugees made incursions into Jersey, advancing by way of Bergen to Rahway and also to the post on Oyster Bank [21] in Newark Bay. Among their prisoners were eight prominent rebels [22] who had gathered in a house and were enjoying music, hard cider, and the company of girls. They had gone there in sleighs, which were brought to Staten Island with horses. This especially incensed the rebels, and they threatened the Refugees. However, the horses come in handy, for nearly one thousand have died for lack of forage. As usual, no thought was given to the erection of a forage magazine until it was too late; nor was any firewood stored.

It is difficult to describe how greatly the garrison and especially the patients in the hospitals and under private care suffered

[20] The German may possibly be translated to mean that one third of the army at Morristown consisted of New Jersey militia.

[21] Oyster Bank is the shore along the east coast of Bergen Point.

[22] Lieutenant Wynantz, New Jersey militia, and eight men of Colonel Jacques' regiment. The sleighs are said to have been brought to New York from Staten Island *over the ice*. See *Royal Gazette*, Jan. 29, 1780.

during the extremely cold winter, for the deep snow made all roads impassable and we could barely clear footpaths. Our need was so great that ships were condemned and torn to pieces, and the trees of the beautiful avenues on York Island as well as the fruit trees had to be cut down ruthlessly. Fresh victuals were hardly to be had, nor did we have the price to pay for them. In short, it was real misery.

Late in the day of the 2nd of February Lieutenant Colonel Norton with the four flank companies of the British Guards, one hundred Hessian infantry from the Erb Prinz and Prinz Carl Regiments, twenty mounted jägers under Captain Mertz, and forty mounted Refugees under Lieutenant Colonel De Lancey of the militia marched from Kings Bridge to Youngs' house,[23] a distance of seventeen English miles, where the rebels had an infantry post of two hundred men.

Very early the following morning the mounted troops allowed themselves to be seen by the rebels, who thought them to be no more than a strong patrol. Hence, about twenty men left the house and posted themselves in a nearby garden, which was fenced in and provided with a barricade on the inside. They did not fire, however, and did not prevent our men from surrounding the house and occupying all the exits. Thereupon the infantry advanced upon the house without platoon fire, forced both the garden and the house, and compelled Lieutenant Colonel Thompson,[24] the commander of the enemy post, to surrender with all his men. The rebels lost forty killed, while others may have burned to death in the house.

Captain Mertz returned on the 4th of February with some ninety prisoners. Not a single man would have escaped had the dragoons been able to get to the footpaths through the deep snow, which had previously been cleared as far as the several buildings at Philipse's Manor. Since this surprise, the nearest rebel outpost has been at the Quaker church on King's Street, where three

[23] The residence of Joseph Youngs was on what is now called the County House Road, about four miles east of Tarrytown, where it intersects the road to Unionville. See Hufeland, *Westchester County during the American Revolution,* p. 324.

[24] Lieutenant Colonel Joseph Thompson, 10th Massachusetts Regiment.

hundred infantry and twenty dragoons are stationed, the latter patrolling no farther than Dobbs Ferry.

As soon as the cold let up and the North River was navigable, his Excellency Lieutenant General von Knyphausen ordered the first winter quarters to be occupied again in good order. The changes had been made only as a precaution against an attack upon Staten Island and Powles Hook during the severe winter.

On the 4th of this month these orders were carried out, except that Lord Rawdon's Volunteers of Ireland went from Staten Island into quarters in Jamaica, Long Island, while von Diemar's Corps of Hussars, which had been stationed between Lloyd's Neck and Oyster Bay, moved to Richmond under the command of Lieutenant Colonel Simcoe.

We have no news yet of Major von Hanstein and the two companies of the Regiment von Lossberg under him. On the 2nd of December last year Colonel von Borck wrote from Charlotte-town, St. John's Island,[25] where he lives quite comfortably with fifty men of his own company and Major von Stein's entire company, for they can obtain all sorts of victuals very cheaply, as may be seen from the enclosed list which he sent to me [missing]. It is not known whether the winter was as severe there as it was here, though he gives us to understand that at Halifax the weather was milder.

Brigadier General McLean is throwing up strong fortifications on the Penobscot River. The inhabitants prove to be more upright than at first, for though they had heeded voluntarily the first manifesto, they became disloyal again as soon as the rebel fleet appeared.

At present the rebel garrison in Portsmouth is stronger than that in Boston, where they are leaving room for the French troops, which they expect without fail to be no less than ten thousand, according to their own accounts. With these reinforcements and the three million florins advanced by Holland, the spirit of the Americans is kept up. However, all these dreams will very soon find quick and clear contradiction.

[25] Now Prince Edward Island.

If negligence could be done away with, and if there were no opportunity for profit, the American contest, strange as are its attendant circumstances, would quickly come to an end; but as it is, we cannot get at the source of the evil, nor is the end in sight. How many have died of the pernicious ague since last fall and how many are still sick can be seen from the returns dispatched. I thank God that I have completely recovered.

After I had finished this account this far, Major General Robertson arrived here on the 21st of this month, ten days after leaving Georgia, where he had arrived some time before with a Cork provision fleet of forty-nine transports, escorted by the *Richmond* and *Raleigh* men-of-war. The letters which the said general brought with him and which were dated in the camp on James Island on the 8th of this month (some of them were addressed to me) contain the following news:

After a passage accompanied by great adversity,[26] the fleet finally reached the coast of Georgia on the 1st of February. Besides the two lost ships mentioned above, two artillery ships sank and the *Anna* was lost. The latter has on board two hundred chasseurs under Captain Hanger,[27] one noncommissioned officer, and ten Anspach jägers. This ship, with the men on board, has run into Barbados harbor, and eighty British artillerymen have been rescued in the Bermudas. Unfortunately, the rebel accounts have been confirmed, but instead of six thousand muskets, twelve thousand went down with some brass 24-pounders and 12-pounders and some mortars.

The fleet remained at Tybee until the 9th of February, taking in fresh water and all the troops of Savannah, except a small detachment under General Prevost, who had not yet departed for his post in St. Augustine. The *Defiance* man-of-war foundered near the harbor, but everything was saved. Some of her artillery and sailors took the place of the heavy train that was lost.

[26] The passage from New York to Savannah, which took thirty-eight days, is described in great detail by Captain Johann Hinrichs of the Jäger Corps. (See Uhlendorf, *Siege of Charleston*, pp. 105–41.)

[27] See 1778, note 100.

On the 11th of February the fleet anchored close to the North Edisto, the troops landing on this and the following day. The militia that had been there until a short time before the landing had fled to Charleston. This city has been evacuated by the residents and occupied by seven thousand men, two thousand of whom are negroes. The pavement in the streets is torn up, and a canal has been dug through the middle of the city uniting the Ashley and Cooper rivers. Thus, the capture of this city will be very difficult.

From the 25th to the 27th of February the army crossed the Stono River to James Island. During this time everything needed to lay siege to the city was taken into camp. Two French and six rebel frigates and some armed ships are stationed at Cooper's Ferry, by which the rebels still have communication with North Carolina. General Paterson [28] was ordered to come from Georgia and St. Augustine by way of the back settlements with fifteen hundred men and four hundred Indians in order to invest Charleston from the other side. On his march he was joined by many loyalists.

On the 28th of February a rebel frigate came close to Fort Johnson and cannonaded the right wing of the army. Two men of Graff's Grenadier Battalion were mortally injured before some trenches could be dug. Now the wing is covered by earthworks.

On the 3rd of this month General Clinton as an authorized royal commissioner issued a manifesto promising a pardon to the rebels for partaking in the rebellion if they would now accept the King's protection.

In the night of the 6th–7th of this month Lord Cornwallis was on detached duty across the Ashley River to Wappoo Island with the light infantry and a British grenadier battalion to attack the rebels, who were about to drive off five hundred head of cattle. However, except for a few men and an officer of the Engineers, the enemy had departed two hours before Lord Cornwallis's arrival, leaving the cattle behind, all of which were taken

[28] Brigadier General James Paterson. Cf. Clinton to Prevost, Feb. 18, 1780, *Carleton Calendar*, II, 91–92.

over to James Island. The places where the magazines were established and where the principal fortifications of the city were built have not remained unknown. According to General Robertson's accounts, the city will soon be taken.

On the 23rd his Excellency Lieutenant General von Knyphausen gave orders that the troops under his command on these islands should hold themselves in such readiness to march that they could leave their quarters at the first notice. Fifty transports were again furnished with sixty days' provisions and anchored so close to the wharves that the embarkation of the troops could proceed with all possible speed.

About ten days ago fourteen spirited refugees took a whaleboat and went to Egg Harbor,[29] where they posed as Jerseyites and also as scouts who had been sent out to gather information about some transports which had sailed from New York. Believing all this, three rebel privateers still in Egg Harbor ran out with a pilot boat. As soon as these ships were out of sight of the whaleboat, it sailed into the Delaware and ran into Maurice River. The refugees captured a ship with a cargo of Indian corn and flour, allowing nine men of the crew to go free on parole. Thence they returned to the Delaware and took nine more ships with the same kind of cargoes. They were compelled to burn eight of them and let the crews go under the same conditions as in the Maurice River. Then they seized three more small vessels loaded with food. They engaged five men from them and thus were able to start out for here with five prizes. Since the wind compelled them to sail too close to Cape May, one of the three small vessels was recaptured, but the rest ran safely into the local harbor on the 21st of this month. In exchange for the fifty-six sailors they paroled, a like number of British sailors is expected to be sent in from Elizabethtown.

In order to surprise an enemy post of three hundred men at Paramus church beyond Hackensack in Jersey, Lieutenant Colonel Howard took four flank companies of British Guards and enough men from Kings Bridge to raise his force to three hundred,

[29] Cf. *New-York Gazette*, March 27, 1780. Gaine refers to the men as refugee sailors.

went up the North River to Philipse's house on flatboats, and crossed over to Jersey in the night of the 22nd–23rd. At the same time, Lieutenant Colonel MacPherson [30] of the local garrison departed with three hundred men and crossed over to Jersey at Weehawken, situated almost straight across the river from the northern part of the city. It was agreed that the two detachments should approach Paramus at the same time. But Lieutenant Colonel Howard came upon the enemy post earlier than did Lieutenant Colonel MacPherson, for the latter met with considerable interference in crossing the North River and also encountered several small rebel pickets on his march through Hackensack.

The rebels in the meantime had taken a position in the graveyard, and their commander, Major Stuart,[31] made a valiant defense. Finally, however, he was compelled to fall back, and on his retreat he encountered Lieutenant Colonel MacPherson's detachment. The heavy firing alarmed a great part of Jersey, and enemy troops approached from all sides in such numbers that our detachments could not hope for further success. They therefore decided to retreat over New Bridge. This gave the enemy so much courage that they followed close upon the heels of the detachments and even made some prisoners. Aside from —— wounded,[32] among them two officers of the British Guards, who, together with sixty-five prisoners and fourteen deserters, came in by way of Powles Hook, we had nine killed and eighteen missing.

With deepest respect I have the honor to commend myself and remain in true reverence [*etc.*]

P.S. It is not generally known yet what troops are to be sent to reinforce General Clinton's army in Carolina. Dittfurth's Regiment will be among them. We are busily engaged now in loading the heavy equipage for all the regiments already before Charleston, since the reinforcements will leave in the near future. Major

---

[30] Lieutenant Colonel Duncan MacPherson, 42nd Regiment. For an account of this excursion see *Royal Gazette*, March 29, 1780, reprinted in *New Jersey Archives,* 2nd Series, IV, 253.

[31] Major Christopher Stuart, 5th Pennsylvania Regiment.

[32] Baurmeister evidently meant to fill in the number later.

General Phillips and Colonels Norton and Cosmo Gordon have returned from Amboy; however, there is still some hope that an exchange of prisoners will be brought about. Major von Stein, who has been here for some time on parole from Reading, will return on the 3rd of April.

: 46 :

[*NEW YORK*

JULY 4, 1780] [33]

The departure of the naval officer Lieutenant Hele [34] offered
a particularly safe opportunity to send to London my account up
to the 18th of May. [35] I hope he has forwarded the letter according
to his instructions. Since General Clinton has an armed ship departing in a few days, the army has been notified to send in all
the letters for Europe. I have the honor to communicate the following:

On the 29th of May the frigate *Iris* sailed into New York
harbor with three prizes. She had left Charleston Bar on the 17th
of May and was destined for Halifax. However, the prizes she had
taken and the short distance from Sandy Hook induced her to run
into this harbor. Thus we received the first news of the reduction
of Charleston. Then, on the 6th of last month Major Crosbie,
General Clinton's aide, arrived and delivered to his Excellency
General von Knyphausen a complete report, whereupon the enclosed *Gazette Extraordinary* appeared [*missing*]. From the said

[33] The date of this letter was established from Baurmeister's letter of September 10, 1780.
[34] Not identified.
[35] Missing from the Von Jungkenn Papers.

348

major, from Adjutant General André, and from General Leslie I learned the following:

On the 12th of May at four o'clock in the afternoon, General Lincoln and all the Continental troops left Charleston. They marched two abreast with shouldered but unloaded rifles, colors cased, to the beating of one drum per battalion, through the outer barrier past General Leslie to a spacious place, and there formed in line, seized their rifles by the butts in an orderly fashion and stacked them, hung their cartouches and bayonets over them, and laid their colors on the drums.

Thereupon they were withdrawn from the place of arms and taken back to the city, for meanwhile the demolished bridge at the outer barrier had been made passable. Two captains per battalion were selected to maintain the strictest order among the prisoners and report the least disorder. The officers were permitted to keep their swords, but since they behaved very insolently soon afterward, they were relieved of them without ceremony.

The militia, too ragged to march out, were disarmed. After pledging loyalty to the government hereafter and obedience to the extent of bearing arms for Great Britain, they were given sufficient provisions and paroled to their homes. The great number of citizens, most of whom had served during the siege, were ordered to assemble with their arms in the public squares. After they had stacked arms, they were declared prisoners of war.

Many Frenchmen had also participated in the defense of the city. These, as well as the French from Cape François and Martinique who had settled there during the course of the rebellion, and the Spanish and Dutch merchants have been particularly declared prisoners and are to be embarked for France at the first opportunity. Whether they will be allowed to sell their homes and plantations is still an open question.

Major General Leslie took possession of the city in the following manner: A detachment of one officer and thirty men formed the van. An equally strong troop of marines followed, one of whom marched at the head and carried the large naval flag. Two British and two Hessian fieldpieces and their train came next.

Then followed General Leslie at the head of a British and Hessian grenadier company. Three English regiments, the 7th, 42nd, and 63rd, formed the rear. The troops moved in with the greatest propriety to the beating of drums and music. As soon as the British naval flag was raised, the ships saluted, which compliment was returned from both sides of the fortification with twenty-one shots.

During the following days lists were prepared to show how much grain, salt provisions, salt, rice, spirits, rum, coffee, sugar, indigo, and cotton the magazines contained. Other commissioners listed the artillery, small-arms, ammunition, and entrenching tools, and a separate commission under the Artillery Captain Collins [36] was appointed to store the guns, many of which had been made in European factories, in a powder magazine. Unfortunately, the storing was not done with the necessary caution; in fact, the whole business was awkwardly done. Without making sure whether the rifles were loaded or not, they threw them on the pile. Barrels of powder and charged shells only lightly crated stood one on top another. A musket went off, and instantly the entire magazine blew up. Meanwhile some hundred loaded rifles were discharged by the heat and increased the loss; the percussion injured men and houses within a large area. Captain Collins, two of his subalterns, some thirty British soldiers, and as many rebels and idle onlookers were instantly killed, and a proportionate number injured.

All the negroes whose masters have been declared prisoners have been listed and are counted in with the booty, which, with the captured ships and the contents of the magazines, will be considerable. According to General Clinton's promise, all the troops participating in the southern expedition are to share in this booty,[37] but he and Admiral Arbuthnot have already renounced their shares. Meanwhile, Major General Leslie tells us that after

[36] Positive identification not made. He embarked with the fleet on the *Russia Merchant*, which carried artillery. This ship became separated from the fleet and later foundered and sank. Captain Collins and his men were rescued by a British privateer and taken to Bermuda. Finally, on April 6 or 7 he and eighty men arrived at Charleston. (See Uhlendorf, *Siege of Charleston*, pp. 51, 89, 239, 241, 297.)

[37] There was no booty. (Cf. following letter.)

the inhabitants had signed a humble address (enclosed herewith) [*missing*], which was answered by a proclamation, the inhabitants were not considered prisoners any longer, and many of their possessions have been returned to them.

Lieutenant Gironcourt,[38] who since the beginning of June has filled the position of the late Captain Martin,[39] whose death is a real loss, will make a plan showing the position of the city of Charleston, its fortifications, the outer forts, and the works raised in front of it by the British during the course of the siege. This plan, together with the necessary explanations, will be sent by the next packet. It will show more clearly how little the rebels must have known of military science to defend themselves so poorly in view of their many excellent advantages, and that we must consider ourselves very fortunate indeed to be masters of the city, especially since the artillery had been lost at sea and had to be replaced by guns taken from the ships. General Lincoln was given permission to follow his dispatches to Congress in person.

On the 17th of June General Clinton arrived at Staten Island with 105 ships, and Admiral Arbuthnot on the *Europe*. With him were the light infantry, the British and Hessian grenadiers, the 42nd Regiment, the Hessian jäger detachment under Major von Wurmb, and the infantry of the Queen's Rangers.

Lord Cornwallis, who was left in command in South Carolina, has the following troops under him: as a garrison in Charleston, the 7th, 63rd, and 64th Regiments, Dittfurth's, Huyn's (but Major General von Huyn [40] has returned to New York ill with consumption), and d'Angelelli's,[41] the last having been ordered up from Savannah. Then, still farther south there are the 23rd, 33rd, and 71st Regiments, the North and South Carolina Volunteers,[42]

[38] Charles Auguste de Gironcourt de Vomecourt, of the Hessian Artillery (*Staats-Calender,* p. 37).

[39] Captain Reinhard Jacob Martin, of the Hessian Engineers, who made some fine maps and plans, of which six are in the Clements Library.

[40] Major General Johann Christoph von Huyn kept a diary during the siege of Charleston. It was translated by the editor of the present volume together with several other diaries and letters of Hessian participants of the siege (Uhlendorf, *Siege of Charleston,* pp. 365–97).

[41] D'Angelelli's Regiment is the old von Rall, which became Woellwarth's and then Trümbach's and finally d'Angelelli's.

[42] Should read: North Carolina Volunteers and South Carolina Loyalists.

Ferguson's Corps (he is now a lieutenant colonel), two battalions of Skinner's, the mounted Legion under Lieutenant Colonel Tarleton, which has grown to five hundred horse, and lastly Lord Rawdon's Irish Volunteers.

As soon as the line of fortifications about the city is tightened and made more regular, which is being done under the supervision of Major Moncrief,[43] who expects to have it finished before the end of October, a force of only two thousand men will be enough to garrison the city and the forts. The entrance to the harbor of Tybee is already strongly fortified, and the Bar is covered by four frigates.[44]

Lieutenant Colonel Tarleton has made a successful excursion through Camden, and there are no armed rebels in the country he swept over. Major General Leslie says that with the occupation of Charleston, the trade with France has been cut off and that the resultant decline in credit is very embarrassing to the Americans and still more so to the French. This is confirmed by the merchants of New York.

I wish I had the space to write an account of the comfortable houses and riches of the Carolinians as well as to describe the obstinacy with which nearly all show themselves to be rebels. But I hope it is their last step and that it is inspired more by shame for having surrendered the city than by ambition.

General Clinton speaks with unfeigned praise of the untiring and fearless behavior of the Hessian grenadiers participating in the siege. The jäger detachment silenced the enemy cannon more than once and killed the artillerymen as soon as they allowed themselves to be seen.[45]

When the Adjutant, Major Crosbie, arrived on the 6th of June, his Excellency General von Knyphausen had just embarked with the following troops, intending to land at Elizabethtown in Jersey: the British Guards, the 22nd, 37th, 38th, 43rd, and 57th Regiments, two battalions of Skinner's, two regiments of Anspach-

---

[43] Major James Moncrief of the Engineers. His name is often erroneously given as Moncrieff.

[44] Baurmeister actually says: "and the Bar covers four frigates."

[45] Cf. Uhlendorf, *Siege of Charleston, passim.*

ers, the entire Anspach and Hessian Jäger Corps, the 17th Regiment of Dragoons, von Diemar's Hussars, the mounted Queen's Rangers, the Leib Regiment, and the Landgraf, Donop's, Bünau's, and Bose's Regiments—a force of about six thousand men. General Governor Robertson and General Tryon went along as volunteers, but those to whom brigades were given were Generals von Lossberg, von Hachenberg, Mathew, Skinner, and Stirling. The last-named had the vanguard.

The march lay through Elizabethtown, through Connecticut Farms [46] to Springfield, where a position in the Short Hills was to be taken with Chatham in front of the right wing, and then, in accordance with circumstances, further toward Morristown or back. It was General von Knyphausen's purpose not to be drawn into any action, but only to look personally into the diverse and favorable reports that have lately been coming in from Jersey— whether the militia was serving any longer and whether the New England brigades would come over at a favorable opportunity and also whether many deserters would come in. These and similar reports have frequently come in to General Robertson, the Governor, and to General Skinner on Staten Island.

Moreover, since Governor Robertson came from England to South Carolina to see General Clinton, it is not unlikely that they agreed before the reduction of Charleston to make an attempt on Washington's weak army corps, without waiting for further news, as soon as Charleston and its entire garrison has surrendered. Since I know that all the troops had already embarked when Major Crosbie arrived and that no decision had been reached as to whether or not this expedition should be carried out, I am constrained to believe that the whole affair was the scheme of Generals Robertson and Skinner.

The troops took with them seven days' provisions and one fieldpiece per battalion, and were allowed only a little equipage. None of these reports was found to be true, however. On the contrary, Brigadier General Maxwell was on the alert in Elizabethtown with a post of eight hundred men and withdrew in good order to Connecticut Farms, alarming the entire country. This

[46] Now Union, New Jersey.

brought the militia together, and they were joined by the Marquis de Lafayette with enough Continental troops to make a force of twenty-five hundred men. At Connecticut Farms the Jägers met with unaccustomed resistance, the rebels holding off our vanguard with fixed bayonets. However, the Leib Regiment and the Regiment von Bünau were even more courageous and put the rebels to flight.

The more we advanced the more it was realized that Washington was always ready to reduce further our still remaining advantage. Connecticut Farms was burned, and on the 8th we returned in good order to Elizabethtown. The enemy followed, and, supposing that the greater part of our troops had already crossed over to Staten Island, fell upon our advanced post, the 22nd Regiment. Their attack was disorderly, and when our post was supported, the rebels withdrew on their own accord to the extreme end of Elizabethtown.

Since the Leib Regiment and the Jäger Corps were out of ammunition, the latter went to Staten Island to get more from the New York magazine. The commandant, General Pattison, then sent the fieldpieces that had been left behind and also four 12-pounders. General Washington then occupied the Short Hills himself, collected his entire force, and had Brigadier Maxwell take a position at Connecticut Farms with one thousand men.

In this situation, everything remained quiet. We learned that Washington was sending his heavy artillery and baggage to West Point by way of Orange-town, intending to follow with his army. This the enemy actually did at ten o'clock at night on the 21st of June. Before they started out, they brought an old heavy iron cannon close to their outpost and, after making a careful patrol, fired three shots at ours, which was a signal that we were quiet and that they could begin their march.

We had built a bridge from Elizabeth Point to Staten Island in order to aid a hurried retreat. Although the rebels were careful not to attack us in battle formation on open ground with the right wing of our troops encamped as far as the lowland before Newark, we nevertheless had to take this precaution, for the militia alone of the rebel hordes, because of their imagined success, had grown in this short time to a force of seven thousand men. They make sudden irregular attacks that resemble surprises and are excellent marksmen. We have not yet learned to meet them the same way and not to offer them our front. It is inconceivable how these people, without being supplied with food, have stuck together and are as steadfast as the Continental troops.

It was General Clinton's intention on his arrival to move into the old camp on the North River in the vicinity of Philipse's house, twenty English miles from New York, and extend his right wing beyond East Chester, including the New Rochelle road. Hence, on the 22nd of June all the troops on Staten Island were embarked again, except the 42nd Regiment and the Queen's Rangers. They crossed the bridge and reinforced his Excellency General von Knyphausen, who, on the 23rd of June, advanced again and chased the rebels through Springfield and across the occupied bridge over the Rahway River. After burning Springfield, he retired again in the afternoon.

The rebels, under the command of Brigadier General Baron von Steuben, kept their position behind strong batteries in the Short Hills. This force consisted of two Continental brigades and about twelve hundred militia. Not a single rebel pursued General von Knyphausen's force, which quietly crossed the bridge at Elizabeth Point. The bridge was demolished the next morning.

Between the 27th and the end of June all the troops went into their present camp, which has already been described, headquarters being in Philipse's house, behind the left wing. The camp is arranged in one line extending through valleys and over hills. Both Sawmill Creek and the Bronx River flow through the line. Beginning with the right wing, the troops are stationed in the following order: on the New Rochelle road, the 17th Regiment of Dragoons; on the road to White Plains at the East Chester Church, von Diemar's Hussars; on their left, the mounted Rangers; in this position the cavalry covers the flank of the British light infantry, on whose left are the British grenadiers; then come the British Guards, the 37th, 38th, 57th, and 42nd Regiments; next, the Leib Regiment, the Landgraf, and von Bose's Regiments, these last three regiments constituting von Lossberg's brigade;

lastly, two regiments of Anspachers and the dismounted Rangers.

His Excellency General von Knyphausen has his quarters in Babcock's house,[47] situated in a valley in front on the road to Philipse's Manor, between the Anspachers and the Hessian grenadier brigade. The pickets of the Hessian grenadiers extend to the North River, and in front of them, on the road to Dobbs Ferry, are stationed the Hessian and Anspach Jäger Corps.

There are no armed rebels this side of the Croton River. Washington has thrown a strong guard around his magazine at Fishkill, raised the garrisons in the forts at West Point to full strength, and gone into his stationary camp at The Clove,[48] having brought along three hundred wagonloads from the Bergen and Essex districts. Great confusion prevails in Philadelphia, and everyone is busy carrying his belongings to safety. There is no lack of victuals and fresh forage, and in East Chester they are making hay.

As a garrison in New York, there remain the Artillery Corps, the 76th Regiment, that of von Donop, and Graff's Grenadier Battalion. Brigadier General Skinner now commands on Staten Island in place of Brigadier General Stirling, who was severely wounded during the Jersey expedition. Besides his own two battalions,[49] he also has under him the 22nd and 82nd Regiments, the latter having been there all along, as well as von Bünau's Regiment. On Long Island are stationed only the militia and the 84th Regiment. The new batteries and redoubts on the island have been finished and now mount artillery.

Not only the frigates, but also the *Europe* man-of-war are cruising with good success, while six frigates have [gone?] to Chesapeake Bay [50]

[47] The rectory of the Reverend Luke Babcock, an ardent loyalist, who died in 1777. His widow continued to live in the house, which was situated on the east bank of the Sawmill River. See Hufeland, *Westchester County*, p. 258.

[48] Smith's Clove.

[49] I.e., Cortland Skinner's Brigade of West Jersey Volunteers, which usually consisted of three battalions.

[50] Rest of manuscript missing.

: 47 :

I had the honor to send my last journal to your Excellency on the 4th of July this year. At that time the army was encamped in one line beyond Philipsburgh on the North River, its right wing extending as far as East Chester. The Hessian General Staff was quartered in Babcock's house. The army remained immobile in this position until the 18th of the same month. The patrols, which scouted beyond Tarrytown, White Plains, North Castle, and Sing Sing did not encounter any armed rebels.

After our movements in Philipse's Manor, General Washington went no nearer West Point than Little Falls on the Passaic, twenty miles from Newark. The greater part of his force is at Horse Neck,[51] and only a few troops have taken position to the west of the Passaic. He experienced a great deal of difficulty in raising the strength of the Continental brigades and in collecting the necessary train between Easton and Morristown to take his provisions (which had been gathered in Pennsylvania, even beyond the Susquehanna) to King's Ferry. Between the 17th and 19th of July General Washington was obliged to go back to Hack-

[51] There is a Horse Neck Bridge in Morris County, New Jersey.

ensack and New Bridge in order to speed up the supplying of
recruits.

According to a general proclamation, all the inhabitants,
irrespective of position, are compelled to appear in person and
either serve six months themselves or furnish acceptable substi-
tutes. Many have resorted to this last means, paying the recruits
eighty Spanish dollars hard money. Unless this is done, the punishment meted out to them is inconceivable. As an illustration, I
mention the following: When his Excellency General von Knyphausen was in Jersey from the 6th to the 23rd of June, Dutchess
County had to raise £30,000, and houses and other property
were confiscated and sold without the least consideration. The
little town of Pequannock, eight miles from Morristown, fared
even worse, for it had to pay £20,000.

On the 9th of July the frigate *Guadeloupe* came in with the
startling news that she had unmistakably sighted, off Cape May,
a French fleet of eight ships of the line, three frigates, and twenty
transports, which, she supposed, would sail into the Delaware.
But after making some inquiries among the American privateers,
Admiral Ternay,[52] who commanded this fleet, sailed to Rhode
Island, and on the 12th of July about six thousand land troops
consisting of the Legion under Colonel Guibert[53] and some
German regiments under the command of Lieutenant General
Rochambeau disembarked on Conanicut. They took possession
of this island in the name of the King of France and with great
solemnity replaced the American flag with their own.[54]

Admiral Graves came to anchor at Sandy Hook with a superior squadron on the 13th and 14th of July. Hurriedly as he
had made the passage from England, it is a pity he could not have
arrived sooner and occupied the harbor of Newport before the
French did. Meanwhile, however, Admiral Arbuthnot had taken
over the command and sailed after the enemy in two divisions
made up of the following ships: the *London,* ninety guns, the
Resolution, Royal Oak, Robust, and *Bedford,* each seventy-four

[52] Charles Henri d'Arsac, Chevalier de Ternay.
[53] Identification not made. The Legion referred to is Lauzun's Legion. Second
in command of this legion was Dillon.
[54] Cf. above, page 324 and note.

guns, the *America, Prudent, Raisonnable,* and *Europe,* each sixty-four guns, the *Renown,* fifty, the *Rainbow, Romulus,* and *Roebuck,* each forty-four; then nine frigates, namely, the *Thames, Iris, Guadeloupe, Delaware, Richmond, Galatea, Camilla, Pearl,* and *Triton;* and lastly two sloops of war, the *Delight* and *Savage.*[55]

On the 23rd of July this fleet blockaded Newport, and by now, the enemy are entrenched up to their ears. General Clinton ordered a number of transports to go up the East River to Whitestone. To cover them, the Queen's Rangers marched to Throg's Neck on the 19th of July; half of them crossed the East River and took position on the Long Island shore.

Some transports sailed up the North River to Philipsburgh, whereupon, on the 21st of July, Lossberg's brigade and the 42nd Regiment embarked, which was done, however, for no other purpose than to mask the embarkation on the East River, where the Queen's Rangers, three hundred dismounted jägers under Captain Ewald, the light infantry, the British and Hessian grenadiers, and the 37th and 38th Regiments embarked.

The ships left Philipsburgh with the tide and anchored later at New York, except that von Bose's Regiment went to Staten Island and occupied the quarters of the 22nd Regiment near Richmond, while this last regiment embarked on the empty transports. After taking on Graff's Grenadier Battalion, too, the loaded transports sailed up the East River to Whitestone, then into Huntington Bay, which was as far as they could sail with the tide. Much as General Clinton had wanted to follow Vice Admiral Arbuthnot to Rhode Island earlier, he was prevented from doing so by continuous east winds. Colonel Robinson's volunteer corps [56] left New York and reinforced the garrison on Staten Island, while the diminished New York garrison was strengthened by the two Anspach regiments.

Major Generals von Lossberg and von Hachenberg remained in New York; Generals Leslie, Mathew, Leland, and von Kospoth,

[55] This list is more complete than any other available; cf., for example, Caesar Rodney, *Letters to and from . . .* , Philadelphia, 1933, p. 23, and Archibald Robertson, *Diary and Sketches in America,* ed. by H. M. Leydenberg, New York, 1930, p. 237.

[56] Beverly Robinson's Guides and Pioneers.

and Colonel von Wurmb [57] as Brigadier of the Landgraf and Leib Regiments were ordered to go on this expedition with General Clinton. His Excellency General von Knyphausen had the command on York Island. General Tryon's brigade, part of von Knyphausen's command, was encamped on the far side of Harlem Creek on the Westchester Heights, where formerly Fort Independence had stood and where now only Redoubt No. 8 remains. This brigade, which was not ordered to participate in the expedition, consisted of the troops that had left the camp at Philipse's Manor July 23rd, namely, the 17th Regiment of Dragoons, von Diemar's Hussars, the rest of Lieutenant Colonel von Wurmb's Jäger Corps, the British Guards, and the 57th and 80th (or Edinburgh) Regiments.

General Washington attempted to bewilder us by all sorts of movements and hinder us in our undertaking. He had the flatboats along the Raritan that had been built two years ago taken down the said river from Brunswick to Amboy and also set in motion the militia stationed between Newark and Elizabethtown. He had two mortars brought up from the artillery park at Easton, and it was rumored that he would attack Staten Island and Powles Hook simultaneously.

General Wayne was ordered to make an attack with sixteen hundred men and six cannon on a little fort which the refugees had built on a wooded height on the far side of the North River opposite Bloomingdale and which they had provided with a blockhouse and four small iron guns in order to be able to cut timber in safety.[58] However, after a cannonade of two and a half hours, the rebels withdrew with a loss of ninety-two killed and wounded.

Eighty-five refugees, inexperienced in war, defended themselves in a spirited manner against the enemy, who were not decent enough to summon them to surrender, but threatened to hang every one of them. The refugees chose Thomas Ward as

[57] Colonel (later Major General) Friedrich Wilhelm von Wurmb of the Leib Regiment. There was also a Lieutenant Colonel (later Colonel) Ludwig Johann Adolph von Wurmb, who commanded the Jäger Corps during much of the war.
[58] The block house was situated at Bull's Ferry. (See *New-York Gazette*, Aug. 14, 1780, reprinted in *New Jersey Archives*, 2nd Series, IV, 578.)

their captain, to whom they vowed to defend themselves to the last man. They had no more than four men killed and eight wounded. This little action is sufficient proof of what the Americans can accomplish when they are determined. General Clinton confirmed Captain Ward's assumed rank and rewarded all the refugees very generously.

Between Paramus and Hopperstown [59] General Washington finally brought together a train of nine hundred two- and four-horse wagons filled with provisions and assembled a force of no more than six thousand Continentals. On the 29th of July he advanced as far as Tappan, and on the following day, to King's Ferry; there he crossed the North River and went into camp at Crompond,[60] which is eight miles from King's Ferry and was occupied by about five hundred militia and two hundred and forty of Sheldon's Dragoons. Washington's outposts extended as far as Sing Sing, this side of North Castle; but he made no attempt to cross the Croton River.

Major General Tryon's brigade had to break camp on the far side of Harlem Creek and take position in the new line. Only Lieutenant Colonel De Lancey with the Refugees remained in Westchester. He had orders to cross the river at Holland's Ferry below Redoubt No. 8 in case he should be dislodged. But the renewed embarkation at Whitestone and the public preparation of other transports on which the garrisons of New York and Staten Island were to be embarked at short notice gave General Washington too much cause for worry to think of landing a large force in the barren Jersey district.

On the other hand, he must have realized that a moderate wind would take us in a short time from the East River into the Connecticut River, where we could land and endanger his rear. This and the fact that the New Englanders levied not even half a brigade of militia were sufficient cause for the small rebel army to set out on the 5th and 6th of this month to reoccupy cautiously

[59] Hopperstown, present Hohokus, Bergen County, New Jersey.
[60] From other accounts it does not appear that Washington went as far inland as Crompond. However, Crompond is on the road from Verplanck's to White Plains, eight miles from the former, and Gaine reports on August 1 that Washington had gone to White Plains.

its former position on the Passaic. Moreover, it saw fit to diminish its burdensome train because the troops were not getting sufficient provisions. This, however, was not owing to a shortage of grain, cattle, and sheep, but to the troops' failure to collect them and erect the necessary magazines, which must be attributed to the lack of their former zeal, confidence, and order.

Everybody is disillusioned, and a disastrous indecision undermines all the American provinces. No matter how this war may end, as long as this mess continues, the people suffer at the hands of both friend and foe. The Americans rob them of their earnings and cattle, and we burn their empty houses; and in moments of sensitiveness it is difficult to decide which party is more cruel. These cruelties have begotten enough misery to last an entire generation. At present it seems that no troop movements will take place before the end of next month, September. Since the French fleet is being blockaded and the French land troops are engaged in fortifying their position, Rhode Island cannot be evacuated. What will happen when the trade winds,[61] which set in the early part of October, no longer allow the ships to lie safely at anchor before Newport harbor, I must describe in a future journal.

General Clinton's intention to sail to Chesapeake Bay with four thousand men, no matter what happens, to find out once and for all whether the Virginians want to be loyalists or not will certainly be carried out. He will undoubtedly return with good news, for the opposition in this province has been so open as to turn down Congress's every request. They are refusing to furnish supplies and raise militia, in spite of a special act of Congress [62] dated June 14th. This act authorized General Gates and Brigadier Generals de Kalb and Caswell [63] to raise an army of eight thousand men in Virginia and Maryland in order to stop the advance of Lord Cornwallis, who returned to Charleston from North Carolina on the 25th of June. The burning heat made all operations

[61] Anti-trade winds? Trade winds extend from approximately 30° N to 30° S lat.

[62] This "act" could not be identified.

[63] Johann Kalb ("Baron de Kalb") was a major general in 1777, and Richard Caswell, commander of the North Carolina militia, seems to have been also a major general.

impossible—another reason why General Gates will be unable to carry out Congress's wishes at this time.

Lieutenant Colonel Tarleton advanced as far as Lynch's Creek. On the 29th of May of this year he attacked and cut down a rebel corps at the Waxhaws. The enemy had one lieutenant colonel, eight captains, fourteen subalterns, one adjutant, one quartermaster, and 293 noncommissioned officers and men killed, and some 50 taken prisoners. Furthermore, Tarleton came into possession of two flags, two 6-pounders, two howitzers, one brass mortar, and thirty-five ammunition and baggage wagons. Our losses were two officers killed, one officer and thirteen men wounded, and some twenty horses killed and wounded. Lieutenant Colonel Tarleton made this attack with 422 horse, since the infantry he had with him could not keep up. In the end, the rebels were pursued as far as Kingston,[64] thirty-five miles from Georgetown.

Before long, Major Hendorff will be able to tell your Lordship from personal observation what the present condition of Charleston is, what kind of a fortification Major Moncrief will build, what success Lieutenant Colonel Ferguson and Major Hanger have had in raising militia in South Carolina, and lastly, how the inhabitants of the city have been moved by the generous return of their property to swear allegiance to the government and give themselves the appearance of zealous Tories.

This act of ours was prompted by the hope that other provinces will follow the example of the Carolinians and have enough confidence in us to give up their rebellious ideas. Otherwise, this righteously gotten booty might as well have been distributed among the troops, as was first promised. To be sure, they do not expect or demand it but certainly they deserve it in view of the many dangers to which they were exposed, particularly since the enemy are unworthy of so much consideration.

The Spaniards have given up the idea of landing at Mobile Point in West Florida. The British ship *Mentor,* coming from Jamaica, captured three provision ships from Havana along that

---

[64] It is not likely that a completely routed enemy would have had to be pursued so far. Buford had surrendered at the Waxhaws.

shore. In order to keep the Indians, those useful auxiliary forces, in good humor, the cargoes were presented to the Creek nation, which put fourteen hundred men under the command of Lieutenant Colonels McIntosh [65] and McGillivray when the Spanish ships landed at Mobile.

The commander of the loyalists in West Florida, Captain Richard Pearis, was so fortunate as to arrange a convention with Brigadier General Williamson's [66] commissioners on the 10th of June. The rebels who had been under arms and the inhabitants of the southern district between the Savannah and Saluda rivers have, accordingly, become subjects of the government again. All the large and small guns were delivered to Ninety-Six, and the garrison of Fort Rutledge, which in times of peace checked the incursions of the Indians, was relieved by new troops. The officers and men and also those persons who had been in the public service of Congress were paroled. A closed battalion of militia at Orangeburg has publicly renounced the rebel service and sworn allegiance to the government. The Waccamaw River has been cleared of all rebel ships, and lively trade is carried on in West Florida, Savannah, and South Carolina.

The British sea force in the West Indies falls short only three sail of having as many ships of the line as the combined enemy fleets, which now number thirty-five ships, though they have not gone to sea as yet with as large and as strong an armament as the British. The action of the 17th of April dampened the well-known British spirit and increased the discord.[67]

Up to the 22nd of May two other engagements took place, and the French alone admit having lost fifteen hundred men in the first and six hundred in the second. Their hospitals on Martinique, Guadeloupe, and Dominica are filled with wounded and sick. Reports from New Providence, which have been confirmed from St. Kitts and Barbados, state that Admiral Rowley has cap-

[65] Captain (not Lieutenant Colonel) William McIntosh was Indian agent in the Southern Department.

[66] Brigadier General Andrew Williamson, Georgia militia, turned traitor July, 1780. He surrendered Ninety-Six to Captain Richard Pearis, a loyalist.

[67] The lost May 18th journal probably had an account of the action of April 17 in the West Indies.

tured twenty-three Spanish transports destined to disembark fresh troops there. General Dalling, Governor of Jamaica, is said to have made several successful landings on the coast of New Spain. Without diminishing the garrison, he is raising a legion, called the Loyal American Rangers,[68] to make these incursions even more effective. Major William Odell has gone down there as a recruiting officer.

French commissaries have bought the necessary train horses in Pennsylvania and the upper part of Jersey and paid for them in cash; but Congress has taken upon itself the particular and troublesome task of furnishing fresh provisions for about twelve thousand allied troops. These large and indispensable amounts can be supplied only by punitive levies, which must now be paid in cattle and sheep. All the horses which the commissaries in New England consider suitable for the four hundred dragoons are being picked up by Colonel Guibert,[69] who, regardless of the wishes of the owners, gives certificates in return.

No more thought has been given to the exchange of prisoners. Lieutenant Colonel Heymell, Major von Stein, and the regimental surgeon Pausch [70] arrived here on parole from Reading some time ago. His Excellency General von Knyphausen was pleased to hear that the noncommissioned officers and men are neither entering the rebel service nor settling down in the country, in spite of the fact that their imprisonment is getting more unbearable every day and their rations are small and poor. Nor are the officers treated much better, for they are believed to be guilty of aiding the escape of the many men who are running away. For this reason the fate of Burgoyne's prisoners in Virginia is even more deplorable. Their main grievances have been communicated in writing by his Excellency to General Clinton with a request for prompt relief.

[68] In the original "Loyal American Rangers" refers to Odell, undoubtedly owing to Baurmeister's garbling of preliminary notes; however, Major William Odell was in charge of this corps.

[69] See 1780, note 53.

[70] Dr. Wilhelm Pausch, Regimental Surgeon of von Knyphausen's Regiment (*Staats-Calender,* p. 33).

On the 25th of April Colonel von Borck sent a letter from Charlottetown on St. John's Island, where the ice had broken only two days before. He is waiting for a transport to take him to Quebec. We have not yet heard from there whether Lossberg's Regiment has arrived. Unfortunately, no one even mentions any more Major von Hanstein and the two companies of the said regiment. The mounted jäger company will soon be about one hundred horse strong, and the cavalry [71] in general have been increased this year to two hundred and forty horse.

The present year is too dry to make much hay, and our stay at Philipse's Manor has been too short to gather more than 150 tons, a ton being 20 hundredweight. Long Island will not be able to provide much. Unless the magazines obtain hay from Halifax, the horses will have another deplorable winter.

Major General von Huyn died on the 25th of July. He was buried according to regulations, Major General von Hachenberg attending to the necessary details. Lieutenant Bornemann of Bünau's Grenadier Company also died in New York. Captain von Eschwege of the Erb Prinz Regiment passed away on the 5th of this month after an attack of colic lasting eighteen hours. He was buried the following day in front of the camp, near Fort Knyphausen. The fever is bearable at present.

When General Clinton was about to sail to Rhode Island, a hospital was established on a transport under the direction of Surgeon General Amelung.[72] In spite of the fact that nothing came of this intended expedition, everything remains in readiness for further orders. Today, the 10th of August, I shall close this journal, for the packet is to sail shortly, although the last announcement is still to be made.

Letters are being called for this very moment. In closing I commend myself to your Excellency. With the greatest respect I shall ever be [etc.]

---

[71] I.e., Hessian cavalry, mostly dragoons.

[72] First Surgeon Johann Amelung of the Hessian Field Hospital service (Staats-Calender, p. 43).

: 48 :

So far this year I have had the honor of dispatching journals to your Excellency on the following dates: March 26th, May 18th, July 4th, and August 11th.[73] I did not send a letter with the transport fleet, which finally set sail on the 4th of this month, because a packet was riding at anchor with orders to take new dispatches to London. Generals Tryon, Mathew, and Pattison and Lieutenant Colonel Faucitt departed on the said fleet. At the same time that the last named was notified of his promotion, he received orders from his general, Loudoun, to return to the Guards.

On the 14th of August the June packet from London was captured off Sandy Hook and all passengers taken to Philadelphia. Captain Wallop [74] of von Knyphausen's Regiment, who has been promoted, was among the passengers. Before being taken from Philadelphia to Lancaster, he sent in a report. On the 2nd of this month the July packet from London arrived safely after a passage of fifty-one days; it brought letters from Hesse, the first since the

---

[73] The journal dated May 18 does not seem to have reached its destination.
[74] The Hon. Bennet Wallop, fourth son of John, Viscount Lymington, and grandson of the 1st Earl of Portsmouth.

middle of March, and thus relieved our anxiety, which was all the
greater because of the loss of the previous packet.

On the 5th of August Admiral Arbuthnot raised the close
blockade of Rhode Island and took a position in the bay of
Gardiner's Island,[75] where even the largest ships can ride out a
storm. His ships are anchored eighteen English miles from New
London and forty from Rhode Island. Our fleet is cruising at present between Block Island, Martha's Vineyard, and the last-mentioned station, and will continue to do so as long as the weather
permits. Five frigates are cruising above Cape Cod to discover
any new enemy ships that may arrive.

The rebels are displeased with the inactivity of the French
on the island, which they occupied alone. The troops that General Heath early brought to their assistance were not allowed to
share in the French provisions, which were to last them for seven
months. On the contrary, the French demanded fresh victuals for
the fleet and the land troops and specified what they were to be.
By orders of Congress, General Heath and his commissaries are
doing everything in their power to comply with their demands.
All the pleasing addresses the Americans make these auxiliary
forces are answered politely, as the enclosed sample will show
[*missing*]. M. Rochambeau refers to his troops as a van and awaits
orders from Washington as soon as the yellow fever in his regiments has let up and a train and horses has been collected. In the
meantime they have completely entrenched and fortified themselves.

General Washington's position extends on the right wing to
Bergen and English Neighborhood, and on the left, to Dobbs
Ferry, where the troops are throwing up trenches on all accessible
parts of the shore. They are also refortifying Fort Lee across the
river from their quarters. General Wayne is in command of the
right wing, and General Poor, of the left. The latter brought a
brigade of New Englanders and erected a blockhouse and new
batteries at Dobbs Ferry but has not mounted any artillery yet.

On the 31st of August the rebels on the west bank of the
North River were no longer to be seen. General Washington had

[75] Reported prematurely (see following letter).

gone into camp with about five thousand men between New Bridge and Hopperstown and ordered General von Steuben to occupy the height behind Bergen with one brigade, so that Morristown and Easton would be covered. If the New England brigade is willing to fill the gap, the latter will have a strong corps set out for Virginia, perhaps under his own command, for Lord Cornwallis left Charleston on the 10th of August, marched to Camden, and there met and defeated General Gates on the 15th,[76] which important news was received at English headquarters by way of Philadelphia on the 5th of this month both in writing and by word of mouth. The dispatches mention eight hundred killed, among them Brigadier General Smallwood,[77] and several thousand wounded and captured. Among the last is Brigadier General de Kalb.[78] Gates, it said, escaped with a small troop of cavalry. General Gates's adjutant is said to have reported this to Congress on the 1st of September. Although repeated confirmation leaves no doubt as to this fortunate event, General Clinton longs to have direct reports now that the packet is about to sail. There were no Hessian troops present.

We have received reports from Charleston that d'Angelelli's Regiment arrived there from Savannah and that Major Matthäus[79] of the said regiment has died. We learned further that von Dittfurth's Regiment already has many sick, that the summer has been unbearably hot—which is also true here—and that many have been overcome by the heat and died of stroke. If the action at Camden turned out as we have heard, then the rebels have only the Pennsylvania and Jersey brigades acting with their army, for the last Maryland brigade was recently marched to Virginia by Brigadier General de Kalb. Eight cannon were also captured in that action.

Several regiments have been under orders to march for this last week, among them von Bose's Regiment, which is stationed on Staten Island. All the fortifications on this island are being increased to twice their strength, and engineers have been appointed

[76] The Battle of Camden took place on August 16, 1780.
[77] Smallwood was at Camden, but was not killed.
[78] De Kalb died August 19, 1780, of injuries received at Camden.
[79] Major Johann Jost Matthäus (Baumeister has Matthias). (Cf. Stryker, p. 390, and *Staats-Calender,* p. 35.)

to keep a constant watch. The discharged Major Pauli was one of them, but there was nothing good in store for him. In his adversity an early death, which occurred on the 5th of this month, was a stroke of good luck. I wish that I had his skill. Lieutenants Lotz and Beerman of von Knoblauch's Regiment [80] likewise passed away, as did also Regimental Surgeon Holdschue [81] of d'Angelelli's regiment. The vexatious fever is beginning to rage again, but not so violently as last year, when no one on the General Staff escaped it. Thanks be to the Lord that his Excellency General von Knyphausen's health has never been impaired. At present War Counsellor Motz [82] and Captain Beckwith [83] are ill. Both are indispensable to the staff, since there is a great deal of work to be done.

The army is anxiously waiting for the recruits. I believe General Clinton will embark just as soon as he learns that the reinforcements are near, for the English regiments are quite weak.

May I once more beg your Excellency to have pity on my helpless sister in Breuna. I wish I might move your Lordship to lighten her terrible burden of having to raise three small sons. Your Excellency could do a great deed of mercy for these orphaned children, whose suffering, due to having lost their father so early, has made me shed many a bitter tear. I hope that Lieutenant Colonel Bretthauer [84] did not deserve such disgrace and punishment as to cause a widow with small children endless suffering. I pray your Excellency to pardon me for showing what I feel for a suffering sister. I would not do it, had I not the greatest confidence in your Excellency, knowing that you are the only one to find ways and means of helping the destitute.

With true reverence I have the honor ever to be [etc.]

[80] Knoblauch's Regiment is the former von Wissenbach.

[81] The *Staats-Calender*, p. 36, has Holzschu (no first names given).

[82] Probably Justin Henrich Motz, Government Counsellor (*ibid.*, p. 105). He sent the official report of the Trenton disaster to the Landgrave (Stryker, p. 229). A Johann Henrich Motz was also a government counsellor (cf. *Staats-Calender*, p. 55), and an H. Motz was secretary to the Hessian general staff.

[83] Captain George Beckwith, who later became aide-de-camp to General Carleton.

[84] Bretthauer was severely wounded at Trenton and died at Dumfries, Virginia. All the officers at Trenton were believed to have been negligent in the performance of their duties.

: 49 :

Although I dispatched a letter on the 10th of this month by a packet which was to have sailed immediately, your Excellency will probably be glad to receive further news by the same packet, which was delayed six days. The enclosed article [*missing*] from the New York *Royal Gazette* will show your Excellency how the Americans inform us of Lord Cornwallis's decisive victory on the 15th or 16th of August. Original letters sent from Portsmouth, Virginia, on the 2nd of this month confirm the defeat of the American troops. Congress itself gives no details of the heavy loss. That the Maryland Continental troops suffered most of all and that General de Kalb, mortally wounded, was taken prisoner are lamented more than anything else in Philadelphia.

On the 7th of August General Gates had sent Congress a flattering report from his headquarters on Little Black Creek,[85] twelve miles from Lynch's Creek and forty from Camden, in which he commented very favorably on the increase of his army. On the 29th, when this report reached Philadelphia, everyone re-

---

[85] There are a Black River and three Black Creeks in South Carolina, but no Little Black Creek; perhaps Baurmeister meant to write "little Black Creek."

joiced, and Congress, for lack of cash, resolved to sell the frigate *Confederacy* to some merchants and put the proceeds at the disposal of General Gates. The shock was all the greater when General Gates's adjutant arrived on the 1st of this month with the news of the defeat.

General Washington has not detached a single man from his army. However, the Pennsylvania militia which had been assembled at Trenton under Mr. Reed, President of War,[86] were sent back to their homes so that a new army could be raised at Portsmouth, Virginia. This army is to reinforce General Gates sufficiently to prevent Lord Cornwallis from following up the advantages of the encounter. At English headquarters they are very anxiously waiting for a direct report, which is expected any hour.

The ships and troops are ready to set out on the expedition to Chesapeake Bay under the command of Major Generals von Lossberg and Leslie, the troops consisting of the entire corps of the British Guards, the rest of the 17th, the 80th, 82nd, 84th, and von Bose's Regiments, Simcoe's and Fanning's corps, and some light dragoons organized by Colonel Watson[87]—three thousand men in all. General Poor of the New England brigade has died, and Brigadier General Maxwell has been cashiered,[88] since he was found guilty of carrying on a suspicious correspondence.

The French on Rhode Island are quiet, and our fleet, superior to theirs, is keeping as close a watch on Newport harbor as possible; but since the trade winds are beginning to blow, Admiral Arbuthnot is expected in the bay of Gardiner's Island any day.

Within the next few days the commissioners will meet again at Amboy and once more attempt to bring about an exchange of prisoners. General Phillips will have the first place on our side, and General Lincoln, on the other. Day before yesterday Captain Wallop, who was promoted in Knyphausen's Regiment, arrived here on parole from Philadephia. Lieutenant Colonel Heymell, Major von Stein, Captain O'Reilly, and Regimental Surgeon

[86] Joseph Reed, President of the Supreme Executive Council of Pennsylvania.
[87] Lieutenant Colonel John Watson Tadwell Watson. See *The Campaign in Virginia, 1781*, comp. and ed. by B. F. Stevens, London, 1888.
[88] According to Heitman, Brigadier General William Maxwell resigned July 25, 1780.

Pausch, who have been here for some time, have received permission to remain longer, and perhaps for good, unless the meeting at Amboy brings no results.

A Spanish packet from Havana was captured in the Bermudas, but all the letters had been consigned to the sea. The last news from the West Indies was received here on the 29th of July and the 5th of August from Barbados and St. Kitts. Whether von Lossberg's Regiment arrived safely at Quebec and whether Colonel von Borck got there from St. John's Island I cannot say for lack of information.

With the greatest respect I have the honor to be [etc.]

P.S. I have been promised two plants of the best variety of magnolia from Philipse's garden, which are to be transplanted here in the first part of November. If they can be transported at that time, I shall attend to it with the greatest diligence and care.

: 50 :

The content of this additional letter will explain why the packet, which was supposed to have sailed on the 10th of September and was subsequently ordered to remain possibly until the 15th, is still riding at anchor. For some time everything has been ready for embarking on the intended expedition; finally, the 28th of September was set as the day of embarkation. However, everything was thwarted by an unexpected turn of affairs:

Since the month of June of this year Brigadier General Arnold has had the command at West Point. He himself was living near Verplanck's Point in a house which, with the surrounding estate, belongs to Colonel Robinson of the provincial troops. This advantageous situation enabled Adjutant General Major André to be in close communication with Arnold. According to agreement, Colonel Robinson and Major André went on board the *Vulture* sloop of war, which lay at anchor in the North River above Fort Lee. From there Major André went up the river alone in a boat to Stony Ferry or Point, where he got into an American boat, and, having previously been provided with a pass signed by Arnold, passed the posts at Verplanck's Point without being stopped. All this occurred on the 24th of last month.

374

Major André left Arnold well informed about everything, for the success of the entire venture depended on his safe return. It was hoped that we would become masters of the forts at West Point so quickly that it would be a complete surprise to Washington. Major André started on his way back through a woods toward Tarrytown, where, on a road unfamiliar to him, he met two militiamen, who were lying in wait to catch a refugee. They stopped Major André and questioned him a long time. In spite of his pass from Arnold and his assurance that he was a French officer, he was compelled to follow them to be delivered to General Arnold.

To make things worse, they met a troop of Lee's Dragoons on the road and behind them General Washington in person, who on the 18th of September had gone to Rhode Island with the Marquis de Lafayette and was now on his way back to Tappan, where the rebels still have their headquarters. Recognized in this fearful predicament, Major André no longer denied his identity. Washington realized the terrible calamity that threatened him and sent an adjutant for General Arnold. The adjutant located the house and found General Arnold willing to accompany him on horseback. Arnold requested the adjutant to remain with the women while he got ready. He could not get his horse saddled quickly enough, and having galloped to below Verplanck's Point, he plunged into a boat, and had himself rowed to the *Vulture* by twelve men, whom he promised substantial reward if they got him there in one hour. He claimed to be carrying a flag of truce on an important matter.

He arrived there safely in fifty minutes, just as a row galley came in pursuit, for the adjutant, finally suspicious of Arnold's long absence, had ordered the row galley to set out after him. She even fired two shots, which, however, were ineffective because of the great distance; besides, the boat was too close to the *Vulture*. Arnold had signaled to Colonel Robinson, so that any attempt of the oarsmen to return after they realized that they were aiding the escape of General Arnold would have been disastrous.

The first thing General Arnold did was to write to Washington warning him to be cautious in his treatment of Major André and asking him to transmit this warning to Congress, which would do well to heed his advice unless it wished to incite him to acts of unbounded revenge. This letter was dispatched by the lieutenant of the *Vulture*, who was treated cordially, but sent back with a mere acknowledgment instead of an answer.

General Arnold was received in New York in a very friendly manner. Everyone laments the fate of Major André and the failure of this important enterprise. Washington shows himself very noble in his reply to General Clinton, in which he says that the case is settled as far as he is concerned, and that he will do nothing to hurt Major André in the eyes of Congress. He is satisfied, he says, with having delivered to Congress a man whose actions will cause him to double his vigilance, and that it would give him no further satisfaction if André were to suffer the extreme penalty, which he indeed deserves. The consequent dispatches sent from headquarters to headquarters and from New York to Philadelphia keep General Clinton exceedingly busy.

Governor Robertson also has his hands full, for General Arnold accused some forty persons in and around New York of being in communication with the rebels. Most of them have already been taken into custody and found guilty at the first hearing.

Major André was taken away from Stony Point under a heavy guard, but we do not know whether he is imprisoned in Philadelphia. He was given permission to ask for his most essential belongings, which were sent to him by way of Powles Hook. On this occasion he was granted leave to write a letter to General Clinton, in which he attempted to console the General, while he himself showed steadfastness in the face of all adversity. It is a pity that it took this extremely capable young man to teach us that we must not be too careless, even with a weak and poorly trained enemy. In the meantime, everyone believes that Major André's chief punishment will be solitary confinement and that the severity of it will be determined by the punishment we mete out to the traitors in New York and St. Augustine—of which I shall report later.

General Arnold will receive the rank of a brigadier general of the provincial troops. He will organize a corps at Jamaica on Long Island, which is to be called Arnold's Loyal Americans.[89] Arnold is a native of New England. In 1761 he was a noncommissioned officer, serving on the side of England against France. After that he became a horse trader and innkeeper in New Providence.[90] At the beginning of the rebellion he offered his services to General Gage in Boston but was refused, and therefore he took service with the rebels, receiving a major's commission. On all occasions he has shown great military talent. On General Putnam's warm recommendations to Congress, he became a lieutenant colonel the latter part of 1774, and a brigadier general early in 1777.[91] At that time, when we were making our attempts on Danbury, it was he who saved the rest of the magazines and drove General Erskine back to his ships with losses. In this encounter, Arnold himself lost two horses, and he shot with his pistol a soldier of the 4th Regiment who was about to bayonet him while he lay on the ground with a wounded foot. In spite of the lameness resulting from this, he served with General Lincoln under General Gates against General Burgoyne, in which campaign he made and carried out the plan to capture this general and his army.

In the summer of 1778, after General Clinton left Philadelphia and Pennsylvania, Arnold became commandant in Philadelphia. The machinations of his enemies, who accused him of deriving unallowed profits from his position, brought about a thorough inquiry into his affairs early in 1779. Although it resulted in his acquittal, he resigned from the service. Having been received into some prominent families in Philadelphia, the Shippens, Allens, and Beekmans—he had married a daughter of the first-named house—Congress was moved to offer him new service, notwithstanding General Washington's coldness. Washington managed to have him put in command over the forts at West

[89] Arnold's corps was called the American Legion.
[90] Arnold was engaged in domestic and in West Indies trade; his home was in New Haven; there are no records available to show whether or not he kept an inn at New Providence, i.e., Nassau, Bahamas.
[91] For Arnold's military appointments see Heitman's *Historical Register*.

Point rather than over the new army in North Carolina, as Arnold had expected. He is only forty-three years old.

My second letter to your Excellency had just been sent from here [92] to New York, very early in the morning of the 15th of September, when we received the news from there that Admiral Rodney with ten ships of the line and several frigates had anchored off Sandy Hook. This is all the information we have of this unexpected appearance. We have learned, however, that on the 14th of August this year a strong fleet of merchantmen left Cape François for France under cover of nineteen ships of the line and many frigates, leaving only La Motte Picquet with fifteen ships of the line at the said cape. The Spanish men-of-war, we are told, have gone to Havana.

Vice Admiral Arbuthnot is still stationed between Rhode and Block islands, and some British frigates are cruising above Cape Cod with great success. New Haven and New London are blockaded, and not a boat can venture to sea from the harbor of Newport, where they are still waiting for the second division from France.

On the 17th of last month General Clinton finally received a report from Lord Cornwallis, for which he had been waiting very anxiously, for the rebels had received news about an engagement as early as the 5th of said month. General Clinton issued no detailed report, which seems all the stranger to many of us, since on the 22nd of September, simultaneously with the festivities commemorating the King's coronation day, a *feu de joie* was fired at six o'clock in the evening by the New York garrison, the entire city militia, and the surrounding forts. Previously this has been intentionally omitted at public rejoicings in spite of all advantages over the rebels.

I have collected only the following facts: After Charleston had fallen into British hands on the 12th of May, after the post at Camden had been established, and Lieutenant Colonel Tarleton had dispersed the rebels on Lynch's Creek and in the Waxhaws district, and Fort Rutledge and Fort Charlotte at Ninety-Six had been occupied, Lord Cornwallis himself returned to Charleston,

[92] I.e., from Morris's house, about twenty miles up the Hudson.

where there was much to be looked after. Moreover, the excessive heat made further activity impossible. Lord Rawdon and Colonel Webster, commander of the 33rd Regiment, remained with the troops as commanders.

Governor Nash of North Carolina gathered the South Carolina refugees together and put them under the command of Colonel Sumter [93] of the militia on the Pedee River. Meanwhile, Brigadier General Caswell had raised two thousand militia in this province and also taken a position on the Pedee. After reinforcing Colonel Sumter, he detached him to the Wateree River, where he successfully surprised and scattered Lieutenant Colonel Tarleton's pickets a quarter of an English mile behind Hanging Rock, inflicting considerable loss. The rebels remained in their newly gained position.

At the beginning of April Congress had detached the two Maryland brigades and the Continentals of the Delaware district under the command of General de Kalb from Washington's army to Philadelphia. Immediately after the reduction of Charleston these troops were ordered to proceed to Hillsboro, North Carolina, under the command of this general. He set out on the march with fifteen hundred men and reinforced his troops with as many more in Virginia. How difficult a march this was may be gathered from the fact that this region as far as the other side of the Roanoke is uninhabited and barren and that the troops carried no provisions. Advancing in small troops, they nevertheless made their way through this wasteland, ever searching for food, arrived at the place of rendezvous, and finally reached Hillsboro at the end of June.

There they found fifteen hundred North Carolinians and one hundred horse under Colonel Armand. Quite unexpectedly, General Gates came with seven hundred Virginians under Brigadier General Stevens [94] and took over the chief command of these forces, which had been lying quiet for a whole month, since pro-

---

[93] Thomas Sumter was made Brigadier General of the South Carolina state troops in July, 1780. The refugees were patriots, of course.

[94] Edward Stevens, Brigadier General, Virginia militia.

visions were entirely lacking. General de Kalb was eager to surrender the command.

In this unpleasant situation General Gates listened to no one but himself, and on the 13th of August he marched to the Pedee as far as Claremont, thirteen English miles from Camden, following the impatient Brigadier General Caswell. On the 14th he reinforced Colonel Sumter with four hundred men, intending to become master of all the passes along the Wateree. Thus communication with Camden was cut off, and the British, if attacked and put to flight, would find as many men in their rear as they had in front. The entire situation seemed favorable for General Gates.

On the 15th of August he could proudly rejoice at seeing the British posts withdraw from Cheraw Hill to Camden. It was only with great difficulty that the British remained masters of both sides of the Wateree Ferry, for the post on the west bank was fiercely attacked by a superior force, which inflicted a loss of seven men killed and some twenty men and Lieutenant Colonel Cary [95] taken prisoners. They were captured while making a futile attempt to save thirty-eight wagons full of flour and rum. The entire garrisons from Forts Rutledge and Charlotte were surrounded and captured on the road to Camden.

Lord Cornwallis joined the army late in the evening of the 14th of August, if indeed a force of less than two thousand men can be called an army. He did not think of rest, but formed his plans before the following morning, communicated them to Lord Rawdon and Colonel Webster, and began his movements on the 15th with the following troops: the 23rd, the 33rd, and the 71st Regiments, the Volunteers of Ireland, the light infantry, the Legion (recruited by Lord Cathcart and now commanded by Lieutenant Colonel Tarleton), one North Carolina regiment, and a corps of South Carolina militia. There were only four fieldpieces,

---

[95] Not identified; probably a loyalist. McCrady, *History of South Carolina in the Revolution, 1775–1780*, pp. 667–68, has Col. Carey and "Carey's Fort," and Sumter to Gates, Aug. 15, 1780, has Col. Cary (Banastre Tarleton, *History of the Campaigns of 1780 and 1781*, Dublin, 1787, p. 151).

and these were at the head of the column under Lieutenant MacLeod.[96]

After a march of barely seven English miles, the advance guards of both armies engaged. General Gates, after having brought all his baggage up to the Waxhaws region, lost no time in meeting Lord Cornwallis in the following formation: Colonel Armand's cavalry was at the head; it was followed by five Maryland fieldpieces, which were covered on the right by the Maryland light infantry under Colonel Porterfield and on the left by the light infantry of the militia under Colonel Armstrong;[97] then came the pickets of the regular army and four cannon; next came the two Maryland and a Delaware brigade under General de Kalb; these in turn were followed by the North Carolina and Virginia militia; and the South Carolina militia formed the rearguard. This was a force of 6,500 men, all of them under the strictest orders. For example, no officer, although accustomed to being attended by orderlies, was permitted to take a single man from the ranks.

General Gates had not expected to meet with the slightest delay in reaching the place where he meant to give battle, which was seven miles from Camden. There he would have had a creek on his right front and an elevation on his left wing, and his army could have occupied the entire field. However, Lieutenant Colonel Tarleton was familiar with the roads leading to this place, and Lord Cornwallis, lying in ambush, routed the vanguard, which caused so much confusion in the first Maryland brigade that it could not be re-formed.

General de Kalb then stationed his troops, as well as the woodland permitted, in the following *ordre de bataille:* The second Maryland brigade was posted on the right wing against a swamp; next in line were the North Carolina and Virginia militia, which had three cannon on their front; all the light in-

[96] John MacLeod, later General Sir John.
[97] Charles Porterfield was a lieutenant colonel in one of the Virginia state regiments (Heitman), and Armstrong (probably John Armstrong) was a major serving with the North Carolina light infantry (cf. Dawson's *Battles of the American Revolution,* New York, 1876, p. 514). Porterfield was mortally wounded and taken prisoner in this engagement.

fantry constituted the left wing, the flank of which was covered
by six cannon; Colonel Armand's cavalry and the first Maryland
brigade formed the reserve.

Lord Cornwallis, who was quicker in forming his troops,
drove the rebel volunteers away from the front and then, with
his light infantry supported by the Volunteers of Ireland, rushed
the enemy's left wing, thus silencing their cannon and routing the
North Carolina troops and Colonel Armand's cavalry. The 23rd
Regiment broke through the center of the Virginia militia, and
then the Marylanders could no longer maintain themselves. They
were the only ones who fought like men. Finally, they also were
compelled to leave their places on the right wing.

Pursued by Lieutenant Colonel Tarleton, they pushed
through dense and dark woods and were not safe even after re-
tiring twenty miles, so close did our cavalry follow upon their
heels. The enemy had eight hundred killed and twelve hundred
taken prisoners, most of whom were wounded. General de Kalb [98]
and Brigadier Gregory [99] were killed, and many commissioned
officers wounded. Moreover, we came into possession of their
artillery, ammunition, tents, and all their baggage.

Colonel Sumter immediately retired into the country fifteen
miles from the Wateree, where he believed himself safe. But on
the 17th of August the light infantry and the Legion, mounted and
dismounted, were ordered to pursue him. They came upon him
so unexpectedly that when the alarm was given, the light infantry
was already in possession of their rifles and two cannon.[100] They
pursued the disarmed rebels five miles, killing 150 and taking 400
prisoners.

The garrison of Ninety-Six was freed from captivity along
with 130 Tories who had been dragged along and sorely maltreated. The best coup of all was the capture of 500 dragoon
horses with accouterments. Most of the wagons found were set
on fire, but the horses were taken along. The English loss in killed

[98] See 1780, note 78.
[99] Isaac Gregory, brigadier in the North Carolina militia, was wounded at
Camden (Heitman).
[100] This action took place at Fishing Creek.

and wounded was somewhat more than 350 men. Among them were three officers killed, two severely wounded, and five slightly wounded.

Lord Rawdon and Colonel Webster particularly distinguished themselves and have received the unstinted praise of Lord Cornwallis, who, he says, is indebted to every man and will ever be grateful for the courage and steadfastness shown. They found thirteen men on parole from Charleston and hanged them on the spot. Among General de Kalb's papers was found an authoritative list of thirty-eight of the most prominent citizens of Charleston, who had been in correspondence with General Gates and had pledged themselves to set the city on fire, open the prisons, and attack the busy garrison as soon as Lord Cornwallis is defeated and routed. These traitors have all been seized and taken to St. Augustine. The rest of the inhabitants of Charleston are so frightened and worried that they will do anything, without reservation, to show their determination to be loyal to the government. They have even organized themselves into companies and formed five battalions.

Lord Cornwallis has not yet advanced beyond Camden. Since his defeat, Colonel Sumter has again appeared on the Pedee River with one thousand volunteers. Caswell is doing everything possible to beat up recruits in North Carolina, for General Gates accused him of forcing him to seek an engagement with Lord Cornwallis too early. Gates retreated alone in great haste by way of Charlotte to Hillsboro, leaving Caswell in Charlotte or Charlotteburg.[101]

In North Carolina, and also in Pennsylvania, petitions signed by about a thousand inhabitants have been sent to Congress asking for an early peace with the mother country. In Paxtang, Lancaster County,[102] Pennsylvania, and in Hunterdon County, New Jersey, the residents have resisted a new levy of militia to be sent to the South, but they had to yield to force and furnish the men. As I write this, we are learning from various sources of a new

[101] The name was Charlotte even at that time.
[102] Now Paxton, Dauphin County; Dauphin County was not separated from Lancaster County until 1785.

action in North Carolina, in which the rebels are reported to have lost another four hundred men.

The troops specified in my letter of September 15th are embarking today on the ships assigned to them. The British Guards in Fort George and Fort Tryon, this side of Kings Bridge, have therefore been relieved by the British light infantry.

Unfortunately, I have to finish my account with the sad news that Major André, found guilty by a court-martial, whose sentence was confirmed by Congress, was hanged as a spy on Monday, the 2nd of October, in the camp at Tappan in the presence of deputies of General Clinton, and that no offer was made. I leave it to your Excellency to judge how exacting and severe a sentence the enemy passes at present and how far, unfortunately, we are from a peace between America and Great Britain.

On the 2nd of this month we finally learned from Quebec that the Lossberg Regiment disembarked near Quebec on the 27th of June and has been quartered in Beauport parish, and also that Colonel von Borck arrived there two weeks after leaving St. John's Island and was given quarters in St. Foy. The field artillery of both regiments has been assigned to the English artillery, and Colonel von Loos has been named a brigadier general by General Haldimand. The 44th Regiment has been sent to Charlesbourg, three English miles from Quebec. At present the 31st Regiment and the remainder of the Hesse-Hanau regiment are in Quebec. All the Brunswickers in that city have been given to Colonel von Loos's brigade.

I cannot say for certain where General Clinton has decided to send the expeditionary force. He is much affected by the loss of the unfortunate Major André. This incident will have serious consequences.

Humbly commending myself to your Excellency and ever striving to be yours with the deepest respect, I remain [*etc.*]

P.S. His Excellency Major General von Lossberg is no longer under orders to go on the expedition; Brigadier General Leslie is to go alone.

: 51 :

General Clinton finds it advisable to dispatch another packet, and the letters for Europe are requested today. The last packet was finally closed on the 10th of this month, although it had been ready to sail since the 10th of September, on which day I had the honor of writing to your Excellency. On the 15th of the same month and also on the 8th of this month [103] I sent additional letters.

From the present part of my journal your Excellency will see that Major General Leslie's corps, when it sailed on the 16th of this month, was weaker than it was originally intended to be, for it consisted only of the following troops: the British Guards, including the four flank companies, the 82nd and 84th Regiments, von Bose's Regiment, and Fanning's and Watson's corps.[104] Colonel von Bischhausen, according to the order, is to serve with them as a brigadier general. The British Guards had to take all their baggage along, for after the Virginia expedition, they are to leave the army and go to England for good.

[103] The October letter is dated the 6th.

[104] Colonel John Watson's corps consisted of the wing companies of the several volunteer corps. In the spring of 1779 he was in command of the wing companies of the Guard regiments.

Some twenty prominent refugees from Virginia embarked with General Leslie, hoping to be of use to him in that province. Nevertheless, General Leslie will not tarry there long, but rather sail to Charleston, where reinforcements are greatly needed because General Greene, who has taken the place of the suspended General Gates, is taking reinforcements from Washington's army to North Carolina. Besides, Generals Stark and Smallwood have brought together a new army of fresh militia on the Pedee River, and the Marylanders have made special efforts to bring their Continental brigades up to full strength, supplying them with all necessities by means of an extraordinary levy.

The rebels claim that Colonel Sumter unexpectedly dashed in between the Pedee and Wateree rivers and completely surprised Lord Rawdon's Irish Volunteers stationed on the Pedee, killing 180 men outright and taking the rest prisoners.[105] This was the reason for the *feu de joie* in Philadelphia on the 23rd and in the camp at Tappan on the following day. Ship's masters and sailors recently exchanged, who arrived here from Philadelphia day before yesterday, confirmed this report. We have had no word from Lord Cornwallis.

On the 15th of this month the Hessian, English, and Anspach recruits arrived. Since the transports were overcrowded, many more men died than usual, and even more had to be sent to the hospitals. I know that your Excellency will receive detailed reports about this, and therefore I shall not enter into details. The recruits already allotted and now in active service are in good condition.

Generals von Bose and von Knoblauch are ready to sail for Charleston and will take with them the recruits, field requisites, accouterments, and baggage—all this under the direction of Lieutenant Colonel von Schuler. The English regiments have the same orders, which proves that General Leslie's corps is to be a part of Lord Cornwallis's army for the time being. His Excellency General von Knyphausen and his suite have been here since the 20th of this month.

[105] Baurmeister refers here to the action at Fish Dam Ford on the Broad River, November 9, 1780, on which he reports in greater detail later.

At present, winter quarters, which, however, will undoubtedly be changed and therefore cannot be considered permanent quarters, are as follows: The garrison of this city consists of the Royal Artillery, the 22nd, the 42nd, the Landgraf, the Erb Prinz, and the Prinz Carl Regiments. On York Island, along the North River is quartered the Leib Regiment; along the East River, the 57th; then comes Mirbach's, which extends as far as McGown's Pass; Colonel Robinson's Corps is in the vicinity of Morris's house; at Fort Knyphausen, von Donop's Regiment; on Laurel Hill, the 76th; and between Fort Knyphausen and Fort Tryon, the 80th (or Edinburgh) Regiment.[106] All these troops are under the command of Major Generals von Lossberg and von Gosen, who have their quarters at Morris's house. On Long Island, at Jamaica and Flushing, are the British and Hessian grenadiers and the Hessian Jäger Corps; at and around Oyster Bay, near Jericho, the 38th Regiment and von Diemar's Hussars; at Denys's Ferry, the 37th Regiment; and at Brooklyn, the light infantry. Before Lieutenant Colonel von Wurmb set out for Oyster Bay, one hundred dismounted jägers were put under the command of the Anspach Captain von Röhder [107] and sent along with General Leslie. On Staten Island are stationed Simcoe's entire corps, the 43rd and von Bünau Regiments, and two battalions of Skinner's.

Thirty-two transports, furnished with sixty days' provisions, are ready to sail. Admiral Rodney's fleet is also ready to sail; but an investigation has been going on in his fleet since the 23rd of this month, for the Admiral has been convinced of bad conduct in the fleet, especially on the part of the captain of the *Yarmouth*.[108] Foreign naval officers have been called as witnesses.

Admiral Arbuthnot is carefully watching the French on Rhode Island. These allies of the rebels have established a hospital for their sea and land forces at Providence. Four deserters arrived from there on the 22nd of this month after working their way through Colonel Sheldon's posts and crossing the Croton River.

---

[106] The 80th or Royal Edinburgh Volunteers.

[107] Eelking-Rosengarten mentions an Anspach Captain Friedrich Wilhelm von Roeder (=Röder).

[108] Captain Nathaniel Bateman (see beginning of following letter and Rodney's *Letters*).

They were very discontented and claim that all their countrymen feel as they do. Other reports confirm the news that the French are putting their artillery aboard their ships again and that, provided they can escape and leave Newport, they will follow the second division (which is coming from France) to Canada.

Until recently, General Heath was the go-between for Congress and the French. I do not know who has this place now that he is commander of the post at West Point. After General Arnold's flight, General Greene commanded there, but at present, as I have already stated, he is on his way to North Carolina. On the 9th of this month General Clinton introduced General Arnold to all the generals here. The latter is now raising a corps of cavalry and infantry which is eventually to be a thousand strong. The officers who have pledged themselves have to furnish a certain number of recruits, varying with their ranks.

My supplementary letter of the 6th of this month gave sufficient information of Major André's fate. To this I will add only the following: Since his fervent request to be shot made no impression, he answered no further questions at the place of execution. He only said to the commanding officer, "Watch and then say that I died courageously enough." [109] Refusing help, he blindfolded himself, slipped the murderous noose around his neck, and jumped from the cart to his death. His servant brought back his uniform and a watch, redeemed for forty guineas, which he had received as a present at the court of Saxe-Gotha. The accompanying note read: "As a token of remembrance for my sister." His death has caused many tears to be shed, and the fact that every British officer wears crêpe is an indication how much his death is lamented.

Among the many prizes that have been brought into the local harbor are three rebel frigates, the *Washington,* twenty-two guns, the *Roebuck,* sixteen, and the *Buckskin,* thirty-two. The frigate *Protector,* twenty-eight guns, which recently ran out of Boston harbor, is being chased, and everyone believes that she

[109] James Thatcher, who witnessed the execution, says in his *Military Journal,* Boston, 1827, p. 223: "I pray you to bear me witness that I meet my fate like a brave man."

will be captured. Admiral Rodney has learned from the West Indies that the French fleet under Count de Guichen,[110] after getting a safe distance out to sea, sent Commodore de Monteil [111] back to Cape François with eight of the best warships, and that Admiral Rowley is very quiet there. We have received no information either of the extent to which the rebellion has progressed in the Spanish American possessions or of General Dalling's success at Fort San Juan.[112]

An exchange of prisoners, it seems, will finally take place insofar as the number of officers and men on the one side can be matched by the other. General Phillips's and General Riedesel's suites have already been exchanged. The former will have for his brigade the British grenadiers, the light infantry, and the 42nd Regiment; the latter will not be able to go to Quebec before spring, and his troops, including the Hesse-Hanauers,[113] will be quartered until then on Long Island. Future journals will give further information.

Arms are being assembled, and it seems that both sides are anxious to put an end to these negotiations, delayed so long by many nasty obstacles, and so to strengthen their forces and make one last attempt. It is likely that the rebels cannot release their prisoners very quickly, for many deserted from the most distant prison camps—some of them were arrested here or there, and a few have come here. If only Major von Hanstein could be located; so far all our inquiries have been fruitless.

Lastly, I must mention that Lieutenant von Dittfurth, formerly of the von Dittfurth Regiment, but since spring serving in von Diemar's Corps of Hussars, communicated to me a letter from his brother, the assessor in Wetzlar, in which he requests War Counsellor Motz [114] to draw up papers renouncing the Dittfurth property turned over to your Excellency. This has been done, but

---

[110] Luc-Urbaine du Bouexic, Comte de Guichen, was a chef d'escadre and a lieutenant general.

[111] Could not be identified.

[112] Not identified; perhaps a fort on the San Juan River, in Nicaragua. Stephen Kemble, in his "Journal" (New York Historical Society Collections, 1884) mentions also a Fort San Juan.

[113] I.e., the exchanged, paroled, or deserted Hesse-Hanau prisoners.

[114] See 1780, note 82.

so far von Dittfurth has not come in to sign these papers in War
Counsellor Motz's presence. Besides, since von Dittfurth's Regiment, as you know, is not here but in Charleston, nothing can be
done by the auditor of the regiment. Lieutenant Juliat is also
serving in the aforesaid corps of hussars. Out of respect to his
great-uncle, the Palatine master of ordnance, von Rottenhausen,
I took it upon myself to help him get to Hesse-Rheinfels to his
family; but the hussar's beaver made him forget the danger he is
in if the rebels capture him.[115] He now repents his new service,
as do also the pitiable deserted Lieutenants Führer and Kleinschmidt, who have sent in very humble requests to be pardoned
and received in our lines again. As soon as I came here, I wrote
Captain von Diemar and asked him to send Lieutenant von Dittfurth over from Jericho to sign the document. When this is done,
I shall dispatch it. General Clinton was inclined to offer him a
lieutenancy in the 60th Regiment, but his reprehensible behavior,
it seems, will indeed thwart all recommendations. Captain Perdot [116] was given a company of light infantry in Watson's corps
of provincials.

With the deepest respect I have the honor ever to be [etc.]

P.S. I am enclosing a *Gazette Extraordinary* [missing] containing
some intercepted rebel letters, from which, among other things,
it may be seen what a pitiful state of affairs the rebels are in at
present. I cannot, of course, vouch for the truth of the statement
that General Starck [117] has encountered Lord Cornwallis with
several corps of North Carolina militia, in spite of the fact that
this news came from Philadelphia and is related with trustworthy
detail. Everyone longs for the arrival of the Cork provision fleet.

[115] Lieutenant Juliat had deserted the Hessian service, joined an American
corps, and then deserted again to serve in von Diemar's free corps, which was
made up largely of deserters.

[116] See 1778, note 135.

[117] Not General John Stark, who was at this time at West Point and in New
Hampshire. Contemporary newspapers fail to give any clue to the identity of this
Stark (Starck). Heitman lists a Robert Stark, Colonel of South Carolina militia in
1775. See also earlier in this letter.

: 52 :

Admiral Rodney boarded his ship on the 6th of this month
for no other reason than to visit the fleet and listen to a reading
of the proceedings against Captain Bateman, which have been
concluded on the *Yarmouth* man-of-war within the last few days.
He did not return to land, but signaled on the 8th, ordering everyone to the fleet. During the night of the 8th–9th, after the fourth
and last impressment of sailors, the ships weighed anchor. The
whole fleet is now riding at anchor off the Hook ready to sail to
the West Indies. Admiral Rowley is still there and has not been
molested by a superior force of enemy ships, but after the hur-
ricanes set in, he will no longer be undisturbed. The French and
Spanish ships, twenty-seven in number, anchored at Cape Nicholas Mole, Hispaniola, as early as the 26th of August to wait for
these storms to pass. At Jamaica everything is quiet. At Fort San
Juan, one hundred men are garrisoned under the command of Sir
Alexander Leith. The rest of the troops have gone on board their
ships, and the many sick have been taken to the most healthful
of the Corn Islands.[118] When the weather becomes better, General

118 The Corn Islands are situated off the coast of Nicaragua.

Dalling will resume his operations. Cumberland Harbor,[119] Cuba, was found to be empty, except for a French privateer, which was burned.

On the 12th of this month we heard the news that the French fleet had sailed away from Rhode Island, but the same evening this report was contradicted on good authority. No doubt, they will undertake it, but whether Admiral Arbuthnot in the harbor at Gardiner's Island will allow it is another question. Should it take place, then the French troops will go into cantonments in Connecticut beyond the Croton River [120] and there wait with the New Englanders for cold weather in order to make an attack on our lines. They are now reproaching each other for not having done this last winter.

General Washington detached the rest of the Maryland Continentals to the Chesapeake on the 16th of last month, October, on which day General Leslie set out for the same place, landing on the shore of Princess Anne County on the 21st of the same month. The following day he took possession of Portsmouth and Norfolk and also of Hampton on the James River. Colonel Howard of the British Guards met with some resistance at Great Bridge and therefore made a halt, intending to attack during the night. The rebels, however, alarmed by their own patrols, fired violently at each other, abandoned the passage of the Great Bridge,[121] and left two cannon behind. Twenty ships loaded with flour and tobacco (among them four armed ships) were found in Chesapeake Bay, and three more at Portsmouth. Among the latter was the recently captured *Sandwich* packet.

On the 7th of this month the frigate *Iris* ran into the said bay after a quick passage from Charleston. Thus General Leslie must have received news of Lord Cornwallis's movements in North Carolina. The last reports received at English headquarters from Charleston are of October 20th. Unfortunately, it is true that Major Ferguson was killed outright in an attack on the rebel

[119] Also called Guantánamo Bay.
[120] Perhaps the Mystic River, which flows through Croton; the Croton River does not touch Connecticut.
[121] Great Bridge is both a long causeway and a village. For an account of Leslie at Portsmouth see *New-York Gazette*, Nov. 20, 1780.

Colonel Sumter.[122] Six hundred militia were taken prisoners, not to mention those killed on the field. At first Colonel Sumter was beaten and in retreat,[123] but as soon as Major Ferguson was killed, Colonel Sumter, who had just received reinforcements, took advantage of the situation and attacked the commanderless mob of ignorant militia, who had scattered too much in pursuing the enemy. Lieutenant Colonel Tarleton and Major Hanger did not participate in this action, but they subsequently stopped Colonel Sumter on his way to the posts this side of the Pedee.

General Greene is en route to North Carolina with a Pennsylvania brigade of the best Continental troops. The question now is whether the governors in the provinces of North Carolina, Maryland, and Virginia will supply General Greene with good troops, artillery, and provisions, which, according to General Gates's bitter complaint, they did not do in North Carolina and Virginia when these necessities could be furnished more bountifully than now.

Intercepted letters from Colonel Hamilton, General Washington's first adjutant, prophesy that all American enterprises will come to a bad end as long as Congress makes the decisions, for they are always too late and never right. The Colonel asserts that if this contest is to be carried on vigorously and to a good end, Congress must entrust the leadership to one person. These and some other letters have been published in New York and are deeply resented by members of Congress, who, it is said, will hold Hamilton responsible. On the 29th of October I had the honor to send your Excellency my last journal.

General Woodford, who was taken prisoner by Lord Cornwallis on the 16th of August this year,[124] was given permission to come to this city because of ill health. He had hardly set foot on land when he died. On the 10th of this month the Cork provision fleet, consisting of fifty-four sail, ran into the harbor, while twenty

---

[122] See page 386 and note 105.

[123] Sumter, since July, 1780, Brigadier General of the South Carolina state troops, was wounded in this action and again on November 20 (Heitman).

[124] Brigadier General William Woodford of Virginia was taken prisoner at Charleston, May 12, 1780. He was exchanged and taken prisoner a second time. He died in captivity November 13, 1780.

such ships arrived safely at Charleston Bar. Our magazines are now well stocked with provisions. Moreover, we have received enough oats to last us ten months.

An exchange of prisoners has been effected only insofar as the officers and men of our side, including the paroled English, Brunswick, and Hesse-Hanau officers of the Convention troops, could be matched. A list of them cannot yet be made, for officers are coming in every day. Admirals Arbuthnot and Rodney no longer exchange rebel naval officers; these are all being transported to England.

This letter will be dispatched by the *Yarmouth* man-of-war. Captain Bateman, her master, has been cashiered and further punishment is left to the Admiralty. Enclosed is an account of Major André's trial,[125] to which are appended some of his letters and one about his character. The other enclosure [*missing*] is an extract from the New Jersey rebel newspapers, so that your Excellency may be informed of the internal conditions of that province.

Much is being written in the rebel newspapers in Boston and Philadelphia about the great importance of the capture of some English ships on their way to the West Indies.[126] The *Ramillies* man-of-war and the frigate *Southampton,* which served as an escort for the captured ships, have, in the meantime, arrived at Kingston, Jamaica. On the 11th of this month the recruits who had embarked for the south still lay at anchor at Sandy Hook.

With the greatest respect and deepest reverence I have the honor to be [*etc.*]

[125] *Proceedings of a Board of General Officers, Held by Order of His Excellency General Washington . . . Respecting Major John Andre, Adjutant General of the British Army. September 29, 1780.* Philadelphia—Printed—New York—Re-printed. James Rivington. 13 pp. [Printed by Order of Congress]. Endorsed: To Adjut. Gen. Major Baurmeister. (Note: The Clements Library has a second copy in the Clinton Papers.)

[126] Clowes (*Royal Navy*, IV, 55) says that of the 63 ships that left for the East and West Indies under convoy of the *Ramillies, Southampton,* and *Thetis* only the warships and eight other ships of the convoy escaped the combined French-Spanish fleet.

On the 13th of last month, November, I had the honor to send your Excellency my last journal. I entrusted it to the British Lieutenant Colonel Hope, who left for England on the *Yarmouth* man-of-war. At that time we knew no more of General Leslie's expedition than that he was encamped at Portsmouth, Virginia, and was exercising his troops by having them fortify the camp, in which activity they were not particularly molested.

We learn from further reports, which were sent on the 27th of November, that this corps embarked again on the 20th of November, left the Chesapeake three days later, and sailed to Cape Fear with a favorable wind. Whether it landed there, or whether Lord Cornwallis had advanced that far, we do not know; but we do know that, after defeating Major Ferguson's corps, the rebels scattered again, for they had brought along only ten days' provisions.

It is said that the cavalry remained with General Sumter on the west bank of the Wateree, whence strong parties boldly sallied forth to molest the British posts on the Pedee. These, however, were always turned back. Finally, Lord Cornwallis advanced

395

with all the troops that could be spared and had Major Wemyss
of the 63rd Regiment again attack General Sumter's outposts on
the 12th of October.[127] After a stubborn resistance, the rebels
maintained their position, and Major Wemyss and twenty-five
men were wounded and taken prisoners. This incident was proclaimed as another victory in Washington's camp in the orders
of the 22nd of November, which also stated, probably erroneously,
that Lord Cornwallis had been taken to Charleston because of illness and that the encircled army was stationed in the vicinity of
Camden under the command of Lord Rawdon.

On the 8th of November Generals Greene and von Steuben
passed Annapolis. The former is to command the army in North
Carolina in place of the suspended General Gates. However, this
army is still in the process of formation, and nothing is known yet
of an indispensable magazine. We are waiting for news, which,
good or bad, will relieve our anxiety.

Yesterday General Arnold embarked with fifteen hundred
men, namely, the 80th Regiment (including the two wing companies), the Queen's Rangers, Colonel Robinson's Corps, one
hundred dismounted jägers under Captain Ewald, and thirty
artillerymen with four British light 12-pounders. General Arnold's
new corps now numbers 182 men, of whom 100 also embarked.
Ensign Balewy,[128] formerly of the Prinz Carl Regiment, is now
serving in this new corps. No one knows where General Arnold
intends to deliver a blow. The rebels have struck his name from
their army rolls. The three militiamen who arrested the unfortunate Major André are to receive two hundred piasters a year in
coin as long as they live. Moreover, they have been advised to
wear a medal struck in their honor, describing their merit and
the gratitude of their country. The 6th of this month was celebrated as a day of general thanksgiving over this incident.

We have heard nothing of Admiral Rodney since he left
Sandy Hook shortly before the middle of November. Admiral
Arbuthnot soon afterwards arrived here in person and counter-

---

[127] Another action on the Broad River.
[128] The *Staats-Calender*, p. 30, gives de Baillivy.

manded and changed what the former had ordered. On the 8th of this month he returned to the fleet, which rode quietly at anchor at Gardiner's Island. His visit was not pleasant while his orders were being carried out. It is the general observation that all changes of this sort during the present war have had an evil effect.

The commanders of the Spanish ships of the line in the West Indies are being severely reproached by their allies for deliberately vacillating and allowing the summer and fall to pass without any decisive action. It is claimed that the enemy should have put us into such a defensive position that they could have spared a fleet of considerable size to make themselves masters of Halifax, which the French on Rhode Island were supposed to have done. The latter, however, remained quietly on and near that island, paying full prices for their provisions, two-thirds in paper and one-third in coin. To this, it seems, the New Englanders are now too much accustomed.

The European newspapers will soon carry detailed accounts of the terrible hurricane which wrought fearful destruction on all the islands in the West Indies at the beginning of October this year. Every nation there has suffered more or less under the convulsions of the elements, and, according to information received from the great merchant of Jamaica, Mr. Stevenson, who has arrived here,[129] offers of peace have probably been made there. This Stevenson witnessed the complete destruction of three parishes in Jamaica. General Vaughan was almost crushed when his house on St. Lucia collapsed. His adjutant, Captain Bell, escaped with a broken leg. At Barbados, three thousand persons were found under the ruins, and the lower part of the city of St. Eustatius was washed away by the swollen sea.

At that time, a Spanish fleet of seventy transports was on its way from Havana with an escort of ten men-of-war to disembark five thousand men at Pensacola. Half of this fleet arrived again before Havana on the 24th of October, the ships being severely

---

[129] Stevenson could not be identified. Perhaps the translation should read: "the great merchant, Mr. Stevenson, who arrived here from Jamaica."

damaged. Nothing is known as yet of the fate of the rest of the ships.

Brigadier General Campbell at Pensacola has profited from this misfortune, for he has long been in need of additional troops on account of rather great losses, especially since the Indians give no assistance without considerable remuneration and, lacking this, will even fight on the other side.

As soon as General Leslie made preparations in Virginia for taking a strong foothold at Portsmouth, Burgoyne's prisoners were removed from Charlottesville to Fort Frederick [130] in Maryland. In the meantime, work on the exchange of prisoners is progressing, partly because the rebel commissioners are now more moderate in their demands for cash to pay the cost of transporting the prisoners from New England to Virginia. The rest of the prisoners will probably be exchanged within a few days. Ten Brunswick officers and Lieutenants Bach and von Lindau of Hesse-Hanau have come in, and Colonel von Gall and Captain Peusch [131] will follow. All these officers are being quartered on Long Island.

The enclosed newspaper [*missing*] shows what we learned from the Albany district under date of November 20th.[132] Reports from that region now come in more frequently than before, but we remain ignorant of their contents. The small magazines which have been erected from Connecticut to Lake Champlain and the sleighs which have been assembled at the stations along this great route make us believe that the rebels and their allies will make use of them this winter.

The frigate *Hussar*, twenty-eight guns, foundered in the rockbound eddies, called Pot and Pan, near Hell Gate, the latter part of November. Only nine sailors lost their lives; the rest saved themselves by swimming to the shores close by.

The weather is tolerable, and there are only a few sick in the hospitals. Since large quantities of fresh food are being brought

---

[130] Now Frederick, Maryland.

[131] Probably Captain Georg Pausch of the Hesse-Hanau Artillery.

[132] Not in the Von Jungkenn Papers. The enclosure was very likely the *New-York Gazette*, the November 20 issue of which contained accounts from Albany.

in from all sides, prices, which have been extremely high, are coming down.

    With the greatest respect I am ever
        Your Excellency's

               Most obedient and devoted servant

                    Carl Baurmeister

New York
December 14, 1780

1781

: 54 :

NEW YORK
JANUARY 22, 1781

Right Honorable Lord,
Gracious High and Mighty Major General:

No packet has left since the 15th of last month, December, when I sent my last. Everything remained quiet until the end of the year; but on the 3rd of this month, late in the evening, some entirely unexpected news came in by way of Powles Hook, namely, that the Pennsylvania troops had revolted near Morristown, dismissed their officers, and refused obedience to Major General St. Clair. These troops had declared as early as the 11th of December that they would no longer serve unless they received their pay in cash, their back pay in coin, complete winter uniforms, and better provisions. They also demanded to be relieved and refused to be obliged ever to serve again. These threats were not heeded, and General St. Clair was in no position to meet any of their demands.

Therefore, at two o'clock on the afternoon of the 1st of this month the revolt began. A noncommissioned officer named Wil-

liams [1] marched sixteen hundred men from the huts at Morristown to Vealtown,[2] twenty-two English miles from Elizabethtown,
having previously spiked or otherwise ruined all the artillery save
four fieldpieces which they took along with sufficient ammunition. Moreover, they burned a grain magazine and took with them
a cattle park of several hundred head. These discontented people,
fortunately, found a small flour magazine at Vealtown, which
supplied them with five days' provisions.

As soon as General Clinton was informed of this, he ordered
the British light infantry and grenadiers, General von Kospoth's
grenadier brigade, and Lieutenant Colonel von Wurmb with the
entire Jäger Corps to Staten Island, apparently in order to gratify
their every want if the revolters should approach needing assistance. Fifty carpenters were also sent to the said island to build a
bridge at Elizabethtown or Amboy. These ingenious preparations
and our expectations were in vain, for Mr. Williams marched his
men between Millstone [3] and Brunswick, where he found food
and cattle to slaughter. He took possession of the boats on the
Raritan and permitted General Wayne his first conference. All
inducements, however, were in vain. Even General Lafayette was
unsuccessful and was satisfied enough to be allowed to stay one
hour with Mr. Williams.[4] Meanwhile, this unruly mob increased
to three thousand men.

The Jersey militia was summoned and ordered to barricade
all the roads to Elizabethtown and Powles Hook. These vigilant
troops arrested two men sent from Staten Island to inquire into
the state of the revolters and to gain Mr. Williams's confidence in

---

[1] Sergeant Williams (no first names given) is mentioned as one of the Board
of Sergeants who negotiated with President Joseph Reed. See W. B. Reed, *Life
and Correspondences of Joseph Reed*, II, 219–36. See also W. H. Smith, *St. Clair
Papers*, Cincinnati, 1882, II, 532–40. Nothing has been found in the *Pennsylvania
Archives*. However, he is probably the John Williams of the 2nd Pennsylvania
Regiment, who had been taken a prisoner at Princeton in 1776, had enlisted in a
loyalist provincial regiment and then deserted to the American forces, whereupon
he was court-martialed for desertion, but pardoned by Washington. See Carl Van
Doren, *Mutiny in January*, New York, 1943.

[2] Now Bernardsville, New Jersey.

[3] Millstone, Somerset County, eight miles from New Brunswick.

[4] Generals Lafayette and St. Clair conferred with the Board of Sergeants (see
Van Doren, *Mutiny in January*, pp. 96, 97).

any case. These two men were taken to Philadelphia as prisoners and were hanged on the 15th instant after a short trial.

Mr. Williams led the Pennsylvanians as far as Bordentown, where President Joseph Reed, then in Trenton, was to negotiate with them in the name of Congress.[5] His conditions were that they march to Cooper's Ferry opposite Philadelphia, where they were to be paid in cash; that those who had served three years were to be mustered out for good, while the rest were to receive their full pay, be clothed, choose their own officers, and serve again under General St. Clair. After making these unreasonable demands, President Reed was compelled to go back across the Delaware. He was told in no uncertain terms that, generally speaking, they would accept seventy-five paper dollars for one piaster, that all the men would have to be mustered out, and that not a single man would leave until their comrades at New Windsor were also paid, clothed, and given better provisions.

This is all the news that I have been able to gather so far (the 19th of this month) about the revolt, which, in my opinion, is based on more than the discontent of the Pennsylvanians. On the 9th of this month General Clinton had the Hessian grenadiers return from Staten Island to New Utrecht on Long Island, and the next day the brigade went into its old quarters at Jamaica and Flushing.

His Excellency General von Knyphausen ordered Major von Stein to Jamaica with one hundred and fifty men, and von Diemar's troop of hussars, who had been at New Utrecht, to Southern Swamp,[6] so that the empty quarters on Long Island would be at least partly occupied. However, after General Clinton had the British light infantry and grenadiers and the Jäger Corps also return from Staten Island to Long Island, Major von Stein and his 150 men returned to the outpost of this city yesterday.

On the 4th of this month Admiral Arbuthnot sent a frigate to London with a report of the revolt. Three hundred mounted

---

[5] For a record of Reed's negotiations with the revolting Pennsylvanians see W. B. Reed, *Life and Correspondence of Joseph Reed, loc. cit.*, and Van Doren, pp. 106–201 *passim.*

[6] Not identified.

French dragoons have gone into winter quarters at Providence, Lebanon,[7] and Hartford, and Colonel Sheldon has taken quarters in Wedderford.[8] Except for fifty militiamen stationed at Horse Neck, no armed rebels are to be found beyond the Croton River as far as Fishkill.

As soon as the French learned of the revolt, all their dragoons assembled on Rhode Island, and by the 12th their unrigged fleet had made ready to sail. On the 8th of this month a French recruiting command left Philadelphia with twenty-eight recruits, among whom were five Hessians and two Anspachers. Three French frigates are so stationed at the main wharf in Philadelphia, not far from the Swedish Church, that the French, the despised allies of the American people, can immediately take flight on them in case of a serious alarm, or rather on two of them, for the third is to cover their retreat. The French are being constantly insulted by the inhabitants.

An officer of the 42nd Regiment and six fellow prisoners found a way to escape from the Philadelphia prison and arrived here on the 17th, faint and naked. I cannot give a description of the misery of the imprisoned soldiers there and wish a thousand times that the rest of the prisoners of von Knyphausen's Regiment were exchanged.

In the night of the 24th–25th of December the rebels were bold enough to row down the North River in three boats to within two miles of this city, intending to capture General Clinton, whose quarters are on the river bank near Fort George [9] and almost completely isolated. However, the tide was so strong and the boats were so far out in the current, that one of them, loaded with combustibles, ran against Powles Hook and the other two were compelled to seek shelter in the inlet at Hohwok.[10] Thus this expedition of Colonel Hamilton, General Washington's adjutant,

[7] Probably Lebanon, New Hampshire.

[8] During January Sheldon was at Hartford, Connecticut, then at Northampton, Massachusetts, and then back again at Hartford. Baurmeister must mean Weathersfield in Hartford County.

[9] Fort George, on Laurel Hill.

[10] The Hook, i.e., Sandy Hook? or Hoboken?

was a complete failure;[11] but, as such incidents always do, it made us take more precautions, and the following day two guns were mounted in the place where Captain von Münchhausen was lodged at the time General Howe was here.

Admiral Arbuthnot has safely got from here to the West Indies. Along with this pleasant news it was reported from Bermuda that Admiral Hood, just arrived from England, was anchored at Barbados. General Clinton has learned in a roundabout way from the rebels that Lord Cornwallis beat them again on the 13th of December, last year, in North Carolina, whereupon he joined forces with General Leslie. We learned through the same channels that General Arnold, who did not leave Sandy Hook until the 21st of December, ran into Chesapeake Bay on the 5th of this month, and then into the James River; that he has destroyed some magazines at Williamsburg and Petersburg; and that he ruined large stores of arms and munitions, especially at the latter place. A confirmation of this may cause another packet to be dispatched, in which case I shall be only too happy to send a detailed report.

Yesterday privateers brought in the news that three French warships and three frigates have run out of Rhode Island and taken a course for the Chesapeake. It is to be hoped that Admiral Arbuthnot has sent as many sail in pursuit of them.

The winter is mild and has not been unhealthful so far. The Commissary of Musters, Mr. Porter, has never found the regiments so complete and healthy as he did at the last muster.

With the deepest respect I have the honor to commend myself to your Excellency and remain, as long as I live [*etc.*]

P.S. Ethan Allen, the Vermont separatist, went as far as Bennington on the 5th of this month with six hundred men, but then retired to Hubbardton, situated twelve miles east of Ticonderoga, which has been made tenable.

11 It was Colonel David Humphreys who led this expedition. For Washington's orders to him (Dec. 23) see *Writings of George Washington* (Ford ed., Washington, 1889–93) IX, 74. Humphreys was ordered to land at Kennedy's house, No. 1 Broadway, corner of Battery Place, and take either Knyphausen or Clinton. (See also Heath's *Memoirs, sub* Dec. 25, and letters from "Hiram," the spy, in *Magazine of American History*, X, 414.)

: 55 :

The last letters for Europe were turned in after a short notice on the 22nd of this month, and the packet set sail soon afterwards. I wrote my letter of that date in the British post office, for there was very little time before the departure of the packet, and I did not want to miss an opportunity to send some news. Tomorrow morning at the latest the empty transport fleet will fall down to Sandy Hook and then proceed to England under escort of the frigate *Clinton*, on which the Hesse-Hanau Brigadier von Gall, his adjutant Count Bickell, Captains von Schachten and Beusch,[12] nine British officers, and the Brunswick Brigadier von Specht have obtained passage. On the transport *Minerva* the Anspach invalids, Captain Lorey, and the former Lieutenant Juliat are embarked. I shall give this part of my journal to Regimental Quartermaster Modell of the Anspachers, who has assured me that he will post it in the first English mail.

The revolt of the Pennsylvanians has not yet come to an end. At Burdent [13] about four hundred men accepted President Joseph

[12] See 1780, note 131.

[13] I.e., Bordentown, New Jersey. However, the agreement was reached at Trenton.

Reed's proposal and were discharged to their homes, but more than two thousand went back to Princeton on the 20th of this month. Moreover, the New Jersey brigade under Colonels Shreve and Dayton at Pompton and Chatham,[14] which is as dissatisfied as the Pennsylvanians ever were, revolted on the 21st and got rid of their officers, rudely maltreating them. These troops gathered at Chatham and fell down to Springfield, where the Jersey militia under Colonels Frelinghuysen and Seely [15] occupied the bridge. However, after a short action, the revolters crossed over, and the militia watched the revolt from a great distance.

Governor Livingston lost no time in quelling this second flare-up. He had in his custody the fines, amounting to £150,000, which the inhabitants of Bergen County had been compelled to pay because its militia refused to leave the county last summer. With this money he paid the revolters their back pay. Moreover, he discharged all those who did not want to serve any longer. Thus, this wanton crowd was satisfied beyond their expectation. Wanting to show their appreciation, they declared that of the eight hundred men all those who were old and had wives (which was about half) would return home, while the rest would serve under Colonel Frelinghuysen with new officers and divided into companies and that they would go into winter quarters at Pompton. This, too, was granted.

We did not publicly show the same interest in the second revolt that we had manifested in the first, though it also appeared to be very favorable. Only Governor Robertson went to Staten Island. However, the 57th, both Anspach, and the Landgraf Regiments have been under orders to march since the 24th of this month. Everything is in a state of ferment with the rebels. During these critical times Washington is compelled to leave the posts at New Windsor and Smith's Clove to inferior soldiers, for he has taken the best to West Point, which he is intent on holding at any price.

[14] Colonel Israel Shreve, 2nd New Jersey Regiment, was stationed at Pompton and Colonel Elias Dayton at Chatham.
[15] Colonel Frederick Frelinghuysen and, apparently, Colonel Silvanus Seely.

In my last letter I reported that the French dragoons suddenly gathered on Rhode Island. Your Excellency will now be pleased to hear that several of the highest French officers, who had gone to Philadelphia at the beginning of last December and from there visited the regions where the British had been stationed under General Howe and where some actions had taken place, were so frightened when they heard of the revolt that they immediately drew together and cautiously retired over King's Ferry. Only the esteemed Lafayette and a Count von Zweibrücken [16] remained with the French ambassador in Philadelphia.

On the 20th of this month three French warships really [17] ran out of Newport. Admiral Graves, who was informed of this at Gardiner's Island, immediately gave orders for four men-of-war to make ready to sail and advise Admiral Arbuthnot. The ships sailed from here on the 22nd.[18] In the meantime Admiral Graves had ordered the men-of-war to run out. Then a terrific north-northwest wind came up, which made the *Culloden* man-of-war founder on Montauk Point, the men being saved, however. The warship *Bedford* would have met the same fate at Fisher's Island if the masts, which held a long time against the storm, had broken sooner. Rudderless and without masts, she was towed to Gardiner's Island by the *Europe* man-of-war the following day. Doubtless other ships pursued the enemy, of whose fate we know nothing, not even their destination.

Admiral Rodney ran out of Barbados with fifteen ships of the line shortly after the middle of December. We learned this from letters from Antigua dated the 20th of last month, which add that this expedition is aimed at Grenada and, also, that no more than five French warships are anchored at St. Vincent.

Letters from merchants in Fredericksburg, Virginia, and others sent from Baltimore to Philadelphia contain the following precise information of General Arnold's operations: He ran into the Chesapeake as early as the 30th of December last year and

[16] More commonly referred to by the French form of his name, de Deux Ponts.

[17] Baurmeister means to imply that his earlier statement (see end of previous letter) was based on less reliable information.

[18] It will be remembered that Arbuthnot had gone to the West Indies because Graves had taken command of the fleet blockading the French fleet at Newport, Rhode Island, thus superseding Arbuthnot.

landed at Williamsburg. He arrived in Richmond very early in the morning of the 5th of this month and burned the magazines and shops, leaving nothing. In the forenoon of the 6th he advanced to Westham, eight miles farther, and there burned the valuable foundries and magazines. However, the inhabitants of Manchester in Powhatan County [19] had concealed the rifles and a great quantity of ammunition.

When these letters were sent, the Governor and General Baron von Steuben were engaged in gathering the militia, which was to go to the general place of rendezvous at Fredericksburg. General Arnold, it seems, at first intended to go there, too, but marched down to Petersburg instead, where, according to the reports, he took possession of the large tobacco magazine. Here it is supposed that he accomplished this, although the rebels make no mention of it. They do say, on the other hand, that the warships that ran out of Rhode Island will sail into the Chesapeake in company with some American armed vessels and that they will make every effort to check General Arnold's progress. We have not yet received any reports from this general, nor have we heard from Lord Cornwallis. Hence, nothing can be said for certain.

In the night of the 21st–22nd of this month General Parsons with a Connecticut Continental brigade was so bold as to approach by way of Horse Neck and Williams's bridge, attack the Refugees' quarters in Westchester, and range as far as Morrisania. At daybreak Lieutenant Colonel James De Lancey collected the scattered Refugees and made the rebels' retreat very uncomfortable. But he could follow them no farther than Williams's bridge, for on the far side of the bridge the greater part of the rebels had taken post under cover of two fieldpieces, in order to give firm support to their returning comrades. Hence, the Refugees fell back, buried sixteen killed, picked up twice as many wounded, and then rebuilt their burned huts. Seventeen men were taken prisoners. General Parsons lost but few or none.

No packet from England has yet arrived, which disturbs General Clinton very much, although yesterday a ship came from Lisbon, making the trip in two days less than eight weeks.

With the deepest respect I have the honor to remain [*etc.*]

[19] Manchester is in Chesterfield County, the next county east of Powhatan.

: 56 :

NEW YORK

FEBRUARY 21, 1781

On the 15th of this month I had the honor to receive your Excellency's gracious letter of October 16th last year, acknowledging the receipt of my journals up to the 4th of July. My last communications were sent on the 22nd and 30th of January, and herewith I continue my account of American events.

General Arnold's reports came in on the 31st of January. The enclosed authorized account [*missing*] is a report of his operations and the subsequent occupation of Portsmouth, which he fortified and still holds. On the 13th of this month we learned from other reports from him that the rebels under Baron von Steuben assembled one thousand men one mile the other side of the Great Bridge, but have made no further move; that our small-craft have been rowed into the Rappahannock River; that he [Arnold] had come into possession of twelve ships with cargoes; and that the other ships, which lay too far up, had been burned.

The post at Portsmouth is very strong indeed, but since almost two thousand French unexpectedly embarked at Rhode Island and set sail for the Chesapeake under cover of four men-of-war, General Arnold will have to double his vigilance. These movements of the French began on the 14th of this month; on the 16th, two days later, a French ship of sixty-four guns was so bold as to cruise two miles off Sandy Hook.

On the 18th General Clinton put the following troops under orders to march: the 17th Regiment of Dragoons, the British and Hessian grenadiers, the light infantry, the 76th Regiment, and the Hessian Erb Prinz Regiment, as well as Major Generals Phillips and von Kospoth. They are furnished with ten days' provisions. All the transports are ready. According to the last order these troops will embark at Denys's Ferry on Long Island and a few here at Fort George.

General Washington himself has not been at New Windsor since the 6th of this month. Not until the 17th did General Clinton hear of his adversary's hurried trip to Rhode Island, where he is said to have planned new and necessary operations with General Rochambeau. It is possible that the rebel commander in chief has cast anchor before the Chesapeake. His presence is needed everywhere, and a deserter of the Jersey militia, who has come in, is trying to assure us that General Washington left Rhode Island after a very short stay and that, with a small escort, he hurried to General Greene, who was defeated by Lord Cornwallis near Hillsboro, North Carolina, on the 25th of January, whereupon Greene made a quick retreat to Virginia via Salisbury. This last news came into English headquarters by way of Philadelphia several days ago.

Regardless of the fact that this deserter's story can be taken as a confirmation of Greene's defeat, no further notice is taken of it. He told us, moreover, of the militia movements on both banks of the North River, beginning at Fishkill, and also that the French Legion under Colonel de Lauzun and Sheldon's Dragoons in Connecticut were ready to march. We shall soon know the designs of the rebels and their allies.

General Clinton's and Admiral Arbuthnot's last declaration to the North American provinces, which was dated December 29th, had a great effect in three parishes in New England as well as in Dutchess and Albany counties, where liberty poles were erected, the British proclamation read and assented to, and the Congressional tax collectors chased away. Thereupon, Ethan Allen, with an escort of twenty-four horse, took courage to ride into Albany, where he found the people open-minded about coming over to the British side.

On the 2nd of this month General Clinton had good news from Governor General Haldimand of Quebec. The messengers were on the way fifty-two days, having come by way of Detroit. The Governor will assemble at the lakes with all possible haste an army of at least eight thousand men, so that he can carry out the plan which General Burgoyne was to have executed. If the British are to become masters of the North River—and without this the rebellion cannot be smothered—the reinforcements expected here must join him at Albany without fail.

General Leslie finally anchored at Charleston on the 16th of December after an uncomfortable passage of almost four weeks. The 82nd and 84th Regiments remained in the city; Colonel Fanning's Corps was ordered to Georgetown; and the rest proceeded to Camden. On the 14th of January Lord Cornwallis began to march on the road to Hillsboro. He detached the 7th Regiment and the 1st Battalion of the 71st Regiment to Ninety-Six, under escort of the Legion under Lieutenant Colonel Tarleton. The rebel General Morgan with eight hundred riflemen had his camp at Grindall's Ford but left his position at Lord Cornwallis's first move and retired to the Broad River, seven miles from Cherokee Ford. On his march to Ninety-Six, Tarleton occupied the rebel camp at Grindall's.

Believing that he had forced General Morgan to retreat and that his force was superior to the rebels', he went in search of General Morgan on the 17th of January. He found him in battle formation at the Cowpens, close to the Pacolet River. Colonel Tarleton had to defend himself as well as he could in a space of four hundred yards. He posted the 7th Regiment on his right, the 1st Battalion of the 71st on his left, and the dismounted Legion in the center. His dragoons covered the flanks. In his rear he had no cover except some baggage, but in front of the left wing of the 7th Regiment he had two light fieldpieces.

The British attack was too furious for the enemy's right wing —nothing withstood the 1st Battalion of the 71st Regiment. Gen-

eral Morgan withdrew and took another position. Since the
Legion did not pursue, Lieutenant Colonel Washington with 240
horse and the Virginia militia under Major Triplett [20] experienced
no difficulty in falling between the dispirited Legion and the two
British regiments, thus putting the Georgia volunteers in a position to capture the two fieldpieces and charge the rear of the 7th
Regiment. Those not killed were captured.

The following is a detailed report of the total losses: 10
officers and 102 noncommissioned officers and soldiers killed; 29
officers and 472 noncommissioned officers and soldiers wounded
and taken prisoners; 2 fieldpieces, 2 flags of the 7th Regiment, all
the guns, 1 field smithy, 35 baggage wagons and their escort, and
70 negroes captured. Tarleton charged Lieutenant Colonel Washington in person, and his horse was shot from under him. A dragoon who parried a blow that Lieutenant Colonel Washington
was about to deal him was lamed. Major Wemyss of the 63rd
Regiment, who has come here to recover from his wounds,
brought this news from Charleston. General Morgan's reports to
Congress were delivered by Major Edward Giles and the volunteer Baron Glasbeech [21] on the 8th of this month.[22] They had left
General Morgan at Cain Creek on the 19th of January. Lieutenant
Colonel Tarleton escaped with a few men and has arrived in Camden. Nothing further is known from South Carolina.

Your Excellency will see from the reports how much illness
prevails there and how many of our men are dying. General Clinton promised last fall to move Knoblauch's Regiment from
Savannah to Georgetown, but so far nothing has been done; nor
have uniforms been sent to the rest of the prisoners of von Knyphausen's Regiment (something more than one hundred men),
who are in dire straits.

[20] Heitman lists many Tripletts from Virginia, but no Major Triplett; Dawson,
Battles of the American Revolution, refers to this Triplett as a major and Lossing,
Pictorial Field Book, and Edward McCrady, *History of South Carolina in the
Revolution, 1780–1783*, New York, 1902, as a captain.

[21] Baron Glasbeech was breveted a captain in the Continental Army March 9,
1781, "in consideration of his merit and services at the Battle of Cowpens" (Heitman).

[22] The dispatches were printed in the *Pennsylvania Packet*, Feb. 10, 1781.

A thorough investigation has been made on the British prison ships into the reputed harsh treatment of the prisoners, of which General Washington has complained. The accusations, which in the absence of Admiral Arbuthnot were examined by Captain Dawson of the *Iris,* have been found to be unjust, and the rebels were censured for spreading these stories as truths simply to stir up the rebellion so much the more. The statements sworn to by the prisoners have been printed and distributed.

Admiral Rodney's enterprise against St. Vincent in the West Indies has been successful. He has been master of the island since the 19th of December, when he made a surprise attack. This has given us hopes that Grenada likewise has been taken.

Admiral Arbuthnot is expected here with the greater part of his fleet. Since the letters will be requested immediately, I must close. With the deepest respect I remain [*etc.*]

: **57** :

In spite of the fact that the packet, which is about to sail after
ng been detained so long, already has two letters for your
llency, one of February 21st and another of the 16th of this
[23] the following interesting events which have occurred
date of my last are of sufficient importance to warrant a
early in the morning of day before yesterday, the 26th
nth, First Midshipman Galgey [24] of the *Royal Oak*
arrived here in an express boat with dispatches from
thnot to General Clinton dated, on board the *Royal*
en Bay, March 21st. Their contents are as follows:
of March, at six o'clock in the morning, the
red the French fleet under Vice Admiral des
es off Cape Charles. It consisted of eight
e frigates, and one sloop of war. Admiral
et was of the same strength, except that he

March 16 is missing.
cation has been impossible. Midshipman Galgey is men-
ork *Gazette*, April 2, 1781, where Arbuthnot's dispatches are

Admiral Chevalier Souchet des Touches.

had one more frigate, maneuvered to have the wind in his favor. The warship *Robust* led the British fleet (enclosed is a list of all the ships),[26] but it was not until twenty minutes after two in the afternoon that the *Robust,* supported by the *Prudent* and *Europe,* opened the attack on the first French warships and, aided by a strong southeast wind, broke the enemy line.

Nevertheless, the enemy ships re-formed in line, taking a position a cable's length from each other. Admiral Arbuthnot approached them in a correspondingly close formation. The enemy admiral's ship, however, had lost her main mast, and the three British ships which had stubbornly attacked during the first engagement became idle.[27] After four o'clock the French fleet disappeared in the fog. The frigate *Medea* joined Arbuthnot's ships, which though signaled to steer for Cape Henry, cast anchor in Lynnhaven Bay the following day. All the ships flew French flags, and so the French commissaries were deceived and sent all their pilots to take the fleet, which they supposed to be theirs, t Yorktown. They became aware of this deception under guns of the frigate *Pearl,* but even more so when they were ta prisoners.

The ships which cover General Arnold's corps at Ports; and which are anchored before the mouth of the Elizab are the following: *Charon,* forty-four guns, *Thames,* guns, *Amphitrite,* twenty-six guns, *Hope,* eighteen gun; *Bonetta,* and *General Monk,* each sixteen guns, the f can, and two galleys, the *Comet* and the *Hussar.*

On the 15th of this month General Arnold ser the *General Monk* up into the bay, and they dro flatboats on which General Lafayette and b barked in the Elk River to cross to the Yo; Annapolis shore. If the Pennsylvanians unde to reach Yorktown, they will have to go over route of one hundred and sixty miles and cross

[26] See end of this letter.
[27] For further details of this action and for losses see pages 4
[28] See *New-York Gazette,* March 26, 1781, for an almost identical

Between the 16th and 19th of this month General Phillips's corps was twice driven back to Sandy Hook by a south wind, but on the 20th the wind was favorable, and the ships got under way. The evening of the 22nd Midshipman Galgey met them sailing under cover of the warship *Chatham* and the frigate *Raleigh* near Cape Charles. Admiral Arbuthnot is said to have remained in Lynnhaven Bay only four days, after which he pursued the enemy, who, on the 17th and 18th, were holding an easterly course.

It is generally supposed that Admiral des Touches has returned to Rhode Island to refit. The *Chatham* and *Charon* men-of-war and the frigates *Thames, Amphitrite, Medea,* and *Raleigh* make the British fleet decidedly superior to the French, and since the French did not succeed in reaching the Chesapeake, and still less in landing their troops at Yorktown, General Arnold's corps is safe again. General Phillips's reinforcements arrived at the right time of the year to derive considerable profit from the post at Portsmouth. Baltimore will be taken, and Maryland with it.

We have no positive reports from Lord Cornwallis. The rebel newspapers claim that he has advanced no further than Halifax, whence he withdrew in three columns by way of Hillsboro. From there, it is said, he sent a detachment to reinforce the post at Wilmington, marched the rest to Salisbury, and had a detachment take post on the Pedee. However, nothing of all this is certain, for, although General Arnold, accompanied by Lieutenant Colonel Simcoe, called on Admiral Arbuthnot on the 21st of this month and at the same time sent in new reports, nothing has been made known; at least, I know of nothing, and since General Clinton has been commander in chief, all inquiries at British headquarters have been fruitless.

The greatest secrecy has become imperative, for the number of those who are secretly rebels (who have become the most dangerous) is, according to the openly professed rebels, greater than Washington's entire army. It is astonishing indeed how these fine enemies are spared and frequently even remain in public business under protection.

The last letters from Charleston were dated on the 1st of this month. The three Hessian regiments, Dittfurth, d'Angelelli, and von Benning,[29] have but few sick. The Brunswick, Anhalt-Zerbst, and Hesse-Hanau recruits, a total of about three hundred men, arrived there the latter part of February.

New propositions have been made for the complete exchange of the Convention troops; so far it has been agreed that the British will leave only one lieutenant colonel, four captains, and ten sub-alterns with their prisoners, and that a proportionate number will remain with the Brunswick and Hesse-Hanau prisoners. The rest of them are on their way here.

From the 19th to the 26th of February General Sumter roamed around a great deal between Monks Corner and the Congaree on the bypaths near Charleston and Camden. However, Colonel Watson, the commander of the wing companies of the volunteer corps, surprised this partisan after he had crossed the Santee on his flight through St. Stephen. General Sumter left behind all his wagons, eighteen killed, and thirty-eight prisoners, and retreated to his old post on the Pedee.[30]

News has come overland from Canada that a rebel corps of five hundred men from the Illinois district has marched to Detroit and stormed the post. A troop of militia and Indians is said to have given them battle and killed most of them on the retreat. After this, a plot was discovered in the garrison, the instigators of which have been sent to Montreal as prisoners.

Privateers have just brought in the news that the French fleet is sailing to Rhode Island, but that they have not yet sighted Admiral Arbuthnot's fleet. In the action of the 16th of this month, he had one lieutenant, two midshipmen, and forty men killed, and eighty-two wounded. The enemy's loss is not yet known.

The stormy and damp, misty weather, which has sent many to bed with breast fever, is letting up. Ensign Pauli of d'Angelelli's Regiment has not arrived yet from his imprisonment in Rutland, where, on the 26th of October last year, he was exchanged along with Colonel Köhler and Lieutenant Studenroth. A memorandum on this matter has been sent to the commissioners of prisoners.

---

[29] Von Benning's Regiment was formerly von Huyn's.
[30] For an account of this action see *New-York Gazette*, March 19, 1781.

Colonel Köhler has become quite weak and feeble during his imprisonment.

Thirty troop transports and sixteen horse transports are again ready to take on troops. All the grenadiers, the 42nd Regiment, three hundred recruits for the provincial corps, and the Jäger Corps are under orders to march. Since the French have been prevented from carrying out their designs in the Chesapeake and since General Arnold has received sufficient reinforcements, nothing but the greatest need, it seems, would take a large body of troops away from here. Everyone fervently hopes that the packet from England will arrive soon.

The lamentations in Philadelphia about the loss of St. Eustatius, Curaçao, and other Dutch islands are beyond all description. These were the only places with which the Americans carried on trade and from which the French at Martinique and Guadeloupe could receive supplies. They were the magazine of the Americans, who in return for their goods received ammunition, guns, cloth, tents, and salt.

A horrible example will be made of the British ships which have so far furnished the enemy with the best supplies with impunity and so shown great faithlessness to their government. Admiral Rodney had the masters of these merchantmen put in irons.

With the greatest respect I have the honor to remain [etc.]

Enclosure

[List of Ships Participating in Action of March 16, 1781] [31]

BRITISH		FRENCH	
1) *London*	90 guns	1) *Le Duc de Bourgogne*	80 guns
2) *Royal Oak*	74 guns	2) *Neptune*	74 guns
3) *Bedford*	74 guns	3) *Conquérant*	74 guns
4) *Robust*	74 guns	4) *Eveillé*	64 guns
5) *Europe*	64 guns	5) *Provence*	64 guns
6) *America*	64 guns	6) *Jason*	64 guns
7) *Prudent*	64 guns	7) *Ardent*	64 guns
8) *Adamant*	50 guns	8) *Fantasque*	64 guns

FRIGATES		FRIGATES	
1) *Pearl*	32 guns	1) *Gentille*	32 guns
2) *Charleston* [32]	32 guns	2) *Surveillante* [33]	32 guns
3) *Iris*	32 guns	3) *Hermione*	32 guns
4) *Guadeloupe*	28 guns		
Sloop of war *Savage*	16 guns	Sloop of war *Guépe*	14 guns

[31] This list appears to be taken from the *New-York Gazette,* March 19, 1781.
[32] Clowes gives *Medea* in place of *Charleston.*
[33] Clowes does not list the *Surveillante.*

: 58 :

The last packet from here to London set sail on the 30th of last month. It had been ready since the 21st of February, on which date I sent a letter, as I did also on the 16th [34] and 28th of March. Thus your Excellency will receive three accounts on the same post day. From today's orders we learn that the dispatches of the British headquarters are to be sent to England on the 28th, the day after tomorrow. I have gathered the following news:

General Phillips had a safe voyage to Chesapeake Bay, landing at Portsmouth on the 26th of March, five days after leaving Sandy Hook. The Marquis de Lafayette, whose plans were completely upset by the sloops of war *Hope* and *General Monk*, gave up his intentions of getting into the York River. He posted his nine hundred Pennsylvanians at the Head of Elk, and then returned to Philadelphia. The two sloops of war ran far up into the West River and burned a nearly completed twenty-gun frigate and nineteen other craft in the shipyards.

On the 19th of March Lieutenant Bickell of the Hessian jäger detachment under Captain Ewald commanded a picket on a tribu-

[34] Apparently lost.

tary of Scott Creek, on the right wing of the Portsmouth line. He sent out a noncommissioned officer with six jägers on a patrol. These men encountered General Muhlenberg's rebel corps, which, deserters tell us, consisted of six hundred infantrymen and one hundred horse. One jäger was killed, another wounded, and the rest of the patrol was captured. The picket was protected only by a deep ditch, which the enemy van attacked in lively fashion. Captain Ewald rushed in with fifteen jägers and defended the post. He was struck in the leg by an almost spent bullet, which, fortunately, could be cut out immediately. He is now well on the road to recovery. One jäger was killed at his side, and another wounded.

General Arnold praised the courageous behavior of the Hessian jägers so much because the maintenance of this post was necessary, lest the entire corps in Portsmouth be exposed to evil consequences. One captain, one subaltern, and twenty-nine men were found killed when General Muhlenberg retired after a stay of four hours.

Admiral Arbuthnot remained in Lynnhaven Bay until the 6th of this month, and cast anchor at Staten Island on the 11th. The *Prudent* man-of-war was severely damaged in the naval action of the 16th of March. The fleet has many sick, and only a few return from the hospital established on Governor's Island—most of them die—which is the reason why the navy has pressed already four times.

Admiral Graves is ready to run out with a force equal to that of the French at Newport, who are again preparing to go to sea. The French fleet returned to anchor again at Rhode Island toward the end of March without being further pursued. They admit having had three hundred killed and wounded in the action. The *Ardent* can no longer be used in the line, and the *Conquérant* and the frigate *Romulus* have to be entirely refitted. Nevertheless, the French can consider themselves fortunate not to have been damaged more by the superior English fleet, which had the wind in its favor, besides. The *Robust* had already encouraged two enemy ships when the *Prudent* came to her support. Then Admiral Graves attacked the enemy line with the *London* and was fortunate enough to bring entire broadsides to bear on the nearby enemy ships. But Admiral Arbuthnot signaled from the *Royal Oak*, fired a few shots across the *London*, and immediately the entire engagement came to an end. Admiral des Touches immediately took advantage of this opportunity, withdrew eastward, and hid in a fog. The following day the British fleet assembled in Lynnhaven Bay.

At the beginning of February of this year the *Romulus* still belonged to the English, but she was attacked and captured off Chesapeake Bay by a French warship and two frigates. General Washington wanted to have the entire French fleet with two thousand land troops at sea at that time on the way to the Chesapeake, but the French could not run out of Newport until the 7th–8th of March. It was sheer luck that they were so late and also that the wind was against them during the action.

A package of letters intercepted at The Clove [35] near New Windsor in Jersey on the 29th of March shows distinctly how much General Washington is displeased with the slow movements of the French. In a letter of March 28th written to his cousin,[36] Lund Washington, at Mount Vernon, Virginia, he says that General Arnold's coup can be attributed solely to the hesitancy of their allies and that consequently but little can be gained from this year's campaign.

Admiral Arbuthnot will go home. The frigates are cruising with considerable success. The *Roebuck* frigate captured the rebel frigate *Confederacy*, thirty-six guns, off the Delaware and brought her in on the 19th of this month. The *Confederacy* and the *Deane* frigates were escorting a merchant fleet of thirty-three sail from Cape François to the Delaware, but after the *Confederacy* and several merchantmen had been captured, the *Deane* sailed to Rhode Island with the French frigate *Hermione*, while the rest of the merchantmen made for Boston. Doubtless, our frigates

---

[35] This account is corroborated by Frederick Mackenzie, who states in his *Diary*, Cambridge, 1930, that Lieutenant John Moody, 4th Battalion New Jersey Volunteers, after hiding for four days near New Windsor, intercepted the post boy five, miles from there. The original letter is in the Clinton Papers, William L. Clements Library. It was printed in Almon's *Remembrancer*, XII, 15.

[36] Baurmeister says "nephew."

which went in pursuit of them will capture several more. There was a French colonel on the *Confederacy* who was to deliver to Congress complete uniforms for five thousand men. The frigate also carried a great quantity of West India goods, which is estimated to be worth £100,000 sterling.

Even more important are the prizes which Admiral Rodney's fleet has taken at the several Dutch islands since the beginning of February. He has twenty-eight ships of the line and some frigates, all of which have been busy plundering the wealthy Dutch. Many British and Irish merchants are reclaiming their ships and wares.[37] The merchants of St. Christopher made their presumptuous claims in writing, not only for themselves, but also for the Europeans.

Admiral Rodney had good reasons for becoming suspicious; he refuses to recognize as noncontraband goods such items as victuals, cloth, blankets, and ship materials of all sorts, and most certainly ammunition and arms from European factories. He sent a party of these friends of America on a ship to London and had a New York merchant hanged. A year ago this man had run into the local harbor with an American ship full of lumber, saying she was a prize. After he had sold the lumber, he loaded both ships full of salt, which he claimed he was taking to Jamaica in the West Indies. Instead, he took his cargoes to Philadelphia, where they were in great need of salt, and then carried on further trade with St. Eustatius. It was this master who was strung up without ceremony. No news has come in from the West Indies since the 11th of this month.

I should now like to give a detailed account of the main action between Lord Cornwallis and General Greene at Guilford Court House, March 15th, but I am unable to obtain the necessary information. At General Clinton's headquarters it is said that the victory was too dearly bought. I myself do not see anything extraordinary in it, for since we made no effort to smother the rebellion at the beginning, when it could have been done at a small cost, the rebels couldn't help but become soldiers. Moreover, their trade is increasing every day.

[37] British merchants kept up their trade with the Dutch West Indies in spite of the war.

General Greene's report, which came into Philadelphia on the 28th of March, was dated March 16th at the Iron Works, ten miles from Guilford.[38] General Greene admits that he was attacked and thoroughly beaten by Lord Cornwallis. His retreat to the Roanoke had deprived Lord Cornwallis of every opportunity of attacking him. The latter had only something over sixteen hundred men, while the rebel army had increased to six thousand. Between the 12th and 14th the enemy advanced from the High Rock Ford to Guilford.

Lord Cornwallis marched to the Deep River, halted at the Quaker Meeting House, and then marched on. He met with the van of the enemy on the main Salisbury Road. General Greene, who had not expected to find the British there, halted his surprised troops and formed his entire force in three lines on wooded rising ground. His first line extended along the edge of the woods, where it could hardly be seen. It was covered by two cannon and consisted of the North Carolina militia battalions under Generals Butler [39] and Eaton. Three hundred yards to the rear of the front line was the second line, namely, the Virginians under Generals Stevens and Lawson.[40] The third line was formed by the Maryland and Virginia Continental brigades commanded by General Huger and Colonel Williams.[41] The flanks, which were held by the sharpshooters, were covered by two light cannon.

General Greene says that the Hessians formed our right wing. This, however, is contradicted in Lord Cornwallis's report, in which he praises von Bose's Regiment, as will be seen from the *Royal Gazette* article which I enclose herewith in the original [*missing*]. This regiment gave proof in every way of the bravery which has characterized it so long. The British Guards on the right of this regiment suffered much from Colonel Washington's and

[38] Greene's report was printed in the *Pennsylvania Packet*, April 3, 1781, with the caption "Camp at the Iron-Works, ten miles from Guilford Court-House, March 16, 1781."

[39] Brigadier General John Butler, North Carolina militia (Heitman).

[40] Major General Edward Stevens and Brigadier General Robert Lawson, both of the Virginia militia (Heitman).

[41] Brigadier General Isaac Huger and Colonel Otho A. Williams, both of the Continental Army.

Lee's cavalry.[42] After von Bose's Regiment had fired one volley, which put the North Carolinians to flight, it met the Marylanders. Then all three lines broke and made room for the 23rd and 33rd Regiments, which in turn permitted the Guards to come into the open. Thus, they succeeded in chasing the rebels beyond the Reedy Fork River, three miles from the battlefield.

General Greene's report says that this action was won by the discipline of Lord Cornwallis's troops. He mentions 1,307 killed, but makes no mention of the wounded; moreover, he does not include the number of cavalry and artillery killed. All his militia disbanded, and when he first assembled his troops at the Iron Works, he had no more than twelve hundred men. The cannon were left on the field, but all the horses had been killed.

Not until the 23rd of this month did General Clinton receive Lord Cornwallis's report of this action, which was sent from Cape Fear.[43] The following is a summary report of our losses: eight British officers killed, and fourteen wounded. Among the former are Colonels Stuart [44] and Webster. Von Bose's Regiment had Captain von Wilmowsky killed, and Captain Eichenbrod, Lieutenants Schwaner and Geisse, and Ensign von Trott [45] wounded, the last severely. Between five hundred and six hundred noncommissioned officers, musicians, and soldiers are estimated to have been killed. No details are given.

With virtually no accouterments and no food in the desolate region between the Deep, Reedy, and Haw rivers, Lord Cornwallis moved along the Haw toward Cape Fear, heading for Wilmington, where he expects to find provisions and hopes to recondition his troops. The small roaming parties had been so frightened that the country between Lord Cornwallis and Cape

[42] "Light Horse Harry" Lee's Dragoons.

[43] Printed in B. F. Stevens, *The Campaign in Virginia, 1781*, and headed "Camp near Wilmington, 10th April, 1781."

[44] Cornwallis's return in Almon's *Remembrancer* gives Hon. Lieut. Col. Stuart of the Guards. The only Stuart or Stewart in the *Army List* (1780) is Hon. James Stewart.

[45] Mackenzie, *Diary*, p. 511, mentions Wilmowsky, Eigenbrodt, Schwaner, Geise, and Ens. de Frott (= Trott?). In the *Staats-Calender* they are listed as Captains Alexander von Wilmowsky and Johann George Eigenbrod, First Lieutenant Johann Jacob Schwaner, Second Lieutenant Johann Josias Geyse, and Ensign Philipp Ernst von Trott.

Fear was open. Moreover, the militia brought together by General Caswell at Newbern had disbanded and gone home. Since Lord Cornwallis dispatched a report to his King, I am confident that a complete account of these important events will appear in the *London Gazette*. Everywhere the rebels feel the weight of their unjust cause. They are well aware of it and do not leave their allies in the dark in this matter.

General Phillips is moving along the James River toward Petersburg. The Hessian Regiment Erb Prinz, Colonel Robinson's Corps, and a detachment of the 76th Regiment under Lieutenant Colonel Fuchs remained posted at Portsmouth and the Great Bridge. We expect good news from there any hour, as well as from Lord Cornwallis about his movements. Everyone in Philadelphia is prepared to fly.

General Washington remains quietly at New Windsor. The enemy are afraid of losing the forts at West Point on the North River; the militia at Albany is being kept in readiness, and the archrebels in Massachusetts Bay have an eye on Lake Champlain. A new chain has been stretched across the North River from Fort Defiance to Fort Constitution, and the redoubts on Butter Hill [46] have been made as strong as possible.

We shall know within a short time what General Clinton expects to do. The fleet, as has been said before, is ready to sail. Battery pieces have been put on board, and thirty transports are ready to take on troops. However, we cannot spare many troops, for small vessels are constantly coming to the Long Island shore, where they burn things, make surprise raids, and never return without carrying out their designs. Some rowboats even came out of the Raritan to below New Utrecht, captured the Brunswick Major von Maybaum [47] and his nephew, Lieutenant von Maybaum, in their quarters, and took them to Amboy. They have only recently been exchanged.

General von Riedesel will soon sail for Quebec with the dragoons who had been imprisoned near Bennington and have been exchanged. They have been joined by some hundred recruits who

---

[46] Butter Hill, Orange County, N. Y.
[47] English accounts have Major von Meibom.

have arrived from Germany to complement that army. Lieutenant Sobbe of the Knyphausen Regiment has departed for Philadelphia with uniforms and money to relieve the wants of the prisoners there. From the reports sent with this packet your Excellency will see that the troops are not at present exposed to any epidemic and that everything is in as good a condition as can be expected. The following detailed report gives the strength of the troops on the three islands and of the garrison:

In New York are both headquarters; the Royal Artillery under Colonel Martin; the 22nd and 42nd Regiments under Brigadier General Leland; the Erb Prinz and Prinz Carl Regiments under General von Hachenberg; and both Anspach regiments under Colonel von Voit.[48]

Supposed
to be in
Virginia
See p 429

On York Island in the new lines are the 57th Regiment; Graff's Grenadier Battalion; the Combined Battalion made up of the exchanged fusiliers; von Knyphausen's Regiment; the convalescents of the Hessian regiments in Charleston, including von Bose's, all of whom are commanded by Major von Stein; and lastly, von Donop's Regiment. Along the North River are the 38th and the Leib Regiments; and along the East River, the Regiment Jung von Lossberg [49] and the Grenadier Battalion von Linsing, which are under the command of Major Generals von Lossberg and von Gosen.

On Long Island are posted the British Grenadiers; the Hessian Jäger Corps; the exchanged troops of the 17th Regiment of Foot; the Hessian Grenadier Battalions von Lengerke and von Loewenstein; [50] the 17th Regiment of Dragoons; the exchanged Brunswick dragoons; the recruits for the German troops at Quebec; and Diemar's Corps of Hussars, which has just been incorporated into the Queen's Rangers and will be sent to Portsmouth on the Chesapeake in the near future. These troops are commanded by Major Generals von Kospoth, De Lancey, and von

[48] August Valentin Voit von Saltzburg: another source has Friedrich August Valentin Voit von Salsburg; the *Carleton Calendar* records several letters signed Voit.

[49] The Jung von Lossberg (i.e., Lossberg, Jr.) Regiment was formerly von Mirbach's.

[50] The Grenadier Battalion von Loewenstein was formerly von Minnigerode's.

Riedesel. The militia on this island amount probably to about eighteen hundred men, among them two hundred and fifty horse. They are commanded by Colonel Axtell.[51]

Brigadier General Paterson is in command on Staten Island, and under him, Brigadier General Skinner. The 43rd Regiment is posted at Richmond; the 37th is on the flagstaff hill; Skinner's two battalions are at Decker's Ferry; von Bünau's Regiment, one of the finest and most complete of the Hessian regiments, is posted in the center of the island. The 54th Regiment is divided over Powles Hook and Sandy Hook, the latter having also a detachment of fifty men from Staten Island on guard duty. A corps of Refugees of three hundred to four hundred men under James De Lancey is posted at Westchester.

In case of need the city will put three thousand men under arms. They are divided into companies and take turns at drilling with arms on Sundays. They have guard houses for night duty and patrol the city between retreat and reveille. The fire companies are extremely well drilled. No sooner is a fire alarm sounded than the pumps are there and the bucket brigade is formed. When we impressed sailors the last time, the fire alarm was sounded so that we should have better success. However, since but little is gained thereby and since the fearful excitement among the inhabitants may have evil consequences, this has since been strictly forbidden.

All the garrisons are drilling with arms. They have been given powder and loaded cartridges so that they can have target practice.

With the greatest respect I have the honor to be [etc.]

P.S. Additional orders of today instructed the local garrison to leave its quarters at seven o'clock this evening and celebrate Lord Cornwallis's victory at Guilford on the 15th of March with three running fires of small arms and cannon along the batteries under

---

[51] William Axtell, of Kings County, N. Y., who owned a mansion at Flatbush. (See Thomas Jones, *History of New York during the Revolution*, New York, 1879, I, 305–09.) The German text leaves some doubt as to whether he commanded all the militia or only the two hundred and fifty horse; most likely he commanded all the militia.

Fort George. Besides, the two Anspach regiments, including their grenadier companies, and also the greater part of the troops of the 17th Regiment of Foot, which have just been exchanged, have been ordered to embark and sail to Charleston. Major General von Kospoth will immediately replace these troops of the New York garrison with the Grenadier Battalions von Lengerke and von Loewenstein.

The Pensacola garrison undertook an attack on Mobile, but the Spanish were prepared for any emergency and the enterprise ended with great losses. Colonel von Hanxleden [52] and several subalterns of the Waldeck regiment were killed. Now we all have reason to expect the news that the Spaniards have made themselves masters there, for they again appeared with ships and troops from Havana. St. Augustine will need a stronger garrison, and Savannah must be more strongly fortified. When I told of the action at Guilford on the 15th of March, I forgot to mention that when Lord Cornwallis started out for Wilmington, lack of transportation compelled him to leave some seventy severely wounded at New Garden. Brigadier General Leland [53] and Colonel Gordon of the Guards will leave here for London the middle of next month, May. I shall be happy if I can send some good news with them.

[52] The form of the Colonel's name is taken from a signed memorial in the Carleton MSS in the William L. Clements Library; Baurmeister calls him Hangsleben. According to Eelking, II, 148, von Hanxleden was killed at Frenchtown on the Mississippi.

[53] Brigadier General Leland was breveted a brigadier general in America only. His regimental rank was that of a lieutenant colonel, 1st Regiment of Foot Guards.

: 59 :

On the 26th of April I had the honor to send your Excellency my last account of American events, and I believed that, in accordance with orders, the packet would depart without delay. However, it seems to have become necessary to postpone the sending of dispatches to Europe until today, which gives me an opportunity to send a supplementary letter.

On the 9th of this month Admiral Arbuthnot's fleet was ready to sail as far as Sandy Hook, where it cast anchor. Disease had reduced the number of sailors on the several ships beyond all proportion. Even by continuous pressing we could not make up the loss. We searched among the inhabitants of Long Island, accepted prisoners, and took men from the transport crews. We had virtually decided to take every tenth man from the privateers, but they sailed away.

Besides the two battalions of Anspachers and the exchanged 17th Regiment of Foot, the 43rd was embarked. These troops will be escorted to the Chesapeake to join General Phillips, who is moving along the James River and has detached General Arnold to the Albemarle [54] to reinforce Lord Cornwallis.[55] The latter is posted near Wilmington, not far from Cape Fear, and is being watched by General Wayne, who has been joined by the Marquis de Lafayette.

General Greene, according to American reports, is on his way to Camden. Apparently, Congress in Philadelphia has agreed that General Greene's report sent from the Deep River on the 28th of March is not to be known except among themselves. He is asking in no uncertain terms for reinforcements, ammunition, and provisions, without which he can do nothing. How much these war necessities are needed at present may be seen from the enclosed letter [missing] by General Washington, which I clipped from a newspaper, and also from the embarrassing questions which have been printed and scattered about in Philadelphia and posted upon the Hall of Congress.[56]

On the 4th of this month one of the most momentous events since the beginning of the rebellion took place in that city, for on that day Congress issued the new paper money, which is guaranteed by all the provinces and is redeemable in 1784 with 5 per cent interest. The merchants are closing their magazines and shops, and the military and civil employees who have been paid in this new paper money are having much mischievous hilarity with it and have demanded of Congress to be paid in hard money, or else to have peace with Great Britain. By the 6th of this month this revolt had spread as far as Princeton. It will certainly have serious consequences, especially if we can give these discontented people timely support.

Lieutenant Sobbe returned from Philadelphia on the 7th, after delivering uniforms and accouterments, blankets, and treaty money to one hundred and twenty-one noncommissioned officers and soldiers of von Knyphausen's Regiment and to twenty-seven Hessians of other regiments. He found them all in great distress, an evil consequence of our having treated our prisoners so badly

---

[54] Albemarle Sound. There is no river by that name.
[55] Arnold's movements were feigned.
[56] Probably handbills distributed by dissatisfied elements to embarrass Congress.

in 1776. Since then we have been unable to appease and assuage the rebels, no matter how good our treatment. Repeated remonstrances have been received coldly and have seldom been answered. Lieutenant Sobbe was carefully watched by an officer.

Congress has reason to distrust the residents of Philadelphia and of all Pennsylvania, just as the British headquarters must watch the inhabitants of this city and the islands. Everyone is in business and anxiously seizes every means, dangerous as it may be, to carry on his trade with profit. For this reason the inhabitants learn all they can about our operations on water and on land, and thus many of our intended movements are betrayed and must be delayed if they are not to be thwarted.

The French fleet has not yet run out of Newport harbor.[57] Part of the land troops have again been embarked, but the greater part, together with the Legion, have been encamped the last few days at White Plains. Another camp has already been selected for them at Fishkill. Their fleet will sail to Boston, where the necessary materials will be found to refit completely.

The frigate *Hermione* succeeded in taking a large cargo of flour from Philadelphia to Rhode Island. She was followed by the rebel frigate *Protector,* twenty-six guns, which also had a cargo of flour. But the frigate *Medea* overtook her off the eastern end of Long Island and captured her, bringing in this valuable prize on the 5th of this month. Three rebel frigates are lying in the Delaware ready to escort twenty-two transports, loaded partly with tobacco for Europe and partly with flour for the Spanish at Havana, where the distress due to shortage of food has become acute. At the end of February they were paying sixty piasters for a barrel of flour on delivery. A barrel of flour as sold by the Pennsylvanians contains 350 pounds, a pound being fourteen [*sic*] ounces.

Now that the Dutch have lost their places in the West Indies, Great Britain's enemies suffer tremendously, the Americans by not being able to exchange their wares for war necessities, and the Spaniards and French by losing a convenient magazine where

[57] Contrary to an earlier report.

they could get provisions whenever Europe could not supply them. These sources are now completely stopped.

The Delaware is still open or, rather, has been kept open. Paul Jones commands the three frigates in the Delaware, the *Ariel*, twenty guns, the *Trumbull*, twenty-eight guns, and the *Congress*, thirty-two guns, he himself being on the *Ariel*. Admiral Arbuthnot will know how to prevent these frigates and the transports going too far out to sea.

Congress has declared the Convention troops at Fredericktown,[58] Maryland, to be prisoners of war. The officers have been sent to Connecticut. The British were marched to York Town, Lancaster, and Peter Little Town.[59] They had hardly reached their destinations when they were brought back to Fredericktown, for it was learned that Colonel Butler had advanced as far as Shamokin on the Susquehanna with sixteen hundred Canadians and Indians. The Brunswickers are under guard in Winchester, and the Hesse-Hanauers at Swedes Spring. The British of Lieutenant Colonel Tarleton's corps, whom General Morgan had captured at the Cowpens, have been in Lancaster for some time. These 411 men were also taken to Fredericktown.[60]

Troops from the West Indies will return to this city,[61] and we are also expecting the long-awaited reinforcements from England. General Clinton is ready to start operations, for which reason his Excellency General von Knyphausen will not go to Morris's house but remain in the city.

On the 12th of this month the occupation of Charleston was celebrated. General Clinton and all the Hessian and British officers in the city, numbering more than two hundred, gathered in the large local tavern. Everyone paid for his own cover.

[58] Now Frederick.

[59] Not identified. Capt. Wiederholdt, in his *Tagebuch*, *sub* Feb. 8, 1777, also mentions "Peter little Town," situated near Hanover, York County, Pennsylvania. Captain Cleve, in his MS journal (Bancroft Collection, New York Public Library, vol. 2, No. 63), *sub* Dec. 25, 1778, calls it the last village in the Province of Pennsylvania (marching to the south).

[60] See Board of War to Colonel Wood and to Reed (*Pennsylvania Archives* IX, 24 and 117, respectively) for orders relative to the movements of the Convention prisoners.

[61] I.e., New York.

Brigadier General Leland will depart on this packet. I shall entrust this letter to Mr. Crowder, paymaster of the local English treasury, who is leaving for good. His place will be filled by Mr. Biddulph.

With the greatest respect, I have the honor to be [*etc.*]

: 60 :

[*NEW YORK*

JUNE 9, 1781] [62]

As soon as the last packet, which was closed on the 14th of
May, was dispatched, it cast anchor at Sandy Hook, whence it
sailed for England just before the end of the month. My journal,
which I had the honor to send your Excellency, extended to the
day the packet was closed. In spite of the fact that a fleet of transports is ready to leave for Cork, another packet is to be closed
today and depart for London without delay. This letter contains
everything I thought worth collecting, most of it consisting of
original newspaper articles [*missing*], which I have numbered.

No. 1 gives an account of the operations from Portsmouth
along the James River to Petersburg, which were begun by General Phillips on the 18th of April but carried on by General Arnold.
Phillips was attacked by a severe fever on the 6th of May. He died
at Petersburg on the 15th and was buried there. Governor General
Robertson was to take over the command at Petersburg; but on
the 28th of May, when he was ready to embark, Brigade Major
Noble [63] arrived here with the pleasant news that Lord Cornwallis

[62] Date given in following letter.
[63] Mackenzie in his *Diary*, II, 531, calls him Lieutenant Noble and aide-de-
camp to Major General Phillips. He died, according to Mackenzie, on May 16.

had left Wilmington at the beginning of May with a large enough force to enable him to arrive at Halifax on the 15th of May without meeting with any interference, and that four days later he crossed the Roanoke into Virginia, where he joined General Arnold not far from Petersburg. Governor Robertson, therefore, remained here. We are now waiting for important news from Virginia.

At Yorktown General Wayne was again mortified by the Pennsylvanians' resistance to his order to march. Five of the fifteen principal revolters were shot to death on the 22nd, but notwithstanding this, the troops cannot be subdued. The Marquis de Lafayette complains especially about the desertion in his brigades at Williamsburg.

No. 2 shows Lord Cornwallis's satisfaction with his troops in the action of the 15th of March.[64]

In my last journal I stated that General Arnold had been detached with a corps from Portsmouth and embarked at North Landing in order to go to Albemarle Sound and effect a junction with Lord Cornwallis.[65] It was only empty ships, however, that made the passage, and these feigned movements were reported overland to the rebels.

On the 20th of May we received some good news from Charleston, which is further explained in No. 3. We do not know what General Greene did after this action.[66] Lord Rawdon was immediately reinforced at Camden by the 64th Regiment and Colonel Watson's corps, which consists of the wing companies of the several volunteer corps. Colonel Balfour, the commandant at Charleston, has organized a troop of fifty horse, all Hessians, under the command of Lieutenant Starckloff of von Benning's Battalion. Ensign Lorey of von Dittfurth's Regiment is serving as cornet with them. They are to patrol the main highways to Camden over which Colonel Sumter now and then makes excursions, which we have not been able to prevent.

---

[64] At Guilford, North Carolina.
[65] See page 433.
[66] Action of April 25, 1781, at Camden.

Colonel Clarke [67] of the 7th Regiment, who heretofore has been commanding at Savannah, has gone to St. Augustine with some provincials and some eighty men of von Knoblauch's Regiment to strengthen the garrison, since a large force of Spaniards has repeatedly attacked Pensacola, though they were beaten back every time. However, it may fall in the near future if General Dalling cannot send reinforcements from Jamaica in the West Indies. Don Galvez [68] is said to be mortally wounded. From the West Indies we hear that Admiral Hood met a superior French fleet and was unable to avoid an engagement, but that he got out of the tight place notwithstanding, and that he had two of his ships, the *Russell* and the *Centaur*, which had been badly damaged, refitted at St. Eustatius. Admiral Rodney has released the British merchantmen and their storehouses which had been confiscated in the Dutch possessions. The correspondence between this admiral and the governor of Martinique, the Marquis de Bouillé,[69] is enclosed as No. 4.[70]

The French fleet at Rhode Island is not yet ready to sail. On the 15th of May, however, Vice Admiral M. de Barras arrived there from Brest by way of Boston, and since then these American auxiliaries have been saying that troops and ships will come over. They are remaining quiet on their island. At White Plains they have only a small force, which has been reinforced by five hundred Americans who have taken post at North Castle. They are beginning to feel a scarcity of salt and flour.

On the 26th of May they held a general muster at Rhode Island; the total number of officers, commissaries, servants, sick, and all those capable of bearing arms amounts to 3,004. Many have succumbed to various diseases, and the action at the Chesapeake also diminished their numbers considerably. On the 23rd of May General Washington had an interview with M. de Barras [71]

[67] Lieutenant Colonel Alured Clarke, who was in command of Georgia and, judging from requisitions and correspondence (*Carleton Calendar,* II, 307), also responsible for East Florida.

[68] Don Bernardo Galvez.

[69] François Claude Amour de Bouillé du Chariol, Marquis de Bouillé.

[70] The correspondence between Rodney and Bouillé was printed in the *New-York Gazette,* May 28, 1781.

[71] Paul François Jean, Comte de Barras, Admiral of the French naval forces.

in Connecticut, after which they went to their respective quarters.

On the 1st of this month another package of mail was seized in Essex County, West Jersey, on the road to Philadelphia, and on the 5th, late at night, it was brought into British headquarters. The letters were of the greatest importance and induced General Clinton to dispatch this packet in such a hurry. In the meantime [72]

[72] MS incomplete.

: 61 :

NEW YORK
JULY 15, 1781

Right Honorable Lord,
Gracious High and Mighty Lieutenant General: [73]

I had the honor to send your Excellency my journal up to the 9th of June with the packet that sailed on the 14th of the same month, when a large number of provision ships also left for Cork. In this letter I humbly continue my report on American events.

On the 10th of June General Arnold, having been taken ill at Portsmouth, returned from Virginia. The great quantities of tobacco, flour, implements of war, and vessels that came into our possession were all claimed by the navy, whereas the captured grain magazines, the loose horses, the cattle, and sheep were to become the property of the army. This allotment of spoils resulted in quarrels and fights between the sea and land forces, so that a decision has been requested from London. The spoils will not be divided until this is received. It is highly desirable that selfish interests be moderated and that the English be governed by a

[73] Von Jungkenn has become a lieutenant general.

genuine concept of liberty during this conflict with the Americans. Only then shall we succeed in our enterprises and make good progress.

General Arnold has completely recovered and has lost nothing in General Clinton's esteem. His command at Portsmouth was taken over by General Leslie. Upon receiving some salutary orders from General Cornwallis after the armies had united at Petersburg, namely, that no officer, whatever his rank may be, can henceforth employ a soldier as a personal servant (such places are to be filled by negroes), that in the future the infantry in battle formation must be arranged in three files and closed squads, and that under no condition will heavy baggage be allowed, his army, consisting of six to seven thousand men, set out on its march and crossed the James River at Westover in the beginning of June. It then advanced to Hanover Court House and crossed the South Anna River, whereupon Lieutenant Colonel Simcoe was detached to Point of Fork at the foot of the mountains and Lieutenant Colonel Tarleton to Charlottesville. The army, however, continued on its march to Richmond, where Lafayette has been stationed. His force being too small, Lafayette retired to Fredericksburg, where it was brought up to eleven thousand men by the corps of Generals Steuben, Wayne, and Muhlenberg.

Lieutenant Colonel Simcoe had expected to find General Steuben, who, however, thought it wise to abandon his magazines after burning everything, destroying several thousand muskets, and blowing up a large store of powder.[74] Nor was anything found in Charlottesville, where the assembled representatives of the Virginia districts were seized. Lord Cornwallis had hoped to get possession of the provision magazine at Albemarle Old Court House.[75] Lafayette, however, hearing of his intention, approached the South Anna by two stolen marches and gained a favorable position on the Mechunk [76] between the British army and Albemarle Old Court House. Thus everything was thwarted, and the

[74] Baron von Steuben was in command of a magazine at Point of Fork, a point of land at the junction of the James and Rivanna rivers.

[75] Albemarle Old Court House was situated above Point of Fork.

[76] The Mechunk Creek is a tributary of the Rivanna, north of its junction with the James River.

troops marched back to Richmond. This occurred from the 15th to the 17th of June.

Three days later the army set out on a five-day march to Williamsburg. Lieutenant Colonel Simcoe and Captain Ewald were in command of the rear guard and at the same time covered the right wing, for the train (loose horses, cattle, and sheep) was large and moved in a single file. On the 25th of June the army, save the rear guard, encamped at Williamsburg without interference.

Early in the morning of the 26th the rear guard was attacked by the rebel Colonel Butler [77] and Major McPherson [78] with five hundred light infantry, three hundred sharpshooters, and one hundred dragoons between Spencer's plantation and New Kent Court House,[79] for Lieutenant Colonel Simcoe had been detained on the Chickahominy River, where he destroyed the boats. Nevertheless, the superior enemy force was prevented from completing its arrangements for a regular attack. Captain Ewald drove the enemy back on their left wing, and the troops on the enemy's right wing, now crowded together, were defeated by the Queen's Rangers. Little quarter was given. One hundred and twenty men and four officers remained on the field, and some twenty were taken prisoners. The rear guard had forty men killed and wounded. Many French officers served as volunteers under Colonel Butler, but again their energetic conduct did not serve as an example for the rebels.

The rebels and their allies will feel the loss of all that was destroyed on the march from Richmond to Williamsburg: a train of French artillery of brass pieces, consisting of ten 24-pounders, four 9-pounders of special length, four 13-inch mortars, and five 8-inch howitzers, as well as a great number of iron cannon of various calibers, muskets, powder, loaded shells, cartridges, fuses, and flints.

[77] The report printed in Almon's *Remembrancer*, XII, 219, is signed "Richard Butler, commanding the advanced light corps."

[78] Probably Major William McPherson of Pennsylvania.

[79] Usually referred to as the action at Spencer's Tavern, or Spencer's Ordinary, which stood at the junction of the roads to Jamestown and Williamsburg.

On the 4th of this month Lord Cornwallis set out for James-town [80] in order to cross the James River there. Lafayette had remained twenty miles from Williamsburg and was encamped at Tyrll's plantation; [81] only a small enemy corps under Major McPherson was frequently seen at New Kent Court House. On the 6th, two days later, the Marquis de Lafayette himself followed with two thousand militia, part of the Continentals, and the Penn-sylvania brigade under General Wayne. But the main body of this enemy corps stopped its advance two miles from our lines in order to avoid a general engagement.

Lord Cornwallis then ordered some closed regiments with their fieldpieces to advance in front of our lines, close to their pickets. In the meantime the army got under arms and formed in two divisions in order to be ready to support the regiments sent out. Thus, the pickets were compelled to withdraw and the enemy was induced to make an attack. However, the militia got almost immediately into the fire of the British light infantry, which was posted on the right wing of the first division. The rebels fell back and left two cannons behind. Lieutenant Colonel Dundas's brigade, consisting of the 43rd, 76th, and 80th Regi-ments, met with considerable resistance on the enemy's right wing until the Pennsylvania brigades broke ranks and took flight everywhere. [82]

The account of this engagement mentions 350 killed but says nothing of the wounded and prisoners. The British lost a lieu-tenant of the 80th Regiment and eleven soldiers killed, and twenty-nine wounded. Lieutenant Colonel Dundas was duly praised by Lord Cornwallis for the part he played in the battle, since the 76th and 80th Regiments went into action for the first

[80] Jamestown was only a ruins then; should probably read "James City," as, indeed, Cornwallis calls it in his letter to Clinton (Clinton Papers, William L. Clements Library).

[81] There are many Tyrrells in Virginia (see E. G. Swem's *Virginia Historical Index*). However, Lee's *Memoirs* (p. 429 of 1869 ed.) says Tyre's plantation and a letter of Lafayette to Pres. Huntington (Almon's *Remembrancer*, XII, 218) is headed "Mr. Tyre's Plantation, twenty miles from Williamsburgh, 27th June, 1781."

[82] This engagement took place at Jamestown Ford, July 6, 1781.

Map of the Southern States During the Revolution. (Redrawn from various sources.)

time [83] and fought under his command like old corps. This is all we know here of the operations in Virginia. The light infantry corps and two regiments are expected here, for the burning summer heat causes inactivity among friend and foe alike. Besides, a different position is to be taken; the magazines are to be taken to Yorktown, and the works at Portsmouth are to be demolished and the city evacuated.

Lord Rawdon was unable to maintain his position at Camden any longer. He drew in all posts with the exception of those at Ninety-Six and Augusta and retired to Monks Corner, thirty-seven English miles from Charleston. The newly organized dragoons had some losses during the retreat. At Mott's house,[84] on the route of march, Lord Rawdon found it advisable to throw up a redoubt to check to some extent the first onrush of the pursuing enemy; but the commanding officer of this redoubt and twenty-five men were forced to surrender. All this occurred early in May.[85]

General Greene, however, has also left the South Carolina border and gone to Halifax to find better provisions on the Roanoke and to be closer to the Virginia army in case he should be needed. Only Brigadier General Morgan, a resourceful partisan, whose excursions have inflicted many losses, remained on the Pedee. Camden was burned.

On the 2nd of June the Cork provision fleet cast anchor in Charleston harbor. It was escorted by the *Warwick* and the *Solebay* men-of-war, which brought in five prizes. The fleet disembarked three Irish regiments, recruits, and implements of war. Thus, both tenable places, Ninety-Six and Augusta, have been sufficiently reinforced. The said provisions fleet left the South Carolina coast as early as the 7th of June, disembarked recruits and provisions in the Chesapeake en route, and sailed into this harbor on the 26th.

[83] The German text is not quite clear; it may be translated "the 76th and 80th were the first to go into action." However, the remark that they fought like old corps seems to bear out the above translation. The two regiments arrived on August 26, 1779, and, judging from Baurmeister's accounts, had not seen action heretofore.

[84] The house of the deceased Jacob Mott (cf. McCrady, *History of South Carolina in the Revolution, 1780–1783*, p. 233).

[85] The action at Fort Mott took place May 12.

With the old and new provisions, the magazines are now provided with salted and dry provisions for fourteen months, counting from the first of this month. Besides, the privateers are bringing in many flour ships from the Delaware. The wood stores are abundant. This year's crop of hay on Long Island is sufficient to feed the horses, and since oats have always been sent from England, it is expected that they will be sent this year.

Since the 14th of June the troops have been encamped on the islands close to this city; only the Jäger Corps is posted in front of the new line on Cock's Hill, this side of Kings Bridge, while the corps of Refugees, five hundred strong, is cantoned between East Chester and Westchester. Besides these, not a single man is outside our line. The quarters of the Hessian General Staff are still in the city.

We have not been ignorant of the fact that General Washington intended to encamp near White Plains at the beginning of this month with fifteen hundred French infantry and three hundred dragoons of these auxiliaries. The French under Count Rochambeau were the first to arrive at the place of rendezvous. They had come from Rhode Island, where one thousand men were left behind under Brigadier Choisy.[86]

The Continental troops, having been increased to four thousand at New Windsor, crossed the North River and passed Sing Sing on the 1st of this month. Part of them remained on flatboats under the command of General Lincoln in order to land in the bay at Philipse's house and march from there to Van Cortlandt's house, which is situated in low land under the former Fort Independence and has the hill of Spuyten Duyvil on its right front. General Washington intended to open the campaign with much vigor and show the French General Staff the narrow limits of the British possessions.

On the 1st instant the worthy Captain Rau went beyond Philipse's house with a patrol and then visited the valley on the right, where Babcock's house [87] stands on the Sawmill River. A

[86] Lieutenant General Claude Gabriel, Marquis de Choisy.
[87] The house of the Reverend Luke Babcock, which was used for Hessian headquarters in the summer of 1780.

number of militia who had gathered in the brush received this patrol with an unexpected fire. Captain Rau was mortally wounded by a shot through the upper part of his body, from which he died two days later. His death is much lamented by the entire Jäger Corps.

Very late on the same day Lieutenant Colonel Emmerich and one hundred picked men took the same route with the intention of capturing a rebel detachment which had come across the North River and landed at Philipse's house. While Lieutenant Colonel Emmerich was away, the Jäger Corps, two hundred foot and thirty horse, set out very early on the 2nd to forage and cover a train of wagons. Lieutenant Colonel von Prueschenck, who was in command, had entrusted the van to Lieutenant Schäffer. The latter detached a noncommissioned officer and ten jägers to reconnoiter, by different routes, the hill of the old Fort Independence. This was before daylight. Lieutenant Schäffer got to within fifteen paces of the rebel detachment, which had formed behind the demolished works, and had to withstand a whole volley.

Lieutenant Colonel von Prueschenck immediately sent back the train so that he might get in the rebels' rear; but he could reach only the raised bastion,[88] where three years before had stood a house which had been fortified by Lieutenant Colonel Emmerich. From this position he attacked the rebels, who, however, were too well covered and were, moreover, supported by a closed battalion. He therefore retired below the Prince Charles Redoubt and had the thirty mounted jägers under Lieutenant Flies[89] charge the pursuing rebels. Since this was effective, Lieutenant Colonel von Prueschenck undertook a second attack, which made the enemy abandon their position in order to gain the height at Devoe's house.[90]

---

[88] The manuscript is not clearly legible, though there seems to be little doubt that the word is meant to be "Reiter," i.e., cavalier, a raised bastion. Accounts of this engagement are printed in Almon's *Remembrancer*, XII, 222, and *New-York Gazette*, July 16, 1781, but they give no further clue.

[89] Second Lieutenant Conrad Flies (*Staats-Calender*, p. 38). The spelling "Files" in the *New-York Gazette*, July 16, is definitely a typographical error.

[90] The house of Daniel Devoe (Hufeland, *Westchester County*).

Immediately thereafter Lieutenant Colonel von Wurmb advanced with the rest of the Jäger Corps. However, no further attacks were made, for on the road to Mile Square, on the height above Williams's bridge, stood a superior enemy force, whose left wing was covered by the three hundred French dragoons.[91] Only one hundred jägers remained posted at Fort Independence; the rest returned to their camp.

On the 2nd of this month Lieutenant Colonel Emmerich discovered many flatboats in Philipse's Bay. He withdrew with the intention of seizing the unmanned boats, but his men fired and betrayed his ambush. He happened upon the flank of an enemy column, and since he was thoroughly familiar with the roads, his detachment succeeded in getting together on Spuyten Duyvil without any loss. Not only that, but he brought in nine prisoners.

In the night of the 2nd–3rd of this month the rebels left our immediate neighborhood and halted at Valentine's Hill. The flatboats returned up the North River with the high tide, and on the 4th the enemy encamped at White Plains. The French have the left wing and are under separate command. According to the most accurate accounts, the entire force consists of seven thousand men.

The real intentions of the French allies are not known to any of us, high or low, and we are constrained to believe that Washington's movements will depend on the turn of affairs in the West Indies and in Virginia. The fleet of Admiral Graves, the present commander of the local fleet (Admiral Arbuthnot has been called back to England), is superior to the French fleet at Rhode Island in ships and good will. The Admiral has finally posted some frigates at the Delaware and furnished escort for transporting General von Riedesel's troops, among whom are those of Anhalt-Zerbst and Hesse-Hanau, as well as part of the 44th Regiment and Alt von Lossberg's. Those of von Knyphausen's Regiment are to remain here under the command of Major von Stein.

When these transports return, Colonel von Borck will come back here with part of the last-mentioned regiment. With this

[91] I.e., the three hundred French dragoons mentioned above.

fleet a ship will sail to Halifax carrying Major Neumann, who will join von Seitz's Regiment, for which he is taking along uniforms and field requisites, for there is not always a good opportunity to do this.

On the 12th of this month 350 Frenchmen landed at Lloyd's Neck, Long Island, but since the refugees in the neighboring Fort Franklin [92] were vigilant and some hundred militia hurried there, these guests returned to their ships after being greeted with grape-shot. Since then, nothing has been seen of them.

On the 4th of this month the first transport with British prisoners arrived here from Pensacola. On the 12th of May General Campbell had been forced to surrender the fort to an army of fifteen thousand men, but not until he had blown up his powder magazine and burned two British ships in the harbor. Fifteen warships and eight frigates, a third of them French, manned by eight thousand marines and sailors, had taken a position along the coast and besieged the fort. Don Galvez granted an honorable capitulation. He himself, as well as all the Spaniards, were very friendly toward the British.

Before leaving Havana the prisoners were induced to agree that they would not serve against the Spaniards and their allies until exchanged. This is the principal point of the capitulation, but at the same time, the most equivocal one. Besides, no time has been set for the exchange; it has been left to the arbitrary decision of the Spaniards, and whenever it does take place it will be for Spanish prisoners as far as possible. But it was not stipulated that after that they would be exchanged for Spanish allies. The transportation and maintenance en route has been at British expense. General Campbell had decided that they were to be brought here, for he could choose any place except Jamaica and St. Augustine.

The Spaniards are met here in the same friendly manner. They are at liberty to sell the goods they have brought along and to buy anything but victuals and war provisions of any kind. They are, moreover, permitted to hold religious services in the City Hall. The merchants are delighted, for the piasters and quad-

[92] A stockade on Lloyd's Neck, named after Governor William Franklin.

ruples [93] will doubtless remain here when the Spanish transports
set sail. They say that Admiral Arbuthnot is a most obliging
Englishman, since he allowed the Philadelphia flour ships to sail
to Havana unmolested. They praise Admiral Rodney for his courage, but assert that he lacks Arbuthnot's finesse. A consuming
jealousy prevails between the Spanish and the French.

The entire force at Pensacola, including servants, women,
children, and sailors, consisted of 1,113. The Waldeck Regiment is
now considerably reduced. It is supposed to have been almost 700
strong but, according to a report of its commander, Lieutenant
Colonel von Horn, it now numbers only 356 men. Among the missing are the many men taken prisoners by the Spaniards during
the repeated attacks and sorties. A fort near New Orleans was
still being defended when the troops left Pensacola.

I can report nothing from the West Indies with certainty. The
small Island of Tobago is said to have been taken by the French,
but the enemy have not succeeded in gaining a foothold on St.
Lucia and have abandoned the artillery and munitions they
landed there.

The regular semiannual muster was held again this month.
The regiments are all in the best of condition. The Hessians are
becoming accustomed to the American climate, but not to the extent of preferring this air in any respect to that of the Fatherland.
Everyone wishes—as much as a soldier has a right to wish—that he
may soon return home.

With the deepest respect I have the honor to be, as long as I
live [etc.]

---

[93] Perhaps cuartos. The Spanish pistareen was at this time frequently cut into
four pieces.

: 62 :

A packet was to have sailed as early as the 16th of this month, and the mail for Europe was called in the day before. However, its departure was delayed, and today's orders state that the packet will be closed tomorrow. Therefore I shall not fail to report to your Excellency the following to supplement my journal closed and delivered on the 15th.

News has been received at General Clinton's headquarters that Augusta, having become completely untenable, has been evacuated, but that Ninety-Six has been made all the stronger. Before his departure from the South Carolina frontier General Greene had undertaken a violent attack on this post, which cost him two hundred men and brought him no gain except an unpursued retreat.[94] This is all that is known, for we have received no letters from Charleston giving further details.

Early in the morning of the 20th a sloop of war came up to Admiral Graves's fleet two miles off Sandy Hook and signaled to

---

[94] Greene's operations against Ninety-Six lasted from May 22 till June 19, 1781. According to Lee's *Memoirs*, p. 377, the siege cost Greene 185 killed and wounded.

the Admiral. The latter had hardly given the countersignal when, fifteen minutes later, he sailed with all his ships eastward into the open sea. Nine officers of the fleet who were in the city had to follow it. Two days later we received a report from Lord Cornwallis from the Chesapeake, which he had sent from Suffolk on the 13th. At the same time we received the news that after the action of the 6th of this month Lord Cornwallis had recrossed the James River undisturbed and that our losses amounted to some eighty men. This is confirmed in letters from Lieutenant Colonel du Puy.

The troops sent here under General Leslie's command by Lord Cornwallis are the following: a corps of light infantry, the Queen's Rangers, the 43rd and 76th Regiments, and the two Anspach regiments, including their grenadier companies. Everyone believes that these troops came to anchor off Sandy Hook late in the evening of the 22nd and that early the following day they followed Admiral Graves. However, we have no certain knowledge, and if it is true, then it is the first time during our operations that any movement has been undertaken in secrecy. It had become virtually impossible to do anything secretly.

This much, however, is certain: The French fleet is poorly manned, and the coast of Rhode Island but little guarded at present. It would therefore be the best time to make a diversion. On the 22nd of this month General Washington moved again from White Plains to Van Cortlandt's heights in order to reconnoiter Harlem Creek and the new works on the plain. He marched by a circuitous route to Morrisania so that he would keep beyond the range of our artillery in Fort No. 8. The Jäger Corps therefore left its camp beyond our new line, in accordance with orders, and the Refugees fled from Westchester.

The following day it was expected that the enemy artillery would make some attempt, but by about six o'clock in the evening no enemy were to be seen. The Refugees went out and seized some stragglers, loose horses, sutlers, and deserters. The enemy had retired to White Plains. They realize that General Rochambeau is right when he contends that their weak army cannot take New York so long as the harbor is open and the rivers free of ice, especially when so little preparation has been made.

The Jäger Corps and the Refugees have again occupied their former posts, and patrols are continually ranging to Rochelle, Valentine's Hill, and along the middle road from Van Cortlandt's house, through the lowland, to Babcock's house on the Sawmill River. The main road to Philipse's house does not need patrolling, for the sloops of war above this house are anchored at strategic places.

The local town militia has again been mustered. Including the five Independent Companies,[95] it now has 3,500 men under arms as well as a company of artillery and artisans. Fifty dragoons have also reported and expect to serve within the lines of this island in case of necessity. The works have been supplied with fresh munitions. Long Island will furnish ten thousand militia.

On the 21st of this month thirty-eight refugees embarked from this island, rowed during the night into the Connecticut, concealed their boats, and made their way to the Middlesex Meeting House.[96] There they took forty saddle horses on which the country people had come to the service, seized the preacher [97] and fifty members of the congregation, reached their vessels with their prisoners and booty in safety, and landed at Lloyd's Neck. The prisoners were brought in day before yesterday. The noteworthy thing about this incident is that for several years the preacher had always carried his rifle to church in order to incite people to take part in the rebellion. At present the following toast is very common among the New Englanders:

> "Here's to the man who felled the tree and turned it into
> charcoal to forge iron for the axe that severed the head
> from the body of Charles I."

General von Riedesel has embarked, and the ships are ready to sail any hour. The Convention troops, now declared prisoners

---

[95] The *Carleton Calendar* has "Independent Companies or Hierlihy's five companies."

[96] See report sent by Lieutenant Colonel Upham to Governor William Franklin, dated July 23, 1781, and printed in the *New-York Gazette*, July 30, 1781. The "Middlesex Meeting House" is not *the* meeting house of Middlesex County but a meeting house of the former parish of Middlesex—today the small township of Darien, Stamford, Connecticut. *then Stamford*

[97] The preacher's name was Moses Mather.

of war, were to have been supplied with uniforms, blankets, and treaty money, for which purpose Captain Gerlach of the Brunswickers departed with these supplies. However, nothing but the money was accepted, and the Captain was told to take the rest back with him. The noncommissioned officers and men, British, Brunswickers, and Hesse-Hanauers, are at present at Reading, but the officers have been sent to East Windsor in Connecticut. They receive miserable treatment and all representations are futile. General Clinton had a separate ship given to General von Riedesel because of his large family and gave him the right of serving as a lieutenant general in Canada.

With constant and deep esteem I have the honor to be [etc.]

P.S. Major Hanger has returned hale and hearty from a voyage and will join Lord Cornwallis in the fall.

: 63 :

Since the 26th of last month, when I humbly dispatched my last report to your Excellency, no great changes have come to my knowledge. However, your Excellency will be pleased to know that the transports with the recruits under Colonel von Benning [98] arrived here safely on the 11th of this month after a voyage of thirteen weeks, and that the recruits were disembarked three days later. A little more than one hundred and thirty sick, most of them suffering from scurvy, of which they will soon be cured, were disembarked earlier and taken to the hospitals. Quantities of fresh vegetables had already been obtained from the gardens, so the maladies incidental to sea voyages could be combatted that much more effectively. Only twenty-two men died during the passage.

The Hessian recruits were distributed over the various regiments on the 14th of this month, the regiments here taking over the recruits for those not here until there is an opportunity to send them to their destination. In the meantime, they will do service, as will also the Brunswick and Anhalt-Zerbst recruits, who

[98] Colonel Friedrich von Benning, who had become chief of von Huyn's Regiment even before his arrival in America.

457

have been sent to Brooklyn, Long Island, to be quartered with the Hesse-Hanau Jäger Corps. The latter is quartered at Flushing, where Lieutenant Colonel Emmerich is to acquaint their commander, Lieutenant Colonel Janeke, with that region, especially with the coast of the East River sound.

These German recruits, together with those for the 60th Regiment, make a reinforcement of three thousand men. General Clinton can now be reconciled to the fact that it was impossible for Lord Cornwallis to detach a corps of four thousand men which had been ordered to come here under General Leslie's command. Lord Cornwallis remonstrated because he did not wish to lose an opportunity to gain possession of Virginia.

After leaving a garrison of British Guards under the command of General O'Hara at Portsmouth, Lord Cornwallis marched his army from Suffolk to Yorktown, contrary to the rebels' expectation, whereupon Lafayette crossed the river at Burwell's Ferry and encamped seven miles further on, at Williamsburg. My next report may therefore contain news about the destruction of Baltimore and further movements toward the Susquehanna.

General Leslie was to have gone to Charleston in the frigate *Blonde* to take over the general command in South Carolina. However, he was taken ill and came to New York. After his recovery he will return to Europe with General Stirling. It is not yet known who will be given the command in that province. On the 31st of July a ship arrived here from Charleston after a passage of nine days and reported that Lord Rawdon had also demolished and evacuated Ninety-Six and had taken a new post at Orangeburg, and that the rebel dragoons under Colonels Lee and Washington had attacked the 19th Regiment posted at Monks Corner, but had been beaten back by the commander and Lieutenant Colonel Coates, with the noticeable loss of seventy dragoons and their horses.

The ships with the above-mentioned recruits were, in the Bermudas, mistaken for a French fleet, and without delay the necessary warning was sent to Barbados and Charleston by courier ships. Here, above all, everyone was very worried about the arrival of a French fleet. Washington's friends faithfully made their reports, so everyone in the rebel camp at White Plains rejoiced. But when the enemy learned that they were British ships and that they brought such large reinforcements, they were all the sadder, particularly because the convoy consisted of only one frigate and two armed ships and because they arrived in such safety and in so short a time.

The French hussars are coming in as deserters with their horses. So far fourteen have arrived; also nine infantrymen, eleven grenadiers, and five artillerymen. Moreover, between the 8th of July and the 15th of this month, thirty-one Americans came in. The militia are running off in disorder into Connecticut for provisions, and Washington can be satisfied if no more than one third fail to return. Sickness is even more reducing their number, which was never more than eight thousand, including their allies.

Admiral Graves is cruising with very good results in the waters between Cape Cod and Rhode Island and as far as the mouth of the Delaware. The frigates *Iris, Medea,* and *Amphitrite* have captured off the Delaware shore the frigates *Trumbull,* thirty-two guns, *Belisarius,* twenty-four guns, and eleven transports with flour and other cargoes, all of them destined for Cape François and Havana.[99] The British frigates went in pursuit of thirteen more transports, which are not likely to escape. To the Philadelphians this will be an irreparable blow, especially since by their loss our provisions are increased. However, we have gained even more by capturing so many sailors, who, being British, have been engaged.

I cannot report any facts from the West Indies, except that if Count de Grasse sends some ships of the line to molest our ships in this harbor, Admiral Rodney will detach a like number. The islands of New York are in a redoubtable state of defense; besides, the rebels have made no preparations for an offensive. We are completely inactive. The summer is mild, and the troops as a whole have never been so well as they are now.

On the 4th of this month an English packet arrived from Falmouth. It brought open letters addressed to French officers in Rhode Island and sent in care of Count Rochambeau. Captain

[99] The *New-York Gazette,* Aug. 13 and 20, gives lists of the captured ships.

Marquard,[100] who at present is with his Excellency General von Lossberg, took charge of them and was treated very kindly at the French outpost. A courteous reply came back for General Clinton.

In my preceding journal I had the honor to state that the non-commissioned officers and soldiers of the Convention troops are quartered at Reading. Of these, thirty-six have returned in the last three weeks by way of Powles Hook. They are poorly guarded and receive miserable food. Five hundred dragoons might get to them by a bold stroke and bring them, one and all, to the Susquehanna and thence to the Chesapeake. But the impracticability of this is evident; the undertaking is dangerous and consequently should not be risked.

Everyone is eager to know how Congress in Philadelphia will account to the Spaniards for the seizure of the last cartel ship, the *St. Joseph* [101] (on its way to New York with Pensacola prisoners) by two privateers, the *Holker* and the *Fair American*. The fact that two British privateers, the *General Arnold* and the *Surprise*,[102] took this supposed booty away from them when they were about to take it into the Delaware will increase the embarrassment of Congress. All the Spanish cartel ships have left this harbor without misgivings, for they were escorted by two armed ships.

The Hessians of the Charleston garrison have very few sick according to reports of July 26th. Captain Egerding [103] of von Dittfurth's Regiment has died. Here, Artillery Captain and Brigade Major Werner [104] also died recently, and his passing is considered a real loss in view of his knowledge of military affairs.

I have just received your Excellency's gracious letter of the 1st of April from Colonel von Benning and find to my satisfaction

[100] Captain Ludwig August Marquard of the Leib Regiment, who had been aide-de-camp to Knyphausen. (Cf. *Staats-Calender*, p. 21.)

[101] Mackenzie, *sub* July 29, calls this cartel ship the *St. Joseph & Joachim*.

[102] The *Surprise* could not be identified.

[103] Captain Ludwig Eggerding, according to the *Staats-Calender*, p. 30. The *New-York Gazette*, Aug. 6, 1781, calls him Edderging in the death notice; Eelking-Rosengarten, quoting this death notice, has Engerding.

[104] The *New-York Gazette, loc. cit.*, says: "Captain Werner of the Hessian Artillery, and Major of Brigade to Gen. Knyphausen." His name was Friedrich Wilhelm Werner, Staff Captain of the Field Artillery Corps in 1779 (*Staats-Calender*, p. 36).

that all my journals up to January 22nd this year have been received.

Admiral Graves came to anchor at Sandy Hook with nine ships of the line the evening of day before yesterday. The *Royal Oak*, a ship of the line, is still cruising with the frigates.

Yesterday the following changes were made in the camps on the islands near the city: The 2nd British and the four Hessian grenadier battalions are encamped at McGown's Pass, and the 1st British Grenadier Battalion on the other side of the East River, at Hallet's Cove, while Major General von Wurmb's brigade and Stein's Combined Battalion, the latter having been stationed at Denys's,[105] are now encamped here before the city. This brigade consists of the Leib Regiment and Prinz Carl's. The Anhalt-Zerbst corps, commanded by Major Luttichow, and the Brunswick recruits under Captain von Woltzogen have gone to Powles Hook, where the 54th Regiment had been. The latter, as well as von Bünau's Regiment, went from Staten Island to Kings Bridge. Brigadier General Skinner remained on that island with two battalions of his regiment.

The rebels' heavy baggage left for Fishkill on the 17th of this month, and the last French deserters informed us that General Washington has placed his army under marching orders. Yesterday evening reports were received from the Chesapeake, but their content has not become known.

With the deepest respect I have the honor ever to remain [*etc.*]

105 I.e., Denys's Ferry.

: 64 :

It was on the 19th of last month, August, that I had the honor to send my last journal to your Excellency. Today, the 24th of September, I have just come from English headquarters, where his Excellency General Clinton told me to inform his Excellency General von Knyphausen that he has just learned from the frigate *Perseverance* that Admiral Digby has arrived, and that a packet will be closed and dispatched this very evening.

I therefore write hurriedly to report to your Excellency that on the 19th and 20th of August General Washington left his camp between Dobbs Ferry and White Plains and crossed the North River with 5,982 men, including 3,560 Frenchmen. He is marching in two columns to Philadelphia by way of Princeton and Trenton and then on across the Schuylkill to the Susquehanna.

Soon after Admiral Hood's arrival we learned that when he left the West Indies with fourteen ships of the line, Comte de Grasse immediately followed with twenty-four ships of the line, that the latter was joined by Admiral de Barras, who came from Rhode Island, and that they are now masters of the Chesapeake. Admiral Graves intended to send nineteen ships of the line to

Yorktown with reinforcements for Lord Cornwallis, but he did not succeed. The warship *Terrible* was burned, and the English fleet returned to New York.

Since the 6th of this month all the grenadiers of the army, the 22nd, 37th, 42nd, and 57th Regiments, the Leib Regiment, and Prinz Carl's have been embarked. But on the 19th all these troops disembarked again on Staten Island, and by this time everything has been brought ashore. Sickness is increasing. Until Admiral Graves's fleet is reinforced, no ships can leave this harbor. Five ships of the line are expected from Newfoundland and four from the West Indies. The next packet, I hope, will carry more favorable news of the English situation in America. At present it looks very bad for Lord Cornwallis's army.

I am writing this in the English post office, for the packet will sail in a quarter of an hour. Lord Rawdon, who was on his way here from Charleston, was captured by Count de Grasse's fleet. The rebels now want him to be turned over to them so that they can hang him, because he caught a paroled rebel lieutenant colonel and hanged him in Charleston.[106]

The boldness and stubbornness of Congress at Philadelphia is unsurpassed at present. All the Brunswick officers will return from their imprisonment next week. The Hesse-Hanau Free Corps has been moved from Flushing to Brooklyn, since more than half of them are ill and forty-six men and one officer have died.

Lieutenant Colonel Graff died yesterday morning from a severe fever.

Once more I beg your Excellency's pardon for writing in such haste. The packet is leaving too soon.

With the deepest respect I have the honor ever to remain [*etc.*]

P.S. The enclosed newpaper [*missing*] tells of General Arnold's expedition to New London.

---

[106] Lieutenant Colonel Isaac Hayne (see following letter). Lord Rawdon was exchanged for Thomas Burke, Governor of North Carolina, who was taken prisoner, September 12, 1781.

: 65 :

On the 25th of last month, September, a sloop of war was sent in the greatest haste to England with dispatches from the British headquarters. The sloop came to anchor at Sandy Hook immediately afterwards. On this occasion I had hardly a quarter of an hour to write a few lines to your Excellency. However, Admiral Digby's safe arrival with his Royal Highness Prince William Henry [107] at this very time detained the sloop of war three days. His Excellency General von Knyphausen obtained permission to send additional letters for Europe to the sloop.

Admiral Digby brought three ships of the line to the fleet, the *Prince George,* the *Canada,* and the *Lion,* as well as the frigate *Perseverance.* Counting these and two men-of-war that have arrived from Jamaica in the West Indies, the *Torbay* and the *Prince William,* Admiral Graves's fleet now numbers twenty-five ships of the line and two fifty-gun ships, exclusive of the frigates, six fire-ships, and four bomb ships. The refitting of the ships has been finished, and the troops landed on Staten Island boarded the

---

[107] Later William IV. In 1779 Admiral Robert Digby was appointed Governor of Prince William Henry. Admiral Digby came to New York as commander in chief of the North American fleet.

transports again on the 11th of this month. They must keep themselves in readiness to be re-embarked on the men-of-war.

I shall once more enumerate the regiments of the corps which
is to go on this important expedition to the Chesapeake: the British and Hessian grenadiers, the 22nd, 37th, 38th, and 42nd English
Regiments, the Leib Regiment, Prinz Carl's, and Lieutenant
Colonel von Wurmb with the Jäger Corps. Generals Clinton, Leslie, von Kospoth, and also von Wurmb are going along.

Only a few troops remain behind, all of them under the command of his Excellency General von Knyphausen. In this garrison
are the 40th, 54th, and 69th Regiments; the Landgraf and von
Bünau's Regiments are encamped before the city; at McGown's
Pass on this island are von Donop's Regiment and Colonel Robinson's Corps; further on, near Morris's house, the mounted jägers
and all the sick and unfit recruits whom the dismounted jägers
could not take along—all under Lieutenant Colonel von Prueschenck.

At Fort Knyphausen are now stationed the Hesse-Hanau
Jäger Corps, which came from Brooklyn two weeks ago; and
finally, also on this island, the Jung von Lossberg Regiment, which
is so posted at the new line that two companies are encamped on
North Hill, two on Laurel Hill, and one in the road at the main
redoubt. The refugees and the militia are posted on Long Island
along the shore of the Sound, and Captain von Wolzogen commands a post of recently arrived Brunswick recruits at Denys's
Ferry.

Major General Skinner is in command on Staten Island,
where his two weak battalions of volunteers and the 57th Regiment are stationed. At Powles Hook the entire Anhalt-Zerbst Free
Corps is garrisoned under the command of Lieutenant Colonel Emmerich. Before Kings Bridge, above Harlem Creek, De
Lancey's Corps of Refugees has been posted for some time. This
corps continually sends vigilant patrols across the Croton River,[108]

---

[108] It seems almost incredible that patrols should range so far, but Mackenzie,
in his *Diary*, *sub* Oct. 18, reports the following: "Nineteen Rebels taken by De
Lancey's Refugees yesterday on the other side of the Croton, were brought to
town this day."

to the left as far as the North River, and to the right as far as Horse Neck, but the patrols do not meet any armed rebels.

The fleet is ready to sail, and with it a packet will depart for England with reports of the events in the Chesapeake. There will be a serious conflict at the entrance of the Bay. Twenty-seven French ships of the line have barricaded the entrance; three more warships and some frigates are anchored in the mouth of the York River, and other frigates are stationed in the James River. Moreover, several French warships are cruising between the Chesapeake and the entrance to the Delaware. Lord Cornwallis's reports were dated the 29th of September and the 5th of this month. His army was then in excellent condition. The land side of Gloucester was still open, but eighteen hundred negroes had finished the entrenchments. The corps of his regular troops is six thousand strong. In addition to these, two thousand marines and sailors have been put under arms.

General Washington and his little suite arrived at Lafayette's quarters as early as the 12th of September. The Marquis de Saint-Simon [109] also arrived there from Hampton, by way of the James River. He commands the three thousand French whom Admiral Comte de Grasse landed at Hampton from his fleet. Comte de Rochambeau reached the Elk on the 14th of September and embarked the French and American troops, only a little more than five thousand men, on flatboats. Lafayette's army at that time numbered six thousand men, so that the entire rebel army, including the Marquis de Saint-Simon's corps, is estimated at fourteen thousand, of whom more than half are militia.

Lord Cornwallis left his lines before the 29th of September to give battle to General Washington, but the enemy preferred to retire quickly. However, they were just as quick to advance again when Lord Cornwallis moved back into his trenches and remained quiet. The houses of Yorktown have been razed, and the British army is cautiously guarding against the consequences of a siege. This is all that is known of the situation on both sides. Frequent councils have been held at the British headquarters, to

[109] Claude-Henri de Rouvroy, Comte de Saint-Simon, the founder of French socialism.

which his Excellency General von Knyphausen is always especially invited.

His Highness Prince William Henry landed at Fort George on
the 25th of September to a salute of twenty-one guns, and took
lodgings with Commodore Affleck.[110] Admiral Digby did not arrive in the city until the following day, and on the 27th a great
reception was held at his Highness's quarters. He also witnessed
the parade and had dinner with General Clinton, who had invited
all the generals.

The following day Governor Robertson gave a dinner in
honor of the Royal Prince, and the militia, four thousand strong,
paraded through the streets. Only on parade days has his Highness been seen in public. He was dressed in a midshipman's uniform and was always on Admiral Digby's right. His Highness
was greatly admired, but never noisily. Governor Robertson, who
has had a promenade laid out on Fort George and a pavilion built
in his garden below the fort, assembled eight of the first ladies of
the city in the pavilion and suggested that they dance. The Prince,
however, only paid the beautiful gathering a general compliment
and avoided any kind of conversation. Admiral Digby forbade all
music, and at half past eight he returned with his Highness to his
quarters at the main guard, which had formerly been occupied
by the commandant, Major General Birch.

A great dinner was given by Admiral Digby on the spacious
warship *Prince George* to the English and Hessian headquarters
on the 30th of September, and the following day the Admiral gave
a reception in his Highness's name to all the officers without distinction. His Highness visited the regions of Kings Bridge, Flatbush, Hell Gate, Powles Hook, and Staten Island, being saluted
at each place. However, he spends most of his time on the above-
mentioned warship, where he painstakingly performs the duties
of a midshipman during the night and day watches.

On the 30th of September Major Barclay of Robinson's Corps
arrived here on a cartel ship from the Chesapeake. He was on his
way here from Charleston and was to have delivered letters in

110 Commodore (later Sir) Edmund Affleck was Commissioner of the Port of
New York during the summer of 1781.

the Chesapeake to Lord Cornwallis when he was captured by the
enemy fleet. But, fortunately, he had thrown all his letters overboard. M. Bougainville [111] expedited his dismissal on parole.

We have learned from him that an action occurred near
Charleston between the 2nd and 10th of September.[112] General
Greene, with five thousand men and two brass 6-pounders attacked Colonel Stewart [113] of the 3rd Regiment, whose force
numbered a little more than two thousand. Colonel Stewart was
outflanked on the right wing, beaten, and taken prisoner. Colonel
Cruger, who had made such a good defense at Camden some
time ago, was in command of the left wing.[114] Much more successful than Colonel Stewart, he gained an advantage over the
enemy's right wing, captured the two cannons, freed all the prisoners, and took about five hundred men.

General Greene left three hundred killed and wounded on
the battlefield. His Continentals followed the flying militia across
the Congaree in good order. The British losses are estimated at
somewhat over forty men. Except for a detachment of Hessians
of 150 men, none of the Hessian regiments from Charleston participated. We do not know yet whether a Hessian detachment got
into the action, for General Clinton has not received a direct report to date. The rebel newspapers are full of generalities about
this engagement. They claim to have gained a victory and lament
the loss of the wounded and captured Colonel Washington.

On the 26th of August this year General Greene issued a
proclamation from his headquarters in Camden in which he
threatened to hang the first British colonel of a regular regiment
he should capture in retaliation for the hanging of Colonel Hayne,
in spite of the fact that the colonel had taken up arms again after
having been paroled as a prisoner and was captured a second time
in an open action. Should the right of retaliation be resorted to in
such an unheard-of manner, many a colonel or other officer may

[111] Louis-Antoine, Comte de Bougainville.
[112] This action took place at Eutaw Springs, September 8, 1781.
[113] Lieutenant Colonel Alexander Stewart (Stevens, *Campaign in Virginia,
1781,* and *Carleton Calendar*).
[114] Dawson, p. 578, says he commanded the center.

be cruelly elevated sooner than could ever have been expected. Hence, Colonel Washington and others, it is reasonable to suppose, will be held as principal hostages. Comte de Grasse was far nobler toward Lord Rawdon than Congress demanded; he refused to surrender him. His Lordship, with Colonel Doyle [115] and his suite, will be sent directly to England as soon as they are paroled.

The frigates *Richmond* and *Iris* were captured by the French fleet in the Chesapeake. They had been ordered to sever the buoys from the cut cables [116] when Comte de Grasse left the Chesapeake and the naval engagement of the 5th of September took place. It is a real loss. On the 21st of September Comte de Grasse earnestly requested all the American vessels in the Chesapeake to have their cargoes on board and be ready to sail at the beginning of this month. The ships were to take to France, under escort, large quantities of tobacco stored between Annapolis and Baltimore. One of several privateers which could observe the Chesapeake from a distance arrived on the 11th of this month and immediately reported that it had seen seventy-one sail southeast of the Chesapeake.

It is not unlikely that since several attacks have been made on Lord Cornwallis which ended very unfortunately, the rebels fear an expedition into the Delaware and have divided their force at Yorktown, so that Philadelphia will not be without protection. It is also surmised that Comte de Grasse is preparing to sail to Rhode Island and Boston with his superior but damaged fleet rather than wait for a decisive battle. On the 6th of this month the Cork provision fleet of thirty-five transports ran safely into this harbor. Now the London provision and merchant fleet is expected to arrive any day.

There is nothing to report about the Spaniards in Havana. Their fleet is not at sea, and St. Augustine is in no danger of being

---

[115] Colonel (later General Sir) John Doyle, 87th Regiment of Foot. See 1782, note 49.

[116] Cf. Clowes, IV, 75: "Rear Admiral Graves, when he appeared off the Chesapeake and the French fleet put to sea to meet him, had reason to suppose that the enemy's ships had slipped, and buoyed their cables. He therefore dispatched the *Iris*, 32, Captain George Dawson, and *Richmond*, 32, Captain Charles Hudson, to cut away the cables from their buoys."

stormed, and even less of being besieged. If the latter should happen, the whole garrison of Savannah will march to its defense.

One hundred and twenty officers of Burgoyne's army, exchanged in Connecticut, arrived in the city a week ago and have been quartered on Long Island. Brigadier General Hamilton was in charge of the British officers, Lieutenant Colonel von Mengers,[117] of the Brunswickers, and Lieutenant Colonel Lentz, of the Hesse-Hanauers. The noncommissioned officers and privates at Reading and Lancaster are gradually running away, so that now not even a thousand are left.

Bilious fever and ague are very common; the hospitals are filling up, and great numbers are dying. The approaching cold weather, it is hoped, will do more for the sick than all the nursing and medicine, for these unavoidable diseases on these islands are due to the change from summer to fall.

Twelve days ago the British frigate *Carysfort* had the good fortune to capture a ship heavily laden with ship's timber and masts on her way from Boston to the Chesapeake. This increased the supply in the local shipyard considerably.

Ten Brunswick and five Hesse-Hanau subaltern officers have been appointed to serve with the Hessian grenadier brigade. The British Brigadier Generals Paterson and Gunning have also been ordered to take part in the impending expedition. They will take with them the grenadier companies of the 40th and 69th Regiments, which came here from the West Indies in Admiral Hood's fleet. The names of the fifteen officers are Lieutenants Rudolphy, Trott, Petersen, de Cramm, Ketner, Feichel, Bornemann, Glaaden, and Ensigns Erich and von Ulmenstein—all Brunswickers; Lieutenants von Trott, von Bischhausen, von Richtersleben, von Wegers, and Ensign Beimerth—Hesse-Hanauers. The enclosure [118] lists the troops which are to be embarked from the transports on the ships of the line for the expedition to the Chesapeake.

With the deepest respect I strive to be [*etc.*]

---

[117] In the *Carleton Calendar* and in Eelking-Rosengarten (p. 251) the name is Mengen, of the Regiment von Riedesel.
[118] See end of this letter.

P.S. On closing this we received news from Lord Cornwallis that he was stormed and bombarded on the 9th, that his sortie was most successful, that hot shot have burned the forty-four-gun ship *Charon* at Gloucester Point and also set fire to two transports. Moreover, four American prizes [119] have just arrived from Philadelphia under escort of the *Nymph,* among them a twenty-four-gun ship, the *Royal Louis de France.*[120]

A fifty-gun ship and the frigate *Blonde* have on board the last recruit detachments and convalescents for Lord Cornwallis's army. Colonel von Cochenhausen and Lieutenant Colonel Thomas [121] are with them.

The two warships *Intrepid,* sixty-four guns, and *Princessa,* seventy guns, have no special troops on board.

[119] Following the preferred use of the word prize, this should read "four British prizes"; in other words, they are American ships that have been captured by the British and are therefore British prizes.

[120] The *New-York Gazette,* Oct. 22, 1781, calls her the *Royal Louis,* "a privateer from Philadelphia."

[121] Lieutenant Colonel Frederick Thomas, 1st Foot Guards.

Enclosure

The troops will embark from the transports on the following ships of the line:

NO.		GUNS	
1)	*Lion*	64	} the Hessian jägers
2)	*Europe*	64	
3)	*London*	96	
4)	*Prince George*	96	
5)	*Barfleur*	90	} two British grenadier battalions
6)	*Bedford*	74	
7)	*Alcide*	74	
8)	*Centaur*	74	
9)	*Resolution*	74	
10)	*Montagu*	74	
11)	*Invincible*	74	} four Hessian grenadier battalions
12)	*Shrewsbury*	74	
	The Frigate *Perseverance*	36	
	Sloop of War *Sybille* [122]	20	
13)	*Ajax*	74	} Hessian Leib Regiment
14)	*Royal Oak*	74	
15)	*Monarch*	74	} Prinz Carl Regiment
16)	*Alfred*	74	
17)	*Torbay*	74	} British 38th Regiment
18)	*Prince William*	64	
19)	*Canada*	74	} British 22nd Regiment
20)	*Robust*	74	
21)	*Belliqueux*	64	} British 37th Regiment
22)	*Prudent*	64	
23)	*America*	64	} British 42nd Regiment
	50-gun ship *Warwick*		

[122] Clowes calls her *Sibyl*.

: 66 :

On the 16th of last month, October, a packet set sail for England from this harbor, and with it were sent the last letters to your Excellency. At the same time Admiral Graves's fleet anchored at Sandy Hook in three divisions and finally departed for the Chesapeake in the night of the 18th–19th of the same month. However, it was too late, and it was all the more regrettable that General Clinton himself should have embarked on the fleet with six thousand men. All this will be explained in the course of this letter.

As soon as General Washington had joined the Marquis de Lafayette's corps at Williamsburg, and the French troops from Comte de Grasse's fleet had arrived from the James River under the command of Brigadier General Saint-Simon, and all preparations had been made, the entire army of nineteen thousand men marched on Yorktown in two columns. The French ships in the York River furnished artillery and munitions.

Lord Cornwallis was prepared in every way for such an attack. He had fortified himself in three lines within the closest confines possible, having finished his preparations before the 5th of September. On the 23rd he attempted to set adrift five transports which had been fitted out as fireships against four enemy warships in the York River. But the French ships cut their cables and sailed out of danger under a press of sail. Not until the 10th of October did the enemy begin a regular attack. The French threw some fourteen hundred bombs into the encampment, while the artillery fired twenty-five hundred cannonshots with noticeable effect. But the works were rebuilt, and all the sorties were successful.

On the 14th of October the enemy doubled their strength for a general attack, but were beaten back with losses. A sally of one thousand men under Colonel Abercromby upon two newly-built enemy redoubts was especially expensive for the French, for they lost during this attack, early in the morning of the 16th of October, in killed alone 229 men, besides having four 24-pounders, seven 16-pounders, and four mortars ruined. The following day, the 17th, immediately after midnight, the British Guards, the light infantry, the 43rd, 76th, and von Bose's Regiments were to cross the York River in boats. But a high wind prevented this undertaking, and the troops returned to their places before noon.

After vainly waiting for relief, Lord Cornwallis could do nothing but capitulate or else see his army completely annihilated. All the redoubts had been taken; not a single line was intact; and the approaches were coming closer and closer. He therefore requested a truce, which lasted from half past two in the afternoon to half past six in the evening. At that time hostilities ceased, and, since the capitulation was agreed upon on the following day, 3,800 men with their small arms and side arms, with music and flying colors, marched out of the fortified camp on the 19th of October and piled their arms. I am enclosing the articles of capitulation [missing] which so far I have seen only in the newspapers.

On the 24th the prisoners of war were marched in three divisions to quarters in Maryland, Virginia, and Pennsylvana. One staff officer will remain with the troops of each nationality; with each two hundred men, a captain, and with each fifty, a subaltern officer. The officers, from Lord Cornwallis down to the least ensign, will be paroled either to Europe or to New York. All the officers' equipage and the baggage of the noncommissioned officers and men remained the undisputed property of the prisoners. A British hospital will remain at Yorktown, for there are many sick there, and even more wounded who cannot be moved. According to one important article, the prisoners will stay together by corps and regiments, and they may and shall receive their uniforms and pay through officers from here, who will be given passes.

The British marines, sailors, and ships were also captured and are the booty of the French fleet. The lost frigates, sloops of war, and small craft amount to 114. It is not known how many killed and wounded Lord Cornwallis had between the 27th of September and the day of the capitulation. The Erb Prinz Regiment had Surgeon Bauer [123] and twenty-three men killed, sixty-two wounded, and three deserters, while von Bose's Regiment had Captain Roll and sixteen men killed and Ensign Spangenberg and forty men wounded. The fieldpieces of this last regiment had been left in Charleston. The two Anspach regiments had much desertion.

The French cannot be praised enough for the obliging pleasantness and sincere soldierly conduct they showed to Lord Cornwallis and his army. The rebels, always faithless to their word of honor, wanted to keep Lord Cornwallis under arrest until a certain Laurens,[124] who is imprisoned in London, should be freed. The *Bonetta* sloop of war was, according to the terms of the capitulation, left at Lord Cornwallis's disposal to send an aide to General Clinton. He was allowed to put as many men on this ship as he pleased and thought feasible, without having her searched. Nevertheless, a rebel colonel wanted to visit this ship before she set sail; but the French commanders resisted publicly this unmannerly interference and told their allies in plain words that such a capitulation must be lived up to in every respect.

When Admiral Graves arrived at the Chesapeake, he found Comte de Grasse's superior fleet of thirty-three ships of the line

---

[123] According to the *Staats-Calender,* p. 30, Dr. Franz August Bauer was the regimental surgeon of the Prinz Carl Regiment. (Cf. *ibid.,* p. 43.)

[124] Henry Laurens, whom Congress had sent to Amsterdam to negotiate a treaty of commerce, was captured aboard ship and imprisoned in London.

and two fifty-gun ships at anchor in a position of defense. Since they were so stationed that he could not attack them without first running past a formidable land battery, he thought it foolhardy to stake everything. Besides, Lord Cornwallis had already capitulated when the fleet sailed from here.

The frigate *Bellisaria* was immediately sent to take the news of this unfortunate turn of affairs to London, and Lieutenant General Leslie was detached to Charleston with two frigates, the *Blonde* and the *Carysfort*. On these ships were also embarked about three hundred men and several British officers who were part of the Charleston garrison. General Leslie had orders to take on board at Wilmington, near Cape Fear, Major Craig,[125] who had been detached there with five hundred men from Charleston at the beginning of this year. Lord Cornwallis had left a hospital at Wilmington with seven hundred sick and a detachment of Anspach jägers under Captain von Röhder. These troops will considerably reinforce the Charleston garrison, which already consists of six British battalions and three Hessian regiments, especially since the fortifications have been put in an excellent condition by the famous Major Moncrief.

We have not yet received an exact account from our side of the engagement with General Greene near Charleston.[126] After this action, the said general remained inactive and at a distance. But since the Marquis de Lafayette was detached to South Carolina with a corps of four thousand men and a train of artillery immediately after Lord Cornwallis's surrender, it is certain that every effort will be made to take Charleston, or at least weaken it. General Washington has also set out to move unopposed into Jersey.

On the 2nd of this month we sighted Admiral Graves's fleet, which disembarked General Clinton and his troops on transports lying in wait off Sandy Hook, after which the fleet immediately ran out to observe the French fleet. This fleet, though superior in number, would prove to be inferior in every respect in case of an engagement, for it is poorly manned, has been unable to make the

[125] Major James Henry Craig, later Sir James.
[126] I.e., at Eutaw Springs.

most needed repairs since the action of the 5th of September,[127] and does not have as many guns as the British fleet. However, I am no mariner, understand nothing about winds, and, consequently, am not a good judge. Nevertheless, I do know the difference between firmness and its counterpart, and lack of the former and too great a portion of the latter cannot but help make our tight situation still worse. Besides, it is discouraging to the most fervent patriot, especially since, with the assistance of the French, the rebels' situation has improved so much that it actually looks as though nothing can change it.

On the 19th of October the English provision and merchant fleet of sixty-one sail ran safely into this harbor under escort of the fifty-gun ship *Centurion,* and on the 28th Colonel von Borck arrived from Quebec with part of von Knyphausen's Regiment. Thus it was confirmed that General von Riedesel arrived at Quebec without mishap and that Governor General Haldimand has detached the Hesse-Hanau Jäger Corps and all the wing companies of the British regiments stationed there to advance on Ticonderoga. On their way they were joined by a body of Indians. We have known for a long time here that in and around Albany everyone lives in fear, and that the militia are astir. Nothing more is known at present.

Lord Cornwallis will leave for England with many officers, and, if possible, directly from the Chesapeake. The Duc de Lauzun [128] is taking the news of their success to France; Lord Rawdon and Colonel Doyle have sailed with him. I shall pass over the general manifestations of joy on the part of the rebels, especially the tumultuous exuberance with which their victory was celebrated in Philadelphia. Nevertheless, the brave and active British have sufficient courage to make this huge mob of malicious, disobedient people pay dearly for all their boldness, if they would only seriously undertake it—so many good and honest men do not lose all hope.

I am unable to send an exact list showing how General Clinton will have the troops go into winter quarters. The cold air is

[127] See 1781, note 116.
[128] Armand Louis de Gontaut Biron, Duc de Lauzun et de Biron.

aiding the recovery of the many sick. This past fall we have suffered a little too much.

Captain von Schaller of the Erb Prinz Regiment has died of illness, and Captain von Gall of the same regiment is still hopelessly ill.

With the deepest respect I have the honor to be [*etc.*]

: 67 :

NEW YORK

DECEMBER 8, 1781

Despite the fact that several officers who will go to Germany along with the invalids can furnish accounts that will surpass the best written report, I have the honor to send your Excellency herewith another account of what has happened here. It was on the 6th of last month, November, when I had the honor to dispatch my last journal with a packet.

On the 25th of November a cartel ship arrived here from the Chesapeake with Anspach, Hessian, and a few English officers, one hundred and eleven in all. Lord Cornwallis and his suite had arrived three days earlier, also on a cartel ship. He refused a guard and ordnance and has not left his quarters except to go to British headquarters. Another ship, which carried ninety-eight British officers and had left the Chesapeake with the first ships, has not come in yet. The constant stiff northwest wind may possibly, if luck is with them, drive this ship to England.[129] If this happens, it is to be hoped that they have sufficient provisions, for the officers did not take the precaution to carry any more than the ordinary store of foodstuffs for the voyage from the Chesapeake

---

[129] The cartel ship was driven to the Bermudas (see postscript to following letter).

to New York. For this reason Lord Cornwallis will board his ship with a great deal of apprehension, for, should such a large number of officers have the misfortune to perish, it would be an irreparable loss.

It is impossible to describe the misery the German officers endured on their ship. They were packed together with two servants for each officer; besides, some fifty persons had concealed themselves in the hold, thus escaping the inevitable revenge of the rebels. No one can explain why several ships were not insisted on, for General Washington is said to have been extremely obliging.

The paroled officers have been quartered at Oyster Bay and its environs. The two captive Hessian regiments, with whom Major Scheer [130] remained, are in Maryland and are quartered with the inhabitants of Fredericktown and the surrounding country within a range of twenty miles. Preparations have been made to send uniforms and pay money to them and also medical supplies for the sick, who were none too well taken care of, as commonly happens when invalids have their wounds dressed and are lifted and carried by strangers who have been enemies and have no compassion. Comfort and gentleness can then play no part, though one hears complaints and rash accusations which are not always justified.

General St. Clair has taken almost two thousand men to South Carolina to reinforce General Greene, who, the latter part of September after the last action,[131] again appeared in the High Hills of Santee, coming from the region above Ninety-Six. A strong detachment from the Charleston garrison under Colonels Fanning and McNeil [132] has advanced as far as Hillsboro, seized Governor Burke [133] of North Carolina, killed Colonel Lutterell,[134] two subalterns, and fifteen men, and took thirteen officers and

[130] See 1782, note 4.

[131] Eutaw Springs, September 8.

[132] Colonels David Fanning and Hector McNeil, both of the North Carolina Loyalists.

[133] Governor Thomas Burke was taken prisoner September 12 (Almon's *Remembrancer*, XIII, 315; *Pennsylvania Packet*, Oct. 4, 1781).

[134] It seems that this must be Lieutenant Colonel John Luttrell (9th North Carolina Regiment), who, however, according to Heitman had retired in 1778.

sixty-two men prisoners, among them the three North Carolina Colonels Drayton, Tuarlton, and Reid,[135] who are guilty of many excesses. Colonel McNeil was killed in this little action, and therefore Colonel Fanning immediately withdrew. However, at Linley's Mills he encountered Brigadier Butler, who was posted there with six hundred men, and was therefore compelled to force a passage, which cost him forty men. The rebel losses were much higher, not to mention the sixty men who were taken prisoners.

On the 20th of September Colonel Fanning arrived at Raft's Swamp without having been further molested. At Wilmington, on the Cape Fear River, he had Major Craig's detachment join him and then set out for Charleston, where he arrived safely with his prisoners. General Leslie has reached that city and is having it fortified still more.

The Spanish do not seem to be eager to besiege Pensacola or take St. Augustine. Their ships and troops did not leave Havana the entire summer.

The New Jersey brigades and the Pennsylvanians in this section appeared again at Morristown at the beginning of the present month. General Washington has been visiting his Virginia estates, where his stepson [136] recently died. Comte de Rochambeau remained behind at Yorktown with five thousand French. His winter quarters extend through Williamsburg as far as Fredericksburg and sideways as far as Hampton. The water side of Yorktown has already been fortified by the French, and preparations have been made to throw up entrenchments on the land side, so that these auxiliaries will be less handicapped in acquiring tobacco, indigo, and rice at first hand and transporting them to France. The mask of unselfishness has already fallen. Of all the European goods that come to Philadelphia, none will be sold until all the French goods have been taken—orders issued by the French ambassador on the 9th of November.

[135] Drayton and Tuarlton could not be identified. Reid is probably Colonel James Read of the North Carolina militia, who had been taken prisoner at Charleston, May 12, 1780, and later exchanged. The *Pennsylvania Packet*, Nov. 24, 1781, reporting from Charleston, gives a detailed account of this action. It mentions "Cols. Drayton, Tuarlston, and Reid," as well as Litterel.

[136] John Parke Custis; Baurmeister calls him Washington's son-in-law.

General Clinton has garrisoned in New York eight Hessian regiments and a single British battalion, the 40th. The Hessian troops are the four grenadier battalions, the Landgraf Regiment, Knyphausen's, Bünau's, and the Combined Battalion under the command of Colonel von Cochenhausen.

The Leib Regiment and Prinz Carl's are still stationed between Denys's Ferry and Brooklyn, just as they were disembarked on Long Island from the ships.[137] They are waiting for the barracks to be built, which will be located at McGown's Pass on this island; but they will probably not be finished and ready to be occupied before the end of February next year. Since we experienced the difficulty of getting winter quarters five times, it seems that we should have learned to begin earlier and build more durable quarters and see to it, most of all, that no avoidable delay is permitted. However, everything continues to drag along. It is a situation about which little can be done, but I can vouch that it requires much self-control to look on calmly, and I am not surprised that the common soldier has become very dissatisfied.

The Canadian expedition beyond the lakes has not been very successful. On the 24th of October a rebel corps gathered under Colonel Willett at Fort Hunter, pursued the British along both sides of the Mohawk, and scattered them in the neighborhood of Fort Herkimer. But it finally made a stand at Warren Bush and captured one of Colonel Willett's guns. The rebels continued their pursuit as far as Canada Creek, for they had burned the British boats on Oneida Creek. At least, so we read in Colonel Willett's report to Lord Stirling at Saratoga and dated Fort Rensselaer, November 2nd, which by Congress's order was printed in the newspapers on the 25th of November.[138]

The French fleet, superior to the British in the number of ships, to be sure, but inferior in every other respect, especially in sailors, left the Chesapeake in great haste at the beginning of November and sailed to Martinique. While stationed in the Chesa-

---

[137] I.e., from the fruitless expedition to Chesapeake Bay.

[138] The report printed in the *New-York Gazette*, Dec. 3, 1781, differs in many details from the report given here.

peake, where he seemed to be apprehensive, Comte de Grasse collected many thousands of strong fascines.

The British fleet lay at anchor here more than ten days. Admiral Graves, however, left earlier on the *Sandwich* for his station at Jamaica in the West Indies, and Admiral Hood then followed him to the same destination. The latter has gained the general esteem of the entire fleet. Admiral Digby remained here in the city with his Highness Prince William Henry. His Highness remains in his quarters, except that he goes riding at times; he does not entertain publicly. Such is our present situation. It is to be hoped that it will improve in the spring; otherwise, we may as well make ready to sail.

With the greatest esteem I have the honor to commend myself to your Excellency and remain with the most profound respect, so long as I live [*etc.*]

P.S. General Arnold finds it advisable to leave us and is taking his family to England. The frigates are bringing in many prizes. In this the British excell at present and gain a great deal in spite of our late heavy losses.

: 68 :

NEW YORK
DECEMBER 25, 1781

On the 8th of this month I had the honor to send your Excellency a letter by the British Captain Willington of the 57th Regiment, who went on board ship that day with Lord Cornwallis, as did also Colonel Köhler, other Hessian officers, and some invalids. However, the fleet destined for Europe could not leave Sandy Hook until the 15th, partly because of contrary winds, but chiefly because of accumulated business in English headquarters, where everything had gotten into disorder.

Hessian recruits, large and small accouterments, and field requisites, also British convalescents and munitions and entrenching tools are being sent to the regiments stationed in Charleston. The transports will be escorted by the warship *Europe* and two frigates. After getting some distance out to sea, the *Europe* will sail for England with dispatches and, incidentally, with our letters.

This humble letter continues my narration of American events. Before I begin, I have the honor to acknowledge the receipt of your Excellency's kind and gracious letter of the 12th of September this year, which came into my hands on the 9th of this month, the October packet from London having arrived very late the day before.

Reports from Charleston dispatched by General Leslie on the 6th of this month contain the following news: Colonel Cruger and 350 men are posted at the Stono; Colonel Stewart is in command of six battalions of British and provincials posted in the lines thrown up across the narrowest part of the Neck between the Ashley and Cooper rivers and provided with three redoubts. General Greene is stationed on the Pedee, where he is raising additional troops and waiting, moreover, for a corps which General St. Clair is bringing. Charleston is so well fortified that they need not worry about an attack from the land side.

The Spaniards in Havana are again preparing for an expedition and, no doubt, will attempt to lay siege to St. Augustine, in which case Colonel Clarke,[139] the present commandant, would get all the reinforcements possible. The garrison of Charleston has a strength of over five thousand men, who are at present in excellent health. Under the famous Major Moncrief of the Engineers, the garrison, it is supposed, will make a spirited defense in case of an attack. While the British Artillery is well organized and disciplined, there is no one who can compare with this engineer in experience, and no one who can succeed him in case he perishes in the danger to which he so frequently and courageously exposes himself.[140]

In the meantime, the army has been extremely quiet here. The Leib Regiment and Prinz Carl's are still on Long Island and are quartered in the barns between Denys's and Brooklyn, where they have made themselves as comfortable as possible, for the building of the barracks at McGown's Pass, on this island, where they are eventually to be quartered, is progressing very slowly because of the cold weather. The inhabitants of this city are filled with great anxiety and are impatiently waiting to learn the news that is expected from London, for their fate depends on getting considerable reinforcements and a superior fleet, without which this island and the city cannot withstand a serious attack.

It has repeatedly been discussed whether or not a citadel should be erected on Brooklyn Heights on Long Island to cover the Sound and the shore of the East River from the island toward

139 See 1781, note 67.
140 Cf. Uhlendorf, *Siege of Charleston, passim.*

the city. However, not a single spade has been dug into the ground; nor have the munitions been renewed, although they have become wet and useless in the works on this island and in the magazines. On Powles Hook casemates are being built, which, late as it may be, will serve us well in any event.

General Washington is making a sojourn in Philadelphia, where the highest personages of the military and the civil establishments of the North American provinces are celebrating—beside themselves with joy. The French gentlemen mingle with these proud Americans with great airs and are demanding gratitude and esteem in too positive a manner. All the tobacco trade of Virginia is now in their hands, the storehouses being along the shore of the Chesapeake. French wares are sold first; the wares of other countries are sold in the Philadelphia market squares only at very high prices; the English wares are the last to be sold.

The Jersey brigade is in cantonments at Morristown in Jersey, and the New York brigade is quartered near Pompton on the highway from Morristown to West Point. The greater part of the French Legion has returned to Connecticut. Lord Cornwallis's hospital has been moved from Yorktown to Fredericksburg,[141] for the French are establishing a depot for all their necessities as well as their own wares at Yorktown. There many merchants of this helpful nation will live. This profitable and domestic settlement cannot help but incite distrust, and the Americans are well aware of the seriousness of the situation they have brought upon themselves.

The Philadelphians are hoping that what the New Englanders are demanding of Congress will come to pass, namely, a truce and settlement with Great Britain before they have to submit to a new ruler.

The departure of the next ordinary packet has been announced for the 6th of next month, January, when I shall send the continuation of my journal. I hope that I shall then be able

---

[141] On October 27, 1781, Washington instructed Timothy Pickering to move the hospital to Fredericksburg, and on November 5 he instructed Thomas Durie to superintend the removal of prisoners from Yorktown to Fredericksburg (Fitzpatrick's *Calendar*, III, 1980, 1990).

to confirm a report that came in from Jersey on the 21st of this month, according to which General Greene, intending to surprise the post on the Stono, was attacked and suffered a total defeat. It sounds good, and we all hope that it is true.[142] After such tidings the British enjoy their breakfast immensely and at present spend the time up to their meal of roast beef on skates. General Clinton has the honor of teaching this art to his Highness Prince William Henry.

With the deepest respect I have the honor to remain

Your Excellency's

Most obedient and devoted servant

Baurmeister

New York
December 25, 1781

P.S. We have not yet received the necessary passports for sending pay money to the prisoners in Philadelphia, nor has a cartel ship been ordered to the Chesapeake to take uniforms and pay to Cornwallis's prisoners.

The ship with the British officers who had been paroled to New York was driven by the storm to the Bermudas and was in hourly danger of being wrecked and lost, so all on board considered themselves lucky in finally reaching Charleston, whence they have been brought here.

[142] It was not true.

1782

: 69 :

Right Honorable Lord,
Gracious High and Mighty Lieutenant General:

Although several letters were dispatched on an armed ship which set sail for Europe on the 25th of January, I did not send the continuation of my journal with it, for I had not collected enough valuable material concerning recent happenings to make my account interesting. Now that another armed ship is to depart for England, I have the special honor humbly to communicate to your Excellency the following news. It will be safely conveyed as far as London by Major Montgomery, who served with the 37th Regiment and was so fortunate as to sell his commission for £4,200 sterling.

On the 12th of this month a sloop of war came to anchor in this harbor. It had made the voyage from Plymouth in seven weeks and carried no letters whatever except some ministerial dispatches for General Clinton. Nine days before this sloop came in, Congress in Philadelphia knew of its arrival and had a summary knowledge of the dispatches it carried. The members of

Congress were amazed that Great Britain was by no means dispirited, but was preparing anew to resist every enemy with all her strength.

From the orders issued by General Clinton on receipt of the London dispatches we can surmise only that for the time being we shall remain on the defensive, and, until we receive reinforcements, await all main attacks behind fortifications. To this end, the troops on Long Island have been instructed to make fascines and send them, five thousand or ten thousand at a time, from Brooklyn along the shore of the East River to Yellow Hook and the Narrows. In this city ground is being broken for new magazines, and at McGown's Pass, on this island, places have been staked out to build the same kind of works between the East and North rivers as have already been erected at Kings Bridge, so that in case a superior force should make an extended defense impossible, we can hold out within our narrow confines.

The accounts from Charleston, Savannah, St. Augustine, and Halifax report no changes. The troops in those places are healthy and well provisioned, and the magazines are full. Our own stores are the largest, especially those of fresh Pennsylvania flour, for between the 9th of December last year and the 21st of this month the British frigates took fifty-two prizes, whose cargoes consisted mostly of flour and tobacco. The captured ships were brought to New York and to Charleston and the Bermudas.

The Philadelphians are seriously making it their business to carry on the flour trade with Havana. Their profit is thereby more than doubled, which shows, incidentally, in what straits the Spanish in Havana are. Only with difficulty can the French agents collect enough flour to maintain the stores at Martinique and other West Indies possessions. They pay their own price, and so far, the Americans have not been pleased to agree to it.

More than forty ships loaded with flour are waiting in the Delaware to go to sea with the last ice floes. Every ship is armed. But since the *Lion* man-of-war and eight frigates and other armed vessels are carefully cruising between the Chesapeake and the mouth of the Delaware, many a contest is likely to ensue. The French are keeping their tobacco ships in the Chesapeake anchored as close to Yorktown as possible. The *Diligente,* forty-four guns, one of the five frigates protecting the Chesapeake, has foundered at Cape Henry with a loss of all but twenty-eight men.

The French troops in Virginia are quiet. They have sent their cavalry, which they have not only increased but also supplied with horses, to South Carolina to serve under General Greene, who has been declared a French major general and at present is posted with two thousand men thirty-six English miles from Charleston. The North and South Carolina militia in his army exist only in name; only a few can be brought together there from the provinces. In the district thirty miles around Camden everything has become desolate and deserted. This has already caused suffering among the rebels and will cause more in the future.

General Greene intends to embarrass the Savannah garrison in the same manner and is having all the inhabitants driven from the upper part of Georgia, beginning at Augusta, leaving nothing but empty houses. His orders are being carried out in the most cruel manner, and many inhabitants lose their lives. The remainder of the 7th Regiment, 182 men, have been sent to Savannah as a reinforcement. The entire garrison is encamped within the works, except for two outer posts stationed at a distance of fifteen and seventeen English miles from the city, namely at Abercorn and Ogeechee.[1] The condition of von Knoblauch's Regiment is now better than it was ever before in this area. Major von Ende immediately started out for there from Charleston with this regiment's share of the recruits. On the 19th of last month Colonel von Benning landed at Charleston after a passage of four weeks. Stormy weather drove one of the ships onto the sandbanks near Cape Hatteras, but the ship suffered no damage.

The troops here appeared in excellent condition at the semi-annual muster, which has just been completed. The Hessian regiments won the approbation of Muster Commissary Porter. Von Bünau's Regiment distinguished itself especially, since the men are young and are equal in height to those of any other regiment.

This regiment is now under orders to relieve the Hanau Free Corps, which is quartered in the huts below Fort Knyphausen and

---

[1] Stevens, *History of Georgia,* locates the first outpost at Ebenezer.

has lost more than one third of its men through illness. One hundred and eighty-three men were absent from the muster, and on the 15th of this month another sixty-three men were reported missing, among them eleven sharpshooters who had deserted. Lieutenant Colonel Janecke, the commander of this corps of volunteers, requested his Excellency General von Knyphausen to send Dr. Michaelis to investigate the cause of all this illness. He found that it was due to the filth in which the men lived, and his only prescription was a plea for cleanliness.

Nothing further is known of the strength of the rebels in Jersey; they are few in number, and only for large sums of hard money can recruits be enlisted from among those who are obliged to serve under the unconsecrated colors. The New Englanders give the most difficulty. They opposed Congress very decisively when under General Washington's name they received orders to furnish more than their share for the impending campaign.

Despite the mandate issued at the insistence of the French ambassador forbidding the sale of English goods in any American province, goods valued at £20,000 sterling have been brought into the Philadelphia harbor from several free ports, and trade with Boston is carried on publicly and without interruption. Taxes are raised only with great difficulty, and the French are giving their sums for nothing.

The news from the West Indies is not at all unfavorable. The French have some twenty sail cruising before St. Kitts and have also disembarked some troops; but their undertaking has been thwarted by Admiral Hood. However, we lack more detailed reports and also confirmation of the rumor that a reinforcement of twelve English warships has arrived in the West Indies. We shall soon know the facts.

Ever since the beginning of this year we have had extremely cold weather.

With the deepest respect I have the honor ever to be [etc.]

: 70 :

I shall humbly dispatch this journal, the continuation of my account of the 26th of February, to your Excellency by the ordinary packet, which is to depart soon.

On the 5th of this month the January packet from London brought European letters dated from September to the end of the year. This belated but nevertheless welcome news from the Old World, which we still consider the best, created a general satisfaction, which could have been diminished only by our not being able to honor any longer in true soldierly spirit his Excellency, the greatly beloved General von Knyphausen. He will probably sail any day, for a flotilla of transports has already been collected, among them the twenty-four-gun ship *Aurora*, on which his Excellency and Captain von Dorrenberg [2] are to embark.

Immediately upon the receipt of the London dispatches, General Clinton held several conferences with the generals of the

[2] His name is variously spelled. It is most likely Ludwig Otto Carl von Dörnberg of the Prinz Carl Regiment, who, however, in 1779 was only a second lieutenant. He is the only officer with even a similar name in the entire Hesse-Cassel military establishment. According to Eelking-Rosengarten he was an aide-de-camp to Knyphausen in 1781 and 1782.

army. It was decided to throw up the first line on this island only one mile in front of the city and in such a way that it will enclose Bunker Hill fort and connect with all the old redoubts. A thousand men of the garrison and five hundred inhabitants of the city have been working day after day on this line. Nothing has been undertaken yet at McGown's Pass or on Long Island. The relief of the Hanau Free Corps has been postponed. Four English regiments are under orders to march, and the necessary transports are waiting to take them to strengthen any post in case of attack.

General Rochambeau has detached six hundred infantry and the Legion, now completely mounted, to reinforce General Greene before Charleston. On the 19th of February the greater part of the Charleston garrison and the troops occupying the line at the Quarter House [3] advanced, and since then we have anxiously been waiting to hear whether General Greene will remain for an encounter with a corps of considerable strength. His devastations in the upper part of Georgia are cruel. The inhabitants have been reduced to misery.

We received mail from the Chesapeake dated the 9th of this month and with it reports from Major Scheer [4] dated Fredericktown, March 2nd. The French quartered in that region have much sickness, owing to their not being accustomed to the climate of Virginia. They do not dare let a single tobacco ship run out alone. They tried it under a Danish flag, but the British frigates and privateers soon found it out.

I stated in my last journal how many prizes had been taken this year. Since then, up to the 23rd of this month, thirty-five more have been brought in, providing the local magazines with 5,226 barrels of flour, 230 pounds to the barrel. Philadelphia merchants had intended to take it to the Spanish in Havana. Five British frigates stationed at Cape Hatteras took as many more prizes and

[3] The Quarter House was situated five miles from Charleston. Cf. G. W. Greene, *Life of Nathanael Greene*, III, 421; Uhlendorf, *Siege of Charleston*, p. 33. During the siege of 1780 it was used as British headquarters for some time.

[4] Fitzpatrick's *Calendar* lists Friedrich Heinrich Schur, Major, Regiment von Bose, writing from Fredericktown, Maryland, November 19, 1781. Eelking, *Die deutschen Hülfstruppen*, II, 252, has Scherr, but Eelking-Rosengarten says Schur. The *Staats-Calender* gives Friedrich Henrich Scheer, a captain in von Bose's Regiment.

are delivering the flour either to Charleston or Savannah. The Bermudas are filled with prizes. Our capture of so many ships with flour is in every respect a very serious loss to the Americans and their friends. It keeps the Spaniards at Havana completely inactive.

At present the larger articles of clothing are being sent to the Erb Prinz and von Bose's Regiments and also to the Anspach troops. The Regimental Quartermaster Ludwig [5] has been commissioned to do this. Sometime ago the Regimental Quartermaster Schmid of von Knyphausen's Regiment was given about a thousand guineas hard money to pay part of the Hessian prisoners in Philadelphia. Contrary to all laws protecting cartel ships, this was taken from him on the coast of Elizabethtown, together with his own money. The necessary report has been made to General Clinton. Meanwhile, the aforesaid regimental quartermaster has again been provided with money and has set out once more.

General Washington is doing his utmost to bring the Continental brigades up to full strength in order to be able to begin activities by the middle of next month, April. He went to West Point in the month of February to inspect the forts, which are commanded by General Heath. Thence he proceeded to Poughkeepsie to confer with Governor George Clinton of the province of New York.

The well-known Allen, owner of all the estates of Vermont, who has declared himself independent, has united with the other enthusiasts of the northern district extending to the southern border of Canada, where the Mohawk unites with the Hudson River. They have decided that, under certain conditions, they will assist Great Britain with five thousand men as soon as Governor General Haldimand undertakes a march from Quebec to the Hudson River. These activities have caused Congress a great deal of worry, and General Washington fears that he will not be able to carry out the plan agreed upon for the next campaign quite so successfully as he had hoped. He is now back in Jersey.

[5] In the *Carleton Calendar* his name is given as Philip Ludewig and in the *Staats-Calender* as Johann Philipp Ludwig, Regimental Quartermaster of the Erb Prinz Regiment.

However, he has requested Governor Trumbull of Connecticut to be ready with three thousand militia of the twelve-months' class to reinforce the garrison at West Point at a moment's notice. The militia of Albany has set out to attack the Vermonters.

The Refugee corps under Colonel De Lancey will have to leave its quarters at Morrisania, since excursions from the Croton River to Morrisania are more likely to be successful in the spring than in the winter and this corps cannot be reinforced for lack of the necessary troops.

According to a capitulation, consisting of seventeen articles, which came in from Philadelphia, there seems to be no doubt that the Island of St. Kitts fell into the hands of the French on the 12th of February, when Fort Brimstone Hill [6] surrendered, and that the small Islands of Montserrat and Nevis met the same fate. But since we learned through the same channel that Admiral Rodney had arrived and that the British fleet in the West Indies had become superior to the French fleet, Admiral Digby is hoping for favorable reports from these waters.

His Royal Highness Prince William Henry is in excellent health. He leaves his quarters but seldom, receives only a few visitors, and accepts but few invitations. Twice a week Admiral Digby gives a great dinner to which all the officers of the garrison down to the rank of captain are invited in turn, and once a week a concert is given in his quarters, on which occasions Captain von Webern [7] is as well liked as he is indispensable.

Two thirds of the immense quantities of British dry goods and other merchandise brought in here November of last year, which the merchants expected to sell at great profit in Virginia and North Carolina, but which, after the failure in the Chesapeake, were stored in the local magazines, have already been exported in spite of all difficulty. Profitable as this permissible smuggling is, it is assuredly harmful to our operations and even

---

[6] American and English accounts do not refer to any works on Brimstone Hill. Some French engravings, on the other hand, show a "Fortresse de Brimstone Hill" (*Recueil des Estampes représentant les différents événemens* [sic] *de la guerre qui a procuré l'indépendence aux États Unis de l'Amérique*, Paris, 1784).

[7] Henrich Carl von Webern was a captain in the 3rd Battalion of Guards, which, however, did not come to America as a unit (*Staats-Calender*, p. 25).

to our defensive activities. It is impossible for the least thing to remain a secret. The irreconcilable enemy receives information about everything and immediately prepares his countermove, while we learn nothing of their preparations or are informed when it is too late. I have said enough and need not go into the various evil consequences.

If I have correctly interpreted my sister's letter, dated Carlshaven, November last year, my humble request has been fulfilled in that she is graciously permitted to live free of charge in the hospital there. With the warmest feeling of gratitude I recognize in this benevolent deed the same gracious kindness which I, enjoying your Excellency's efficacious protection, shall praise as long as I live. With this unalterable conviction I have the honor to be with the deepest respect [*etc.*]

: 71 :

On the 27th and 28th of last month, April, packets arrived from England with the February and March letters from Europe, and I was honored with your Excellency's gracious letter of the 4th of February of this year.

On the 5th of this month the New British commanding general, Carleton, landed after a short passage of twenty-five days, and now General Clinton is ready to embark on the frigate *Pearl* with his Excellency General von Knyphausen. Brigadier Generals De Lancey and Bruce [8] and some twenty British officers will also avail themselves of this opportunity, for a considerable number of empty transports is returning to Ireland under escort of this frigate and two armed ships. Captain von Dürrenberg and Lieutenant Schmidt of his Highness Prinz Carl's Regiment are also sailing. The former will be able to give your Excellency a detailed account of the straits we are in, which may change for the better or may, on the other hand, become still worse. He will report to your Excellency on the following topics:

[8] Probably Brigadier General James Bruce, who had come to New York on leave from Halifax in April, 1782 (*Carleton Calendar*).

1) The inactivity of the army before and since the capture of Lord Cornwallis's corps.

2) What little attention has been paid to the new and promising ferment among the Vermonters and their neighbors as far as the southern border of Canada in spite of the fact that Congress has been seriously alarmed and General Washington found it necessary to go to Albany and Poughkeepsie several times during February and the first part of March. His army, barely six thousand Continentals, is quietly quartered in Jersey and is satisfied that the militia everywhere is ready to march at a favorable moment or in case of necessity.

3) With what success ships from this harbor have been cruising during the past winter and continue to do so off the Chesapeake, at the mouth of the Delaware, at Cape Hatteras, in the waters of the Bermudas, and from Halifax to Penobscot, from which last the Bostonians suffered a great deal.

4) How greatly the Spaniards in Havana have suffered from our capture of the ships running out of Philadelphia—which robbed the entire Spanish force stationed there of Pennsylvania flour and filled the magazines of our tenable places for eighteen months.

5) Our fortifications at New York and on the neighboring islands and concerning the good condition of the army; that the British fleet in the West Indies is stronger than the French fleet; that, since Jamaica is being threatened, General Clinton has sent General O'Hara to Charleston to sail to that island with the 19th and 30th Regiments to give the enemy greater opposition. These arrangements, however, were contrary to the content of the British dispatches sent from London in March and delivered here the 28th of April which announced the coming of General Carleton and ordered General Clinton, in case he should leave prior to General Carleton's arrival, to turn over the command to Governor General Robertson.

6) The condition of the garrisons at Charleston and Savannah. General Wayne has taken post at Ebenezer; the last two outposts at Abercorn and Ogeechee have been abandoned, and the enemy have sent detachments as far as Savannah. There some-

thing strange occurred after there had been a great deal of desertion, especially in von Knoblauch's Regiment: a detachment of "Creekers," [9] people who live along the little rivers and who, in return for provisions, have taken up arms in behalf of the government, pursued five Hessian deserters, caught them seven miles from the city, and as they would accept no pardon,[10] shot them on the spot. There has been no desertion since then.

7) A New Jersey refugee hanging an American without provocation and General Washington demanding an explanation in haughty and threatening terms. It is a regrettable incident, and I shall take the liberty to report the outcome in due time.

8) General Carleton's short voyage and arrival; his arrangements to introduce economy in the army by bringing with him a commissary general; his liberating two imprisoned American staff officers; his sending a flag of truce to General Washington and Congress; and the conjectures publicly made about an early truce and peace or else the earnest resumption of warfare. I shall not fail to report in detail everything that can be said about this with certainty.

Finally, Captain Durrenberg can tell your Excellency at length and much more vividly than I can in this letter how much the army and the inhabitants lament the departure of his Excellency General von Knyphausen.

A soldier must not be discouraged by any change or adversity or the various hardships incidental to his profession.

But we are all too far from home and our original ranks have thinned so much that it is impossible to be as unconcerned as a soldier should be. I fervently hope that his Excellency General von Lossberg will enjoy good health long enough to be honored with unfaltering obedience to the end of this war—only then shall we be able to bear it all.

Once more I humbly thank your Excellency for having kindly granted my request and permitting my sister to live in the hospital

[9] Creekers, people who live along "little rivers" (=creeks), as Baurmeister says? or Creek Indians? or possibly "Crackers"?

[10] I.e., contingent probably upon their return to the colors.

at Carlshaven until the end of this war. I shall never forget this benefaction, nor any other. With the deepest respect I commend myself to your Excellency's further protection and remain with true reverence as long as I live [*etc.*]

: 72 :

NEW YORK
JUNE 15, 1782

I sent a letter dated the 10th of last month by Captain von Dürrenberg, which no doubt will furnish your Excellency some guidance in questioning the Captain about details of our present situation.

General Carleton's first orders contained the principal point of his instructions, namely that the economy of the entire army is to be in the hands of a commissary general, Brook Watson, whom General Carleton brought with him, and that all the superfluous and ever-idle hands in the office of the commissariat are to be dismissed without the least delay being felt in the various duties.

Accordingly, all the magazines were turned over to Commissary General Watson, and he was given general specifications of all the field requisites. The directors of the various departments were notified that the ships, boats, wagons, and horses which they had acquired at their own expense were to be surrendered to the commissary general, since these necessities were no longer to be rented out and paid for by the King, but were to be acquired by the commissary general and maintained at the King's cost.

Henceforth, the Treasury will no longer furnish the directors of the commissariat with sums of £20,000 and more for the purchase of firewood, coal, and forage, as well as barrack furnishings and bedstraw. The troops will receive these provisions as heretofore, but only on contract. The vouchers and quotations will be examined by a commission and authorized for payment. General Carleton himself is president of this commission, and every British staff officer has a seat and a voice in it.

This institution has become highly necessary and will be very beneficial in the future. Our enemies, who have become too familiar, will suffer from it as much as will all those Hurrah patriots who have been tolerated so generously and who have lived such a carefree and immune life at the expense of the fat English moneybag. This wholesome change seems very strange indeed to all those who have been earnestly warned to be nothing more than real soldiers, not merchants, ever again.

On the 20th of May and the following day General Carleton ordered the following troops on York and Long islands to pass in review before the city: the British Artillery, the 40th and 42nd Regiments, the Leib Regiment, the Landgraf, Prinz Carl's, Donop's, Knyphausen's, and Bünau's Regiments, and the four Hessian grenadier battalions. The general air and propriety of these troops received the sincere approbation of the commanding general. He expressed his pleasure with the strength of each battalion in a compliment paid to Major General von Kospoth, for his Excellency General von Lossberg was prevented from being present by a slight ailment, from which he has since recovered. On the 21st of May he reviewed at Bedford on Long Island, the 17th Regiment of Dragoons, the King's American Dragoons, Arnold's Corps, the remainders of Simcoe's Corps and the Legion, two battalions of British grenadiers, the 38th and 54th Regiments, Colonel Robinson's Royal American Regiment of foot,[11] the 3rd Battalion of De Lancey's, the Hessian and Anspach Jäger Corps (including last year's 170 recruits belonging to the latter), the Anhalt-Zerbst Battalion, and, lastly, the Brunswick and Hesse-Hanau recruit detachments. There, too, General Carleton was

[11] Colonel Beverly Robinson's Regiment of Loyal Americans.

extremely well satisfied with the troops. Since the provincial corps were so weak, however, the commanders were asked to look around diligently for recruits and send in without delay detailed accounts of the recruiting money received, how it was spent, and who received rations. This will cause much explanation. Later exact and detailed specifications were drawn up as to who is entitled to receive rations and who not. In order to prevent dishonesty, the receipts are countersigned in the districts where the troops are stationed.

The commanding general's aides are Major von Wilmowsky [12] of the Prinz Carl Regiment, Captain Conway,[13] and Lieutenant Rotten.[14] His train consists of a coach, three saddle horses, and six servants. Since the quarters in this city will no longer be paid for by the King, General Carleton will leave the large house of his predecessor and move to another. Until fall he will be encamped with the troops on this island. Orders have already been issued, and we are hourly waiting for instructions to pitch tents. He frequently visits the outposts, watch parades, and hospitals.

Twice a week the British headquarters is open for any kind of business, but urgent matters are taken care of without delay. A new spirit pervades the entire command of the army. General Carleton himself has declared that since this war was caused by the boundless disobedience of the North American colonies, it must be waged against the rebels and not against the British Treasury.

The enclosed paper [*missing*] contains the notification advising General Washington of General Carleton's presence and sentiments. The proceedings against the refugee [15] are not over yet; he is being rigorously examined and will, no doubt, be punished. General Washington's threats and impatience have carried him so far as to arrest a captain of the British Guards, named Charles

---

[12] Major Wilhelm von Wilmowsky, Prinz Carl Regiment.

[13] The *Army Lists* have an Hon. George Conway (b. 1763), seventh son of Francis Seymour Conway, 1st marquess of Hertford. In 1782 he is listed as a lieutenant. However, the *British and American Register with an Almanac for 1782*, New York, 1781, p. 71, lists the Hon. Captain Conway as an aide to Clinton.

[14] Lieutenant John Rotten, 47th Regiment of Foot.

[15] See letter dated May 10, 1782 (No. 71) item 7.

Asgill, a prisoner of war at Lancaster, whom he threatens to hang if the refugee is not turned over to him.

So bold have the Americans become since 1776 (when we, unfortunately, introduced indulgence and leniency) that it is to be feared that the unrelenting rebel commander will carry out his cruel intention in order to set the refugees at variance with the British and frighten the loyalists to such an extent that we can no longer recruit among them. The members of Congress are afraid of this barbarian, who has succeeded in having only petty and insignificant men elected to Congress from the several provinces. The president and secretary of Congress owe their offices to his influence and must blindly agree in order to retain their posts. This is the reason why all overtures for peace are in vain, regardless of the fact that trade in Boston and Philadelphia is paralyzed.

Since Admiral Rodney has won a complete victory over the French fleet near Guadeloupe in the West Indies and we have nothing to fear in these quarters during the present year, we would gain a decided advantage for next year if we were strong enough in other respects to occupy Rhode Island again and then cruise off Cape Cod as we now cruise off the Delaware and the Chesapeake. However, since General Rochambeau has left Yorktown with two thousand men and is on his way to the North River, I fear that he will hold his advantage.

Somewhat over a thousand French remained behind on the shores of the Chesapeake to cover their many tobacco ships, which are still at anchor and are protected only by two land batteries and the frigate *Romulus*. The French had intended to set sail in July, when Comte de Grasse was to detach part of his fleet to blockade New York. The fifty-gun ship *Warwick* has been sent to the Chesapeake with five frigates, and since Captain Elphinstone [16] is an enterprising seaman, Admiral Digby has hopes that he will succeed.

On the 28th of May the said ship returned here from a six weeks' cruise with his Royal Highness Prince William Henry and brought in eleven prizes. The Prince has had a serious accident,

[16] The Hon. George Keith Elphinstone, master of the *Warwick*.

dislocating his right arm in a fall. This was not discovered by the ship's surgeon. Here, however, the very painful operation of setting the bones has been successfully accomplished. Admiral Digby's anxiety cannot be described.

On the 22nd of April a Spanish squadron under Don Cagigal [17] left Havana and sailed to the Bahama Islands. As early as the 8th of May it had taken New Providence, which Lieutenant Colonel Maxwell,[18] with a garrison of two hundred and fifty men, could not prevent. He and the garrison are being taken to England as prisoners of war at the expense of the Spanish. But after it became known that the French fleet of Comte de Grasse had been defeated, Don Cagigal was quickly called back. A Spanish account has it that the French lost twelve ships of the line, that the Count himself was taken, and that everything is blamed on Commodore Bougainville and his party.

On the 10th of this month Colonel von Wurmb and his corps marched from Flushing to Huntington to cover the cavalry horses taken to pasture there, while the 1st British Grenadier Battalion went to Flushing to take the place of this corps. The provincials took post at Powles Hook, which the 22nd Regiment had vacated for its new post at Richmond on Staten Island.

The prisoners of Lord Cornwallis's army, especially the British, find opportunities to escape in groups of from ten to thirty men. Of the light infantry alone, forty-two have arrived, twenty-two of whom came at one time in a boat from Egg Harbor to Sandy Hook. General Carleton gave fifty guineas to the leader who made the escape possible and rewarded handsomely all those who did anything to help. This liberality will certainly bear fruit, for there is no nation in the whole world that can compete with the Americans in real insatiable greed for money, and I do not understand why this greed has not been appealed to in a flattering manner long ago.

[17] Juan Manuel Cajigal y Montserrate, according to Spanish encyclopedias. Documents published in Almon's *Remembrancer,* XIV, 148 *et seq.,* are signed Cagigal. Hill, in his *Catalogue of the . . . Papeles procedentes de Cuba,* also spells the name Cagigal.

[18] The articles of capitulation give the following: "John Maxwell Esq., Captain-General, Governor and Commander in Chief of the Bahama Islands, Chancellor, Vice-Admiral and Ordinary of the same, and a Lieutenant-Colonel in his Majesty's army."

Before the end of last month Lieutenant Ungewitter of the Erb Prinz Regiment arrived here on parole from Maryland by way of Lancaster and Reading. He had left the two Hessian regiments at Fredericktown in excellent condition. The Regimental Quartermaster Ludwig had arrived there to deliver uniforms and pay money, but he has not yet returned to New York.

The reports from Charleston and Savannah, which extend to the month of May, mention no changes. General Greene is observing the former from behind Dorchester. He has obtained provisions for his weak corps from the district beyond the Hills of Santee. Even more insignificant is General Wayne's force at Ebenezer, whence he sends strong patrols as far as Savannah.

Nearly thirty transports left this harbor on the 28th of May and sailed to Martha's Vineyard, where, under cover of two frigates, they will take on board four thousand head of cattle and an even greater number of sheep, which have been gathered together on the island from Connecticut and sold to our commissaries through go-betweens.

General Carleton did not have us celebrate Admiral Rodney's victory by a *feu de joie*. This, however, was done on the 4th of this month, the birthday of the King of Great Britain, when the artillery at Fort George fired a salute at twelve o'clock noon, the ships an hour later, and this garrison and all the posts on the neighboring island lit fires at half past seven.

We have just received orders that the troops are to encamp in suitable places tomorrow, the 16th of June, that forty new cartridges per man will be furnished, and that each man is to retain twenty old ones for target practice. Work on the new fortifications on this island and on Long Island was discontinued on the 16th of May, but it will be resumed after the troops are encamped, since another thirty thousand fascines have been made. The regiments, battalions, and the Jäger Corps, continue to be in good health. None of our drill time was interrupted by bad weather.[19]

With the deepest respect I have the honor ever to be [*etc.*]

[19] Baumeister, probably carelessly, wrote "good weather."

: 73 :

On the 15th of June this year I had the honor to send your Excellency by packet my last journal, which extended to that date. Since a frigate is about to sail for London with dispatches from General Carleton, I shall continue my news of the army from my dutiful observation.

On the 16th of June the troops that had spent the winter in quarters and huts made camp on the islands near this city. The Hessian grenadier brigade took a position to cover the British headquarters, two and one-half English miles from the city. Major General von Bischhausen's brigade, consisting of von Knyphausen's Regiment and the remainders of the captured Erb Prinz and von Bose Regiments, is nearest the said headquarters. The Landgraf and von Bünau Regiments under Major General von Hachenberg are encamped on the East River, one and a half miles from the city; the 37th, 40th, and 42nd British Regiments under Brigadier Abercromby have their camp on the bank of the North River, four miles from the city; to the right of the British and extending as far as Jones's house [20] is Major General

20 Nicholas Jones's house "Woodlawn."

von Wurmb's brigade, the Prinz Carl and the Leib Regiments. On North Hill and Laurel Hill, under Major General von Gosen, are von Donop's and Jung von Lossberg's Regiments and the 17th Regiment of Dragoons. The Hesse-Hanau Free Corps left its huts below Fort Knyphausen and moved into the empty barracks at McGown's Pass. This corps has finally recovered from its siege of illness, with a loss of from sixty to seventy men deceased in each company.

Major General Paterson is in command on Long Island. Brigadier Bruce with the 38th, the 54th, and part of the 60th Regiment is encamped near Bedford; Fox's [21] and Brownlow's [22] British Grenadier Battalions have their camp at a place called Ireland's Heights [23] on the Flushing road; the 2nd Anhalt-Zerbst Battalion, the Waldeck Regiment, the last Anspach recruits, and some picked men of the old corps are encamped at Brooklyn under the Hesse-Hanau Colonel Lentz, under whom are also the escaped Brunswick prisoners, the exchanged officers, the Brunswick recruits under Captain von Wolzogen, and the Hesse-Hanau jäger recruits under Lieutenant von Bünau; the 3rd Battalion of De Lancey's, Colonel Robinson's Corps, the remainders of Simcoe's and Tarleton's Corps, and the Pennsylvania and Maryland loyalists are at Denys's under the command of Colonel Ludlow of the provincials. However, on Long Island the troops did not encamp at the given places on the 16th of June, but rather on the 29th of July, after Lieutenant General Campbell and the Pensacola garrison had been exchanged. The said lieutenant general will be commander in chief at Charleston in place of Lieutenant General Leslie. The 22nd and 57th Regiments and Arnold's troop of dragoons are encamped on Staten Island under Brigadier Marsh.[24] From this island a captain and forty men are detached to Sandy Hook as guards, being relieved every four weeks. Brigadier Skinner has the post at Powles Hook with the 1st and 3rd battalions of his provincial regiment.

[21] Henry Edward Fox, Lieutenant Colonel, 2nd Grenadiers.
[22] Charles Brownlow, Lieutenant Colonel, 1st Grenadiers.
[23] Not identified.
[24] The *Carleton Calendar* gives "Brig. Gen. Marsh [supposed James]."

Throughout the summer Colonel von Wurmb with the entire
Jäger Corps, including the Anspach jägers, covered the pastures
at Oyster Bay, Cow Bay, Great Neck, and, of late, at Flushing,
but since the 3rd of this month he has been posted at Denys's,[25]
for a French fleet of thirteen ships of the line, three frigates, and
one sloop of war, all under the Marquis de Vaudreuil,[26] arrived
on the Virginia coast from the West Indies on the 25th of July
and anchored in the Chesapeake, as we learned here on the 1st
of this month. The militia of the city and the Island of New York
have been doing garrison duty since the 17th of June, but the inhabitants are not employed in the work of fortification, this being
done by the army. The citadel on the East River on this island
and the one on Brooklyn Heights on Long Island will be finished
soon, and the old fortifications on the North River have been
repaired.

A sum of £4,000 sterling has been saved each day through
the new economy. The enclosed list [*missing*] will show the reduction in wagons and the number retained, and also the regulations about rations. No one is entitled to provisions who is not
actually in service in the army. Those who have been entitled to
them under the name of refugees receive cash compensation.
Severe punishment will be meted out to anyone who attempts to
make a profit—which was formerly allowed as a fair practice.
Promptly at eleven o'clock the daily orders are dictated at headquarters to the brigade majors and adjutants. At this time, too,
the reports are made and promptly dealt with, so that one seldom
has to wait till the next day.

In this situation everything is quiet on our side, and the
foraging to Westchester County by way of Kings Bridge meets
with no interference. The rebels are also quiet; they are reducing
their train and dismissing militia.

[25] The Von Jungkenn Papers contain the following letters from von Wurmb
dated Long Island, 1782: Jericho, March 17; Flushing, May 7; Camp near Cedar
Swamp, June 11; Denyses, Aug. 5. There is a Cow Neck (now Manhasset); Cow
Bay could not be identified; however, the *Atlantic Neptune*'s chart of Huntington
Bay, Long Island, shows a Cow Harbor on the eastern side of the bay.
[26] Louis Philippe de Rigaud, Marquis de Vaudreuil.

In the early part of May the Connecticut Continental brigade revolted at West Point [27] because of lack of pay and uniforms. It started out for Hartford to lay its claims before the recently assembled council but was stopped. The ringleaders were hanged on the spot, and the rest were satisfied to receive the most needed articles of clothing. The members of the Hartford council, however, are just as displeased this year as is their brigade, for Congress has again increased the taxes. Since the first assessment of 1778, the council has been unable to collect any taxes. One hundred and fifty-eight towns in the eastern part of New England sent no representatives to this year's council sessions. Their example was followed by the western counties of Berkshire, Hampshire, and Worcester even more emphatically.

The French troops who were in Virginia are now on the Susquehanna near Lancaster, no longer under General Rochambeau but under General Vioménil.[28] Where they will go from there is not yet known.

On the 29th of July the British frigate *Santa Margarita* [29] met the French frigate *Amazone* off Cape Henry, and after an engagement lasting an hour and a half, the enemy frigate struck her flag, having lost her captain, three officers, and seventy men killed, and three officers and some seventy men wounded. However, after the *Amazone* had been in British possession for eleven hours, she was recaptured by an eighty-gun ship. Captain Salter of the *Santa Margarita* hardly had time to take his men and the French officer and some sixty Frenchmen from the *Amazone*.[30] He learned from the prisoners that the *Amazone* belongs to the

[27] According to Heath's *Memoirs, sub* May 6, the mutiny did not develop. The plan was for soldiers to walk off at reveille, march to Fishkill, seize cannon, and march on to Hartford to demand "their due" from the council. This plan was divulged by a faithful soldier, whereupon several men were seized and confined "and one suffered."

[28] Charles Joseph Hyacinthe du Houx, Marquis de Vioménil. He was Marechal de Camp.

[29] The *Santa Margarita*, 36 guns, Captain Elliot Salter, had been captured from the Spaniards.

[30] The *Amazone* was a 36-gun ship. Captain Salter's report to Admiral Digby, Aug. 1, 1782, was printed in Almon's *Remembrancer*, XIV, 274. Salter says that he recalled his men from the prize when the French fleet hove in sight. Clowes makes a similar statement.

fleet of the Marquis de Vaudreuil, who was planning to sail to Boston; that, before leaving Cape François, this fleet had escorted fourteen ships of the line to Havana; that in May and June the rest of the French warships had escorted transport fleets to France; that only two ships of the line, two fifty-gun ships, three frigates, and two sloops of war are stationed at Martinique, while only two ships of the line are left at Cape François; and, lastly, that the warship *Le Palmier* has been condemned.[31]

The greater part of Admiral Rodney's fleet is expected in New York. A French sixty-four-gun ship which had been sent from Boston to Martinique with a valuable cargo of masts and ship materials was fortunately captured by the British and sold for the benefit of the fleet at Kingston, Jamaica, for £30,000 sterling, which will amply suffice to refit the entire British fleet.

At Portsmouth, not far from Boston, the Americans have built and launched a seventy-four-gun ship, called the *America*, which is flying the flag of Commodore Chevalier Paul Jones. Frigates and armed ships are under construction in all the shipyards. The port cities of New Haven, New London, Newport, Baltimore, and Boston are displeased with Congress's refusal to exchange the seamen imprisoned here. Admiral Digby's recommendations and Congress's stubborn answers were published in the newspapers. However, the said port cities were so bold as to send some British seamen here under a flag of truce, in exchange for whom the same number were immediately sent to them.

Many prisoners of Lord Cornwallis's corps are escaping and arriving here without mishap. The handsome rewards given those who bring in prisoners are a great enticement and bring excellent results.

In the middle of June the Regimental Quartermaster Ludwig of the Erb Prinz Regiment returned safely from his trip to the imprisoned regiments at Fredericktown in Maryland. He delivered the large and small accouterments as well as the pay money to Major Scheer without any unpleasant interference.

---

[31] Clowes does not know what happened to this ship; he says that she disappears in 1780.

Foreigners, especially those dealing in British goods, are no longer permitted to carry on private trade. The southern provinces have been warned of this very emphatically. On the other hand, there is no trade carried on with the French: no American likes French merchandise. The Frenchman's way of doing things is and will continue to be unpopular with the Americans, who will always be imbued with the British spirit.

The Spaniards' sudden departure from the Bahama coasts after the fall of New Providence gave the privateers an opportunity to capture several Spanish transports and take them to St. Augustine with land troops. In this manner 450 Spaniards were paroled to Havana as prisoners. The garrison at St. Augustine is in excellent condition; the trade of the inhabitants with South Carolina and Georgia and with the southern Indians in that vicinity has grown to considerable proportions during the last six years, and for this reason ten thousand armed men from Florida have offered their services to the governor to aid in the defense of St. Augustine in case of attack.

On the 1st of July the fortified town of Lunenburg, ten miles [32] west of Halifax, was attacked by a hundred rebels. After plundering the houses and burning the blockhouse, they were dissuaded from burning the town by a ransom of £1,000 sterling. The enemy had come from Boston in five privateers and landed unnoticed at Read Head,[33] two miles from Lunenburg. Two hundred men of von Seitz's Regiment arrived from Halifax on three armed ships, but too late to keep the enemy from taking the town.

It is certain that Savannah has been evacuated, but we have no reliable information on how Brigadier Clarke embarked the garrison, or when he arrived at Charleston. General O'Hara did not sail all the way to Jamaica from Charleston with the 19th and 30th Regiments. While still on the high seas he learned of the defeat of the French fleet, and, in accordance with his supplementary instructions, seems to have landed at Antigua. Detailed

[32] Baurmeister means German miles; one German mile equals about four and one-half statute miles. Almon's *Remembrancer*, XIV, 259, giving an account of the following, says "ten leagues from Halifax." (The account appears also in the *Boston Gazette*, July 15, 1782.)

[33] See Memorial from Sufferers at Lunenburg (*Carleton Calendar*, III, 305).

rebel accounts report that the British are now in possession of Puerto Rico. But since, unfortunately, there never has been any regular communication with the West Indies, the accounts from those quarters are not always well founded.

The General Assembly of Georgia, which is zealous in its support of Congress, adjourned at Augusta on the 2nd of May. The governor of the province was authorized to give General Wayne a gratuity of 4,000 guineas to buy an estate in Georgia, wherever it pleased him. Last spring the generals of the South Carolina militia of both sides agreed not to wage war between the 15th of April and the 15th of June in the arable district, sixty English miles in diameter, between the Savannah and the Santee rivers, so that the crops could be harvested without interference. Solemnly as this truce [34] was agreed to on the Saltketscher,[35] the rebels broke it as early as the 25th of May by making an attack from this outpost, called Four Holes, [36] on our post on the Edisto.

The Indian incursions across the Pennsylvania frontier are murderous and devastating, and Colonel Crawford, who set out with five thousand men, was repeatedly beaten in June near Fort Sandusky on Lake Erie, only a few of his men escaping the Indians to recross the Ohio.[37] The Americans living in the farthest part of Pennsylvania committed great cruelties against the Moravians some time ago, and the Indians, who live among these Moravians on friendly terms, have been on the warpath against the Pennsylvanians since then and have carried their vengeance very far.

On the 18th of July the Cork provision fleet of twenty-eight sail came to anchor here under escort of the frigates *Vestal* and *Jason.* Our store of provisions has never been so plentiful as it

---

[34] No such truce is mentioned anywhere in the literature, nor in the Wayne-Leslie letters (William L. Clements Library). Leslie proposed a general truce in the spring of 1782, but it was rejected by Greene and the legislatures of the southern states.

[35] Not definitely identified. A Saltketcher Bridge is mentioned in William Johnson's *Life and Correspondence of Nathanael Greene,* Charleston, 1822, and the *Carleton Calendar* has Saltketchers.

[36] Four Holes could not be identified.

[37] Colonel William Crawford, of Virginia, was burned at the stake June 11, 1782 (Heitmann).

now is. For some time our cruising frigates and privateers have been very successful in bringing in prizes. But the French warship *Eveillé* with the frigate *Cybèle* have cleared the Chesapeake and the Delaware to some extent, and the French transports with tobacco and flour now set sail for France and Martinique under their protection without interference.

All the British prisoners and officers here on parole are being sent to England, as are also the rest of the Guards and Lord Rawdon's Volunteers of Ireland. The field artillery of the army drilled in July. General Carleton was well pleased with the drill of Lieutenant Colonel Eitell [38] and Captain Krug and ordered every British regiment to be provided with two fieldpieces and an artillery detachment such as the Hessians have.

Immediately after the departure of his Excellency General von Knyphausen, Brevet Major Beckwith was asked to serve as adjutant to General Carleton and was consequently released by General von Lossberg.

The regular June packet, which had set sail from Falmouth on the 18th of June, arrived here on the 31st of July. On the 2nd of this month General Carleton and Admiral Digby sent a letter (enclosed herewith) [*missing*] to General Washington, after which proclamation every man was put under arms. We are anxiously waiting for developments; the militia watches have ceased; the 42nd Regiment has moved into the city; and a frigate is waiting for an answer. Whatever I learn will follow at the end of this letter.

On the 24th of July the Regimental Quartermaster Schmidt of Knyphausen's Regiment was sent to Philadelphia with pay money and small accouterments for the prisoners. He found some ninety soldiers in the new jail of that city and immediately supplied them; several had hired their services out. About the 20th of July the Board of War had sent a rebel lieutenant colonel to this prison to tell the prisoners that his Britannic Majesty would no longer take care of the prisoners and would make no reimbursements for provisions, for which reason it had been decided

---

[38] The *Carleton Calendar* records several documents and bills certified by H. H. Eitell. In the *Staats-Calender* he is shown as Hans Henrich Eitel.

to hire them out for three years. For this they were to receive
thirty pounds currency, and then, after swearing never to leave
the North American states, they were to receive complete freedom
and the protection of the law. Sergeant Wolf of the Alt von Lossberg Regiment and Quartermaster Wiegand of Knyphausen's
Regiment [39] replied to this proposal in the name of the faithful
prisoners in a polite yet determined manner. Besides, Sergeant
Wolf sent in a written declaration to the effect that even the worst
miscreant must be provided with bread and fresh water, and that
henceforth, no Hessian prisoner would demand any more than this
sparse diet. Thus the intended sale failed completely; but instead
of twenty men per room, thirty men were packed together, which
makes the condition of these people even worse. Eight hundred
and eighty-two English prisoners in Philadelphia endured their
misery within even narrower confines.

The aforesaid regimental quartermaster returned from Philadelphia with these reports on the 8th of this month by way of
Dobbs Ferry on the North River, where he found about two
battalions of rebels. When he left Philadelphia on the 5th of this
month, reports had come in from Baltimore, dated the 3rd, according to which the French corps had moved from the Susquehanna
to Baltimore and was again under orders to march. Reports from
Jersey cause General Carleton to fear that Powles Hook is not
sufficiently garrisoned. Colonel Lentz and his brigade therefore
moved into this post yesterday from Brooklyn, while the two
British grenadier battalions were ordered to go into the camp at
Brooklyn.

Brigadier General Clarke and the Savannah garrison arrived
today in the East River on twenty-one transports. He had lain at
anchor before Charleston for two days and there received his
orders to land his munitions and a part of the provincials in the
said city and then proceed to New York. St. Augustine likewise
was greatly reinforced without interference before Savannah was
evacuated. Von Knoblauch's Regiment is short one captain, two

---

[39] Apparently a mistake (see above). A Carl Wiegand was quartermaster of
the Waldeck Regiment according to Eelking-Rosengarten (p. 348), who has Earl
Wiegand (a typographical error).

subalterns, and some hundred and seventy noncommissioned officers and men.

The letters are being called for since the frigate is to fall down to Sandy Hook before night, whence she is to sail as soon as General Carleton sends the last letters he is holding back in expectation of an answer from Congress. Brigadier Generals Dalrymple [40] and Gunning will embark on this frigate just before she sails. I hope to be able to obtain further information and send it by this frigate.

With the deepest respect I have the honor ever to be [*etc.*]

[40] William Dalrymple (d. 1807) was at this time Quartermaster General in America. In 1777 he became a colonel in the army, though he was still a lieutenant colonel in his regiment, the 14th Foot. In November, 1782, he was made a major general. The *Army Lists* do not record whether or not he had the rank of a brigadier general in the summer of 1782.

: 74 :

I had the honor to send your Excellency the last portion of my journal on the 10th of last month, August. Congress in Philadelphia has not yet replied. I am therefore unable to append its decision or report what General Carleton and Admiral Digby, pursuant to their instructions, communicated to Congress in regard to their hoped-for independence and the exchange of prisoners. Finally, there appeared a resolution advising General Washington that it was considered unwise to enter into a discussion of any such proposals, that, on the contrary, everyone was warned to remain at his post as watchful and ready as ever before, but that, notwithstanding this, General Washington might appoint commissioners to confer with the British on the exchange of prisoners. As early as the 13th of August an English ship appeared in the Delaware with 260 American prisoners, and five days later, another, and on the 19th three such ships arrived in Boston Bay. I am enclosing a printed copy of the Congressional resolution [missing].

When I finished my last journal, the Savannah garrison had already arrived on twenty transports under convoy of the two frigates *Adamant* and *Assurance,* and the troops had been stationed on Long Island. Later von Knoblauch's Regiment was transferred to the local garrison and mustered. It had 298 men under arms and seemed in good condition in spite of the fact that it suffered greatly from the intense heat of the province of Georgia and consequently lost much of its strength.

General Carleton has ordered this regiment, the remainder of the 7th Regiment, Colonel Robinson's Corps, and the New York Volunteers to do garrison duty in the city. The greater part of the army is encamped on this island in two lines and a reserve. The very unusual drought is drying up all the springs, for which reason the Hessian grenadiers and the brigades of Major Generals von Hachenberg and von Bischhausen have not yet moved to their stations. Von Knoblauch's Regiment is in Major General von Bischhausen's brigade.

On the 13th of August the French squadron under M. de Vaudreuil sailed into Boston Bay. The very high tide misled the pilots. The warship *Magnifique,* seventy-four guns, completely foundered on Lovell Island, and five other ships suffered considerable damage to their keels when the tide went out. Three ships of this squadron immediately sailed to Portsmouth to make repairs. Congress was so polite as to offer M. de la Luzerne [41] its recently built and only seventy-four-gun ship, the *America,* in place of the foundered *Magnifique,* for permanent use in his Most Christian Majesty's service, which offer was accepted.

The news of the arrival of M. de Vaudreuil's [42] fleet in Boston Bay was brought in by the *Chatham* frigate. Admiral Digby ordered the *Carysfort* frigate to be stationed in the Sound and all other frigates to cruise with the *Lion* man-of-war. His Royal Highness Prince William Henry followed on the fifty-gun ship *Warwick* immediately after celebrating his birthday on the 21st of August.

[41] Anne-César, Chevalier de la Luzerne, had succeeded Gérard de Rayneval as French minister to the United States in 1779.

[42] Louis Philippe de Rigaud, Marquis de Vaudreuil, made lieutenant general of the French naval forces, August 14, 1782. He was at this time commander of the French fleet on the New England coast. A younger brother, Louis, was commander of a squadron.

Late on the 10th of August General Carleton had Colonel
Lentz's brigade cross over in boats from Long Island to Powles
Hook, and the following day woodcutters proceeded beyond
Bergen under cover of a strong detachment. Within a short time
we had the necessary firewood for the winter, while the surround-
ing country furnished hay and straw, without any disturbance.
After this the said brigade, except the 2nd Anhalt-Zerbst Bat-
talion, left this post again.

On Long Island the Brunswickers and Hesse-Hanauers prepared for their voyage to Quebec, which they made toward the
end of August. The Waldeck Regiment has been transferred to
Brooklyn. Before the end of last month, namely on the 18th and
25th of August, we received the pleasant news from Halifax that
the transports carrying the recruits of the German auxiliaries,
those with the English recruits, and also some merchantmen had
come to anchor there, and that they were detained by the governor because he did not know whether M. de Vaudreuil was still
in the Chesapeake or not. Pursuant to General Carleton's orders,
these recruits are expected any day.

On the 23rd of August the *Lively* sloop of war came in from
the West Indies with dispatches from Admiral Pigot,[43] announcing that he would soon arrive. Admiral Hood arrived here
on the 3rd of this month on his ship, the *Barfleur,* accompanied by
two other frigates, the *Jupiter* and the *Champion,* and two days
later Admiral Pigot and Commodore Affleck followed with the
entire fleet, consisting of twenty-six ships of the line, one fifty-gun
ship, six frigates, one sloop of war, and two fireships.

Admiral Drake [44] came to anchor at Staten Island with eight
ships of the line, four frigates, and the fireships (which were
joined by five fireships from this harbor), took in fresh water,
and disembarked his sick on Governor's Island. This was also done
by the entire fleet, and the hospitals on this island are now filled
with eighteen hundred seamen.

[43] Admiral Hugh Pigot, who in 1782 became commander in chief in the West
Indies, superseding Admiral Rodney.
[44] Rear Admiral Sir Francis Samuel Drake.

We are expecting at least an expedition to Portsmouth in New Hampshire. M. de Vaudreuil has asked for five thousand Americans to reinforce his land troops in order to be able to occupy Boston harbor. The French who were stationed in Virginia passed through Philadelphia last week and crossed the Delaware at Trenton. Although the number of their sick increased during this extremely hot weather, this corps is continuing its march to Verplanck's Point to join General Washington, who has assembled all the Continentals at Fishkill and is likewise in motion.

We shall soon know whether the preparations on our side will be of a serious nature and whether General Washington will appear before Kings Bridge and even threaten a siege in order to keep our army together, despite the facts that the entire American force does not amount to six thousand Continentals (your Excellency already knows the strength of the French) and that the militia, as we all know very well, is disbanding everywhere and refuses to serve longer. The enemy, it seems, lack the chief necessities, namely, provisions and money. Admiral Pigot will not take up quarters on land, but will remain on the *Formidable*. Admiral Rowley has the command at Jamaica.

A great number of prizes have again been taken and brought in here, among them the French sloop of war *L'Aigle*,[45] which was to carry dispatches from the West Indies to M. de Vaudreuil in the Chesapeake, and also the rebel privateer *General Greene*.[46] The fleet brought in nine prizes, and some twenty were lately taken into St. John, Antigua, by the frigates *Rotterdam* and *Magicienne*.[47] General O'Hara, on arriving at Antigua from Charleston, found orders to send the 19th and 30th Regiments to St. Lucia. Several transports and their provision ship got too far into the southern current and were lucky enough to land their troops, three companies of the 19th and four companies of the 30th Regiment, on St. Croix. The sloop of war *Thorn*, which was

[45] The capture of the sloop *L'Aigle* was reported in the *Pennsylvania Packet*, Aug. 31, 1782.

[46] Captured by Captain Lutwidge of the *Perseverance* (*ibid.*, Sept. 10, 1782).

[47] Captured from the French, September 2, 1781, by Andrew Snape Douglas of the *Chatham* (Clowes).

captured at Boston in the spring, has been retaken near Halifax.[48]

The reports from Charleston extend up to the 15th of August. Two days earlier Major Doyle [49] of the Irish Volunteers and his detachment had returned from the Santee, bringing with them six hundred tierces of rice from a captured magazine. On the 7th of August it was intimated to the inhabitants that the garrison would soon evacuate the city, and the refugees were offered East Florida as a place to live. Most of the inhabitants are already negotiating with General Greene and the governor of South Carolina to be permitted to remain, either for good or for a specified time, on just terms and without being disturbed. An arrogant and uncertain answer has increased the embarrassment of these poor people still more.

Since the arrival of the last English packet, on the 4th of this month, and while Admiral Pigot was here, two ships were separately dispatched to Charleston, and it is reported that the evacuation is not to take place. However, I don't know anything for certain about this. The merchants claim it is true, and they know much, for a British war is inseparable from commerce. In this the British and the Americans were never enemies.

On the 14th of August Major Ross, who commands at Fort Oswego, sent three of his most trusted spies by different routes to the Albany district to obtain information and then proceed to New York, if possible; but they were caught,[50] and nothing certain can be reported of that region. It is reported from Richmond in Virginia that Fort Pitt has been stormed and that preparations have been made to lay siege to it. As soon as the Fishkill region is cleared again, we shall receive more accounts and learn the truth about the reported siege of Fort Pitt.[51]

General Carleton gave orders on the 25th of August that every officer, in accordance with his rank, should arrange his field

[48] Reported in the *Pennsylvania Packet, loc. cit.*

[49] Colonel, later General Sir John Doyle, together with Lord Rawdon, was captured by de Grasse's fleet on his way from Charleston to New York. After being paroled, he sailed for Europe on the French ship carrying the news of Cornwallis's surrender. He was exchanged, and returned to resume activities in South Carolina.

[50] Major John Ross's intercepted instructions were printed in the *Pennsylvania Packet*, Aug. 27, 1782.

[51] Apparently a mere rumor.

equipage in such a manner that it can be transported in an expedition either by sea or by land, since no superfluous horses, carriages, and effects would have room in any movement. Brigadier Abercromby has been appointed Quartermaster General in place of Brigadier Dalrymple.

The present letters and dispatches from the army and the fleet will be carried by the frigate *Southampton*.

The fever has taken hold of the army just as it did in the fall of 1779; not more than two thirds in each regiment are well enough to do service, and the number of sick increases each day. The oldest jäger captain, von Hagen, died suddenly on the 8th of this month. Major von Stamford has had a hard time escaping the extreme danger of a chest illness. Captain von Zengen was also seriously ill. Yesterday rainy weather set in, which promises a change to humid air.

With the deepest respect I have the honor to be [*etc.*]

P.S. Tomorrow, the 13th, Lieutenant General Campbell and the lieutenant governor of this province will go to Tappan, where the commissions for the exchange of prisoners will begin negotiations.

: 75 :

On the 12th of last month I had the honor to conclude another part of my journal and to dispatch it to your Excellency by the frigate *Southampton*. Since another ordinary packet is to sail for England tomorrow, I take this opportunity to send another account of local events.

On the 14th of September Major General von Hachenberg took over the command at Powles Hook. Von Knoblauch's Regiment followed him to the said post, for Brigadier Skinner had taken two of his provincial battalions with him to Long Island, one of which was to occupy Denys's Ferry and the other, Brooklyn again, the Waldeck Regiment having been transferred to New York for garrison duty.

On the 23rd of September his Excellency General von Lossberg left New York with the Hessian grenadier brigade and the brigade now commanded by Major General von Bischhausen and went into camp along the North River between Jones's house and Bloomingdale. Hence, the inhabitants of New York and vicinity were again called upon to do the greater part of the garrison duty in the city, to which they objected because on the 3rd of August

General Carleton had declared and proclaimed the independence of the states, with the results that not only militia service stopped but British jurisdiction as well, although the administration of justice, insofar as it could be carried out under martial law, has never ceased.

Then General Carleton once more demanded that a part of the inhabitants begin to serve again, which they were willing to do on condition that only 180 men be called on for a daily city guard. For this reason Brigadier General Skinner and his two battalions had to return from Long Island to the city and complete the garrison. Because of the drought, the long siege of hot weather, and the consequent drying up of the springs, the troops could not encamp in regular order on this island. The enemy, however, did not compel us to occupy camps in which we would have been uncomfortable for lack of water.

Between the 8th and 12th of September General Washington moved from Fishkill to Verplanck's Point. Two days later General Rochambeau and his suite were received in the rebel camp with great honors. His corps had remained in camp at Chatham five days in order to collect the stragglers, whereupon it marched to Haverstraw and crossed the North River at King's Ferry on the 16th; it made a halt at Peekskill and then joined forces with the rebels at Crown Point or Crompond.[52] On the 25th part of the enemy army crossed the Croton River, whence Sheldon's Dragoons advanced to Dobbs Ferry, while a large train of wagons spread out as far as Sing Sing and foraged in the whole region, whereupon they returned to camp and remained quiet. General Washington has with him all the Continental brigades except the one from Albany.

We learned from two deserters that no militia have been called out, that Washington's army, including the French, is twelve thousand strong, and that the French and half of the Continentals are to march to Canada under Lord Stirling's command as soon as the fleets leave the North American coast. This, however, does not seem plausible. On the contrary, General Carleton expects to learn that General Rochambeau and his corps will hasten to

[52] It was at Crompond.

Boston to embark on the fleet of Admiral Vaudreuil, who has again been compelled to condemn an eighty-gun ship. This admiral sent a flag of truce to New York with 133 sailors to be exchanged. From them we learned of the rumor that M. Vaudreuil will make an attempt on the post at Penobscot. However, Admiral Digby's frigates at this station are too much on their guard to let such an enterprise succeed.

His Royal Highness Prince William Henry undertook a cruising trip to the coast of Nova Scotia on the fifty-gun ship *Warwick*, commanded by Captain Elphinstone, and thence, the middle of September, to the mouth of the Delaware. There the *Warwick* encountered the French frigate *L'Aigle*, forty-four guns, with thirty 24-pounders mounted on one deck. This frigate was accompanied by the armed vessel *La Gloire*, which escaped with the help of an English pilot who had been captured on the *Racoon* sloop of war and was treacherous enough to show them the passage for 500 louis d'or. The Duc de Lauzun and several officers and passengers escaped to Philadelphia with the greater part of the cash on board the frigate *L'Aigle*. The frigate, however, could neither be navigated nor sunk. Four captured Englishmen stopped up all the holes. Count La Touche [53] surrendered to the frigate *Vestal*, twenty-eight guns. The total cash is said to have amounted to 90,000 louis neufs, of which at least a third was taken, along with an extremely rich booty of silk goods, lace, and galloons, all consigned to the ambassador, M. de la Luzerne.

Count La Touche had come to take over the command of twelve French and American frigates on this coast. He had on board 650 men, 250 of whom were to go aboard the captured British frigate *Guadeloupe*, which his brother was to have commanded. This frigate was repaired in Baltimore last summer.

Two days later the *Sophie*, a ship of twenty-four guns, was captured by the *Lion* man-of-war at the mouth of the Delaware. She also is a rich prize, having a cargo of cloth for uniforms for the Continentals of the provinces of Pennsylvania and Jersey, copper plates for three frigates, a quantity of merchandise con-

[53] Louis René Madelène le Vassor, Comte de la Touche Treville, who commanded the frigate *L'Aigle*.

signed to Philadelphia, and a complete supply of accouterments for the horses of the French Legion under the Duc de Lauzun.

Admiral Drake is still riding at anchor at Staten Island, and 162 transports are ready to sail to Charleston in two divisions. Twenty transports previously went down the Sound as far as Whitestone to procure fresh water for all the transports—so great has been the shortage of water.

The reports from Charleston extend to the 7th of September. According to the August report the three Hessian regiments stationed there had almost six hundred sick, among them twenty-two officers. Ensign Wetzell of Dittfurth's Regiment died. However, the maladies are not of a serious nature. General Leslie has had the lines at the Quarter House razed and all the heavy artillery put on board the ships. Major Doyle of the Irish Volunteers with a detachment from Charleston made several successful sallies, and recent reports from there have it that the said major beat back an attack by a certain Colonel Laurens,[54] who was supported by Colonel Armstrong,[55] and that both the colonels and many others were killed, while Major Doyle is said to have lost only five men.

Six merchantmen from Jamaica in the West Indies arrived in Charleston on the 22nd of August. Two days earlier they had left a British Jamaica fleet of merchantmen consisting of eighty sail fifty leagues from Charleston. The fleet was escorted by seven ships of the line under Admiral Graves. At that time Admiral Graves had already taken possession of three very rich French prizes. The frigate *Amphion* of this station, which was so bold as to cruise to the waters of Havana, took a Spanish ship with a cargo of coined silver and silver bullion consigned to the merchants of Cadiz.

The British and Hessian recruits who arrived at Halifax, as well as the merchandise from London, have not come in yet. Some

[54] Colonel John Laurens, killed in this action, usually referred to as the affair at Combahee Ferry.

[55] Not definitely identified. The accounts of Greene, Gist, and Almon's *Remembrancer* (XV, 29–30) make no mention of an Armstrong. It seems improbable that it could be Major John Armstrong who took part in the actions at Eutaw Springs (McCrady, *History of South Carolina, 1780–1783*, p. 448) and at Camden.

of the last ships from London had sailed to Charleston and, being unable to unload there, came to New York. A great deal of merchandise of the kind they carried has already arrived in New York from Charleston, where it has become very difficult to get underwriters to take further risks.

The negotiations for the exchange of prisoners at Tappan under Lieutenant General Campbell came to an end the very first day. The rebel commissioners demanded that the said general authorize the speedy payment of an immense sum, which they claimed to have spent on the prisoners since the beginning of the war. Upon receipt of this sum of money the exchange was to begin. They showed little appreciation for the recent release of Americans in England, whom they gladly received, but for whom they are unwilling to exchange a single man. General Campbell therefore returned on the 28th of September.

Since then his Excellency General von Lossberg has been soliciting a passport, so that articles of uniform and pay money can again be sent to Major Scheer in Fredericktown. All the Hessians who served under Lord Cornwallis from his departure from Camden until their imprisonment at Yorktown, are now also at Fredericktown. Nothing could be more desirable than that the wretched creatures in the Philadelphia prison be allowed to join this largest group of our prisoners, for they suffer a great deal.

General Carleton's headquarters are on the East River, seven miles from New York. The field service is regulated as follows: Two brigadiers or colonels, accompanied by two staff officers, make daily inspections; the password is given out at headquarters at ten o'clock in the morning, an hour after the guard has mounted.

Good provisions, wood, and bedstraw are furnished in sufficient quantity, and extra attention is given to the care of the many sick. General Carleton intends to have a special hospital built for the sick officers of the army, where they will receive adequate care without charge. British doctors who, contrary to orders, accept remuneration from officers after they have recovered are subject to severe punishment. All the barracks are being repaired, and several new ones are being built near New York.

The requisites and furnishings for them are already in store at the commissary general's.

In the meantime, very rigid economy prevails. Since the 1st of May of this year undreamed-of sums have been saved, from which great profit will be derived in the future.

Day before yesterday, the 4th, the army turned out in excellent order. His Royal Highness Prince William Henry and all the admirals reviewed it and showed great satisfaction. The Hessian regiments are now beginning to drill, too.

With the greatest respect I have the honor ever to be [*etc.*]

: 76 :

Although the packet dispatched last took in all the European mail on the 6th of last month, October, and sailed to Sandy Hook the same day, it did not depart until the 15th, i.e., nine days later, having been held there by Admiral Pigot. Since then, on the 21st and 26th of the same month, two English packets have arrived and delivered letters from London. General Carleton divulges nothing of their content. He has ordered the troops to be ready to move into winter quarters and announced that an exact list of all quarters will be published. The recruits for the army who reached Halifax have not yet come in. The Brunswick recruits, however, have been transported to Penobscot, where Brigadier Campbell [56] has taken over the command. He has 650 men with him, divided between the two recently built forts. Moreover, 460 refugees left New York harbor on the 6th of October to establish themselves and their wives and children between Penobscot and Casco Bay. The government provided these families, 1,128 men, women, and children, with clothes, a year's supply of food, implements, arms, and the necessary ammunition. The incoming refugees are to be provided for in this manner from time to time.

[56] Brigadier General John Campbell.

General Leslie in Charleston has been ordered to send all South and North Carolina refugees to the governor of St. Augustine, who is to furnish them with quarters. We do not know as yet the time for the evacuation of Charleston. Admiral Pigot crossed the bar below Sandy Hook on the 26th of October, and by nine o'clock in the morning his two divisions, consisting of sixteen ships of the line, were already out of sight of the pilot boats. He will have the British regiments and corps from Charleston join him and take them with him to the West Indies. At this time I have no knowledge of the destination of the Hessian regiments under General von Bose. Admiral Hood and Commodore Affleck will remain in New York harbor with the third division of Pigot's fleet. The French fleet at Boston has not yet refitted. *Le Fantasque,* a seventy-four-gun ship, has been condemned and sold.

Between the 21st and 27th of October the rebels and their auxiliaries left their camp at Crompond and Verplanck's Point, the Americans going to Fishkill, and the French marching to Boston in two divisions by way of Hartford and Providence. The French Legion, however, remained encamped at Danbury, and Sheldon's Dragoons are still occupying a post beyond the Croton River. Among the many prizes brought in was a ship with twenty-eight horses which French commissaries had bought in Pennsylvania and which were sold in New York. General Washington will go into winter quarters at Morristown again, and occupy Pompton, but not Orange-town, so that he may have that many more troops to leave at West Point.

The French ambassador in Philadelphia was greatly worried at the beginning of October and told Congress of his fears that it might be negotiating a separate treaty with Great Britain, whereupon the enclosed declaration appeared in print.[57] Notwithstanding, General Rochambeau did not encamp with the rebels, and a noticeable coolness has prevailed between the two nations throughout this campaign.

General Carleton has ordered the parties roaming along the western frontier of Pennsylvania and consisting mostly of Indians

---

[57] Baurmeister neglected to enclose this newspaper clipping (see beginning of next letter). It is not in the Von Jungkenn Papers.

to withdraw. However, in August of this year three hundred Indians found ways and means to creep on as far as the settlement of Lexington in Kentucky County,[58] burning and killing everywhere. Small militia detachments under the famous Colonel Todd pursued the Indians and fell into an ambush, where the Colonel, five officers, and forty-two men were killed.[59] The northern Indians make many raids of this sort and commit many excesses.

Since great severity is being used in all the provinces in the collection of the imposed taxes of eight million dollars (still without results), many a conflict ensues here and there. The obstinate ones are placed under arrest and then liberated by force, which the governors and magistrates make little attempt to prevent. It will, therefore, be a long time before the said sum is collected. At the beginning of September no more than $107,906 had been brought into the federal treasury, and because the collectors are exposed to such danger, no one dares serve in this capacity any longer.

In accordance with General Carleton's orders, everyone in the entire Hessian contingent, including the recruits in Halifax, has been given strong woolen cloth for a pair of long winter trousers, and orders have been given for the soldiers to receive weekly rations of fresh meat. On the other hand, a new reduction in forage will be made when the troops go into winter quarters. The economy under Commissary General Brook Watson is beyond conception. Sickness has completely let up, and the number of those who died is tolerable. This can be ascribed only to the extremely good order and care in the hospitals.

With the deepest respect, I have the honor to hope for your Excellency's continued protection and remain with all reverence [etc.]

P.S. Major Neumann of von Seitz's Regiment has been detached from Halifax to Penobscot with the Zerbst, Anspach, Waldeck,

---

[58] Kentucky County was created by the Virginia assembly on December 31, 1776.
[59] Colonel John Todd was killed at Blue Licks, Kentucky, August 18, 1782.

and Hanau recruits. On the 28th of last month the chief War Commissary Harnier arrived here from Halifax. This letter will be carried by Captain Conway, an aide to General Carleton, who is sailing on the frigate *Carysfort* with express orders. Major von Stamford, God be praised, has completely recovered.

: 77 :

[*NEW YORK*
NOVEMBER 18, 1782]

I had the honor to send your Excellency my last journal, extending to the 1st of this month, on the frigate *Carysfort,* which set sail the same day. Since this frigate shipped too much water, she was detained until the 6th for the necessary repairs at the last place of anchorage, Sandy Hook. Today an ordinary packet will depart for London, and I shall not miss this opportunity to report humbly the course of local events. Being in a great hurry, I neglected to enclose the newspaper clipping referred to in my last journal, for which I ask your forgiveness. I shall therefore send it in this letter, along with a list of winter quarters.[60]

Between the 3rd and the 11th, inclusive, of this month the army broke camp by brigades and immediately marched to the designated places. Colonel von Wurmb's brigade was the last, for a general foraging expedition had been undertaken to Philipse's Manor and was accomplished without interference; therefore our forage magazine has increased considerably. The dry summer and the low prices which Commissary General Watson offered the farmers made it difficult to obtain the scarce fodder. The said

[60] Both enclosures are missing.

536

Hon. Watson is now planning to reduce the train and the number of small craft (convenient vessels on the North and East rivers).

On the 3rd of this month his Royal Highness Prince William Henry and Admiral Hood went on board the *Barfleur* man-of-war to follow Admiral Pigot to the West Indies with the third division. On the 12th of October Admiral Rowley sent a sloop of war from Jamaica to New York, and on the 10th of this month the dispatches were delivered. They reported that the French ships have joined the Spanish fleet at Havana and that a landing is being threatened on Jamaica; that Governor General Campbell,[61] having learned on the 26th of August that the Spaniards were planning an attack on Cape Gracias a Dios [62] and are keeping themselves in readiness, thought it wise to get ahead of them. Consequently, an expedition to attack the Spanish at Black River [63] was immediately entrusted to Colonel Despard. He had with him only eighty American Rangers [64] under Major Odell. Commodore Parry [65] covered the disembarkation with the fifty-gun ship *Preston* and five frigates. Five hundred negroes and six hundred Mosquito Indians immediately put themselves under the command of the British in order to take vengeance on the Spaniards, against whom they had many grievances. However, the Spanish governor did not wait for an attack, but surrendered with the garrison, which consisted of the Guatemala Regiment, 742 in all, who were sent to Omoa [66] as prisoners of war, much to the displeasure of the Indians and negroes. Besides quantities of artillery, small arms, and ammunition, a large sum of money was taken in the blockhouse at Black River.

On the 14th a schooner arrived from St. Lucia and reported that twelve ships of the line had been sighted from the island and

[61] Archibald Campbell, Major General and Governor of Jamaica.

[62] Cape Gracias a Dios, on the northmost tip of Nicaragua.

[63] The town of Black River is situated on the southwestern coast of Jamaica.

[64] The Loyal American Rangers, a corps raised in the West Indies in 1780. The *Carleton Calendar*, III, 267, has Odell's American Rangers.

[65] Probably Francis Parry, later rear admiral. A notice of the expedition sailing from Jamaica appeared in Almon's *Remembrancer*, XV, 31. The report mentions six frigates and their armor. The *Royal Gazette*, Nov. 13, 1782, also has an account of the Black River expedition under the command of Colonel Despard, "Commodore Parry, commanding the King's squadron."

[66] Omoa, Honduras.

that they were taken to be French ships since their course was southeast. The French fleet in Boston Bay still rode at anchor there on the 6th of this month. The warship *Triomphant* cannot refit there for the time being because of lack of the necessary materials. A ship with these necessities was sent from Virginia to Boston, but was captured on the 8th off the Chesapeake by the privateer *Surprise* and brought in here.

General Rochambeau and his infantry have arrived in Boston and are ready to embark. As soon as we have assurance of this, the 38th, 40th, and 57th British Regiments will go on board the transports lying in wait. The French Legion has left Danbury and gone into winter quarters at Wilmington on the Delaware. General Washington remains quiet and is kept busy only by the indignant garrisons at West Point. The men in Fort Defiance, particularly, demanded uniforms and back pay from Brigadier General Howe in a tumultuous manner. Except for two small posts beyond the Croton River Bridge, no rebels are to be found.

The last reports from Charleston were dated October 17th. The 64th Regiment and two provincial corps have embarked with all their belongings and set sail for the West Indies. The remainders of the 23rd, 33rd, and 71st Regiments are expected to go to Halifax, and the Hessian regiments to New York. General von Bose's quarters have already been [67]

[67] MS incomplete.

: 78 :

As a token of my obedience, your Excellency will receive by the present packet the continuation of the journal which I closed and dispatched on the 18th of November.

Captain Asgill of the British Guards arrived here unexpectedly from Jersey on the 19th of November and was able to leave for London with the said packet. Congress was induced by urgent representations to order General Washington not to commit a second crime by executing this innocent officer, but, rather, to set him free.[68] The enclosure [*missing*] discusses this matter in greater detail.

Admiral Lord Hood, with fourteen ships of the line, left this harbor on the 23rd, and the Bar, two days later. Everyone believed that he was already halfway to the West Indies, when it was learned that he had come to anchor in Gardiner's Bay and was cruising as far as Newport. The French squadron in Boston Bay is by no means ready to sail, and General Rochambeau has moved into winter quarters extending from Boston to Providence. There are no enemy garrisons on Rhode Island.

[68] See page 506.

In the bay between Elizabeth Point and Long Neck Point, commonly called Greenwich Inlet, the rebels are keeping three hundred boats ready. We know of no reason for this. It seems improbable that the French troops are planning an excursion to Canada. The New Englanders were notified from Boston to keep their militia in readiness. But the militia does not obey any more; nor does anyone from New England care about Congress's orders.

Several armed ships have arrived in quick succession with dispatches from France to Congress, the contents of which are said to be unpleasant. One such express ship meant to run into Boston Bay on the 28th of November, but, losing her course in a snow storm, foundered on Boon Island.[69] However, her crew and the dispatches were saved.

Admiral Pigot notified us of his safe arrival in the West Indies, and immediately after we had learned this, a ship from St. Lucia arrived here on the 10th of this month after a voyage of twenty-two days. She brought the following news: A warship of forty-four guns was so fortunate as to capture a French ordnance ship at St. Lucia; the Marquis de Bouillé has arrived at Martinique from France with four thousand land troops and as many ships of the line as he had frigates, one half of which he had speedily sail for Santo Domingo with 2,500 troops.

Lord Howe dispatched a sloop of war to Admiral Pigot on the 7th of October informing him that the siege of Gibraltar had been raised a few days before. This was confirmed by a ship from Cadiz, which brought a detailed account of this happy event to Boston on the 26th of November. General Carleton does not permit the publication of extraordinary gazettes; otherwise the loyalists in this section would have celebrated the event.

Unless the *Narcissus*, twenty-four guns, which sailed direct from England to Charleston and arrived on the 21st of November with orders for General Leslie, carried counterorders regarding the evacuation of the city, it took place on the 10th of this month. The last reports from there are of the 18th of last month. One

[69] The *Atlantic Neptune* shows a Boon Island off York Harbor. The *New-York Gazette*, Dec. 18, 1782, reports the stranding of the *Argo*, eighteen guns, coming from Nantz (Nantes) near Old York Harbor because of snow on November 28.

week before, namely, on the 10th, the Royal Rangers [70] and the North and South Carolina corps were transported from Charleston to St. Augustine. Since the garrison of Fort Johnson on James Island consisted only of the remainders of the Guards and the 33rd Regiment, the rebels were so bold as to attack it on the 16th of November, but were beaten back with losses. This induced General Leslie to throw up some new redoubts to ward off the first onrush. Emissaries of the rebels have spread the rumor in Charleston that the garrison is to be taken to the West Indies. This caused much desertion, despite the fact that every precaution was taken.

The Brunswick and Hanau prisoners at Reading have repeatedly been urged either to enter into three years' servitude with farmers, who will pay eighty Spanish dollars per man, or else serve in Washington's army for eight pounds recruiting money and under the conditions that every noncommissioned officer keep his rank, and that at the close of the war everyone be given a hundred acres of land and freedom.

On the 9th and 11th of this month twenty-three Brunswickers and Hanauers arrived here from their imprisonment, assuring us that more will follow. Some discontented prisoners have been induced to go over to the enemy's side by such shallow and unfounded arguments that I shall not take the pains to write them down. But the Americans have a knack of attaining their ends by persuasion as well as by money. General Washington's army would have had all its companies full strength if ten pounds sterling had been offered per man. There were people who repeatedly offered their wholehearted services for this undertaking, but that dreadful brigade of the army made up of commissaries voiced strenuous objections. To be sure the present economy [71] has done away with these robbers, who, however, retain quiet possession of their treasures and bear their mild fate very comfortably.

Within the last few days, Regimental Quartermaster Flachshaar of von Bose's Regiment finally set out for Fredericktown with small accouterments and blankets for Major Scheer. In Lan-

[70] Apparently the 60th (or Royal American) Regiment.
[71] Add: "in the British forces."

caster he is to receive the necessary money to pay off the imprisoned regiments to the end of this year. He has also taken over the provisioning of the other German prisoners in proportion. Captain Armstrong [72] of the English army will take along several thousand blankets to help out all the prisoners, regardless of nationality. The small accouterments have arrived from Halifax, but not the recruits. The invalids of the army will leave for England before this year is out. Captain Krug will take those of the Hessian army to Cassel.

Daily working parties of two hundred men resumed work on the citadel on this island on the East River three weeks ago.

With the deepest respect I have the honor to remain as long as I live

Your Excellency's

Most obedient and devoted servant

C. Baurmeister

New York
December 14, 1782

[72] Captain William Armstrong of the 64th Regiment (*Carleton Calendar*).

1783

: 79 :

Right Honorable Lord,
Gracious High and Mighty Lieutenant General:

I owe your Excellency the continuation of my journal from January 18 [1] to date. Not until the 9th of this month did General Carleton announce in daily orders that a warship is to depart this afternoon for London and will carry ordinary letters to Europe as well as his dispatches. Therefore, I shall not fail to send my humble account of the news I have collected.

The troops on the three islands and in the city have remained quiet and motionless in their quarters. The only changes to be noted are that the entire 17th Regiment of Dragoons has been moved into the city and that the mounted Hessian Jäger Company is now stationed in Jamaica on Long Island.

The instructions for the strictest economy keep the British headquarters and the commissariat constantly at their labors. Most of those who formerly did this work were discharged, and

[1] The journal of January 18 was apparently lost.

only a few of them have been reappointed to assist Commissary General Watson. The refugees will receive pay to the end of this month only, after which they may either return to their old homes or be transported to Nova Scotia.

The provincials have been notified that they must expect some reduction. For this purpose every battalion has been ordered to prepare its rolls in two columns, showing, from the first officer to the last man, whether they want to escape this reduction, or be transported to Nova Scotia without expense to themselves, or, lastly, return to their former homes with three months' pay. The established provincial officers are excluded from this arrangement and will receive half pay.

A considerable number of local families who have good reason to fear vindictive treatment from Congress should we evacuate New York have likewise received free transportation to Nova Scotia and new homes on the Bay of Fundy, at a place called Port Roseway.[2] Although no public orders have been given for the evacuation of New York, the following changes indicate that our time here is very limited: Our stores are diminishing, and, contrary to custom, no preparations are being made to replenish the magazines; a train of thirty-six pieces of field artillery, together with the equipage belonging with it, is ready to be embarked, although the rest of the heavy artillery remains in the fortified places.

All the American prisoners have been dismissed on parole. Some sixty men, well clothed, were taken over to Elizabethtown on the 25th of January. Two weeks earlier a refugee patrol near Kings Bridge had seized a militiaman from Tarrytown who, in 1780, had captured Adjutant General Major André. This man was also set free and was at the head of the said group of prisoners. As soon as General Carleton learned that the British Artillery Major Traille had taken the church bells of Charleston and that several other things had been wrongfully purloined from the homes of that city, he issued strict orders that everything must be returned by an express ship.

2 Now Shelburne, Nova Scotia.

A public general order of the 18th of February (enclosed as No. 1),[3] which promises restitution of property to the escaped inhabitants, causes American staff officers and other officers to come to the city. They make their claims and have their property restored to them. The loyalists are still waiting for a similar proclamation from Congress, and General Washington is as yet undecided whether to follow General Carleton's noble example and dismiss an equal number of prisoners. To what extent the kindness on our side and the insensibility on the other are genuine, or whether they are mere politics at the cost of suffering people, have become real riddles.

Since the 17th of December we have had no direct reports from Great Britain. This has given rise to rumors about a general peace. Consequently, all commerce has stopped, and even commercial credit has been affected. Admiral Digby, however, takes no notice of all this and is not so inactive as we are. His frigates bring in one prize after another, thus causing great suffering among the Americans and also among their allies proportionately.

French transports loaded with Virginia products are vainly riding at anchor along the Chesapeake shore. The frigates *Romulus* and *Guadeloupe* were to serve as an escort to France as early as December of last year; however, they did not dare undertake the trip. The capture of the frigate *Sibylle* and the resulting serious dispute between the French and British captains is reported in the newspaper clipping marked No. 2. The French captain has been released from his arrest, and Captain Russell will give him satisfaction.[4]

Discord prevails at present both in Congress and in Washington's small army. Jealousy among themselves daily increases the distrust of their allies, and so the foundation just laid for the new,

---

[3] None of the enclosures referred to in this letter is in the Von Jungkenn Papers.

[4] The *Sibylle* had suffered damage in a storm during which she jettisoned twelve of her guns. When the British frigate *Hussar*, Captain Thomas M. Russell, hove in sight off the Chesapeake, she hoisted a British flag and allegedly misused distress signals. As soon as the *Hussar*, supposing her disabled, had come within close range, "the *Sibylle* fired a broadside at the British frigate and ran on board her." After the *Sibylle* had been taken, Captain Russell broke the sword of her captain, Kergarion Locmaria, and placed him in close confinement. (Clowes, IV, 93.)

though too vast, state has already been undermined. Nor can anything be done about it, for their finances, the mainspring, remain paralyzed. The resignation of the financier Mr. Morris [5] and the resultant criticism (marked Nos. 3 and 4) will make this clear.

The French ambassador in Philadelphia finally induced Congress to undertake an excursion from Albany to Fort Oswego, for which Colonel Willett and six hundred men were selected. Their provisions followed them on sleighs to the Mohawk at the beginning of this year. A body of Indians formed their vanguard, but during snow storms the guides lost their way, and Colonel Willett got too far to the left, below Lake Ontario. Some twenty men froze to death, and half of the detachment were so crippled by the cold that they remained behind. The rest returned to Albany in sorrowful condition and without having accomplished anything.

The French are accusing the Americans of not having been seriously interested in the expedition. This accusation, together with some bold irregularities—I shall mention only two—increases the hatred in Philadelphia toward the French.

The French frigate *Emeraude* failed in her duty to an American merchant fleet in the West Indies. Instead of protecting the merchantmen and animating them to fight against the British frigate *Jason*, which had hove in sight and was preparing to attack, the *Emeraude* made off, giving as an excuse that the British ship was a three-decker and not a frigate.

Another instance: A negro threw a snowball into a sleigh full of merrymaking Frenchmen, hitting one of them, for which the boy was immediately shot. Five Frenchmen paid with their lives for this, while some thirty still feel more or less the blows of an angry mob that quickly gathered. No one knows where this would have ended had not two French frigates, heavily manned, been ready to fire their cannon in case the revolt did not subside instantly.

[5] Robert Morris resigned from his post as Superintendent of Finance in January, 1783, but was induced to continue in this position until November, 1784, when he retired.

icans, many of them are greatly disturbed again for fear that even there no liberty can be enjoyed by those whom Congress has threatened to persecute to the end of their lives. The lot of these unfortunate families is very sad and uncertain.

General Governor Robertson will take a frigate to London day after tomorrow. Should the adjutant sent to General Washington return with more definite information regarding the speedy departure of the army, I shall seize this opportunity to report it to your Excellency. Since ships can now make the trip to Europe in safety, I suppose that I shall have an opportunity nearly every week to send an account of important developments.

Commissary General Watson will select the best dragoon horses tomorrow to make the train complete, so that, at the time of a general embarkation, we shall have no shortage of horses. No other preparations will be made until General Grey's arrival. General Carleton is having the work on the citadel on the East River on this island continue, and also that on Long Island between Yellow Hook and Brooklyn. The remainder of the dragoon horses, including those of the Hessian Jäger Company, are to be sold.

Regimental Quartermaster Flachshaar sent reports from Lancaster, dated the 27th of February, informing us that, after overcoming a few difficulties, he succeeded in making his deliveries to the imprisoned regiments; but he himself has not returned yet. Collecting the prisoners and preventing desertion in the regiments stationed here will require double care and watchfulness. Immediately after the rumor of an impending peace, some men escaped here and there. They have been captured and severely punished. But since the promises are so alluring, it will be difficult to prevent all desertion.

With the greatest respect I shall always be [etc.]

: 81 :

The last part of my journal was sent to your Excellency on the 13th of this month by an ordinary packet. Since another packet is to sail this month, I shall humbly report the following under today's date:

Five days after Captain Stapleton, General Carleton's adjutant, returned from General Washington's quarters, Colonel Humphreys, adjutant to General Washington, arrived at the British headquarters to confer with our commissioners and make the necessary preparations for an exchange of all the prisoners, after which he returned to Windsor.[12] The British Guards imprisoned in Lancaster, 309 men in all, arrived in Philadelphia as early as the 12th of this month, but why these prisoners, together with those held in that city, have not come in yet I cannot say. Nor do I know whether anything has been done toward releasing the prisoners held in Maryland. Brigadier General Clarke, Lieutenant Colonel du Puy,[13] Captain von Eschwege, and Lieutenant

12 I.e., New Windsor, New Jersey.
13 A Major Johann Christian du Puy is listed in von Bose's Regiment in 1779.

Reinecke [14] are under orders to set out at a moment's notice to meet these prisoners. General Carleton will go up the North River in a boat today to confer with General Washington at Dobbs Ferry.[15]

On the 27th of this month a fleet with nearly ten thousand refugees set sail for Nova Scotia. Colonel Thompson's North American Dragoons [16] left for Halifax at the same time. With them were a detachment of the 82nd Regiment; the escaped Brunswick prisoners under Lieutenant Peters, consisting of the said lieutenant, one auditor, three noncommissioned officers, three surgeons, eight hautboyists, one provost and his assistants, one tent servant, one drummer, one fifer, and forty-nine soldiers; and the escaped Hesse-Hanauers, namely, one surgeon, seven noncommissioned officers, one drummer, and forty soldiers.

On the 24th of this month two men of von Knyphausen's Regiment arrived in the city after buying their freedom at £30 currency per man. The following day thirty men of this regiment sent a petition from Jersey to his Excellency General von Lossberg asking that they be liberated from their servitude. They were bought out of prison by a man in whose iron works they must labor until they have earned the sums paid by him.[17] Other German soldiers have been bought out of prison by charitable women, _haw!_ but they got married and thus completely fulfilled the intentions of the Americans.

General Carleton is not likely to permit a single man to remain behind; but whether Congress or General Washington will be able to put into effect his orders in that respect among the inhabitants remains to be seen. No matter how serious an attempt is made, many will object strenuously because we have taken so many negroes. Moreover, the Americans, unfortunately, made an objectionable difference between those who are still actually imprisoned, those who have escaped from prison and returned to

[14] Later his name is given as Reinking; Fitzpatrick's *Calendar* lists a letter signed Carl Reinking.

[15] He did not go until May 7 (see following letter).

[16] King's American Dragoons, commanded by Colonel Benjamin Thompson, Count Rumford.

[17] See pages 561, 575 and 580.

their provinces, and those who have been prisoners and have voluntarily settled in the country. Nothing can be said about this, however, until the prisoners return.

General Carleton is setting a good example to the Americans. All the negroes except those proved to have been bought and certified are being sent back. Furthermore, no one who has come in since March, 1782, is recognized as a refugee. Those who were embarked between the 16th and 24th of this month have been examined by commissioners representing both sides. Even their debts have been paid. Moreover, the archive registers and other papers appropriated now and then during the war have been returned. On the other hand, the Americans are not at all willing to live up to the articles of peace.

Another six thousand loyalists have assembled and have been promised to be transported to Nova Scotia. The loyalists of the districts of Rhode Island and Providence are fleeing to the southern border of Canada. The negroes who returned to their masters are being treated so cruelly that it is beyond description. Almost five thousand persons have come into this city to take possession again of their former property. We had leased out their houses and kept them in repair. Now the owners are shameless enough to demand back rents, whereas they ought to strive to express their gratitude to General Carleton for having the kindness to let them return and offer them the free possession of their houses. This is being overlooked, but double guards, the patrols meeting between the posts, keep a close watch over this crowd of insolent inhabitants.

The adjutants general, the staff officers of the day, the brigade majors, and the two captains separately detached to the wings of the line make the rounds during the night. Work on the fortifications on this island and on Long Island continues in full swing. No artillery has been moved out of the works yet, nor have the horses of this train been sold. The horses of Thompson's Dragoons and of the Hessian Jäger Company as well as a hundred horses of the 17th Regiment of Dragoons have been sold, since they were unfit for further use.

Admiral Digby does not have a single frigate or warship at sea; nor does he have any ships ready to sail to Europe. On the 14th of this month the frigate *Santa Margarita* cast anchor at Fort George, thirty-two days after leaving Jamaica, where she had left Lord Hood's squadron while the rest of the fleet under Admiral Pigot was cruising near St. Lucia. His Royal Highness Prince William Henry is at Kingston, Jamaica.

On the 20th of this month the French sloop of war *Triomphe* ran into this harbor and surrendered some prisoners. This is the same sloop of war which was dispatched from Cadiz by Admiral d'Estaing under Captain du Quesne's command to proclaim the peace. After a stay of two days, this ship took advantage of the first favorable wind to depart, ostensibly for Brest.

The British merchants who remained in Charleston, of whom there are 119, had received permission to stay only until the last day of March, but, after sending a petition to the governor, they were allowed another twelve months. Sixty-five of these gentlemen have even gone further than that and asked for citizenship, which has been granted. Fifty-eight British merchants have settled in Georgia on the same footing. These merchants have already acquired most of the trade and have put the French merchants completely out of business, which was particularly easy when the French refused credit and their bills were protested. This situation has already arisen in Boston, where they are waiting for British merchandise.

So far no Frenchman has come to New York to start in business. The Duc de Lauzun, Comte Dillon,[18] and Count Nassau [19] are expected to arrive here any day. In the meantime, General Carleton is very reluctant to give army officers permission to go to Philadelphia for fear that they might be insulted. This has already been the lot of some provincial officers.

If we can believe a Maryland newspaper from Baltimore, Captain Kimm of the Erb Prinz Regiment has taken his life in an attack of despondency. We are fortunate in having prevented

---

[18] Théobald, Comte de Dillon, who was second in command in Lauzun's Legion.
[19] Perhaps Charles Henri Nicolas, Duc de Nassau-Siegen.

desertion so far, although the Jägers have had some as well as the Landgraf Regiment, which is stationed in Brooklyn in an open place on an open island where it cannot be sufficiently guarded.

With the deepest respect I have the honor to be as long as I live [*etc.*]

: 82 :

NEW YORK

MAY 24, 1783

Since an ordinary packet is ready to sail, I have the honor to send the continuation of my journal, the last part of which was dispatched on the 29th of last month, April, when Captain von Diemar of the 60th Regiment of North Americans started on a six months' leave, going to London on the privateer *Vigilant*.

On the 4th of this month General Carleton finally went up the North River to Dobbs Ferry on the frigate *Perseverance*. Two adjutants, his secretary, and Lieutenant Governor Elliot constituted his suite, and the sloop of war *Terrier* followed his frigate.[20] On the 5th an adjutant was sent to General Washington, who was at Lawrence's house [21] across from Dobbs Ferry, and the following forenoon General Carleton and his suite crossed to the opposite bank, where General Washington's carriage was waiting to take his guests to his quarters. Four companies of American light infantry were encamped there as a guard. The two generals discussed no particular topic, but carried on a general public conversation. Immediately after the noon meal, the British returned

[20] I. N. Phelps Stokes, *Iconography of Manhattan Island*, vol. 5, *sub* May 6, 1783, quoting William Smith, mentions the yacht *Greyhound*.
[21] Not identified. Hamilton Fish, *George Washington in the Highlands*, mentions the Hesbrook house at Newburgh.

to their frigate, while a salute of thirteen guns was fired in their honor.

General Washington and a small suite visited on board the frigate on the 7th; he remained until after the noon meal and also had the honor of being saluted by thirteen guns at the end of his visit. On that day General Carleton had a severe attack of fever and ague. Consequently, he had to remain in bed, and General Washington was alone with him for several hours. On the 8th General Carleton returned to the city, and for the last few days he has been rid of the fever.

Upon receipt of passes from General Lincoln, Brigadier Clarke, Lieutenant Colonel du Puy, Captain Marquard (this captain took the place of Lieutenant Gironcourt,[22] who was ill), Captain von Eschwege of the Hesse-Hanauers, and Lieutenant Reinking of the Brunswickers set out on a trip to Philadelphia to take charge of the surrendered prisoners. Nevertheless, the first group of Burgoyne's prisoners was not complete; only 1,000 Englishmen, 407 Brunswickers, and 67 Hesse-Hanauers arrived on Staten Island on the 9th and 10th. Besides these, there were 33 noncommissioned officers and men of von Knyphausen's Regiment, some of the Jäger Corps, and some of the Alt von Lossberg Regiment.

Lieutenant Colonel du Puy, who makes every effort to assemble the scattered troops of von Knyphausen's Regiment, has had little success so far. The Brunswickers are claiming 250 more men, and the Hesse-Hanauers are 90 men short. Two Brunswick officers and 110 soldiers are still at Rutland, near Boston. The above-mentioned exchanged prisoners have already embarked and will sail without delay, the British to Halifax and the Germans to Quebec. The rest of the prisoners of Cornwallis's army are expected to arrive on Staten Island any day, for they were to have been in Philadelphia as early as the 22nd of this month. The Erb Prinz and von Bose Regiments will be quartered on Long Island, the former at Bedford and the latter at Hempstead.

[22] Charles Auguste de Gironcourt de Vomecourt was married on August 10, 1783, to Elizabeth Corne, daughter of Captain Corne of New York (*New-York Gazette*, Aug. 18, 1783).

The Regimental Quartermaster Flachshaar has returned. He brought with him Major Scheer's reports of April, according to which he has only a few sick and very few deserters. I wish the last few reports of the Jäger Corps did not indicate so much desertion;[23] in the regiments this does not mean very much.[24] The Prinz Carl Regiment has had several deserters, all of them native Hessians. The opportunity for desertion in this regiment is very favorable, for it is quartered in a brewery before the city and close to the North River, where many fishing boats lie along the shore. In these boats the men easily cross the river with the help of women.

In Jersey these rash people are given no such reception as they imagined. They are compelled to enlist and are being transported to Virginia, whose militia has already advanced to the Great Kanawha River in order to stop the Shawnee Indians at the fords.

These Indians, who are divided into three tribes and live in great numbers along the Wabash, have been on the warpath against the Virginians since 1775. On the 20th of March they crossed the Quasioto Mountains[25] and proceeded to the Clinch River, captured Fort Hamlin, and destroyed all the houses in the district encircled by the Kanawha River. Furthermore, they threatened to kill the people living along the James River and destroy their property, claiming that they are not honest traders and that they have turned their envoys back after maltreating them.

On the 14th of this month we evacuated Fort No. 8, which is situated on the Heights of Morrisania, on the other side of Harlem Creek. At present the so-called Charles Redoubt at Kings Bridge is our most advanced outpost. All the refugees waiting for the second transportation to Nova Scotia, i.e., four thousand persons, have left Morrisania and moved closer to the lines of this island. These loyalists are being fearfully maltreated by the Americans

---

[23] The Jäger Corps were the élite of the Hessians in America.

[24] The regiments had many non-Hessian Germans, most of them probably secured by press gangs.

[25] Quasioto, i.e., Cumberland Mountains.

and cannot hope for peace and protection. More of their property is being confiscated every day.

On the other hand, the levying of taxes causes much disturbance everywhere. At the end of April the Continental troops demanded thirty months' back pay. Consequently, Congress ordered the Board of War to command the governors of the several provinces to raise the money the first part of this month. The New England states have refused to do this but offered to pay off their Continental troops as soon as General Washington discharges them and sends them home. His army, however, is not yet dismembered, and the troops want satisfaction in their present place.

The French Legion under Duc de Lauzun embarked at Wilmington on the 11th of this month and left for France on the 15th, so no French soldiers are left in North America, though the number of French merchants and adventurers still to be encountered is all the greater. They have already spread as far as New York. A certain Chevalier de Chaulme [26] has offered to serve the generals as *maître d'hôtel* or *homme de chambre*, or, if necessary, in an even more menial post.

These people are turned back, as are also the inhabitants who have recently come in and who, after having been away seven years with evil intent, were nevertheless invited to come back to take peaceful possession of their houses and live side by side with the refugees who have been occupying their houses in return for small sums. But as soon as the rebels returned, they told the refugees to clear out and pay back rent besides. General Carleton immediately ordered the refugees to remain in the houses and the trouble-making newcomers to leave the city within one week, which the majority of them are compelled to do. In the meantime, large quantities of food are being brought in by way of the North River, and the enormous food prices have declined considerably.

Admiral Lord Hood's squadron is expected here. Admiral Drake with seven ships of the line has already left the West Indies; but we do not know when Admiral Pigot will follow. All the

[26] Not identified, probably an adventurer.

transports that can be dispensed with in the West Indies are to be used in evacuating St. Augustine.

An expedition under the provincial Major Deveaux from St. Augustine to New Providence had the good fortune to bring about the capitulation of the Spanish garrison of 611 men immediately after its arrival on the 7th of April. Major Deveaux had only 300 men and two cannons. This Bahama island, however, had already been ceded to England, and it is fortunate that nothing further has occurred and that neither side had any loss.

The General Commissariat is again collecting firewood to replenish the magazines; straw is being brought in for bedding, and large quantities of flour have been purchased in Baltimore for Nova Scotia and this city.

The fortifications were completed on the 20th of this month. The Hessian regiments and the grenadier battalions stopped drilling today, and the men have not even been furnished with gun powder.

With the deepest respect I shall always remain [*etc.*]

P.S. On the 9th of this month his Excellency General von Lossberg proclaimed a general pardon, effective until the 1st of August this year. On the 14th the Anspachers followed his example, making their pardon valid up to the same date.

: 83 :

On the 24th of last month I had the honor to write and dispatch to your Excellency another part of my journal, but General Carleton found it necessary to detain the packet. I am unable to tell what his principal reason was. One of the reasons, however, was the difficulty experienced in obtaining a large enough loan from the merchants. Up to the 23rd of May, when the British Treasury offered 5 per cent interest, it procured only small sums; then, after the rate of interest was set at 10 per cent until the end of the month, £200,000 sterling was obtained in two days.

The following are the most noteworthy events that took place between the 24th of May and this morning: The captive troops of Lord Cornwallis's army continued to arrive on Staten Island up till the 27th of May. Major Scheer is greatly worried about having had 240 deserters since his departure from Fredericktown, namely, 136 in the Erb Prinz Regiment and 104 in von Bose's. The Anspachers had 512, and the British, because of their greater number, had even more. These desertions are due only to the scattering of printed invitations and previous persuasion on the part of the inhabitants, who have resorted to every possible inducement.

Of von Knyphausen's Regiment, 140 men have not yet returned. Lieutenant Colonel du Puy arrived from Philadelphia within the last few days. In spite of every effort, he did not succeed in obtaining the release of the men bought out of captivity. Moreover, there is no hope of the escaped prisoners ever returning, unless they come in voluntarily after the proclamation of the general pardon.

Brigadier General Clarke is before Congress demanding that the articles of peace be carried out in every detail in this respect; one-sixth of the prisoners of Burgoyne's army have not come in yet because of such reasons. The state of affairs is serious in every respect, for while the prisoners are being begged for and gathered, the standing army has more desertion than ever before, which the reports show only too clearly.

In spite of the fact that the Americans have permission to conceal the branding marks of rebels, they are incapable of acting like a recognized nation. Although their behavior is not inimical, they are, nevertheless, filled with envy and scorn. These vices explain everything they do. Although their acts will bring them to grief before long, they are by no means frightened by well-meant warnings.

They are driving away thousands of the wealthiest inhabitants from each province by their continued confiscation of large estates. Congress is acquiring houses, other property, and capital. Those who are not royalists suffer almost as much from overtaxation. The oppressed are still waiting for relief; everything is in ferment. Under this burden everyone looks at his neighbor with silent doubt, wondering whether to unite with him in revolt against this tyranny or come to ruin in this sad state of affairs.

General Washington was lately asked by Congress (it never gives orders to him) to reduce the Continental Army to four thousand men and to discharge the rest with three months' pay, to be given them in small installments. But this general and his entire army want to receive all their pay at one time and disband. No one wants to be separated from the rest. This decision, more positive than any Congressional act, not only increases the amount due for pay, but augments even more the worries of this great, though always insignificant, council.

Contrary to Congress's intentions and orders, South Carolina and Virginia have opened their harbors to all British merchantmen. Boston takes British and Irish merchandise in preference to any other, and its harbor is not visited by many foreign flags. Danish ships from St. Croix have twice been turned away at Sandy Hook, and on their way out they were joined by ships from Ostend that intended to cast anchor in this harbor. Everyone is disconcerted because the London packet has not yet arrived.

The extent of commerce with Great Britain along the American coast has not yet been determined, and it would seem that other nations would profit in trade from the nonexistence of such an agreement. That this is not the case is due to the Americans' decided preference for British merchandise. The merchants of other countries, especially those of France, assure everyone in the maritime towns that taste for British wares is a pernicious prejudice, but to no avail. The Americans are not deceived by such make-believe. To be sure, they appreciate the spirit they have acquired from the French and are malicious enough to give crude expression to the cunning they have learned; but these crude people lack the manners to be able to conceal the deep-seated hatred they feel toward the French. Dr. Franklin has warned Congress to guard carefully against any French encroachments. Washington always kept a certain distance from these auxiliaries and whenever General Rochambeau made a proposal, asked time to think it over.

Colonel Armand was promoted to the rank of a brigadier by the Americans and authorized to establish a regiment of one thousand men, all foreigners—in other words, deserters. Subsequently, an act of Congress forbade this corps, or any other regiment, to enlist foreigners at any time.

General Carleton has ordered one pound of powder to be given each man and an equal amount to the field artillery, an indication that drilling will be resumed. So far no orders have been given to make camp, but they are expected. The Hesse-Anspach Jäger Corps and the Hesse-Hanau Free Corps were transferred from Long Island to McGown's Pass on this island on the 29th of May in order to guard against desertion. The provincials who were heretofore stationed in Flushing have been quartered at Huntington, while the 33rd and 38th Regiments have gone to Flushing. The 40th and 57th Regiments have taken quarters in the huts on Laurel Hill.

In the army as well as in Admiral Digby's fleet preparations are being made to celebrate with every show of joy the birthday of His Majesty the King of Great Britain on the 4th of this month. The merchants of this city also will give expression to their joy, since they earn so much money in a few hours with the rate of interest set at 10 per cent.

With the deepest respect I shall always be [etc.]

: 84 :

NEW YORK
JUNE 17, 1783

The ordinary packet had hardly made ready to sail to London on the 1st of this month when a packet arrived from England after a very short passage. By this packet I had the honor to receive your Excellency's highly esteemed letter of the 13th of February this year, which assured me that no part of my journal from the 12th of September to the 18th of November of last year failed to arrive. Now that his Excellency General von Bose is leaving, I shall dispatch the continuation of my journal, the last part of which I had the honor to conclude and send on the 1st of this month.

On the 2nd of this month General Carleton requested the embarkation lists of all auxiliary corps. It is apparent from these that the corps of Hessian troops will require about ninety transports, figuring one and a half tons to the man, if the entire corps is to sail at one time, rather than in two divisions. However, there are no ships available now, for the second group of refugees is being transported to Port Roseway. Only twenty-three transports could be spared from Jamaica in the West Indies. No embarkation of German troops can be expected before the end of next month, and even then ships for only eight thousand men can be brought together.

The released prisoners of Burgoyne's army are still aboard the ships riding at anchor. After these troops have left the harbor, the Brunswickers and Hesse-Hanauers will sail for England, and the British to Quebec. Two Brunswick officers and about a hundred men are still in Rutland near Boston.

Brigadier General Clarke arrived from Philadelphia on the 13th of this month without having accomplished anything. His representations to set free all those who were sold for a three-year period and are working here and there as slaves (for example, the thirty-five men of von Knyphausen's Regiment who are digging in the iron mines at Mount Hope in Jersey) seem to have made no impression whatever.

Although General Carleton, while commander in chief, did his utmost to be obliging toward Congress, the provinces of Virginia, Georgia, and North and South Carolina have bestowed on him the undeserved name of disturber of the peace. They are demanding through their Congressional delegates the immediate surrender of all escaped negroes or else a definite sum of money for each negro not returned.

General Clinton's repeated proclamations while he was the chief in command permitted the negroes to leave their plantations and follow the army. Half of them are no longer alive, and the greater part of the rest have gone on board the ships. The small number still here refuse to be delivered in so unwarrantable a manner. They insist on their rights under the proclamation, and General Carleton protects these slaves, although those who desire to return may do so.

The fact that we took these negroes away is the principal reason that the Americans were struck by the unreasonably revengeful thought of buying our men out of prison, contrary though it is to the law of nations, or else luring them to desertion. These wicked people have lately been extraordinarily successful in their attempts to cause desertion among the German troops, as may be seen from the reports.

At the beginning of this month a Continental battalion occupied the passes in East Chester and Westchester above Kings Bridge, ostensibly to put a stop to the hostile incursions from that region to Morrisania, where some refugees are still living. The real reason, however, is to enable the lieutenant governor of the province of New York to carry out the confiscation of Philipse's Manor [27] without interference. General Carleton took no particular notice of it. All such acts as well as the accounts of the evicted Americans who came in are recorded at headquarters in every detail. These records make up the greater part of the dispatches sent to London each week.

The lately released prisoners of Lord Cornwallis's corps have again been armed and are serving in the quarters. The munitions in the several magazines have been carefully examined, and everything that had gone to ruin was immediately replaced. Moreover, every man received the proper number of cartridges, and the whole army was given powder for small arms and fieldpieces, whereupon drilling was resumed. General Carleton will attend the last day of drill.

Ships of foreign nations still stay away from this harbor. Only two Spanish merchantmen have run in and are attempting to buy from the British agents those of the dispensable ships which Admiral Digby had captured from the French and rebels and have not yet been sold. According to express orders, they are to be sold preferably to Spaniards, and these merchants and the ships' equipage receive all consideration.

St. Augustine has not yet been evacuated, as has been learned from the frigate *Cyclops*, which arrived here on the 15th of this month after a voyage of eighteen days. There is no recent news from the West Indies.

The favorable conditions offered by the government to the refugees and others who are interested in settling in various districts of Nova Scotia have induced many to make the attempt. Some of the officers of the auxiliary corps will undoubtedly remain

---

[27] Manor, or manors? Baurmeister uses the English word, in a corrupted form, with a dative plural ending (following the preposition "von"). Perhaps "estates" would be a better translation.

behind, and the foreigners [28] among these troops are very eager to be mustered out, for on their return they would be without any means of subsistence, especially those who are undersized and old. Those who have learned a trade are receiving very substantial offers. If everyone were given what all kinds of inducements have led him to expect, the number of embarrassed soldiers would be beyond all concept.[29]

Considering all this, the extraordinary amount of desertion is justifiable, if there were room for such excuses. In the meantime, there is no letup in watchfulness, but there are many ways in which the disloyal are tempted to desert.

With deepest respect I remain [etc.]

[28] By "foreigners" Baurmeister means those who are not subjects of the princes under whose colors they fought.

[29] A literal translation; Baurmeister's meaning is not clear.

: 85 :

NEW YORK
JULY 25, 1783

From the 1st of this month until the evening of the 26th I was in the provinces of Jersey and Pennsylvania, whither I had been sent in order to look into the situation of the German soldiers who are employed here and there. For this purpose, I had been furnished with a letter from General Carleton to the American War President, General Lincoln,[30] and also with other instructions.

The mission was undertaken at the request of his Excellency General von Lossberg, who had sent several memoranda to General Carleton to induce him to collect the soldiers bought out of captivity. I am unable to say why General Carleton never answered in writing, but it finally pleased him to have his adjutant, Major von Wilmowsky, tell his Excellency General von Lossberg to order me to proceed to Philadelphia with a letter to General Lincoln.

Although such requests are ordinarily received with eagerness, I knew well enough that my efforts, the expense of the trip, and, above all, the time consumed would be in vain. If anything satisfactory is to be accomplished in this strange situation among

[30] Major General Benjamin Lincoln was Secretary of War, 1781 to 1783.

572

even stranger people, it must be done by the commanding general of the army and no one else. The following report of my partly finished business will prove that I was right.

On the 1st of the month I was unable to proceed further than Elizabethtown, but I arrived in Philadelphia late in the evening of the following day. According to my instructions, I stopped an hour at Princeton, where Congress has been established since the 24th of last month, June. President Boudinot had fled there from Philadelphia with all the members of Congress because they could not fulfill their promise to pay the mutinous Pennsylvania Continental brigade, which was ready to carry out its serious threats against this great American council.

President Boudinot gave me permission to continue my journey through Pennsylvania and directed me to Governor Dickinson in Philadelphia. I learned at the same time that General Lincoln had gone to Richmond in Virginia and was expected back on the 8th of this month. His adjutant, Major Jackson, who is Secretary of the War Council [31] and conducted the General's business during his absence, read General Carleton's letter and immediately ruled as follows: (1) The War Council has no jurisdiction over the Hessian, Brunswick, and Hesse-Hanau soldiers who have been sold out of imprisonment to the inhabitants. (2) Whether the soldiers are released or not depends entirely upon the owners of these men and upon the desires and intentions of the foreign soldiers. (3) No German soldiers may return to the British army unless the owners are reimbursed in cash for their outlay.

The President confirmed these decisions, adding, however, that since the British Generals Howe and Clinton allowed American prisoners to languish in prisons and then authorized provincial officers to recruit among these wretched people as they saw fit, since the several admirals on the New York station have treated many seamen cruelly and impressed them, and since, moreover, no exchange of prisoners could be effected in spite of five meetings with the British commissioners, the War Council had been authorized to treat the British auxiliaries in the same manner.

[31] Major William Jackson, Assistant Secretary of War.

To this he added that if his Excellency General von Lossberg wanted to get possession of these prisoners, the Americans would be so kind as to permit it in return for a cash payment of £30 Pennsylvania currency per man, conditional on an investigation which would have to be made to determine whether these German soldiers really desired to return, for America held open her arms to people of all nations in welcome and protection.

The French ambassador M. de la Luzerne was present during this conversation. He had just arrived in Princeton from his country estate situated on the Schuylkill, three miles from Philadelphia, and conferred in the college building with the President before the assembled Congress without any ceremony whatever. He heard my answer to the President, namely, that whatever the British generals and admirals had done could not possibly serve as an example, for at that time the Americans under arms were looked upon only as disobedient subjects, and the prisoners, in view of this, were treated well enough. This, however, made no impression, nor did it affect the friendly treatment I enjoyed everywhere and have every reason to praise.

Governor Dickinson in Philadelphia had no objections to my riding out to Lancaster and Reading. I therefore went from Philadelphia to Darby, Kennett Square, Downingtown, Pequea, Bethlehem, and Lancaster. In these places and on the farms I found one hundred and sixty-two Brunswickers and thirteen Hasse-Hanauers, most of them married and settled on their own land. Thirty-nine Brunswickers showed a desire to return, but none of the Hesse-Hanauers. I visited these places between the 6th and 8th.

On the 10th I started out from Philadelphia for Reading. The prescribed route was the following: from Philadelphia to Germantown, Swedes Ford, Potts Grove, and Reading. I found eighty-four men, all Brunswickers save eight from Hesse-Hanau. On the way back I rode by way of the Delaware Mills in Bucks County, where I found another twenty-three Brunswickers and also two deserters from the Regiment von Knyphausen. All these men demanded their freedom with the exception of six Hanauers and the two Hessian deserters.

In Philadelphia I discovered fifty-two Hessian deserters, but could do no more than let them read a copy of the general pardon, and even in doing this I had to be very cautious. The greater part of them had been talked into desertion and now wish to be allowed to return. Of the Brunswickers at the Delaware Mills, thirteen men had escaped on the 29th of June, but the provincial Colonel Bird recaptured them between Newark and Elizabethtown.[32]

I next went to Mount Hope in Jersey to see the thirty-five men of von Knyphausen's Regiment who are working in the iron works. I found only twenty-seven men. Some of the missing eight had escaped to New York, but two had worked themselves free and settled in Philadelphia.

I returned to New York with the owner of the iron works on the 16th of this month. His Excellency General von Lossberg sent a letter with my report to General Carleton, in which he asked permission to enter into negotiations with this man, whose name is Faesh,[33] with a view of paying him as much in cash for these twenty-seven men as they still owe in labor until the expiration of their third year, for only in this way can we get possession of these twenty-seven men again. This was done on the 18th of this month, and today, as I conclude this humble letter, he has not yet received a reply, in spite of the fact that I mentioned it to him again on the 22nd.

Meanwhile, in order to lose no time, his Excellency General von Lossberg asked the said Faesh to prepare an itemized statement, showing how much each of the twenty-seven men will have received in cash by the end of this month and how much each has still coming to him, and also how large a sum they still have to work off between the 1st of August and the end of the three-year period.

[32] It seems that these Brunswickers merely attempted to escape and that they were put in the Newark jail.

[33] John Jacob Faesh (or Faesch). In *New Jersey Archives*, 2nd Series, V, 299, there appears an advertisement for iron from Mount Hope Furnace over the name of John Jacob Faesh. See also Stryker, pp. 215–16. Stryker says that Faesh had emigrated from Hesse-Cassel in 1766 and was under contract with Congress to make cannon and shot.

His answer is now expected; it will certainly arrive before the one due from General Carleton. His Excellency General von Lossberg will then buy these men's freedom, for the most part with his own resources, that is, if Mr. Faesh was serious in his offer and the American War Council does not retract its word.

The incidental information which I gathered in Philadelphia and in most of the other places seemed to be pleasing to English headquarters, and I was asked to submit reports on the following topics to General Carleton:

A sergeant major had led the Pennsylvania brigade in Philadelphia in front of the City Hall. In this rebellious mob were six officers in the uniforms of common soldiers. The President was about to escape but was captured and taken with all firmness before the assembled Congress. The officers were later arrested.

In spite of Congress's promise to pay the Pennsylvanians in three installments, nothing has been paid them. To avoid its obligations, Congress established itself in Princeton and asked General Washington for a brigade for protection. The brigade of Massachusetts Bay under Major General Howe and Brigadier Paterson [34] left the army at Newburg and marched, fifteen hundred strong, through Morristown, Princeton, Trenton, Bristol, and Frankford and encamped on the 7th of this month on the Germantown road, three and a half miles from Philadelphia.

Governor Dickinson, in accordance with the decision of the Pennsylvania Council, was to forbid General Howe to enter Pennsylvania and order him to stop at Trenton, but this was left undone. This brigade had six pieces of artillery and every night posted pickets half an hour's march in front in the direction of the city. An indescribable bitterness has since prevailed in Philadelphia and in the province. Congress and its behavior is not spared in public opinion; faith in General Washington has diminished considerably; the party of former Governor Reed is active in all the Pennsylvania counties; and a general revolt is feared. The French embassy and the Bank fear for their safety. In this tumult I left Philadelphia.

[34] Brigadier General John Paterson (breveted Major General Sept. 30, 1783) of the Continental infantry.

There are some forty Dutch merchantmen there, nine ships from Ostend flying the imperial flag, five Spanish ships which, however, had been rented by the Swedes, four Danish ships from St. Croix, three from Hamburg, two from Bremen, one from Emden, and, lastly, eight English and seven Irish ships. These last are permitted to fly their country's flag, while the British flags must be struck at Gloucester Point in the Delaware, because the American flag has been insulted in New York.

All European merchandise finds a ready sale for hard cash, for no domestic products are to be found in Philadelphia with the possible exception of flour and lumber, which, however, only the Spanish and Dutch can accept. When I was in Philadelphia, there were six Portuguese ships at anchor. Two of these departed with cash, using rocks for ballast. They took American seamen to complete their crews. This was also done by the Dutch, who, however, set out for the West Indies with cargoes of flour, which they will trade there for rice, tobacco, and indigo.

The Virginians, always jealous of the Pennsylvanians, are equally void of all honesty in trade and cheat their neighbors almost as much as the Marylanders cheat the Carolinians. They consider the Chesapeake theirs and have complete confidence in the French. On the 29th of May this year the Portuguese agent Francisco [35] received orders to buy up all the iron ships' cannon of four, nine, and eighteen pounds caliber.

Running into the Delaware is made more difficult each year by the chevaux-de-frise,[36] which cannot be raised and now form an island in the middle of the river, opposite Gloucester Point and extending toward the city. Thus the river bed, ordinarily very wide, has been made considerably narrower and shallower.

The wares and merchandise that find a ready sale, particularly with the Pennsylvania farmers, are scythes, sickles, cutting knives, unworked steel, grindstones, linen of all sorts, and salt. The Irish make a great profit selling linen, and the English cannot supply enough cloth.

[35] Not identified.
[36] See illustration on page 161.

When American products ordered for Europe are ready for shipment, the Dutch ships take them at half rates, whereas American ships cannot carry them even at full rates. This is quite a blow. Besides, it costs two-thirds more to produce such merchandise as nails, iron wares, shoes, leather, hats, and silk goods in America than it costs to import them from Europe. No one thinks of building any warships.

The immense sums owed to France cause everyone worry, for there is no money to pay back the borrowed capital. Consequently, Congress gladly condones the confiscation of property in the provinces, hoping to derive some benefit from it. In general, however, this policy is very harmful, since the provinces are thereby depopulated, the people of the northern provinces moving to Nova Scotia and those of the southern provinces migrating to the Ohio. To sum up in a few words, everything has gone to ruin, and experiencing the evil consequences thereof will be the lot of the North American people for a long time.

I saw General Gates in Philadelphia. He had just returned from a trip to the region above Albany, whither he had been sent to exhort the Indians to be peaceful. He found the old Indians obliging, but the young chieftains ready for war and cruel expeditions. His report contains the important statement that these Indians are still given presents and provided with munitions from Canada.

Now that all the small auxiliary corps, except two Anspach regiments, have already departed and these two regiments are ready to embark, some troops will encamp at McGown's Pass on this island next week. Von Knyphausen's and von Bünau's Regiments will then move in front of the city, while the Vacant, the Erb Prinz, Bose's, von Knoblauch's, and von Benning's Regiments will come from Long Island and go into garrison in the city.

On the 21st a frigate arrived from England with special dispatches, and today a frigate will depart for England with an answer. All the warships and frigates in New York harbor are under orders to sail.

With the deepest respect I have the honor ever to be [etc.]

: 86 :

On the 25th of last month I had the honor humbly to send your Excellency the last part of my journal. The changes that have occurred since then will be sent by the *Minerva,* whose master, Captain Hall, has undertaken to post this letter in London.

The orders given some time ago to the troops on York Island to be ready to move into camp were countermanded on the 27th of July. On the other hand, the troops on Long Island were ordered to encamp the 1st to the 3rd, inclusive, of this month between Newtown Creek and Bedford. They had hardly done so, when eight Hessian regiments were ordered to prepare for embarkation to Europe, which is to take place the day after tomorrow, the 12th.

I am enclosing an *ordre de bataille,*[37] showing the encampment of the troops at Bedford. On the 4th of this month they were joined by the 57th Regiment, 492 strong, which had come from Staten Island and took position in the second line. The 54th and 37th Regiments have marched to Kings Bridge, while the 40th Regiment was transferred from there to the garrison of this city.

[37] See end of this letter.

Moreover, the North Carolina and Maryland Loyalists took post on Long Island at Denys's Ferry while the Vacant, the Erb Prinz, and von Bose's Regiments were stationed at the redoubts near Brooklyn.

Also enclosed is an embarkation list [*missing*]. Doctor Lauckhard [38] and the necessary orderlies will sail on the hospital ship to care for the sick. Doctor Nooth, the chief British doctor, has taken great pains to provide every comfort.

On the 8th of this month Lieutenant Unger [39] of von Knyphausen's Regiment returned from Mount Hope in Jersey, whither he had been sent to redeem the twenty-seven Hessians and two Hesse-Hanauers. He brought with him twenty-one Hessians and one Hesse-Hanauer, the other seven having no greater desire than to remain in Jersey.

At present there are no extra ships in the harbor destined to sail to Europe, nor shall we be able to sail to our coast in September. It is very likely, however, that the rest of the Hessian corps will depart this coming October, for on the 8th of this month Captain Andrew Campbell, arrriving from Havana on the *Dragon* after a passage of eighteen days, reported that some twenty transports would come here from the West Indies. Besides, an even greater number of ships is expected from Nova Scotia within the next few days.

Captain Campbell also brought the news reported in the enclosed newspaper clipping,[40] all of which was confirmed this morning by a British merchantman which had left Jamaica in the West Indies only sixteen days ago.

General Washington and General Baron von Steuben left their camp at Newburgh and went to Crown Point with a small suite. The former returned to the army by way of Albany on the 28th of July, and General Steuben proceeded to the new Canadian

[38] A Dr. Lauchard (no first name given) is listed in the *Staats-Calender*, p. 43.

[39] An ensign Ungar (without given names) is listed in von Mirbach's Regiment in 1779 (*Staats-Calender*, p. 34), and Eelking-Rosengarten, p. 313, lists an ensign Ferdinand Ungar in the Knyphausen Regiment.

[40] Clipping from a New York loyalist newspaper, dated Aug. 9 [1783], summarizing news received from Captain Andrew Campbell, of the *Dragon*, relative to a revolt in Panama and the movements of Spanish ships, partly owing to the revolt.

border to find suitable places to establish garrisons, which are to extend from Lake Champlain to the mouth of the Mississippi River. The American Congress is still in Princeton, and General Howe's brigade of New England Continentals remains encamped before Philadelphia, which increases the bitterness in Pennsylvania from day to day.

With the deepest respect I remain as long as I live [etc.]

P.S. The death of Captain Hartterd of the Prinz Carl Regiment is very much regretted. It was a sad accident that caused his death. He was walking with other officers along a street in front of his quarters on the North River when he was run down by a racing horse. He died the following morning at eight o'clock.[41]

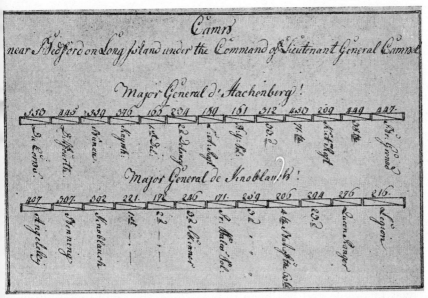

Plan of Encampment near Bedford, Long Island. Enclosed in Baurmeister's Letter of August 16, 1783. This seems to be the official plan sent from British headquarters.

[41] The *New-York Gazette*, Aug. 13, 1783, has a death notice. The captain's name is given as Theodor Hart Harkert. Apparently Theodor Hartm[ann] Hartert (*Staats-Calender*, p. 29).

: 87 :

On the 10th of this month I took advantage of a good opportunity to send to your Excellency, as far as London, the continuation of my journal, based on dutiful observation. Since the frigate *Bellisaria* is to leave the New York harbor tomorrow and sail to Portsmouth, it is my pleasure to acknowledge the receipt of your Excellency's gracious letter of the 15th of May this year.

On the 12th of this month the London packet *Sandwich* delivered its dispatches on the sandbanks below Sandy Hook. This ship had missed its course and was compelled to remain on the banks for two days.

On the 15th the eight Hessian regiments got under sail. Their embarkation took place on the 12th and 13th, and since the wind was favorable and has been so ever since, they will undoubtedly make the passage in a short time. We have been advised from Halifax that on the 5th of this month von Porbeck's Regiment and the recruits left for Europe with the recruit transport.

On the 24th the Leib Regiment left its camp on Long Island and encamped on this island close to the city. On the other hand, the British grenadier battalion, the 23rd Regiment, and a detach-

582

ment of dragoons went to Huntington, for lately so many robbers have been coming across the Sound from Connecticut that these troops were needed at that post. The commander of the grenadiers has been ordered not only to scatter these bands but to have every thief they catch hanged without much ceremony.

Brigadier General Martin, chief of the British field artillery, is very busy removing cannon from the works to the ordnance ships, which he began doing as soon as the reduction of the British troops commenced. I enclose a list [*missing*] showing the plan according to which the regiments destined to go to Nova Scotia are to embark in the near future.

The following field regiments are to be reduced to four hundred men before they are transported to England: the 17th Dragoons, the 7th, 22nd, 23rd, 38th, 40th, 43rd, 70th, 74th, 76th, 80th, and 82nd. The 17th Regiment of Dragoons and the 70th to 82nd Regiments, inclusive, have already been advised that they will be entirely reduced after reaching England.

If some of the men in these last regiments wish to enlist in one of the regiments that is to serve in Nova Scotia, they are to receive five guineas levy money immediately. Moreover, those who wish to remain behind in America or accept land in Nova Scotia will receive permission to do so.

The provincial and other volunteer corps are to disband entirely, except that four of these corps, which are now being disbanded on Long Island, may take land in Nova Scotia, the officers to be put on half pay, though without army rank.[42] This is also a prerogative of Colonel Thompson's recently organized dragoon regiment,[43] whose horses were sold in April. Some officers, noncommissioned officers, and 140 men have been assigned quarters on the St. John River. The four discharged corps are Fanning's, Colonel Donkin's, Colonel Tarleton's, and Colonel Simcoe's.

The 3rd and 4th battalions of the 60th Regiment, as well as the entire 84th Regiment, have the same prospect. Their noncom-

---

[42] The German text is not perfectly clear; it might possibly be translated to mean that the officers alone may settle in Nova Scotia, though the text immediately following seems to bear out the correctness of the above translation.

[43] The King's American Dragoons.

missioned officers and men will receive free transportation and maintenance to England or Nova Scotia, in which latter case they will also receive grants of land. Those who wish to remain in America have been ordered to draw pay until the 25th of October and two weeks' maintenance and have been told to cross the lines in groups of three. Only a few have chosen to remain in America. Most of them desire to go to Nova Scotia, whither the provincial corps noted below will be transported as units and where they will disband.

Pay and maintenance will stop for officers and men alike, but land will be distributed to them in accordance with their rank. Likewise, those in these corps who wish to remain in America will be mustered out and given two weeks' provisions; none of them have been offered passage to England. The names of these provincial corps are the detached Garrison Battalion, whose 1st Battalion is in the Bermudas, the New York Volunteers, the 1st, 2nd, and 3rd Battalions in New Jersey Volunteers, the 1st and 2nd Battalions of De Lancey's, the Prince of Wales' Americans, the Pennsylvania and Maryland Loyalists, and the Guides and Pioneers.

As soon as this reduction is completed, the volunteer corps will be transported with the six regular regiments. Some of the artillery and armament will go with them. Lieutenant General Campbell will have the command in Nova Scotia.

His Excellency General von Lossberg has been assigned a transport which is being prepared for him and his suite. Where the ships for the British and Hessian troops are to come from is still unknown. Since the month of October is considered the best time to make the passage from here to Europe, everybody hopes that our departure will not be delayed longer than that.

The reduction of the army is being carried out with unexpected order. This is especially remarkable since the inhabitants of this city and the greater part of those on the neighboring islands are emigrating at the same time. These people, together with those in Connecticut and Jersey who have announced themselves to be refugees, number twenty-two thousand and consist of entire families. This great number will be transported to Port Roseway,

Annapolis Royal, and the St. John River before the British and Hessians leave.

Governor Clinton of the province of New York has publicly told the committees to stop persecuting the refugees and confiscating their property. He has even made arrangements for an investigation to ascertain whether the confiscated property can rightly be withheld from the former owners. Just as this move is, the populace contests its justice, and so nothing is done.

General Washington left the army on the 19th of this month with his bodyguard and went into quarters at Rocky Hill, five English miles from Princeton. Major General McDougall is now in command of the army,[44] and the forts at West Point have been entrusted to Brigadier General Knox.[45]

Preparations are being made in the American camp to hold peace celebrations as soon as the final peace is concluded. Then the army will want to have a dictator, and who knows what else it will want to make of General Washington in spite of his chosen absence from the army. It is being freely talked of in Philadelphia.

The impotent Congress is at Princeton waiting until New York has been evacuated, whereupon it will move here. General Howe's brigade is still encamped before Philadelphia.

The Dutch merchants are departing with their ships without having sold their merchandise, for they extend no credit, while the British and Irish merchants give three, six, and twelve months' credit and are consequently selling their wares. Moreover, American seamen are hiring themselves out on Irish ships and would do the same on English ships if they could obtain a time limit to their engagement. This the British are unwilling to grant, but the Irish make this concession.

A few days ago Captain Sutherland of the 55th Regiment arrived here from Antigua in the West Indies. On the 2nd of this month the French had not surrendered a single British island captured by them. According to the Captain's statement, their land forces do not exceed three thousand men. A ship from St. Augustine arrived at Sandy Hook on the 22nd and gave its dispatches

[44] Alexander McDougall was, of course, not made commander in chief.
[45] Henry Knox was then a major general.

for General Carleton to the pilot. I believe that no one so far has learned their contents. Preparations are being made there, too, for a speedy evacuation.

General Haldimand has his borders closely guarded, so that no one can pass the lines unnoticed. He refuses any kind of communication and is ordering the people nearby to remain quiet until the actual conclusion of peace.

Desertion among us has almost entirely ceased. On the other hand, the Hessians remaining in Maryland are returning in even smaller numbers; only a nine-inch soldier [46] of Prinz Friedrich's Regiment,[47] General von Hachenberg's Company,[48] has come in.

On the 27th, i.e., last Wednesday, at six o'clock in the morning, General von Hachenberg died in this city.[49] He had been declining in health for some time, and there was little hope of his recovery. He was buried the following day. Everything was done according to regulations, the Leib Regiment forming the guard of honor.[50] General Carleton, the British generals, staff officers, and other officers honored the deceased by accompanying the body to the garrison church, where interment took place.

Before I conclude I must tell your Excellency that a ship from Rotterdam arrived in Philadelphia on the 9th of this month, after a passage of forty days, with some emigrants from the Upper

[46] A nine-inch soldier is a soldier 5 feet 9 inches tall. According to the Prussian system a man had to measure at least five feet to become a soldier. Someone 5 feet 10½ inches was then considered very tall.

[47] Baurmeister must mean the Erb Prinz Regiment, which was taken with Cornwallis's army at Yorktown and imprisoned in Maryland. The Landgrave of Hesse-Cassel was Prinz Friedrich; before his ascension to the throne he was the hereditary (=Erb) prince of Hesse-Cassel. (The then hereditary prince was Prince Wilhelm.) On the other hand, it is not improbable that the name of the regiment had just been changed. The *Carleton Calendar*, *sub* Aug. 5, 1783, speaks of the Erb Prinz Regiment as the Late Prince Hereditaire Regiment. There was in the regular military establishment in 1779 a Prinz Friedrich Regiment of Dragoons, which, however, did not serve in America—all very confusing.

[48] One of the companies in the Erb Prinz Regiment may have been named in von Hachenberg's honor, since he had been at the head of this regiment. On the other hand, it is not impossible that Baurmeister's thoughts were ahead of his pen and that he was already thinking of General von Hachenberg, whose death he reports two lines further on.

[49] An obituary and eulogy appeared in the *New-York Gazette*, Sept. 1, 1783.

[50] "Leib" means "body"; the Leib Regiment were the (body) guard. The French term, frequently used in military correspondence, muster rolls, and returns, is "Regiment du Corps."

Rhine. Before admitting them, the governor asked Congress for instructions. Prior to the rebellion such Europeans frequently came to Philadelphia, especially in the fall. For free transportation and maintenance they bound themselves, as it were, to the ships' masters, who in turn sold them into servitude in Philadelphia for a certain number of years, after which they were given the rights of citizenship. However, since times have noticeably changed and people are emigrating from Jersey and Pennsylvania to the Ohio River, the admittance of indigent people will become more difficult.

Brigadier General Birch, till now commandant of New York, will go to London on the same frigate that carries these letters. His place has been taken by Brigadier General Musgrave. The latter is so pleased with the Hessians' drill, that he has asked for a corporal to instruct the British regiments in this garrison in the simple movements of presenting arms, taking the gun by the butt, and shouldering it, all following the file leader, for the majors of the Hessian regiments command the reviews.

With the deepest respect I remain so long as I live [*etc.*]

: 88 :

NEW YORK

OCTOBER 5, 1783

When on the 30th of last month, August,[51] I had the honor to send your Excellency an account of the events up to that date, I did not suppose that the army would remain this long in New York and on the neighboring islands. Even now nothing definite can be said about the time of departure from North America, although every preparation is being made.

The refugees began to embark on the 16th of September; forty-eight transports filled with these exiles are ready to sail to Nova Scotia within the next few days. Lieutenant General Campbell is under orders to embark any hour with the following regiments, which are already under his sole command and are to be distributed over Nova Scotia: the 17th, 33rd, 37th, 42nd, 54th, and 57th. The 42nd Regiment and five companies of the 37th are sailing with the refugee transports, earlier than the rest. Three companies of this last regiment have been sent to St. Augustine. I see no reason why troops should be sent to East Florida at this time. They are not, in my opinion, sent in compliance with a request from the governor of that province, who is said to have

[51] Apparently Baurmeister expected to post the letter in September.

asked for reinforcements so that the evacuation of the several places might be carried out with that much more order.

For a long time the Hessian corps has been under orders to embark. His Excellency General von Lossberg had been assigned a good ship, but it was used for the transportation of the 42nd Regiment. Now, ships neither for the Nova Scotia regiments nor for the Hessians are in the harbor. The daily orders, however, admonish us to keep in readiness.

General Carleton puts the blame on Congress for not having left with his army long ago, for he had received very emphatic orders from London not to evacuate New York until all the refugees had been taken to safety and put in possession of new homes. However, since Congress has so little influence in the provinces where the loyalists can no longer live and since the number of these unfortunate people increases daily, the evacuation cannot take place at this time.

The Americans have finally been convinced by General Haldimand that the places on the Canadian border cannot be surrendered during the present year and that for the time being they cannot think of intercourse with Canada. General von Steuben has been asked to go to Lake Champlain on this business, at the latest during the latter part of May, if it should be agreeable to Congress.

General Washington lives near Princeton, like a private individual. If, as is generally said, he gave prestige to the American army, it is certain that his frequent presence near Princeton is lending some dignity and respect to the declining Congress. As a matter of fact this great council has never been so little respected and revered as it now is, especially in New England, where the prescribed taxes cannot be collected. This is now also the case in Pennsylvania, where Congress's flight from Philadelphia is considered an unpardonable mistake. Besides, the Pennsylvanians were the first to realize that the members of Congress were misappropriating the money gained from the sale of confiscated property.

In view of the present misgovernment, General Washington could obtain anything he might want, even the crown of North

America. The people are ready to offer it to him, but so far he has shown no desire for this gift of fortune, if, indeed, it is one.

The British Treasury here is in possession of great sums of cash. The many wealthy inhabitants of this city and Long Island gladly surrendered their wealth at 2½ per cent discount, and now the Americans also come with considerable sums which they entrust to the Treasury at the same rate, so that they will not have to turn them over into the empty purse of the avaricious Congress, and so lose them forever.

Since the winter of 1781, when the Bostonians provisioned Admiral Vaudreuil's fleet in return for promissory notes which were returned unpaid and have since been presented to Congress for payment, their allies are always welcome when they have cash, but not when they can offer nothing but notes. This is true not only in Boston but also in Philadelphia and Baltimore.

The boldest thefts occur in this city and along the road from here to Kings Bridge, and on Long Island robbery is even more common. All the roads are open. Everyone knows that British liberty has often extended beyond the limits of fairness and has led to disastrous results, but North American liberty has no limits whatever. Everything that wickedness is capable of is being perpetrated by this profligate people. The result must be inevitable ruin.

General Carleton's tasks are many and commensurate with his talents. The evacuation alone is a troublesome business. To have gained the profound respect of the Americans he must possess rare qualities. It is a pity that he is the last in command, for he always has a trick in reserve, but unfortunately he is too late to smother the enemies of Great Britain.

With the deepest respect I have the honor to be [etc.]

: 89 :

NEW YORK

OCTOBER 28, 1783

I have the honor humbly to submit to your Excellency, by a packet which is to leave for London immediately, an account of the events that have taken place since I sent my last report.

All the transports except twelve are here to take on board the rest of the Hessian corps as soon as orders are given. Each ship is completely provisioned for six months. The magazines of the city contain supplies for only three more weeks, counting from the 26th of this month. The train, already greatly reduced, will cease to exist after the 31st. Everything brought in is carried by boats, for which reason von Lengerke's Grenadier Battalion has been transferred from the East River to Powles Hook, while von Platte's [52] has been quartered at McGown's Pass, on this island.

General Carleton is waiting only for a packet from England with an answer to his reports, which were dispatched by his secretary, Morgann, on the 6th of July. Congress, however, is by no means urging the speedy departure of the army; nor did it send a definite answer to General Carleton's letter of August, in which

[52] Friedrich von Platte was in command of the Grenadier Battalion formerly commanded by von Graff and before then by von Köhler. In 1779 he is listed as a major in von Bünau's Regiment (*Staats-Calender,* p. 42).

he gave it to understand that the delay in evacuating the city was caused by having so many loyalists to take care of.

France's serious admonition to Congress, and the still more emphatic one from Spain, that it must comply with every article prescribed in the preliminary peace, causes a great and irremediable stir in Congress, for, if the confiscated property is to be returned and old as well as new debts are to be paid to England and other powers, the embarrassment of the Americans will be great indeed, and only the stronger nations will be able to enforce their demands. The corrupt conditions in America do not permit of any improvement in this regard. The members of Congress are well aware of this and could no longer withhold it from the French ambassador.

Colonel Gordon of the 80th Regiment died suddenly at his post at Kings Bridge several days ago, whereupon Colonel von Wurmb received that command. On the 23rd of this month the American detachment of 150 men left Westchester. It had also maintained a post at Kings Bridge, on the far side of the bridge, while a British post was stationed on this side.

Last week General Carleton refused to allow a French officer of the Engineers to stay in the city overnight. He had come from West Point and was expecting the same friendly reception that had always been given to officers who went from the city to those forts and who, on returning, were filled with praise for the sincere courtesy of the Americans.

The late transportation of British regiments and refugees to Nova Scotia did not take place without shipwreck. The transport ship *Martha* foundered [53] near the Tusket River [54] in the Bay of Fundy. Of the 356 Maryland refugees, 72 were saved. The transport *Bridgewater* on which the Queen's Rangers had embarked is still missing. This ship was last seen at Cape Sable.

[53] Cf. *Carleton Calendar*, IV, 439. The return of the disaster was made by Lieutenant Colonel Richard Hewlett, Oct. 3, 1783.

[54] There is a Tusket River in Yarmouth County, Nova Scotia, which empties into Townshend Bay, at the southeastern extremity of the Bay of Fundy; however, there is also an island channel by that name in Townshend Bay. Since, according to Colonel Hewlett's report, the *Martha* was wrecked "on a ledge of rock of the Seal Islands," Baurmeister must mean the channel.

We hope to be supplied with better transports. Then the continuous northwest wind will be good enough for an uncomfortable but very fast voyage to the British coast.

The Irish emigration to North America is very heavy. Around the 10th of this month three ships came into Philadelphia with emigrants from that country. There are several free negro families living in Philadelphia. One of the better situated of these bought two young Irishmen for five years' compulsory service by paying for their transportation. This occurrence was very provoking to the old Irish settlers. They threatened to kill the bold negro if he did not immediately free the two Irishmen upon having the purchase price refunded to him and if the governor did not immediately proclaim a law that a freed slave could never hold slaves. This incident stirred Philadelphia for two days and moved the governor to enact a law in accordance with the will of the people.

The Dutch ambassador van Berckel has arrived in Philadelphia but has not yet had a public audience with Congress.

On the 5th of this month I had the honor to send my last communication to your Excellency.

With the deepest respect I am as long as I live
Your Excellency's

Most humble and faithfully devoted servant

Baurmeister

New York
October 28, 1783

784

: 90 :

PORTSMOUTH [ENGLAND]

JANUARY 15, 1784

Right Honorable Lord,
Gracious High and Mighty Lieutenant General:

When, after a passage of forty days, his Excellency General von Lossberg and his suite came to anchor in this harbor on the *Duchess of Gordon* transport on the 25th of last month, December, I was unable to send your Excellency a letter with the first shipment of mail to Cassel because of continuous seasickness. Now that another packet is to leave, I can no longer deny myself this honor.

I shall not describe the very uncomfortable winter voyage, during which the raging storms and a heavy sea could easily have caused one shipwreck after another, a passage, however, which, taking everything into consideration, can by no means be called the worst imaginable. It has greatly enriched the experience of the soldiers, for they will always remember these days of peril, and, since no unfortunate accidents occurred, their memories will be pleasant. For this reason, too, I hope that the missing transports will arrive on this coast by and by.

His Excellency General von Lossberg is hourly expecting a second report from the Honorable Major General von Wurmb, stationed at Chatham. Besides the *Grand Duchess of Rusye*,[1] which ran into Plymouth harbor, three transports were still missing at Chatham on the 1st of this month, namely, the transport *Palliser* with Lieutenant Colonel Platte and part of his battalion, the transport *Molly* with Colonel von Loewenstein, and the second hospital ship, *Jane*, with Chief Surgeon Amelung. These ships belong to Major General von Wurmb's division.

The last division, under orders of Major General von Gosen, left Sandy Hook on the 25th of November and consisted of the Jäger Corps, von Lengerke's Grenadier Battalion, and von Donop's and the Jung von Lossberg Regiments. This division is ordered to land here, and the men are to be quartered in the barracks at Hilsea, about one hour from here, where Lengerke's entire Grenadier Battalion, Major von Wurmb with two jäger companies, and Colonel Heymell with two companies of von Donop's Regiment went into quarters on the 11th of this month. Major von Wurmb of the last-named regiment and the whole Jung von Lossberg Regiment have arrived in the Downs and have probably disembarked at Chatham, but our commanding general has received no reports about it.

The following are still missing: Colonel von Wurmb with two jäger companies and the war treasurer Lorentz,[2] all of whom embarked on the transport *Mars*;[3] Lieutenant Colonel Prueschenck with two companies; and Major General von Gosen and Colonel Hinte with the rest of the Donop Regiment, with whom is also Chief War Commissary Harnier.

The barracks are very well fitted out. The officers, from the regimental commanders down to the lowest rank, have good quarters, but without furniture, coal, or light, while the noncommissioned officers and men are well supplied with these necessi-

---

[1] *Grand Duchess of Russia?* Not identified.

[2] Probably Richard Lorentz, paymaster of the Hessian forces. There was also a Johann Georg Lorentz, Commissary General and Counsellor of War, who died in New York July 2, 1781.

[3] Not clearly legible, as the word is partly written over another word not completely erased.

ties. His Excellency the General and his suite, who had remained on board their ship, took quarters in this city on the 10th of this month, each man paying his own expenses. The coast and harbor towns in England are expensive; hence the weekly outlay for quarters is high. War Counsellor Motz lives with me, and it costs each of us twenty-eight shillings a week. If only we could have left America sooner, so that we might have proceeded to the coast at Bremerlehe without further delay! The expense of our sojourn in this kingdom could then have been saved, but now, nothing can be done about it.

Colonel von Keytel [4] and Major von Eschwege with two and a half companies of the Leib Regiment have been in this harbor since the 25th of December. Admiral Montagu,[5] the commander of the harbor, had received definite instructions from the First Secretary of the Admiralty, Mr. Stephens, to stop all transports coming from America with troops. Even though it had been decided that the Hessian troops were to spend the winter at Dover Castle, Chatham, and here, and though Colonel von Keytel's ship belonged to the division of Major General von Wurmb and therefore had to follow Captain Wachs's transport (which was also in this harbor), no one could persuade the old Admiral Montagu to permit this ship to sail. Finally, however, the agent for transports in this harbor, Captain Berry,[6] accomplished it on the 10th of this month. Another difficulty arose when the master of the ship, who had entered into the negotiation of family business in London, refused to sail until his affairs were settled. God be praised, such reasons are valid only in this country and in no other.

Colonel von Keytel might have come to great grief through a fall on the deck of the ship on the 26th of December. He sprained his right foot and injured the small long-bone.[7] His regimental surgeon reset the dislocated bones, and all signs promise a complete recovery. He wants to remain on board the ship.

[4] Probably Henrich Walrab von Keudel of the Landgraf Regiment (*Staats-Calender*, p. 27). His name is spelled Keutel in letter dated Sept. 28, 1779 (No. 42).

[5] Admiral John Montagu, commander in chief at Portsmouth, 1783–86.

[6] Not identified.

[7] Fibula.

Admiral Digby has arrived in Portland Road, near Dartmouth. The ships that came in yesterday with English troops had left the frigate *Ceres,* which carried General Carleton, in the Channel.

His Excellency General von Lossberg has his own general's guard here, which comes in from Hilsea, where one officer, two noncommissioned officers, and forty men are on barracks guard, and one noncommissioned officer and twelve men on guard at the powder magazine at Portsea Lines Bridge,[8] near the barracks.

The vice governor of this city, Lieutenant General Smith [9] of the Marines, did not consent to our making contracts with the local bankers, as did the English troops, additional payments being made by his Majesty the King, but directed us to apply to the War Office in London. This has been done, and an answer is expected.

All the officers' baggage had to be taken from the ships directly to the Customs House for inspection, from which there was no escaping. His Excellency General von Lossberg was compelled to leave behind the silver that did not have an English trademark. It must remain there until permission has been granted from other quarters to bring it in without having to pay duty.

The desire of those holding offices in this city really to please the Hessian troops deserves to be praised. A merchant of Gosport, near this city, who is dependent on the bankers Van Rotton [10] in London, has offered to advance money to anyone requesting it. His Excellency General von Lossberg has helped out von Lengerke's Grenadier Battalion with nearly £200 sterling of his own. However, since Colonel von Loewenstein in a letter of the 12th of this month (announcing his arrival at Dover Castle), referring to a letter of the 8th of this month (addressed to Chatham and received by Major General von Wurmb), repeats his demand for pay, his Excellency General von Lossberg has ordered the Regimental Quartermaster Zinn of von Donop's Regiment to borrow a

---

[8] A floating bridge between Portsmouth and Gosport.
[9] Major General Henry Smith.
[10] The banking house of Van Rotton was the London agent of the Landgrave of Hesse-Cassel.

small sum from the merchant Carver in Gosport, hoping that the war commissariat will land at one place or another and repay this sum.

The said Colonel von Loewenstein now probably has his battalion together at Dover Castle, for Captain Wachs as well as Captain Mondorff's company sailed for that place more than a week ago.

With the deepest respect I have the honor to be [*etc.*]

: 91 :

PORTSMOUTH [ENGLAND]

APRIL 1, 1784 [11]

With today's mail for Hesse, the last that will be sent, I have the honor to inform your Excellency that tomorrow, the 2nd, the Hessian troops quartered in the Hilsea Barracks will embark and depart for Bremerlehe with the first favorable wind without further delay. The troops quartered in other places will also embark tomorrow and start on their way home.

We should have embarked several days sooner if the parliamentary elections had not taken place and, according to custom, the troops been obliged to clear the barracks and take quarters in distant places.

The military as well as the civil authorities of Portsmouth have given candid expression to their satisfaction with the orderly behavior of the troops during their stay in England. On the other hand, we, too, have every cause to be very grateful for their desire to please us, and we are convinced that their wishes for a happy return to the Fatherland are sincere.

[11] It is very likely that Baurmeister wrote several letters between January 15 and April 1, and that he also received some letters from Baron von Jungkenn. Perhaps they related in part to private business, such as the purchase of sheep and horses mentioned later. For this reason they may have been extracted from the war correspondence proper.

The two horses for His Serene Highness Prince Friedrich have been embarked and furnished with ample forage. Forage has also been provided for the generals and staff officers who are taking along horses. I have been waiting for the Spanish sheep in vain; apparently Major von Kutzleben [12] is hesitating because of the continued cold. Day after tomorrow, or else Sunday the 4th, wind permitting, the transports will set sail, and we hope that our passage to the beloved German coast will be a short one, so that without delay we shall be able to report further on our wanderings, which, God be praised, will soon end.

With the deepest respect I remain [etc.]

[12] Major Christian Moritz von Kutzleben, resident minister at the English court, whom Baurmeister succeeded in 1793.

: 92 :

A week ago today his Excellency General von Lossberg embarked with the troops that had been stationed in the Hilsea Barracks, but because of unfavorable wind the ships have been unable to set sail. In order to make more room, five of our transports fell down to Spithead on the 6th, where they came to anchor again. There they will be less handicapped in reaching the North Sea with the first favorable wind.

I received permission to spend this forenoon in the city, where I met the young naval Captain Affleck, who is about to depart for London overland. He had just returned from the West Indies on the sloop of war *Le Duc de Chartres* [13] and had landed at St. Helen's. [14] He is good enough to take this hastily written letter along and mail it. I hope your Excellency will not be displeased at receiving further news of our situation.

The agent of this harbor, Captain Berry, received letters from Chatham dated the 7th, according to which the Hessian troops there had embarked but had not got under way.

[13] Taken from the French in April, 1782 (Clowes).
[14] On the Isle of Wight.

604

Von Lengerke's Grenadier Battalion had barely embarked when Lieutenant von Trott, Senior, of the Grenadier Company of the Prinz Carl Regiment died, after suffering a long time with consumption. He was buried in Portsmouth on the 3rd of this month in accordance with regulations.

With the deepest respect I remain [*etc.*]

P.S. I had the honor to receive your Excellency's esteemed letter of the 17th of March, day before yesterday.

: **93** :

BREMERLEHE [GERMANY]
APRIL 20, 1784

On the 9th of this month I had the honor to write once more
to your Excellency from Portsmouth, for I had permission to leave
the ship and go to the city, where I found a naval officer ready to
travel to London.

In that letter I reported that contrary wind forced all the
Hessian troops, which had been embarked since the 1st, to remain
at anchor.

On the 11th of this month, when the wind became more
favorable, we weighed anchor, and the six transports departed
from Portsmouth. Changeable April weather and a southwest
wind carried the little fleet through the Channel. We passed the
Downs on the 13th and ran into the Weser with the tide on the
16th of this month without the least untoward incident.

Von Loewenstein's Grenadier Battalion had arrived two days
earlier. On the 16th it was mustered on the ships and then transferred onto nine vessels, on which it was to run up to Bremen,
whence the larger Weser ships will take all the returning troops as
far as Münden, Hanover.

On the 17th the troops that had arrived from Portsmouth were mustered on the transports and, like von Loewenstein's Grenadier Battalion, sent to Bremen. The British Major Gunn and the Hanoverian Major Niemeyer are in charge of transporting the Hessian troops, in which they are assisted by the Hanoverian Captains v. d. Osten and von Kettenbourg.

I have nothing to report about the troops under the Honorable Major General von Wurmb; we know of no reason for their being so late in arriving. The jäger companies that spent the winter at Sheerness [15] have not come in yet either. Yesterday the wind was northwest, and this morning it is still blowing approximately the same, which makes us hope that the Chatham ships will arrive today. However, the transportation of these troops to Bremen may be somewhat delayed, since the small vessels must return from Bremen after taking the first troops there.

If the transportation of all the troops is arranged as well as the march commissaries have told us, both in writing and by word of mouth, there will be no further delay, which would be very advantageous. But, we shall see. Major Gunn gladly listens to the representations of the Hanoverians and believes that he can justify having inadvertently caused the Crown of England greater expense by sending the Hessian troops home on the Weser instead of having them march through the Electorate,[16] where they would suffer from scarcity of provisions.

Day after tomorrow the two saddle horses for his Serene Highness Prince Friedrich will be sent from here by way of Hanover, Einbeck, and Münden. They were safely disembarked with several others on the 17th, although such debarkations are sometimes dangerous.

At the local post station I found a letter from your Excellency dated September 17th of last year.

With the deepest respect I have the honor to be [etc.]

[15] At the mouth of the Medway.
[16] The Electorate of Brandenburg.

: 94 :

BREMERLEHE [GERMANY]
APRIL 23, 1784

When on the 20th of this month I had the honor to inform your Excellency of our long-hoped-for arrival here, Major General von Wurmb had not yet come in with the Hessian troops that had spent the winter under his command at Chatham. However, they arrived that very afternoon, without any of their ships having met with the slightest misfortune.

Yesterday, the British Major Gunn mustered the Jäger detachment, von Donop's Regiment, and von Linsing's Grenadier Battalion. This first division was then transferred to other ships and taken as far as Blexen, where they are still lying at anchor since the southwest wind threatens to drive them ashore. The wind is so strong that even with the tide Fegesack [17] cannot be reached. This morning a boat belonging to the *Admiral Parker* transport had the misfortune to capsize with two sailors, who were drowned.

Tomorrow the Leib Regiment and Platte's Grenadier Battalion will be mustered; on the 26th, the Erb Prinz and Prinz Carl Regiments, and on the 28th, the Jung von Lossberg. On this last

[17] A small town on the Weser, about ten miles northwest of Bremen.

608

day the General Staff, too, will leave Bremerlehe on two vessels assigned to it. However, if the present wind should continue, all these arrangements may be upset, especially if the troops have to remain on the vessels more than twenty-four hours, for they are issued only a day's provisions from the transports and cannot be reached where they are lying at anchor. I fear that the march commissaries' arrangements for transporting the Hessian troops up the Weser will not be entirely satisfactory.

With the deepest respect I have the honor to remain
Your Excellency's

Most obedient and faithfully devoted servant

Baurmeister

Bremerlehe
April 23, 1784

List of Holographs and Copies,
with Designations of Writers

1–LS *, Copyist A; last paragraph in Baurmeister's hand

2–LS, Copyist B; last paragraph and complimentary closing in Baurmeister's hand

3–ALS †

4–Holograph ‡ journal

5–Fragment of holograph journal

6–ALS

7–LS, Copyist C; last paragraph in Baurmeister's hand

8–ALS

9–Copyists D and E (E begins: "On the 16th of September . . .")

10 to 12–ALS

13–LS, Copyist D

14–LS, Copyist F

15 and 16–LS, Copyist D

17–ALS

18–Journal, Copyist G

19 and 20–ALS

21–LS, Copyist H; last paragraph in Baurmeister's hand

22 and 23–ALS

24–LS, Copyist D; last paragraph in Baurmeister's hand

25–ALS

26 and 27–LS, Copyist H

28 to 31–ALS

32 and 33–LS, Copyist I

34 and 35–ALS

36–LS, Copyist I

37–ALS

38–LS, Copyist G; postscript in Baurmeister's hand

39–ALS

40–LS, Copyist J; last paragraph in Baurmeister's hand

41 to 44–ALS

45–LS, Copyist D; postscript in Baurmeister's hand

46–Fragment of holograph letter

47 to 59–ALS

60–Fragment of holograph letter

61 to 76–ALS

77–Fragment of holograph letter

78 to 94–ALS

* LS: Letter signed (by author)
† ALS: Autograph letter signed, i.e., letter in hand of and signed by author
‡ Holograph: In author's hand

Index

(Abbreviations: Am.–American, Americans; Br.–British; Fr.–French; Ger.–German; Hess.–Hessian)

Abercorn, Ga., 493, 501
Abercromby, Robert, 162, 279, 474, 510, 525
Abington, Pa., 119, 120, 137
Adams, John, 40, 47
Adams, Samuel, 40
Affleck, Edmund, 467, 522, 533, 604
Agnew, James, 33, 57, 62, 69, 86, 111, 121
Albany, N.Y.: 196, 223, 231, 240, 281, 283, 289, 328, 337, 414, 477, 548, 580; loyalists vs. patriots, 87; militia, 191, 429, 498; garrison strength, 251, 337; Washington at, 501, 580-81. –County, 240; inhabitants resist tax collectors, 335, 413; brigade not part of Washington's army, 527. –District, 398, 524, 578
Albemarle Old Court House, N.C., 443
Albemarle Sound, 434, 439
Alden, Ichabod, 240
Alexander, William. See Stirling, Earl of
Allen, Ethan, 407, 413, 497
Allentown, N.J., 183, 184, 189
Amboy, N.J.: 47, 58, 73-90 passim, 191, 240, 295, 303, 347, 360, 372, 373, 404, 429. –Ferry, 33. (See also Perth Amboy.)
American Army—
    General: Shortage of powder, 39; generals praised, 40; leaves Rhode Island, 77; increases, 86; form of attack, 86; situation not good, 140; discord between commanders, 243, 252; and paper money, 252. –Continentals, 154, 157, 191, 203, 205, 206, 237, 252, 270, 348, 354, 355, 357, 361, 445, 448, 468, 497, 523, 562. –Desertion, 44-288 passim, 339, 346, 378, 459, 527. –Distribution, 250, 251-52. –Encampments, 40, 44, 49, 65, 66, 87, 175, 215. –Intelligence, 26, 75, 96, 134, 139, 162, 176, 226, 435, 491, 499. –Losses, 34-481 passim, 529. –Officers, 39, 40, 140, 336. –Recruits and recruiting, 261, 263, 275, 281, 357-58, 370, 494. –Soldiers, 39, 40, 426, 528

    Services: Artillery, 115, 117, 138, 174, 186, 192, 208, 268, 554. –Cavalry, 369, 395, 428. –Dragoons, 104, 105, 109, 129, 134, 138, 148-72 passim, 191, 196, 216, 221, 222, 231, 251, 258, 342, 382, 444. –Infantry, 129, 183, 208, 251, 342, 444, 559. –Riflemen (sharpshooters), 34, 36, 37, 175, 427, 444.
    Provincial Corps: Armand's (Pulaski's Legion), 154, 202, 205, 226, 312, 325, 381. –Baylor's Dragoons, 220. –Lee's Dragoons, 54, 74, 375, 429, 458. –Morgan's Riflemen, 184. –Moylan's Dragoons, 298, 312, 333. –Sheldon's Dragoons, 312, 361, 413, 522
    Militia: 119, 124, 134, 139, 146, 164-65, 218, 240, 317, 354-55, 406, 468; disband, 54, 124-25, 146, 187, 191, 193, 204, 211, 215, 261, 326, 386, 428, 459, 523; Patterson's corps, 125, 134; Lacey's brigade, 168; raising of, 154, 165, 275; not to be drawn on for Continental battalions, 206; at White Plains, 267; in Lincoln's force, 324; praised, 354-55; on Pedee River, 386; along North River, 424; in Lafayette's corps, 445; make up half of army before Yorktown, 466, 481; reduced, 512; refuse to serve, 523. (See also names of states.)
    Corps and Armies:
    Gates's, 191, 219, 369-72, 381, 383.
    Greene's, 480, 485, 509; makes attempts to occupy Rhode Island, 203, 208; Lafayette with corps, 208; reinforcements, 334, 443, 480, 493, 496; at Guilford, 426-28; at Eutaw Springs, 468; and northern Georgia, 493, 496; near Charleston, 496.
    Lafayette's, Continentals in, 354; desertion, 439; at Yorktown, 466, 473; detached to Charleston, 476.
    Muhlenberg's, 224, 443.
    St. Claire's, 480.
    Steuben's, 443.

The last reports from the West Indies were sent from St. Lucia on the 19th of January. Since Admiral Hughes's arrival at Barbados with nine ships of the line, the British West Indies fleet under Admiral Pigot numbers forty-two ships of the line, of which seventeen were cruising under Admiral Hood northeast of Hispaniola at the time the reports were sent. At Havana there are ten Spanish ships of the line under the command of Don Solano [6] ready to sail to Cape François to join a French squadron from Martinique. Four of Don Solano's ships of the line and three of his frigates are reported to be cruising between Cape San Antonio (Cuba) and Cape Catoche (Yucatan) [7] in order to cover the Spanish ships before Cartagena [8] and make the passage to and from Jamaica unsafe. But Admiral Pigot, aware that these prepartions were ineffective, took no notice of them. The British troops sent from Charleston to Jamaica arrived safely, and now that island is in a good state of defense.

The Charleston troops that came to New York also received forage money and cloth for winter trousers. Lieutenant Colonel du Puy has gone to Long Island to muster Dittfurth's, d'Angelelli's, and von Benning's Regiments. The sick brought along by the several regiments are gradually recovering; the rest of the troops continue to be in good health during this persistently cold winter weather. Captain Krafft is ready to sail to Halifax in order to re-organize his company. He will be accompanied by a noncommissioned officer from each regiment, who will join the recruits at Halifax. In spite of the severe weather of Halifax and its environs, the number of recruits has noticeably decreased, and a dangerous illness still prevails among them. Major von Stamford, who has had several serious relapses, earnestly wishes that his son may come here. But according to the last report, he is ill with a bilious fever.

General Carleton is present every day at the watch parade and visits the hospitals once a week.

[6] Rear Admiral José Solano.
[7] The two capes are situated directly across from each other, being separated by the Yucatan Channel.
[8] Cartagena, Colombia.

The prisoners of Burgoyne's army who were compelled to take service are still finding ways to escape. So far, some seventy Brunswickers and as many Hesse-Hanauers have gathered here and are waiting to be transported to Halifax under the command of Captain von Eschwege, in accordance with the orders of the 5th of this month. Regimental Quartermaster Flachshaar of von Bose's Regiment has not yet returned from Maryland.

With the deepest respect I have the honor to remain [*etc.*]

: 80 :

I had the honor to send the last continuation of my journal on the 16th of March, when General Carleton sent dispatches to London. The following day the January packet arrived, and on the 6th of this month, the February packet. With the first I had the honor to receive your Excellency's gracious letter of the 14th of November of last year, from which I learned that my journal sent from time to time up to the 10th of August [9] had arrived and that it was graciously received.

Today an ordinary packet will leave for London with the news that the peace proclamation, which arrived here from London on the 8th of this month, has been publicly read in front of the City Hall by the town major of the local garrison and that an armistice went into effect immediately. All the outposts have been notified of it; Admiral Digby has called in the privateers, and an adjutant [10] has been sent to General Washington with letters, though he has not returned yet.

Since General Carleton's proclamation of the 18th of February, advising the inhabitants of this city and the nearby islands

[9] The August, 1782, letter is dated the 19th.
[10] Captain John Stapleton, Deputy Adjutant General (see below).

who have left their homes since the beginning of the rebellion that they can take possession of their homes and property again, unmolested, a great number of such people have returned. For this reason our quarters will be more confined and scarcer after the 1st of May. Despite the fact that the city was crowded already and great numbers poured in when the armistice was proclaimed, everything remained as quiet as it was before. Many even showed signs of being seriously displeased with all the liberty granted them and with the separation from England. How this change is received in New England will not be known before another month has passed.

On the 24th of March a secretary of Congress arrived from Philadelphia with letters for General Carleton and Admiral Digby, informing them that the French ambassador in Philadelphia has received news of the peace from Count d'Estaing by a flagship [11] dispatched expressly from Cadiz. No further notice was taken of this here. The many prizes taken by the privateers before the Delaware and near New London before the 2nd of this month are recognized.

Not until yesterday did dispatch ships depart for Halifax and St. Augustine with the news that the war is over. The ship sent to the latter place also carries orders that the garrison is to be withdrawn. However, when this is to take place, how the established provincial corps are to be distributed to Canada, Halifax, and the West Indies, and when they will leave here is known no more than what preparations are to be made for the departure of the entire army. All this will be worked out quickly after General Grey's arrival, which has already been announced by the January packet.

At present there are here only fifty-one transports, one sixty-four-gun ship, fifteen frigates, and nineteen armed ships. Twenty-nine of the transports belong to private individuals and will be held in readiness for their flight. Most of the evicted persons have escaped to Port Roseway in the Bay of Fundy, where they have been advised to settle. But since the Canadian border has been established close to the said bay, to the advantage of the Amer-

[11] The *Triomphe* sloop of war (see following letter).